Birnbaum's 94
Spain

A BIRNBAUM TRAVEL GUIDE

Alexandra Mayes Birnbaum
EDITORIAL CONSULTANT

Lois Spritzer
Executive Editor

Laura L. Brengelman
Managing Editor

Mary Callahan
Senior Editor

Patricia Canole
Gene Gold
Jill Kadetsky
Susan McClung
Beth Schlau
Associate Editors

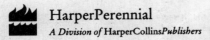 HarperPerennial
A Division of HarperCollinsPublishers

To Stephen, who merely made all this possible.

FIRST EDITION

ISSN 0749-2561 (Birnbaum Travel Guides)
ISSN 1055-565X (Spain)
ISBN 0-06-278113-8 (pbk.)

93 94 95 96 97 CC/CW 10 9 8 7 6 5 4 3 2 1

Cover design © Drenttel Doyle Partners
Cover photograph © Michael Busselle/Tony Stone Images

BIRNBAUM TRAVEL GUIDES

Bahamas, and Turks & Caicos
Berlin
Bermuda
Boston
Canada
Cancun, Cozumel & Isla Mujeres
Caribbean
Chicago
Disneyland
Eastern Europe
Europe
Europe for Business Travelers
France
Germany
Great Britain
Hawaii
Ireland
Italy
London

Los Angeles
Mexico
Miami & Ft. Lauderdale
Montreal & Quebec City
New Orleans
New York
Paris
Portugal
Rome
San Francisco
Santa Fe & Taos
South America
Spain
United States
USA for Business Travelers
Walt Disney World
Walt Disney World for Kids, By Kids
Washington, DC

Contributing Editors

Carmen Anthony
David Baird
F. Lisa Beebe
Frederick H. Brengelman
Kevin Causey
David Cemlyn-Jones
Thomas de la Cal
Dwight V. Gast
Judith Glynn
Rochelle Goldstein
Maureen Griffin
Arline Inge
Donald A. Jeffrey
Emily Kadin
Robert Latona
Charles Leocha
Robert Levine

Howell Llewellyn
Jan S. McGirk
Erica Meltzer
Jeanne Muchnick
Joan Kane Nichols
Clare Pedrick
Mark Potok
Richard Schweid
Allan Seiden
Frank Shiell
Richard Slovak
Tracy Smith
Brook Hill Snow
Paul Wade
Dan Whitman
David Wickers
Mark Williams

Maps

B. Andrew Mudryk

Contents

Getting Ready to Go

Practical information for planning your trip.

Useful Words and Phrases

The Cities

Thorough, qualitative guides to each of the 13 cities most often visited by vacationers and businesspeople. Each section offers a comprehensive report on the

*city's most compelling attractions and amenities —
highlighting our top choices in every category.*

Diversions

*A selective guide to a variety of unexpected
pleasures, pinpointing the best places in which to
pursue them.*

Directions

*The most spectacular routes and roads; most
arresting natural wonders; and most magnificent
castles, manor houses, and gardens — all organized
into 13 specific driving tours.*

Foreword

Separately and together, my husband Steve Birnbaum and I made many a circuit around Spain. During our early visits, the almighty American dollar seemed to stretch the full length and breadth of the Iberian Peninsula and having a limited amount of cash in our pockets was, in truth, a plus. We took buses rather than trains, and walked everywhere with the enthusiasm and fervor of pilgrims heading to Santiago de Compostela. In spite of recent skyrocketing costs in several Spanish cities, both of us developed a fondness for Spain that we never lost.

Perhaps it is because Spain is at once a part of Europe and yet very distinctive and different from the other members of the European community. Just a brief turning of the pages in this guide will demonstrate the diversity that thrives in Spain between the Pyrenees and the Strait of Gibraltar. The idea that Spain is a single, homogeneous nation is one of travel's least justifiable assertions, and the atmosphere and ambience that flourish across this extremely variegated country are, in themselves, among the prime targets that draw visitors. At least half a dozen distinct "nations" coexist under the Spanish flag — each demanding strict attention — and one of the joys of traveling to and through Spain is the constant feeling of surprise and discovery.

Obviously, any guidebook to Spain must keep pace with and answer the real needs of today's travelers. That's why we've tried to create a guide that's specifically organized, written, and edited for the more demanding modern traveler, one for whom qualitative information is infinitely more desirable than mere quantities of unappraised data. We think that this book, along with all the other guides in our series, represents a new generation of travel guides — one that is especially responsive to modern needs and interests.

For years, dating back as far as Herr Baedeker, travel guides have tended to be encyclopedic, much more concerned with demonstrating expertise in geography and history than with a real analysis of the sorts of things that actually concern a modern tourist. I think you'll notice a different, more contemporary tone to our text, as well as an organization and focus that are distinctive and more functional. Early on, we realized that giving up the encyclopedic approach precluded our listing every single route and restaurant, a realization that helped define our overall editorial focus. Similarly, when we discussed the possibility of presenting certain information in other than strict geographic order, we found that the new format enabled us to arrange data in a way that best answers the questions travelers typically ask.

Travel guides are, understandably, reflections of personal taste, and putting one's name on a title page obviously puts one's preferences on the line. But I think I ought to amplify just what "personal" means. I don't believe in the sort of personal guidebook that's a palpable misrepresentation on its face. It is, for example, hardly possible for any single travel writer to visit thousands of restaurants (and nearly as many hotels) in any given year and provide accurate appraisals of each. And even if it were physically possible for one human being to survive such an itinerary, it would of necessity have to be done at a dead sprint, and the perceptions derived therefrom would probably be less valid than those of any other intelligent individual visiting the same establishments. It is, therefore, impossible (especially in a large, annually revised and updated guidebook *series* such as we offer) to have only one person provide all the data on the entire world.

I also happen to think that such individual orientation is of substantially less value to readers. Visiting a single hotel for just one night or eating one hasty meal in a random restaurant hardly equips anyone to provide appraisals that are of more than passing interest. We have, therefore, chosen what I like to describe as the "thee and me" approach to restaurant and hotel evaluation and, to a somewhat more limited degree, to the sites and sights we have included in the other sections of our text. What this really reflects is a personal sampling tempered by intelligent counsel from informed local sources, and these additional friends-of-the-editor are almost always residents of the city and/or area about which they are consulted.

In addition, very precise editing and tailoring keep our text fiercely subjective. So what follows is the gospel according to Birnbaum, and it represents as much of our own taste and instincts as we can manage. It is probable, therefore, that if you like your cities stylish and prefer hotels with personality to high-rise anonymities, we're likely to have a long and meaningful relationship.

I also should point out something about the person to whom this guidebook is directed. Above all, he or she is a "visitor." This means that such elements as restaurants have been specifically picked to provide the visitor with a representative, enlightening, stimulating, and above all pleasant experience. Since so many extraneous considerations can affect the reception and service accorded a regular restaurant patron, our choices can in no way be construed as an exhaustive guide to resident dining. We think we've listed all the best places, in various price ranges, but they were chosen with a visitor's enjoyment in mind.

Other evidence of how we've tried to tailor our text to reflect modern travel habits is most apparent in the section we call DIVERSIONS. Where once it was common for travelers to spend an urban visit seeing only the obvious sights, the emphasis today is more likely to be directed toward pursuing some special interest. Therefore, we have collected these exceptional experiences so that it is no longer necessary to wade through a pound or two of superfluous prose just to find unexpected pleasures and treasures.

Finally, I also should point out that every good travel guide is a living enterprise; that is, no part of this text is carved in stone. In our annual revisions, we refine, expand, and further hone all our material to serve your travel needs better. To this end, no contribution is of greater value to us than your personal reaction to what we have written, as well as information reflecting your own experiences while using the book. Please write to us at 10 E. 53rd St., New York, NY 10022.

We sincerely hope to hear from you.

Alexandra Mayes Birnbaum

ALEXANDRA MAYES BIRNBAUM, editorial consultant to the *Birnbaum Travel Guides,* worked with her late husband Stephen Birnbaum as co-editor of the series. She has been a world traveler since childhood and is known for her lively travel reports on radio on what's hot and what's not.

Spain

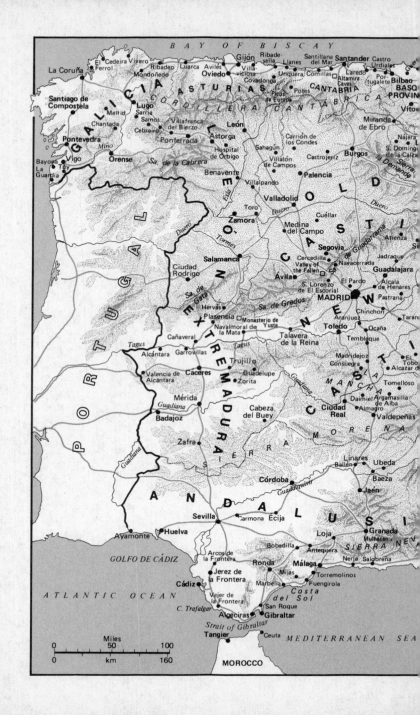

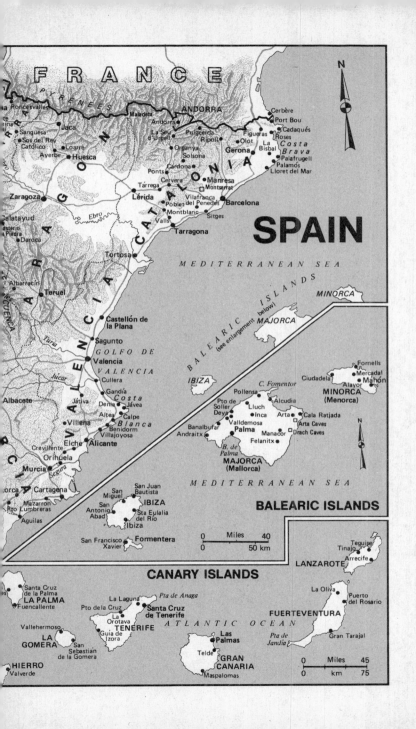

How to Use This Guide

A great deal of care has gone into the special organization of this guidebook, and we believe it represents a real breakthrough in the presentation of travel material.

Our text is divided into four basic sections in order to present information in the best way on every possible aspect of a vacation to Spain. Our aim is to highlight what's where and to provide basic information — how, when, where, how much, and what's best — to assist you in making the most intelligent choices possible.

Here is a brief summary of what you can expect to find in each section. We believe that you will find both your travel planning and en route enjoyment enhanced by having this book at your side.

GETTING READY TO GO

A mini-encyclopedia of practical travel facts with all the precise data necessary to create a successful trip to and through Spain. Here you will find how to get where you're going, plus selected resources — including useful publications, and companies and organizations specializing in discount and special-interest travel — providing a wealth of information and assistance useful both before and during your trip.

THE CITIES

Our individual reports on the 13 Spanish cities most visited by travelers and businesspeople offer a short-stay guide, including an essay introducing the city as a historic entity and a contemporary place to visit; *At-a-Glance* material is actually a site-by-site survey of the most important, interesting, and sometimes most eclectic sights to see and things to do; *Sources and Resources* is a concise listing of pertinent tourism information, such as the address of the local tourist office, which sightseeing tours to take, where to find the brightest nightspot or hail a taxi, which shops have the finest merchandise and/or most irresistible bargains, and where to play tennis or golf. *Best in Town* lists our choices of the best places to eat and sleep on a variety of budgets.

DIVERSIONS

This section is designed to help travelers find the best places in which to engage in a variety of exceptional — and unexpected — experiences for the mind and body without having to wade through endless pages of unrelated text. In every case, our particular suggestions are intended to guide you to that special place where the quality of experience is likely to be highest.

DIRECTIONS

Here are 13 itineraries that range all across Spain, along the most beautiful routes and roads, past the most spectacular natural wonders, through the most historic cities and countrysides and the most idyllic islands. DIRECTIONS is the only section of this book that is organized geographically, and its itineraries cover the touring highlights of Spain in short, independent journeys of 3 to 5 days' duration. Itineraries can be "connected" for longer sojourns or used individually for short, intensive explorations.

To use this book to full advantage, take a few minutes to read the table of contents and random entries in each section to get a firsthand feel for how it all fits together. You will find that the sections of this book are building blocks designed to help you put together the best possible trip. Use them selectively as a tool, a source of ideas, a reference work for accurate facts, and a guidebook to the best buys, the most exciting sights, the most pleasant accommodations, the tastiest foods — *the best travel experience* that you can possibly have.

Getting
Ready to Go

When to Go

In Spain, the months of May, June, and September offer the most comfortable weather, although mild weather is not uncommon in the coastal regions during February and November. Winters on the Spanish *meseta* can be piercingly cold and windy, but in the summer the weather resembles that of the drier parts of the southwestern US. Summers in the Costa del Sol and the Costa Blanca can be extremely hot. Much of the country is dry, although there is considerable variation in rainfall between regions.

The peak travel period generally is from mid-May to mid-September, but travel during the off-season (roughly November to *Easter*) and shoulder seasons (the months immediately before and after the peak months) also offers relatively fair weather and smaller crowds. During these periods, travel also is less expensive.

The *Weather Channel* (2600 Cumberland Pkwy., Atlanta, GA 30339; phone: 404-434-6800) provides current weather forecasts. Call 900-WEATHER from any touch-tone phone in the US; the 95¢ per minute charge will appear on your phone bill.

Traveling by Plane

SCHEDULED FLIGHTS

Leading airlines offering flights between the US and Spain include *Air France, American, British Airways, Continental, Delta, Iberia Airlines of Spain, KLM, Sabena, TAP Air, TWA,* and *United.*

FARES The great variety of airfares can be reduced to the following basic categories: first class, business class, coach (also called economy or tourist class), excursion or discount, and standby, as well as various promotional fares. For information on applicable fares and restrictions, contact the airlines listed above or ask your travel agent. Most airfares are offered for a limited time period. Once you've found the lowest fare for which you can qualify, purchase your ticket as soon as possible.

RESERVATIONS Reconfirmation is strongly recommended for all international flights. It is essential that you confirm your round-trip reservations–*especially the return leg* — as well as any flights within Europe.

SEATING Airline seats usually are assigned on a first-come, first-served basis at check-in, although you may be able to reserve a seat when purchasing your ticket. Seating charts often are available from airlines and are included in the *Airline Seating Guide* (Carlson Publishing Co., PO Box 888, Los Alamitos, CA 90720; phone: 310-493-4877).

SMOKING US law prohibits smoking on flights scheduled for 6 hours or less within the US and its territories on both domestic and international carriers. These rules do not apply to nonstop flights between the US and international destinations. A free wallet-size guide that describes the rights of nonsmokers is available from *ASH* (*Action on Smoking and Health;* DOT Card, 2013 H St. NW, Washington, DC 20006; phone: 202-659-4310).

SPECIAL MEALS When making your reservation, you can request one of the airline's alternate menu choices for no additional charge. Call to reconfirm your request 24 hours before departure.

BAGGAGE On a major international airline, passengers usually are allowed to carry on board one bag that will fit under a seat or in an overhead bin. Passengers also can check two bags in the cargo hold, measuring 62 inches and 55 inches in combined dimensions (length, width, and depth) with a per-bag weight limit of 70 pounds. There may be charges for additional, oversize, or overweight luggage, and for special equipment or sporting gear. Note that baggage allowances may vary for children (depending on the percentage of full adult fare paid) and on domestic and intra-European routes abroad. Check that the tags the airline attaches are correctly coded for your destination.

CHARTER FLIGHTS

By booking a block of seats on a specially arranged flight, charter operators frequently offer travelers bargain airfares. If you do fly on a charter, however, read the contract's fine print carefully. Charter operators can cancel a flight or assess surcharges of 10% of the airfare up to 10 days before departure. You usually must book in advance (no changes are permitted, so invest in trip cancellation insurance); also make your check out to the company's escrow account. For further information, consult the publication *Jax Fax* (397 Post Rd., Darien, CT 06820; phone: 203-655-8746).

DISCOUNTS ON SCHEDULED FLIGHTS

COURIER TRAVEL In return for arranging to accompany some kind of freight, a traveler may pay only a portion of the total airfare and a small registration fee. One agency that matches up would-be couriers with courier companies is *Now Voyager* (74 Varick St., Suite 307, New York, NY 10013; phone: 212-431-1616).

Courier Companies
Courier Travel Service (530 Central Ave., Cedarhurst, NY 11516; phone: 516-763-6898).
Discount Travel International (169 W. 81st St., New York, NY 10024; phone: 212-362-3636; and 940 10th St., Suite 2, Miami Beach, FL 33139; phone: 305-538-1616).

Excaliber International Courier (c/o *Way to Go Travel,* 6679 Sunset Blvd., Hollywood, CA 90028; phone: 213-466-1126).

F.B. On Board Courier Services (10225 Ryan Ave., Suite 103, Dorval, Quebec H9P 1A2, Canada; phone: 514-633-0740).

Halbart Express (147-05 176th St., Jamaica, NY 11434; phone: 718-656-8279).

International Adventures (60 E. 42nd St., New York, NY 10165; phone: 212-599-0577).

Midnight Express (925 W. High Park Blvd., Inglewood, CA 90302; phone: 310-672-1100).

Publications

Insider's Guide to Air Courier Bargains, by Kelly Monaghan (The Intrepid Traveler, PO Box 438, New York, NY 10034; phone: 212-304-2207).

Travel Secrets (PO Box 2325, New York, NY 10108; phone: 212-245-8703).

Travel Unlimited (PO Box 1058, Allston, MA 02134-1058; no phone).

World Courier News (PO Box 77471, San Francisco, CA 94107; no phone).

CONSOLIDATORS AND BUCKET SHOPS These companies buy blocks of tickets from airlines and sell them at a discount to travel agents or to consumers. Since many bucket shops operate on a thin margin, before parting with any money check the company's record with the Better Business Bureau.

Bargain Air (655 Deep Valley Dr., Suite 355, Rolling Hills, CA 90274; phone: 800-347-2345).

Council Charter (205 E. 42nd St., New York, NY 10017; phone: 800-800-8222 or 212-661-0311).

International Adventures (60 E. 42nd St., New York, NY 10165; phone: 212-599-0577).

Travac Tours and Charters (989 Ave. of the Americas, New York, NY 10018; phone: 800-872-8800 or 212-563-3303).

Unitravel (1177 N. Warson Rd., St. Louis, MO 63132; phone: 800-325-2222 or 314-569-0900).

LAST-MINUTE TRAVEL CLUBS For an annual fee, members receive information on imminent trips and other bargain travel opportunities. Despite the names of these clubs, you don't have to wait until literally the last minute to make travel plans.

Discount Travel International (114 Forest Ave., Suite 203, Narberth, PA 19072; phone: 215-668-7184).

Last Minute Travel (1249 Boylston St., Boston, MA 02215; phone: 800-LAST-MIN or 617-267-9800).

> **Moment's Notice** (425 Madison Ave., New York, NY 10017; phone: 212-486-0500, -0501, -0502, or -0503).
>
> **Spur-of-the-Moment Cruises** (411 N. Harbor Blvd., Suite 302, San Pedro, CA 90731; phone: 800-4-CRUISES in California; 800-343-1991 elsewhere in the US; or 310-521-1070).
>
> **Traveler's Advantage** (3033 S. Parker Rd., Suite 900, Aurora, CO 80014; phone: 800-548-1116 or 800-835-8747).
>
> **Vacations to Go** (1502 Augusta, Suite 415, Houston, TX 77057; phone: 713-974-2121 in Texas; 800-338-4962 elsewhere in the US).
>
> **Worldwide Discount Travel Club** (1674 Meridian Ave., Miami Beach, FL 33139; phone: 305-534-2082).

GENERIC AIR TRAVEL These organizations operate much like an ordinary airline standby service, except that they offer seats on not one but several scheduled and charter airlines. One pioneer of generic flights is *Airhitch* (2790 Broadway, Suite 100, New York, NY 10025; phone: 212-864-2000).

BARTERED TRAVEL SOURCES Barter is a common means of exchange between travel suppliers. Bartered travel clubs such as *Travel World Leisure Club* (225 W. 34th St., Suite 909, New York, NY 10122; phone: 800-444-TWLC or 212-239-4855) offer discounts to members for an annual fee.

CONSUMER PROTECTION

Passengers with complaints who are not satisfied with the airline's response can contact the US Department of Transportation (DOT; Consumer Affairs Division, 400 7th St. SW, Room 10405, Washington, DC 20590; phone: 202-366-2220). If you have a complaint against a local travel service, contact the Spanish tourist authorities. Also see *Fly Rights* (Publication #050-000-00513-5; US Government Printing Office, PO Box 371954, Pittsburgh, PA 15250-7954; phone: 202-783-3238).

Traveling by Ship

Your cruise fare usually includes all meals, recreational activities, and entertainment. Shore excursions are available at extra cost, and can be booked in advance or once you're on board. An important factor in the price of a cruise is the location and size of your cabin; for information on ships' layouts and facilities, consult the charts issued by the *Cruise Lines International Association* (*CLIA;* 500 Fifth Ave., Suite 1407, New York, NY 10110; phone: 212-921-0066).

Most cruise ships have a doctor on board, plus medical facilities. The US Public Health Service (PHS) also inspects all passenger vessels calling at US ports; for the most recent summary or a particular inspection report, write to Chief, Vessel Sanitation Program, National Center for Environmental Health (1015 N. America Way, Room 107, Miami, FL 33132; phone: 305-536-4307). For further information, consult *Ocean and Cruise*

News (PO Box 92, Stamford, CT 06904; phone: 203-329-2787). And for a free listing of travel agencies specializing in cruises, contact the *National Association of Cruise Only Agencies* (*NACOA;* PO Box 7209, Freeport, NY 11520; phone: 516-378-8006).

Numerous ferries link the Spanish mainland with the Balearic and Canary islands and with Morocco. Nearly all of them carry both passengers and cars and most routes are in service year-round.

Cruise Lines

Classical Cruises (132 E. 70th St., New York, NY 10021; phone: 800-252-7745 in the US; 800-252-7746 in Canada; or 212-794-3200).

Costa Cruises (80 SW 8th St., Miami, FL 33130; phone: 800-322-8263 for information; 800-462-6782 for reservations).

Crystal Cruises (2121 Ave. of the Stars, Los Angeles, CA 90067; phone: 800-446-6645).

Cunard (555 Fifth Ave., New York, NY 10017; phone: 800-5-CU-NARD or 800-221-4770).

Diamond Cruise (11340 Blondo St., Omaha, NE 68184; phone: 800-333-3333).

Epirotiki Lines (551 Fifth Ave., New York, NY 10176; phone: 212-599-1750 in New York State; 800-221-2470 elsewhere in the US).

Ocean Cruise Lines (6301 NW 5th Way, Suite 4000, Ft. Lauderdale, FL 33309; phone: 800-556-8850).

Odessa America Cruise Company (170 Old Country Rd., Mineola, NY 11501; phone: 800-221-3254 or 516-747-8880).

P&O Cruises (c/o *Express Travel Services,* Empire State Bldg., Suite 7718, 350 Fifth Ave., New York, NY 10118; phone: 800-223-5799 or 212-629-3630).

Princess Cruises (10100 Santa Monica Blvd., Los Angeles, CA 90067; phone: 800-421-0522).

Royal Cruise Line (1 Maritime Plaza, Suite 1400, San Francisco, CA 94111; phone: 800-792-2992 in California; 800-227-4534 elsewhere in the US).

Royal Viking Line (95 Merrick Way, Coral Gables, FL 33134; phone: 800-422-8000).

Seabourn Cruise Line (55 Francisco St., Suite 710, San Francisco, CA 94133; phone: 800-929-9595).

Swan Hellenic Cruises (c/o *Esplanade Tours,* 581 Boylston St., Boston, MA 02116; phone: 800-426-5492 or 617-266-7465).

Ferry Companies

Flebasa (*Fletamentos de Baleares, S.A.;* 1 Edificio Faró, San Antonio, Ibiza 07820, Spain; phone: 71-342871).

Trasmediterránea (2 Calle P. Muñoz Seca, Madrid 28001, Spain; phone: 1-431-0700; or Estación Marítima, Barcelona 08039, Spain; phone: 3-317-4262).

Traveling by Train

The government-owned and -operated *Red Nacional de los Ferrocarriles Españoles (RENFE)*, also known as *Spanish National Railways*, operates an 8,000-mile railway system. *RENFE* trains include the high-speed *Alta Velocidad Español (AVE)*, as well as *Euro City (EC)* and *Intercity (IC)* trains, express trains like the *Talgos* and *Electrotren*, and the slower *"expresos."* Car carrying trains, called *AutoExpresos* in Spain, are another convenience.

Most Spanish trains have both first and second class cars. Meal service ranges from traditional dining cars to vendors dispensing sandwiches and beverages from a cart. Some trains also provide sleeping accommodations, such as *couchettes* (coach seats of a compartment converted to sleeping berths) and *wagons lit*, or sleepers (bedroom compartments providing one to three beds). Baggage often can be checked through to your destination or can be checked overnight at most stations. Travel as light as possible — porters and self-service carts are often scarce.

International and long-distance railway tickets in Spain *must* be purchased from *RENFE* sales offices, which often — but not always — are found at major train stations. Sales offices often are centrally located in towns and cities; auxiliary offices throughout the country offer more limited services. Electronic vending machines dispensing tickets are increasingly common. Domestic and international tickets usually are sold separately. You can buy your rail tickets before leaving the US either from travel agents or from *RENFE*'s North American representative, *Rail Europe* (226-230 Westchester Ave., White Plains, NY 10604; phone: 800-4-EURAIL). *Rail Europe* can make reservations for train trips of 3 hours or more in duration, including overnight excursions. Reservations — which are advisable during the summer and other peak travel periods — can be made up to 2 months prior to the date of travel. Various discount excursion tickets and rail passes also are available, including the Eurailpass, which is good for train travel throughout much of Europe. Note that most rail passes must be purchased before you leave the US. Some special *RENFE* trains provide full-day or weekend sightseeing excursions for tourists. Information and reservations for current excursions can be obtained in Madrid at travel agencies or *RENFE* offices. A company offering packaged rail tours is *Accent on Travel* (112 N. 5th St., Klamath Falls, OR 97601; phone: 503-885-7330 in Oregon; 800-347-0645 elsewhere in the US).

FURTHER INFORMATION

Rail Europe (address above) offers a *Travel Guide*, as well as brochures on the Eurailpass and train travel in Spain. The *Thomas Cook European Timetable*, a compendium of European rail services, is available in bookstores and from the *Forsyth Travel Library* (PO Box 2975, Shawnee Mission, KS 66201-1375; phone: 800-367-7984 or 913-384-3440). Other useful resources include the *Eurail Guide*, by Kathryn Turpin and Marvin Saltz-man (Eurail Guide Annuals, 27540 Pacific Coast Hwy., Malibu, CA 90265) and *Europe by Eurail,* by George Wright Ferguson (Globe Pequot Press, PO Box 833, Old Saybrook, CT 06475; phone: 203-395-0440).

Traveling by Bus

The public bus service in Spain is well developed, but is best for short day trips. Buses go from Madrid to many cities and towns throughout the country. There are bus stations in all major cities, including several in Madrid and Barcelona.

In Spain, the buses are run by a number of privately owned companies, and tickets are purchased in the bus station. Seats cannot be reserved — tickets for a given trip are sold on a first-come, first-served basis at bus stations or (in towns where there are none) at local stores acting as ticket agents. The ticket generally is good only for that ride on that day. Toilet facilities are likely to be provided only on the newer buses on long-distance trips, and air conditioning, though common, is not universal — particularly on rural routes.

Some small regional companies offer bus tours conducted by English-speaking guides; information on these tours often is available from local tourism authorities. In addition, many US tour operators offer more extensive, all-inclusive motorcoach tours. Tour operators offering such packages to Spain are listed below.

Traveling by Car

Driving is the most flexible way to explore Spain. To drive in Spain, a US citizen needs a US driver's license. Although it is not required, an International Driver's Permit (IDP) — available from US branches of the *American Automobile Association (AAA)* — is strongly recommended. Proof of liability insurance also is required and is a standard part of any car rental contract. (To be sure of having the appropriate coverage, let the rental staff know in advance about the national borders you plan to cross.) If buying a car and using it abroad, you must carry an International Insurance Certificate, known as a Green Card (*Carta Verde* in Spain), which can be obtained from your insurance agent or through the *AAA*.

Driving in Spain is on the right side of the road and those coming from the right at intersections have the right of way. Pedestrians, provided they are in marked crosswalks, take precedence over all vehicles. (Unfortunately, such laws are not always observed.) Exceptions include priority roads, marked by a sign with a yellow diamond on it; these have the right of way until the diamond reappears with a black bar and the right of way reverts to those coming from the right. Pictorial direction signs are standardized under the International Roadsign System, and their meanings are indicated by their shapes: Triangular signs for danger; circular signs for instructions; and rectangular signs for information.

Distances are measured in kilometers (1 mile equals 1.6 kilometers; 1 kilometer equals .62 mile) and speeds are registered as kilometers per hour (kph) on the speedometer. In Spanish towns, speed limits usually are 60 kph (about 38 mph). The speed limit is 120 kph (75 mph) on *autopistas,* or toll highways; 100 kph (about 62 mph) on *carreteras nacionales,* or main roads; and 90 kph (56·mph) elsewhere, unless otherwise marked. Pay attention to parking signs in large cities. If you park in a restricted zone, you may return to find a wheel "clamped," which renders the car inoperable and involves a tedious — and costly — process to get it freed. For additional information, consult *Euroad: The Complete Guide to Motoring in Europe* (VLE Ltd., PO Box 444, Ft. Lee, NJ 07024; phone: 201-585-5080).

MAPS

In the US, free maps can be obtained from the Spanish tourist authorities. The best road maps for touring are available from Michelin Guides and Maps (PO Box 3305, Spartanburg, SC 29304-3305; phone: 803-599-0850 in South Carolina; 800-423-0485 elsewhere in the US). Freytag & Berndt maps cover most major destinations throughout Europe; they can be ordered from *Map Link* (25 E. Mason St., Suite 201, Santa Barbara, CA 93101; phone: 805-965-4402). The *American Automobile Association (AAA;* address below) also provides some useful reference sources, including an overall planning map of Europe, regional maps of Spain, the *Travel Guide to Europe,* and *Motoring in Europe.*

AUTOMOBILE CLUBS AND BREAKDOWNS

To protect yourself in case of breakdowns while driving to and through Spain, and for travel information and other benefits, consider joining a reputable automobile club. The largest of these is the *American Automobile Association (AAA;* 1000 AAA Dr., Heathrow, FL 32746-5063; phone: 407-444-7000). Before joining this or any other automobile club, check whether it has reciprocity with Spanish clubs such as the *Federación Española de Automóvil* (67 Av. Menéndez Pelayo, Madrid 28003, Spain; phone: 1-573-5600).

GASOLINE

Gasoline is sold in liters (about 3.7 liters to 1 gallon). Leaded and diesel fuel are more widely available than unleaded fuel.

RENTING A CAR

You can rent a car through a travel agent or international rental firm before leaving home, or from a regional or local company once in Europe. Reserve in advance.

Most car rental companies require a credit card, although some will accept a substantial cash deposit. The minimum age to rent a car is set by the company; some impose special conditions on drivers above a certain age. Electing to pay for collision damage waiver (CDW) protection will add to the cost of renting a car, but releases you from financial liability for the vehicle. Additional costs include drop-off charges or one-way service fees. One way to keep down the cost of car rentals is to deal with a car rental consolidator, such as *Connex International* (phone: 800-333-3949 or 914-739-0066). A national car rental company with offices throughout Spain is *Atesa* (phone: 1-572-0151 or 3-237-8140).

International Car Rental Companies

Auto Europe (phone: 800-223-5555).

Avis (phone: 800-331-1084).

Budget (phone: 800-472-3325).

Dollar Rent A Car (known in Europe as *Eurodollar Rent A Car;* phone: 800-800-4000).

Europe by Car (phone: 212-581-3040 in New York State; 800-223-1516 elsewhere in the US).

European Car Reservations (phone: 800-535-3303).

Foremost Euro-Car (phone: 800-272-3299).

Hertz (phone: 800-654-3001).

Kemwel Group (phone: 800-678-0678).

Meier's World Travel (phone: 800-937-0700).

National (known in Europe as *Europcar;* phone: 800-CAR-EUROPE).

Thrifty (phone: 800-367-2277).

Package Tours

A package is a collection of travel services that can be purchased in a single transaction. Its principal advantages are convenience and economy — the cost is usually lower than that of the same services bought separately. Tour programs generally can be divided into two categories: escorted or locally hosted (with a set itinerary) and independent (usually more flexible).

When considering a package tour, read the brochure *carefully* to determine what is included and other conditions. Check the company's record with the Better Business Bureau. The *United States Tour Operators Association* (*USTOA;* 211 E. 51st St., Suite 12B, New York, NY 10022; phone: 212-944-5727) also can be helpful in determining a package tour operator's reliability. As with charter flights, always make your check out to the company's escrow account.

Many tour operators offer packages focused on special interests such as the arts, nature study, sports, and other recreations. *All Adventure Travel* (PO Box 4307, Boulder, CO 80306; phone: 800-537-4025 or 303-499-1981) represents such specialized packagers; some also are listed in the *Specialty*

Travel Index (305 San Anselmo Ave., Suite 313, San Anselmo, CA 94960; phone: 415-459-4900 in California; 800-442-4922 elsewhere in the US).

Package Tour Operators

Abercrombie & Kent (1520 Kensington Rd., Oak Brook, IL 60521; phone: 708-954-2944 in Illinois; 800-323-7308 elsewhere in the US).

Abreu Tours (317 E. 34th St., New York, NY 10016; phone: 800-223-1580 or 212-532-6550).

Adventure Center (1311 63rd St., Suite 200, Emeryville, CA 94608; phone: 510-654-1879 in northern California; 800-227-8747 elsewhere in the US).

Adventures in Golf (29 Valencia Dr., Nashua, NH 03062; phone: 603-882-8367).

AESU (248 W. Quadrangle, Village of Cross Keys, Baltimore, MD 21210; phone: 800-638-7640 or 410-323-4416).

American Airlines FlyAAway Vacations (phone: 800-832-8383).

American Express Vacations (offices throughout the US; phone: 800-241-1700 or 404-368-5100).

AutoVenture (425 Pike St., Suite 502, Seattle, WA 98101; phone: 800-426-7502 or 206-624-6033).

Bacchants' Pilgrimages (475 Sansome St., Suite 840, San Francisco, CA 94111; phone: 415-981-8518).

Blue Marble Travel (c/o *Odyssey Adventures,* 89 Auburn St., Suite 1199, Portland, ME 04103; phone: 800-544-3216 or 207-878-8650).

Brendan Tours (15137 Califa St., Van Nuys, CA 91411; phone: 800-421-8446 or 818-785-9696).

Butterfield & Robinson (70 Bond St., Suite 300, Toronto, Ontario M5B 1X3, Canada; phone: 800-387-1147 or 416-864-1354).

Caravan Tours (401 N. Michigan Ave., Chicago, IL 60611; phone: 800-CARAVAN or 312-321-9800).

Cavalcade Tours (2200 Fletcher Ave., Ft. Lee, NJ 07024; phone: 800-356-2405 or 201-346-9061).

Continental Grand Destinations (phone: 800-634-5555).

Cycling Through the Centuries (PO Box 877, San Antonio, FL 33576; phone: 800-245-4226 or 904-588-4132).

Dailey-Thorp (330 W. 58th St., New York, NY 10019-1817; phone: 212-307-1555).

Delta's Dream Vacations (phone: 800-872-7786).

DER Tours (11933 Wilshire Blvd., Los Angeles, CA 90025; phone: 800-937-1234).

Equitour (PO Box 807, Dubois, WY 82513; phone: 307-455-3363 in Wyoming; 800-545-0019 elsewhere in the US).

Exodus (9 Weir Rd., London SW2 OLT, England; for information, contact their US representative, *Force 10 Expeditions,* PO Box 34354, Pensacola, FL 32507; phone: 800-922-1491).

Extra Value Travel (683 S. Collier Blvd., Marco Island, FL 33937; phone: 800-336-4668 or 813-394-3384).

Fishing International (PO Box 2132, Santa Rosa, CA 95405; phone: 800-950-4242 or 707-539-3366).

FITS Equestrian (685 Lateen Rd., Solvang, CA 93463; phone: 805-688-9494).

Frontiers International (PO Box 959, 100 Logan Rd., Wexford, PA 15090; phone: 412-935-1577 in Pennsylvania; 800-245-1950 elsewhere in the US).

Globus and Cosmos (5301 S. Federal Circle, Littleton, CO 80123; phone: 800-221-0090 or 800-556-5454).

Golfing Holidays (231 E. Millbrae Ave., Millbrae, CA 94030; phone: 800-652-7847 or 415-697-0230).

Himalayan Travel (112 Prospect St., Stamford, CT 06901; phone: 800-225-2380).

Ibero Travel (69-24 Loubet St., Forest Hills, New York, NY 11375; phone: 800-263-0200).

In Quest of the Classics (316 Mission Ave., Oceanside, CA 92054; phone: 800-227-1393 or 619-721-1123 in California; 800-221-5246 elsewhere in the US).

Insight International Tours (745 Atlantic Ave., Suite 720, Boston, MA 02111; phone: 800-582-8380 or 617-426-6666).

InterGolf (PO Box 500608, Atlanta, GA 31150; phone: 800-468-0051 or 404-518-1250).

ITC Golf Tours (4134 Atlantic Ave., Suite 205, Long Beach, CA 90807; phone: 800-257-4981 or 310-595-6905).

Jet Vacations (1775 Broadway, New York, NY 10019; phone: 800-JET-0999 or 212-247-0999).

Marsans International (19 W. 34th St., Suite 302, New York, NY 10001; phone: 800-777-9110 or 212-239-3880).

Maupintour (PO Box 807, Lawrence, KS 66044; phone: 800-255-4266 or 913-843-1211).

Melia International (c/o *MI Travel,* address below).

MI Travel (450 7th Ave., Suite 1805, New York, NY 10123; phone: 212-967-6565 in New York State; 800-848-2314 elsewhere in the US).

Mountain Travel-Sobek (6420 Fairmount Ave., El Cerrito, CA 94530; phone: 510-527-8100 in California; 800-227-2384 elsewhere in the US).

Olson Travelworld (970 W. 190th St., Suite 425, Torrance, CA 90502; phone: 800-421-2255 or 310-354-2600).

Past Time Tours (800 Larch La., Sacramento, CA 95864-5042; phone: 916-485-8140).

Path Tours (25050 Peachland Ave., Suite 201, Newhall, CA 91321; phone: 800-843-0400 or 805-255-2740).

Perry Golf (8302 Dunwoodie Pl., Suite 305, Atlanta, GA 30350; phone: 800-344-5257 or 404-641-9696).

Petrabax Tours (97-45 Queens Blvd., Suite 600, Rego Park, NY 11374; phone: 800-367-6611 or 718-897-7272).

Plus Ultra Tours (174 7th Ave., New York, NY 10011; phone: 212-242-0393 in New York State; 800-242-0394 elsewhere in the US).

Prospect Music and Art Tours (454-458 Chiswick High Rd., London W4 5TT, England; phone: 44-81-995-2151 or 44-81-995-2163).

Skyline Travel Club (376 New York Ave., Huntington, NY 11743; phone: 516-423-9090 in New York State; 800-645-6198 elsewhere in the US).

Spanish Heritage Tours (116-47 Queens Blvd., Forest Hills, NY 11375; phone: 800-221-2580 or 718-520-1300).

Take-A-Guide (11 Uxbridge St., London W8 7TQ, England; phone: 800-825-4946 in the US).

Thomas Cook (Headquarters: 45 Berkeley St., Piccadilly, London W1A 1EB, England; phone: 44-71-408-4191; main US office: 2 Penn Plaza, 18th Floor, New York, NY 10121; phone: 800-846-6272 or 212-967-4390).

Trafalgar Tours (11 E. 26th St., Suite 1300, New York, NY 10010-1402; phone: 800-854-0103 or 212-689-8977).

Travcoa (PO Box 2630, Newport Beach, CA 92658; phone: 800-992-2004 in California; 800-992-2003 elsewhere in the US; or 710-476-2800).

Travel Concepts (62 Commonwealth Ave., Suite 3, Boston, MA 02116; phone: 617-266-8450).

TWA Getaway Vacations (phone: 800-GETAWAY).

Unitours (8 S. Michigan Ave., Chicago, IL 60603; phone: 800-621-0557 or 312-782-1590).

Wide World of Golf (PO Box 5217, Carmel, CA 93921; phone: 408-624-6667).

Wilderness Travel (801 Allston Way, Berkeley, CA 94710; phone: 800-368-2794 or 510-548-0420).

X.O. Travel Consultants (38 W. 32nd St., Suite 1009, New York, NY 10001; phone: 800-262-9682 or 212-947-5530).

Insurance

The first person with whom you should discuss travel insurance is your own insurance broker. You may discover that the insurance you already carry protects you adequately while traveling and that you need little additional coverage. If you charge travel services, the credit card company also may provide some insurance coverage (and other safeguards).

Types of Travel Insurance

Baggage and personal effects insurance: Protects your bags and their contents in case of damage or theft anytime during your travels.

Personal accident and sickness insurance: Covers cases of illness, injury, or death in an accident while traveling.

Trip cancellation and interruption insurance: Guarantees a refund if you must cancel a trip; may reimburse you for the extra travel costs incurred in catching up with a tour or traveling home early.

Default and/or bankruptcy insurance: Provides coverage in the event of default and/or bankruptcy on the part of the tour operator, airline, or other travel supplier.

Flight insurance: Covers accidental injury or death while flying.

Automobile insurance: Provides collision, theft, property damage, and personal liability protection while driving your own or a rented car.

Combination policies: Include any or all of the above.

Disabled Travelers

Make travel arrangements well in advance. Specify to all services involved the nature of your disability to determine if there are accommodations and facilities that meet your needs. Regularly revised hotel and restaurant guides, such as the *Michelin Red Guide to Spain and Portugal* (Michelin Guides and Maps, PO Box 3305, Spartanburg, SC 29304-3305; phone: 803-599-0850 in South Carolina; 800-423-0485 elsewhere in the US), use a symbol of access (a person in a wheelchair) to point out accommodations suitable for wheelchair-bound guests.

Organizations

ACCENT on Living (PO Box 700, Bloomington, IL 61702; phone: 309-378-2961).

Access: The Foundation for Accessibility by the Disabled (PO Box 356, Malverne, NY 11565; phone: 516-887-5798).

American Foundation for the Blind (15 W. 16th St., New York, NY 10011; phone: 800-232-5463 or 212-620-2147).

Holiday Care Service (2 Old Bank Chambers, Station Rd., Horley, Surrey RH6 9HW, England; phone: 44-293-774535).

Information Center for Individuals with Disabilities (Ft. Point Pl., 1st Floor, 27-43 Wormwood St., Boston, MA 02210; phone: 800-462-5015 in Massachusetts; 617-727-5540 or 617-727-5541 elsewhere in the US; TDD: 617-345-9743).

Mobility International USA (*MIUSA;* PO Box 3551, Eugene, OR 97403; phone: 503-343-1284, both voice and TDD; main office: 228 Borough High St., London SE1 1JX, England; phone: 44-71-403-5688).

National Rehabilitation Information Center (8455 Colesville Rd., Suite 935, Silver Spring, MD 20910; phone: 301-588-9284).

Paralyzed Veterans of America (*PVA;* PVA/ATTS Program, 801 18th St. NW, Washington, DC 20006; phone: 202-872-1300 in Washington, DC; 800-424-8200 elsewhere in the US).

Royal Association for Disability and Rehabilitation (RADAR; 25 Mortimer St., London W1N 8AB, England; phone: 44-71-637-5400).

Society for the Advancement of Travel for the Handicapped (SATH; 347 Fifth Ave., Suite 610, New York, NY 10016; phone: 212-447-7284).

Travel Information Service (MossRehab Hospital, 1200 W. Tabor Rd., Philadelphia, PA 19141-3099; phone: 215-456-9600; TDD: 215-456-9602).

Tripscope (The Courtyard, Evelyn Rd., London W4 5JL, England; phone: 44-81-994-9294).

Publications

Access Travel: A Guide to the Accessibility of Airport Terminals (Consumer Information Center, Dept. 578Z, Pueblo, CO 81009; phone: 719-948-3334).

Air Transportation of Handicapped Persons (Publication #AC-120-32; US Department of Transportation, Distribution Unit, Publications Section, M-443-2, 400 7th St. SW, Washington, DC 20590).

The Diabetic Traveler (PO Box 8223 RW, Stamford, CT 06905; phone: 203-327-5832).

Directory of Travel Agencies for the Disabled and *Travel for the Disabled,* both by Helen Hecker (Twin Peaks Press, PO Box 129, Vancouver, WA 98666; phone: 800-637-CALM or 206-694-2462).

Guide to Traveling with Arthritis (Upjohn Company, PO Box 989, Dearborn, MI 48121).

The Handicapped Driver's Mobility Guide (*American Automobile Association,* 1000 AAA Dr., Heathrow, FL 32746; phone: 407-444-7000).

Handicapped Travel Newsletter (PO Box 269, Athens, TX 75751; phone: 903-677-1260).

Handi-Travel: A Resource Book for Disabled and Elderly Travellers, by Cinnie Noble (*Canadian Rehabilitation Council for the Disabled,* 45 Sheppard Ave. E., Suite 801, Toronto, Ontario M2N 5W9, Canada; phone: 416-250-7490, both voice and TDD).

Incapacitated Passengers Air Travel Guide (*International Air Transport Association,* Publications Sales Department, 2000 Peel St., Montreal, Quebec H3A 2R4, Canada; phone: 514-844-6311).

Ticket to Safe Travel (*American Diabetes Association,* 1660 Duke St., Alexandria, VA 22314; phone: 800-232-3472 or 703-549-1500).

Travel for the Patient with Chronic Obstructive Pulmonary Disease (Dr. Harold Silver, 1601 18th St. NW, Washington, DC 20009; phone: 202-667-0134).

Travel Tips for Hearing-Impaired People (*American Academy of Otolaryngology,* 1 Prince St., Alexandria, VA 22314; phone: 703-836-4444).

Travel Tips for People with Arthritis (*Arthritis Foundation,* 1314 Spring St. NW, Atlanta, GA 30309; phone: 800-283-7800 or 404-872-7100).

Traveling Like Everybody Else: A Practical Guide for Disabled Travel-

ers, by Jacqueline Freedman and Susan Gersten (Modan Publishing, PO Box 1202, Bellmore, NY 11710; phone: 516-679-1380).

Package Tour Operators

Accessible Journeys (35 W. Sellers Ave., Ridley Park, PA 19078; phone: 215-521-0339).

Accessible Tours/Directions Unlimited (Lois Bonnani, 720 N. Bedford Rd., Bedford Hills, NY 10507; phone: 800-533-5343 or 914-241-1700).

Beehive Business and Leisure Travel (1130 W. Center St., N. Salt Lake, UT 84054; phone: 800-777-5727 or 801-292-4445).

Classic Travel Service (8 W. 40th St., New York, NY 10018; phone: 212-869-2560 in New York State; 800-247-0909 elsewhere in the US).

Dialysis at Sea Cruises (611 Barry Pl., Indian Rocks Beach, FL 34635; phone: 800-775-1333 or 813-596-4614).

Evergreen Travel Service (4114 198th St. SW, Suite 13, Lynnwood, WA 98036-6742; phone: 800-435-2288 or 206-776-1184).

Flying Wheels Travel (143 W. Bridge St., PO Box 382, Owatonna, MN 55060; phone: 800-535-6790 or 507-451-5005).

Good Neighbor Travel Service (124 S. Main St., Viroqua, WI 54665; phone: 608-637-2128).

The Guided Tour (7900 Old York Rd., Suite 114B, Elkins Park, PA 19117-2339; phone: 800-783-5841 or 215-782-1370).

Hinsdale Travel (201 E. Ogden Ave., Hinsdale, IL 60521; phone: 708-325-1335 or 708-469-7349).

MedEscort International (ABE International Airport, PO Box 8766, Allentown, PA 18105; phone: 800-255-7182 or 215-791-3111).

Prestige World Travel (5710-X High Point Rd., Greensboro, NC 27407; phone: 800-476-7737 or 919-292-6690).

Sprout (893 Amsterdam Ave., New York, NY 10025; phone: 212-222-9575).

Weston Travel Agency (134 N. Cass Ave., PO Box 1050, Westmont, IL 60559; phone: 708-968-2513 in Illinois; 800-633-3725 elsewhere in the US).

Single Travelers

The travel industry is not very fair to people who vacation by themselves—they often end up paying more than those traveling in pairs. Services catering to singles match travel companions, offer travel arrangements with shared accommodations, and provide useful information and discounts. Also consult publications such as *Going Solo* (Doerfer Communications, PO Box 123, Apalachicola, FL 32329; phone: 904-653-8848) and *Traveling on Your Own,* by Eleanor Berman (Random House, Order Dept., 400 Hahn Rd., Westminster, MD 21157; phone: 800-733-3000).

Organizations and Companies

Club Europa (802 W. Oregon St., Urbana, IL 61801; phone: 800-331-1882 or 217-344-5863).

Contiki Holidays (300 Plaza Alicante, Suite 900, Garden Grove, CA 92640; phone: 800-466-0610 or 714-740-0808).

Gallivanting (515 E. 79th St., Suite 20F, New York, NY 10021; phone: 800-933-9699 or 212-988-0617).

Globus and Cosmos (5301 S. Federal Circle, Littleton, CO 80123; phone: 800-221-0090 or 800-556-5454).

Insight International Tours (745 Atlantic Ave., Suite 720, Boston, MA 02111; phone: 800-582-8380 or 617-426-6666).

Jane's International and Sophisticated Women Travelers (2603 Bath Ave., Brooklyn, NY 11214; phone: 718-266-2045).

Marion Smith Singles (611 Prescott Pl., N. Woodmere, NY 11581; phone: 516-791-4852, 516-791-4865, or 212-944-2112).

Partners-in-Travel (11660 Chenault St., Suite 119, Los Angeles, CA 90049; phone: 310-476-4869).

Singles in Motion (545 W. 236th St., Riverdale, NY 10463; phone: 718-884-4464).

Singleworld (401 Theodore Fremd Ave., Rye, NY 10580; phone: 800-223-6490 or 914-967-3334).

Solo Flights (63 High Noon Rd., Weston, CT 06883; phone: 203-226-9993).

Suddenly Singles Tours (161 Dreiser Loop, Bronx, NY 10475; phone: 718-379-8800 in New York City; 800-859-8396 elsewhere in the US).

Travel Companion Exchange (PO Box 833, Amityville, NY 11701; phone: 516-454-0880).

Travel Companions (Atrium Financial Center, 1515 N. Federal Hwy., Suite 300, Boca Raton, FL 33432; phone: 800-383-7211 or 407-393-6448).

Travel in Two's (239 N. Broadway, Suite 3, N. Tarrytown, NY 10591; phone: 914-631-8301 in New York State; 800-692-5252 elsewhere in the US).

Older Travelers

Special discounts and more free time are just two factors that have given older travelers a chance to see the world at affordable prices. Many travel suppliers offer senior discounts — sometimes only to members of certain senior citizen organizations, which provide other benefits. Prepare your itinerary with one eye on your own physical condition and the other on a topographical map, and remember that it's easy to overdo when traveling.

Publications

Going Abroad: 101 Tips for Mature Travelers (*Grand Circle Travel,* 347 Congress St., Boston, MA 02210; phone: 800-221-2610 or 617-350-7500).

The Mature Traveler (GEM Publishing Group, PO Box 50820, Reno, NV 89513-0820; phone: 702-786-7419).

Take a Camel to Lunch and Other Adventures for Mature Travelers, by Nancy O'Connell (Bristol Publishing Enterprises, PO Box 1737, San Leandro, CA 94577; phone: 510-895-4461 in California; 800-346-4889 elsewhere in the US).

Travel Tips for Older Americans (Publication #044-000-02270-2; Superintendent of Documents, US Government Printing Office, PO Box 371954, Pittsburgh, PA 15250-7954; phone: 202-783-3238).

Unbelievably Good Deals & Great Adventures That You Absolutely Can't Get Unless You're Over 50, by Joan Rattner Heilman (Contemporary Books, 180 N. Michigan Ave., Chicago, IL 60601; phone: 312-782-9181).

Organizations

American Association of Retired Persons (*AARP;* 601 E St. NW, Washington, DC 20049; phone: 202-434-2277).

Golden Companions (PO Box 754, Pullman, WA 99163-0754; phone: 208-858-2183).

Mature Outlook (Customer Service Center, 6001 N. Clark St., Chicago, IL 60660; phone: 800-336-6330).

National Council of Senior Citizens (1331 F St. NW, Washington, DC 20004; phone: 202-347-8800).

Package Tour Operators

Elderhostel (PO Box 1959, Wakefield, MA 01880-5959; phone: 617-426-7788).

Evergreen Travel Service (4114 198th St. SW, Suite 13, Lynnwood, WA 98036-6742; phone: 800-435-2288 or 206-776-1184).

Gadabout Tours (700 E. Tahquitz Canyon Way, Palm Springs, CA 92262; phone: 800-952-5068 or 619-325-5556).

Grand Circle Travel (347 Congress St., Boston, MA 02210; phone: 800-221-2610 or 617-350-7500).

Grandtravel (6900 Wisconsin Ave., Suite 706, Chevy Chase, MD 20815; phone: 800-247-7651 or 301-986-0790).

Insight International Tours (745 Atlantic Ave., Suite 720, Boston, MA 02111; phone: 800-582-8380 or 617-426-6666).

Interhostel (UNH Division of Continuing Education, 6 Garrison Ave., Durham, NH 03824; phone: 800-733-9753 or 603-862-1147).

OmniTours (104 Wilmont Rd., Deerfield, IL 60015; phone: 800-962-0060 or 708-374-0088).

Saga International Holidays (222 Berkeley St., Boston, MA 0211€
phone: 800-343-0273 or 617-262-2262).

Money Matters

The basic unit of Spanish currency is the *peseta* (abbreviated pta.). It i
distributed in coin denominations of 1, 5, 10, 25, 50, 100, 200, and 50
pesetas. Paper money is issued in bills of 100, 200, 500, 1,000, 2,000, 5,000
and 10,000 pesetas.

Exchange rates are posted in international newspapers such as th
International Herald Tribune. Foreign currency information and relate
services are provided by banks and companies such as *Thomas Cook
Foreign Exchange* (for the nearest location, call 800-621-0666 or 312-236
0042), *Harold Reuter and Company* (200 Park Ave., Suite 332E, New
York, NY 10166; phone: 212-661-0826), and *Ruesch International* (for the
nearest location, call 800-424-2923 or 202-408-1200). In Spain, you wil
find the official rate of exchange posted in banks, airports, money exchange houses, hotels, and some shops. Since you will get more pesetas for
your US dollar at banks and money exchanges, don't change more than
$10 for foreign currency at other commercial establishments. Ask how
much commission you're being charged and the exchange rate, and don't
buy money on the black market (it may be counterfeit). Estimate your
needs carefully; if you overbuy, you lose twice — buying and selling back.

TRAVELER'S CHECKS AND CREDIT CARDS

It's wise to carry traveler's checks while on the road, since they are replace-
able if stolen or lost. You can buy traveler's checks at banks and some are
available by mail or phone. Although most major credit cards enjoy wide
domestic and international acceptance, not every hotel, restaurant, or
shop in Spain accepts all (or in some cases any) credit cards. (Some cards
may be issued under different names in Europe; for example, *MasterCard*
may go under the name *Access* or *Eurocard,* and *Visa* often is called *Carte
Bleue.*) When making purchases with a credit card, note that the rate of
exchange depends on when the charge is processed; most credit card
companies charge a 1% fee for converting foreign currency charges. Keep
a separate list of all traveler's checks (noting those that you have cashed)
and the names and numbers of your credit cards. Both traveler's check and
credit card companies have international numbers to call for information
or in the event of loss or theft.

CASH MACHINES

Automated teller machines (ATMs) are increasingly common worldwide.
Most banks participate in one of the international ATM networks; card-
holders can withdraw cash from any machine in the same network using
either a "bank" card or, in some cases, a credit card. At the time of this

writing, most ATMs belong to the *CIRRUS* or *PLUS* network. For further information, ask at your bank branch.

;ENDING MONEY ABROAD

Should the need arise, it is possible to have money sent to you via the services provided by *American Express* (*MoneyGram;* phone: 800-926-9400 or 800-666-3997 for information; 800-866-8800 for money transfers) or *Western Union Financial Services* (phone: 800-325-4176). If you are down to your last cent and have no other way to obtain cash, the nearest US Consulate will let you call home to set these matters in motion.

Accommodations

For specific information on hotels, resorts, and other selected accommodations see *Best in Town* in THE CITIES, *Checking In* in DIRECTIONS, and sections throughout DIVERSIONS.

?ARADORES

This network of state-owned inns consists of converted palaces, castles, convents, and other historic structures, as well as more modern–but nevertheless colorful — establishments, from mountain chalets to houses in the tile-roofed, whitewashed style of an Andalusian village. All are set in picturesque locations and have restaurants that specialize in regional cuisine. Reservations are strongly recommended and can be made through travel agents or *Marketing Ahead* (433 Fifth Ave., New York, NY 10016; phone: 212-686-9213).

RELAIS & CHÂTEAUX

Although most members of this association are in France, the *Relais & Châteaux* association, which consists of two groups of members–*Relais & Châteaux* (hotels and other accommodations) and *Relais Gourmands* (restaurants) — has grown to include establishments in numerous countries. Currently, there are about 12 members in Spain; all maintain very high standards in order to retain their memberships, as they are reviewed annually. An illustrated catalogue of properties is available from *Relais & Châteaux* (11 E. 44th St., Suite 707, New York, NY 10017; phone: 212-856-0115).

RENTAL OPTIONS

An attractive accommodations alternative for the visitor content to stay in one spot is to rent one of the numerous properties available throughout Spain. For a family or group, the per-person cost can be reasonable. To have your pick of the properties available, make inquiries at least 6 months in advance. The *Worldwide Home Rental Guide* (369 Montezuma, Suite 297, Santa Fe, NM 87501; phone: 505-984-7080) lists rental properties and managing agencies.

Rental Property Agents

At Home Abroad (405 E. 56th St., Suite 6H, New York, NY 10022-2466; phone: 212-421-9165).

Europa-Let (92 N. Main St., Ashland, OR 97520; phone: 800-462-4486 or 503-482-5806).

Hideaways International (PO Box 4433, Portsmouth, NH 03802-4433, phone: 800-843-4433 or 603-430-4433).

Interhome (124 Little Falls Rd., Fairfield, NJ 07004; phone: 201-882-6864).

International Lodging Corp. (300 1st Ave., Suite 7C, New York, NY 10009; phone: 212-228-5900).

Rent a Home International (7200 34th Ave. NW, Seattle, WA 98117; phone: 206-789-9377).

Rent a Vacation Everywhere (*RAVE;* 383 Park Ave., Rochester, NY 14607; phone: 716-256-0760).

VHR Worldwide (235 Kensington Ave., Norwood, NJ 07648; phone: 201-767-9393 in New Jersey; 800-633-3284 elsewhere in the US).

Villas International (605 Market St., Suite 510, San Francisco, CA 94105; phone: 800-221-2260 or 415-281-0910).

HOME EXCHANGES

For comfortable, reasonable living quarters with amenities that no hotel could possibly offer, consider trading homes with someone abroad. The following companies provide information on exchanges:

Home Base Holidays (7 Park Ave., London N13 5PG, England; phone: 44-81-886-8752).

Intervac US/International Home Exchange (PO Box 590504, San Francisco, CA 94159; phone: 800-756-HOME or 415-435-3497).

Loan-A-Home (2 Park La., Apt. 6E, Mt. Vernon, NY 10552; phone: 914-664-7640).

Vacation Exchange Club (PO Box 650, Key West, FL 33041; phone: 800-638-3841 or 305-294-3720).

Worldwide Home Exchange Club (138 Brompton Rd., London SW3 1HY, England; phone: 44-71-589-6055; or 806 Brantford Ave., Silver Spring, MD 20904; phone: 301-680-8950).

HOME STAYS

The *United States Servas Committee* (11 John St., Room 407, New York, NY 10038; phone: 212-267-0252) maintains a list of hosts throughout the world willing to accommodate visitors free of charge. The aim of this nonprofit cultural program is to promote international understanding and peace, and *Servas* emphasizes that member travelers should be interested mainly in their hosts, not in sightseeing, during their stays.

Time Zones

Spain is in the Greenwich Plus 1 time zone, often called Central European Time, which means the time is 6 hours later than it is in east coast US cities. The time in the Canary Islands is 1 hour earlier than on the mainland. Spain moves its clocks ahead an hour in late spring and an hour back in the fall, although the exact dates of the changes are different from those observed in the US. Spanish and other European timetables use a 24-hour clock to denote arrival and departure times, which means that hours are expressed sequentially from 1 AM.

Business Hours

Throughout Spain, most businesses and shops are open Mondays through Fridays from 9 AM to 1 or 2 PM, and then from 3 or 4 PM until 7 or 8 PM. Many shops also are open on Saturdays from 9 AM to 1 PM. In small towns and villages, shops may close on a weekday at 1 PM; others may skip the early closing and simply not open on Mondays or another day of the week. Larger stores in shopping centers generally stay open through midday and may close as late as 9 PM.

In Spain, weekday banking hours are from 8:30 or 9 AM to 2 PM.. Some banks may be open on Saturdays from 9 AM until 1 PM; Saturday hours are less common during the summer. Major airport banks may be open 7 days a week.

Holidays

In Spain, the public holidays are as follows:

New Year's Day (January 1)
Epiphany (January 6)
Good Friday (April 1)
Labor Day or *May Day* (May 1)
Assumption Day (August 15)
Spain's National Day (October 12)
Constitution Day (December 6)
Immaculate Conception (December 8)
Christmas Day (December 25)

Note that *Corpus Christi* (June 5, this year) no longer is an official public holiday in Spain.

Mail

Most post offices in Spain are open weekdays from 8 or 9 AM to 2 PM and from 5 PM to 9 PM. Some branches also are open on Saturdays from 9 AM to 12:30 or 1 PM. Stamps *(sellos)* can be bought at post offices and at authorized tobacconists *(estancos)*. Letters can be deposited in mail boxes on the street (these are mustard yellow colored, with a red stripe), but it is better to mail letters (and certainly packages) directly from post offices. If your correspondence is especially important, you may want to send it via one of the international courier services, such as *Federal Express* or *DHL Worldwide Express*.

You can have mail sent to you care of your hotel (marked "Guest Mail, Hold for Arrival") or to a post office (c/o *Lista de Correos,* the Spanish equivalent of "General Delivery"). *American Express* offices also will hold mail for customers ("c/o Client Letter Service"); information is provided in their pamphlet *Travelers' Companion.* US Embassies and Consulates abroad will hold mail for US citizens *only* in emergency situations.

Telephone

Direct dialing and other familiar services are all available in Spain. The number of digits varies somewhat within the country (generally 7 digits in major cities and 6 digits elsewhere in Spain). The procedure for calling Spain from the US is to dial 011 (the international access code) + 34 (the country code) + the area code (if you don't know this, ask the international operator) + the local number. To call the US from Spain, dial 07 (the international access code) + 1 (the US country code) + the US area code + the local number. To make a call between Spanish cities, dial 9 + the area code + the local number. To call a number within the same area code, just dial the local number.

Public telephones are widely available. In metropolitan areas, long distance calls also can be made from offices of *Telefónica,* Spain's national telephone company. You can use a telephone company credit card number on any phone, but pay phones that take special phone cards are increasingly common. Phone cards are sold at post offices and at *Telefónica* branch offices.

Long-distance telephone services that help you avoid the surcharges that hotels routinely add to phone bills are provided by *American Telephone and Telegraph (AT&T Communications,* International Information Service, 635 Grant St., Pittsburgh, PA 15219; phone: 800-874-4000), *MCI* (323 3rd St. SE, Cedar Rapids, IA 52401; phone: 800-444-3333), *Metromedia Communications Corp.* (1 International Center, 100 NE Loop 410, San Antonio, TX 78216; phone: 800-275-0200), and *Sprint* (offices throughout the US; phone: 800-877-4000). Some hotels still may charge a fee for line usage.

AT&T's *Language Line Service* (phone: 800-752-6096) provides interpretive services for telephone communications in Spanish. Also useful are the *AT&T 800 Travel Directory* (available at *AT&T Phone Centers* or by calling 800-426-8686), the *Toll-Free Travel & Vacation Information Directory* (Pilot Books, 103 Cooper St., Babylon, NY 11702; phone: 516-422-

2225), and *The Phone Booklet* (*Scott American Corporation*, PO Box 88, W. Redding, CT 06896; phone: 203-938-2955).

Important Phone Numbers
  Long-distance operator (calls within Spain): the area code + 003.
  International operator: 008 for calls within Europe; 005 for non-European calls.
  Local and countrywide information: 003.
  Emergency assistance: 091.

Electricity

Like most other European countries, Spain runs on 220-volt, 50-cycle alternating current (AC). Thus, travelers from the US will need electrical converters to operate the appliances they use at home, or dual-voltage appliances, which can be switched from one voltage standard to another. (Some large tourist hotels may offer 110-volt current or may have converters available.) You also will need a plug adapter set to deal with the different plug configurations found in Spain.

Staying Healthy

For information on current health conditions, call the Centers for Disease Control and Prevention's *International Health Requirements and Recommendations Information Hotline:* 404-332-4559.

Travelers to Spain — and to Western Europe in general — do not face the same health risks entailed in traveling to many other destinations around the world. Tap water generally is clean and potable in metropolitan and tourist areas throughout Spain. Ask if the water is meant for drinking, but if you're at all unsure, bottled water is readily available in stores. Do not drink water from freshwater streams, rivers, or pools, as it may be contaminated. Milk is pasteurized throughout Spain, and dairy products are safe to eat, as are fruit, vegetables, meat, poultry, and fish. Because of Mediterranean pollution, however, all seafood should be eaten cooked, and make sure it is *fresh,* particularly in the heat of the summer, when inadequate refrigeration is an additional concern.

Spain is famous for its beaches, but it's important to remember that the sea can be treacherous. When you are swimming, be careful of the undertow (a current running back down the beach after a wave has washed ashore), which can knock you down, and riptides (currents running against the tide), which can pull you out to sea. If you see a shark, swim away quietly and smoothly. Also beware of eels, Portuguese man-of-war (and other jellyfish), sea urchins, and razor-sharp coral reefs — although Spain's coral reefs are not extensive. Though rare, bites from snakes, spiders, and — in southern Spain — the occasional scorpion can be serious and should be treated immediately.

Spain has socialized medicine, and medical care is free (or relatively inexpensive) for Spanish citizens, but this does not apply to travelers from the US. There are both public and private hospitals. *Policlínicas,* or clinics, are for less serious medical matters; however, the staff may not speak English, and you generally need an appointment. Ask at your hotel for the house physician or for help in reaching a doctor or contact the US Consulate.

There should be no problem finding a 24-hour drugstore in any major Spanish city. Each pharmacy is part of a local network, so that there always should be a drugstore somewhere that is open. Closed pharmacies often have a sign in the window that provides the location of a pharmacy that is open — the name and address follow the words *farmacias du servicos.* A call to a local hospital also may produce this information.

In an emergency: Go directly to the emergency room of the nearest hospital, dial the emergency number given above, or call an operator for assistance.

Additional Resources

International Association of Medical Assistance to Travelers (*IAMAT;* 417 Center St., Lewiston, NY 14092; phone: 716-754-4883).

International Health Care Service (440 E. 69th St., New York, NY 10021; phone: 212-746-1601).

International SOS Assistance (PO Box 11568, Philadelphia, PA 19116; phone: 800-523-8930 or 215-244-1500).

Medic Alert Foundation (2323 Colorado Ave., Turlock, CA 95380; phone: 800-ID-ALERT or 209-668-3333).

TravMed (PO Box 10623, Baltimore, MD 21285-0623; phone: 800-732-5309 or 410-296-5225).

Consular Services

The American Services section of the US Consulate is a vital source of assistance and advice for US citizens abroad. If you are injured or become seriously ill, the Consulate can direct you to sources of medical attention and notify your relatives. If you become involved in a dispute that could lead to legal action, the Consulate is the place to turn. In cases of natural disasters or civil unrest, Consulates handle the evacuation of US citizens if necessary.

The US Embassy is located at 75 Calle Serrano, Madrid 28006, Spain (phone: 1-577-4000). There are two US Consulates, one at 23-25 Paseo Reina Elisenda, Barcelona 08034, Spain (phone: 3-280-2227) and the other at 11-3 Lehendakari Agirre, Bilbao 48014, Spain (phone: 4-475-8300).

The US State Department operates a 24-hour *Citizens' Emergency Center* travel advisory hotline (phone: 202-647-5225). **In an emergency, call 202-647-4000 and ask for the duty officer.**

Entry Requirements and Customs Regulations

ENTERING SPAIN

A valid US passport is the only document a US citizen needs to enter Spain (as well as the nearby principality of Andorra) for a stay of up to 3 months as a tourist. Visas are required for study, residency, or work, and are good for up to 1 year. US citizens should inquire at the Spanish Embassy or the nearest Spanish Consulate well in advance of a proposed trip. Proof of substantial means of independent financial support during the stay is pertinent to the acceptance of any long-term–stay application.

You are allowed to enter Spain with the following duty-free: 200 cigarettes, 50 cigars, or 250 grams of tobacco, 1 bottle of wine, and 1 bottle of liquor. Personal effects and sports equipment appropriate for a pleasure trip also are allowed.

RETURNING TO THE US

You must declare to the US Customs official at the point of entry everything you have acquired in Spain. The standard duty-free allowance for US citizens is $400; if your trip is shorter than 48 continuous hours, or you have been out of the US within 30 days, it is cut to $25. Families traveling together may make a joint declaration. Antiques (at least 100 years old) and paintings or drawings done entirely by hand are duty-free.

A flat 10% duty is assessed on the next $1,000 worth of merchandise; additional items are taxed at a variety of rates (see *Tariff Schedules of the United States* in a library or any US Customs Service office). With the exception of gifts valued at $50 or less sent directly to the recipient, items shipped home are dutiable. Some articles are duty-free only up to certain limits. The $400 allowance includes 1 carton of (200) cigarettes, 100 cigars (not Cuban), and 1 liter of liquor or wine (for those over 21); the $25 allowance includes 10 cigars, 50 cigarettes, and 4 ounces of perfume. To avoid paying duty unnecessarily, before your trip, register the serial numbers of any expensive equipment you are bringing along with US Customs.

Forbidden imports include articles made of the furs or hides of animals on the endangered species list. In addition, you must obtain a permit from the Ministerio de Cultura, Subdirección General de Protección del Patrimonio Histórico (Plaza del Rey, Madrid, Spain 28004; phone: 1-532-5089) to take archeological finds or other original artifacts out of Spain.

For further information, consult *Know Before You Go; International Mail Imports; Travelers' Tips on Bringing Food, Plant, and Animal Products into the United States; Importing a Car; GSP and the Traveler; Pocket Hints; Currency Reporting;* and *Pets, Wildlife, US Customs;* all available from the US Customs Service (PO Box 7407, Washington, DC 20044). For tape-recorded information on travel-related topics, call 202-927-2095 from any touch-tone phone.

DUTY-FREE SHOPS AND VALUE ADDED TAX Located in international airports, duty-free shops provide bargains on the purchase of foreign goods. But beware: Not all foreign goods are automatically less expensive. You *can* get a good deal on some items, but know what they cost elsewhere.

Value Added Tax (VAT) — called *IVA* in Spain and *IVT* in the Canary Islands — is a tax added to the purchase price of most goods and services, and visitors usually are entitled to a refund. For information about minimum purchase requirements and refund procedures, contact the Spanish Tourist authorities.

For Further Information

In the US, branches of the **National Tourist Office of Spain** are the best sources of travel information. Offices generally are open on weekdays, during normal business hours.

National Tourist Offices of Spain

California: San Vincente Plaza Bldg., 8383 Wilshire Blvd., Suite 960, Beverly Hills, CA 90211 (phone: 213-658-7188).

Florida: 1221 Brickell Ave., Suite 1850, Miami, FL 33131 (phone: 305-358-1992).

Illinois: Water Tower Place, 845 N. Michigan Ave., Suite 915E, Chicago, IL 60611 (phone: 312-642-1992).

New York: 665 Fifth Ave., New York, NY 10022 (phone: 212-759-8822).

Useful Words
and Phrases

Useful Words and Phrases

Unlike the French, who tend to be a bit brusque if you don't speak their language perfectly, the Spanish do not expect you to speak their native tongue, but appreciate your efforts when you try. In many circumstances, you won't have to, because the staffs at most hotels, tourist attractions, and museums, as well as at a fair number of restaurants, speak serviceable English, which they are eager to use. Off the beaten path, however, you will find at least a rudimentary knowledge of Spanish very helpful. Don't be afraid of misplaced accents or misconjugated verbs. Most people will do their best to understand you and will make every effort to be understood.

Although there are several languages spoken throughout Spain, including *Gallego* (in the Galician region), *Catalan* (in Catalonia), and *Euskera* (in the Basque country), the majority of the population is fluent in the most common language, Castilian Spanish. The spelling of Castilian Spanish is a very reliable guide to pronunciation, with only some minor dialect variations.

You also might consider taking a course in Spanish before you go. Language courses are offered at most adult education and community colleges. *Berlitz,* among others, has a series of teach-yourself language courses on audiocassette tapes. They are available for $15.95 from Macmillan Publishing Co., 100 Front St., Riverside, NJ 08075 (phone: 800-257-5755).

The list below of commonly used words and phrases can help get you started.

Greetings and Everyday Expressions

Good morning! (also, Good day)	*Buenos días!*
Good afternoon/evening (when arriving)	*Buenas tardes/noches*
Hello	*Hola*
How are you?	*Cómo está usted?*
Pleased to meet you. (How do you do?)	*Mucho gusto en conocerle.*
Good-bye	*Adiós*
So long	*Hasta luego*
Goodnight (when leaving)	*Buenas noches*
Yes	*Sí*
No	*No*

Please	*Por favor*
Thank you	*Gracias*
You're welcome.	*De nada.*
I beg your pardon. (Excuse me.)	*Perdón.*
I'm sorry.	*Lo siento.*
It doesn't matter.	*No importa.*
I don't speak Spanish.	*No hablo español.*
Do you speak English?	*Habla usted inglés?*
I don't understand.	*No comprendo.*
Do you understand?	*Comprende?/Entiende?*
My name is . . .	*Me llamo . . .*
What is your name?	*Cómo se llama?*

miss	*señorita*
madame	*señora* (married)
	doña (unmarried)
mister	*señor*

open	*abierto/a*
closed	*cerrado/a*
entrance	*entrada*
exit	*salida*
push	*empujar*
pull	*tirar*
today	*hoy*
tomorrow	*mañana*
yesterday	*ayer*

Checking In

I have a reservation.	*He hecho una reserva.*
I would like . . .	*Quisiera . . .*
a single room	*una habitación sencilla*
a double room	*una habitación doble*
a quiet room	*una habitación tranquila*
with bath	*con baño*
with shower	*con ducha*
with a sea view	*con vista al mar*
with air conditioning	*con aire acondicionado*
with balcony	*con balcón*
overnight only	*sólo una noche*
a few days	*algunos días*
a week (at least)	*una semana (por lo menos)*
with full board	*con pensión completa*
with half board	*con media pensión*

| Does that price include . . . | *Está incluido en el precio . . .* |
| breakfast? | *el desayuno?* |

taxes?	*los impuestos?*
VAT (Value Added Tax)?	*IVA?*
Do you accept traveler's checks?	*Acepta usted cheques de viajero?*
Do you accept credit cards?	*Acepta tarjetas de crédito?*
It doesn't work.	*No funciona.*

Eating Out

ashtray	*un cenicero*
(extra) chair	*una silla (adicional)*
table	*una mesa*
bottle	*una botella*
cup	*una taza*
plate	*un plato*
fork	*un tenedor*
knife	*un cuchillo*
spoon	*una cuchara*
napkin	*una servilleta*
hot chocolate (cocoa)	*un chocolate caliente*
black coffee	*un café solo*
coffee with milk	*café con leche*
cream	*crema*
milk	*leche*
tea	*un té*
fruit juice	*un zumo de fruta*
lemonade	*una limonada*
water	*agua*
mineral water	*agua mineral*
(carbonated)	*(con gas)*
(non-carbonated)	*(sin gas)*
orangeade	*una naranjada*
beer	*una cerveza*
port	*oporto*
sherry	*jerez*
red wine	*vino tinto*
white wine	*vino blanco*
cold	*frío/a*
hot	*caliente*
sweet	*dulce*
(very) dry	*(muy) seco/a*
bread	*pan*
butter	*mantequilla*
bacon	*tocino*
eggs	*huevos*

hard-boiled	huevos duros
soft-boiled	huevos pasados por agua
fried	huevos fritos
scrambled	huevos revueltos
omelette	tortilla

honey	miel
jam/marmalade	mermelada
orange juice	zumo de naranja
pepper	pimienta
salt	sal
sugar	azúcar

| Waiter! | Camarero! |

I would like	Quisiera
a glass of	un vaso de
a bottle of	una botella de
a half bottle of	una media botella de
a carafe of	una garrafa de
a liter of	un litro de

The check, please.	La cuenta, por favor.
Is a service charge included?	Está el servicio incluido?
I think there is a mistake in the bill.	Creo que hay un error en la cuenta.

Shopping

bakery	la panadería
bookstore	la librería
butcher shop	la carnicería
camera shop	la tienda de fotografía
delicatessen	fambrería
department store	almacén
grocery	la tienda de comestibles
jewelry store	la joyería
newsstand	el quiosco de periódicos
pastry shop	la pastelería
perfume (and cosmetics) store	perfumería
pharmacy/drugstore	la farmacia
shoestore	la zapatería
supermarket	el supermercado
tobacconist	el estanco

inexpensive	barato/a
expensive	caro/a
large	grande
larger	más grande

too large	demasiado grande
small	pequeño/a
smaller	más pequeño/a
too small	demasiado pequeño/a
long	largo/a
short	corto/a
old	viejo/a
new	nuevo/a
used	usado/a
handmade	hecho/a a la mano
Is it machine washable?	Es lavable a máquina?
How much does it cost?	Cuánto cuesta esto?
What is it made of?	De qué está hecho?
camel's hair	pelo de camello
cotton	algodón
corduroy	pana
filigree	filigrana
lace	encaje
leather	cuero
linen	lino
silk	seda
suede	ante
synthetic	sintético/a
wool	lana
brass	latón
copper	cobre
gold	oro
gold plate	lámina de oro
silver	plata
silver plate	plata chapada
stainless steel	acero inoxidable
tile	azulejo
wood	madera

Colors

beige	beige
black	negro/a
blue	azul
brown	moreno/a
green	verde
gray	gris
orange	naranjo/a
pink	roso/a
purple	morado/a
red	rojo/a

white	*blanco/a*
yellow	*amarillo/a*
dark	*oscuro/a*
light	*claro/a*

Getting Around

north	*norte*
south	*sur*
east	*este*
west	*oeste*
right	*derecho/a*
left	*izquierdo/a*
Go straight ahead.	*Siga todo derecho.*
far	*lejos*
near	*cerca*
gas station	*la gasolinera*
train station	*la estación de ferrocarril*
bus stop	*la parada de autobuses*
subway station	*la estación de metro*
airport	*el aeropuerto*
tourist information	*información turística*
map	*el mapa*
one-way ticket	*un billete de ida*
round-trip ticket	*un billete de ida y vuelta*
track	*la vía*
platform	*el andén*
first class	*primera clase*
second class	*segunda clase*
smoking	*fumar*
no smoking	*no fumadores*
gasoline	*gasolina*
regular leaded	*gasolina normal*
super leaded	*gasolina super*
extra leaded	*gasolina extra*
unleaded	*gasolina sin plomo*
diesel	*gasóleo*
Fill it up, please.	*Llénelo, por favor.*
oil	*el aceite*
tires	*los neumáticos*
Where is . . . ?	*Dónde está . . . ?*
Where are . . . ?	*Dónde están . . . ?*
How far is it from here to . . . ?	*Qué distancia hay desde aquí hasta . . . ?*

Does this train go to . . .?	*Va este tren a . . .?*
Does this bus go to . . . ?	*Va este autobús a . . . ?*
What time does it leave?	*A qué hora sale?*

Danger	*Peligro*
Caution	*Precaución*
Detour	*Desvío*
Do Not Enter	*Paso Prohibido*
No Parking	*Estacionamiento Prohibido*
No Passing	*Prohibido Adelantar*
One Way	*Dirección Unica*
Pay Toll	*Peaje*
Pedestrian Zone	*Peatones*
Reduce Speed	*Despacio*
Steep Incline	*Fuerte Declive*
Stop	*Alto*
Use Headlights	*Encender los faros*
Yield	*Ceda el Paso*

Personal Items and Services

aspirin	*aspirina*
Band-Aids	*tiritas*
condoms	*preservativos*
sanitary napkins	*unos paños higiénicos*
shampoo	*un champú*
shaving cream	*espuma de afeitar*
soap	*el jabón*
tampons	*unos tampones higiénicos*
tissues	*unos pañuelos de papel*
toilet paper	*papel higiénico*
toothbrush	*un cepillo de dientes*
toothpaste	*pasta de dientes*

barbershop	*la peluquería*
beauty shop	*el salón de belleza*
dry cleaner	*la tintorería*
hairdresser (salon)	*la peluquería*
launderette or laundry	*la lavandería*
post office	*el correo*
postage stamps	*sellos*

Where is the bathroom?	*Dónde está el baño?*
The bathroom door will say:	
for the men's room	*Caballeros*
for the women's room	*Señoras*

Days of the Week

Monday	*Lunes*
Tuesday	*Martes*
Wednesday	*Miércoles*
Thursday	*Jueves*
Friday	*Viernes*
Saturday	*Sábado*
Sunday	*Domingo*

Months

January	*Enero*
February	*Febrero*
March	*Marzo*
April	*Abril*
May	*Mayo*
June	*Junio*
July	*Julio*
August	*Agosto*
September	*Septiembre*
October	*Octubre*
November	*Noviembre*
December	*Diciembre*

Numbers

zero	*cero*
one	*uno*
two	*dos*
three	*tres*
four	*cuatro*
five	*cinco*
six	*seis*
seven	*siete*
eight	*ocho*
nine	*nueve*
ten	*diez*
eleven	*once*
twelve	*doce*
thirteen	*trece*
fourteen	*catorce*
fifteen	*quince*
sixteen	*dieciséis*
seventeen	*diecisiete*
eighteen	*dieciocho*
nineteen	*diecinueve*
twenty	*veinte*
thirty	*treinta*

forty	*cuarenta*
fifty	*cincuenta*
sixty	*sesenta*
seventy	*setenta*
eighty	*ochenta*
ninety	*noventa*
one hundred	*cien*
one thousand	*mil*
1994	*mil novecientos noventa y cuatro*

The Cities

Barcelona

Seeing a circle of men and women move in simple, slow steps to the music of flute and drum around a sun-drenched square on a Sunday afternoon provides an almost visceral understanding of Barcelona and its people. This regional dance, the *sardana* — once described by a poet as a dance "of people going forth holding hands" — is indicative of the sense of community and passion for music that is typical of Barcelona.

Barcelona has long been a great Mediterranean port and Spain's "Second City," but its strongest identity is as the capital of the fiercely individualistic and communal Catalan people. It has served as a stronghold of Catalan nationalism in more repressive times, and the locus of Catalan representation vis-à-vis the government of Madrid in freer ones. There always has been a strong regional identity and pride here. After the death of Generalísimo Francisco Franco in 1975, the native Catalan language, no longer suppressed (as it was under Franco), quickly regained its place as the dominant one of the region. Streets and place-names were changed back from Castilian to Catalan, and with the democratic constitution of King Juan Carlos, the region of Catalonia — encompassing the provinces of Barcelona, Gerona (Girona in Catalan), Lérida (Lleida), and Tarragona — was designated one of the country's 17 *comunidades autónomas* (autonomous communities).

Given its position across the Pyrenees from France, Barcelona has a history and language that link it as much to France as to Spain. Catalan, the lilting language of the region, is derived from the French *langue d'oc,* or Provençal, and is spoken in French Catalonia as well.

The history of Barcelona dates back to 218 BC, when Hamilcar Barça, a powerful Carthaginian (and Hannibal's father), founded Barcino. The Romans developed the town, throwing up walls, parts of which can still can be seen. The Visigoths fought over it in the 5th century; the Moors in the 8th century. In 801 Barcelona was conquered by Charlemagne, and it became the dividing line between Christian Europe and Muslim Spain. During the 9th and 10th centuries, local lords, the Counts of Barcelona, became strong enough to establish their independence and drive the Moors from the lands to the south, and by 1100 Barcelona had dominion over all of Catalonia. When Ramón Berenguer IV, a 12th-century Count of Barcelona, married an Aragonese heiress and became King of Aragon, the city became the capital of the combined Catalonian and Aragonese kingdom.

At one point, Barcelona was a major Mediterranean power, a force whose might can be felt even today in the medieval streets of the city's old Gothic quarter, the Barri Gòtic. During the 1400s, Barcelona rivaled Genoa and Venice in Mediterranean trade. At the end of the 15th century it was assimilated into the new Spain of Ferdinand and Isabella. The discovery of the New World, however, proved disastrous for Catalonia. As trade moved from east to west, Cádiz and other Spanish ports on the Atlantic rose in importance, and Barcelona declined.

Thereafter, the question of Catalan autonomy became a consistent theme in Barcelona's history, and the city and region often picked the wrong team in making a stand against the rest of Spain. They rose up against the Spanish crown during the Thirty Years War in the 17th century and failed in an attempt to set up an independent nation. In the early 18th century, they backed the Hapsburgs in the War of the Spanish Succession, prompting the victorious Bourbons to put an end to what Catalonian autonomy remained. Only in the late 19th and early 20th centuries did Barcelona begin to recoup. Success in industry fostered a cultural revival — the *Renaixença* — and a newfound sense of Catalan identity. Architects such as Antoni Gaudí i Cornet (1852–1926) and his contemporaries designed and raised buildings of astonishing creativity in new city quarters. Barcelona was as much a center of Art Nouveau as Paris or Vienna, although here the style was called *Modernisme*. Catalan and non Catalan artists such as Joan Miró, Pablo Picasso, and Juan Gris, attracted by the city's life and color and the spirit of its people, made it a meeting place. Political radicalism flourished, and Barcelona became the capital of a short-lived autonomous Catalan government set up in 1932. Then, during the Spanish Civil War, it became the seat of the Republican government from November 1937 until its fall to Franco's Nationalists in January 1939.

Today, Barcelona, the most European of Spanish cities, is big (pop. 1,755,000), rich, and commercial. Catalans are famous throughout Spain for their business acumen, and young people seeking commercial advancement are drawn here from all parts of the Iberian Peninsula. In addition to being the country's major port and second-largest city, Barcelona is the publishing and literary capital of Spain.

Barcelona has become a favored destination for Europeans who like their big cities to have more than just a cathedral and an art museum. Scores of good restaurants attest to the Barcelonan love of good food and the variety of the regional dishes. Chic designer fashion boutiques attract visitors, as do some of the finest modernist buildings in Europe, including the works of Gaudí and the Palau de la Música Catalana, the embodiment of *Modernisme*. The latter building also reflects the city's love of music; many residents belong to choral societies and choirs, and the young usually join societies to learn regional dances such as the *sardana*.

Barcelona spent hundreds of millions of dollars as host of the *1992 Olympic Games* to let the world know it is ready for the 21st century. In addition to being a feast of sport, the games triggered a massive cleanup and rebuilding: Working class areas like Vall d'Hebron now have sports facilities and the *Olympic Village* remains as a living community. The city has spent over $100 million on the construction of 20 new hotels and built a $150-million terminal at El Prat Airport that is capable of handling over 12 million passengers a year.

But while impressive, all the *Olympic*-inspired construction fails to capture the essence of the city. To find this, you might walk through the Barri Gòtic some evening at dusk, when voices are sometimes heard softly singing medieval madrigals as though the spirits of the past were alive. Such moments embody the true spirit of Barcelona.

Barcelona At-a-Glance

SEEING THE CITY

There are excellent panoramic views of Barcelona, its harbor, the foothills of the Pyrenees, and the Mediterranean (on a clear day you can see the island of Majorca, some 125 miles away) from the top of Tibidabo, a 1,745-foot hill on the northwest side of the city. Tibidabo is crowned with an amusement park; a quasi-Gothic church (built early in this century), which is lit up at night; and a needle-like, 800-foot-tall telecommunications tower designed by noted British architect Norman Foster as a symbol of Barcelona's perception of itself as "the city of the future." To get to Tibidabo, take the *FFCC* train to Avinguda del Tibidabo, change to the *tramvia blau* (blue tram; operating from 7:05 AM to 9:35 PM daily), and take it one stop to Peu del Funicular, where you can take the funicular to the *Tibidabo Amusement Park*. Check the park's opening hours with the tourist office before setting out, however, because it's not open every day and it closes fairly early. At other times, do as the locals do and get off after the tram ride and walk across the square at the foot of Tibidabo to *La Venta* (Plaça Dr. Andreu; phone: 212-6455), an old café expanded into a large restaurant with an attractive terrace, where the contemporarily accented Catalan and Basque dishes are decent but pricey. Or stop for drinks at one of the bars across the square. The *Mirablau* and *Merbeyé* both offer panoramic views of the city, especially dramatic at night, and a lively clientele.

SPECIAL PLACES

The city's oldest buildings of historic and artistic interest are located in the Barri Gòtic, or Gothic Quarter, the old medieval heart of Barcelona. Just southwest of the Barri Gòtic is the city's most colorful and animated promenade, La Rambla (or Las Ramblas), alternately sordid and sophisticated as it stretches from the Plaça de Catalunya down to Barcelona harbor. In 1858, after the walls of the old city had been razed, Barcelona expanded north and west into the Eixample (Ensanche in Castilian — literally "enlargement" or "expansion"), a grid pattern of wide streets and boulevards designed by visionary city planner Ildefons Cerdà. The Avinguda Diagonal and the Gran Via de les Corts Catalanes, two of modern

Barcelona's major streets, cut across this chessboard, which is the city's special pride because of the unparalleled late 19th- and early 20th-century Modernista architecture found here, including a number of Gaudí's most interesting works. To the south of the Barri Gòtic and the Eixample, beginning to rise almost at the foot of La Rambla, is Montjuïc, the city's playground, with several museums, illuminated fountains, a sports and recreation area, and the site of the *1992 Olympic* complex. Buildings put up to house exhibitions for the *1929 World's Fair* still scale its slopes, and at the summit, the huge *Palau Nacional* (National Palace) overlooks the sea.

BARRI GÒTIC

CATEDRAL DE BARCELONA Barcelona's cathedral, dedicated to Saint Eulàlia, the 4th-century Barcelona-born martyr who is one of the city's patron saints, is an excellent example of Catalan Gothic architecture. It was begun in 1298 on the site of two earlier cathedrals. Though most of the present-day cathedral was completed by the mid-15th century, the façade and spired cupola that rises over it were added between 1887 and 1913, although they follow the original plans. The interior is laid out in classic Catalan Gothic form, with three aisles neatly engineered to produce an overall effect of grandeur. The church is comparatively bright inside, thanks to the flickering of thousands of votive candles and the shafts of light pouring through the stained glass windows.

In the enclosed choir are 14th- and 15th-century wooden stalls bearing the coats of arms of the Knights of the Golden Fleece. Also worthy of note is the 16th-century choir screen depicting scenes from Saint Eulàlia's life. The saint is interred in a crypt in front of the High Altar. The chapel of St. Benedict (the third one beyond the caskets) is among the most notable of the many in the cathedral; it contains the nine-panel *Altarpiece of the Transfiguration* by the 15th-century Catalan artist Bernat Martorell. Another of the cathedral's treasures is the 15th-century polychrome tomb of Saint Raymond of Penyafort.

The adjoining cloister is a homey surprise. Reached from within the cathedral through the Santa Llúcia chapel or through doors from the street, it is an oasis of greenery, full of palm trees and inhabited by numerous pigeons and a gaggle of geese who reside beside a fountain and a pool. The cathedral is open daily from 7:45 AM to 1:30 PM and from 4 to 7:45 PM; the museum is open from 11 AM to 1 PM. Admission charges to the enclosed choir and to the museum. Plaça de la Seu (phone: 315-3555).

PALAU DE LA GENERALITAT (PALACE OF THE CATALAN GOVERNMENT) This 15th-century Gothic structure was the seat of the ancient Catalonian parliament and now houses the executive branch of Catalonia's autonomous government. Among the notable rooms are a 15th-century Flamboyant Gothic chapel; the Chapel of St. George, with splendid 17th-century vaulting; and the 16th-century Saló de Sant Jordi (St. George Room), in which the most important decisions of state have been handed down over the centuries. Unfortunately, this is a working building and is not open to the public, but arrangements can be made to see it, on weekends only, by appointment. Contact the Protocolo (public relations) office. Plaça de Sant Jaume (phone: 402-4600).

CASA DE LA CIUTAT (CITY HALL) Like the Palau de la Generalitat across the square, this structure, also known as the Ajuntament, is another fine example of Gothic civil architecture. The façade on the square is 19th-century neo-classical, however. Walk along the Carrer de la Ciutat side to see the building's original 14th-century Flamboyant Gothic façade. Since this, too, is a working building, its interior, including the restored Saló del Consell de Cent (Chamber of the Council of One Hundred) and the Saló de Sesion (Session Chamber), can be seen only on Sundays from 10 AM to 1:30 PM. No admission charge. Plaça de Sant Jaume (phone: 402-7000).

PALAU REIAL MAJOR (GREAT ROYAL PALACE) This is the former palace of the Counts of Barcelona, who ruled the Catalan-Aragonese Confederation — and through it much of the Mediterranean world — from the 12th through the 15th centuries. Actually a complex of buildings, dating mostly from the 14th century but built on 12th-century foundations, it is most notable for its Saló de Tinell (Dining Hall), which is over 50 feet high and 110 feet long, and is defined by 6 immense arches spanned by wooden beams. The Catalan Parliament met here for several years in the 1370s, and it is popularly believed that Columbus was presented to King Ferdinand and Queen Isabella here to report his discovery of the New World. The room is closed to the public unless there is a concert or exhibition; then it is worth the price of admission just to see it and the stylized painting of the Catholic Monarchs sitting on the palace's great steps, surrounded by the heroic Columbus and the American Indians he brought home on his return voyage. The palace is entered from the Plaça del Rei, a small and beautiful square almost completely surrounded by buildings, with a flight of shallow rounded stairs in one corner. The acoustics are excellent here, and the landing atop the stairs is sometimes used as a stage for jazz or chamber concerts. Plaça del Rei.

MUSEU D'HISTÒRIA DE LA CIUTAT (MUSEUM OF CITY HISTORY) The city's history museum, on Plaça del Rei, is housed in the Casa Clariana-Padellàs, a 16th-century Gothic merchant's house. Begin a tour in the basement, where pathways thread through an actual excavated section of Roman Barcelona, past remains of houses, storerooms, columns, walls, and bits of mosaic pavement. Upstairs rooms contain paintings, furniture, and municipal memorabilia, including the 16th-century Gran Rellotge, one of the six clocks that have occupied the cathedral bell tower. The museum also incorporates part of the Palau Reial Major. Open Tuesdays through

Saturdays from 10 AM to 8 PM, Sundays from 10 AM to 2 PM; closed Mondays. No admission charge for children under 18. Entrance on Carrer del Veguer (phone: 315-1111).

MUSEU FREDERIC MARÈS Located in another part of the Palau Reial Major, this is an important collection of medieval art, particularly sculpture, which was donated to the city by Frederic Marès, a prominent local sculptor. The painted wooden religious statues, peculiar to this part of Spain, are outstanding. On the upper floors, a display of artifacts ranging from costumes and combs to pipes and purses invites visitors to discover what everyday life was like in old Catalonia. Open Tuesdays through Saturdays from 10 AM to 5 PM; Sundays from 10 AM to 2 PM; closed Mondays. Admission charge. 5-6 Plaça de Sant Iu (phone: 310-5800).

MUSEU PICASSO Although Pablo Picasso lived in France for 69 years, Barcelona was where he spent his student days, and it occupied a warm place in his heart throughout his life. The museum was founded in 1963 when Jaime Sabartés, a native of Barcelona and friend of Picasso's, presented his collection of the master's work to the city. Picasso himself donated 58 paintings. Housed in the beautiful 15th-century Palau Agüilar, which is nearly as interesting as the artist's works, the museum is not strictly within the Barri Gòtic, although it's quite near. A lovely Gothic-Renaissance courtyard opens to the roof, surrounded by tiers of arcaded galleries with pointed arches and slender columns. Lithographs and early works from the artist's years in Málaga and Barcelona constitute most of the collection, but there are a few special pieces. One is the large exhibition of 44 variations of *Las Meninas,* the famous Velázquez painting in Madrid's *Prado.* Also notice examples of Picasso's warm and unpretentious ceramic work. One section of the museum is devoted to small changing exhibitions of works by other artists. Open Tuesdays through Saturdays from 10 AM to 8 PM; Sundays and holidays from 10 AM to 3 PM; closed Mondays. No admission charge for children under 18. 15 Carrer de Montcada (phone: 319-6310).

MUSEU TÈXTIL I DE LA INDUMENTÀRIA (TEXTILE AND COSTUME MUSEUM) The beautiful 14th-century palace of the Marquis of Llió holds a fascinating collection of fabrics and men's and women's everyday and ceremonial dresses from the 18th to the 20th century. Open Tuesdays through Saturdays from 10 AM to 5 PM; open mornings only on Sundays and holidays; closed Mondays. No admission charge for children under 18. 12 Carrer de Montcada (phone: 310-4516).

ESGLÉSIA DE SANTA MARIA DEL MAR (CHURCH OF SAINT MARY OF THE SEA) At the foot of the Carrer Montcada, where it meets Passeig del Born, is the back of what many consider to be the most beautiful Gothic church in Barcelona, if not in all Spain. Once the preserve of the city's wealthy shipbuilders and merchants, the church dates mostly from the 14th century. Walk around to the front entrance on the Plaça Santa Maria and note the perfectly proportioned and simply (but attractively) detailed façade. The interior of the church draws its great beauty from its simplicity and its high, slender proportions.

PALAU DE LA MÚSICA CATALANA (CATALAN CONCERT HALL) Also not far from the Barri Gòtic, this is quintessential *Modernisme,* the Catalan variation on the Art Nouveau theme. Designed by Lluís Domènech i Montaner and built from 1905 to 1908, this concert hall is every bit as colorful as anything designed by the more famous Gaudí. But it's also less bizarre and, therefore, in the opinion of many, more beautiful — Gaudí himself is said to have likened it to what heaven must be like. The interior, which was renovated and expanded by noted Barcelona architects Oscar Tusquets and Carlos Díaz, is illuminated partially by an elaborate stained glass dome, and is full of mosaics and rife with ceramic rosettes, garlands, and winged beasts. Tours are given in several languages and schedules vary, but attendance at a portion of a rehearsal by the *Barcelona Municipal Orchestra* often is included. Call for details. Or just amble in with the crowd on evenings when there is a performance and admire the foyer, a lovely space full of brick pillars that rise to ceramic capitals. In summer, when there are no concerts or tours don't fail to walk by the equally colorful exterior. Carrer d'Amadeu Vives (phone: 268-1000).

EIXAMPLE

PASSEIG DE GRÀCIA Running from Plaça de Catalunya to Plaça de Joan Carles I, where it is cut off by Avinguda Diagonal, this is the widest boulevard in the grid-patterned enlargement that grew up in the 1860s and 1870s after Barcelona's old walls were torn down. Lined with boutiques, banks, hotels, cinemas, and art galleries, it links the Barri Gòtic to what once was the old village of Gràcia, and it provides a pleasant backdrop for a stroll. Note the *fanals-banc,* combined lampposts and mosaic benches. Of much greater interest, however, are the Modernista buildings located here, three of them in one block alone, between Carrer del Consell de Cent and Carrer d'Aragó, the so-called *manzana de la discórdia,* or "block of discord," as it was named by locals shocked by the clashing of avant-garde styles.

CASA LLEÓ-MORERA On the corner of Passeig de Gràcia and Carrer del Consell de Cent, this is one of the three noteworthy Modernista buildings occupying the "block of discord." Designed by Domènech i Montaner, and built in 1905, at the peak of the Catalan Modernista movement, it has stone balconies carved in flower designs and winged lions. The façade is monochromatic, but step across the street to see the ventilator on top, which looks like an elaborate bonnet with a green, pink, and yellow flowered hat band. 35 Passeig de Gràcia.

CASA AMATLLER AND CASA BATLLÓ These two buildings, both designed as apartment complexes, make up the remainder of the "block of discord." The Casa Amatller (41 Passeig de Gràcia), completed in 1900, was designed by

Josep Puig i Cadafalch, perhaps the best-known and most prolific of Modernista architects and designers after Gaudí and Domènech i Montaner. The building contrasts dramatically with its immediate neighbor, the Casa Batlló (43 Passeig de Gràcia), which was designed by Antoni Gaudí, leader of the Modernista movement. Built circa 1907, it's a fairy-tale abode with mask-shaped balconies, sensuous curves in stone and iron, and bits of broken tile in its upper levels. Both buildings are closed to the public.

CASA MILÀ Only a few blocks from the "block of discord," on the other side of the Passeig de Gràcia is this apartment house, which is regarded as the classic example of Gaudí's Modernista architecture. Popularly known as La Pedrera (the "stone quarry"), this sinuous yet geometric building seems to be making an almost sculptural attempt to distance itself from the harsh, square lines of its turn-of-the-century neighbors. Barcelona novelist Joan Perucho once wrote that the Casa Milà "gives the impression of a mountain eroded by the wind and the rain, excavated right into its entrails by the piercing blast of atmospheric accident." Be sure to visit the rooftop terrace with its strange chimney caps. Conducted tours take place Mondays through Saturdays at 10 and 11 AM, noon, and 1 PM; there is no charge. There is no elevator, but the 6 flights of stairs are worth the effort to see details of doorknobs and banisters en route. 91 Passeig de Gràcia (phone: 215-3398).

FUNDACIÓ ANTONI TÀPIES (ANTONI TÀPIES FOUNDATION) Designed by Lluís Domènech i Montaner in an early Modernista style with Mudéjar (medieval Hispanicized Muslim) overtones, this museum houses a major collection of the internationally acclaimed, still-living Catalan artist's works — paintings, drawings, sculpture, assemblages, and ceramics. There also is a research library, as well as a basement gallery devoted to shows by other artists and photographers. But perhaps the main attraction is the huge Tàpies sculpture of metal wire and tubing on the roof of the building, taking up the entire width of the façade and adding 40-plus feet to its height. It's called *Cloud and Chair*, and you may love this bizarre construction or hate it, but if you're walking along the opposite side of the street, near Passeig de Gràcia, you certainly won't fail to notice it. Open Tuesdays through Sundays from 11 AM to 8 PM. Admission charge. 255 Carrer d'Aragó (phone: 487-0315).

PARC GÜELL Originally planned as a real estate development by Gaudí and his friend Count Eusebio Güell, a noted Barcelona industrialist and civic leader, Parc Güell is now a public park, located to the north and west of Eixample. At its core, resting on 86 pillars and edged with an undulating stone bench "upholstered" with a mosaic quilt of broken glass and tiles, is a plaza that was meant to be the development project's marketplace. Only two of the development's houses — the gingerbread cottages flanking the park entrance — were ever built; a third, not designed by Gaudí but his home for the last 2 decades of his life, has been turned into the *Casa-Museu Gaudí,* containing drawings, models, furniture, and a number of his belongings. South of the park, the Passeig de Gràcia ambles past some impish turn-of-the-century houses. Parc Güell is open daily from 10 AM to dusk; the museum is open from 10 AM to 2 PM and from 4 to 7 PM; closed Saturdays. Admission charge to the museum. Bus No. 24 up Passeig de Gràcia leads to the Carretera del Carmel entrance, which is close to the museum, and also not far from the main entrance (with pavilions) located at Carrer de Llarrad and Carrer d'Olot. Metro line No. 3 runs from the intersection of Passeig de Gràcia and the Diagonal to Plaça Lesseps (two stops); the main entrance is about a 6-block (uphill) walk from there.

TEMPLE EXPIATORI DE LA SAGRADA FAMÍLIA (CHURCH OF THE HOLY FAMILY)

Antoni Gaudí was killed in a tram accident in 1926 before he could complete this religious edifice, his most famous and controversial work — and a structure that has come to be an emblematic symbol of Barcelona in much the same way that the Eiffel Tower is of Paris or Big Ben is of London. Begun in 1884 by Francesc de Pau Villar in a neo-Gothic style, in 1891 it was taken over by Gaudí, who changed the style dramatically. La Sagrada Familia is in the great Gothic tradition of Flamboyant swirls, jutting gargoyles, allegorical façades — and lifetimes of construction. Gaudí's estimate that the completion of his final project would take 200 years may prove to be overly optimistic. Under construction for more than a century, the church still doesn't have four complete walls or a roof.

Only the Nativity Façade — with its tall spires, stained glass windows, and sculpted figures of the Virgin Mary, Joseph, and the infant Christ — was actually completed before Gaudí died. Construction on the Passion Façade, on the Carrer de Sardenya side, was begun in 1952. Still to come are a central dome, to rise more than 500 feet, along with several smaller domes.

Take the elevator (or the stairs) up the Nativity side to the dizzying heights of the spires for views of the city and close-ups of the amazing architectural details. Steps go even higher, but beware if you suffer from vertigo (or from claustrophobia, as the stairways are dark and close). The audiovisual show in the *Museu Monogràfic,* located in the crypt, traces the history of the church. There's also a scale model of the structure as it will be one day, although we may never be able to compare it to the real thing. Open daily from 9 AM to 9 PM in July through August; from 9 AM to 6 PM in September through March; and from 9 AM to 7 PM in April through June. Admission charge, plus an additional charge for the elevator (which operates from 10 AM to 1:45 PM and from 3 PM until shortly before the cathedral closes). Plaça de la Sagrada Família; entrance on Carrer de Sardenya (phone: 455-0247).

FONTS LLUMINOSES These illuminated fountains, designed by Carles Buïgas for the *1929 International Exposition,* look like Hollywood special effects. The pavilion built for the fair was designed by noted Modernista architect Enric Català i Català and his associates, under the supervision of Josep Puig i Cadafalch. Shows here feature the interplay of colored lights, jets of water, and music. For hours, which change frequently, call Barcelona Informació (phone: 010). There are no shows from January through March. Between Plaça d'Espanya and Montjuïc.

POBLE ESPANYOL (SPANISH VILLAGE) Built for the *1929 International Exposition* and revitalized for the *1992 Olympics,* this is a 5-acre model village whose streets and squares are lined with examples of traditional buildings from every region of Spain, most of them re-creations of actual structures, from Galician *casonas* (cottages) to whitewashed Andalusian villas with wrought-iron grilles. A walk through the "town" illustrates the diversity of Spanish architecture and offers a chance to see traditional artisans at work — their carvings, pottery, glass, leather, and metalworks are sold in the village's 35 shops. There also is an interesting *Graphic Arts Museum,* with displays of printing and engraving equipment both old and new, and samples of posters, playing cards, hand-printed books, and other items; and a *Museum of Popular Arts, Industry, and Tradition,* containing historical and ethnological material from all over Catalonia and other parts of Spain, including a reconstructed antique pharmacy. The grounds open daily at 9 AM, and close at 4 AM on Sundays, 8 PM on Mondays, and at 6 AM the rest of the week; shops, restaurants, museums, and other enterprises within the village keep their own, shorter hours. (*Torres de Avila,* a nightclub with a fantasy-land interior and rooftop terrace, opens at 10 PM and is rarely animated before midnight.) Admission charge. Av. del Marquès de Comillas (phone: 325-7866).

MUSEU D'ART DE CATALUNYA (MUSEUM OF CATALONIAN ART) Occupying a portion of the Palau Nacional, and now being remodeled by Italian architect Gae Aulenti (who turned an unused train station in Paris into the magnificent *Musée d'Orsay*), this museum is often referred to as "the *Prado* of Romanesque art." Its collection of Romanesque and Gothic altarpieces and sculpture is superb, but its chief treasure, a series of 12th- and 13th-century frescoes removed by Italian craftsmen from dank little churches in the Pyrenees and reinstalled magnificently here, is unparalleled in the world. The museum also contains works by Tintoretto, El Greco, Zurbarán, and the Catalan painter Antoni Viladomat. The museum is officially closed for renovations, but special exhibits are frequently mounted, and the public admitted. Mirador del Palau, Parc de Montjuïc (phone: 423-6199).

FUNDACIÓ JOAN MIRÓ (JOAN MIRÓ FOUNDATION) Set up in an ultramodern building designed by the late Catalan architect Josep Lluís Sert, this is a light, airy tribute to Catalonia's surrealist master, Joan Miró (who died in 1983 and is buried nearby in the Montjuïc cemetery). Numerous painted bronze sculptures are displayed on terraces of the museum's upper level; in the galleries are works in various styles and mediums, including a haunting *Self Portrait,* which the artist began in 1937 and did not finish until 1960. The *Fundació* hosts frequent special exhibitions, and also has a library, a well-stocked art bookstore, and a very good snack bar. Open Tuesdays through Saturdays from 11 AM to 7 PM; Thursdays until 9 PM; Sundays and holidays from 10:30 AM to 2:30 PM. Admission charge. Plaça Neptú, Parc de Montjuïc (phone: 329-1908).

MUSEU ARQUEOLÒGIC (ARCHAEOLOGICAL MUSEUM) Exhibits include relics found in the excavation of the Greco-Roman city of Empúries on the Costa Brava; other remnants of Spain's prehistoric cultures; and a fine collection of Carthaginian, Greek, Iberian, Roman, and Visigothic artifacts, mosaics, and sculptures, most of them found in present-day Catalonia and the Balearic Islands. There also is an archaeological library. Open Tuesdays through Saturdays from 9:30 AM to 1 PM and from 4 to 7 PM; Sundays and holidays from 10 AM to 1 PM. No admission charge. Carrer de Lleida (phone: 423-2149).

PAVELLÓ BARCELONA Designed by world-famous architect Mies van der Rohe as the German pavilion for the *1929 International Exposition,* this sleek, spare, very contemporary building has been called one of the landmarks of modern architecture. Among the meager furnishings are a sensuous standing nude sculpture by Georg Kolbe and two prototype examples of the Barcelona chair — probably the most famous chair design of our century, done originally for this space and first sat in (according to tradition) by Alfonso XIII, the last King of Spain before the Franco era. Disassembled and put into storage in the 1930s, the pavilion was rediscovered after 50 years and re-created in 1986. Open daily from 8 AM to 8 PM; from 8 AM to noon in June, July, and August. No admission charge. Av. del Marquès de Comillas.

ANELLA OLÍMPICA (OLYMPIC RING) Some 63 years after hosting the *1929 International Exposition* on its slopes, Montjuïc was designated as the principal site for the *1992 Summer Olympics.* The sports facilities within the *Olympic Ring,* from which there is a panoramic view of the Mediterranean, include the main 70,000-seat *Estadi Olímpic* (Olympic Stadium), built for the *International Exposition* but completely remodeled in the late 1980s by a team of top Catalan and Italian architects. Within the *Olympic Ring* are the 17,000-seat domed *Palau d'Esports Sant Jordi* (St. George Sports Palace), designed by noted Japanese architect Arata Isozaki, and the *Piscines Municipals B. Picornell* (B. Picornell Municipal Pools), open-air pools with seating for 5,000. The Universitat d'Esport (University of Sport) was built by controversial architect Ricardo Bofill and his associate Peter Hodgkinson in a neo-classical–post-Modernista style.

MUSEU MILITAR (MILITARY MUSEUM) Since time immemorial, there has been a fortress at the top of Montjuïc, and the 17th- and 18th-century castle currently occupying the spot now houses military uniforms, toy soldiers, models of castles and fortresses, and a collection of 17th- to 19th-century firearms. The castle can be reached by road as well as aboard the Montjuïc *telèferic,* a cable car (see *Getting Around*). The museum is open Tuesdays through Saturdays from 10 AM to 2 PM and from 4 to 7 PM; Sundays and holidays from 10 AM to 7 PM. Admission charge. The *telèferic* is in operation daily in summer; on Saturdays, Sundays, and holidays in winter. Parc de Montjuïc (phone: 412-0000).

ELSEWHERE

LA RAMBLA This is the city's favorite, and liveliest, promenade — the main artery feeding its animated street life. Originally a drainage channel (a *rambla* is a watercourse), it is now a wide, tree-lined pedestrian esplanade, with a single lane of traffic and a sidewalk on each side, running at a gentle downhill angle from the Plaça de Catalunya to the harbor. Though popularly known simply as La Rambla or Las Ramblas, the boulevard in fact changes its name en route (Rambla dels Caputxins, Rambla de Sant Josep, Rambla de Canaletes, and so on). A brisk 20-minute trot will cover it all, from the Plaça de Catalunya to the harbor, but the whole idea is to take it much more slowly, examining the flower stands, thumbing through books and magazines at the numerous newsstands (which sell everything from Arabic-language newspapers to German brides' magazines), reading a favorite newspaper or magazine at a sidewalk café, or merely strolling and chatting with friends amidst the inevitable din. Notice the sidewalk mosaic by Miró at the Plaça de Boqueria, and be sure to visit *La Boqueria,* the city's extraordinary main food market (see below). You'll also pass the *Teatre del Liceu* (at the corner of Carrer de Sant Pau), one of Europe's great opera houses, which is closed for renovation until next year.

On the right side of La Rambla (facing the sea), almost to the harbor, is the new *Centre d'Art Santa Mònica* (phone: 412-2279), not a museum but a beautiful contemporary art exhibition space designed by Albert Viaplana and Helio Piñón on the site of a former convent. Hours vary according to the shows. Also see Gaudí's first major work, the Palau Güell (3 Carrer Nou de la Rambla; phone: 317-3974), a few steps off La Rambla and now serving as the *Museu de les Arts de l'Espectacle* (Museum of Performing Arts; phone: 317-3974) and the *Institut del Teatre* (Theater Institute). The Palau Güell offers guided tours at 10 AM, 11 AM, noon, and 1PM; closed Saturdays, Sundays, and holidays. Admission charge.

| **SEEING RED** | Just off the port, the triangle between La Rambla and the Avinguda del Paral·lel, with its little alleyways, is known as the Barri Xinès, literally "Chinese district" or "Chinatown" — but it is actually the red-light district and should be avoided at night, when it can be quite dangerous. |

A BOQUERIA Officially known as the *Mercat de Sant Josep,* this is one of the most attractive and richly stocked public food markets in Europe. A huge, covered 19th-century ironwork structure that looks quite a bit like a turn-of-the-century French train station, it features displays of the finest food products of Catalonia and the rest of the world in an abundance and variety that are simply breathtaking. Mountains of bright vegetables, mounds of earthy mushrooms, oceans worth of fish displayed on ice, treasure chests of candied fruit and nuts, thick screens of sausages dangling from the butcher stalls — it's one glorious sight and smell after another. Merchants are happy to sell a single piece of fruit or a tiny bag of olives or almonds, so even the casual visitor can sample the wares. The market building itself is open 24 hours a day, but the individual shops and stands are open mostly from 8 or 8:30 AM to 2 or 3 PM Mondays through Saturdays.

WATERFRONT Barcelona is by far the largest port in Spain, and has become a port of call for major international cruise ships. The Moll de la Fusta (Wooden Wharf, though it isn't made of wood — its name honors a wooden pier that once stood nearby), the quay where the Barri Gòtic meets the harbor, now boasts a pedestrian promenade complete with palm trees, park benches, and unusual-looking contemporary bridges, as well as a row of indoor/outdoor restaurants and bars. Most locals consider most of these restaurants too expensive to patronize, so just stop in for *tapas* and a drink.

MONUMENT A COLOM (COLUMBUS MONUMENT) Barcelonans are very fond of Christopher Columbus, who allegedly first reported on his discovery of the New World to King Ferdinand and Queen Isabella in this city. This 200-foot-high column-and-statue at the harbor end of La Rambla, anchoring one end of the Moll de la Fusta, is the tallest tribute in the world to the noted explorer. Together with Antoni Gaudí's Temple Expiatori de la Sagrada Família, it is an emblematic symbol of Barcelona. Take the elevator to the top floor for an extraordinary view. Open late June to late September from 9 AM to 9 PM daily; the rest of the year, open Tuesdays through Saturdays from 10 AM to 2 PM and from 3:30 to 6:30 PM, Sundays and holidays from 10 AM to 7 PM. Admission charge. Plaça Porta de la Pau.

MUSEU MARÍTIM (MARITIME MUSEUM) The old low, stone buildings with the gables behind the Columbus Monument are the Drassanes Reials (Royal Shipyards), fine examples of medieval Catalan industrial architecture. Built in the 13th and 14th centuries, they are believed to be the largest intact medieval shipyards in the world. Ships carrying the red-and-yellow Catalan flag to the far corners of the world were launched from these yards years before Columbus's bold discovery. Fittingly, the city's *Maritime Museum,* considered one of its finest, now occupies the yards. The immense and varied collections include old maps (including one drawn by Amerigo Vespucci) and navigational instruments, ships' figureheads, models of ancient fishing boats, freighters and other vessels. Open Tuesdays through Saturdays from 9 AM to 1 PM and from 4 to 7 PM; Sundays and holidays from 10 AM to 2 PM. Admission charge. 1 Plaça Porta de la Pau (phone: 318-3245).

BARCELONETA Created in the early 18th century on what had been an empty spit of land jutting into Barcelona harbor, lively "Little Barcelona" was originally a resettlement area for citizens who had been displaced by the huge citadel built by Philip V to keep rebellious Barcelonans in line. Today, it is virtually its own little town, bustling and colorful, and almost romantically tacky. The Passeig Nacional, lined with bars and every kind of eating establishment imaginable, forms the area's waterfront promenade on the city side. Behind it is a grid of streets strung with laundry drying from balconies and encompassing a few leafy plazas stretching to the Platja de la Barceloneta, the beach on the Mediterranean side. Though the beach was cleaned up in time for the *Olympics,* it is still rather dirty and run-down — a fact that doesn't stop thousands of local citizens from frequenting it in hot weather. Somewhat to the north is Poble Nou (or New Village), an industrial, working class quarter, much of which was torn down to construct the *Olympic Village.* A new beach, the Platja de Sant Martí, with breakwaters creating two large coves, has been constructed at Poble Nou, with half a million tons of sand added by barge. Some people swim at these beaches; others claim the water is still too polluted. To reach Barceloneta, walk all the way around the waterfront from the Columbus Monument past the Moll d'Espanya; take the subway (Line No. 4) to the Barceloneta stop and walk from there; take any of several buses; or take the Barceloneta *teleferic.* Poble Nou may be reached via the No. 6 or No. 92 bus, or by subway (Line No. 4), four stops past Barceloneta.

PARC DE LA CIUTADELLA This open space was created just over 100 years ago for the *International Exhibition* of 1888, on the site of the hated citadel built by Philip V in 1716 and razed in 1868. Popular with Barcelonans, the park features gardens, an artificial lake with an elaborate fountain and cascade (co-designed by Antoni Gaudí early in his career), and a zoo (phone: 309-2500) that's home to Snowflake, said to be the only albino gorilla in captivity. There's also the Palau de la Ciutadella, which houses the Catalan Parliament and the *Museu d'Art Modern* (Museum of Modern Art; see below); the *Museu de Zoologia* (Zoology Museum), housed in a Modernista building by Domènech i Montaner (open Tuesdays through Sundays from 10 AM to 2 PM; no admission charge for children under 18); and the *Museu de Geologia* (Museum of Geology), Barcelona's oldest museum, with a large mineral collection and paleontology exhibits (open Tuesdays through Sundays from 10 AM to 2 PM; no admission for children under 18).

MUSEU D'ART MODERN (MUSEUM OF MODERN ART) Housed in the Palau de la Ciutadella, the collection includes a few works by such well-known Catalan artists as Dalí, Miró, and Tàpies, but is occupied mostly by 19th-century and early 20th-century paintings, graphic works, and sculptures by such less famous but talented local artists as Ramón Casas (a great portraitist), Santiago Russinyol, Isidre Nonell, Miguel Utrillo, Pau Gargallo, and Josep-Maria Sert — all of whom deserve more attention today than they are generally accorded. The museum is open Tuesdays through Saturdays from 9 AM to 7:30 PM; Sundays from 9 AM to 3 PM; and Mondays from 3 to 7:30 PM. No admission charge for children under 18. Plaça de las Armes (phone: 319-5728).

EXTRA SPECIAL The Sierra de Montserrat lies 40 miles (64 km) northwest of Barcelona, in the geographical and spiritual heart of Catalonia. The many legends that surround Montserrat, which inspired Wagner's opera *Parsifal*, undoubtedly arose from the strangely unreal appearance of these impressive mountain peaks. Tucked within the mountains is the Benedictine monastery whose Marian shrine has attracted pilgrims for over 700 years. *La Moreneta* (The Black Madonna), a polychrome statue of the Virgin Mary that dates from the 12th century, represents the spiritual life of the province and is central to Catalan unity. The basilica where the Virgin sits is open daily from 6 AM to 8 PM. No admission is charged, but a donation is welcome. The monastery's famous *Escolania*, a boys' choir that claims to be the oldest in the world, sings at 1 PM each Sunday and on special occasions. There is also a museum at the site, open daily from 10:30 AM to 2 PM and from 3 to 6 PM. Admission charge (phone: 845-0251). From the monastery, paths and funiculars lead to the Santa Cova, the cave where the statue is supposed to have been found, and to the isolated hermitages of Sant Miguel, Sant Joan, and Sant Jeroni. The belvedere provides breathtaking views that stretch from the Pyrenees to the Balearic Islands.

Sources and Resources

TOURIST INFORMATION

From June 24 to September 30, brochures, maps, and general information are available at the Palau de la Virreina (658 Gran Via de les Corts Catalanes; phone: 301-7443; open weekdays from 9 AM to 7 PM and Saturdays from 9 AM to 2 PM) and in the Barri Gòtic (at the Ajuntament, Plaça de Sant Jaume; open weekdays from 9 AM to 9 PM, Saturdays from 9 AM to 2 PM June 24 to September 30). The tourist information office at Barcelona Sants Station is open daily, year-round, from 8 AM to 8 PM, while the office at El Prat Airport's international arrival hall (phone: 478-4704) is open Mondays through Saturdays from 9:30 AM to 8 PM, Sundays until

3 PM. A branch at the Estació de França is open daily from 8 AM to 8 PM. The "Casacas Rojas," red-jacketed tourist guides who patrol popular areas such as the Barri Gòtic, the Passeig de Gràcia, and La Rambla, supply on-the-spot information from approximately mid-June to mid-September. The US Consulate is at Passieg Reina Elisenda (phone: 280-2227).

LOCAL COVERAGE The tourist offices provide good free maps and brochures. The weekly *Guía del Ocio* and monthly Barcelona city magazine, *Vivir en Barcelona,* both available at newsstands, provide comprehensive listings of museums, nightspots, restaurants, and other attractions, although not in English (the latter does include some information in English in high-season editions). Watch the news in English on TV3 during the summer.

TELEPHONE

The area code for Barcelona is 3. If calling from elsewhere in Spain, dial "9" before the area code and the local number.

GETTING AROUND

AIRPORT Barcelona's airport for both domestic and international flights is El Prat (phone: 379-2762), located 7½ miles (12 km) southwest of the city, or about 30 minutes from downtown by taxi; the fare ranges from about $12 to $22. Trains run between the airport and Barcelona Sants Central Railway Station, connecting with the subway lines, every 20 minutes; the trip takes 15 minutes and the fare is approximately 60¢. *Iberia's* shuttle (*Puente Aereo*) has flights to and from Madrid every half hour to every hour throughout the day. There is an *Iberia* office at 30 Passeig de Gràcia (phone for domestic reservations: 301-6800; for international reservations: 302-7656; for information: 301-3993).

BOAT Ferries operated by *Trasmediterránea* leave Barcelona for the Balearic Islands daily in summer, less frequently in winter. The company is located at 6 Avinguda Drassanes (phone: 317-6311); departures are from the Moll de Barcelona pier near the Columbus Monument. *Golondrinas,* or "swallow boats," making brief sightseeing jaunts in the harbor (out to the breakwater and back) depart from directly in front of the monument from 10:30 AM to 9 PM during June, July, and August; Sundays and holidays the hours are from 11 AM to 7 PM. During the rest of the year the boats run from 11 AM to 6 PM. The trip takes only about 15 minutes; buy the ticket from the office at the water's edge (phone: 310-0342).

BUS Although more than 50 routes crisscross the city, the system is easy to use, since each stop is marked with a map of the routes that pass there. The best deal for the visitor is *Bus Cien,* the No. 100 bus that constantly circles around 12 well-known sites, including the cathedral and the Sagrada Família. A flat-rate, full-ticket (bought on the bus) lets you get on and off as often as you like, and also entitles the bearer to a discount at museums (about $2.25 for 1 day, $6.50 for 3 days, $9.50 for 5 days). The route operates only in high season, however, from approximately mid-June to mid-September. At other times, buy a 10-ride ticket (called T-1, or Targeta Multiviatge) at a reasonable price. It's valid on all buses, as well as on the subway, the funicular to Montjuïc, and the *tramvia blau* (blue tram) to Tibidabo. (A 10-ride T-2 ticket is good for the subway, the funicular, and the *tramvia blau,* but not for the bus.) Buy the tickets at the public transport kiosk in the Universitat Estació (*Metro L1*) or at the Sants Estació (*Metro L5*), where the *Guía del Transport Públic de Barcelona* (Guide to Barcelona's Public Transportation) also is available, or just buy tickets at any subway station. After boarding the bus (enter through the front doors), insert the ticket in the date-stamping machine. For city bus information, call 412-0000.

There is also bus service every 15 minutes between Plaça Catalunya and the airport Mondays through Fridays from 5:30 AM to 10 PM, and on Saturdays, Sundays, and holidays from 6 AM to 10 PM. From the airport, the bus runs Mondays through Fridays from 6:25 AM to 11 PM, and on Saturdays, Sundays, and holidays from 6:45 AM to 10:15 PM. The fare is less than $4.

Long-distance domestic and international buses also serve the city. For information on tickets and departure points, call 412-0000.

CAR RENTAL Cars are useful for day trips outside Barcelona, but usually are more trouble than they are worth for touring within the city. All the major international and local car rental firms have offices at the airport.

FUNICULARS AND CABLE CARS In addition to the funicular to Tibidabo (see *Seeing the City*), there is a funicular making the climb from the Paral-lel subway stop up to Montjuïc, where it connects with the Montjuïc *telèferic* (cable car) that swings out over the *Montjuïc Amusement Park* and makes one interim stop before depositing passengers at the castle, belvedere, and restaurant at the top. The funicular, cable car, and amusement park are in operation daily in summer; in winter, only on Saturdays, Sundays, and holidays. Another *telèferic* connects Barceloneta with Miramar, at the foot of Montjuïc, making an interim stop at the Torre de Jaume I on the Moll de Barcelona. The trip is a spectacular one across the harbor — passengers swing out over the cruise ships and hang over the water as though in a slow-moving airplane. Rides begin at noon.

SUBWAY A "Metro" sign indicates an entrance to Barcelona's modern, clean subway system. There are four lines (*L1, L3, L4,* and *L5*), all easy to use. Individual rides cost about 60¢, but the 10-ride ticket (T-2, or Targeta Multiviatge) is much better buy for multiple trips; it can be purchased at any subway station and is valid on the funicular to Montjuïc and the *tramvia blau* as well, but not on the buses.

TAXI Taxis can be hailed while they cruise the streets or picked up at one of the numerous *paradas de taxi* (taxi ranks) throughout the city. For *Radio Taxi,* call 490-2222. During the day, *Lliure* or *Libre* in the window indicates that a cab is available; at night, a green light shines on the roof. The city is divided into various fare zones, and fares generally are moderate.

TRAIN Barcelona is served by trains operated by *RENFE* (Spanish National Railways) and by trains operated by *Ferrocarrils de la Generalitat de Catalunya (FFCC).* There are four railway stations, all undergoing long-term refurbishment. Local, national, and international departures constantly are being changed, so it is vital to check and double-check before any journey. The stations are Estació Barcelona Sants, at the end of Avinguda de Roma, the main station for long-distance trains within Spain; Estació de França, on Avinguda Marquès de l'Argentera, for international trains; Estació Passeig de Gràcia, on Passeig de Gràcia at Carrer d'Aragó; and Estació Plaça de Catalunya. For fare and schedule information, contact *RENFE* at Barcelona Sants or call the 24-hour-a-day information service (phone: 490-0202).

SPECIAL EVENTS

Religious holidays and saints' days are occasions for numerous festivities in Barcelona, many of them associated with elaborate pageantry and also (since food is very important in Catalan life) with special pastries, confections, or other foodstuffs. The *Cavalcada de Reis* (Cavalcade of Kings) is held on January 5 with a parade of floats from the waterfront to Montjuïc commemorating the journey of the Wise Men (or Three Kings) to visit the baby Jesus. *Carnaval* commences every year on *Dijous Gras* (Fat Thursday), the week before *Ash Wednesday,* and runs for 6 days and nights with nonstop parades, concerts and theatrical performances, costume balls, and ceremonial gluttony (a traditional dish of the holiday is a stew of pigs' trotters, veal, pork loin, sausage, and hard-boiled eggs). On March 19, the *Festa de Sant Josep* (Feast of St. Joseph), Valencian residents of Barcelona recreate the *fallas,* or ritual bonfires, for which their own city is famous, and everybody eats *crema catalana,* Catalan "burnt cream" (custard with a caramelized sugar topping), also known as *crema de Sant Josep.* On April 23, the *Festa de Sant Jordi* (Feast of St. George, the patron saint of Catalonia), Barcelonans traditionally give gifts to one another — books to friends, roses to lovers (real or hoped for). The Sunday after the *Festa de Sant Jordi* is the *Día Universal de la Sardana* (Universal Day of the Sardana), celebrated all over Catalonia, and dedicated to performances of the region's evocative traditional dance and its accompanying music. Bonfires, fireworks, dancing, and revelry mark the nights before the *Festa de Sant Joan* (Feast of St. John) and *Festa de Sant Pere* (Feast of St. Peter), on June 23 and 28, respectively, and every bakery dispenses its version of the *coca de Sant Joan,* a large rectangular pastry covered with candied fruit, on the former occasion. On Thursdays from June through September, the

Guardia Urbana (City Police) don scarlet tunics and white plumed helmets for a riding exhibition at 9 PM at the Pista Hipica La Fuxarda in Montjuïc. The narrow streets of the Gràcia neighborhood are elaborately and colorfully decorated for the *Festa Major de Gràcia* (Main Feast of Grace); for a week beginning on August 15 there are open-air concerts and theatrical performances. September 11 is *La Diada,* Catalonia's national day commemorating the defeat of the Catalans at the hands of Philip V and the fall of Barcelona in 1714. *La Festa de la Mercé* (The Feast of Our Lady of Mercy) is Barcelona's most extravagant annual festival. The feast day itself is September 24, but the week leading up to it is great fun — noisy, exhausting, and full of general gaiety. Included in the festivities are folk dancing, wine and gastronomic fairs, free concerts (often by major international stars) in squares and other public spaces all over the city, fireworks displays, *casteller* (human pyramid) competitions, and such other observances as a Ball de Gegants or Giants' Ball (with parades of flamboyantly costumed papier-mâché figures 15 feet high and more), and the remarkable Correfoc, or Fire Run, in which crowds ceremonially confront and try to turn aside fireworks-wielding teams of men and women dressed as dragons, devils, and other fantastical characters. *Christmas* is heralded by the 2-week *Fira de Santa Llúcia,* when stalls selling greenery, decorations, gifts, and figurines for *Christmas* crèches are set up in front of the Gothic cathedral and the Sagrada Família.

MUSEUMS

Barcelonans love museums, and the city has many more to be proud of in addition to those listed in *Special Places.*

CENTRE CULTURAL DE LA FUNDACIÓ CAIXA DE PENSIONS (CULTURAL CENTER OF THE CAIXA DE PENSIONS FOUNDATION) Though not strictly speaking a museum, this beautiful exhibition space is a must for art lovers; there is always a well-mounted and sophisticated show here, and there are chamber music concerts in an enclosed garden area, plus a contemporary-style arts bookshop and café. The building itself is one of Modernista architect Josep Puig i Cadafalch's best, with hints of Moorish and Catalan Gothic architecture incorporated seamlessly into the turn-of-the-century façade. Open Tuesdays through Saturdays from 10 AM to 8 PM; Sundays and holidays from 11 AM to 3 PM. Admission charge. 108 Passeig de Sant Joan (phone: 258-8905).

MUSEU DELS AUTÓMATES (MUSEUM OF AUTOMATONS) A collection of mechanical dolls and animals, amusement park figures, and model trains. Open only when the *Tibidabo Amusement Park* is open: Saturdays, Sundays, and holidays from 11 AM to 8 PM. Admission charge to the park includes the museum. Parc del Tibidabo (phone: 211-7942).

MUSEU DEL CALÇAT ANTIC (ANTIQUE SHOE MUSEUM) A two-room collection of antique shoes, including 1st-century slave sandals and 3rd-century shepherd's footwear, and a collection of famous people's shoes. Open Tuesdays through Sundays and holidays from 11 AM to 2 PM. Admission charge. Plaça Sant Felip Neri (phone: 302-2680).

MUSEU DE LA CIÈNCIA (SCIENCE MUSEUM) A popular, hands-on museum with a small planetarium and an innovative children's section, which features experimental exhibits about the body, matter, communication, and movement. Open Tuesdays through Sundays and holidays from 10 AM to 8 PM. Admission charge. 55 Carrer Teodor Roviralta, off Avinguda del Tibidabo (phone: 212-6050).

MUSEU ETNOLÒGIC (ETHNOLOGICAL MUSEUM) Particularly good collections of ritual and religious art and everyday objects from Japan, New Guinea, and Afghanistan. Open Tuesdays through Saturdays from 10 AM to 5 PM; Sundays from 10 AM to 2PM; closed Mondays. No admission charge for children under 18. Passeig Santa Madrona (phone: 424-6807).

MUSEU DEL FUTBOL CLUB BARCELONA (BARCELONA SOCCER MUSEUM) One of the most popular attractions in this sports-mad town, a small museum of trophies and videos highlighting the local soccer club's illustrious history — located in the 120,000-seat *Estadi Camp Nou,* the largest stadium in Europe. Open from November through March on Tuesdays through Fridays from 10 AM to 1 PM and from 4 to 6 PM, and weekends from 10 AM to 1 PM; from April through October open Mondays through Saturdays from 10 AM to 1 PM and from 3 to 6 PM. Open holidays from 10 AM to 1 PM. Admission charge. *Estadi Camp Nou,* Carrer Arístides Maillol (phone: 330-9411).

MUSEU MONESTIR DE PEDRALBES (PEDRALBES MONASTERY AND MUSEUM) A 14th-century Gothic church known for its stained glass windows, choir stalls, unusual 3-story cloister surrounded by galleries, and its overall elegant simplicity of design. This gem of medieval architecture also contains an impressive collection of Italian-influenced Catalan paintings and other art. At press time, there were plans to make the monastery the new, permanent home of 80 paintings and eight sculptures from the renowned Thyseen–Bornemisza art collection now in Madrid's *Prado.* Open Tuesdays through Sundays from 10 AM to 2 PM. No admission charge for children under 18. 9 Baixada del Monestir (phone: 203-9282).

MUSEU DE LA MÚSICA (MUSEUM OF MUSIC) An odd collection of antique musical instruments from many countries, dating from the 16th century to the present, in a Modernista building by Puig i Cadafalch. Open Tuesdays through Sundays from 10 AM to 2 PM. No admission charge for children under 18. 373 Av. Diagonal (phone: 416-1157).

MUSEU TAURÍ (MUSEUM OF BULLFIGHTING) A collection of bullfighters' costumes and other memorabilia, including trophies, posters, and bull-ranch branding irons. Open daily from 10 AM to 1 PM and from 3:30 to 7 PM in

April through September. Admission charge. 749 Gran Via de les Corts Catalanes (phone: 245-5803).

SHOPPING

Barcelona has been a textile center for centuries, and it always has been a good place to buy leather goods. More recently, it's become a source of up-to-the-minute fashion as well.

Passeig de Gràcia and Rambla de Catalunya are lined with elegant shops selling leather goods, furs, accessories, and jewelry for men and women, as well as with boutiques carrying Spain's *moda joven* (young fashion). More boutiques are housed in shopping centers or indoor arcades, of which the best known is the original *Bulevard Rosa* (55 Passeig de Gràcia) — an entire city block filled with 100 shops selling everything from clothing and hats to unusual jewelry and paper goods. This complex has been so successful that two other *Bulevard Rosas* have opened — a much smaller complex with 40 stores (474 Av. Diagonal), and a 4-story wonderland of fashion, design, and miscellaneous ephemera (609-615 Av. Diagonal, in the Pedralbes district). The small *Diagonal Center* (584 Av. Diagonal) is also very pleasant and filled with good shops. Also at the same address is the government-sponsored *Centre Permanent d'Artesania* (phone: 215-7178 or 215-5814), where changing exhibitions of crafts by contemporary Catalan artists and artisans are held. What's on display is for sale, although it can't be taken away until the show closes. For more traditional crafts, however, don't fail to visit the *Poble Espanyol*, the model village on Montjuïc, where there are some 35 stores featuring pottery, carvings, glassware, leather goods, and other typical folk crafts made by artisans from every region of Spain. Also visit the Ribera–El Born quarter around the *Picasso Museum* on Carrer de Montcada, known as the artists' and craftsmen's quarter.

There are two *El Corte Inglés* stores (Plaça de Catalunya; phone: 302-1212, and 617 Av. Diagonal; phone: 419-5206) in the city. Part of the country-wide department store chain, they're known for quality in everything from Lladró porcelain and leather gloves to other clothing, records, and books; best of all, they are open during the long Spanish lunch hour. In general, department stores are open from 10 AM to 8:30 PM; smaller shops close between 2 and 4:30 PM. All are closed — *Tancat* in Catalan — on Sundays.

Somewhat smaller, but still carrying wide range of merchandise, are the two *Galerias Preciados* stores (on Porta de l'Angel; phone: 317-0000, and Plaça Francesc Macià; phone: 419-6262). Top avant-garde Spanish clothing designers are represented, as well as everyday goods from children's clothes and toys to food.

A visit to at least one of the city's markets is a colorful must, whether *La Boqueria* food market (see *Special Places*) or the *Mercat de Santa Caterina* (Carrer Francesc Cambó, near the Gothic cathedral), where the fresh, tempting produce puts big-city supermarkets to shame. *Els Encants* is the principal Barcelona flea market (held Mondays, Wednesdays, Fridays, and Saturdays from dawn until dusk). Formerly held on the Plaça de les Glòries Catalanes, at press time it was slated to be moved to a new, as-yet-to-be announced location. (Check with the tourist office.) An outdoor art market is on the Plaça de Sant Josep Oriol on Saturdays from 10 AM to 10 PM and Sundays from 10 AM to 3 PM in September through July. Spend Sunday mornings in Plaça Reial among the stamp and coin collectors (9 AM to 2:30 PM) or at the *Mercat de Sant Antoni,* leafing through old books and magazines (10 AM to 2 PM). There is an unusual organic food market, featuring bread, cheese, honey, tea, and such from the nearby mountains, on Saturdays, Sundays, and holidays from 10 AM to 2 PM on the Plaça de la Sagrada Família.

More than 150 antiques shops are spread along the narrow streets of the Barri Gòtic in Barcelona. Major periods as far back as the 12th century are represented. One of the best shops is *Alberto Grasas* (10 Carrer Banys Nous and 10 bis Carrer Palla; phone: 317-8838), which sells antique paintings, furniture, and decorative objects, principally porcelain. For ceramics, one of the city's top showrooms is *Arturo Ramón* (25 Carrer Palla; phone: 302-5974). Its prize possessions include 18th-century furniture, as well as the highly prized ceramics from Manises. Look out for the monthly *subastas* (sales) at *Sotheby's* (2 Passeig Domingo; phone: 215-2149). A Barri Gòtic antiques market, formerly held on the Plaça Nova, now takes place on the Plaça del Pi every Thursday (except during August) from 10 AM to 10 PM. See also *Antiques and Auctions* in DIVERSIONS.

It is no coincidence that Catalonia has the highest literacy rate in Spain and can claim to be the only city in the country where the patron saint's day (*St. George's Day,* April 23) is celebrated with gifts of books to friends. In Barcelona, it sometimes seems as if there's a bookshop on every block. A good collection of English-language books can be found at *BCN Books* (277 Arago; phone: 487-3123) and *The English Bookshop* (52 Calaf; phone: 200-4147). For secondhand books in English, try *K.O. and Simon's* (13 Calle La Granja; phone: 238-3086).

Other shops worth exploring:

ADOLFO DOMÍNGUEZ Menswear from one of Spain's internationally recognized designers. 89 Passeig de Gràcia (phone: 215-7638).

ARTESPANYA A high-quality choice of Spanish crafts, from handmade glass and leather goods to tables and chairs. 75 Rambla de Catalunya (phone: 215-2939).

BD EDICIONES DE DISEÑO Showroom for one of the top Spanish interior design firms. Furniture and accessories by major contemporary figures, as well as licensed reproductions of design classics by Gaudí, Josef Hoffman, and other 20th-century designers. 291-293 Carrer de Mallorca (phone: 258-6909).

CAMILA HAMMI Furniture, tableware, and decorative objects from the 1940s and 1950s, plus an exhibition space for contemporary Catalan artists. 197 Carrer del Rosselló (phone: 218-2211).

CAMPER Women's shoes and handbags, the latest in styles and colors. Popular with the younger disco and nightclub set. 5 Av. Pau Casals (phone: 209-5846), 248 Carrer Muntaner (phone: 201-3188), and 246 Carrer de València (phone: 215-6390).

DOS Y UNA A glorified souvenir shop, full of Mariscal T-shirts, plus miniatures of Gaudí buildings and other local memorabilia. 275 Carrer del Rosselló (phone: 217-7032).

E. FUREST Classy men's clothing both neo-traditional and contemporary, from a wide selection of Spanish, other European, and even American designers. 3 Av. Pau Casals (phone: 203-4204), 12 Passeig de Gràcia (phone: 301-2000), 468 Av. Diagonal (phone: 218-2665), and 609 Av. Diagonal (phone: 419-4006).

ELEVEN The largest selection of men's and women's shoes in Barcelona, more than 2,000 styles, from traditional to way-out. 466 Av. Diagonal (phone: 218-4558).

ENRIC MAJORAL Unusual handmade jewelry in silver, gold, oxidized bronze, and even plastic. 19 Carrer de Laforja (phone: 238-0752).

GRÀFIQUES EL TINELL A sort of antique stationery store, with recently minted notepaper, letterheads, bookplates, prints, and the like, many hand-colored and/or made from original 18th- and 19th-century woodblocks and engraving plates. 1 Carrer Freneria (phone: 315-0758).

GROC Trendy designer Tony Miró's own boutique, with men's clothing and chic and expensive ladies' evening and daywear, plus Miró shoes and Chelo Sastre jewelry. Will make to order in 15 days, but 20% is added to ready-to-wear prices. 103 Rambla de Catalunya (phone: 215-0180) and 385 Carrer de Muntaner (phone: 202-3077).

JEAN PIERRE BUA Fashion by young designers, from Catalonia and elsewhere in Europe. Look for Roser Marcé's "modern classics" for men and women. 469 Av. Diagonal (phone: 439-7100).

JOAQUÍN BERAO Contemporary jewelry, often avant-garde, in an award-winning interior. 277 Carrer del Rosselló (phone: 218-6187).

JORGE JUAN Well-priced women's shoes and handbags in distinctive designs. 125 Rambla de Catalunya (phone: 217-0840).

LAIE Attractively designed bookshop/café, specializing in books on the arts and humanities, with a particularly good section on the cinema. The upstairs café has a terrace, and books and newspapers for browsing. 85 Carrer de Pau Claris (phone: 318-1739).

LOEWE Spain's best-known and most expensive purveyor of fine leather goods 5 Passeig de Gràcia (phone: 216-0400). There are two other locations, one specializing in men's fashions, 570 Av. Diagonal (phone: 200-0920), and the other in women's apparel, 8 Carrer Johann Sebastian Bach (phone: 202-3150).

LA MANUAL ALPARGATERA Handmade rope-soled espadrilles in contemporary colors and designs. 7 Carrer d'Avinyó (phone: 301-0172).

MARGARITA NUEZ Sophisticated women's clothing in the finest fabrics. 3 Carrer de Josep Bertrand (phone: 200-8400).

MATRÍCULA The latest in men's and women's clothing and accessories from Yamamoto, Rifat Ozbek, and noted Spanish designer Sybila, among other names. 24 Carrer de Pau Claris (phone: 201-2308) and at Bulevard Rosa de Pedralbes, 609-615 Av. Diagonal (phone: 419-1100).

PILMA A large selection of contemporary home furnishings, Spanish and otherwise, including kitchen utensils, luggage, and fabrics. 403 Av. Diagonal (phone: 416-1399) and 1 Carrer de València (phone: 226-0676).

SARA NAVARRO Elegant, original, contemporary-style shoes and good-quality leather jackets and other accessories. 598 Av. Diagonal (phone: 209-3336).

TEMA Fashions by Spanish designers Manuel Piña, Jesús del Pozo, and Jorge Gonsalves (a favorite of Queen Sofía). 10 Carrer Ferran Agulló (phone: 209-5165).

TERESA RAMALLAL Stylish women's clothing, accessories, and shoes. 17 Carrer Mestre Nicolau (phone: 201-3998).

TOCS Large, well-stocked bookshop, specializing in art, design, and architecture books. Also a wide selection of magazines, stationery and other paper goods, and CDs and cassettes. 341 Carrer del Consell de Cent (phone: 215-3121).

TRAU Where society girls go for posh glad rags. 6 Carrer Ferran Agulló (phone: 210-4268).

2 BIS Amusing "popular art" pieces, including overweight terra cotta beauties and papier-mâché infants, as well as tabletop-size papier-mâché replicas of the fierce-looking *dracs* (dragons) that are featured in the Correfoc, or Fire Run, during Barcelona's annual *Festa de la Mercé* (Feast of Our Lady of Mercy). Also some serious glassware and plates. Near the Gothic cathedral. 2 Carrer del Bisbe Irurita (phone: 315-0954).

VIGARES A small but good selection of leather goods at tempting prices (including riding boots for about $90). 16 Carrer de Balmes (phone: 317-5898).

VINÇON Barcelona's number-one design and home furnishings store, it carries gifts and trinkets, kitchen gadgets, glassware and plates, fabrics, furniture and lighting, food and design books, and many other items. There is a delightful terrace upstairs, and an exhibition space with changing art shows. 96 Passeig de Gràcia (phone: 215-6050).

SPORTS AND FITNESS

In addition to the *Olympic Ring* facilities built for the *1992 Summer Olympics,* the city boasts many major facilities, including the 120,000-seat *Estadi Camp Nou,* Europe's largest sports stadium, and the *B. Picornell Municipal Pools* on Montjuïc. Other possibilities for the sports-minded include the following:

BULLFIGHTING Catalans claim to abhor bullfighting and, in fact, most of the spectators in the arena are Spaniards who have moved to the area — or tourists. The gigantic *Plaça Monumental* (743 Gran Via de les Corts Catalanes) has fights on Sundays from April to late September at 6:30 PM. Additional fights are held on Thursdays in August at 6:30 PM. Advance tickets are available (at 24 Muntaner, at the corner of Carrer d'Aribau; phone: 453-3821). The city's other bullring, *Les Arenes,* at the other end of the same avenue, is now used for pop shows and exhibitions.

FITNESS CENTERS *Squash Diagonal* (193 Carrer de Roger de Flor; phone: 258-0809) has a pool, sauna, and gym, in addition to squash courts. *Sport Dyr* (388 Carrer de Castillejos; phone: 255-4949) has four gyms, including a weight room, a sauna, and massage. A gym for women only (2 Av. de Roma; phone: 325-8100) also offers a sauna, a swimming pool, and a solarium, as well as aerobics sessions and beauty treatments.

GOLF There are several golf courses around Barcelona, including the *Real Club de Golf El Prat* (phone: 379-0278), 10 miles (16 km) southwest of town near the airport, and the area's best course, used on the European pro tour; *Club de Golf Sant Cugat* (Sant Cugat del Vallès; phone: 674-3908; fax: 675-5152), 12½ miles (20 km) away and hard to find in the hilly suburbs to the west; and *Club de Golf Vallromanes* (phone: 568-0362; fax: 568-4834), 15½ miles (24 km) along the Masnou-Granollers road.

JOGGING Parc de la Ciutadella, near the center of town, has a good track. The paths surrounding Montjuïc also are popular jogging spots.

SOCCER The major passion of born and bred Barcelonans. The *Fútbol Club (F.C.) Barcelona* embodies the spirit of Catalonia, especially when the opponent is longtime rival *Real Madrid.* The world's greatest stars are signed up to play for the club, and infants are enrolled as club members at birth. More than 120,000 fans regularly attend home games, played at the *Estadi Camp Nou* (Carrer Arístides Maillol; phone: 330-9411). *Espanyol,* the other, less popular "major league" club in town, plays at *Sarrìa Stadium* (2 Ricardo Villa; phone: 203-4800).

SWIMMING Take a dip in the waters that hosted the *1992 Olympic* swimming events at *Piscines Municipals B. Picornell* (on Montjuïc, near the main stadium; phone: 325-9281). The cost is about $6 an hour. Open Mondays through Fridays from 7 AM to 10 PM; Saturdays from 7 AM to 9 PM; Sundays from 7:30 AM to 2 PM. Although the locals go to the beach at Barceloneta, the water is polluted and swimming is not recommended near the city.

TENNIS Courts may be available at the *Vall d'Hebron Municipal Tennis Centre* (178 Passeig Vall d' Hebron; phone: 427-6500, 427-8561) or *Real Club de Tenis de Turó* (673 Av. Diagonal; phone: 203-8012). The nearby seaside town of Castelldefel, a few miles beyond the airport, is the site of many tennis clubs that rent courts to non-members. It's fun to play there, then go to the beach.

THEATER

The city has a strong theatrical tradition in Catalan, but it still embraces foreign playwrights such as Shakespeare and Chekhov. At the *Teatre Lliure* (Free Theater; 47 Carrer Montceny; phone: 218-9251), Fabia Puigserver's cooperative troupe is so dynamic that language is no barrier when the works are familiar. Another Catalan troupe, the *Companiya Flotats,* led by Josep Maria Flotats, whose repertoire tends to be lighter, though still socially aware, will move into the national theater, part of the Plaça de les Arts complex being built near the Plaça de les Glòries Catalanes. Experimental theater can be seen in the impressive *Mercat de les Flors* (59 Carrer de Lleida; phone: 426-2102), the old Flower Hall built on Montjuïc for the *1929 International Exposition.* Higher up the hill, the *Teatre Grec* (Passeig Santa Madrona, Montjuïc; phone: 243-0062), an open-air amphitheater, hosts a festival every June and July, with classic Greek tragedies and other works. Many companies from around the world now make appearances. At press time, the city's main opera house, *Gran Teatre del Liceu* (facing La Rambla with the box office at 1 Carrer de Sant Pau; phone: 318-9173), was closed for renovation until next year.

MUSIC

Barcelona is a music center year-round. From November through May, opera and ballet dominate, but there is a festival of some sort every month, from medieval music in May to the *International Music Festival* in October. The *Palau de la Música Catalana* (just off Via Laietana, at the corner of Carrer de Sant Pere Més Alt and Carrer d'Amadeu Vives; phone: 268-1000) is a gem of Art Nouveau style (see *Special Places*). The *Orquestra Ciutat de Barcelona* (Barcelona Municipal Orchestra), among other groups, can be heard here. There are two concert halls being built in the Plaça de les Arts complex, located near Plaça de les Glòries Catalanes.

NIGHTCLUBS AND NIGHTLIFE

Barcelona has plenty of action, but be careful while roaming through the most popular after-dark centers, since the city also has its share of muggers and purse snatchers. Be wary of thieves on motorcycles and mini-bikes, who snatch purses from pedestrians and out of cars parked or stopped at traffic signals. The city's pubs, bars, and cafés begin to fill up between 10 and 11 PM, but these establishments merely serve as a warm-up for the clubs and discotheques, which open even later and only kick into high gear at 1 or 2 AM. For flamenco, try *El Cordobés* (35 Rambla; phone: 317-6653), *Andalucía* (27 Rambla; phone: 302-2009), and *El Patio Andaluz* (242 Carrer d'Aribau; phone: 209-3378). Shows are continuous from 10 PM to 3 AM, but really get going after midnight, when the performers and the audiences are both warmed up. Popular discotheques include the *Up and Down* (179 Carrer de Numancia; phone: 204-8809), with loud music downstairs and a restaurant and a more "sophisticated" club upstairs; and *Studio 54* (64 Av. del Paral-lel; phone: 329-5454), a weekends-only favorite, boasting lots of elbow room and the best light show in town. For sheer spectacle and good music (no dancing), *Los Torres de Avila* (Av. de Marquès de Comillas, Poble Espanyol, Montjuïc; phone: 424-9309) features an astral theme, with an electric moon circling the wall in sync with the music on one side, and an electric sun setting slowly on the other. Elegant yet whimsical, *Tragaluz* (5 Passeig Concepctió; phone: 487-0621) is fun, lively, and definitely chic. For hot jazz, try the live jams at *Hot Club Otto Zutz* (15 Lincoln; phone: 238-0722). At the *Gran Casino de Barcelona* (Sant Pere de Ribes, 26 miles/42 km from the city near the seaside town of Sitges; phone: 893-3666), you have to be over 18, with a passport for identification, to enjoy the dining and gambling in a 19th-century setting.

Best in Town

CHECKING IN

Though Barcelona always was short on hotel space, the *1992 Olympics* spurred an expansion that resulted in the addition of 5,000 hotel rooms to the city's previous 14,000-room-plus hotel capacity. The newest property, slated to open at press time, is Ritz-Carlton's *Hotel Arts* (47 Rambla de Catalunya; phone: 488-2854; 800-241-3333 for reservations in the US), a 455-room high-rise luxury hotel located near the Ramblas, which has a formal restaurant, a café, and two swimming pools.

Expect to pay more than $300 a night for a double room at a hotel listed below as very expensive, between $190 and $300 for a double room at a hotel listed as expensive, between $75 and $190 at one listed as moderate, and less than $75 at an inexpensive hotel. All telephone numbers are in the 3 area code unless otherwise indicated.

VERY EXPENSIVE

Barcelona Hilton Situated on a tree-lined avenue in one of the most stylish parts of the city, this hotel's architecture is modern, the decor classic, cozy, and restful. This establishment has 300 rooms, including several executive floors, one of which is reserved exclusively for women. Popular with business travelers, in addition to a health club, there are with 15 meeting rooms for up to 1,000, an English-speaking concierge, foreign currency exchange, English-speaking secretarial services, audiovisual equipment, photocopiers, computers, translation services, plus 24-hour room service and express checkout. 589 Av. Diagonal (phone: 419-2233; in the US, 800-445-8667; fax: 419-5003).

Ritz Built in 1919, this deluxe, recently refurbished aristocrat boasts a new face, and once again lives up to its reputation for superb service in an elegant, charming atmosphere. A favorite meeting place — especially for afternoon tea, which is served in the lounge with a string quartet softly playing — this is the hotel of choice of many international celebrities. All 314 rooms have high ceilings and air conditioning. There also is a fine restaurant. Amenities include 24-hour room service, 8 meeting rooms that hold from 20 to 500 people, an English-speaking concierge, foreign currency exchange, English-speaking secretarial services, audiovisual equipment, photocopiers, a translation service, and express checkout. 668 Gran Via de les Corts Catalanes (phone: 318-5200; fax: 318-0148).

EXPENSIVE

Almirante This small, modern hostelry is in the center of the city near the cathedral. There are 80 oversize rooms with luxury bathrooms and TV sets. Amenities include 24-hour room service, 6 meeting rooms for up to 80, an English-speaking concierge, foreign currency exchange, English-speaking secretarial services, a photocopier, and translation services. 42 Via Laietana (phone: 268-3020; fax: 268-3192).

Avenida Palace Polished brass and fancy carpets lend a tasteful, Old World atmosphere to this deluxe property. The 229 rooms are air conditioned, cheerful, and quiet, with color TV sets and mini-bars. The public areas are adorned with sedate paintings, fine reproductions, and interesting antiques. There is a gym and a sauna, 5 meeting rooms that hold up to 300, an English-speaking concierge, foreign currency exchange, English-speaking secretarial services, audiovisual equipment, photocopiers, computers, translation services, 24-hour room service, and express checkout. The staff is well trained and extremely attentive. 605 Gran Via de les Corts Catalanes (phone: 301-9600; fax: 318-1234).

Calderón Another longtime Barcelona favorite with the business crowd, its generously proportioned 244 rooms are air conditioned, and most have been equipped with the conveniences and services frequent business travelers expect. There are 10 meeting rooms, an English-speaking concierge, foreign currency exchange, English-speaking secretarial services, audiovisual equipment, photocopiers, translation services, and express checkout. The rooftop swimming pool, sauna, and sun terrace command a splendid view of the city. 26 Rambla de Catalunya (phone: 301-0000; fax: 317-4453).

Claris The former 19th-century Vedruna Palace, with its original regal façade intact, has been renovated with marble floors and teak paneling. Owner Jordi Clos owns the most important collection of Egyptian art in Spain, and he has installed 70 pieces of it in a 2nd-floor gallery of the hotel. There are Egyptian or Indian pieces of art in the 124 rooms; the hotel also boasts 2 restaurants, a bar, a swimming pool, a sauna, and parking facilities, plus an English-speaking concierge and foreign currency exchange. 150 Carrer Pau Claris (phone: 487-6262; in the US, 800-888-4747; fax: 487-8736).

Colón A renovated old favorite in the Barri Gòtic, right in front of the cathedral. Clean and pleasantly decorated, it has 146 air conditioned, high-ceilinged rooms, including 10 on the sixth floor with terraces (3 of these — 2 doubles and a single — face the cathedral). Amenities include 24-hour room service; 1 meeting room for up to 100 people; an English-speaking concierge; foreign currency exchange; and translation services. 7 Av. de la Catedral (phone: 301-1400; fax: 317-2915).

Condes de Barcelona Modernista outside and modern inside, it's in a striking Art Nouveau building that was transformed into a luxury hotel in the mid-1980s, and proved so popular that it is already undergoing an expansion. The 100 air conditioned rooms and suites contain all the expected amenities. Its location in the heart of the Eixample is ideal, and its *Brasserie Condal* is a good dining spot. There are 5 meeting rooms with a capacity of 20 to 225 people, an English-speaking concierge, foreign currency exchange, English-speaking secretarial services, audiovisual equipment, photocopiers, and translation services. 75 Passeig de Gràcia (phone: 487-3737; fax: 487-1442).

Derby This is an elegant establishment done in hushed colors, with diffused lighting and impressive wood trim and ornamentation. The 117 air conditioned rooms have private baths; those on the top floor have large terraces. There are 3 meeting rooms for up to 50 people, an English-speaking concierge, foreign currency exchange, English-speaking secretarial services, a photocopier, and translation services. The intimate piano bar adds an extra special touch. Affiliated with Best Western. 21 Carrer de Loreto (phone: 322-3215; in the US, 800-528-1234; fax: 410-0862).

Diplomatic Dedicated to businesspeople with its excellent conference facilities, this modern 217-room establishment is conveniently located near the Pedrera and the Passeig de Gràcia shops. Amenities include 24-hour room service, 5 meeting rooms that hold up to 500 people, an English-speaking concierge, foreign currency exchange, English-speaking secretarial services, audiovisual equipment, photocopiers, computers, translation services, and express checkout. 122 Carrer de Pau Claris (phone: 488-0200 fax: 488-1222).

Duques de Bergara Stepping into the foyer, you'll find yourself 100 years back in time. Located next to the Plaça de Catalunya, this charming hotel boasts marble floors, pillars, cut-glass mirrors, molded ceilings, and 56 modern and stylish rooms. Amenities include 24-hour room service, 2 meeting rooms, an English-speaking concierge, foreign currency exchange, English-speaking secretarial services, and photocopiers. 11 Bergara (phone 301-5151; fax: 317-3442).

Gran Hotel Havana This luxury establishment has a neo-classical façade, but a completely modern interior featuring a dramatic 6-story central atrium lined with shops, a piano bar, and a restaurant. Its 141 rooms are decorated with Italian marble and are equipped with satellite television. On the top floor are 10 deluxe suites and a private terrace garden. Other amenities include a concierge, 4 large meeting rooms, audiovisual equipment, fax machines, and translation services. 647 Gran Via de les Corts Catalanes (phone: 412-1115; fax: 412-2611).

Meliá Barcelona Sarrìa Near Plaça de Francesc Macià, this is a favorite with businesspeople. All 312 rooms are air conditioned and have king-size beds. The executive Piso Real floor features its own concierge. Amenities include 24-hour room service, 9 meeting rooms, an English-speaking concierge, foreign currency exchange, English-speaking secretarial services, audiovisual equipment, photocopiers, and translation services. 50 Av. de Sarrìa (phone: 410-6060; in the US, 800-336-3542; fax: 321-5179).

Le Meridien Barcelona A large (210-room), imposing link in the international chain, it provides expected standards of comfort and service. The Renaissance Club rooms on the top 4 floors are the finest accommodations, featuring computer terminals. Ideally located near the Barri Gòtic, it has 2 restaurants. Other amenities include 24-hour room service, an English-speaking concierge, foreign currency exchange, English-speaking secretarial services, audiovisual equipment, photocopiers, computers in its business center, translation services, 10 meeting rooms, and express checkout. 111 La Rambla (phone: 318-6200; in the US, 800-543-4300; fax: 301-7776).

Presidente This 156-room modern, luxury establishment is located away from the center of town but is, nevertheless, bustling with businesspeople, film stars, and other personalities. Amenities include 24-hour room service, 3 meeting rooms holding up to 150, an English-speaking concierge, foreign currency exchange, English-speaking secretarial services, audiovisual equipment, photocopiers, and translation services. 570 Av. Diagonal (phone: 200-2111; fax: 209-5106).

Princesa Sofía Big, bustling, and modern, this convention-oriented hotel has an indoor swimming pool, a gym, a sauna, and restaurants. It could be anywhere in the world, but is out near the university and the *Estadi Camp Nou.* The 511 air conditioned rooms, decorated in contemporary style, have large tile bathrooms, direct-dial telephones, color TV sets, and mini-bars. Other amenities include 24-hour room service, 28 meeting rooms, an English-speaking concierge, foreign currency exchange, English-speaking secretarial services, audiovisual equipment, photocopiers, computers, translation services, and express checkout. Plaça de Pius XII (phone: 330-7111; fax: 330-7621).

Rey Juan Carlos I Named for the King of Spain, this modern property, near the university and the upscale Pedralbes neighborhood, has 375 rooms and 37 suites, all surrounding a large, open atrium. Facilities include 24-hour room service, English-speaking secretarial services, 6 meeting rooms, foreign currency exchange, a health club and outdoor swimming pool, 3 restaurants (one of which is Japanese), and 2 bars. 661-667 Av. Diagonal (phone: 448-0808; fax: 448-0607).

Rivoli Rambla Conveniently situated on La Rambla, within easy walking distance from the Barri Gòtic, the Plaça de Catalunya, Passeig de Gràcia, and the waterfront. The 87 rooms are furnished in low-key contemporary style, with remote-control TV sets, room safes, mini-bars, and personal computers in the suites. There is a small fitness center, an attractive restaurant called *Le Brut,* showcasing specialties from all over Spain, a rooftop terrace, and the *Blue Moon* piano bar. 128 Rambla dels Estudis (phone: 302-6643; for reservations, 412-5053; fax: 317-5053).

MODERATE

Espanya A well-priced hotel with an Art Nouveau dining room in a 19th-century building. It has antique plumbing, but it's clean, with 84 rooms on the edge of the Barri Gòtic. 9 Sant Pau (phone: 318-1758; fax: 317-1134).

Gala Placidia An economical apartment complex, it has 31 suites with small bedrooms, sitting rooms with fireplaces, dining areas, and refrigerators. 112 Via Augusta (phone: 217-8200; fax: 217-8251).

Majestic A Barcelona classic affiliated with Best Western, with 335 air conditioned rooms with TV sets, in-room English-language movies, built-in hair dryers, and mini-bars. There is also a gym, a sauna, and a rooftop swimming pool, plus 24-hour room service, 9 meeting rooms, an English-speaking concierge, foreign currency exchange, English-speaking secretarial services, audiovisual equipment, and photocopiers. The location, in the heart of the Eixample (opposite the *Condes de Barcelona*), amid restaurants, shops, and Art Nouveau buildings, couldn't be better. 70 Passeig de Gràcia (phone: 488-1717; in the US, 800-528-1234; fax: 418-8880).

Oriente Right on La Rambla, so reserve a room at the back. Built in 1842, with fancy public rooms, its Old World charm has worn a bit thin, but its central location just about compensates. There are 142 rooms. 45 La Rambla (phone: 302-2558; fax: 412-3819).

Rialto In the heart of the Barri Gòtic, this simple but stylish place has 128 rooms, all air conditioned. 42 Carrer de Ferrán (phone: 318-5212; fax: 315-3819).

INEXPENSIVE

Gaudí Renovated and rather spartan, but handy for Montjuïc, the port, and the Barri Gòtic. There are 73 rooms; those on the top floor have great views of Montjuïc and the Gothic cathedral. 12 Carrer Nou de la Rambla (phone: 317-9032; fax: 412-2636).

Jardín Overlooking two of the most picturesque squares in the Barri Gòtic, this 100-year-old establishment is simple, but scenic. Half of its 38 rooms have private baths. 1 Plaça de Sant Josep Oriol (phone: 301-5900; fax: 318-3664).

Nouvel Conveniently located on a pedestrians-only street near the top of La Rambla and the Plaça Catalunya, it has 76 air conditioned rooms. 18-20 Carrer Santa Anna (phone: 301-8274).

EATING OUT

Barcelonans are serious about eating, often taking coffee and a pastry for breakfast in a café or *cafeteria* (in Spain this word means a kind of sit-down coffee shop; our idea of a cafeteria is called a "self-service"); a Spanish-style omelette or a ham-and-cheese sandwich between 11 AM and noon; a late lunch (many restaurants don't even open until 2 PM); a round of *tapas* (see below) later in the day to take the edge off the appetite; and an even later dinner, beginning at 10 or 10:30 PM. (In the heat of the summer, and on weekends, this could be 11 PM.)

Barcelona boasts restaurants of every kind, including French, Italian, German, Chinese, Japanese, Argentinean, Ecuadoran, Lebanese, and even American, as well as establishments serving specialties of the Basque country, Andalusia, Navarra, and virtually every other Spanish region. But as Catalan self-pride has blossomed, so has interest in and respect for the traditional cooking of Catalonia, as well as contemporary improvisations on the theme. Catalan food is unusual, and not much like other Spanish culinary idioms. Codified as early as the 14th century, influenced by the Romans, Visigoths, and Moors (and later by the French and Italians), it is exuberant, voluptuous, dense, baroque, and definitively Mediterranean. It freely and skillfully mixes fish and fowl, meat and fruit, garlic and chocolate; it adds nuts and aromatic spices to its savory sauces; combines salted fish (especially anchovies and salt cod) with fresh; and constructs elaborate culinary fantasies around pigs' trotters, snails, wild mushrooms, and squid — sometimes all in the same pot. It has remained closer to its medieval roots than any other Western European cooking today, but at the same time has admitted influences from Italy, France, even Asia, updating itself without losing its ancient soul. *Sarsuela,* an everything-but-the-kitchen-sink soup, or stew of fish and shellfish, is something of a tourist dish, often made with products past their prime. Instead, try the simpler *suquet,* a stew made with potatoes and just one or two varieties of fish. Paella, originally from Valencia, to the south, is popular in Barcelona; the version called *paella Parellada,* named for a local dandy, is a specialty, made without bones or shells. *Arròs negre,* or black rice, made with inkfish (similar to squid but more flavorful), is a delicacy from the Costa Brava, well interpreted at several Barcelona restaurants. The most basic Catalan dish is *escudella i carn d'olla,* a hearty stew of sausage, beans, meatballs, and assorted vegetables — best eaten on chilly winter days. The classic Catalan snack food is *pa amb tomàquet* (bread with tomato), simply good country bread moistened with olive oil and the juice of fresh tomatoes, usually accompanied by plump Costa Brava anchovies or mountain ham. *Crema catalana,* the ubiquitous caramel custard with the burnt-sugar top, often concludes a meal.

Expect to pay $60 or more for a dinner for two, including wine, in restaurants classified as expensive, $30 to $60 in establishments in the moderate range, and under $30 in inexpensive places. It's always a good idea to check for the daily fixed-price menu — the *menú del día* — which all restaurants are required to offer. All telephone numbers are in the 3 area code unless otherwise indicated.

For an unforgettable dining experience, we begin with our culinary favorites, followed by our recommendations of cost and quality choices listed by price category.

DELIGHTFUL DINING

Eldorado Petit A proud recipient of the National Gastronomy Award, owner Lluís Cruanyas made a big hit with his first restaurant of the same name, in Sant Feliu de Guixols on the Costa Brava, before opening this culinary shrine in the Catalan capital. Situated in one of Barcelona's elite neighborhoods, the menu combines local and 'rench dishes in a "new Catalan" style. For starters, try the shrimp salad vinaigrette, or the cold cod salad with cilantro and thyme. Entrées include *bacalao* wrapped in bell peppers, scallops with leeks julienne, salmon lasagne, and goose liver and duck liver pâtés. Dessert specialties include exquisite homemade ice creams and sherbets. There is also a walk-through wine cellar. Closed Sundays and the first 2 weeks in August. Reservations essential. Major credit cards accepted. 51 Carrer de Dolors Monserdá (phone: 204-5506).

Neichel This dining spot boasts two Michelin stars and a dedicated local following. Owner Jean-Louis Neichel serves Catalan specialties with a French flair, among them rare slices of duck breast lavished with juniper berries and wild raspberries, lobster salad garnished with quail eggs and truffle strips, a wonderful seafood platter of *merluza*, mollusks, and freshwater crab in two tasty sauces, filet of sea bass in cream of sea urchin, fish pot-au-feu with wine, and the best pastry cart in all of Spain. When the taste buds crave something French, this luxurious and elegant restaurant is the place to visit. Closed August, Sundays, holidays, *Christmas Week*, and *Holy Week*. Reservations necessary. Major credit cards accepted. 16 bis Av. de Pedralbes (phone: 203-8408).

Racó de Can Fabes Nestled in the foothills of Montseny Mountain just north of the city, this highly creative restaurant, hidden away in an old stone house, is another of the very few two-Michelin-star restaurants in the area. (In fact, it is rumored to be the next Spanish establishment in line for a third one.) Rustic, yet refined, the Relais Gourmands establishment focuses on Mediterranean fare, with specialties making wide use of local ingredients — particularly indigenous truffles and other funghi, as well as herbs — in outstanding dishes such as *raviolis de gambas al aceite de ceps* (prawn ravioli with porcini mushrooms) and *lomo de cordero con hierbas del Montseny* (loin of lamb with local herbs). Closed Sunday nights, Mondays, 2 weeks at the end of January, and the first 2 weeks in July. Reservations necessary. Major credit cards accepted. 6 Carrer de Sant Joan, Sant Celoni (phone: 867-2851).

EXPENSIVE

Agut d'Avinyó A favorite for both lunch and dinner, this beautiful multilevel restaurant in the Barri Gòtic has whitewashed walls, oak plank floors, and antique furnishings. Its traditional Catalan food — especially the duck with figs — is excellent. The award-winning owner-hostess, Mercedes Giralt, lends her considerable charm to it all. Closed Sundays, *Holy Week,* and the month of August. Reservations necessary. Major credit cards accepted. 3 Carrer de la Trinitat (phone: 302-6034).

Azulete Imaginative international dishes are served here, and the house, with its gardens and fountain, is a delight. The dining room of this former mansion is actually a glass-enclosed garden, with tables arranged around a decorative pool, surrounded by lush vegetation. Specialties include tiny medallions of pork, crowned with mushroom purée, and broiled *lubina* (sea bass) with fresh dill. For dessert, try figs with strawberry-scented honey. Closed Saturdays at lunch, Sundays, holidays, the first 2 weeks in August, and from *Christmas* through *New Year's*. Reservations necessary. Major credit cards accepted. 281 Via Augusta (phone: 203-5943).

Beltxenea When he opened it on the premises of the former *Ama Lur* restaurant, owner-chef Miguel Ezcurra was reviving the tradition of Basque cooking in Barcelona. His new approach to the typical dishes of northwest Spain offers a change from Catalan food. Fish in spicy sauce is a specialty. Closed Sundays, and Saturdays at lunch. Reservations necessary. Major credit cards accepted. 275 Carrer de Mallorca (phone: 215-3024).

Casa Isidre Miró's favorite restaurant in Barcelona while he was alive, this contemporary-and-traditional Catalan place offers impeccable seafood of many kinds. Choose from *espardenyes* (a kind of sea slug eaten only in this part of Catalonia), fava bean salad, foie gras from the Costa Brava (which is very good), and superb calf's brains, among other delicacies. Recently awarded one Michelin star, it boasts good wines, too, and the best selection of armagnacs in town. Closed Sundays, holidays, *Christmas Week, Holy Week,* and from mid-July to mid-August. Reservations are essential and should be made at least 2 days in advance. Major credit cards accepted. 12 Carrer de les Flors (phone: 241-1139).

Casa Leopoldo A longtime favorite among Barcelonans, this family-run eatery features beautifully tiled walls and the freshest of seafood. Take a taxi: While the restaurant is top-shelf, the neighborhood is not. Closed Sunday dinners, Mondays, and during August. Reservations advised. Major credit cards accepted. 24 Carrer de Sant Rafael (phone: 441-3014).

Florián One of the city's most imaginative and consistent contemporary-style dining spots, modern-Mediterranean rather than strictly Catalan in style, but with plenty of local flavors (and flavor) anyway. Wild mushrooms and beef from bullring bulls are specialties. Rosa Grau cooks, while Xavier García-Ruano, her husband, minds the art-filled dining room. There are good wines, often reasonably priced. Closed Sundays, *Holy Week,* 2 weeks in August, and *Christmas.* Reservations necessary. Major credit cards accepted. 20 Carrer de Bertran i Serra (phone: 212-4627).

Gorría This first-rate old-line Barcelona dining establishment specializes in the food of Navarra. Though there are some good seafood dishes (including sautéed cod cheeks in garlic sauce), the best choices here are roasted meat, sausages, and anything involving white or red beans. Closed Sundays and during August. Reservations necessary. Major credit cards accepted. 421 Carrer de la Diputació (phone: 245-1164).

Hispania A Catalan classic in a large roadside villa about a 20-minute drive up the coast from Barcelona, offering light salt cod beignets, stuffed cabbage rolls with *botifarra* sausage, pig's trotters stewed with lentils, *suquet* of monkfish and clams, and wonderful *crema catalana,* among other dishes. It's definitely worth the trip. Closed Sunday nights, Tuesdays, *Holy Week,* and during October. Reservations necessary. Major credit cards accepted. 54 Carretera Reial, Arenys de Mar (phone: 791-0457).

Nostromo Named (rather curiously) for Joseph Conrad's silver-grubbing South American dock foreman, this place boasts a bar and a nautical-theme bookshop upstairs and a good-looking dining room below. Ideas sometimes exceed execution in the young-minded kitchen here, but the warm tongue and lentil salad, the salt cod *de la catedral* (topped with puréed tomatoes and souffléed garlic mousseline), and the chicken and shrimp *canalons,* among other dishes, are excellent. Closed Saturdays for lunch, and Sundays. Reservations advised. Major credit cards accepted. 16 Carrer de Ripoll (phone: 412-2455).

La Odisea This attractive, art-filled restaurant (whose owner-chef, Antonio Ferrer, is also a well-known local poet) offers an imaginative assortment of Catalan and French-influenced dishes. Some things work better than others, but among the outstanding items are the marinated monkfish and vegetable salad, the classic *fideus* noodles fish stock, and the remarkable stuffed rabbit loin with apple-honey *allioli* (garlic sauce). There's a good wine selection, including numerous private labels. Closed Saturdays, *Holy Week,* and during August. Reservations advised. Major credit cards accepted. 7 Carrer de Copons (phone: 302-3692).

Oliana An upscale spinoff of *L'Olivé* (see below), with a light, airy, very handsome upstairs dining room and an ample menu of Catalan specialties — including both the old standbys served at *L'Olivé* and such newer items as red peppers stuffed with hake and black-eyed peas sautéed with anchovies and onions. Closed Sundays. Reservations advised. Major credit cards accepted. 54 Carrer de Santaló (phone: 201-0647).

Els Perols de l'Empordà Excellent traditional cooking from the Empordà region of Catalonia — whence come many of the best and most unusual Catalan dishes. Duck (for which the Empordà is famous) is a specialty, the *escupinya* clams from Minorca are a revelation, and the rice dishes (including *arròs negre*) are glorious. Closed Sunday nights, Mondays, and *Holy Week.* Reservations necessary. Major credit cards accepted. 88 Carrer de Villaroel (phone: 323-1033).

Quo Vadis Muted paneling, soft lights, and harmonious decor provide a pleasing ambience at this top establishment. Service is solicitous and the highly original international cuisine is excellent. Closed Sundays. Reservations advised. Major credit cards accepted. 7 Carrer de Carmen (phone: 317-7447).

Via Veneto A grand, serious place with a rather silly interior — mock–Art Nouveau, padded in black leather — but excellent food, much of it genuinely Catalan. One traditional — and excellent — dish is a remarkable boneless pig's trotters stuffed with ground pork and herbs, wrapped in caul fat, and braised with wild mushrooms. The wine list is one of the best in town, especially strong in Rioja. Closed Saturdays and Sundays for lunch, and August 1 through 20. Reservations necessary. Major credit cards accepted. 10-12 Carrer de Ganduxer (phone: 200-7024).

Antigua Casa Solé Also known as *Can Solé,* one of the relatively few non-tourist-trap seafood restaurants in portside Barceloneta, simple and always crowded. The choice of fish and shellfish changes daily. Closed Saturday nights, Sundays, the first 2 weeks of February, and the first 2 weeks of September. Reservations advised. Major credit cards accepted. 4 Carrer de Sant Carles (phone: 319-5012).

Arcs de Sant Gervasi One of Barcelona's favorite dining spots in the bustling neighborhood near Plaça de Francesc Macià. Try the gratin of eggplant, ham, and tiny shrimp, or the slices of rare duck with zucchini mousse and sliced pears. Open daily. Reservations advised. Major credit cards accepted. 103 Carrer de Santaló (phone: 201-9277).

Asador de Aranda North-central Spanish food, which means lots of rich sausages, grilled meat, suckling pig, and homemade bread, in one of the city's most notable Modernista buildings — a veritable urban castle of a place, built between 1903 and 1913 by Joan Rubió i Bellvé. Closed Sunday nights. Reservations advised. Major credit cards accepted. 31 Av. del Tibidabo (phone: 417-0115).

La Bona Cuina The decor looks a bit like a Modernista parlor, with walls paneled in dark wood, lace curtains at the windows, and a huge Art Nouveau mirror, all gold swirls with a golden peacock on top, dominating the room. In the Barri Gòtic, behind the cathedral, it unabashedly caters to tourists, but delivers good Catalan food, especially fish and seafood, and good value. Open daily. Reservations advised. Visa accepted. 12 Carrer Pietat (phone: 315-4165).

Can Majó Slightly fancier than other seafood spots in the neighborhood, and specializing in seafood-based rice dishes of several kinds. The *suquet* (fish and potato stew) is excellent as well. Many Barcelonans say this is the best eatery in Barceloneta. Closed Sunday and holiday nights, Mondays, and August. Reservations advised. Major credit cards accepted. 23 Carrer Almirall Aixada (phone: 310-1455).

Los Caracoles At first glance this bustling, jovial place looks like a tourist trap, but the good solid Catalan cooking can be impressive. Try *los caracoles* (snails) or the chicken that's always roasting on rotisseries outside; the langostinos are fresh and delicious. Open daily. Reservations necessary (but, even so, you'll have to wait during rush hours). Major credit cards accepted. 14 Carrer dels Escudellers (phone: 302-3185).

Chicoa An attractive folkloric interior and a large menu of well-cooked traditional Catalan specialties are featured here. There are a number of excellent interpretations of *bacalao,* or salt cod (try the sampler plate). Closed Saturdays, Sundays, and during August. Reservations necessary. Major credit cards accepted. 73 Carrer d'Aribau (phone: 253-1123).

El Gran Café A big, warm, turn-of-the-century bistro in the Modernista style, featuring café-society piano music in the evenings, and decent food from a menu that is part traditional Catalan and part contemporary. Featured items include a tart filled with ratatouille-like *escalivada,* monkfish sautéed with scampi, and sweetbreads and kidneys in anchovy-cream sauce. Closed Sundays, holidays, and August. Reservations advised. Major credit cards accepted. 9 Carrer d'Avinyó (phone: 318-7986).

Mordisco For a taste of post-modern Barcelona, this trendy eatery boasts contemporary interior design, paintings by Mariscal on the walls, and a simple Catalan-French menu full of imaginative salads and meat dishes. Closed Sundays. Reservations necessary. Major credit cards accepted. 265 Carrer del Rosselló (phone: 218-3314).

Network Café With a TV set at every table, loud rock music, and trendy decor, it's not surprising that this place attracts a young, well-heeled crowd. Its menu is generally continental, offering such hard-to-find-in-Spain dishes as curried chicken salad and guacamole. Downstairs, there's a lively bar with billiard tables. Open daily for lunch and dinner. Reservations advised. Major credit cards accepted. 616 Av. Diagonal (phone: 201-7238).

L'Olivé Pure, straightforward Catalan cooking in a simple but attractive setting. Bread with tomato and anchovies, marinated salt cod, stewed calf's head with ratatouille-like *samfaina,* and veal with mushrooms are among the typical specialties. Closed Sundays. Reservations necessary. Major credit cards accepted. 171 Carrer de Muntaner (phone: 430-9027).

Passadís del Pep Tiny, hard to find (it's hidden down a long corridor off a busy square), and always jam-packed with local politicians and businessmen. The cooking is home-style and seafood is the specialty. Menus exist, but regulars (and astute first-timers) just ask for little tastes of whatever's particularly good that day. Closed Sundays and holidays. Reservations necessary. Major credit cards accepted. 2 Plaça de Palau (phone: 310-1021).

Pekin The place to satisfy your cravings for Peking duck (the specialty of the house, natch), this attractive place, with its dark walls covered with sheets of burnished copper, also serves a variety of other Peking and Cantonese dishes. Closed Sunday nights. Reservations advised. Major credit cards accepted. 202 Carrer Rosselló (phone: 215-0177).

El Raïm A tiny place, hard to locate, with a guestbook filled with famous names, and a kitchen offering plain, hearty, absolutely unadorned Catalan specialties — often including *escudella i carn d'olla,* this region's monumental version of pot-au-feu. Closed Sunday nights. Reservations necessary. Major credit cards accepted. 6 Carrer de la Pescateria (phone: 323-1033).

Senyor Parellada A good-looking place near the *Museu Picasso,* built around the atrium of an early iron-frame Modernista building. Owner Ramón Parel lada comes from a restaurant family — his grandfather once ran *Set Portes* and his father had the well-known *Fonda Europa* in the suburb of Granollers — and standards of food and service are high here. The menu is almost exclusively Catalan, with occasional contemporary improvisations. Closed Sundays and holidays. Reservations advised. Major credit cards accepted. 37 Carrer Argenteria (called Calle Platería on some maps; phone: 315-4010).

Set Portes Also known as *Siete Puertas,* and more or less *La Coupole* of Barcelona — a big, bright, bistro or brasserie kind of place, dating from the mid-19th century. The paellas and other rice dishes and simple roasted meat (goat chops, for instance) aren't bad, but people go here more for the piano and the lively atmosphere than for the cooking. Tour buses stop here regularly — the atmosphere is worth it. Open daily. Reservations advised. Major credit cards accepted. 14 Passeig de Isabel II (phone: 319-3046). Moderate.

Ticktacktoe A combination billiard parlor and restaurant, in a sort of delicate post-modern mode. Some dishes are rather precious — salmon tartar with baby eels, strawberries with black pepper — but the thin noodles with clams and the filet mignon with wild mushroom sauce are delicious, the dining room is luminous, and the scene is animated. Closed Sundays and holidays, and from August 7 to 31. Reservations necessary. Major credit cards accepted. 40 Carrer de Roger de Llúria (phone: 318-9947).

INEXPENSIVE

Bar Pinocho Not a restaurant at all, but a little stand with nine or ten stools in *La Boqueria,* Barcelona's great covered market. Somehow, though, the closet-size kitchen manages to produce market-fresh traditional Catalan food — black rice, stewed calf's head, salt cod in cream sauce, and the like — as good as that at most of the white-tablecloth eateries in town. Breakfast and lunch only (the stewed calf's head is a popular dish even at breakfast!). Closed Sundays. No reservations. No credit cards accepted. *La Boqueria* (phone: 317-1731).

Café de la Ribera Near the Plà de Palau, this airy bi-level café is a real find. Noisy, bustling, and very popular with the under-30 crowd, it features a *menú del día,* usually seafood-oriented. The walls are covered with framed watercolors, posters, and black-and-white photographs; there's often a line of people waiting to get in. Closed Sundays. No reservations. No credit cards accepted. 6 Plaça de les Olles (phone: 319-5072).

Les Corts Catalanes A wonderful vegetarian delicatessen, located 1 block from the Passeig de Gràcia, serving everything from vegetable lasagna to cheese and spinach empanadas. Open daily. No reservations. Visa accepted. 603 Gran Via de les Corts Catalanes (phone: 301-0376).

Egipte Very popular and definitely bohemian, serving students and artists. One branch is located behind *La Boqueria* market, so order the dish of the day for some of the freshest food in town (this one is closed Sundays); both have long menus of Catalan specialties. No reservations. Visa accepted. 3 Carrer de Jerusalem (phone: 317-7480) and 79 La Rambla (phone: 317-9545).

Los Immortales A Barcelona version of one of the most famous pizzerias in Buenos Aires. Pasta and other dishes are served, too. Closed Sundays and August. No reservations. Major credit cards accepted. 27 Carrer Marc Aureli (phone: 202-3579).

Quatre Gats The third incarnation of the popular café near the Barri Gòtic. The original, which opened in 1897 in this landmark Modernista building designed by Puig i Cadafalch, was a hangout for artists and writers of the Catalan Modernista movement, and Picasso had his first show here. There's café-society ambience still, especially in the pretty dining room, behind the café: Art Nouveau lamps, wrought-iron and marble tables, potted palms, and a candelabra on the baby grand. The menu is a limited one of unpretentious Catalan dishes (try the special *Quatre Gats* salad for a new twist on diet food). Open daily. No reservations. Visa accepted. 3 Carrer de Montsió (phone: 302-4140).

Tortilleria Flash-Pan Owned by the proprietor of *Set Portes,* and specializing in *tortillas* — not the Mexican kind, but torte-like Spanish omelettes, 101 varieties in all. Open daily until 1:30 AM. No reservations. Major credit cards accepted. 25 Carrer de la Granada del Penedès (phone: 237-0990).

TAPAS BARS

The Catalans did not invent *tapas,* the Spanish equivalent of dim sum; the Andalusians did. And many Catalans consider this kind of eating to be too frivolous to be worth their time; they like to sit down at a table with a knife and fork and plenty of real food. Nonetheless, Barcelona has numerous *tapas* bars, catering both to locals and to immigrants from other parts of Spain (Andalusia included). You can eat *tapas* as a snack to stave off hunger waiting for Spain's late mealtimes, or you can make an entire dinner of them. This latter is what the Spanish call a *tapeo:* It consists of making the rounds of *tapas* bars, downing a drink (beer, sherry, and wine are common choices) at each, and sampling these delicious snacks.

Many of Barcelona's *tapas* bars are found along or just off La Rambla, and in the area surrounding the *Museu Picasso.* Some of the more popular choices are beyond this zone, however, including *José Luis* (520 Av. Diagonal; phone 200-8312), which offers a wide selection of seafood and some of Spain's finest hams; *Casa Fernández* (46 Carrer Santalo; phone: 201-9308), a great place to sample a variety of beers, including their own brand; *Jamón Jamón* (off Plaça de Francesc Macià at 4 Carrer del Mestre Nicolau;

phone: 209-4103), which serves what its name ("Ham Ham") implies, and it serves the best, from Jabugo; *Mundial* (1 Plaça Sant Agustín; phone: 331-2516), which specializes in seafood; *Belvedere* (in a quiet alleyway off Passeig de Gràcia, at 3 Passatge Mercader; phone: 215-9088), which offers a nice terrace and a wide selection; and *Bodega Sepúlveda* (173 Carrer de Sepúlveda; phone: 254-7094), where the proprietor's own wine accompanies cheese in oil and little salads. Don't avoid *tapas* bars because their floors look "dirty": Throwing crumpled napkins on the floor is the tradition, and in fact the messier a floor looks, the better a place usually is.

BARS AND XAMPANERIES

Barcelona is a hard-drinking town, and in addition to the usual cafés, hotel bars, restaurants, cocktail lounges, and such, has a large number of old-style "American" bars specializing in 1930s-style cocktails, and a good many newer places called *xampaneries* (singular: *xampaneria*), devoted to "xampany," or champagne — which usually means Catalonia's own champagne-method *cava* sparkling wine, often very good.

Among the best cocktail bars are *Antiquari* (13 Carrer Veguer; phone: 315-3109), a secret of the Barri Gòtic, near the Plaça del Rei, beautifully furnished with old-style chairs and tables, a sturdy wooden bar (dispensing fine mixed drinks), antique tiles, and even bits of Roman wall visible in the basement lounge; *Boadas* (1 Carrer del Tallers; phone: 318-8826), on the corner of La Rambla, a tiny triangular-shape bar that has great cocktails, opened in 1933; *Dos Torres* (300 Via Augusta; phone: 203-9899), a handsome, easy-going drinking spot in a well-decorated Modernista mansion with a terrace that is extremely popular in summertime; and *Ideal Scotch* (89 Carrer d'Arribau; phone: 253-1028), a big, warm, popular Anglo-American–style bar with a formidable array of single-malt Scotch whiskies, opened in 1931 and presided over by well-known personality Josep Gotarda — known as "El Rey Gotarda," supposedly the local king of cocktail making. Top *xampaneries* include *La Cava del Palau* (10 Carrer Verdaguer i Callis; phone: 310-0938), just down the street from the *Palau de la Música Catalana* and featuring a wide choice of sparklers and excellent anchovies and duck-breast ham to nibble on, as well as piano music in the evenings; *El Xampanyet* (22 Carrer de Montcada; phone: 319-7003), near the *Museu Picasso,* beautifully tiled and serving sparkling cider in old-fashioned bottles in addition to *cava;* and *Xampu Xampany* (702 Gran Via de les Corts Catalanes; phone: 232-0716), which adds a number of complicated specialty drinks to the list of sparkling wines available.

Barcelona also boasts a number of what can only be called dance bars — trendy places with contemporary-style interiors by some of the city's best designers and architects, full of young people, with loud rock music — although dancing is usually downplayed (these aren't discos per se) — and lots of drinking and flirting. If this sounds like your sort of thing, two worth visiting are *Nick Havana* (208 Carrer del Rosselló; phone: 215-6591), the original of the genre and much copied; and *Velvet* (161 Carrer de Balmes; phone: 217-6714), small, rather loony, and fun. Other possibilities in the same style: *292, Otto Zutz, KGB, Network, Rosebud, Universal Bar,* and *Zeleste.* The Eixample area has a greater concentration of bars than other neighborhoods.

Burgos

Burgos lies between the Spanish *meseta* (plateau) and the foothills of the Cantabrian and Iberian cordilleras, about 150 miles (240 km) due north of Madrid and 95 miles (152 km) due south of the Atlantic coast at Santander. The city has been an important crossroads for centuries, and thrives in a setting that — combining tableland and mountain, wheatfields and pine woods — is particularly characteristic of inland Spain. Although a relatively young city, dating from the 9th century, Burgos nevertheless boasts a rich and colorful history as an outpost for troops fighting on the Moorish frontier, and later as the capital of the kingdom of Castile.

Burgos is probably best known for its most famous native son, Rodrigo Díaz de Vivar, Spain's national hero, more commonly known as El Cid Campeador, a much-romanticized hero who was born in the tiny village of Vivar, just north of Burgos, and became a legend of the Reconquest. Following his victory over the Moors in 1081, El Cid was expelled from Castile by Alfonso VI, who was jealous of the soldier's popularity and distrusted him, even though the hero was married to Doña Jimena, the king's cousin. As an exiled soldier of fortune, El Cid joined the forces of the Moorish King of Zaragoza, and subsequently fought *against* the same Christian forces he had once led. His sympathies soon switched again, and in 1094 he led 7,000 Christian knights to a stunning victory over the Moors at Valencia, where, 5 years later, he met his death. His brave widow held Valencia until 1102, when she burned the city before it was overrun by the Moors, then returned to Castile with her husband's remains.

El Cid was eventually immortalized in the great, anonymous 12th-century Castilian epic poem *El cantar del mio cid,* a tender but mostly fictional account of the mercenary's exploits. Today, he and Doña Jimena are buried side by side in the Cathedral of Burgos, after centuries of peaceful rest in the Monastery of San Pedro de Cardeña, several miles east of town. A simple tombstone just outside the front entrance to the monastery pays tribute to El Cid's loyal horse, Babieca, reputedly buried here. The hero's presence still pervades the city, evidenced by the striking statue of him in the Plaza de Miguel Primo de Rivera.

While El Cid was making the name of Burgos known to the Moors, the city also was gaining renown among medieval Christians as a major stopping point for pilgrims on their way to the shrine of St. James in Santiago de Compostela. This great mass movement had begun in earnest in the 10th century, and as it grew, so did Burgos. The cathedral, begun and completed for the most part in the 13th century, became the city's focal point, and over the years has come to be recognized as one of the world's most important landmarks of Gothic architecture and sculpture. The cathedral is a living testament to the wealth of Burgos in the 13th century, when a powerful group of sheep farmers, known as the Mesta, generated an unprecedented amount of commerce by selling their merino wool both locally and abroad. Burgos was a center of the wool trade, a fact that is recalled by its name, which derives from the "burghers," or middle class merchants, who gave rise to the towns of the Middle Ages.

The 13th and 14th centuries were periods of extraordinary splendor, during which the construction of churches, monasteries, and homes grew under the influence of bishops and abbots and with the patronage of kings and noblemen. During the 15th and 16th centuries, the city achieved further spectacular development, thanks in part to its economic wealth, which attracted corps of painters, sculptors, and architects.

After the 16th century, Burgos began to decline. Only in this century did it return to the fore, this time infamously, as the capital of the Civil War regime of Generalísimo Francisco Franco. In 1936, the Nationalist movement was spawned in Burgos, where it was said that "even the stones are nationalist." Yet despite adverse historical circumstances and its share of warfare, Burgos has retained a wealth of artistic relics that few Spanish cities or provinces can surpass.

Burgos At-a-Glance

SEEING THE CITY

The best way to get a panoramic view of Burgos is to walk or drive up to the remains of the old castle, which is just above the cathedral. To reach it on foot, begin in Plaza de Santa María, in front of the cathedral, take the steps up to the Iglesia de San Nicolás, and turn left onto Calle Fernán González; at the triumphal arch, take the stairs leading upward to the top. The castle is nothing but a ruin, having been blown up by departing Napoleonic troops in the early 19th century, but it's possible to climb carefully to the top of the walls (although it's not encouraged) and behold Burgos, majestically spread out below.

SPECIAL PLACES

The major sights are clustered in the Old Town, a relatively small area on one side of the Arlanzón River. Its central features are the arcaded Plaza Mayor (Plaza de José Antonio on some maps), just west of which, at the foot of the castle hill, is the impressive Gothic cathedral. South of the cathedral is the Plaza del Rey San Fernando; from it, the Arco de Santa María, a massive gate with semicircular towers, opens onto the beginning of the Paseo del Espolón, one of the most beautiful and pleasant riverside promenades in Spain. Just in front of the gate, the Arlanzón is crossed by the Puente de Santa María (Santa Maria Bridge). The main sights of Burgos are within easy walking distance of this core, although most people will want to take public transportation to the Monasterio de las Huelgas and the Cartuja de Miraflores (Convent of Miraflores).

CATHEDRAL The cathedral in Burgos is the third-largest in Spain, following those of Seville and Toledo, but it was the country's first great Gothic cathedral. Begun in 1221, the structure was largely designed by Master Enrique, who also built the Cathedral of León. The first mass was said 9 years later, although the church was not finished for several more centuries. The main body of the church, mostly completed in the 13th century, is in a simpler Gothic style than that represented by such 15th-century additions as the two west front spires or the Capilla del Condestable (Constable's Chapel). Both of these latter are wondrously Flamboyant Gothic. Yet while the cathedral's plàn was originally based on French models, and both French and German architects collaborated in its construction, its design and decoration are in the finest Spanish tradition.

Before going inside, walk down to the Plaza del Rey San Fernando, from where a flight of stairs leads up to what is considered the most beautiful of the church's four entrances, the Puerta del Sarmentál, or Sarmental Door, in French Gothic style. Inside, massive columns rising to the vaulted dome at the crossing of the transept appear to stretch to the heavens, and the dome — colorless, opaque glass in an eight-pointed star shape amid ornate Plateresque stone carving — is as jewel-like as a giant rhinestone pin. Light shining through the windows, the screens, and the skylight and glinting off the grillwork all make the building appear as if it were made mostly of air. In the floor under the dome is the tomb of El Cid and his wife, Doña Jimena, sandwiched between the 16th-century Renaissance Capilla Mayor (Main Chapel, or High Altar) and altarpiece (the Infante Don Juan, one of Alfonso X's sons, and other members of the royal family are in tombs at the foot of the altar) and the 16th-century walnut choir stalls. Both the choir and the high altar are surrounded by a giant grille. The gilded staircase on the north side of the cathedral, a 16th-century Renaissance design by Diego de Siloé, is one of the church's treasures.

The cathedral has 19 chapels, not all of which are on view at any given time. Foremost is the octagonal Capilla del Condestable, behind the Main Chapel. In the small room just off the chapel is a painting of Mary Magdalene, attributed to Leonardo da Vinci (it's behind closed doors in a cupboard — ask the attendant to open it). Also noteworthy are the beautifully carved cloister doors; they lead into the 13th-century cloister, built on 2 levels, and adjoining chapel and chapter house, which function as the cathedral museum. Here the treasures include the 16th-century *Christ at the Column* sculpture by Diego de Siloé, considered a masterpiece of Spanish expressionism, and the silver carriage that transports the gold monstrance in the city's *Corpus Christi* procession.

One of the cathedral's lighter facets is the famous 16th-century Papamoscas (Flycatcher), a clock with automated figures high up above the central aisle. On the hour, a figure to the right rings a bell causing the Flycatcher's mouth to open in a grimace (catching flies in the summer, hence the name). The cathedral is open daily from 9:30 AM to 1 PM and from 4 to 7 PM. Admission charge to the cloister. Plaza de Santa María (phone: 204712).

IGLESIA DE SAN NICOLÁS An unusual, mostly 15th-century Gothic church just up the stairs from the Plaza de Santa María, it has a magnificent altarpiece by Francisco de Colonia, dating from 1505. Carved in stone are some 48 scenes from the Bible and from the life of the saint, made up of hundreds of figures. On either side of the altar and on the sides of the church are haunting Gothic tombs. The church also contains some interesting 16th-century Flemish paintings. Don't spare the 100 pesetas for illumination — it's well worth it. Open daily from 9 AM to 2 PM and 5 to 9 PM. Calle Fernán González.

ARCO DE SANTA MARÍA When Burgos was a walled city, this was its main gateway, fed by the main bridge over the Arlanzón River. It dates from the 14th century (although there was an earlier, 11th-century gate here), and was remodeled in the 16th century. Pictured in its niches are some famous figures from local history: Count Diego Rodríguez Porcelos, the city's 9th-century founder, flanked by judges, on the lower level; Count Fernán González, the 10th-century founder of the County of Castile, flanked by the Holy Roman Emperor Charles V and El Cid, on the upper level. Plaza del Rey San Fernando.

MUSEO ARQUEOLÓGICO (ARCHAEOLOGICAL MUSEUM) Set up in the Casa de Miranda, a 16th-century mansion that features an elegant 2-story courtyard with a fountain in the center, the collection embraces finds from prehistoric times through the present day. Roman artifacts include ceramics, weapons, glass bowls, and household items. There also is an interesting presentation on the region's Roman road system and a small display of Visigothic items. The medieval section houses the Gothic tomb of Juan de Padilla, the Franciscan missionary. Open Mondays through Fridays, from 10 AM to 1 PM and from 4:45 to 7:15 PM; Saturdays, from 11 AM to 1 PM. Admission charge. 13 Calle Miranda (phone: 265875).

MUSEO MARCELIANO SANTA MARÍA The museum occupies the former Augustinian Monastery of San Juan, now fully restored and converted into a palace of the arts. The upstairs houses 165 works by Santa María, a local 19th- and 20th-century Impressionist painter, including portraits and colorful landscapes of the surrounding countryside. Open Tuesdays through Saturdays from 10 AM to 2 PM and from 5 to 8 PM; Sundays from 10 AM to 2 PM. Admission charge. Plaza de San Juan (phone: 205687).

CASA DEL CORDÓN A fine example of secular, rather than ecclesiastic, Gothic architecture of the 15th century, the *Casa del Cordón* is the building where, in April 1497, the Catholic Monarchs met Christopher Columbus after his return from his second trip to the New World. Beautifully restored, it now belongs to the bank that financed its restoration and is open to the public during banking hours, Mondays through Fridays from 9 AM to 2 PM. Plaza de Calvo Sotelo.

ESTATUA DEL CID (EL CID STATUE) This statue of the Burgalese hero astride Babieca, his faithful steed, is so centrally located that visitors come upon it again and again as they explore the city. A contemporary work (1954) in bronze, it bristles with energy. Plaza de Miguel Primo de Rivera.

ENVIRONS

MONASTERIO DE LAS HUELGAS What originally was a royal summer palace was converted into a Cistercian convent for nuns of aristocratic and royal lineage by Alfonso VIII and his English wife, Eleanor, in 1187. This eventually became one of the most important and powerful convents in Europe. The buildings and artwork reflect a wealth of changing architectural styles and influences from Romanesque and Mudéjar to Renaissance and Plateresque. The church has a rather simple façade with a square tower. Inside, note the unique 16th-century revolving pulpit that allowed the priest to address both sides of the church, which is divided by a wall that is also a carved Renaissance-style altarpiece. Beyond side aisles containing tombs of Alfonso VIII, Eleanor, and other royal personages are cloisters, rooms with stone ceilings carved Moorish-style, a small room with a wonderful wooden *artesonado* ceiling, and, at the end, the *Museo de Telas Medievales* (Museum of Medieval Textiles). On display here, among other things, are garments found in the only one of the church's tombs left unsacked over the centuries, that of Don Fernando de la Cerda (1225–75), son of Alfonso X.

Unfortunately, all of the above can be seen only on a fast guided tour, which is conducted exclusively in Spanish. Open Tuesdays through Saturdays from 11 AM to 1:15 PM and from 4 to 5:15 PM; Sundays and holidays from 11 AM to 1:15 PM. Admission charge. Located in a residential district about 1 mile (1.6 km) west of the city center. Av. del Monasterio de las Huelgas (phone: 201630).

CARTUJA DE MIRAFLORES (CONVENT OF MIRAFLORES) In the mid-15th century, King Juan II gave the land here to the Carthusians to build a monastery, which he chose as the final resting place for himself and his second wife, Isabel of Portugal (they were the parents of Queen Isabella of Castile). He died in 1454 and work on the church was carried out largely by their daughter, in the late Gothic style that came to be known as Isabeline. Visitors to the church pass through a grating into the Coro de los Hermanos (Brothers' Choir), with Renaissance choir stalls beautifully carved with reliefs of saints, then through the Felix Coeli Porta into the Coro de los Padres (Fathers' Choir), with Gothic choir stalls carved with arabesques. Ahead stands the dual tomb of the king and queen, with an intricately sculpted alabaster base and reclining figures of the monarchs on top, carved by sculptor Gil de Siloé. He also sculpted the tomb of Isabella's brother on the adjacent wall. (The Infante Don Alfonso was "accidentally' dropped off the Alcázar walls in Segovia in 1468, allowing Isabella to become heiress to the Spanish throne.) Siloé, with the help of Diego de la Cruz, was also responsible for the church's magnificent, immense wood altarpiece, whose sculptured, polychromed, and gilded biblical scenes are crowded with figures. Note the Last Supper, in the lowest row to the left. King Juan II is depicted in the scene to the left of it; Queen Isabel is in a corresponding position to the far right. Open Mondays through Saturdays from 10:15 AM to 3 PM and from 4 to 6 PM; Sundays and holidays from 11:20 AM to 12:30 PM and from 1 to 3 and 4 to 6 PM. No admission charge. Located a little over 2 miles (3 km) east of the center, the monastery is best visited by car, taxi, or, in July and August, by bus. The return trip, down a slight incline along a paved path, is an easy 45-minute walk. If walking *to* the monastery, just cross to the southern side of the river and follow Paseo de la Quinta east.

BRIVIESCA This medieval town, just 25 miles (40 km) northeast of Burgos on the main highway (N1), is well worth a visit. The 14th-century Colegiata de Santa María (Church of Colegiata de Santa María), with its exquisite Renaissance façade, is a fine example of Christian Castilian architecture. The town is also the site of the San Martín church, built in the 15th century, and the 16th-century Santa Clara church; both draw large crowds of religious art enthusiasts. Treat yourself to lunch at the 14th-century *El Concejo* inn (14 Plaza Mayor, Briviesca; phone: 591686), where roast lamb is the specialty.

EXTRA SPECIAL There are promenades all along the river in Burgos, on both sides. The Paseo del Espolón, which runs from the Arco de Santa María to the Plaza de Miguel Primo de Rivera, is truly a treat. A walkway lined with park benches and topiary bushes, a parallel allée of sycamore trees, a sprinkling of fountains, a gazebo, and statues — along with a fair share of the milling citizenry — are all found here. The *paseo* — the communal stroll — is still an important part of Burgalese life, so why not join the crowd?

Sources and Resources

TOURIST INFORMATION

There are two tourist offices in Burgos. The main Oficina de Información y Turismo (7 Plaza de Alonso Martínez; phone: 203125 or 201846) is open Mondays through Fridays from 9 AM to 2 PM and from 4:30 to 6:30 PM; Saturdays from 10 AM to 1:30 PM. A second office, the Asociación de

Fomento del Turismo (1 Calle San Carlos; phone: 201844 or 208960), is open Mondays through Saturdays from 10 AM to 2 PM and from 4:30 to 7:30 PM; and Sundays from noon to 2:15 PM. Both provide general information brochures on Burgos (in English), as well as a detailed city map.

LOCAL COVERAGE *Diario de Burgos,* the local Spanish-language daily newspaper, contains schedules of activities and events in and around the city.

TELEPHONE

The area code for Burgos is 47. If calling from elsewhere in Spain, dial "9" before the area code and local number.

GETTING AROUND

Walking is the easiest and most enjoyable way to get around in Burgos. Most of the major sights are within a relatively compact area. A car, taxi, or bus, however, will be useful for excursions to the sights in the environs and beyond.

BUS Burgos has a good city bus system, with stops at or near the major sights and most hotels. A bus for the Monasterio de las Huelgas departs approximately every half hour from Plaza de Miguel Primo de Rivera, stopping at several bridges en route before turning away from the river; take the bus marked Barrio del Pilar. In July and August, there also is service connecting the center with the Cartuja de Miraflores approximately every hour; take the bus marked Fuentes Blancas from the same plaza. Burgos's main station for long-distance buses is at 4 Calle Miranda (phone: 205575), just across the river from the Arco de Santa María. There is daily service to León, Santander, Madrid, Soria, and San Sebastián; schedules are printed in the *Diario de Burgos,* and are often more convenient than those for the trains.

CAR RENTAL There are several choices: *Atesa* (Av. General Vigón; phone: 223803); *Avis* (5 Av. Generalísimo Franco; phone: 205813); and *Hertz* (10 Calle Madrid; phone: 201675).

TAXI Taxis are available at stands throughout the city, or they can be flagged on the streets. To call a cab, try dialing 203055, 203088, or 262862, which correspond to centrally located cabstands at Plaza Santo Domingo de Guzmán, Calle Conde de Jordana, and Plaza de Vega, respectively.

TRAIN The train station (Plaza de la Estación; phone: 203560) is across the river, at the end of Avenida Conde de Guadalhorce, a 15-minute walk from the cathedral. Burgos is on the main rail line connecting Irún and Madrid, with daily service to Pamplona, Vitoria, Bilbao, Valladolid, and other towns and cities. There also is less frequent service to Zaragoza, Palencia, León, and La Coruña. Tickets can be bought at the station or at *RENFE's* downtown office (21 Calle Moneda; phone: 209131), open weekdays from 9 AM to 1 PM and 4:30 to 7:30 PM.

SPECIAL EVENTS

There are two particularly festive occasions that fill up the town. The first, the *Feast of Corpus Christi,* in late May or early June, and *Curpillos,* the day following it, are marked by picturesque processions. The second, the *Feast Day of St. Peter and St. Paul,* on June 29, is an excuse for a week of celebration known as the *Fiesta de Burgos,* featuring parades, bullfights, sports competitions, and folkloric performances, and a host of other activities that can include anything from mime, ballet, and concerts to model airplane contests and fireworks. Detailed information on these events can be obtained from the tourist information offices.

SHOPPING

Burgos's main shopping district spreads from the cathedral to the Plaza Mayor and up to Plaza de Alonso Martínez, including the streets between Calle Santander and Calle Lain Calvo. The major department store, *Galerías Preciados* (two entrances: 4 Calle Almirante Bonifaz and 9 Calle Moneda; phone: 205846), is open Monday to Saturday from 9 AM to 2 PM and from 4:30 PM to 8 PM. In general, shopping hours are from 10 AM to 2 PM and 5 to 8 PM, Mondays through Saturdays.

CACHARRERÍA A wide variety of handicraft work in tin and copper. 16 Calle La Puebla (phone: 277329).

CON REY Costume jewelry with personality, mainly a Spanish one. 19 Calle Lain Calvo (phone: 260209).

HIJOS DE FÉLIX SEBASTIÁN Fine leather boots and wineskins. 11 Calle Merced (phone: 206661).

VAQUERO Handbags, wallets, briefcases, belts, umbrellas, plus cuff links and costume jewelry. 7 Calle Almirante Bonifaz (phone: 204791).

SPORTS AND FITNESS

The major public sports and recreation complex, *El Plantió* (Calle Vitoria; phone: 220001), has tennis courts and a municipal swimming pool. Open daily from 10 AM to 9 PM.

FISHING With the disappearance of the river crayfish, trout has become the most important catch in Burgos and its surrounding areas. The Arlanzón River yields trout and barbel. Also see *Fishing* in DIVERSIONS.

HUNTING Wild boar abound in the forests of the Burgos countryside, and roe deer are commonly sighted in the National Game Reserve of the Sierra de la Demanda. For information about hunting licenses, inquire at the main tourist office (see above).

NIGHTCLUBS AND NIGHTLIFE

After dark, life in Burgos is lively and very youth-oriented, with most of the activity in the bars and cafés of the Old Town. Calle de la Llana de

Afuera, behind the cathedral, is a center of activity, where bar and café crowds usually spill out onto the street. Popular discotheques include *Pentágono* (2 Calle Conde de Jordana; phone: 202834); *La Finca* (Paseo de la Isla; phone: 234810); *Armstrong* (13 Calle Clunia; phone: 227266); and *Trastos* (9 Calle Huerto del Rey; no phone).

Best in Town

CHECKING IN

Burgos offers an excellent selection of hotels in various price ranges, most within a short walk of the cathedral. Expect to pay $95 or more for a double room listed as very expensive; $65 to $95 at a hotel listed as expensive; $40 to $65 at a moderately priced hotel; and less than $40 at an inexpensive one. All telephone numbers are in the 47 city code unless otherwise indicated.

VERY EXPENSIVE

Almirante Bonifaz Noted for its high standards of comfort and service, it has 79 air conditioned rooms, a bar-cafeteria, even a bingo room. It's centrally located, in the midst of banks and stores. 22-24 Calle Vitoria (phone: 206943; fax: 202919).

Condestable One of the grand old dames of Burgos, a favorite with bullfighters (among others), also centrally located on one of the main business streets. Some of the 85 rooms retain the Old World elegance — ornate beds, overstuffed chairs, wallpaper that takes you back in time — that made the hotel's reputation; others have been modernized with off-white walls and contemporary furniture. 8 Calle Vitoria (phone: 267125; fax: 204645).

Landa Palace The best in the Burgos area and one of Spain's best hotels, this Relais & Châteaux hostelry is a world of its own. Set 2 miles (3 km) from the city center on the road to Madrid, it's a self-contained establishment of 42 rooms and suites decorated with antiques, some of them in the stone tower of a 14th-century castle. An indoor/outdoor swimming pool is at the bottom of a circular stone staircase, its indoor portion protected by soaring, skylighted Gothic vaulting. The restaurant (see *Eating Out*) is a room of equally Gothic splendor. Carretera Madrid–Irún, Km 236 (phone: 206343; in the US, 800-677-3524; fax: 264676).

EXPENSIVE

Cordón The 35 rooms are large, comfortable, and clean, and the location is favorable. There is no restaurant, but some of Burgos's best eating places are just steps away. Staff members speak little English. 6 Calle de la Puebla (phone: 265000; fax: 200269).

Fernán González Just across the bridge from the Arco de Santa María, overlooking the river. The 66 rooms are quiet, modern, and comfortable, the overall decor a medley of dark woods, fascinating antiques, and ancient balconies. There's a hotel dining room for guests, plus a bright, beautiful à la carte restaurant (see *Eating Out*). 17 Calle Calera (phone: 209441).

Mesón del Cid This Best Western–affiliated property occupies a lovely 15th-century house directly opposite the cathedral. The 28 rooms are well appointed, with a rustic, old-fashioned look and private bathrooms with brass fittings; most of them are graced with an excellent view of the cathedral's western façade. Only the public areas are air conditioned. Parking can be a problem, but the hotel will provide a garage for an added charge. The restaurant is a longtime Burgos favorite (see *Eating Out*). 8 Plaza de Santa María (phone: 208715; in the US, 800-334-8484; fax: 269460).

MODERATE

Conde de Miranda Across the bridge from the Arco de Santa María and attached to the bus station, this place is convenient and the area is safe at all hours. Nothing fancy, but the 14 rooms have private baths and offer simple yet comfortable furnishings. 4 Calle Miranda (phone: 265267).

Norte y Londres Centrally located, the 50 rooms here are clean and comfortable, offering lots of Old World charm. Count on the friendly staff to provide good service. 10 Plaza de Alonso Martínez (phone: 264125; fax: 277375).

INEXPENSIVE

HOSPEDERÍA DE SAN PEDRO CARDEÑA Located about 6½ miles (11 km) south of Burgos, this restored 9th-century Cistercian monastery offers 30 simple but comfortable rooms, all with private baths. It's still run by monks and guests have to be in by 9 PM, but for about $15 a day for full board and lodging it's a bargain. Monasterio de San Pedro Cardeña (phone: 290033).

EATING OUT

Burgos and the surrounding Castilian provinces are renowned for traditional lamb and pork dishes, especially *cordero asado* (roast suckling lamb) and *cochinillo asado* (roast suckling pig). For starters, try Burgos soup, a tasty broth made of chopped lamb and crayfish tails. Other local favorites include *olla podrida* (stew), *picadillo de cerdo* (finely chopped pork), *morcilla de Burgos* (rice-stuffed blood sausage), fresh trout, *chanfaina a la cazuela* (hash), *caracoles* (snails), and *callos a la burgalesa* (tripe). Candied egg yolks are a popular sweet. Dinner for two with wine will cost $45 or more in restaurants listed as expensive, $25 to $45 in moderate restaurants, and $25 or less at inexpensive ones. All telephone numbers are in the 47 city code unless otherwise indicated.

EXPENSIVE

Casa Ojeda Some say they've had the meal of their lives here. Going strong since 1910, the establishment encompasses a traditional, regional restaurant upstairs, a popular and appealing *tapas* bar — *cafetería* downstairs, and a fancy-food store next door. The decor is charming, the ambience everything it should be, the experience (we think) worth the cost. Restaurant closed Sunday evenings (but the snack bar stays open). Reservations advised. Major credit cards accepted. Entrances at 5 Calle Vitoria and on Plaza de Calvo Sotelo (phone: 209052).

Los Chapiteles Enjoy *tapas* in the bar before settling down at one of the heavy, dark tables in the smartly rustic dining room. The menu is a regional one, stressing various grilled lamb and pork dishes. Closed Wednesdays and Sunday evenings. Reservations necessary. Major credit cards accepted. 7 Calle General Santocildes (phone: 205998).

Fernán González In luxurious surroundings where diners sit on balconies overlooking an interior patio bar, this hotel restaurant has won a good reputation for its imaginative food and excellent wine cellar. Specialties include French beans with truffles and foie gras, sole cooked in a shellfish sauce, and Burgos cabbage with pork knuckles. Reservations advised. Major credit cards accepted. 17 Calle Calera (phone: 209441).

Landa Palace Burgos's finest restaurant is in the hotel of the same name, 2 miles (3 km) from the center of town. It specializes in local Castilian dishes, and is perhaps best known for lamb baked in a wood-fired oven. The food is wholesome, the portions of good size, the service a study in Spanish exuberance, and the dining area itself is a lovely Gothic room with a 12-foot chandelier hanging from the vaulted ceiling. Open daily. Reservations advised. Major credit cards accepted. Carretera Madrid–Irún, Km 236 (phone: 206343).

Mesón del Cid Within the splendor of the 15th-century building housing the *Mesón del Cid* hotel, this Burgos tradition features a downstairs bar and several dining rooms on the upper levels that convey a feeling of medieval rusticity, along with offering excellent views of the cathedral. The fare includes sumptuous salads, fish, and steaks. Try the *solomillo* (sirloin) or the chef's special *merluza* (hake). Closed Sunday nights and February. Reservations advised. Major credit cards accepted. 8 Plaza de Santa María (phone: 208715).

Ribera del Duero In the center of town, this place serves traditional Castilian fare in two elegant, antiques-filled dining rooms at the top of a beautiful winding staircase. Closed Sundays and some holidays. Reservations necessary on weekends. Visa and MasterCard accepted. Plaza Santo Domingo de Guzmán (phone: 208513).

MODERATE

Angel Small, frequented by locals, it's up behind the cathedral, with its main dining room built against a section of the Old Town wall. Its own white stucco walls are accented with handsome wrought-iron fixtures. Castilian and fish dishes are the fare. Closed Sundays. Reservations advised. No credit cards accepted. 36 Calle Fernán González (phone: 208608).

El Buen Vantar Also up behind the cathedral; pass the unpretentious bar and head downstairs to the dining room, which is actually outdoors, covered by an awning. This is a popular place with the lunchtime crowd because of its picturesque setting, and it's cool and appealing at night, when part of the awning is rolled back to reveal the stars. The food is regional, well prepared, and very reasonable. Closed Mondays at lunch. Reservations advised. No credit cards accepted. 41 Calle Fernán González (phone: 206116).

Mesón de los Infantes Pleasantly tucked into a corner just downhill off the Plaza del Rey San Fernando, this dining spot offers more fine Castilian specialties such as *olla podrida* and *lentejas medievales,* "medieval lentils." There are tables outdoors for summer dining. Open daily. Reservations advised. Major credit cards accepted. Calle de Corral de los Infantes (phone: 205982).

Rincón de España Another choice spot for fine regional cuisine, which is served in an elegant dining room decorated with ceramic tiles or, weather permitting, on the large, awning-covered terrace looking overlooking the cathedral. Though this has the perfect location to draw busloads of sightseers, it is packed with both locals and visitors. Closed Mondays. Reservations necessary. Visa accepted. 11 Calle Nuño Rasura (phone: 205955).

INEXPENSIVE

Bonfin Self-Service Located at the base of the stairs that descend from the west front of the cathedral, this cafeteria-style eatery has a wide range of entrées, as well as simple salads and sandwiches. A good choice for a quick meal between sightseeing stops. Open for lunch and dinner daily. No reservations or credit cards accepted. Calle Cadena y Eleta (phone: 206193).

Hermanos Alonso Simple food and surroundings make this a favorite of the student crowd. The chicken, veal, and lamb dishes, all very good, are served in large helpings. Closed Thursdays. No reservations or credit cards accepted. 5 Calle de la Llana de Afuera (phone: 201711).

TAPAS BARS

Burgos has literally hundreds of *tapas* bars, as well as many cafés and restaurants that also serve *tapas. Casa Ojeda* (see above) and *Bar La Cabaña Arandina* on a pedestrian street leading from Plaza Mayor (12 Calle Sombrerería; phone: 261932) are considered by many to be the best *tapas* bars in town. Both offer huge selections, which include *boquerones* (pickled anchovies); *pinchos* (skewers) of meat, fish, mushrooms, calamari, mussels, and sausage; *tortillas;* pickled vegetables, and much more. Two other favorites are *Bodega Riojana* (9 Plaza de Alonso Martínez; phone: 260719), a crowded corner eatery with a counter and a few tables where an amazing variety of edibles is consumed, including some in miniature casseroles called *cazuelitas,* and *Pancho* (15 Calle San Lorenzo; phone: 203405), on a pedestrian street, where delicacies include baked stuffed mussels, mushrooms sautéed in garlic, and potato salad.

Córdoba

The low-slung city of Córdoba sprawls along a sleepy, shallow stretch of the Guadalquivir River, 90 miles (143 km) upstream from Seville and 103 miles (165 km) northwest of Granada. Of the three great medieval Andalusian capitals, it is Córdoba that best preserves its Moorish legacy. The city's incomparable treasure, the Mezquita or Great Mosque, is a forest of stone pillars and arches so vast that a full-blown cathedral, built by Christian conquerors who ripped out the heart of the mosque to accommodate it, seems lost in the shadowy aisles. Strange bedfellows, the mosque and cathedral are a fascinating expression of the amalgam of Moslem and Christian elements that is Spain.

One of the greatest attractions in Spain, the Mezquita stands in the Judería, a quarter of the city where the pattern of narrow winding streets has not changed since Córdoba flourished under the rule of the opulent Umayyad caliphs in the 8th to the 11th centuries. At the height of its splendor under the Arabs, who had wrested the territory from the Visigoths in 711, Córdoba was the capital of all Iberia, a city second in luxury and power only to glittering Constantinople. A pilgrimage to its Great Mosque is said to have equaled a journey to Mecca. Chroniclers of the day wrote of a city of half a million people, with 300,000 homes and palaces, 700 mosques, and hundreds of ritual baths. The same city that in Roman times had been home to Seneca the Elder and his son Lucius Annaeus Seneca, tutor of Nero, but which had declined under the Visigoths, became once again, under the Arabs, a center for scholars, scientists, and philosophers. It had the first university in Europe, a library with 400,000 handcopied volumes, and legendary pleasure palaces. The silverwork and tooled leathers from its workshops were world famous. The glory days of the Arabs in Córdoba lasted until 1031, when political infighting among the leaders led to the disintegration of the caliphate of Córdoba. Seville then became the capital of the Iberian Peninsula.

Today, Córdoba is a quiet provincial city of 295,000, its economy sustained by mining from the nearby mountains and by agriculture from the surrounding plains. Conveniently compact, it has clearly defined old and new sections, which makes it an easy town to tour. Exploring its historic districts absorbs most of any visitor's time, but exploring its broad, tree-lined boulevards and up-to-date central core is a pleasant plus.

There are comfortable hotels in the city (and the recently built *Convention Center* is an attempt to lure business folk), but despite this, many visitors make do with an afternoon stopover at the Mezquita on a trip between Seville and Madrid. However, Córdoba is worth a stay of at least 2 days, if only for the chance to drive out to the nearby excavations of the Medina Azahara, a country palace and royal city built by a 10th-century caliph. It takes time to browse Córdoba's famous flower-filled patios, to explore the Judería, to loll in Queen Isabella's gardens in the Alcázar, to watch the black-and-white cows grazing on the marshy river islands by the Roman Bridge. Those interested in Renaissance churches, palaces, and monuments will be occupied for several days. All the while, the romantic can fuel their dreams by sleeping and eating in centuries-old buildings that now serve as hotels and restaurants in the heart of the Judería. In Córdoba, if you so choose, you truly can live in the past.

Córdoba At-a-Glance

SEEING THE CITY

The bell tower of the Mezquita, due to reopen this year after a 2-year reconstruction project, is the best place to take the measure of Córdoba. It's open every day, and the extra fee to climb it (in addition to the Mezquita's admission charge), is worth it, especially because the tower affords a bird's-eye view of the Mezquita's roof with the cathedral rising out of it. Bordering the Mezquita to the north and northwest are the humble tile roofs of the Judería, enclosed on the west by restored Arab walls. The bridge near the foot of the Mezquita is the Puente Romano (Roman Bridge), leading over the Guadalquivir to the Torre de la Calahorra, a 14th-century fortress, and to working class suburbs on the south side of the river. Running west along the near riverbank are the golden walls and gardens of the Alcázar. They end near the Puente San Rafael, the city's main approach bridge, which feeds traffic into the major north-south avenues, Paseo de la Victoria and Avenida República Argentina. Farther north is the Plaza de las Tendillas, Córdoba's downtown hub, where the chimes of the main clock are strummed flamenco guitar chords; beyond, the residential El Brillante district rises gently toward the hills. North and east of the Mezquita are the beautiful Renaissance church towers, monasteries, and palaces that proliferated after the 13th-century Christian Reconquest, as well as 11 columns of an excavated Roman temple right beside the prizewinning modern white marble building that houses Córdoba's City Hall.

SPECIAL PLACES

Though its easygoing atmosphere is easy to love, Córdoba's casual attitude toward opening and closing times, especially for the less-visited attractions, can disrupt the best-made tourist plans. Be sure to check on hours and days of opening when you arrive. Generally, summer hours are from 9:30 or 10 AM to 1:30 or 2 PM and from between 4 and 6 PM to 7 or 8 PM. (Afternoon hours begin earlier in winter.) Museums are closed on Sunday afternoons and Mondays. Because of the city's compact layout, all the sights below, except the Medina Azahara and others situated in the environs, are within walking distance of each other.

LA MEZQUITA (GREAT MOSQUE) This 1,200-year-old masterwork by a succession of caliphs is so vast that not even the enormous Catholic cathedral built in its center can destroy the impact of its "forest" of pillars and red-and-white candy-striped Moorish horseshoe arches. In fact, as seen from the Puerta de las Palmas (Palm Door), which leads into the mosque from the Patio de los Naranjos (Orange Tree Court), the phantasmagoric rows of columns stretching in every direction screen out the florid cathedral in their midst. Visit the ancient mosque first and leave the cruciform Gothic-Renaissance church section for last.

The Puerta del Perdón (Pardon Door), next to the bell tower on Calle Cardenal Herrero, is the main entrance to the mosque, although at present visitors enter at the ticket gate on Calle Magistral González Francés. Before going in, be sure to make a full circuit of its crumbling walls to see all the old mosaic-decorated entranceways (some long since blocked up).

Note that the now-murky interior of the mosque was originally open to light and air on all sides. When Abd-er-Rahman I built the first section in 785, each row of marble columns ran straight out to its own row of orange trees in the forecourt. It was only after King Ferdinand III conquered Córdoba in 1236 that the Christians closed in the mosque and lined the walls with Catholic chapels. The mosque's minaret was rebuilt as a bell tower in the 16th century, when more than 60 of its columns were torn out to erect a proper cathedral in its heart.

Abd-er-Rahman I's original square mosque was enlarged on three occasions, as Córdoba grew in size and importance in the Muslim world. By the 10th century, it covered its present 6 acres. More than 800 pillars stood along its aisles, for the most part antique classical pillars, some left from the Visigoth Christian church and the Roman temple that previously stood on the site, and others taken from structures as far away as Italy, France, North Africa, and Constantinople. Since these secondhand columns were of unequal lengths, the builders raised the brick and marble flooring of the mosque and "planted" the columns at various depths to maintain a uniform height on which to support the arches. This illusion of pillars growing right out of the floor combines with a profusion of leafy Corinthian capitals to underscore the forest image.

The addition made to the mosque by Alhakem II in 961 — the southwest corner, containing 10 rows of exquisite alternating rose and blue marble columns and the most dazzling of its holy shrines — represents the high point in caliphate art. Here, against the south wall, is the holy Mihrab, a glistening alcove indicating the direction of Mecca. Framed by an arch of golden and polychrome Byzantine mosaics, it was the repository of a bejeweled Koran copied by a caliph's own hand and anointed with his blood. Just in front of the alcove, on the site of a former mihrab, is the Mudéjar Capilla Villaviciosa (Villaviciosa Chapel), whose stalactite ceiling and plaster lacework are visible only through a locked grille.

The much-maligned cathedral — which even the Holy Roman Emperor Charles V, who authorized its construction, deplored after seeing how it had disfigured the mosque — has some magnificent details. Its 18th-century mahogany choir stalls are among Europe's most elaborate. The big hanging lamp before the altar is a fine example of 17th-century Cordoban silverwork.

The Mezquita is open October through December, from 10 AM to 1:30 PM and from 3:30 to 5:30 PM; January through September, from 10 AM to 1:30 PM and from 4 to 7 PM. Admission charge; there is a separate fee to climb the bell tower. Calle Cardenal Herrero (phone: 470512).

JUDERÍA (JEWISH QUARTER) North and west of the Mezquita, Córdoba's Judería is a medieval Old Town where Arabs and Jews once lived side by side. The former homes of two of the world's greatest thinkers, the Jewish philosopher-physician Maimonides and the Arab philosopher-mathematician Averroës are located here. Today the neighborhood is no longer Jewish or Arab, and the whitewashed houses — some of which date from caliphate times — are now the residences of middle class and wealthy Cordobans. About a third of a mile of restored town wall, lighted till dawn, runs beside a moat and gardens along Calle Cairuán, at the neighborhood's western edge. A bronze statue of Seneca stands at the northern end of the wall, beside the Puerta de Almodóvar, a gate that once protected the city with an iron portcullis and is the principal western entrance to the Judería.

SINAGOGA (SYNAGOGUE) Pass through the Puerta de Almodóvar and turn right down Calle de los Judíos to one of only three synagogues in Spain to survive the Inquisition. (Toledo has the other two, which are grander.) Note the niche where the holy scrolls were kept and the 14th-century Mudéjar plasterwork along the upper walls and balcony where the women were sequestered during worship. Open Tuesdays through Saturdays from 10 AM to 2 PM and from 3:30 to 5:30 PM; open 10 AM to 2 PM on Sundays. Admission charge. Calle de los Judíos (no phone).

MUSEO MUNICIPAL DE ARTE TAURINO (MUNICIPAL MUSEUM OF BULLFIGHTING ART) The city maintains this display in the 12th-century home of Maimonides (whose seated statue is nearby in the Plaza de Tiberiades). Most of the museum is devoted to bullfighting: posters, photos, swords, trophies, suits of light (jeweled suits for toreadors), and stuffed heads of bulls that were dispatched by famous Córdoba-born toreros. Such individual superstars as Manolete and native son, El Cordobés have whole rooms devoted to their costumes (some bloodstained) and personal possessions. Open Tuesdays through Saturdays from 10:30 AM to 1:15 PM and from 5 to 7:45 PM May through September; from 10:30 AM to 1:15 PM and from 4 to 6:45

PM October through April; open Sundays 10:30 AM to 1:15 PM year-round. Admission charge. Plazuela de Maimónides (phone: 472000).

CALLEJA DE LAS FLORES (ALLEY OF FLOWERS) The loveliest lane in the Judería offers a postcard view of the Mezquita bell tower framed by flowers. It's just northeast of the Mezquita, reached from Calle Bosco off Calle Cardenal Herrero.

CASA DEL INDIANO (THE INDIAN'S HOUSE) Near the Puerta de Almodóvar and also known as the Casa de las Ceas, this was once a great Arab palace, but now only its 15th-century façade remains. Walk through the portal to see the small, upper-crust residential enclave of new Andalusian houses installed in the area once occupied by the palace proper. Calleja del Indiano.

ALCÁZAR DE LOS REYES CRISTIANOS (FORTRESS OF THE CHRISTIAN MONARCHS) Much of the beauty of this fortress is in its outer walls and three remaining towers rather than in the interior living quarters. Ferdinand and Isabella were in residence during the later stages of their conquest of Granada, but the Alcázar has been a prison for most of its grim history. King Boabdil of Granada, the legendary king whose surrender marked the end of Moorish rule in Spain, was held captive here; the local headquarters of the Inquisition was located here from the 15th until the 19th century. The Alcázar then became a provincial prison, which it remained until it underwent restoration after the Spanish Civil War. Enter the complex under the archway of the Torre de los Leones (Tower of the Lions), then turn left into the clean-lined Gothic palace, where artifacts such as a sword of 11th-century Castilian hero El Cid are displayed. Magnificent Roman murals from the 1st century line the walls of the royal salon, now used for concerts; down steep stairs are the crumbling walls of underground Moorish baths, with typical Arab star-shaped skylights.

The fortress's centerpiece, the Patio Morisco (Moorish Court), endowed with twin pools and an ivy-covered grotto, leads to the Arab-walled Alcázar gardens, filled with more pools, fountains, rose gardens, and orchards. Before leaving the Alcázar, walk the ramparts and climb the three stone towers remaining from the original four: The Torre de los Leones is the oldest and most interesting because of its Gothic dome, but the other two, El Río (River) and Homenaje (Homage), also command sweeping views. The Alcázar is open daily from 9:30 AM to 1:30 PM and from 5 to 8 PM in the summer; 5 to 7 PM in the winter; the gardens are lighted on summer evenings until midnight. Admission charge. Camposanto de los Mártires (phone: 472000).

PUENTE ROMANO (ROMAN BRIDGE) Just along the river from the Alcázar and easily recognized by its 16 characteristic arches, this was built by the Roman Emperor Augustus in the 1st century BC, although few traces of the original structure remain after centuries of destruction and rebuilding. The restored 16th-century triumphal arch, Puerta del Puente, guards the main

Córdoba side of the bridge and is flanked by the Triunfo de San Rafael column, one of a dozen homages to the city's guardian archangel. Another statue of the saint (this one 17th-century) stands at the bridge's halfway point, its base blackened by wax from candles burned by passing worshipers. What's left of the Arabs' old water-powered stone flour mills can be seen in the river; the giant wooden waterwheel on the Alcázar side is a replica of one that used to scoop up river water to irrigate the fortress gardens.

TORRE DE LA CALAHORRA (CALAHORRA TOWER) In the 14th century, King Henry II constructed this stone fortress at the south end of the Puente Romano to ward off attacks by his hated half brother, Peter the Cruel, who built the Alcázar of Seville. The well-preserved cruciform tower was erected over an old Arab fort. It's now a city historical museum where a slide show about Córdoba and Andalusia is shown daily at 11 AM, noon, 1, 3, and 4 PM October through April; 10:30 and 11:30 AM, 12:30, 6, and 7 PM in the summer. The museum is open daily from 10:30 AM to 6 PM October through April; from 10 AM to 2 PM and from 5:30 to 8:30 PM in the summer. Admission charge. Puente Romano (phone: 293929).

MUSEO ARQUEOLÓGICO (ARCHAEOLOGICAL MUSEUM) Extensively restored in recent years, this museum, a short walk northeast of the Mezquita, is worth seeing both for its beautiful old multi-patioed 16th-century palace and its important collection, which begins with stones from Neolithic times. The history of Andalusia is written in its Roman and Moorish treasures. Some of the most appealing objects, such as the famous stylized bronze stag, come from the ruins of the Medina Azahara outside Córdoba. Open Tuesdays through Saturdays from 10 AM to 2 PM and from 6 to 8 PM mid-June through mid-September; from 5 to 7 PM in the winter; open mornings only on Sundays. Admission charge. Plaza Jerónimo Páez (phone: 471076).

PLAZA DEL POTRO This famous square east of the Mezquita takes its name from the diminutive statue of a rearing colt (*potro*) atop the 16th-century fountain in its center. The austere plaza, walled in by the former Hospital de la Caridad (Charity Hospital) on one side and by an old inn, the *Posada del Potro,* on the other, looks just as it must have in the 16th and 17th centuries. Cervantes mentioned the big white *posada* in *Don Quixote* — it's where Sancho Panza endures the blanket toss. It now functions as a cultural center, featuring changing exhibitions.

MUSEO DE BELLAS ARTES (MUSEUM OF FINE ARTS) The museum, with its restored blue-tile trim and black wrought-iron grilles, stands at the end of a manicured sculpture garden reached through the archway of the 15th-century Hospital de la Caridad. Its creditable collection of statues and paintings includes works by such famous painters as Murillo, Zurburán, and Córdoba's own Valdés Leal. Open Tuesdays through Saturdays from

10 AM to 2 PM and from 6 to 8 PM June to September; from 5 to 7 PM the rest of the year; open 10 AM to 1:30 PM on Sundays. Admission charge. Plaza del Potro (phone: 473345).

MUSEO JULIO ROMERO DE TORRES Recently reopened after an extensive face-lift, this frescoed building, part of the *Museo de Bellas Artes* complex, is devoted to the works of the saccharine 1920s painter Julio Romero de Torres, whose father was the curator at the *Museum of Fine Arts*. Torres's romantic portrayals of Gypsy women and especially his *Naranjas y Limones* (Oranges and Lemons), a portrait of a topless woman, are the big draw. Open Tuesdays through Saturdays from 9:30 AM to 1:30 PM and from 5 to 8 PM in the summer; from 4 to 7 PM October to May; open mornings only on Sundays. No admission charge. Plaza del Potro (phone: 491909).

PLAZA DE LAS TENDILLAS The heart of downtown Córdoba, this is a huge square on a gentle hill, lined with banks, cafés, and shops. At the northern end of the square, Avenida Cruz Conde leads down to the city's main shopping area; at the southern end, Calle Jesús y María leads to the Mezquita.

CRISTO DE LOS FAROLES (CHRIST OF THE LANTERNS) Don't miss this towering 18th-century stone crucifix surrounded by wrought-iron lanterns in a stark, narrow square. It's particularly moving at night when the lanterns are lit. Inside the small, white church on the square — the Iglesia de los Dolores (Church of the Sorrows) — is Córdoba's most venerated virgin, the tearful, gold-crowned Virgen de los Dolores, displayed above the altar against a background of glowing blue light. Plaza de los Dolores.

PALACIO-MUSEO DE VIANA (VIANA PALACE-MUSEUM) This enchanting ancestral palace of the Marqués de Viana, with a dozen breathtaking patios and 52 lavish rooms (of nearly 100) on view, is one of the best-kept and most efficiently managed attractions in Córdoba. A brochure in English describes a self-guided tour of its magnificent interconnected patio gardens, which are its star feature; a guard leads visitors through the house itself, which is a complete museum of the aristocratic Andalusian lifestyle, fully furnished and decorated with the family's art collection and possessions. Allow about 2 hours to see both house and gardens. Open from 9 AM to 2 PM in the summer and from 10 AM to 1 PM and 4 to 6 PM October through May; from 9 AM to 2 PM on Sundays year-round; closed Wednesdays and the first week of June. Admission charge. Plaza de Don Gome (phone: 482275).

MUSEO ETNOBOTÁNICO (ETHNOBOTANICAL MUSEUM) Set among the pavilions and greenhouses in the Botanical Gardens, this 2-year-old museum focuses on the 500-year exchange of vegetable species between the Amerindian and Mediterranean cultures. Exhibits include a profusion of Iberian and Latin American plants, as well as traditional farming implements and interpretive videos. Open daily from 10:30 AM to 2:30 PM and from 5:30 to 7:30

PM in summer; from 4 to 6 PM in winter. Admission charge. Av. de Linneo (phone: 200018).

ENVIRONS

MEDINA AZAHARA A dry, olive-dotted Sierra foothill 4 miles (6 km) west of Córdoba is the site of the extensively excavated and delightfully restored pleasure palace and city built by Abd-er-Rahman III for his favorite wife, Azahara, in 936. Clearly marked paths descend through a terraced town that once housed 20,000 royal retainers and served as the seat of Córdoban government for 70 years. No expense was spared in laying out its royal palace, great mosque, 400 houses, army barracks, royal mint, gardens, fish ponds, orchards, fountains, heavy fortifications, and ornate gateways, spread over 275 acres. Excavation began in 1914 and proceeded fitfully until recent years, when the pace was stepped up. Much of what the visitor sees are foundations and ruined shells of buildings; but the magnificent, colonnaded Dar al-Mulk, or royal apartment complex, with delicate plasterwork, intricate stone carving, and majestic proportions, has already been roofed over and is being meticulously reconstructed. Medina Azahara is open Tuesdays through Saturdays from 10 AM to 2 PM and from 6 to 8:30 PM in the summer; from 4 to 6:30 PM in the winter; Sundays from 10 AM to 2 PM year-round. Admission charge (phone: 234025). To reach the site by car, take Avenida de Medina Azahara out of town to the C431 highway.

LAS ERMITAS Scattered in the hills 8 miles (13 km) northwest of town are a baker's dozen Christian hermits' cells known as Las Ermitas. Their existence may go back as far as the 4th century, although the hermits who occupied them were organized into a monastic order only in the 17th century. The community finally died out in the 1950s, and the cells have fallen into disrepair, but the site is still evocative. Donation suggested. The grounds are reached via Avenida del Brillante. The tourist office can supply driving directions.

EXTRA SPECIAL Don't be shy about gazing into Córdoba's patios. In the narrow streets of the Judería, a quarter that hasn't been Jewish for over 500 years, front doors are left ajar with a purposeful carelessness and a studied pretense of privacy. So lean through the head-wide crack or peer through the convenient gaps in the vines that veil the iron gate into the preening patios inside. They are tiled oases, green-filled refuges from the Andalusian sun, which bounces glaringly off the whitewashed walls of Córdoba's North African–style houses. They are lovingly tended — water burbles from hoses and laps lavishly onto plants, flowers, and white-and-blue patterned ceramic floors. During an annual festival in May, Cordobans shed their coyness, open their doors wide, and bare their patios to the judges, who award a city prize to the best.

If the door to the forecourt is open, that's an invitation to look through the wrought-iron *cancela* (grille) into the family's private world, fragrant with geraniums, roses, carnations, orange and lemon trees, sweet basil, and jasmine. Some outstanding beauties are around Plaza de Juda Levi, especially at 6 Calle Albucasis, where one of the most visited patios in town displays walls studded with pots of blazing geraniums. Take Calle Buen Pastor (be sure to stop at No. 2) and continue to Calle Leiva Aguilar. There's another cluster of prize winners across from the Alcázar gardens, on Calle San Basilio and surrounding streets. Ask at the tourist office for a patio tour map.

Sources and Resources

TOURIST INFORMATION

The recently refurbished Oficina Municipal de Turismo (Municipal Tourist Office), in the heart of the Judería (Plaza de Juda Levi; phone: 472000), is open from 9 AM to 2 PM weekdays, closed weekends. A blackboard outside lists the city's principal sights and hours of opening, as well as special events. The Oficina de Turismo de la Junta de Andalucía, just west of the Mezquita inside the Palacio de Congresos (at 10 Calle Torrijos; phone: 471235), has information on all of Andalusia and is open weekdays from 9:30 AM to 2 PM and from 5 to 7 PM in summer; weekdays from 3:30 to 5:50 PM in the winter; Saturdays from 10 AM to 1 PM year-round. Both offices have helpful English-speaking personnel, and many free useful guidebooks and leaflets, mostly in Spanish (though still comprehensible for address, hours, and maps). Since there is no satisfactory guidebook for the Mezquita, a local guide schooled in the subtle complexities of this fascinating structure is recommended. Licensed English-speaking guides can be hired at guide headquarters (12 Calle Torrijos; phone: 487602). A half-day bus and walking tour of the city is offered by *Viajes Vincit* (1 Calle Alonso de Burgos; phone: 472316).

LOCAL COVERAGE The local daily read by Cordobans is the *Córdoba.* The weekly *El Mercadillo,* also in Spanish, carries listings of theatrical and special events.

TELEPHONE

The area code for Córdoba is 57. If calling from another part of Spain, dial "9" before the area code and local number.

GETTING AROUND

AIRPORT Córdoba's municipal airport, 5½ miles (9 km) from town, has an extremely limited flight schedule, since most people arrive by bus, train, or car. For flight information, check with *Iberia* at 3 Ronda de los Tejares (phone: 478928 or 472695).

BUS Green-and-white city buses cover the town. Tourists rarely use them, however, because it's possible to walk almost everywhere and taxi fares are low. There is no central bus terminal for intercity buses and no central information number. The tourist office has up-to-date schedules; or, for information on buses to Madrid and Barcelona, call 472352; for Seville, call 472352; for Málaga and Granada, call 236474.

CAR RENTAL Among the firms represented are *Avis* (at the airport and at 32 Plaza de Colón; phone: 476862); *Hertz* (at the airport and at the railroad station; phone: 477243); and *Europcar* (at the airport and at Avenida República Argentina, in front of the *Meliá Córdoba* hotel; phone: 233460). Convenient parking for the Mezquita and the Judería can be found along the Paseo de la Victoria (a street attendant collects a small fee) or at the river at Plaza del Triunfo, where there's a guarded lot.

HORSE AND CARRIAGE A popular way to see the Judería, though coaches can't enter some of its alleyways. Drivers are entertaining guides. *Coches de caballo* are for hire around the Mezquita and the Alcázar.

TAXI Call for a cab (phone: 470291) or hail one in the street.

TRAIN The inaugural route of Spain's new high-speed train system — the Madrid–Seville — passes through Córdoba, and the city's railroad station (on Av. de América) has been appropriately refurbished. Seville is now just 40 minutes away, and Madrid a 2-hour trip. Tickets can be purchased downtown at the *RENFE* office (10 Ronda de los Tejares; phone: 475884). For train information, call 490202.

SPECIAL EVENTS

The famous *Fiesta de los Patios* draws visitors to the city during the first 2 weeks in May. Everyone goes from one private patio to another admiring walls literally covered with gorgeously planted flowerpots, and prizes are awarded for the best displays. At the same time, public plazas are decked with flowers and flowered crosses. This is followed by the annual *Feria de Nuestra Señora de la Salud — Feria* for short — held the last week in May. Córdoba's fair is especially festive because of its location in the heart of town: *Casetas* (private tents for entertaining) and the midway Ferris wheel, merry-go-round, and snack stands run the length of the Jardines de la Victoria, and flamenco contests, concerts, ballet performances, parades, fireworks, and displays of Cordoban horsemanship fill the streets. The annual *Festival de la Guitarra Paco Peña,* a celebration of flamencos and Spanish classical guitar, which attracts leading musicians, including the locally born Peña, is held for 2 weeks in July. Information is available at the Centro de Flamenco Paco Peña (Plaza del Potro; phone: 470329).

SHOPPING

With prices of most goods generally high, the things to look for are local products, notably silver filigree jewelry and fine tooled leather. Silver shops with affordable filigree jewelry can be found around the Mezquita and especially along Calle Deanes, as can a jumble of souvenir stands selling toreador dolls, fans, caftans, brass trays, embossed leather wallets, handbags, and hassocks. At Córdoba's finest leather shop, *Meryan* (2 Calleja de las Flores; phone: 475902), the *guadamecil* (hand-embossed and tinted leather) goods are done in the Renaissance style; the handwork is painstaking and magnificent, and prices on the larger pieces run into the thousands. Wander up and down the stairs in this centuries-old mansion to inspect leather chairs, chests, wall hangings, maps, picture frames, and even some wooden pieces, and ask to see the workshops surrounding the serene white marble patio. The more affordable leather bags and wallets that many visitors end up buying here are of excellent quality but not made by the shop. Silversmiths, leatherworkers, woodworkers, weavers, ceramists, and other craftspeople sell their wares in *El Zoco,* the municipal crafts market opposite the synagogue in the Judería. The latest addition to this old complex is the avant-garde *Arte Zoco* cooperative art gallery facing Calle de los Judíos (phone: 204033), which offers silver filigree items. The *Librería Sefarad* (4 Calle Romero, Judería; phone: 296262) houses Spain's only shop devoted to Sephardic Jewry, including folk songs and books in Ladino — the old Spanish dialect spoken by Spanish Jews before their final expulsion from the country in 1492.

For general purchases and boutique fashions, shop the Avenida Cruz Conde area off Plaza de las Tendillas. The city's major department store, the *Galerías Preciados* (32 Ronda de los Tejares; phone: 470267), is another place for general shopping; it has a convenient cafeteria, too.

SPORTS AND FITNESS

BULLFIGHTING May is the season at the *Plaza de Toros* (Gran Vía del Parque), although there are occasional corridas during the rest of the year. Arrange for tickets through your hotel.

GOLF The *Club de Golf Los Villares* (5½ miles/9 km north of town via Av. del Brillante; phone: 474102) has an 18-hole course, a practice course, a restaurant, a swimming pool, and tennis courts. Visitors may use the facilities; call for reservations.

HORSEBACK RIDING Try the *Club Hípico,* Carretera Santa María de Trassiera (phone: 271628).

JOGGING Beautiful suburban roads await guests of the *Parador de la Arruzafa* (see *Checking In*); for those staying in town, there's early-morning jogging in the Jardines de la Victoria.

SOCCER The *Club de Fútbol de Córdoba* plays at the *Estadio Arcángel* (Calle Venerable Juan de Santiago) — but Córdoba hasn't been proud of its home team lately.

SWIMMING Short of a quick trip to the Costa del Sol, the best bet is to stay at one of the few hotels in Córdoba equipped with a pool. The good ones are at the *Melia Córdoba, Las Adelfas,* and the *Parador de la Arruzafa;* the pool at *Los Gallos Sol* is small for laps. The *Club de Golf Los Villares* also has a swimming pool (see "Golf," above).

TENNIS The *Parador de la Arruzafa* and *Las Adelfas* have tennis courts for guests. Another option is the *Club de Golf Los Villares* (see above), which can be used by non-members.

THEATER AND MUSIC

Plays (some by national touring companies), dance performances, and classical, flamenco, and pop concerts come to the refurbished, century-old *Gran Teatro* (Av. del Gran Capitán; phone: 480237 or 480644). American and British films in original-language version are just about the only entertainment offered in English and are arranged by the *Filmoteca de Andalucía* (phone: 481835) on an unpredictable basis. The films are usually shown at Escuela de Profesores on Calle Doña Veringuila (phone: 480624). In summer, the municipal orchestra gives Sunday concerts in the Alcázar gardens. Check the weekly *El Mercadillo* for listings or consult the daily newspaper.

NIGHTCLUBS AND NIGHTLIFE

Except during the *Feria* in May, Cordobans stick pretty close to home at night. Nevertheless, count on finding life after dark in the city center at Plaza San Ignacio de Loyola, off Avenida Menéndez y Pelayo, where, in fair weather, yellow and white café umbrellas sprout in front of the Iglesia San Hipólito. You can do your own *sevillanas* to live combos at the crowded *La Caseta* (4 Plaza San Ignacio de Loyola; phone: 412967), which also offers dinner and *tapas,* and disco. Best from 10 PM to 4 AM, although this lively spot is open earlier (closed Sundays). Or have snacks, wine, or beer at the contemporary little pubs, bars, and bodegas (liquor shops selling drinks) along the square. Oddly, for one of the homes of flamenco, there's only one nightspot in Córdoba with regular flamenco shows. The *Cardenal Restaurante-Tablao Flamenco* in front of the Mezquita bell tower (14 Calle Cardenal Herrero; phone: 480346) features the fast flamenco footwork.

Bar hopping is a good way to end a day in the Judería. Join the neighborhood people at the hospitable bar in *Casa Rubio* (5 Puerta de Almodóvar; phone: 290064), or enjoy *tapas* and beer in its postage-stamp patio (closed Wednesdays). Then cross the street to the minuscule and impeccable *Casa Salinas* (there's no number, but you'll see the sign; phone:

290846), a longtime musicians' hangout, and munch the house specialty, *pescaitos fritos* — *tapas* of crisp fried fish. At the Calle de la Luna entrance to the Judería, Cordobans dance *sevillanas* within the 150-year-old, 3-foot-thick walls of *Mesón de la Luna* (Calle de la Luna) and at *Mesón Murillo* (just across the way). There's also a convivial crowd to be found at the venerable *Bar Mezquita* (24 Calle Cardenal Herrero), across from the front of the mosque.

Best in Town

CHECKING IN

Córdoba's charms are centered around the Judería, so try for one of the atmospheric hotels there. If they're all booked, don't despair — the city is so compact that even a hotel in the modern section is close to the center. But it's essential to book early for the month of May, when the *Patio Festival,* the *Feria,* and the bullfighting season, occur. The hotels noted are all air conditioned. Expect to pay from about $90 to $130 for a double room in those listed as expensive, from $70 to $90 in those listed as moderate, and from $40 to $70 in the inexpensive ones. All telephone numbers are in the 57 area code unless otherwise indicated.

EXPENSIVE

Adarve An updated Moorish villa just across the street from the Mezquita, it has 103 rooms, but it seems much smaller and more intimate. The central courtyard is enchanting. Some rooms have French doors opening onto the courtyard; others face the weathered walls of the mosque. There's a coffee shop, but for lunch and dinner, the hotel uses the *Mesón Bandolero* restaurant (see *Eating Out*), which is under the same ownership. Full room and board are possible. There also is a garage. 15 Calle Magistral González Francés (phone: 481102; fax: 474677).

Las Adelfas This establishment is splendidly located near the *Parador de la Arruzafa* (see below) on a gentle hill overlooking the city. The façade is South American–colonial. Inside, it is brightly lit and spacious; paintings and sculpture adorn every space. It has 101 rooms, a restaurant, a pool, tennis courts, and conference rooms. Paseo de la Arruzafa (phone: 277420; fax: 272794).

Husa Gran Capitán A recently refurbished, efficient international property filled with tour groups. It's on the outskirts of the city across from the railroad station (double window glass muffles the noise), but still only a short cab ride to the Judería, and a comfortable haven when closer places are booked. It has 100 rooms, a restaurant, and a garage. 5 Av. de América (phone: 470250; fax: 474643).

Maimónides Across the street from the Mezquita, it has a somber elegance, with Renaissance Spanish decor. There are 83 comfortable rooms; only breakfast is served, but the *Mesón Bandolero* restaurant is two steps across a narrow alley from the lobby (see *Eating Out*). There's also a parking garage. 4 Calle Torrijos (phone: 471500; fax: 483803).

Melia Córdoba The city's "grand hotel" lacks architectural flair, despite the recent opening of an extension, but boasts an ideal location, a big-hotel lobby, an extremely helpful staff, 147 well-appointed rooms, a cocktail lounge, the elegant *Restaurante del Palacio,* boutiques, and a large swimming pool. A garage is expected to open this year, ending guests' parking problems. Jardines de la Victoria (phone: 298066; in the US, 800-336-3542; fax: 298147).

Occidental This delightful converted seminary set in the hills is now a 153-room hotel. Amenities include a swimming pool, 2 tennis courts, and 2 restaurants; all rooms have a color TVs and mini-bars. It's a 10-minute drive from the city center and from the high-speed Madrid–Seville train station. 7 Calle Poeta Alonso Bonilla (phone: 400440; in New York City, 212-838-3322; elsewhere in the US, 800-332-4872; fax: 400439).

Parador de la Arruzafa The former garden of *arruzafa* (date palms) of Abd-er-Rahman I, first builder of the Mezquita, is the expansive country club setting of Córdoba's government-run *parador,* although the structure itself is of fairly recent vintage. Located 2 miles (3 km) from town, it has terraces overlooking spacious lawns and gardens leading down to a big swimming pool and 2 tennis courts. Many of the 94 rooms have balconies. Cab service is available. Av. de la Arruzafa (phone: 275900; in the US, 212-686-9213; fax: 280409).

MODERATE

Albucasis Close to the Mezquita, this delightful little property occupies an old mansion that has been stylishly restored in Mudéjar fashion. Spotlessly clean, with friendly service, it has 15 rooms and a charming patio, and it's popular among visiting university staff. Breakfast only. Closed in July. 11 Calle Buen Pastor (phone: 478625).

Cisne Simple but sparkling, this hostelry is in the modern section of the city, near the railroad station, a short cab ride to the Judería; it has 44 rooms and a cafeteria. 14 Av. Cervantes (phone: 481676; fax: 490513).

Los Gallos Sol Just a short cab ride from the Old Town is a comfortable 7-story high-rise with upbeat, colorful decor, a token rooftop swimming pool, a popular lobby cafeteria, and a restaurant. Many of its 115 simple, tweedy rooms face a charming avenue; others have patio views. 7 Av. de Medina Azahara (phone: 235500; in the US, 800-336-3542; fax: 231636).

El Triunfo This 70-room *hostal,* right by the river at the foot of the Mezquita, is one of the best hotels in the Old Town. All rooms have TV sets, and the very reasonable restaurant, is usually filled with European tourists. Reserve early. 79 Calle Cardenal González (phone: 475500; fax: 486850).

INEXPENSIVE

Boston Tidy and comfortable, this little *hostal* of 40 rooms overlooks the hubbub of Plaza de las Tendillas. No restaurant, but there is a pleasant cafeteria. Reserve early. 2 Calle Málaga (phone: 474176; fax: 478523).

Marisa A simple refuge with 28 rooms in a prime location across from the shrine of the Virgen de los Faroles at the Mezquita. Breakfast, but no restaurant. 6 Calle Cardenal Herrero (phone: 473142; fax: 474144).

EATING OUT

Córdoba's most intriguing restaurants and *tapas* bars cluster around the Mezquita, although there are also some well-frequented places in the modern city that are convenient to hotels outside the Judería. As elsewhere in Andalusia, the local cuisine is Arab influenced, but here the Arab accent comes to the fore in dishes rich in almonds, honey, figs, candied fruits, oranges, pine nuts, and sweet, fragrant Arab flavorings. Then there are the dishes Cordobans say they originated, among them *salmorejo,* a thick, waterless tomato gazpacho. The city's most famous culinary contribution is *pastel cordobés,* sometimes called *tarta Manolete,* a flat, round pastry with a honey-sweetened *cabello del ángel* (angel hair) pumpkin filling. Be sure to taste the local Montilla-Moriles wines, ranging from dry white *finos* to sweet Pedro Ximénez dessert wines. The Montilla-Moriles wine country to the south produces twice as much sherry-like wine, made by the *solera* system, as is made in Jerez.

Expect to pay $55 or more for a 3-course meal for two with local wine at restaurants listed as expensive, and from $35 to $55 at those listed as moderate. All telephone numbers are in the 57 area code unless otherwise indicated.

EXPENSIVE

Almudaina Elegant Andalusian dining in one of the intimate lace-curtained salons of a 15th-century palace or in the brick-lined, glass-roofed central courtyard. Try the *solomillo al vino tinto* (pork loin in wine sauce) or *merluza en salsa de gambas* (hake with shrimp sauce), and for dessert, order the chef's renowned tropical fruit sorbet or the *pudín de limón y almendras* (semi-frozen lemon-almond crème). Closed Sunday nights. Reservations necessary. Major credit cards accepted. Across from the Alcázar, at 1 Plaza Camposanto de los Mártires (phone: 474342).

El Bosque An indoor-outdoor suburban dining spot on the sloping road to the *Parador de la Arruzafa* (see *Checking In*). Well-heeled Córdoba congregates here — for a *copa* (glass of wine) while the lights of the city below are coming on, or for an elegant dinner later. Try *pez bosque con pisto y gambas* (swordfish with vegetables and prawns). Closed Mondays and January. Reservations unnecessary. Major credit cards accepted. 134 Av. del Brillante (phone: 270006).

El Caballo Rojo Consistently well-executed regional dishes, served by patient, red-jacketed waiters accustomed to foreigners, make this big, friendly place across from the mosque the most popular spot in Córdoba for first-time visitors. (It's also probably Andalusia's most famous restaurant.) Bypass the ground-floor bar and head upstairs to the bright dining rooms, where Andalusian specialties are displayed on a big buffet, and while sipping your complimentary aperitif of the local dry white montilla wine, ponder the choices: thick *salmorejo* (gazpacho), *sopa de ajo blanco* (milk-white garlicky gazpacho with chopped apples, raisins, and ground almonds), *rape mozárabe* (monkfish with raisins and brandy), and *cordero a la miel* (lamb shanks in honey sauce). A 4-foot-high dessert trolley bears flan and other delights, but if you haven't tried *pastel cordobés*, this is the place. Open daily except December 24. Reservations advised. Major credit cards accepted. 28 Calle Cardenal Herrero (phone: 475375).

El Churrasco When it comes to that one big meal in Córdoba, this low-key place, with the best white wine selection in Andalusia, gives the showier *El Caballo Rojo* a run for its money. Locals join tourists in this unassuming house on a Judería side street, tempted by the patio dining, the sumptuous *tapas* bar, and the signature dish, *churrasco* (charcoal-grilled pork loin in savory sauce), plus other grilled meat and fish dishes. Closed August. Reservations necessary. Major credit cards accepted. 16 Calle Romero (phone: 290819).

Mesón Bandolero Rough brick arches, furnishings in tooled leather and old wood, tables set with hammered-brass service plates — this is a restaurant on a grand scale. It's set in an old palace next to the Mezquita, and has, besides the lavish indoor dining rooms, a spacious canvas-shaded patio where songbirds in filigree cages sing among the four palm trees. The menu is elegant international, with local touches such as *salmorejo* (gazpacho), *rabo de toro* (oxtail stew), and *ensalada de perdiz en escabeche* (marinated partridge salad). Next door to the *Maimónides* hotel. Open daily. Reservations advised. Major credit cards accepted. 8 Calle Medina y Corella (phone: 485176).

MODERATE

Azahar Vaguely Arab in style, and in vogue, it's often crowded with discerning locals. Try the excellent *crema de cangrejos al brandy* (crab purée with brandy sauce) and *bonito al txakolí* (fresh tuna in Basque white wine). Closed Sunday nights and the second half of August. Reservations necessary. Major credit cards accepted. 10 Av. de Medina Azahara (phone: 414387).

El Burlaero The modest outdoor dining court and cozy restaurant here are easiest to find by walking through *El Caballo Rojo* to the outdoor staircase in back and turning right up the stairs. A budget sleeper, this place serves simple, well-prepared Cordoban cooking, such as *carne de monte* (Andalusian wild boar stew). Open daily; closed the second half of November. Reservations unnecessary. Major credit cards accepted. The restaurant's front entrance is at 5 Calleja La Hoguera (phone: 472719).

Da Vinci You'll be off the tourist track here at the city's leading pizzeria, which also serves good fish and meat dishes cooked in a new wood-fired oven. Take a seat in the pocket-size plaza in front of the restaurant, or in the dark, cozy dining rooms. Open daily. Reservations advised. Major credit cards accepted. 6 Plaza de los Chirinos (phone: 477517).

Pic-Nic Extremely popular and highly regarded by locals, although it's hard to tell from the unpromising name, façade, and dull commercial courtyard where the restaurant's located. But inside, the menu is imaginative, and it's a casual place to taste typical Andalusian food without much protocol. Try *solomillo a la pimienta y al Pedro Jiménez* (sirloin steak with pepper in local white wine). Closed Sundays. Reservations advised. Major credit cards accepted. 16 Ronda de los Tejares (phone: 482233).

Granada

Of all the fabled landmarks in the world, none stands in a more gorgeous setting than the magnificent Alhambra, the hilltop fortress-palace of the Nasrid kings, the last Muslim rulers of Spain. Snow-capped peaks of the nearby Sierra Nevada form a natural tapestry behind its golden walls, and below, a mosaic of Granada's Moorish-Christian towers spreads like a magic carpet over a fertile plain. Granada has much more to offer than the Alhambra, but it's worth the trip alone to visit this UNESCO World Heritage site — Spain's second-biggest attraction, after the *Prado* in Madrid.

In its Roman days and up through the early Muslim period, Granada languished on history's sidelines. But the city came into its own during the 13th century, when the Moors began to lose their grip elsewhere in Andalusia. After Córdoba and Seville fell to Christian rule, Granada became the last surviving Islamic capital in Spain. Moors by the thousands flocked to the city, transforming it into a center of artists and craftsmen. The Alhambra was their masterpiece. Through ensuing centuries, this wonder of the world cast its spell over writers, painters, and musicians, including the American author Washington Irving and two of Granada's most famous sons, the composer Manuel de Falla and the poet-playwright Federico García Lorca.

The final triumph in the Christians' 781-year struggle to regain Moorish-held Spain took place on January 2, 1492, when the last Muslim king, Boabdil, handed over the keys to the city to Ferdinand and Isabella and rode tearfully off into the mountains with the queen mother, Ayesha. ("You weep like a woman for what you could not defend as a man" were her immortal words of consolation to her son.) The Catholic Monarchs installed their thrones in the Alhambra and set about christianizing the city, creating the architectural mix that is still in evidence. Isabella ordered the construction of the cathedral and its Capilla Real, the finely wrought Royal Chapel, where the marble tombs of the royal pair, as well as her crown and jewel box, can be seen today. Muslim mosques were converted to Christian uses. Unfortunately, many fine Moorish buildings have been destroyed, but a walk through the twisted, narrow streets of the Albaicín, an old Arab neighborhood on a hill across from the Alhambra, gives a pretty good idea of what the city once was like.

Granada continued to flourish into the 16th century, then sank back into relative obscurity once again. Today it's a city of about 265,000 people, with an economy that depends on its rich agricultural valley, as well as on nonindustrial enterprises such as banking, education, and tourism. Sightseeing in Granada is delightful. The absence of heavy manufacturing sections and the existence of only a scattering of garish modern buildings in the busy downtown area confer a small-town, open-air feeling to the streets. The large student population at the University of Granada keeps the city young, and Granada's famous and unavoidable Gypsy women — those wheedling entrepreneurs who press carnations and fortunes on passersby at the cathedral and on the Alhambra hill — add to the city scene. The *granadinos* shoo them off with a firm "no," but visitors don't get off so easily. Nonetheless, the Gypsies have a long history here, and local residents are accepting of their ways. They are part of Granada, and few people would want any part of this colorful, exotic city to change.

Granada At-a-Glance

SEEING THE CITY

This is a city of many views, but the "postcard" picture of the Alhambra set against mountains that are snow covered most of the year is from Plaza San Nicolás in the Albaicín. Within the Alhambra walls, the Torre de la Vela in the Alcazaba (see below) affords a panorama of city, plains, and mountains.

SPECIAL PLACES

Granada is divided neatly into upper and lower towns. Two prominent hills facing each other across the narrow gorge of a river — the Río Darro — compose the upper city. On the southern hill are the Alhambra and the adjoining Generalife (the summer palace and gardens of the Nasrid kings). On the northern hill is the old Arab quarter, the Albaicín, now a fascinating residential district. An even taller satellite hill leads off from the Albaicín to the dusty Sacromonte Gypsy district, a warren of small white houses trailing out to a rocky mountainside pockmarked with abandoned Gypsy caves.

The main descent from the Alhambra is a narrow road, Cuesta de Gomérez, that drops directly down to the Plaza Nueva, where the lower city begins. The plaza is the eastern end of the principal east-west artery, Calle de los Reyes Católicos, which meets the principal north-south artery, Gran Vía de Colón, at the circular Plaza de Isabel la Católica. A much-photographed bronze statue of the enthroned Queen Isabella offering the Santa Fé agreement to Columbus graces this major intersection; the document, named for the nearby town where it was signed, authorized the epochal voyage to the New World. Calle de los Reyes Católicos then continues west, passing within a few short blocks of the cathedral, the Capilla Real, and other downtown sights, en route to Puerta Real, the hub of the city's business, shopping, and hotel and restaurant district.

Note that the opening hours listed below for Granada's monuments, churches, and museums are for the months of March through September; winter afternoon hours generally are shorter, and times are subject to change.

THE ALHAMBRA COMPLEX

Spain's last remaining fortress-palace built for a Moorish sovereign stands atop the Alhambra hill, girded by more than a mile of ramparts that appear in the distance like a golden shield. Behind these walls is what amounts to a royal city, at the core of which is the Alhambra's crown jewel, the Casa Real (Royal Palace) — actually a series of three palaces leading from one to the other as if they were one building. Within their fountained courtyards and fanciful halls, whose scalloped windows frame vistas of the Albaicín and Sacromonte, the sultans conducted state business and housed their families and harems.

The Alhambra was abandoned for centuries until Washington Irving wrote *Tales of the Alhambra* in 1832 after a stint as an attaché in the US Embassy in Madrid (he was later Ambassador to Spain). The book focused world attention on this neglected treasure and prompted Spain to begin restoration; most of the present plasterwork, mosaics, and inlaid wood are skillful reproductions.

An Alhambra visit takes at least one full day (on the run), and it's wise to arrive at opening time, because as the day progresses, the lines of people waiting to walk through the palaces get longer — these famous rooms and courtyards are surprisingly small.

The main approach to the fortress is via the steep Cuesta de Gomérez and through the Puerta de las Granadas (Pomegranate Gate), which signals the entrance to the Alhambra's cool, elm-forested grounds. Beyond the main entrance, bordering the Plaza de los Aljibes (Square of the Cisterns), are the fortifications of the Alcazaba and the Arab royal palaces (Casa Real). The Alhambra admission ticket includes visits to these two, as well as the Generalife, which is outside the Alhambra walls; Charles V's palace, which is within the walls, can be entered without paying any admission charge, although there is a separate charge for its museums.

ALCAZABA The oldest part of the Alhambra — dating back to the 9th century — this rugged medieval fortress had been part of the hill's defenses before construction began on the royal palaces across the square. Climb the most spectacular of its towers, the Torre de la Vela (Watch Tower), for a view directly down into the Plaza Nueva and out as far as the Sierra Nevada.

MEXUAR This is the first of the three palaces that make up the Casa Real. From the outside, it appears to be a simple stucco residence, but it was actually the headquarters of the sultan's ministers. The first main council chamber, the Hall of the Mexuar, was converted to a chapel in the 17th century, hence the coat of arms of Castile beneath the Moorish ceiling of marquetry and plaster restorations. The room is a tame introduction to the splendors of the Alhambra, but its dazzling mirador suggests the mesmerizing world to come, and the spectacle builds as visitors pass through another council chamber, the Cuarto Dorado (Golden Room), to the Patio del Mexuar, one of the palace's smallest but most admired spaces.

PALACIO DE COMARES (COMARES PALACE) This was the royal palace proper, named for the stained glass that once decorated its windows. Its centerpiece is the Patio de los Arrayanes (Court of the Myrtles), graced with an oblong fishpond running its length between symmetrical myrtle hedges. The tower with the balconies (to the right upon entering the patio) is a remnant of a seraglio that was partially destroyed to make room for Charles V's palace behind it. Opposite is the Torre de Comares, a fortification tower that houses the magnificent Salón de Embajadores (Hall of the Ambassadors), the Moorish kings' throne room. Perfectly square, and clothed in lacy plaster arabesques and brilliant mosaics, this is the largest room in all three palaces. Its domed *artesonado* ceiling is a geometric depiction of the firmament comprising more than 8,000 separate pieces of painted wood. The Hall of Ambassadors is separated from the court by an antechamber, the Sala de la Barca (Hall of Benediction) which has an intricate, inlaid cedar ceiling.

PALACIO DE LOS LEONES (PALACE OF THE LIONS) The final palace, built around the famous Patio de los Leones (Court of the Lions), was the royal residence. The court's 124 slim marble columns, each with a subtly different design carved into its capital, are said to represent a palm oasis in the desert. In the center is a fountain, its basin supported by 12 gray marble lions, possibly representing the hours of the day, the months of the year, or the signs of the zodiac. At one time, it is said, water flowed from the mouth of a different lion each hour of the day. The lions no longer spout, but the fountain is filled, as are the four narrow channels (representing the four rivers of paradise) that run across the pebbled courtyard floor. The channels were designed to carry used household water from fountains in the living quarters surrounding the court, and on at least one occasion — when Boabdil's father ordered a mass beheading of suspected traitors among a group of nobles called Abencerrajes — the water ran red. The heads were thrown into the fountain of what came to be known as the Sala de los Abencerrajes, the room to the right upon entering the patio. Note the room's stalactite plasterwork ceiling with high inset windows, then go directly across the courtyard to the Sala de las Dos Hermanas (Hall of the Two Sisters), which has an even more extravagant dome. This room, named for two marble slabs set in the floor near the entrance, was reserved for the sultan's wife and was inhabited at one time by Boabdil's mother, Ayesha. Off the room is the Sala de los Almeces (Room of the Windows), with the jewel-like Mirador de Lindaraja, or Mirador de Daraxa, the sultana's private balcony. The windows are low to the ground so the queen could gaze into her private cypress garden, the Patio de Lindaraja, from a couch of floor pillows. At the far end of the Court of the Lions is the Sala de los Reyes (Hall of the Kings), surprising for its unusual 14th-century ceiling paintings, probably by Christian artists. Downstairs from the Court of the Lions, the Patio de Lindaraja leads to the sumptuous Sala de

Baños (Royal Baths), where the sultan surveyed his women from balconies. Small star-shaped windows in the ceiling let in light and allowed steam to escape. Washington Irving's furnished rooms, where he began his book about the Alhambra, are upstairs in the Patio de la Reja (Window-Grill Patio). They're opened by special request only.

ALHAMBRA GARDENS The Jardines de Partal (Partal Gardens), which occupy an area that once held the kitchen garden of the palace servants and contain the Torre de las-Damas (Ladies' Tower), with a delicate porticoed mirador at its base, are passed upon leaving the royal palaces. From here, visitors can choose their own path among the lily pools, fountains, waterfalls, and flower beds that parallel the fortress wall and its succession of towers. Or, by following the fortifications to a footbridge across a narrow gorge, they can proceed directly to the Generalife. (This can also be reached from outside the Alhambra through a ticket gate at the parking lot off Avenida de los Alixares.)

GENERALIFE The Generalife — the word (pronounced Hay-nay-rah-*lee*-fay) derives from the Arabic for "Garden of the Architect" — was the summer home of the Nasrid rulers. Though the remnants of its simple white palace and pavilions are appealing, the main attractions are the colorful terraced flower gardens, cypress-lined walkways, the pools, and the miradors from which the potentates could catch the country breezes while keeping an eye on the Alhambra below. The Patio de la Acequia (Patio of the Canal) within the palace walls, however, is an ancient plant-filled paradise with rows of fountain jets sending arcs of dancing waters over a long, narrow pool. The sunken amphitheater was built in the 1950s (see *Theater and Music*).

PALACIO DE CARLOS V The Holy Roman Emperor Charles V, who so loved Granada that at one point he planned to hold court here, built himself a grandiose Italianate palace right next to the delicate medieval Moorish palaces in the Alhambra. This majestic interloper, designed by Pedro Machuca, a student of Michelangelo, has been admired for its beautiful proportions and hated for its unsuitable location from the very start. The perfectly square exterior hides a spectacular circular 2-story courtyard open to the sky — a dome in the style of the Pantheon in Rome was originally intended. Inside are two museums. The *Museo Hispano-Musulmán* (Museum of Hispano-Muslim Art) contains fragments of original marble and tile from the Alhambra and other ancient city buildings, as well as jewelry and ceramics. The *Museo Provincial de Bellas Artes* (Provincial Fine Arts Museum) contains painting, sculpture, and stained glass primarily by Granadan artists from the 15th to the 20th centuries. The *Museo Hispano-Musulmán* (phone: 226279) is open from 10 AM to 2 PM; closed Sundays and Mondays. The *Museo Provincial de Bellas Artes* (phone: 224843) is open from 10 AM to 2 PM; closed Sundays and Mondays. There is an admission charge to both museums (separate from the Alhambra's charge — see details below); there's no admission charge for the palace.

PARADOR SAN FRANCISCO Also within the walls of the complex, this convent founded by Ferdinand and Isabella in the 15th century, is now a government-run *parador* and restaurant (see *Checking In*).

Hours for the Alhambra complex are Mondays through Saturdays from 9 AM to 8 PM, and Sundays from 9 AM to 6 PM (no admission charge after 3 PM) from April through September; Mondays through Saturdays from 9 AM to 6 PM, and Sundays from 3 to 6 PM (no admission charge) from October through March. Visits to the illuminated complex can be made Tuesdays, Thursdays, and Saturdays from 10 PM to midnight, April through September; Saturdays only from 10 PM to midnight the rest of the year. Admission to the Alhambra (phone: 227527) includes admission to the Generalife (phone: 222616). The ticket is good for 2 days.

ELSEWHERE IN THE UPPER CITY

CASA-MUSEO MANUEL DE FALLA The composer Manuel de Falla's charming whitewashed house on the Alhambra hill has been kept as it was during his lifetime. A typical Granadan villa, or *carmen,* it has a bright blue front door and a garden awash with roses. De Falla's piano, furniture, manuscripts, photos, and mementos are on display. Open from 10 AM to 2 PM and from 4 to 6 PM; closed Sundays and Mondays. Admission charge. Across from the *Alhambra Palace* hotel on Antequerela Alta (phone: 229421).

ALBAICÍN AND SACROMONTE These are Granada's oldest neighborhoods, dating back to medieval times. Even after the Reconquest, Moors continued to populate this Old Quarter. Now a residential area in the early stage of gentrification, it can be reached by a fascinating walk from Plaza Nueva up the Carrera del Darro, which becomes Paseo del Padre Manjón before turning left up the Cuesta de Chapiz. En route, it passes several landmarks: El Bañuelo (Moorish Baths; 33 Carrera del Darro), officially open at no charge all day but in reality sometimes closed; the ornate 15th-century Casa de Castril (housing the *Museo Arqueológico,* open from 10 AM to 2 PM; closed Mondays; 41 Carrera del Darro; phone: 225640); the 16th-century Convento de Santa Catalina de Zafra (43 Carrera del Darro); and, farther along on Cuesta de Chapiz, the Casa del Chapiz, a quintessential *carmen* that is now a college of Arab studies. Make a right turn at Camino del Sacromonte to climb the dusty streets, lined with sunbaked houses, into the Sacromonte Gypsy district, or continue along the Cuesta de Chapiz into the heart of the Albaicín. The long, steep road is rough going, especially on a hot summer day, but you can't go wrong by choosing any route either up or down through the neighborhood's narrow streets of red-roofed houses and walled gardens.

CAPILLA REAL (ROYAL CHAPEL) For King Ferdinand and Queen Isabella, to die in Granada was a triumph, and the Capilla Real (Royal Chapel) serves as their eternal gilded trophy (as well as their mausoleum). For 7 centuries, Spain had belonged to the Moors, and Granada was their last stand. So when the Catholic Monarchs finally conquered the city, they undertook the construction of a small chapel. This Gothic-Plateresque treasure is now downtown Granada's greatest attraction. The cathedral beside it (see below) did not yet exist when the royal couple began construction on their final resting place in 1504 — and because the chapel was not yet complete at their deaths (Isabella died in 1504, her husband in 1516), the two were buried initially at the Convento de San Francisco (now the *parador*) at the Alhambra. They were moved when the new chapel was completed by their grandson and successor, the Holy Roman Emperor Charles V, in 1517. Visitors enter through the Lonja (Exchange House), an adjoining building on Calle de los Oficios, the narrow pedestrian street alongside the cathedral.

Note the graceful frieze on the chapel's façade, one of many decorative variations on the royal initials and crest that appear throughout the building. Inside, a wrought-iron *reja* (grille) crafted by Bartolomé de Jaén separates the nave of the cruciform chapel from the apse. Behind the grille is an elaborate carved wood altarpiece, with scenes from the conquest of Granada, including Boabdil's farewell, along its base. To the right (as you face the altar) are the recumbent Carrara marble figures of Ferdinand and Isabella, sculpted by Domenico Fancelli of Florence in 1517; to the left are marble effigies of Juana la Loca and Felipe el Hermoso (Joan the Mad and Philip the Handsome — the parents of Charles V), sculpted by Bartolomé Ordóñez in 1520. Stairs at the royal feet lead to a crypt containing four lead caskets where the royal remains actually lie — plus a smaller one for a royal grandchild.

Isabella's prodigious collection of paintings, many by Flemish masters, as well as her scepter, her ornate jewel chest, her dainty filigree crown, Ferdinand's sword, and church vestments are on display in the chapel's sacristy. Above the chapel's exit doorway is a copy of a famous painting of Boabdil's surrender to Isabella; in it, she wears the filigree crown. Open daily from 10:30 AM to 1 PM and from 4 to 7 PM. Admission charge. Calle de los Oficios (phone: 229239).

CATEDRAL (CATHEDRAL) After the lush, dark intimacy of the Capilla Real, the cathedral's white interior, flooded with light from high stained glass windows, overwhelms with a stark grandeur. Begun in 1523, it was originally meant to be Gothic in style, but during the 150 years of its construction, under principal architects Diego de Siloé and Alonso Cano, a Renaissance church took shape. Outside, be sure to view Cano's 17th-century main façade, on the west along Plaza de las Pasiegas, and the Puerta del Perdón, a notably elaborate side entrance facing north on Calle de la Cárcel. The visitors' entrance at Gran Vía de Colón leads to the ambulatory around the golden Capilla Mayor, or chancel, where a 150-foot dome is ringed by a double tier of stained glass windows and by enormous scenes from the Life of the Virgin painted by Cano. Notice the polychrome figures at prayer on either side of the main arch: These are Ferdinand and Isabella, who commissioned the cathedral to celebrate the Reconquest but died before they saw a stone placed. Numerous glittering side chapels grace the church; don't miss the extravagantly carved and gilded Capilla de Nuestra Señora de la Antigua (or Capilla Dorada) on the north wall. Open daily from 10:30 AM to 1 PM and from 4 to 7 PM. Admission charge. Gran Vía de Colón (phone: 222959).

ALCAICERÍA (SILK MARKET) At one time, the old Moorish silk market in Granada covered an entire quarter and was among the most important markets in the Muslim world. It burned down in the 1800s, but a small part of it near the cathedral has been rebuilt as a tiny 3-street tourist bazaar crammed with gaudy souvenir shops and stands. Reach it from Calle Zacatín.

PLAZA DE LA BIB RAMBLA This big, busy square, where the Moors once thronged for tournaments and horse shows, is now bright with flower stalls and café table umbrellas. All Granada pauses here, near the cathedral, for *tapas,* beer, or platefuls of *churros* — long, skinny crullers just made for dipping into cups of thick hot chocolate.

CORRAL DEL CARBÓN (HOUSE OF COAL) A Moorish horseshoe arch leads into the gray stone courtyard of this building, which originally was an inn — the Grand Hotel of 14th-century Arab Granada — and subsequently a warehouse, a theater, and an apartment house. Now it houses Granada's branch of *Artespaña,* the government-run handicrafts company that has shops throughout Spain. 40 Calle Mariana Pineda (phone: 224550).

MONASTERIO DE SAN JERÓNIMO (MONASTERY OF ST. JEROME) The first monastery to be founded in Granada after the Reconquest, this huge establishment has both a private and a public cloister, the latter a magnificent space with double tiers of arcaded ambulatories surrounding an orange grove. The 16th-century monastery church, is one of Diego de Siloé's greatest buildings. Open daily from 10 AM to 1:30 PM and from 3 to 6 PM. Admission charge. 9 Calle Rector López Argüeta (phone: 279337).

IGLESIA DE SAN JUAN DE DIOS (CHURCH OF ST. JOHN OF GOD) Widely considered Granada's most beautiful place of worship because of its dazzling gilded chancel, this 18th-century baroque church is part of a complex that includes the 16th-century Hospital de San Juan de Dios. (The latter still functions as a hospital, but have a look at its frescoed courtyards and magnificent staircase with *artesonado* ceiling.) Open daily from 9 to 11 AM and from 6:30 to 9 PM. Calle San Juan de Dios (phone: 275700).

NUESTRA SEÑORA DE LAS ANGUSTIAS (OUR LADY OF PERPETUAL SORROWS) This charming Renaissance church in the downtown shopping district honors the city's patron saint. The church's carved wood statue of the Virgin, bearing Christ in her arms, is carried through the city during *Holy Week.* Open daily for mass; since times vary, check at your hotel. Carrera de la Virgen (phone: 226393).

LA CARTUJA (CARTHUSIAN MONASTERY) The daily routine of the monks is dramatically documented in the well-preserved refectory, capitular hall, and other common rooms of this great 16th-century religious center. The depictions of martyrdom, painted by a monastery friar, are bloodcurdling. In contrast, the monastery church is enchanting. The sacristy, an 18th-century addition, is an airy surprise, with rococo plasterwork and brown and white marble whose colors are swirled like a chocolate sundae. On the northern outskirts of town, about 10 minutes by cab (or take the No. 8 bus). Open daily from 10 AM to 1 PM and from 3 to 6 PM. Admission charge. Camino de Alfácar (phone: 201932).

Sources and Resources

TOURIST INFORMATION

The city's Oficina de Turismo is at 10 Plaza de Mariana Pineda (phone: 226688), while the provincial office is off Plaza de la Bib Rambla (2 Calle Libreros; phone: 225990). Both offices are open from 10 AM to 1:30 PM and from 4 to 7 PM; closed Saturday afternoons and Sundays. An English-speaking staff can answer questions, but printed information in English is sketchy. At the Alhambra, on the other hand, information services are excellent. Visitors are provided with well-annotated maps of the Alhambra and Generalife, and there is a selection of books for sale. Tour guides for both the Alhambra and downtown attractions are available in the ticket building at the Alhambra's Puerta del Vino entrance (phone: 229936).

LOCAL COVERAGE For those who read Spanish, the local daily paper, *El Ideal,* is a source of local and national news, information on entertainment and cultural events, and the *fútbol* scores. The weekly *El Faro* also contains an entertainment guide.

TELEPHONE

The area code for Granada is 58. If calling from within Spain, but outside the Granada area, dial "9" before the area code and local number.

GETTING AROUND

Those traveling by car won't have to park it for the duration of their stay, because Granada, unlike other ancient Andalusian cities, is fairly easy to navigate. Those without a car will find that the city's big red buses go everywhere, although except for hard climbs up the Alhambra and Albaicín hills, you'll probably prefer to walk.

AIRPORT Granada Airport is 10½ miles (17 km) west of the city (phone: 233322). *Iberia Airlines* has an office in town (2 Plaza de Isabel la Católica; phone: 221452).

BUS City bus routes are well marked at stops in the downtown area. The most useful ones for visitors are No. 2, which goes to the Alhambra and the Generalife, and No. 7, which goes to the Albaicín. Fare is 80 pesetas (exact change not required). Intercity buses depart from several terminals, depending on the bus line. The Alsina Graells Sur station (97 Camino de Ronda; phone: 251358), serving other points in Andalusia and Madrid, is the main one; the *Bacoma* line terminal in front of the train station (12 Av. de los Andaluces; phone: 234251) is the departure point for buses to Alicante, Valencia, Barcelona, and Madrid. *Bonal* buses (Av. de la Constitución; phone: 273100) go to the Sierra Nevada ski slopes.

CAR RENTAL *Avis* (31 Calle Recogidas; phone: 252358; and at the airport; phone: 446455), *Hertz* (7 Calle Luis Braille; phone: 251682), and *Europcar* (Plaza de Mariana Pineda, Edificio Cervantes; phone: 295065) are among the firms represented.

TAXI Hail one on the street or call *Radio-Taxi* (phone: 151461) or *Tele-Taxi* (phone: 280654).

TRAIN The train station is located some distance north of the center on Avenida de los Andaluces. Tickets can be bought there or at the *RENFE* office (at the corner of Calle de los Reyes Católicos and Calle Sillería; phone: 223119). For all train information, call 271272.

SPECIAL EVENTS

Granada's most unique celebration, the *Día de la Toma* (Day of the Capture), on January 2, commemorates the day in 1492 when the Muslim ruler, Boabdil, turned the city over to Ferdinand and Isabella, thereby completing the Christian Reconquest of Spain. Granada marks the day with a parade and the tolling of the bell installed in the Alhambra by Ferdinand and Isabella, and the flag of the Catholic Monarchs hangs from City Hall. On May 3, *Cruces de Mayo* (Crosses of May), there is dancing in the streets and plazas, which are bedecked with crosses covered with spring flowers. A much bigger event, the *Feast of Corpus Christi,* observed in June, features a glittering holy procession that displays the monstrance Isabella gave the cathedral, and costumed *granadinos* who ride horseback through downtown traffic. The fiesta goes on for 10 days, complete with bullfights, a flamenco festival, and a sprawling fair with blazing midway. Granada's renowned annual *Festival Internacional de Música y Danza* runs for 3 weeks bridging June and July (see *Theater and Music*).

SHOPPING

The booty includes ceramics, particularly the typical blue-and-white Fajalauza pottery (which took its name centuries ago from the city gate where the pottery workshops and factories were clustered); marquetry items — boxes, trays, and other wooden objects inlaid with wood, shell, or ivory; woven rugs and blankets; jewelry; copper pots; leather bags; and some of Spain's finest guitars, sold from stock or made to order (which may take anywhere from a week to several months). Crafts and souvenir shops are concentrated at a few popular tourist locations, so shopping is easy. Downtown, visitors browse the Alcaicería, off Calle Zacatín. In the vicinity of the Alhambra, fine craftsmen, as well as souvenir shops, line the lower section of the Cuesta de Gomérez approach. The Albaicín is also a good place for shopping. The two major nationwide department store chains both have branches in Granada: *Galerías Preciados* (13 Carrera del Genil; phone: 223581) and *Hipercor* (97 Calle Arabial; phone: 292161). Also, on pleasant weekends, the promenade along Carrera del Genil turns into an outdoor bazaar, blossoming with booths selling paintings, leatherwork, ceramics, jewelry, and souvenirs.

ANTONIO GONZÁLEZ RAMOS A standout for marquetry objects. 16 Cuesta de Gomérez (phone: 227062).

ARTESPAÑA The Granada outlet of the nationwide, government-operated company displays local and regional crafts and furniture in a handsome 2-story showroom at the rear of the courtyard in the Corral del Carbón. 40 Calle Mariana Pineda (phone: 224550).

CERÁMICA ALIATAR Local designs in ceramics. 18 Plaza de Aliatar (phone: 278089).

CERÁMICA ARABE A fine selection of typical Fajalauza platters and bowls (but the store doesn't ship). 5 Plaza San Isidro (phone: 201227).

EDUARDO FERRER CASTILLO The craftsman who taught most of the other guitar makers in Granada. 26 Cuesta de Gomérez (phone: 221832).

EDUARDO FERRER LUCENA Fine craftsmanship in leather. 19 Calle del Agua, Albaicín (phone: 279056).

TALABAR Elegant leather handbags and wallets. 2 Puente Verde (phone: 286786).

TEJIDOS ARTÍSTICOS FORTUNY Handwoven bedspreads, rugs, and drapes. 1 Plaza Fortuny (phone: 224327).

V. MOLERO MARTÍNEZ Another outstanding shop for marquetry. 8 Calle Santa Rosalia (phone: 111356).

SPORTS AND FITNESS

BULLFIGHTING Though the corrida has lost popularity here, the season of Sunday bullfights runs from mid-March to October, with daily events during the *Feast of Corpus Christi* in June. The *Plaza de Toros* (Av. de Doctor Olóriz) is near the soccer stadium. Tickets can be purchased downtown on

Calle Escudo del Carmen behind the Ayuntamiento (City Hall) from 5 to 9 PM on the day of the bullfight.

HIKING Follow the joggers to the Parque de Invierno (see below). Serious hikers can follow the route of the snow carriers who brought ice from the mountains to the Alhambra. The tourist office has trail maps.

JOGGING To jog along nearby mountain roads lined with olive groves, take the No. 2 bus beyond the Alhambra to Cementerio (the hilltop cemetery at the end of the line) for the entrance to the Parque de Invierno, the city's favorite outdoor recreation and picnic area.

SKIING The ski slopes at Solynieve (phone: 249100), the southernmost ski resort in Europe, are less than an hour's drive (about 20 miles/32 km) southeast of Granada along a well-tended mountain road. At more than 11,000 feet, Solynieve's snows never melt; up-to-date facilities include cable cars, chair lifts, ski shops, restaurants, and hotels, as well as the *Parador de Sierra Nevada* (phone: 480200), with a cheery bar and restaurant, above the town. For bus transportation from Granada, call *Bonal* buses (phone: 273100); for slope, weather, and highway conditions, call 480153.

SOCCER Ask at your hotel or consult the newspaper for game schedules at Granada's *Estadio de los Cármenes* (on Av. de Madrid). *Fútbol* season runs from September to mid-June.

SWIMMING Because the city is so close to resort towns of the Costa del Sol, few of the hotels have pools. Two that do are *Los Alixares* and *Los Angeles,* but they're for guests only. The *Neptuno* sports complex, located downtown (Calle Arabial; phone: 251067), has two pools open to the public.

TENNIS Courts are for rent at the *Neptuno* sports complex (see *Swimming*).

THEATER AND MUSIC

Gypsy *zambras,* flamenco *tablaos,* and jazz are part of the music scene (see *Nightclubs and Nightlife*), as are classical concerts at the *Auditorio Manuel de Falla* (Paseo de los Mártires, near the Alhambra; phone: 228288). The auditorium, rebuilt after a fire and acoustically acclaimed, also is the principal indoor venue for the city's renowned *Festival Internacional de Música y Danza,* which runs from late June through early July. For the 3 weeks of the festival's duration, Granada is treated to a round-robin of daily performances not only indoors but also in the courtyard of the Palace of Charles V and in the outdoor theater at the Generalife. Among those doing the honors are ensembles such as the *Spanish National Orchestra* and the *Spanish National Ballet,* plus orchestras, ballet companies, chamber groups, and soloists from around the world. For an advance schedule of events, contact the festival office (Casa de los Girones, 1 Ancha de Santa Domingo, Granada 18009; phone: 225441) or branches of the National Tourist Office of Spain in the US (see GETTING READY TO GO).

NIGHTCLUBS AND NIGHTLIFE

Granada's biggest nighttime draw — and its biggest disappointment — are the *zambras,* Gypsy song-and-dance fests put on in cave dwellings hollowed out of the Sacromonte hill. Not so many years ago, the Gypsies danced for their own pleasure, but the shows have now deteriorated into tawdry commercial ventures, where there's more emphasis on selling souvenir fans and castanets than on artistry. A nightclub bus tour run by *Viajes Meliá* (44 Calle de los Reyes Católicos; phone: 223098) goes to several caves and is one way to see them; another is to have a taxi drive slowly along the Camino del Sacromonte while you choose one that intrigues you. Don't wander around alone after dark in this neighborhood.

For something closer to a Seville-style *tablao* (flamenco song and dance performance), book the show at *La Reina Mora* (Mirador de San Cristóbal; phone: 278228), in the Albaicín. *Jardines Neptuno,* a garden nightclub (downtown on Calle Arabial; phone: 251112), has flamenco and regional dance and song. Because it's near the university, the section of Calle Alarcón that runs into Plaza Alberto Einstein and includes Calle Martínez de la Rosa has wall-to-wall discotheques, jazz clubs, bars, and burger, pizza, and fried-fish places jammed with young people.

A more sophisticated disco scene prevails at the *Club Cadí* in the *Luz Granada* hotel and at *Granada-10* (13 Calle Cárcel Baja). Or try *Oxford 2* (25 Calle del Gran Capitán) or *Distrito 10* (5 Calle del Gran Capitán). Go late. The watering holes around the Campo del Príncipe provide nightlife or *tapas* nearer the Alhambra. Among them, the 2-story *Patio Rossini Quesería Bar* (15 Campo del Príncipe) is particularly charming. (Ask for a *tabla variada,* a cheese board that also includes pâtés, hams, sausages, and olives — priced by weight.) And make sure to have at least one drink on the terrace of the *Alhambra Palace* hotel, with a view of the city lights glistening at your feet.

Best in Town

CHECKING IN

Choosing a hotel in Granada means deciding between the forested heights of the historic Alhambra hill and the "real life" of the city below. The hilltop choice offers rustic charm, inspiring views, a feeling of the distant Moorish past, and easy walking access to the Alhambra itself. A downtown hotel offers a better acquaintance with Granada's Renaissance period and a greater selection of shops and restaurants. Either way, it's hard to go wrong. Fast, efficient transportation shuttles visitors freely between upper and lower Granada for a full range of sightseeing, shopping, and dining. Expect to pay $85 and up for a double room in a hotel listed as expensive and between $50 and $75 in a moderate place. All telephone numbers are in the 58 city code unless otherwise indicated.

For an unforgettable experience, we begin with our favorite *parador*, followed by our recommendations of cost and quality choices of hotels, listed by price category.

A SPECIAL HAVEN

Parador San Francisco Because Granada's Alhambra Palace is one of the most visited sites in Spain, it's no wonder that this *parador*, located within its sprawling complex, is booked months in advance. The building is a former Franciscan monastery, founded by Queen Isabella when she was in Granada with the king, sending troops against the Moors (she and Ferdinand were even temporarily buried here). The 39-room *parador* has meandering corridors, carved bedroom doorways reminiscent of 18th-century monks' cells, and religious statues. Rich Moorish purples and golds decorate the public rooms. Other features include gardens, a convention hall, and an outdoor café overlooking the Alhambra. Expensive though it is, the wait for rooms is from 6 months to a year, depending on the season, but cancellations do come up; ask for a room in the old wing. The restaurant serves Spanish and Andalusian specialties (see *Eating Out*). In the Alhambra (phone: 221441; in the US, 212-686-9213; fax: 222264).

EXPENSIVE

Alhambra Palace This grand old baronial establishment on the Alhambra hill is an easy stroll to the Alhambra entrance, and many of its 132 high-ceilinged, old-fashioned (but air conditioned) rooms have a view of the city from token balconies. The huge lobby and lounges, with plaster curlicues and tiled dadoes aping the real Alhambra, provide a meeting place for locals and visiting dignitaries. The concierge and staff snap to attention when approached. A palatial dining room serves buffet and from-the-menu dining. 2 Calle Peña Partida (phone: 221468; fax: 226404).

Luz Granada A 174-room businesspeople's hotel, it stands on the sweeping Avenida de la Constitución, somewhat out of the way for Alhambra-bound tourists. It offers the comforts of air conditioning, an international restaurant, an American-style cocktail lounge, boutiques, and a discotheque. 18 Av. de la Constitución (phone: 204061; fax: 293150).

Melia Granada The city's largest hotel, it's within a stone's throw of the downtown sights. There are 197 air conditioned rooms, a restaurant, a cocktail lounge, a coffee shop, and lobby boutiques. 7 Calle Angel Ganivet (phone: 227400; in the US, 800-336-3542; fax: 227403).

Princesa Ana With a white marble and peach-colored interior, this luxurious oasis has 61 air conditioned rooms and an undistinguished restaurant. Popular with European business executives, it's down the street from the *Luz Granada* and a couple of blocks from the railroad station. 37 Av. de la Constitución (phone: 287447; fax: 273954).

MODERATE

Los Alixares The last hostelry up the Alhambra hillside above the Generalife is a charmless modern structure without Andalusian flavor, but it does have a swimming pool and sun deck, and European tour groups love it. The 162 air conditioned rooms (plus a restaurant) are a short cab or bus ride from downtown Granada. Av. de los Alixares (phone: 225506; fax: 224102).

Los Angeles This place requires a short — but steep — hike to the Alhambra. The hotel's name may have no connection with the American city, but the flashy balconies and big heated swimming pool fairly scream Hollywood. The 100 air conditioned rooms are furnished in a comfortable modern fashion. 17 Cuesta Escoriaza (phone: 221424; fax: 222125).

Guadalupe By the side of a steep road across from the upper entrance to the Generalife, this modest hostelry is high enough above the city to give guests a country feel. There are 42 air conditioned rooms and a small restaurant; bus to downtown. Av. de los Alixares (phone: 223423; fax: 223798).

Kenia A favorite with old Granada hands, this 16-room gem occupies a gracious old mansion at the foot of the Alhambra hill, near the Campo del Príncipe. Ask for a room in the back, away from the street; the ones in the front tend to be noisy. The owner has furnished the lobby and parlor with family antiques, and each guest's itinerary gets his personal attention. There's also a charming restaurant. 65 Calle Molinos (phone: 227507).

Victoria The silver dome and Parisian façade of this graceful dowager have been a landmark at the bustling Puerta Real for more than a century. The 69 air conditioned rooms have been renovated, but the lavish period chandelier and potted palms in the tiny lobby remain, as does the aristocratic turn-of-the-century ambience that keeps the restaurant and bar popular with *granadinos*. Though the traffic is noisy, the downtown location is great, with easy bus access to the Alhambra. 3 Puerta Real (phone: 257700; fax: 263108).

EATING OUT

The fruitful fields and orchards surrounding the city, the game-rich mountains nearby, and the waters of the Mediterranean not far away make Granada's menus as notable for their fresh ingredients as for the excellent food preparation. One of the most famous local dishes is *habas con jamón,* a simple casserole of locally grown fava beans with ham. Most cooks won't use the prized ham from Trévelez, dried in the crisp Sierra Nevada air, but if you want to be your own judge in the ongoing contest between Trévelez lovers and aficionados of Seville's Jabugo ham, try slivers of Trévelez for *tapas,* with a fresh local wine (huétor, huescar, or albondón are names to note) or with one of the plentiful Jerez wines. The city's convent kitchens, famous for their egg-yolk-based and sugared cookies and candies, help satisfy the local sweet tooth. Expect to pay $40 and up for a three-course meal for two with local wine in the restaurants listed below as expensive, from $25 to $40 in places described as moderate, and from $15 to $25 in inexpensive spots. All telephone numbers are in the 58 city code unless otherwise indicated.

EXPENSIVE

Alhacena de las Monjas A sophisticated restaurant blending nouvelle cuisine and old Arab recipes to produce an elegant dining experience that's hard to match anywhere. Tuxedo-clad waiters serve in the gleaming whitewashed cellar of a 16th-century house as guests nibble on crusty Arab breads and choose such dishes as *pimientos rellenos de bacalao en salsa de azafrán* (peppers stuffed with salt cod in saffron sauce) and *cordero Alhacena de las Monjas* (lamb shank in a prune, carrot, and wine sauce). An old Arab dessert, *cogollo de lechuga con miel de caña* (hearts of romaine lettuce with orange slices in a burnt sugar sauce), is among the fascinating offerings, but there's also the house *tarta,* an airy cheesecake topped with honey and *crème anglaise.* Closed Sundays. Reservations necessary. Major credit cards accepted. 5 Plaza del Padre Suárez (phone: 224028).

Chikito Choose indoor dining in a historic building, once a meeting place for Federico García Lorca and the El Reconcillo band of intellectuals, or pick the restaurant's shady outdoor café across the street. Shoppers and businesspeople keep both spots filled. Try the *zarzuela de pescado* (seafood casserole), or selections from the outstanding *tapas* bar. Closed Wednesdays. Reservations unnecessary. Major credit cards accepted. 9 Plaza del Campillo (phone: 223364).

El Corral del Príncipe The outdoor tables crowded (especially on Sunday mornings) with homegrown yuppies mark the entrance to one of Granada's most spectacular eating places — a remodeled movie palace whose Andalusian interior is lavish with Moorish brass chandeliers and urns. The full range of Granadan cuisine is available. There's also a bar with lots of action, dancing on the former theater stage, and a late-night flamenco show. Open daily. Reservations advised. Major credit cards accepted. Campo del Príncipe (phone: 228088).

Cunini Pass through the long bar and choose your meal from the tempting fish market display. Well-heeled *granadinos* come here for the food, not for atmosphere or solicitous service (neither is to be found in this restaurant's plain, pine-paneled rooms). The menu lists almost a hundred fish and shellfish dishes, in addition to meats. For starters, try the *ensalada de hueva* (a cold fish roe salad) or the *pipirrana de chanquetes* (matchstick-size baby fish in tomato vinaigrette). Closed Mondays. Reservations advised. Major credit cards accepted. 14 Pescadería (phone: 250777).

Parador San Francisco A leisurely three-course lunch in the *parador*'s spacious dining room — within view of the rose gardens and the Generalife hill beyond — is a delightful way to break a visit to the Alhambra. Among the Spanish and Andalusian specialties served here for lunch and dinner are the gazpacho, *choto alpujerrano* (stewed kid), and *rape mozarabe* (angler fish in an herb sauce). Open daily. Reservations unnecessary. Major credit cards accepted. At the Alhambra (phone: 221441).

Ruta de Veleta This luxurious roadhouse restaurant on the way to Solynieve is worth the 4½-mile (7-km) trip. Feast on first-rate pheasant, partridge, roast suckling pig, and a cornucopia of other Spanish and international dishes, and enjoy the finest old rioja wines. Even the dining room ceiling, hung with row upon row of ceramic mugs in the typical blue-and-white floral pattern of Granada, is sensational. Closed Sunday evenings. Reservations advised. Major credit cards accepted. Carretera de la Sierra Nevada, Km 5.5, Cenes de la Vega (phone: 486134).

Sevilla Brigitte Bardot, El Cordobés, and Andrés Segovia have eaten here, and the menu is printed in three languages — you get the idea. But the food is tasty and authentic. Dine in one of the tiled dining rooms or on the narrow terrace, actually an alley, across from the frescoed walls of La Madraza, the old Arab university. Granadan specialties include *cordero a la pastoril* (spicy shepherd's lamb stew), *rape a la granadina* (monkfish in a shrimp, pine-nut, and mushroom sauce), and a dessert of *nueces con nata y miel* (the Arab-inspired nuts with cream and honey). Closed Sunday evenings. Reservations advised. Major credit cards accepted. 12 Calle de los Oficios (phone: 221223).

MODERATE

Casa Manuel Ring the doorbell to gain admission to this old mansion in a neighborhood of elegant hillside residences. The walk down the long front hall to the dining rooms, the china-filled antique sideboards, and the informal, home-style cooking, with desserts baked by the owner's wife, make you feel more like a guest than a customer. Closed Sundays. Reservations unnecessary. No credit cards accepted. Calle Blanqueo de San Cecilio, off Campo del Príncipe (phone: 229617).

Los Manueles Trévelez hams hang over the noisy bar in this friendly *taberna* in an alley off Calle de los Reyes Católicos. Spaniards and foreigners alike flock to the tile and wrought-iron accented dining rooms, where the menu runs to Andalusian specialties. It's great in summer, when the tables spill outdoors. Open daily. Reservations unnecessary. No credit cards accepted. 4 Calle Zaragoza (phone: 223415).

Mesón Antonio Anyone in town from October through June should make a beeline for this homey eatery — and be hungry. After finding the humble house off Campo del Príncipe (even cab drivers have to inquire), go through the patio and upstairs to a simple dining room with an open kitchen. There, before cavernous wood-burning ovens, Antonio delivers sizzling platters of gratinée leeks, beef tongue in tomato sauce, and roast lamb, while his wife fries potatoes and stirs an intense seafood bisque at the range. There are also reasonably priced, fine old rioja wines. The couple speaks excellent English. Closed Sunday evenings and July, August, and September. No reservations. No credit cards accepted. 6 Calle Ecce Homo (phone: 229599).

INEXPENSIVE

Polinario The buffet on the patio or a *bocadillo* (sandwich) and beer at the bar make for a quick lunch just outside the Alhambra. The cooking doesn't merit raves, but the location is convenient. Closed evenings. No reservations. No credit cards accepted. 3 Calle Real de la Alhambra (phone: 222991).

Madrid

When King Philip II proclaimed Madrid the capital of Spain and all her colonies in 1561, he said that he chose it because of the "healthy air and brilliant skies" and because, "like the body's heart, it is located in the center of the Peninsula." As a result of Philip's proclamation, what had been an insignificant Castilian town of 17,000 suddenly burst into being as the cosmopolitan nucleus of the Spanish Empire. One of Europe's youngest capitals, Madrid grew fast, and today the city is a glamorous metropolis of approximately 4 million people. More than ever, it is ebullient, outgoing, fun-loving, proud, stylish, and creative, a city intensely lived in and adored by its varied mosaic of inhabitants. Throughout its history, a great proportion of its residents have been born elsewhere in Spain, a country of various and diverse cultures. Yet soon after their arrival, they feel "adopted" and become as genuinely *madrileño* as native sons and daughters.

Madrileños love to be out on the streets, where walking or strolling — the *paseo* — is an activity in itself, rather than just a means of getting somewhere. And Madrid's artistic-creative surge of the late 1970s and early 1980s — *la movida* — sparked a rebirth of indoor and outdoor café society. Stylish *madrileños* congregate at *terrazas* (cafés) along Paseo de Recoletos and the Castellana day and night, chatting, eating, drinking, and gossiping. Crowded late-night, Spanish-style pubs, specializing in high-decibel rock or soothing classical music, line Calle de las Huertas, one of the liveliest streets in the old part of town. Amazingly, this street is also occupied by the early-17th-century Convent of the Trinitarias, where cloistered nuns live and embroider, and where Miguel de Cervantes is buried. In the old section of Lavapiés, families gather to eat, drink, and chat with their neighbors at simple restaurants with sidewalk tables. The *tertulia,* an age-old Madrid custom, brings experts and devotees together for informal discussions. At the *Café Gijón, tertulias* are generally about theater or literature; art is the favorite topic at the *Círculo de Bellas Artes* lounge; and bullfighting and bull breeding are discussed at the bar of the *Wellington* hotel.

When it's time for the midday *aperitivo* around 1 PM (when stores, offices, and many museums close), thousands of *tapas* bars, *tabernas,* and swank cafés become jammed for a couple of hours until lunchtime, when they suddenly empty and the restaurants fill up. Around 4 or 5 PM (when the stores, offices, and museums reopen), the restaurants become vacant — it's customary to go somewhere else for coffee or cognac — and the bars and cafés are reactivated. They reach another peak when it's *aperitivo* time again, around 8 PM (as stores, offices, and museums close for the day). At dinnertime, around 10 PM, the restaurants fill up once more. Then it's time for a movie, concert, theater performance, jazz at a café, or a stroll.

Madrid boasts the longest nights of any Spanish city — even though in midsummer the sun doesn't set until almost 11 PM. Discotheques don't get started until 1 or 2 AM, and at many, the action continues until 7 AM. Then it's time for a typical Madrid breakfast of thick hot chocolate with *churros* (sticks or loops of crisp fried dough). Nevertheless, for *madrileños,* the city isn't a vacation spot — it's a place for hard work as well as for play.

There are many Madrids. In fact, the city is sometimes referred to in the plural — *los madriles* — because of its various facets. In addition to nocturnal Madrid, daytime Madrid, and seasonal Madrid, there are different architectural and historical Madrids.

Not much remains of medieval Moorish Madrid, and even less is known — although legends abound. In 852, the Emir of Córdoba, Muhammad I, chose the strategic ravine top above the Manzanares River (where the Royal Palace now stands) as the site for a fortified Alcázar (castle) to guard the route between Toledo and Alcalá de Henares against the reconquering Christians. The Moors called it Magerit (later mispronounced as Madrid by Castilians), meaning "source of flowing water," referring to water from the nearby Sierra de Guadarrama.

Magerit began to grow, and the Moors built and rebuilt walls to enclose it, keeping up with its random expansion. Fragments of these old walls, as well as sections of underground passageways to the Alcázar, have been uncovered as recently as the 1970s — a major site can be seen at Cuesta de la Vega, near the Royal Palace. Other well-preserved remnants of medieval Moorish Magerit are the house and tower of the Lujanes family and the adjacent Periodicals Library building, both at Plaza de la Villa; the Mudéjar tower of the Church of San Nicolás de los Servitas, slightly to the north of the plaza; the Mudéjar tower of the Church of San Pedro el Viejo, on the site of what may have been the original mosque of La Morería (the Moorish Quarter), to the south of the plaza; and La Morería itself, a zone of winding alleys around Plaza del Alamillo.

In 1083, King Alfonso VI and his Christian troops reconquered Madrid and took up residence in the Alcázar. The *madrileño* melting pot expanded with the subsequent influx of Christians into what then became medieval Christian Madrid, and more walls were built to surround it.

In addition to raising the city's rank to capital of Spain and moving the throne and court from Toledo, King Philip II of the Hapsburg House of Austria (1556–98) launched what is known as Madrid de los Austrias, or the Madrid of the Hapsburgs. This is the charming and picturesque section of Old Madrid around the Plaza Mayor. Into the 17th century, the nobility built mansions, the clergy founded churches, convents, monasteries, and hospitals, and merchants, artisans, and innkeepers set up shop. Hapsburg Madrid grew into a labyrinth of meandering, narrow cobblestone streets and tiny squares lined with severe buildings of stone, brick, and masonry, topped by burnt-red tile roofs. The Spanish Empire was at its zenith, and the *siglo de oro* (golden age) of Renaissance literature flourished in Hapsburg Madrid. Streets, squares, and statues bear the names of Cervantes, Lope de Vega, Tirso de Molina, Quevedo, and Calderón de la Barca, all of whom lived here.

The city continued fanning southward, creating such *barrios* (neighborhoods) as Lavapiés and Embajadores, lively with *tabernas, mesones* (inns), vendors, organ-grinders, and artisans. The *castizo* (genuine) and uniquely *madrileño* personality of these barrios and their colorful people were the inspiration of many of the 18th- and 19th-century *zarzuelas* (traditional Spanish operettas) — such as *La Verbena de la Paloma* — that are presented outdoors during the summer at La Corrala, located at Plaza Agustín Lara. *Castizo* Madrid also inspired many of Goya's paintings depicting *majos* and *majas* (nicknames for *madrileños* and *madrileñas*), such as *Majos on a Balcony, The Kite, The Wedding,* and *The Parasol.* Anyone visiting Madrid in May and the first half of August should stroll around these *barrios castizos* to see *madrileños* of all ages bedecked in traditional costumes, dancing the graceful *chotis* in the streets, and enjoying the *verbenas* (fairs) from nightfall into the wee hours.

When the Hapsburg dynasty died out at the end of the 17th century, King Philip V, grandson of France's King Louis XIV, was the chief claimant to the throne of Spain. After a war of succession, he established the Bourbon dynasty as the legitimate heir to the kingdom in 1770. The Bourbon monarchs began the new century by setting out to create a splendid new European capital worthy of their neo-classical French models. When the medieval Alcázar burned down, Philip V commissioned top architects to replace it with a grandiose palace comparable to Versailles. Expansion to the east of old Hapsburg Madrid, with wide avenues and large squares laid out in geometric configuration, transformed Madrid into a model city of the Enlightenment. The city's urban renewal, embellishment, and social progress culminated with the reign of *madrileño* King Carlos III, "the Construction King of the Enlightenment," known affectionately as the "King-Mayor." Carlos commissioned Juan de Villanueva to design the neo-classical *Natural Science Museum,* which later became the *Prado Museum,* and the adjacent Botanical Gardens. The exquisite tree-lined Paseo del Prado, with its Neptune, Apollo, and Cibeles fountains by Ventura Rodríguez; the monumental Puerta de Alcalá (then marking the eastern end of the city); and the immense Hospital General de San Carlos (now the *Museo Nacional de Arte Reina Sofía,* Spain's museum of modern and contemporary art) are among the legacies of Carlos III.

The steady progress of the city and the country foundered in 1808, when Napoleon was encouraged to invade Spain because of the weakness of Carlos IV, the next Bourbon king. The French succeeded in the invasion after ruthlessly executing Spanish resisters on May 2, a tragedy immortalized by Goya in his famous paintings now in the *Prado.* At the Plaza de la Lealtad on Paseo del Prado, a memorial obelisk with an eternal flame commemorates *el dos de mayo* (the second of May).

Napoleon forced the crowning of his brother, Joseph Bonaparte, as King of Spain. In his quest for open space for ongoing urban renewal, Joseph Bonaparte tore down picturesque chunks of Hapsburg Madrid, including much of the Retiro Park Palace and a church in the small Plaza de Ramales that contained the grave of Velázquez. But the Spanish War of Independence led to the expulsion of the French and the return to the throne of a Bourbon king, Fernando VII, in 1813.

In the last third of the 19th century, Romantic Madrid spread farther northward. Aristocratic palatial mansions graced the elegant Salamanca district, where today some of Madrid's finest shops and boutiques line Calles Serrano and Velázquez. Paseo del Prado extended north to become Paseo de Recoletos and, still farther north, Paseo de la Castellana. By the early 20th century, a transportation problem arose: There was no street connecting the new outlying districts of Salamanca and Argüelles. The solution was to chop through part of Old Madrid and construct a new thoroughfare, the Gran Vía.

The instability of the monarchy during the early 20th century led once again to political upheaval. Alfonso XIII finally abdicated in 1931 to avoid a civil war. But the Socialist Republican government's decentralization plan and reform measures aroused strenuous right-wing opposition, which resulted in insurrection and, in 1936, the Spanish Civil War. Much of Madrid, which remained aligned with the Republican government, was blown to pieces at the hands of Generalísimo Francisco Franco's Nationalist forces. During the nearly 40 years of Franco's dictatorship, Madrid's spirit and creativity were stifled. Franco's death in 1975, the restoration of the monarchy, and the institution of a representative, democratic government brought about a dramatic surge of activity in many facets of the city, from construction to culture.

As a result of Madrid's designation as the European Capital of Culture in 1992, the city now boasts several major new attractions. The Triángulo del Arte (Triangle of Art) encompasses the *Museo Nacional de Arte Reina Sofía* (Queen Sofía National Museum of Art); the refurbished *Prado Museum;* and the *Prado*'s Palacio de Villahermosa annex, remodeled and reopened in 1992 to exhibit the 830 paintings of the Thyssen-Bornemisza Collection, considered to be the world's second-most-important private art collection after that of the Queen of England. Next to the new *Auditorio Nacional* on Calle Príncipe de Vergara, another newcomer, the *Museo de la Ciudad* (Museum of the City), has exhibits that trace the evolution of Madrid. Flanking the Plaza Mayor (Main Square), the 17th-century *Casa de la Panadería* has been refurbished and opened as a cultural center. The restored 19th-century Palacio de Linares in the Plaza de Cibeles has been given a new name — the Palacio del Quinto Centenario — and converted into the *Museo de América* (Museum of America), a cultural and diplomatic center devoted to Spain's relationship with Latin America. Already in operation are major sections of Madrid's new convention and exhibition center, the *Parque Ferial Juan Carlos I,* a vast, multifaceted urban project near Barajas International Airport, whose completion date is the year 2000. In addition, after years of renovation and transformation, the *Teatro Real* is scheduled to reopen this year as *Teatro de la Opera,* one of Europe's premier opera houses.

But Madrid has yet to boast a completed cathedral. Under construction now for an entire century, the Catedral de la Almudena, named for the patroness of the city, is located in the Plaza de la Armería facing the Royal Palace. Once it is finished, it will enjoy the distinction of being the oldest "new" cathedral in Europe. Until then, however, visitors to Madrid will have plenty to see, both old and new, in this multifaceted, modern capital that retains so much of its rich history and traditions.

Madrid At-a-Glance

SEEING THE CITY

For a wonderfully romantic view of Madrid, watch the sun set from the 25th-floor roof garden and pool of the *Tryp Plaza* hotel (see *Checking In*). The vivid "Velázquez sky," portrayed in the artist's famous paintings, is usually tinted with a golden hue. Looking over the "sea of tile" rooftops, visitors will see a fine view of the Royal Palace and, to the north, the distant Sierra de Guadarrama. The hotel's terrace and pool are open daily during the summer months; there's an admission charge.

SPECIAL PLACES

The bustling Puerta del Sol, "kilometer zero" of the Spanish road network, and the Plaza de Cibeles traffic circle are two focal points at the heart of Madrid. The Atocha railroad station and traffic circle mark the southern extremity of this zone, the Royal Palace and Parque del Retiro form its western and eastern borders, respectively, and Plaza de Colón marks its northern limit. One major tree-lined avenue, with three names, bisects the entire city from top to bottom. Its southern section, between Atocha and Plaza de Cibeles, is called Paseo del Prado. From Cibeles north to Plaza de Colón, its name is Paseo de Recoletos. At Plaza de Colón, it becomes the long Paseo de la Castellana, which runs through modern Madrid to the north end of the city beyond Plaza de Castilla and the Chamartín railroad station. The two major east–west arteries are Calle de Alcalá and the Gran Vía; the latter angles northwest to Plaza de España.

The best way to see Madrid is by walking; many picturesque areas can be seen only on foot. A good stroll is from Puerta del Sol to Plaza Mayor, then downhill to Plaza de Oriente. Good maps of the city are provided free of charge at the tourist offices. Most museums close on Mondays, some at midday, and smaller ones for the entire month of August.

PLAZA MAYOR This grandiose main square, which is closed to vehicular traffic, is easily missed if you don't aim for it and enter through one of the nine arched entryways. Built during the 17th century by order of King Philip III, it is the quintessence of Hapsburg Madrid — cobblestones, tile roofs, and imposing austere buildings. The plaza became the stage for a wide variety of 17th- and 18th-century spectacles — audiences of more than 50,000 witnessed hangings, burnings, and the decapitation of heretics, as well as canonizations of saints, jousting tournaments, plays, circuses, and even bullfights. The 477 balconies of the surrounding buildings served as spectator "boxes" — not for the tenants, but for royalty and aristocrats. Beautifully refurbished, the Plaza Mayor is still lively, but with tamer entertainment — *la tuna* (strolling student minstrels), other amateur musicians, artists, and on-the-spot portrait painters selling their works, as well as summer concerts and ballets, and outdoor cafés for watching it all. Myriad shops, many over a century old, line the arcades around the plaza. On Sunday mornings, philatelists and numismatists set up shop in the arcades, to the delight of stamp and coin collectors. During the yuletide season, numerous stands sell lovely *Christmas* ornaments. Visitors can easily lose their sense of direction inside this vast enclosure, so it's helpful to know that the bronze equestrian statue of Philip III in the center is facing east (toward the *Prado Museum*). The legendary Arco de Cuchilleros entrance is at the southwest corner.

PUERTA DEL SOL This vast oblong plaza is the bustling nerve center of modern Madrid life. Ten streets converge here, including the arteries of Alcalá, San Jerónimo, Mayor, and Arenal. Near the curb in front of the building's main entrance, a famous emblem in the sidewalk marks "kilometer zero," the central point from which all Spanish highways radiate, and from which their distance is measured. Directly across the plaza stands the venerated bronze statue of the *Oso y el Madroño* (the bear and the madrona berry tree), the symbol and coat of arms of Madrid since the 13th century.

MUSEO NACIONAL DEL PRADO (PRADO MUSEUM) One of the world's supreme art museums, the *Prado* is a treasure house of over 4,000 universal masterpieces, most of which were acquired over the centuries by art-loving Spanish monarchs. The wealth of Spanish paintings includes famous works by El Greco (including the *Adoration of the Shepherds*), Zurbarán, Velázquez (including *The Spinners* and *Maids of Honor*), Murillo, Ribera (including the *Martyrdom of St. Bartholomew*), and Goya (including his renowned *Naked Maja* and *Maja Clothed*). On the ground floor, a special section is devoted to the tapestry cartoons designed by Goya for the palace-monastery at San Lorenzo de El Escorial (see *Extra Special*) and to his extraordinary *Disasters of War* etchings, which represent his thoughts and comments on Spain's War of Independence. Visitors also will find Goya's stunning *Second of May* and *Third of May* canvases. Vast rooms are devoted to Italians Fra Angelico, Botticelli, Raphael, Correggio, Caravaggio, Titian, Tintoretto, and Veronese. Other rooms display paintings by Flemish and German masters such as Rubens, van der Weyden, Hieronymus Bosch (including *The Garden of Earthly Delights*), Memling, Dürer, and Van Dyck. From the Dutch are works by Rembrandt, Metsu, and Hobbema. French art is represented by Poussin, Lorrain, and Watteau, and the English by Reynolds, Gainsborough, and Lawrence.

The neo-classical *Prado* building was originally a natural science museum, conceived by Carlos III. In 1819, King Fernando VII converted it into a museum to house the royal art collection. In addition to the main *Prado*, or Villanueva Building, the museum includes two annexes. One, the Casón del Buen Retiro, resembles a small Greek temple, and is just up a hill from the Goya statue that stands at the *Prado*'s north façade. It was once the stately ballroom of the 17th-century Royal Retiro Palace complex, which was destroyed during the French occupation of Madrid. It now contains the *Museum of 19th-Century Spanish Painting*. The other annex, the splendid Villahermosa Palace, is diagonally across Plaza Cánovas del Castillo (the square with the Neptune Fountain) from the main building. Its spacious interior has been redesigned by architect Rafael Moneo to house a major portion of the vast Thyssen-Bornemisza Collection, 830 paintings considered one of the most important privately owned art collections in the world. Officially on a 10-year loan (that began in 1992) to the museum, the collection is believed likely to be sold to Spain. (At press time, 80 paintings and eight sculptures from the collection were slated to be moved to the Monastery of Pedralbes in Barcelona.)

The *Prado* collection is so vast that it is impossible to savor its wonders in a single visit. If time is limited, it is best to select a few galleries of special interest, or enlist the services of one of the extremely knowledgeable government-licensed free-lance guides at the main entrance. The guides are more readily available in the early morning, and their fee is about $12 per hour. Reproductions from the *Prado*'s collection, postcards, and fine arts books are sold at the shop inside the museum. There is a bar-restaurant on the premises. The *Prado* is open Tuesdays through Saturdays from 9 AM to 7 PM; Sundays and holidays from 10 AM to 2 PM. Closed Mondays, *New Year's Day, Good Friday, May 1, November 1,* and *Christmas.* One admission charge grants access to the main building and the annexes. Paseo del Prado (phone: 420-2836).

JARDÍN BOTÁNICO (BOTANICAL GARDEN) The garden was designed in 1774 by Juan de Villanueva, the same architect who designed the *Prado Museum,* whose south façade it faces. Twenty manicured acres contain some 30,000 species of plants and flowers from Spain and throughout the world. Carlos III commissioned the project as part of his urban refurbishment program. By his order, therapeutic and medicinal plants and herbs were distributed free to those in need. Between the *Prado* and the entrance to the garden is the small Plaza de Murillo, which has a bronze statue of the 17th-century painter and the "Four Fountains" of mythological triton cherubs playing with dolphins. Open daily from 10 AM to 7 PM (later in summer). Admission charge. On Paseo del Prado at Plaza de Murillo (phone: 420-3568).

PALACIO REAL (ROYAL PALACE) The Moors chose a strategic site overlooking the Manzanares River to build their Alcázar, or castle-fortress. After the 11th-century Reconquest, Christian leaders renovated it and moved into it, and Philip II made it the royal residence after proclaiming Madrid the capital of Spain in 1561. After the Alcázar was destroyed by fire on *Christmas Eve*, 1734, a new palace was built. It took 26 years to complete the colossus of granite and white limestone, with walls 13 feet thick, over 2,800 rooms, 23 courtyards, and magnificently opulent interiors. At the north side are the formal Sabatini Gardens; and down the slopes on the west side is the Campo del Moro — 20 acres of forest, manicured gardens, and fountains, now a public park. The palace's main entrance is on the south side, through the tall iron gates leading into an immense courtyard called the Plaza de la Armería (armory), a setting for the pageantry of royal occasions. The imposing structure at the courtyard's south end is the Catedral de la Almudena, honoring the patroness of the city.

The palace is seen by guided tour, with different sections covered on different tours, led by Spanish- and English-speaking guides. The King and Queen of Spain live in the Palacio de la Zarzuela, on the outskirts of Madrid, but the Palacio Real still is used for official occasions and is closed to the public at those times, which are not always announced in advance. Normally, opening hours are Mondays through Saturdays from 9:30 AM to 5:15 PM; Sundays and holidays from 9 AM to 2:15 PM. Admission charge. Plaza de Oriente (phone: 559-7404).

PLAZA DE ORIENTE This square is bordered by the east façade of the Royal Palace (*oriente* in Spanish means East) and the *Teatro Real* (Royal Theater), scheduled to reopen this year as *Teatro de la Opera*. In the center of the plaza stands the 9-ton bronze equestrian statue of King Philip IV, based on a drawing by Velázquez.

MUSEO NACIONAL DE ARTE REINA SOFÍA (QUEEN SOFÍA NATIONAL MUSEUM OF ART) This gargantuan 18th-century building was Madrid's Hospital General de San Carlos until 1965. Following a tremendous reconstruction project, the building was inaugurated in 1986 as a museum devoted to contemporary art, named in honor of the present Queen of Spain. Since then, it has taken its place among the world's leading contemporary art galleries and modern art museums. The museum's collection encompasses that of the former *Museo Español de Arte Contemporáneo* (Spanish Contemporary Art Museum), which consists of 3,000 paintings, 9,000 drawings, and 400 sculptures, including works by Picasso, Miró, Dalí, Gris, and Julio González. A recent addition to its still-growing permanent collection is Picasso's monumental *Guernica* (moved here from the *Prado*). The museum also contains the most important contemporary art libraries in Spain, including state-of-the-art braille facilities, videos, photography collections, research systems, and workshops. Throughout the year, prominent exhibitions are scheduled at the museum's two landmark annexes in Retiro Park, the *Palacio de Velázquez* and *Palacio de Cristal.* Open from 10 AM to 9 PM; Sundays from 10 AM to 2:30 PM; closed Tuesdays. Admission charge. 52 Calle Santa Isabel (phone: 467-5062).

PLAZA DE CIBELES Dominating Madrid's favorite traffic circle is the fountain and statue of the Greek fertility goddess Cibeles, erected during the reign of "King-Mayor" Carlos III. It's a Madrid custom to "say hello to La Cibeles" upon arriving in town. The massive, wedding-cake, turn-of-the-century Palacio de Comunicaciones (the city's central post and telecommunications office) on the plaza is so imposing that it almost overshadows Cibeles.

PARQUE DEL RETIRO (RETREAT PARK) During the early 17th century, this was a royal retreat and the grounds of both a royal palace complex and a porcelain factory, then on the outskirts of town. Now Madrid's public park, the Retiro covers 300 peaceful acres of forest, manicured gardens, statuary, fountains, picnic grounds, and cafés. On a sunny Sunday afternoon, all of Madrid comes to jog, hug, gossip, or walk the dog around the lakeside colonnade. Art exhibitions are held at the park's *Palacio de Cristal,* a 19th-century jewel of glass and wrought iron, and at the *Palacio de Velázquez,* named for its architect, not for the painter. During the summer, at 10 PM and midnight, classical and flamenco concerts are staged in the Cecilio Rodríguez Gardens (Menéndez Pelayo entrance), and the outdoor cinema (entrance on Alfonso XII) features Spanish and foreign (including US) films. We recommend savoring a *coupe royale* — a deluxe ice cream — among the statues of kings. The park's loveliest entrance is through the wrought-iron gates at Plaza de la Independencia, also referred to as the Puerta de Alcalá.

PLAZA DE LA VILLA One of Madrid's most charming squares, its architectural diversity makes it especially interesting. Dominating the west side, the 17th-century neo-classical Casa de la Villa, also called the Ayuntamiento (City Hall), was designed by Juan Gómez de Mora, the same architect who planned the Plaza Mayor. Its carillon chimes the hour with *zarzuela* melodies and plays 20-minute concerts every evening. Along the back of the square is the 16th-century Plateresque Casa de Cisneros palace, built by the nephew of, and heir to, the cardinal regent of the same name. On the east side are the old Periodicals Library, with a large Mudéjar doorway, and the massive medieval Lujanes Tower, one of the oldest in Madrid (King Francis I of France was once imprisoned here). Separating these two structures, the tiny Calle del Codo (Elbow Street) angles down to the tranquil Plaza del Cordón, which is surrounded by historic noble mansions. The City Hall's splendid museum collection is open to the public every Monday (except holidays) from 5 to 7 PM, with free tours escorted by guides from the Madrid Tourist Board. Plaza de la Villa (phone: 588-0002).

MUSEO DE LA REAL ACADEMIA DE BELLAS ARTES DE SAN FERNANDO (MUSEUM OF THE SAN FERNANDO ROYAL ACADEMY OF FINE ARTS) Housed in a splendid 18th-century palace just east of the Puerta del Sol, the academy's permanent collection comprises some 1,500 paintings and over 800 sculptures. There are works by El Greco, Velázquez, Zurbarán, Murillo, Goya, and Sorolla, as well as by Italian and Flemish masters. Open Tuesdays through Fridays from 9 AM to 7 PM; Saturdays, Sundays, and Mondays from 9 AM to 3 PM; during the summer, 9 AM to 2 PM daily. Admission charge. 13 Calle de Alcalá (phone: 522-1491).

CONVENTO DE LAS DESCALZAS REALES (CONVENT OF THE BAREFOOT CARMELITES) Behind its stark stone façade is an opulent interior filled with an astonishing wealth of artistic treasures and ornamentation bestowed by kings and noblemen. Founded in 1559 by Princess Juana of Austria, sister of Philip II, the convent welcomed disconsolate empresses, queens, princesses, and *infantas,* including Juana's sister María, Empress of Germany. The grandiose stairway is a breathtaking example of *barroco madrileño,* every centimeter lavishly decorated with frescoes and carved wood. Art treasures include works by El Greco, Zurbarán, Titian, and Sánchez Coello, as well as Rubens tapestries. From the windows of the upper floor is a lovely view over the tranquil rooftop garden, where the cloistered nuns grow their vegetables as they have for centuries. Visitors are escorted by resident Spanish-speaking guides; tours in English should be arranged in advance through the Madrid Municipal Tourist Office (see *Tourist Information*). Hours vary according to the season, and are limited because the cloistered nuns often use the museum sections in their daily life; in general opening hours are Tuesdays through Saturdays from 10 AM to 1:30 PM. The admission charge includes the tour. Plaza de las Descalzas Reales (phone: 559-7404).

CONVENTO DE LA ENCARNACIÓN (CONVENT OF THE INCARNATION) Built by order of Queen Margarita of Austria, wife of King Philip III, this Augustinian convent was founded in 1616. Designed in the severe classical style by Juan Gómez de Mora, its façade gives no clue to the bounteous religious and secular art treasures inside. The dazzling reliquary room displays some 1,500 religious relics contained in priceless gold and silver urns and jeweled cases. Among them is a vial of the blood of St. Pantaleón, which is said to liquefy every year on his birthday, July 27. This is another active cloistered convent, so individuals and groups must be escorted by resident guides; tours in English can be arranged in advance through the *Office of Museums* (phone: 248-7404). Open Tuesdays through Saturdays from 10 AM to 1:30

PM. The admission charge includes the tour. Plaza de la Encarnación (phone: 247-0510).

MUSEO MUNICIPAL (MUNICIPAL MUSEUM) Devoted to the history of Madrid, this fine museum will enhance any visitor's awareness of the city's evolution, culture, and personality. It is filled with art, furnishings, porcelains, photographs, engravings, and meticulously detailed maps and models of the city during the 17th, 18th, and 19th centuries. The museum building, declared a National Monument in 1919, was originally an 18th-century hospital, and its elaborately ornate churrigueresque entrance is a memorable sight. Open Tuesdays through Saturdays from 10 AM to 2 PM and 5 to 9 PM; Sundays from 10 AM to 2:30 PM. Admission charge. 78 Calle Fuencarral (phone: 522-5732).

MERCADO PUERTA DE TOLEDO What used to be Madrid's old Central Fish Market (*mercado*) has been transformed into a sparkling showcase of fine Spanish handicrafts, art, antiques, jewelry, fashion, and interior design. Within the complex, the *Café del Mercado* is a lively nightspot. The market is also the setting for concerts, recitals, and art and photography exhibitions. Regularly scheduled video projections include a "bird's-eye view" of Madrid past and present. At the courtyard entrance is a functional Monument to Time: a giant sculptured combination sundial and lunar clock, considered the world's largest. The market is adjacent to the Puerta de Toledo, one of the ancient city gates, dominated by a 19th-century neoclassical triumphal arch. Open daily, with dining, drinking, and entertainment going on into the wee hours. No admission charge. 1 Ronda de Toledo (phone: 266-7200).

REAL FÁBRICA DE TAPICES (ROYAL TAPESTRY FACTORY) Established early in the 18th century, this factory-museum continues to use authentic traditional techniques in producing handmade Spanish tapestries and rugs. In addition to the permanent collection, visitors can see the workshops and watch master artisans at work weaving tapestries from cartoons by Goya and other artists, knotting luxuriant rugs, or doing intricate restoration work. Rugs and tapestries can be purchased by special order, and even can be custom-made from the customer's own design. Open Mondays through Fridays from 9:30 AM to 12:30 PM; closed August. Admission charge. 3 Calle Fuenterrabía (phone: 551-3400).

MUSEO DEL EJÉRCITO (ARMY MUSEUM) An amazing array of more than 27,000 items related to battle throughout Spain's history — uniforms, armor, cannon, swords (including one belonging to El Cid), stupendous collections of miniature soldiers, and portraits of heroines and heroes — are displayed here. Housed in the vast, baroque interior of one of the two surviving buildings of the 17th-century Royal Retiro Palace complex, this museum is well worth seeing — while it lasts. Plans have been laid for the ever-expanding *Prado Museum* to take over this palatial building, and for the collection to be moved in a couple of years to a new venue at the Ministry of Defense complex in the Moncloa district. Open daily from 10 AM to 2 PM; closed Mondays. Admission charge. 1 Calle Méndez Núñez (phone: 522-8977).

MUSEO ARQUEOLÓGICO NACIONAL (NATIONAL ARCHAEOLOGICAL MUSEUM) The star among the Iberian and classical antiquities is the enigmatic *Dama de Elche,* a dramatic Iberian bust of a priestess, or perhaps an aristocrat, estimated to have been sculpted during the 4th century BC. Also on display are basket weavings and funeral objects of early Iberians, as well as Neolithic, Celtic, ancient Greek, Roman, and Visigothic artifacts and handicrafts. In the garden at the entrance is an underground replica of the famous Altamira Cave and its prehistoric paintings. Open Tuesdays through Saturdays from 9:30 AM to 8:30 PM; Sundays and holidays from 9:30 PM to 2:30 PM. The admission charge includes entrance to the *National Library* (see below), at the opposite side of the same building. 13 Calle Serrano (phone: 577-7915).

BIBLIOTECA NACIONAL (NATIONAL LIBRARY) With more than 6 million volumes, this is one of the world's richest libraries. It was inaugurated in 1892 to commemorate the quadricentennial of the Discovery of America. Statues of Cervantes, Lope de Vega, and other illustrious Spaniards of letters stand at the classical columned entrance. Scheduled and seasonal exhibits of publications and graphics are held in the ground floor galleries. Open Tuesdays through Saturdays from 10 AM to 9 PM; Sundays and holidays from 10 AM to 2 PM. The admission charge includes entrance to the *National Archaeological Museum* at the opposite side of the same building. 20 Paseo de Recoletos (phone: 575-6800).

CASA DE CAMPO Once the private royal hunting grounds, this 4,300-acre forested public park on the right bank of the Manzanares River is a playground for *madrileños* and visitors alike. It has a zoo (complete with a panda), picnic and fair grounds (important trade fairs and conventions are held here), and a giant amusement park, *Parque de Atracciones,* with rides and entertainment at an outdoor theater rife with a spirited carnival atmosphere. Other highlights include a concert stadium, an all-encompassing sports complex, a small lake, and the bullpens of La Venta de Batán (for bullfight practice and previews of the bulls). The zoo is open daily in April through September; Saturdays, Sundays, and holidays only in October through March. The amusement park is closed in winter and closed Mondays the rest of the year. Admission charge to attractions. The park is easily reached by bus, metro, taxi, or the *teleférico* (cable car) that runs from Paseo del Pintor Rosales in Parque del Oeste (not far from Plaza de España). Casa de Campo (phone: 463-2900).

BASÍLICA DE SAN FRANCISCO EL GRANDE (BASILICA OF ST. FRANCIS THE GREAT) A few blocks south of the Royal Palace, this neo-classical church is one of the largest and most richly decorated in Madrid. Another project of King Carlos III, it was designed by the city's finest 18th-century architects. Six side chapels (the first on the left was painted by Goya) line its circular interior, which is topped by a cupola 108 feet in diameter. The museum inside the church contains a wealth of religious art. Museum hours are Tuesdays through Saturdays from 11 AM to 1 PM and 4 to 7 PM; closed holidays. Admission charge to the museum. Plaza de San Francisco (phone: 265-3800).

| EXTRA SPECIAL | Some 30 miles (48 km) northwest of Madrid is the colossal monastery-palace of El Escorial, which reflects the fervent, yet often brutal, Catholicism of 16th-century Spain. King Philip II built the Real Monasterio de San Lorenzo de El Escorial — El Escorial for short — in thanksgiving for his victory over the French at Saint-Quentin in 1557. The lean architecture of this royal and religious complex in the mountains bears the mark of Philip's asceticism, but the collection of works by such artists as Ribera, El Greco, Velázquez, Titian, Veronese, and Bosch in the *Nuevos Museos* (New Museums) is sinfully opulent. The small, monastic chambers in the Palacios (Royal Apartments), from which Philip governed the Spanish Empire for 14 years (1584–98), provide a stark contrast to the splendor of the rest of the structure. The monastery also houses the Panteón de los Reyes (Royal Pantheon), which contains the remains of 26 Spanish monarchs, as well as a library with 40,-000 priceless volumes and 4,700 manuscripts. El Escorial is easy to reach by car; there is also frequent train and bus service between Madrid and the contiguous town of San Lorenzo de El Escorial, which is charming and well worth seeing.

Nearby, to the north, is the Valle de los Caídos (Valley of the Fallen), an astonishing memorial to those who died in the Spanish Civil War. A huge basilica containing the tombs of soldiers from both sides has been hollowed into a mountain. Generalísimo Francisco Franco, who ordered the monument's construction, also is buried here. A granite cross stands 500 feet in the air atop the mountain peak. For additional information on both these places, see the *Madrid Region* route in DIRECTIONS.

Sources and Resources

TOURIST INFORMATION

Information, maps, and brochures can be obtained from the Oficina Municipal de Turismo (Municipal Tourist Office; 3 Plaza Mayor; phone: 266-5477). Information on the city, the rest of the province, and all of Spain also is available from the tourist information office of the Comunidad de Madrid (Province of Madrid, 2 Duque de Medinaceli; phone: 429-4951), near the *Palace* hotel. Other information offices run by the province are at Torre de Madrid, Plaza de España (phone: 541-2325), at Barajas Airport, and at the Chamartín train station.

The US Embassy is at 75 Calle Serrano (phone: 576-3400 or 576-3600).

LOCAL COVERAGE *ABC* and *El País,* among Spain's most important Spanish-language dailies, cover local, national, and international events, plus arts and entertainment listings. The *Guía del Ocio* ("Leisure Guide"), in Spanish, is the most complete weekly guide to restaurants, entertainment, culture, and sports.

TELEPHONE

The area code for Madrid is 1. If calling from elsewhere within Spain, dial "9" before the area code and local number.

GETTING AROUND

AIRPORT Aeropuerto de Barajas, 10 miles (16 km) from downtown Madrid, handles both international and domestic flights. It is about a 20-minute taxi ride from the center of the city, depending on traffic; the fare will run about $12. (Note that taxis charge an additional 40¢ for picking up passengers at the airport, as well as another 20¢ per bag. There also is a 40¢ surcharge for all rides at night, from about 11:30 PM to 6 AM, and all day on Sundays and holidays.) Public buses run every 15 minutes between the airport and the air terminal in the center of the city under Plaza de Colón; the buses are yellow and are marked "Aeropuerto," and the one-way fare is 275 pesetas. *Iberia Airlines* has two offices: one at the *Palace* hotel, and another at 130 Calle Velázquez (phone for domestic reservations: 411-1011; phone for international reservations: 563-9966). *Iberia*'s *Puente Aéreo* (Air Bridge) runs 1-hour flights to Barcelona, leaving every 10 minutes.

BUS Excellent bus service is available throughout Madrid. Normal service operates from 6 AM to midnight; between midnight and 6 AM, there is service every 30 minutes from Plaza de Cibeles and Puerta del Sol. Signs clearly marking the routes are at each bus stop. Individual bus tickets are bought from the driver and cost 125 pesetas per ride. Discounted "bonobus" passes, good for ten rides, cost 490 pesetas, and can be bought at *Empresa Municipal de Transportes (EMT)* kiosks all over the city, including one on the east side of Puerta del Sol and another at the south side of Plaza de Cibeles; upon boarding the bus, insert the pass into the date-stamping machine behind the driver. For information on the city bus system, call *EMT* at 401-9900. Madrid has several bus stations from which long-distance buses depart; the Estación Sur de Autobuses (17 Calle Canarias; phone: 468-4200), serving Andalusia and other points south, is the largest.

CAR RENTAL All major international and Spanish firms are represented; most have offices at Madrid's Aeropuerto de Barajas, and some are based at the Chamartín and Atocha train stations. Agencies in the city include *América* (23 Calle Cartagena; phone: 246-7919); *Atesa* (59 Gran Vía; phone: 247-0202; and 25 Calle Princesa; phone: 241-5004); *Avis* (60 Gran Vía; phone: 247-2048; and in the airport terminal under Plaza de Colón; phone: 576-2862); *Europcar* (29 Calle Orense; phone: 445-9930; and 12 Calle García de Paredes; phone: 448-8706); *Hertz* (88 Gran Vía; phone: 248-5803; and in the *Castellana Inter-Continental Hotel,* 49 Paseo de la Castellana; phone: 319-0378); and *Ital* (31 Calle Princesa; phone: 241-9403).

SUBWAY Madrid's metro is efficient and clean and in operation from 6 AM to 1:30 AM. Stops along all ten lines are clearly marked, and color-coded maps are easy to read. Tickets are purchased from machines and inserted into electronic turnstiles, or they're bought at pass-through booths. (Do not discard the ticket until the end of the ride.) Discounted ten-ride tickets also are available (450 pesetas); buy these at metro stations. For subway information, call 435-2266.

TAXI Metered cabs are white with a diagonal red line. If a cab is available, it will have a windshield sign that says *libre* and an illuminated green light on its roof. Fares are moderate. Taxis can be hailed on the street, picked up at cabstands, or summoned by phone; call *Radio-Teléfono Taxi* (phone: 247-8200); *Radio-Taxi* (phone: 404-9000); or *Tele-Taxi* (phone: 445-9008).

TOURS Companies offering half-day motorcoach tours of the city, as well as excursions to surrounding sights, include *Juliá Tours* (68 Gran Vía; phone: 541-9125); *Pullmantur* (8 Plaza de Oriente; phone: 541-1805); and *Trapsatur* (23 Calle San Bernardo; phone: 542-6666). *Juliá Tours* also can be booked in the US through their US representative, *Bravo Tours* (182 Main St., Ridgefield Park, NJ 07760; phone: 800-272-8764).

TRAIN The two major stations of the *RENFE* (Spanish National Railway) are Chamartín at the north end of Madrid (north of Plaza de Castilla) and Atocha at the south end (near Plaza Emperado Carlos V). Both serve long-distance trains, as well as commuter trains to surrounding areas. West of Plaza de España, a third station, Príncipe Pío (also called Estación del Norte), serves some lines to northern Spain. *RENFE*'s main city ticket office is located at 44 Calle de Alcalá (phone: 429-0518 for information; 429-8228 for reservations). Tickets also can be purchased at the train stations and at *RENFE*'s Nuevos Ministerios (Paseo de la Castellana and Calle de Villa Verde Raimundo Fernández) and Recoletos stations (Paseo de Recoletos).

On Saturdays and Sundays from May through mid-October, *RENFE* operates a restored 19th-century–style train, *Tren de la Fresa* (Strawberry Train), which makes excursions to the famous strawberry growing town of Aranjuez. See the *Madrid Region* route in DIRECTIONS for details.

RENFE's new bullet train, the *AVE* (Alta Velocidad Española), makes the trip to Seville in 2½ hours, departing every hour on the hour. Prices vary according to the time of day, and there are 3 classes of service: *turista, preferencia* (business class), and *club* (first class). One-way fares range from 6,000 pesetas (*turista,* off-peak) to 16,500 pesetas (*club,* rush hour). Reservations should be made in advance at *RENFE* offices or through one of the many travel agencies scattered throughout Madrid.

SPECIAL EVENTS

Madrid has a distinctive, exuberant way of celebrating Spain's national holidays, as well as its own year-long calendar of local fairs and festivals. *Madrileños* go all out for *Carnaval,* a week-long nonstop street fiesta of parades and dancing that climaxes on *Ash Wednesday* with the allegorical *Entierro de la Sardina* (Burial of the Sardine). The *International Festival of Theater and Film* is held in April. On the *Second of May,* at Plaza 2 de Mayo in the Malasaña district, processions and events commemorate the city's uprising against the invading French, which Goya portrayed so dramatically. But even more *madrileño* are the *Fiestas de San Isidro* — 10 days of nonstop street fairs, festivals, concerts, special daily bullfights, and more, all in celebration of Madrid's patron saint, whose feast day is on May 15. On June 13, the *Verbena de San Antonio* (St. Anthony's Fair) takes place at the shrine of San Antonio de la Florida, with outdoor singing and dancing and traditional drinking from the fountain.

Madrid is extra lively during the summer, despite the mass exodus of summer vacationers. During July, August, and early September, the city government presents *Veranos en la Villa* (Summers in the "Town"), 2-plus months of countless cultural events featuring international superstars and local talent — ballet, symphonic music, opera, jazz, rock, pop, salsa, *zarzuelas,* films, and many diverse exhibitions — in open-air and theater settings throughout the city. There are also colorful *verbenas* (street fairs) on the feast days of three of Madrid's most popular saints: San Cayetano (August 3), San Lorenzo (August 5), and La Virgen de la Paloma (August 15). In the *barrios castizos* (authentically typical neighborhoods, such as Lavapiés, Embajadores, and Puerta de Toledo), *madrileños* dress in the traditional attire of *chulos* and *chulapas* reminiscent of 19th-century *zarzuelas.* They gather at lively street fairs to eat, drink, and dance the *chotis* and *pasodoble,* enjoying folk music performances, organ-grinders, processions, and *limonada* (not lemonade, but a kind of white-wine sangria). The world class *Madrid International Jazz Festival* is held in late October and/or early November.

From October to the beginning of December, the *Fiesta de Otoño* (Autumn Festival) presents an abundance of concerts and performances by top international and Spanish companies at Madrid theaters and concert halls. November 9 celebrates the day of Madrid's patroness, La Virgen de la Almudena. During the *Christmas* season, the city is bedecked with festive lights, and the Plaza Mayor fills with countless stands selling decorations, figurines for Nativity scenes, candies, wreaths, and *Christmas trees*. On *New Year's Eve*, throngs gather at the Puerta del Sol to swallow one grape at each stroke of the clock at midnight, wishing for 12 months of good luck in the new year. The *Christmas* season lasts until *The Feast of the Epiphany*, January 6, on the eve of which is the *Cabalgata de los Reyes*, the procession through the city streets by the gift-giving Three Wise Men.

As if all of this weren't enough, each barrio expresses its individual personality with its own fiestas and *festivales* throughout the year.

MUSEUMS

The city's major museums are described in *Special Places*. Included in the following list of additional museums are certain churches that, because of their high artistic quality, should not be overlooked. Note that the hours of many museums may vary during the summer, and smaller museums may be closed during July and August. The *Office of Museums* will be able to supply the latest information (phone: 248-7404).

BASÍLICA DE SAN MIGUEL An unusual 18th-century church with an air of Italian baroque in its convex façade and graceful interior. Open daily. 4 Calle de San Justo.

CASA-MUSEO DE LOPE DE VEGA (LOPE DE VEGA HOUSE-MUSEUM) The home and garden of Spain's great golden age dramatist. Hours are extremely erratic; it's best to call in advance. Closed Sundays. Admission charge. 11 Calle Cervantes (phone: 429-9216).

CATEDRAL DE SAN ISIDRO This imposing 17th-century church was *temporarily* designated the Cathedral of Madrid in 1885, pending the completion of the Catedral de la Almudena — which has been under construction for over a century. The entombed remains of St. Isidro, patron saint of Madrid, and those of his wife, Santa María de la Cabeza, sit on the altar. Open daily. 37 Calle Toledo.

ESTUDIO Y MUSEO SOROLLA (SOROLLA STUDIO AND MUSEUM) The house in which Joaquín Sorolla, the Valencian Impressionist "Painter of Light," lived, worked, and died in 1923. The studio and library remain intact. There's also a collection of his works. Open daily from 10 AM to 3 PM; closed Mondays. Admission charge. 37 Calle General Martínez Campos (phone: 410-1584).

IGLESIA Y CONVENTO DE SAN JERÓNIMO EL REAL (CHURCH AND CONVENT OF ST. JEROME) This giant Gothic temple overlooking the *Prado* was built by order of King Ferdinand and Queen Isabella in 1503. Worth a look from the outside, it is closed for massive renovation, and is not scheduled to reopen in the near future. 19 Calle Ruiz de Alarcón.

MUSEO CERRALBO The palatial 19th-century mansion of the Marqués de Cerralbo houses an important collection of art, antiques, ceramics, tapestries, and ancient artifacts. Outstanding among the paintings are works by El Greco, Ribera, Velázquez, Zurbarán, and Van Dyck. Open from 10 AM to 2 PM and 4 to 6 PM; closed Mondays and in August. Admission charge. 17 Calle Ventura Rodríguez (phone: 547-3646).

MUSEO DE LA CIUDAD (MUSEUM OF THE CITY) This relatively new museum testifies to the evolution of Madrid. Open 10 AM to 2 PM and 5 to 7 PM; Saturdays and Sundays from 10 AM to 2 PM. 140 Calle Príncipe de Vergara (phone: 588-6582).

MUSEO DE FIGURAS DE CERA (WAX MUSEUM) An international gallery of historic personages, including celebrity bullfighters and such fictional Spanish notables as Don Quixote and Sancho Panza. Open daily from 10:30 AM to 1:30 PM and 4 to 8 PM. Admission charge. Centro Colón (phone: 308-0825).

MUSEO LÁZARO GALDIANO Named for its founder, whose palatial mansion houses his extraordinary collection of art, jewelry, ivory, and enamel. Open from 10 AM to 2 PM; closed Mondays and in August. Admission charge. 122 Calle Serrano (phone: 561-6084).

MUSEO NACIONAL DE ARTES DECORATIVAS (NATIONAL MUSEUM OF DECORATIVE ARTS) Four floors of furniture, porcelains, jewelry, Spanish tiles and fans, a full Valencian kitchen, and handicrafts from the 16th through 19th centuries. Open Tuesdays through Fridays from 10 AM to 3 PM; Saturdays and Sundays from 10 AM to 2 PM; closed in summer. Admission charge. 12 Calle Montalbán (phone: 521-3440).

MUSEO NACIONAL FERROVIARIO (NATIONAL RAILROAD MUSEUM) Madrid's first train station, Estación de las Delicias, now is a museum complete with intact antique trains, royal cars, and other predecessors of the modern railroad. From May through mid-October, the restored 19th-century *Tren de la Fresa* ("Strawberry Train"; see *Train* above) departs here on 1-day excursions to Aranjuez. Open Tuesdays through Saturdays from 10 AM to 5 PM; Sundays and holidays from 10 AM to 2 PM. Admission charge. 61 Paseo de las Delicias (phone: 227-3121).

MUSEO PANTEÓN DE GOYA (PANTHEON OF GOYA, ALSO CALLED ERMITA DE SAN ANTONIO) Goya painted the magnificent religious frescoes on the dome and walls of this small 18th-century church, which was to become his tomb. Open Tuesdays through Fridays from 10 AM to 2 PM and 4 to 8 PM; Saturdays and Sundays from 10 AM to 2 PM; closed Mondays and holidays. No admission charge. Glorieta de San Antonio de la Florida (phone: 542-0722).

MUSEO ROMÁNTICO (ROMANTIC MUSEUM) Paintings, furniture, and decor of 19th-century Madrid, housed in an 18th-century mansion. Open Tuesdays through Saturdays from 10 AM to 6 PM; Sundays from 10 AM to 2 PM. Closed August. Admission charge. 13 Calle San Mateo (phone: 448-1071).

MUSEO TAURINO (BULLFIGHTING MUSEUM) An important collection of bullfighting memorabilia. Open Mondays through Fridays from 9 AM to 3 PM; during bullfighting season (May through October), open Sundays and closed Mondays. Admission charge. Plaza de Toros Monumental de las Ventas, 237 Calle de Alcalá (phone: 255-1857).

TEMPLO DE DEBOD A gift from the Egyptian government in the 1970s, this 2,500-year-old Egyptian temple was shipped to Madrid in 1,359 cases and reassembled, towering over a reflecting pool. Theater and music performances are held here in summer. Open daily from 10 AM to 1 PM; holidays from 10 AM to 3 PM. No admission charge. Parque del Oeste.

SHOPPING

Madrid's 54,000 stores and shops offer everything imaginable, from high fashion to flamenco guitars. Handicrafts, fine leather goods, embroidery, ceramics, Lladró porcelains, art, and antiques are among the enticing buys available throughout the city. Everything goes on sale twice a year — after *Christmas* (which in Spain means January 7, the day after *Epiphany*) and during the summer. The big summer sales (*rebajas*) begin in July, and prices are reduced even more during the first 3 weeks of August. Shops generally open at 9:30 AM, close from 1:30 to 4:30 PM for lunch and the siesta, and close for the night at 8 PM. The huge flagship stores of Spain's two major department store chains — *El Corte Inglés* (3 Calle Preciados; phone: 532-8100) and *Galerías Preciados* (1 Plaza de Callao; phone: 522-4771) — are next to each other in the pedestrian shopping area between the Gran Vía and Puerta del Sol. Unlike most retailers, they remain open during the lunch and siesta hours, and they provide special services for tourists, such as English-speaking escorts to accompany shoppers and coordination of shipping services to hotel or home. Branch stores of *El Corte Inglés* are at 56 Calle Princesa, 76 Calle Goya, and 79 Calle Raimundo Fernández Villaverde (the biggest of all, just off the Castellana). Branches of *Galerías Preciados* are at 10-11 Calle Arapiles, 87 Calle Goya, 47 Calle Serrano, and at the *Centro Comercial Madrid 2* (also known as *La Vaguada*) in northern Madrid.

Near the two department stores, four stores specializing in fine china, porcelain (especially Lladró), and Majórica pearls line the Gran Vía: *Souvenirs* (11 Gran Vía, near Calle de Alcalá; phone: 521-5119); *Vinvinda* (44 Gran Vía, near Plaza de Callao; phone: 213-0514); *Regalos A.R.* (46 Gran Vía; phone: 522-6869); and *La Galette* (67 Gran Vía, near Plaza de España; phone: 248-8938). Window shopping is a favorite pastime along Calle Serrano, which is full of elegant boutiques and galleries, as is the Plaza Mayor area.

As in other European capitals, Madrid's antiques shops are often found clustered in certain areas. Antiques row is the Calle del Prado, near the *Prado*. Worth a look is *Luis Rodríguez-Morueco* (16 Calle del Prado; phone: 429-5757), which feature treasures from the 16th, 17th, and 18th centuries. On the first Sunday of every month, the *Wellington* hotel (8 Calle Velázquez) hosts an antiques fair featuring an array of jewelry, books, and furniture. For more concentrated antiques browsing and buying, try *Centro de Anticuarios Lagasca* (36 Calle Lagasca). It has 11 antiques shops under one roof, including *Luis Carabe* (phone: 431-5872), which has an interesting collection of crystal. Also browse along Calle Serrano, where many antiques shops are located; the 5-story *Central de Arte Antigüedades* (5 Calle Serrano) houses 50 shops with honored reputations. For fine ceramics, try *Abelardo Linares* (11 Plaza de las Cortes; phone: 432-4962). *Alcocer* (5 Calle Santa Catalina, 68 Calle Pelayo, and 104 Calle Hortaleza) is a fourth-generation antiques dealer specializing in furniture, paintings, and other objects, including antique Spanish silver. The bibliophile also can savor the experience of *Luis Bardón Mesa* (3 Plaza San Martín; phone: 521-5514), which counts among its 50,000 volumes masterpieces by authors such as Cervantes, Lope de Vega, and Calderón de la Barca. Also try *Librería del Callejón* (4 Callejón de Preciados; phone: 521-7167). See also *Antiques and Auctions* in DIVERSIONS.

Other places to browse or buy include the rebuilt *Mercado Puerta de Toledo* (see *Special Places*), a converted fish market where more than 150 shops, boutiques, and galleries are filled with the finest in Spanish handicrafts, art, fashion, antiques, jewelry, housewares, and food products. *La Galería del Prado* (phone: 429-7551), a sparkling addition to the *Palace* hotel (7 Plaza de las Cortes), is a glamorous assembly of 38 top fashion boutiques, art galleries, jewelers, and gift shops, as well as a fancy food shop, a beauty salon, bookstore, and a buffet-style restaurant. Still another shopping mall is *Moda Shopping* (40 Av. General Perón), just off the Castellana, with more than 60 establishments selling everything from high fashion to sporting goods, plus plenty of restaurants and bars. *Madrid 2* (Av. Monforte de Lemos), also known as *La Vaguada,* is an enormous 350-shop complex, complete with movie houses, restaurants, discos, amusement rides, and parking for 4,000 cars.

El Rastro, Madrid's legendary outdoor flea market (open Sundays and holiday mornings only), spreads for countless blocks in the old section of the city, beginning at Plaza de Cascorro and fanning south along Ribera de Curtidores to Ronda de Toledo. Hundreds of stands are set up to sell everything from canaries to museum-piece antiques, and bargaining, preferably in Spanish, is customary. (Guard wallets and purses from pickpockets.) The *Cuesta de Moyano,* on a stretch of Calle de Claudio Moyano (along the south side of the Botanical Gardens), has a string of bookstalls selling new, used, and out of print books. It's open daily, year-round. On Sunday mornings, the arcades of the Plaza Mayor overflow with stamp and coin dealers, buyers and sellers.

Other recommended shopping spots:

ADOLFO DOMÍNGUEZ The boutique of the innovative Spanish celebrity designer whose daring women's fashions illustrate his "wrinkles (in the fabric, that is) are beautiful" philosophy. 4 Calle Ortega y Gasset (phone: 576-0084).

ANTIGUA CASA TALAVERA Authentic regional hand-crafted ceramics and dinnerware from all over Spain fill this small shop just off the Gran Vía, near Plaza de Santo Domingo. 2 Calle Isabel la Católica (phone: 247-3417).

ARTESPAÑA Government run, with a wide range of handicrafts and home furnishings from all over Spain. 3 Plaza de las Cortes, 14 Calle Hermosilla, 33 Calle Don Ramón de la Cruz, and *Centro Comercial Madrid 2–La Vaguada* (phone for all locations: 413-6262).

EL AVENTURERO A small bookstore specializing in guidebooks, maps, books on the art of bullfighting and other Spanish subjects, with an ample selection in English, too. Just off Plaza Mayor at 15 Calle Toledo (phone: 266-4457).

CANALEJAS Top-quality men's shirtmakers, specializing in the classic European formfitting cut. 20 Carrera de San Jerónimo (phone: 521-8075).

CASA BONET Featuring a variety of handmade embroidery, including beautiful items from Palma de Mallorca. The prices are very reasonable. 76 Calle Núñez de Balboa (phone: 575-0912).

CASA DE DIEGO Founded in 1858, this old-time store makes hand-painted fans — and frames for displaying them — as well as canes and umbrellas. Two locations: 12 Puerta del Sol (phone: 522-6643) and 4 Calle Mesonero Romanos (phone: 531-0223).

CASA JIMÉNEZ Another store specializing in fans and *mantones de manila,* fine lace shawls. 42 Calle Preciados (phone: 248-0526).

CASA DEL LIBRO Madrid's biggest book store. 29 Gran Vía (phone: 521-1932). A newer branch, with 4 floors, is at 3 Calle Maestro Vitoria (phone: 521-4898).

CERÁMICA EL ALFAR They carry a large assortment of regional ceramics and earthenware. Glazed-tile reproductions of famous Spanish paintings are a specialty. 112 Calle Claudio Coello (phone: 411-3587)

CORTEFIEL A leading purveyor of men's and women's fashions and accessories. 40 Calle Serrano (phone: 431-3342). Branches at 178 Paseo de la Castellana (phone: 259-5713) and 27 Gran Vía (phone: 247-1701) specialize in men's fashions only, while those at 146 Paseo de la Castellana (phone: 250-3638) and 13 Calle Preciados (phone: 522-6567) cater exclusively to women.

FERNANDO DURÁN One of the city's most prestigious shops for antique furniture, sculpture, china, and a wide variety of silver items. 11 Calle Conde de Aranda (phone: 431-3806).

GIL, SUCESOR DE ANATOLÍN QUEVEDO Spanish and international celebrities purchase work-of-art shawls, mantillas, and embroidery at this generations-old establishment. 2 Carrera de San Jerónimo (phone: 521-2549).

GRITOS DE MADRID A fine ceramics shop owned by master craftsman Eduardo Fernández, and featuring his works. He is responsible for the restoration of Madrid's interesting hand-illustrated tile street signs, and his ceramic mural of 17th-century Madrid hangs in the City Hall's museum collection. 6 Plaza Mayor (phone: 265-9154).

HORNO DEL POZO Established in 1830, this small shop has the best *hojaldres* (puff pastries) in town. 8 Calle del Pozo (phone: 522-3894).

JOSÉ RAMÍREZ They have supplied *madrileños* with fine classical and flamenco guitars for generations. 2-5 Calle Concepción Jerónima (phone: 227-9935).

LEPANTO Fashions, luggage, and accessories, in leather. 3 Plaza de Oriente (phone: 242-2357).

LOEWE Fine leather fashions for men and women, as well as accessories and luggage. At several locations: 8 Gran Vía, 26 Calle Serrano, and at the *Palace* hotel; the shop at 34 Calle Serrano carries men's fashions exclusively (phone for all locations: 435-3023).

MANUEL CONTRERAS One of the city's largest collections of guitars and other musical instruments. 80 Calle Mayor (phone: 248-5926).

MANUEL HERRERO A popular leather outlet, offering a wide selection and good prices. 7 and 23 Calle Preciados (phone: 521-2990).

MATY For dance enthusiasts: authentic regional (including flamenco) costumes for men, women, and children. Dance shoes and boots are also sold. 2 Calle Maestro Vitoria (phone: 479-8802).

MÉXICO II There are over 200,000 books here from the 16th century to the 18th, as well as drawers full of historical prints and maps. 17 Calle Huertas (phone: 532-7664).

MUSGO Five row houses joined together as one huge store and filled with contemporary clothing and furnishings. 36 Calle Hermosilla (phone: 431-5510).

PLATA MENESES Spain's leading silver manufacturer, featuring a huge line of giftware and place settings, which fill two showrooms. 3 Plaza de Canalejas (phone: 429-4236).

SESEÑA Founded in 1901, this store manufactures a fine line of capes for men and women. 23 Calle Cruz (phone: 531-6840).

TURNER ENGLISH BOOKSHOP An impressive collection of English, French, and Spanish titles. 3 Calle Génova, on Plaza de Santa Bárbara (phone: 319-2037).

SPORTS AND FITNESS

BASKETBALL Madrid plays host to much of the finest basketball in Europe. The city is represented by such teams as *Real Madrid* and *Estudiantes* and also is the home of the Spanish National and Olympic squads. The most important games are played at the *Palacio de Deportes* (99 Calle Jorge Juan; phone: 401-9100), and at the *Polideportivo Magariños* (127 Calle Serrano; phone: 262-4022).

BULLFIGHTING Madrid's bullring, *Plaza de Toros Monumental de las Ventas,* (in the Ventas neighborhood), seats 22,300 people. The season runs from mid-May through October. Tickets may be purchased the day of the event at a counter at 3 Calle Vitoria (near the Puerta del Sol), at the bullring, or through a hotel concierge.

FISHING There are fishing reserves along the Lozoya, Madarquillos, Jarama, and Cofio rivers not far from Madrid. They are populated mostly by trout, carp, black bass, pike, and barbel. The Santillana reservoir is good for pike. For season and license information, contact the *Dirección General del Medio Rural,* 39 Calle Jorge Juan (phone: 435-5121).

FITNESS CENTERS Madrid has 27 municipal gymnasiums; for information on the one nearest your hotel, call 464-9050. Many major hotels also have gyms and fitness centers.

GOLF The Madrid area boasts a number of excellent golf courses. Below are the best choices.

TOP TEE-OFF SPOTS

Club de Golf de Las Lomas–El Bosque Built in the early 1970s, this pleasantly rambling 18-hole, par 72 course offers some deceptive challenges. Eleven of its fairways and greens lie against, or very close to, a manmade lake and stream. Villaviciosa de Odón, Apartado 51 (phone: 616-2170 or 616-2382).

Real Club de la Puerta de Hierro Founded at the turn of the 20th century, this prestigious club occupies a slope studded with pines and oaks. There are two 18-hole courses (known as *Course I* and *Course II*), and several holes are crossed by bridle paths. Av. Miraflores (phone: 316-1745).

Real Sociedad Hípica Española de Campo This 18-hole course, founded in 1932, is 2½ miles (4 km) from Madrid near the right bank of the Manzanares River in Casa de Campo. One of Madrid's best, it hosted the *World Cup* in 1975 and the *Spanish Open* in 1957, 1960, and 1982. The course is characterized by very narrow fairways, flanked by oak trees, which lead to elevated greens protected by bunkers. There also is a 9-hole course. 6 Calle Fernanflor (phone: 429-8889).

In addition, there's the *Club de Campo Villa de Madrid* (Carretera de Castilla; phone: 207-0395), with 18-hole and 9-hole courses; the Jack Nicklaus–designed 18-hole course at the *Club de Golf La Moraleja* (7 miles/11 km north of town along the Burgos–Madrid highway; phone: 650-0700); and the 18 holes of the *Nuevo Club de Golf de Madrid* (at Las Matas, 16 miles/26 km west of town via the Carretera de La Coruña; phone: 630-0820). The *Federación Española de Golf* (9 Calle Capitán Haya; phone: 555-2682) has details on most of the area's facilities; hotels also can provide information regarding the use of the clubs by non-members.

HORSE RACING The *Hipódromo de la Zarzuela* (4 miles/7 km north of the center, along Carretera de La Coruña; phone: 207-0140) features Sunday afternoon races during spring and fall meetings. Buses for the track leave from the corner of Calles Princesa and Hilarión Eslava.

JOGGING Parque del Retiro and *Casa de Campo* both have jogging tracks.

SKIING The mountain resort *Puerto de Navacerrada* (37 miles/60 km north of Madrid; phone: 852-1435) has 12 ski runs and 6 lifts.

SOCCER One of Spain's most popular teams, the capital's *Real Madrid,* plays its home games at the *Estadio Santiago Bernabéu* (1 Calle Concha Espina; phone: 250-0600), while its rival, *Atlético de Madrid,* takes the field at the *Estadio Vicente Calderón* (6 Paseo Virgen del Puerto; phone: 266-4707).

SWIMMING Many hotels have pools, but Madrid also has 150 public swimming pools, including those indoors and outdoors at *Casa de Campo* (Av. del Angel; phone: 463-0050). Another nice pool is at *La Elipa* (Av. de la Paz; phone: 430-3358), which also has an area set aside for co-ed nude sunbathing. For information on other municipal pools, call 463-5498.

TENNIS Among the hundreds of public and private tennis courts in town are the 35 courts at the *Club de Campo Villa de Madrid* (Carretera de Castilla; phone: 207-0395) and the 28 courts of the *Club de Tenis Chamartín* (2 Calle Federico Salmón; phone: 250-5965).

THEATER

Theater productions are in Spanish. Anyone fluent and interested in the Spanish classics should check the *Guía del Ocio* for what's on at the *Teatro Español* (25 Calle del Príncipe; phone: 429-6297). Nearby, at *Teatro de la Comedia* (14 Calle del Príncipe; phone: 521-4931), the *Compañía Nacional de Teatro Clásico* (National Classical Theater Company) also puts on a fine repertoire of classic Spanish plays, as well as modern ones and foreign adaptations. The *Teatro Nacional María Guerrero* (4 Calle Tamayo y Baus; phone: 319-4769) is still another venue for both modern plays and classics of the Spanish and international repertoires. For the strictly modern and avant-garde, there's the *Centro Nacional de Nuevas Tendencias Escénicas* (National Center of New Theater Trends), housed at the *Sala Olimpia* (Plaza de Lavapiés; phone: 237-4622). Madrid is a city of film buffs, but if you feel like taking in a film and your Spanish is not good enough for the latest Almodóvar, note that foreign films aren't usually dubbed into Spanish — look for "V.O.," meaning *versión original,* in the ad. *Cine Doré,* also known as the *Filmoteca Española* (3 Calle Santa Isabel; phone: 227-3866), has all the avant-garde foreign films; *Alphavilla* (14 Calle Martín de los Heros; phone: 248-4524) is another possibility. Ballets, operas, and *zarzuelas* (or operettas — some *zarzuelas* resemble musical comedy, others light opera) present fewer difficulties for non-speakers of Spanish. Check listings for the restored *Teatro Nuevo Apolo Musical de Madrid* (1 Plaza Tirso de Molina; phone: 369-0637), home base for director José Tamayo's *Nueva Antología de la Zarzuela* company; *Teatro Lírico Nacional de la Zarzuela* (4 Calle Jovellanos; phone: 429-8225), which hosts opera, ballet, and concerts, as well as traditional *zarzuela;* and the *Centro Cultural de la Villa* (Plaza de Colón; phone: 575-6080), which presents both theater and *zarzuela.*

MUSIC

Bolero and fandango are the typically Castilian dances and flamenco is Andalusian, but it is the latter most tourists want to see and hear, so there are numerous excellent flamenco *tablaos* (cabarets) in Madrid. Some of the best are *Corral de la Morería* (17 Calle Morería; phone: 265-1137), a simply furnished cellar in the Old City; *Café de Chinitas* (7 Calle Torija; phone: 548-5135), an intimate club frequented by Madrid's beautiful people; *Torres Bermejas* (11 Calle Mesonero Romanos; phone: 532-3322), a dinner-theater considered by many to put on the most authentic flamenco show in town; and *Venta del Gato* (about 5 miles/8 km outside Madrid on the road to Burgos, 214 Av. de Burgos; phone: 776-6060). *Café Central* (10 Plaza del Angel; phone: 468-0844) offers live music nightly (jazz, classical, salsa, or folk) as well as late dinner. Madrid's main hall for classical concerts is the *Auditorio Nacional de Música* (146 Calle Príncipe de Vergara; phone: 337-0100), the home of the *Orquestra Nacional de España* (the Spanish National Orchestra) and the *Coro Nacional de España* (the Spanish National Chorus). Symphonic, choral, chamber, and solo works are offered in either of its two theaters during a season that stretches from May to October. The opera season, which runs from January through May, brings a host of performances to the *Teatro Lírico Nacional de la Zarzuela* (see *Theater* above). The *Teatro de la Opera* (Plaza de Oriente; phone: 547-1405), formerly the *Teatro Real,* was set to reopen at press time and will host international opera performances. Classical music can also be heard at several other locations, including the *Fundación Juan March* (77 Calle Castelló; phone: 435-4250). For a list of theaters presenting *zarzuela,* Spain's traditional form of operetta, see *Theater* above.

NIGHTCLUBS AND NIGHTLIFE

Nightlife in Madrid can continue long into the early morning hours. Cover charges at cabarets and nightclubs include one drink, dancing, and floor shows that are becoming more risqué by the minute. Top choices include *Scala–Melia Castilla* (43 Calle Capitán Haya; phone: 571-4411) and *Florida Park* (in the Parque del Retiro; phone: 573-7804). For a night of gambling, dining, dancing, and entertainment, the *Casino Gran Madrid* has it all (it's 20 minutes from downtown at Torrelodones, with free transportation from 6 Plaza de España; phone: 856-1100). The latest dance rage in Madrid is the *sevillanas*. *Madrileños* have adopted the delightful dance music of their Andalusian cousins as their own and, by popular demand, *sevillanas* music plays at many discos. Among the best of dozens of *salas rocieras* — nightclubs dedicated to dancing and watching the *sevillanas* — are *El Portón* (25 Calle López de Hoyos; phone: 262-4956), *Al Andalus* (19 Calle Capitán Haya; phone: 556-1439), *La Caseta* (13 Calle General Castaños; phone: 419-0343), and *Almonte* (35 Calle de Juan Bravo; phone: 411-6880). *La Maestranza* (16 Calle Mauricio Legendre, near Plaza de Castilla; phone: 315-9059) features star *sevillanas* performers in its floor shows and also serves outstanding Andalusian dishes. Some discotheques and boîtes run two sessions a night, at 7 and 11 PM until the wee hours. Among the more popular are *Pachá* (11 Calle Barceló; phone: 446-0137) and *Joy Eslava* (11 Calle Arenal; phone: 266-3733), where ballroom dancing is now the fad. There's late dining and an energetic downstairs disco at *Archy* (11 Calle Marqués de Riscal; phone: 308-2736), while the latest gathering spot for the glitterati is *Teatriz* (15 Calle Hermosilla; phone: 577-5379). The *Cervecería Alemana* (6 Plaza Santa Ana; phone: 429-7033), a tavern that's an old Hemingway hangout, remains a favorite nightspot. In the *Mercado Puerta de Toledo,* the *Café del Mercado* swings with late-night live jazz, and salsa dancing starts at 2 AM on weekends (1 Ronda de Toledo; phone: 265-8739); *Cock* (16 Calle Reina; no phone) draws an avant-garde set. *Madrileños* love to *pasear,* or stroll along the streets, and from April through October thousands of *terrazas* — outdoor cafés lining plazas, parks, and avenues — are jumping with nocturnal activity. Late revelers usually cap the evening with thick hot chocolate and *churros* at *Chocolatería de San Ginés* (in the alley behind San Ginés church), open all night.

Best in Town

CHECKING IN

Modern Madrid boasts over 50,000 hotel beds in more than 800 establishments, with accommodations ranging from "grand luxe" to countless *hostales* and *pensiones*. Reservations are nonetheless recommended, especially between May and September and during such special events as national and local festivals, expositions, and conventions. Expect to pay $190 to $250 and up a night for a double room in a hotel listed as very expensive, from $125 to $175 in an establishment listed as expensive, from

$50 to $115 in a moderately priced hotel, and $40 or less in an inexpensive one. All telephone numbers are in the 1 area code unless otherwise indicated.

VERY EXPENSIVE

Ritz The epitome of elegance, luxury, and Belle Epoque grace, this impeccably maintained classic opened in 1910. Built at the behest of King Alfonso XIII, its construction and decoration were overseen by César Ritz himself. No two of the 156 air conditioned rooms and suites are alike, but all are adorned with paintings, antiques, and tailored handwoven carpeting from the Royal Tapestry Factory. Jacket and tie are appropriate for men in the bar and the exquisite *Ritz* restaurant, one of Madrid's finest (see *Eating Out*). The casual *Ritz Garden Terrace* also offers delightful dining, cocktails, and *tapas*. Business facilities include 24-hour room service, meeting rooms for up to 500, an English-speaking concierge, foreign currency exchange, secretarial services in English, audiovisual equipment, photocopiers, computers, cable television news service, translation services, and express checkout. 5 Plaza de la Lealtad (phone: 521-2857; in New York City, 212-838-3110; elsewhere in the US, 800-223-6800; fax: 232-8776).

Santo Mauro This exquisite addition to Madrid's supreme echelon of *gran lujo* hotels is located in what was originally the turn-of-the-century palatial mansion of the Duques de Santo Mauro, and then the Philippine Embassy. Centrally situated in the elegant Almagro-Castellana section, the French-style building was faithfully restored to its original style. The interior decor, created by Madrid's hottest designers, is the last word in Art Deco. The 36 rooms, mostly suites, all feature a compact disc and cassette stereo system and satellite TV (VCRs are available on request). In keeping with the pampered surroundings, other facilities include a sauna, indoor swimming pool, summer terrace restaurant, and in the mansion's original library, the *Belagua* restaurant (see *Eating Out*). Business facilities include 24-hour room service, an English-speaking concierge, foreign currency exchange, photocopiers, translation services, and express checkout. 36 Zurbano (phone: 319-6900; fax: 308-5417).

Villa Magna A Park Hyatt hotel, this 194-room property is set amid landscaped gardens in the heart of aristocratic Madrid, right around the corner from the US Embassy. A multimillion-dollar remodeling project added unequaled luster — and technology — to the spacious, air conditioned rooms. The *Champagne Bar* boasts one of Europe's finest selection of the bubbly, and the *Villa Magna* restaurant is celebrated for its imaginative specialties (see *Eating Out*). Richly decorated private salons accommodate meetings and banquets. Business facilities include 24-hour room service, meeting rooms for up to 250, an English-speaking concierge, foreign currency exchange, secretarial services in English, audiovisual equipment, photocopiers, computers, cable television news service, translation services, and express checkout. 22 Paseo de la Castellana (phone: 578-2000; in the US, 800-233-1234; fax: 575-3158, for reservations; fax: 575-9504, to reach hotel guests).

Villa Real Among Madrid's newer establishments, its design and atmosphere embody Old World grace; marble, bronze, handcrafted wood, works of fine art, and antique furnishings create a seignorial interior decor. All 115 luxurious rooms and suites are air conditioned and feature satellite TV and 3 or more high-tech telephones. Elegantly furnished top-floor duplexes have 2 bathrooms — 1 with a sauna, the other with a Jacuzzi — and large private balconies overlooking the Spanish Parliament Palace, the Neptune Fountain, and the *Prado*'s Villahermosa Palace annex. The hotel's choice setting — between Paseo del Prado and Puerta del Sol — couldn't be better. Business facilities include 24-hour room service, meeting rooms for up to 300, an English-speaking concierge, foreign currency exchange, secretarial services in English, audiovisual equipment, photocopiers, computers, cable television news service, translation services, and express checkout. 10-11 Plaza de las Cortes (phone: 420-3767).

EXPENSIVE

Barajas This hotel, close to Madrid's Barajas International Airport, offers 230 air conditioned rooms with TV sets, plus a garden swimming pool, a bar, a restaurant, and a health club. Free transportation is provided to and from the airport terminals. Business facilities include 24-hour room service, meeting rooms for up to 675, an English-speaking concierge, foreign currency exchange, secretarial services in English, audiovisual equipment, photocopiers, computers, cable television news service, translation services, and express checkout. 305 Av. Logroño (phone: 747-7700).

Castellana Inter-Continental Its 310 air conditioned rooms, all with modern accoutrements, are large and nicely decorated in pleasant pastels. Adjacent to the stately, marble-pillared lobby are car rental, airline, and tour desks, boutiques, a health club, and a business services department. *Los Continentes* restaurant and *La Ronda* piano bar are agreeable spots for meeting and eating. Business facilities include 24-hour room service, meeting rooms for up to 350, an English-speaking concierge, foreign currency exchange, secretarial services in English, audiovisual equipment, photocopiers, computers, cable television news service, translation services, and express checkout. 49 Paseo de la Castellana (phone: 410-0200; in the US, 800-327-5853; fax: 319-5853).

Eurobuilding A well designed modern complex off the northern section of the Castellana near the *Convention Center* and *Estadio Santiago Bernabéu*. In addition to the 421-room hotel building, the *Eurobuilding 2* tower comprises 154 apartment-style units. All rooms and apartments are air conditioned. There also are 2 swimming pools, a health club, a hair salon, stores, and 4 restaurants. Business facilities include 24-hour room service, meeting rooms for up to 900, an English-speaking concierge, foreign currency exchange, secretarial services in English, audiovisual equipment, photocopiers, computers, cable television news service, translation services, and express checkout. 23 Calle Padre Damián (phone: 457-1700; in the US, 800-645-5687; fax: 457-9729).

Holiday Inn Madrid This modern and busy establishment with 344 air conditioned rooms has a swimming pool, health club, gymnasium, shopping arcade, and restaurants. It is near the *Azca* shopping and commercial complex, the *Convention Center, Estadio Santiago Bernabéu,* and the Castellana. Business facilities include meeting rooms for up to 450, an English-speaking concierge, foreign currency exchange, secretarial services in English, audiovisual equipment, photocopiers, computers, cable television news service, translation services, and express checkout. 4 Plaza Carlos Trías Bertrán (phone: 597-0102; in the US, 800-465-4329; fax: 597-0292).

Meliá Castilla Nearly 1,000 air conditioned rooms in a modern high-rise just off the Castellana in northern Madrid's business section. Facilities and meeting rooms cater primarily to executive travelers. There is a swimming pool, a gym, a sauna, a shopping arcade, several restaurants and bars, and the *Scala–Melia Castilla,* a Las Vegas–style nightclub. Business facilities include 24-hour room service, meeting rooms for up to 800, an English-speaking concierge, foreign currency exchange, secretarial services in English, audiovisual equipment, photocopiers, computers, cable television news service, translation services, and express checkout. 43 Calle Capitán Haya (phone: 571-2211; in the US, 800-336-3542; fax: 571-2210).

Meliá Madrid Ideally located near the Plaza de España and very well run, this gleaming white, modern building has 266 tastefully decorated rooms with air conditioning and TV sets. The dining room, grill, bar, and *Bong Bing* discotheque are popular meeting places. There is also a gym, a sauna, and conference facilities complete with state-of-the-art audiovisual equipment. Business facilities include 24-hour room service, meeting rooms for up to 380, an English-speaking concierge, foreign currency exchange, secretarial services in English, audiovisual equipment, photocopiers, computers, cable television news service, translation services, and express checkout. 27 Calle Princesa (phone: 541-8200; in the US, 800-336-3542; fax: 541-1988).

Miguel Angel Conveniently located on Paseo de la Castellana, this 304-room property combines modern luxuries with 17th-, 18th-, and 19th-century paintings, tapestries, and furniture. Most rooms have balconies, and all offer TV sets. Facilities include a health club with sauna, Jacuzzi, gymnasium, and heated, indoor swimming pool. There are 2 restaurants and a bar. Business facilities include 24-hour room service, meeting rooms for up to 650, an English-speaking concierge, foreign currency exchange, secretarial services in English, audiovisual equipment, photocopiers, computers, cable television news service, translation services, and express checkout. 31 Calle Miguel Angel (phone: 442-8199; in the US, 800-423-6902; fax: 442-5320).

Palace This aristocratic Madrid landmark maintains its Belle Epoque elegance while offering the utmost of modern facilities in the spacious 518 air conditioned rooms and suites. Located in the heart of the city, the hotel overlooks the Neptune Fountain and Paseo del Prado. The lobby, embellished with trompe l'oeil painting, leads to a cozy lounge, which is topped by an immense painted-glass rotunda — an inviting setting for cocktails or informal dining at *El Ambigú,* with a musical backdrop of piano and violin until 2 AM.. On the ground floor is the *Galería del Prado,* a collection of more than 40 fine boutiques, galleries, and shops, as well as *La Plaza,* a self-service restaurant. Business facilities include 24-hour room service, meeting rooms for up to 1,500, an English-speaking concierge, foreign currency exchange, secretarial services in English, audiovisual equipment, photocopiers, computers, cable television news service, translation services, and express checkout. 7 Plaza de las Cortes (phone: 429-7551; in New York City, 212-838-3110; elsewhere in the US, 800-223-6800; fax: 429-8655).

Suecia Expansion of this Swedish-managed hotel has added modern rooms and suites within the same building, but the original ones are still well maintained and very comfortable. All 67 rooms, old and new, are air conditioned and have TV sets. Hemingway lived here, enjoying the great advantage of the location — on a quiet street just west of Paseo del Prado, around the corner from Calle de Alcalá. Smoked salmon and smorgasbord are main attractions in the *Bellman* restaurant. Business facilities include meeting rooms for up to 150, an English-speaking concierge, foreign currency exchange, secretarial services in English, audiovisual equipment, computers, and translation services. 4 Calle Marqués de Casa Riera (phone: 531-6900; in the US, 800-528-1234; fax: 521-7141).

Tryp Fénix This Madrid aristocrat once again is counted among the city's finest. Ideally situated on the tree-lined Castellana at Plaza de Colón, it has 216 air conditioned rooms and up-to-the-minute amenities enhanced by an air of sparkling elegance. Business facilities include 24-hour room service, meeting rooms for up to 200, an English-speaking concierge, foreign currency exchange, secretarial services in English, audiovisual equipment, photocopiers, computers, translation services, and express checkout. 2 Calle Hermosilla (phone: 431-6700; fax: 576-0661).

Wellington Classic and nicely located in the Salamanca district, with fine boutiques, galleries, and the Parque del Retiro practically at the doorstep. All of the spacious 258 rooms are air conditioned, with TV sets. In summer, the outdoor swimming pool and the garden, with its restaurant, bar, and health club, are lively gathering spots. Business facilities include 24-hour room service, meeting rooms for up to 250, an English-speaking concierge, foreign currency exchange, secretarial services in English, audiovisual equipment, photocopiers, computers, translation services, and express checkout. 8 Calle Velázquez (phone: 575-4400; fax: 576-4164).

MODERATE

Alcalá On the north edge of Parque del Retiro and Plaza de la Independencia, in the genteel Salamanca district, it is within easy walking distance of fine shops and restaurants on Calle Serrano, as well as the *Prado* and other museums. All 153 air conditioned rooms have TV sets. The restaurant serves Basque specialties. Business facilities include meeting rooms for up to 60, an English-speaking concierge, foreign currency exchange, secretarial services in English, audiovisual equipment, photocopiers, computers, and translation services. 66 Calle de Alcalá (phone: 435-1060; in the US, 800-528-1234; fax: 435-1105).

Arosa Although it's on the bustling Gran Vía, it has the charm, peaceful mood, and personalized service of a small luxury establishment. The 126 air conditioned rooms, no two exactly alike, are tastefully decorated; luxurious bathrooms feature built-in hair dryers and fabulous showers in the bathtubs. The atmosphere is delightful in the bar, lounge, and restaurant. Business facilities include an English-speaking concierge, foreign currency exchange, and translation services. 21 Calle de la Salud (phone: 532-1600; in the US, 800-528-1234; fax: 531-3127).

Carlos V Conveniently located in the lively pedestrian area between the Gran Vía and Puerta del Sol, near the Convento de las Descalzas Reales and *El Corte Inglés* department store. There are 67 air conditioned rooms. Business facilities include an English-speaking concierge and foreign currency exchange. 5 Calle Maestro Vitoria (phone: 531-4100; in the US, 800-528-1234; fax: 531-3761).

Carlton This establishment is in a unique location in the southern part of central Madrid, near the Atocha train station complex, as well as within easy walking distance of the *Queen Sofia Art Center–National Museum*, the Botanical Gardens, and the *Prado*. All of the 133 air conditioned rooms have TV sets. Business facilities include 24-hour room service, meeting rooms for up to 200, an English-speaking concierge, foreign currency exchange, secretarial services in English, audiovisual equipment, photocopiers, computers, and translation services. 26 Paseo de las Delicias (phone: 239-7100; fax: 227-8510).

Don Diego A well-kept *pensión* near the Parque del Retiro in Madrid's lovely Salamanca district. The 58 rooms are nicely furnished, and several have ample balconies. There is a TV lounge and a bar that serves sandwiches and breakfast. 45 Calle Velázquez (phone: 435-0760).

Emperador Centrally located right on the Gran Vía, all 232 rooms are air conditioned and have color TV sets. Unusual among the many hotels in the immediate area, it boasts a rooftop garden with a swimming pool and excellent views of the city. Business facilities include 24-hour room service, meeting rooms for up to 200, an English-speaking concierge, foreign currency exchange, secretarial services in English, audiovisual equipment, photocopiers, computers, and translation services. 53 Gran Vía (phone: 413-6511; fax: 247-2817).

Escultor Conveniently located near the Castellana in a quiet residential area, its 82 air conditioned, apartment-style units offer separate sitting rooms with TV sets, complete kitchens, and mini-bars. Business facilities include meeting rooms for up to 250, an English-speaking concierge, foreign currency exchange, secretarial services in English, audiovisual equipment, photocopiers, computers, and translation services. 5 Calle Miguel Angel (phone: 410-4203; in the US, 800-528-1234; fax: 319-2584).

Galiano A converted mansion, complete with marble floors, antique paintings, tapestries, and carved-wood furniture in the lobby and lounge. On a tranquil side street just off the Castellana and Plaza de Colón, it has 29 comfortable singles, doubles, and suites. Breakfast and TV sets are optional. There is an English-speaking concierge. 6 Calle Alcalá Galiano (phone: 319-2000).

Mayorazgo Excellent service and 200 well-appointed, comfortable, air conditioned rooms just a step from the central Gran Vía. The hotel's dining room serves breakfast, lunch, and dinner. Business facilities include meeting rooms for up to 300, an English-speaking concierge, foreign currency exchange, secretarial services in English, audiovisual equipment, photocopiers, computers, and translation services. 3 Calle Flor Baja (phone: 247-2600; fax: 541-2485).

Puerta de Toledo Away from major hotel clusters, it is located on the fringe of picturesque Old Madrid, facing the Triumphal Arch of the Puerta de Toledo and near the *Mercado Puerta de Toledo*. Its 160 rooms are air conditioned, comfortable, and well maintained. There is a modest restaurant serving lunch and dinner on the premises. 4 Glorieta Puerta de Toledo (phone: 474-7100; fax: 474-0747).

Reina Victoria Run by the Tryp hotel chain, this 201-room remodeled Madrid classic was built in 1923 and designated a building of National Historic Interest. Its unaltered 6-story façade, elaborate with pilasters, turrets, wrought-iron balconies, and bay windows, dominates the entire west side of the picturesque Plaza Santa Ana. The *Bar Taurino* revives the hotel's decades-old tradition as a rendezvous for bullfighters, breeders, and aficionados. A formal restaurant serving breakfast, lunch, and dinner is on the premises. Business facilities include meeting rooms for up to 500, an English-speaking concierge, foreign currency exchange, secretarial services in English, audiovisual equipment, photocopiers, computers, and translation services. 14 Plaza Santa Ana (phone: 531-4500).

Serrano Small and tasteful, refined and immaculate, on a quiet street between the Castellana and the boutique-lined Calle Serrano. Its marble-floored lobby is comfortably furnished and richly decorated with antiques (including a large 17th-century tapestry) and huge arrangements of fresh flowers. All 34 rooms are air conditioned and have TV sets. No restaurant, but snacks and sandwiches are available at the bar. Business facilities include an English-speaking concierge, foreign currency exchange, and translation services. 8 Calle Marqués de Villamejor (phone: 435-5200; fax: 435-4849).

Tryp Ambassador Formerly a 6-story noble mansion, this fine 181 room hotel has all the latest conveniences and is located near the *Teatro de la Opera,* Plaza de Oriente, and the Royal Palace. The restaurant serves Spanish and international fare. Business facilities include 24-hour room service, meeting rooms for up to 290, an English-speaking concierge, foreign currency exchange, secretarial services in English, audiovisual equipment, photocopiers, computers, translation services, and express checkout. 5 Cuesta Santo Domingo (phone: 541-6700).

Tryp Plaza Located within the gigantic Edificio España landmark building of the early 1950s, this hotel with 306 rooms (all air conditioned) is usually swarming with tour groups. The 26th-floor swimming pool and terrace restaurant offer marvelous panoramic views of the city. Business facilities include 24-hour room service, meeting rooms for up to 500, an English-speaking concierge, foreign currency exchange, secretarial services in English, audiovisual equipment, photocopiers, computers, and translation services. 2 Plaza de España (phone: 247-1200; in the US, 800-645-5687; fax: 248-2389).

INEXPENSIVE

Jamic A small 19-room pension centrally located across the street from the *Palace* hotel and near the *Prado.* Some of the rooms have full bath, others just offer sinks. Breakfast is served in a small dining room. 4 Plaza de las Cortes (phone: 429-0068).

Lisboa This well run residential *hostal* has 23 rooms, all with recently renovated private baths, plus maid service, a TV lounge, and an elevator. The location — just off the Plaza Santa Ana in charming Old Madrid, yet a short walk to the *Palace,* the *Ritz,* and the *Prado* — is terrific. English is spoken and credit cards are accepted. Fine restaurants of all price ranges line the street. 17 Calle Ventura de la Vega (phone: 429-9894).

EATING OUT

Madrileños eat the main meal of their day during the work break from 2 to 4 PM. An early-evening snack (*merienda*), such as wine and *tapas, chocolate con churros,* or coffee and sweets, takes the edge off appetites until a light supper is eaten after 10 PM. For those who can't adjust to the Spanish schedule, there are always *cafeterías* and snack bars, and many restaurants start serving dinner at about 8:30 PM to accommodate non-Spaniards. There are over 3,000 restaurants in Madrid. Dinner for two with wine will cost $130 or more at restaurants described below as very expensive; from $70 to $115 at places listed as expensive; between $30 and $60 at moderate eateries; and $25 or less at inexpensive ones. Most restaurants offer a set menu (*menú del día*), a complete meal for an economical price. Some restaurants include the 6% Value Added Tax in their menu prices. Check beforehand whether the menu says *IVA incluido* or *IVA no incluido*. All telephone numbers are in the 1 area code unless otherwise indicated.

For an unforgettable dining experience, we begin with our gustatory favorites, followed by our recommendations of cost and quality choices listed by price category.

DIVINE DINING

La Gamella This intimate restaurant, one of Madrid's best, is dedicated to new Spanish cuisine. American owner-chef-host Richard Stephens, also an instructor at Madrid's famed Alambique School of Gastronomy, imaginatively combines choice ingredients in such dishes as slices of cured duck breast in Belgian endives with walnut oil or *pastel de chorizo fresco y pimientos rojos* (Spanish sausage and red pepper quiche) for starters, followed by such delights as turbot in wild mushroom sauce with a fresh tomato *coulis*. Irresistible desserts and a fine wine list add up to an adventure in taste. Closed Sundays, holidays, and August. Reservations advised. Major credit cards accepted. 4 Calle Alfonso XII (phone: 532-4509).

El Mentidero de la Villa Just off the bustling Castellana, this delightful intimate restaurant, decorated with classic and modern touches, offers inventive food and efficient and friendly service. Award-winning Japanese chef Ken Sato has created a distinctive French menu with Spanish and Japanese culinary influences. The salads are superb, as is *pato con manzana* (duck with apple), and *rollo de primavera con puerros y gambas* (spring rolls with leeks and shrimp). For dessert, try the homemade chocolate mousse. Closed Sundays. Reservations advised. Major credit cards accepted. 6 Calle Santo Tomé (phone: 419-5506).

Príncipe de Viana Owner Iñaki Oyarbide, another of Madrid's top restaurateurs, and son of *Zalacaín*'s famous proprietor (see below), offers fine Basque-Navarrese specialties (the menu changes from season to season) served in a relaxed, elegant atmosphere. Loyal customers include the crème de la crème of Madrid's financial community. Closed Saturdays for lunch, Sundays, and from mid-August through the first week of September. Reservations advised. American Express and Visa accepted. 5 Calle Manuel de Falla (phone: 259-1448).

Zalacaín Probably the finest restaurant in all of Spain, it was the first in the country to win three Michelin stars. Imaginative Basque and French haute cuisines are served here, with particular emphasis on seafood. Try the fish and shellfish soup and the pig's feet stuffed with lamb. Owner Jesús Oyarbide often travels to the Rioja, Navarre, and Aragon regions in search of new ingredients and additions to his wine cellar. Luxuriously decorated, the restaurant shimmers with polished silver, gleaming glass, and fresh flowers. Impeccable service and an irresistible dessert cart also contribute to a memorable dining experience. Closed Saturdays for lunch, Sundays, August, *Easter Week,* and holidays. Reservations necessary (call at least 2 days in advance). American Express, Visa, and Diners Club accepted. 4 Calle Alvarez de Baena (phone: 261-4840).

VERY EXPENSIVE

Horcher Operated for generations by the Horcher family, this remains one of Madrid's most elegant dining places, serving continental fare with an Austro-Hungarian flavor. Dining here is an indulgence that should include such delicacies as *chuletas de ternasco a la castellana* (baby lamb chops), endive salad with truffles, and crêpes Sir Holten for dessert. Diners might even try the classic goulash. Closed Sundays. Reservations necessary for lunch and dinner. American Express, Visa, and Diners Club accepted. 6 Calle Alfonso XII (phone: 522-0731).

Jockey A Madrid classic, intimate and elegant, and a recipient of the National Gastronomy Award. The continental cuisine is superb, as are traditional dishes such as *cocido madrileño,* a savory stew. Other specialties include *perdiz española* (partridge), *lomo de lubina* (filet of sea bass), and *mousse de anguila* (eel mousse). Closed Sundays and August. Reservations necessary. Major credit cards accepted. 6 Calle Amador de los Ríos (phone: 319-1003).

Ritz The sumptuous restaurant of the luxurious *Ritz* hotel serves French as well as traditional *madrileño* cuisine. The separate *Ritz Garden Terrace* offers more casual dining, or simply afternoon tea or *tapas.* Open daily for breakfast, lunch, and dinner. Reservations necessary. Major credit cards accepted. 5 Plaza de la Lealtad (phone: 521-2857).

Villa Magna The remodeling of Madrid's *Villa Magna* hotel placed its restaurant among the city's finest. Cristóbal Blanco, the prize-winning chef, designs such nouvelle delicacies as grilled scallops with caviar in basil sauce. The china was designed by Paloma Picasso. The *Champagne Bar* dispenses 252 French and Spanish vintages. Open for breakfast, lunch, and dinner. Reservations necessary. Major credit cards accepted. 22 Paseo de la Castellana (phone: 261-4900).

La Basílica Once an old baroque church, this elegant restaurant serves international, nouvelle, and Spanish cuisines in the see-and-be-seen main dining room or in secluded alcoves. It's located on a narrow street in Old Madrid, near Plaza Mayor. Closed Saturdays at lunch and all day Sundays. Reservations essential. Major credit cards accepted. 12 Calle de la Bolsa (phone: 521-8623).

Belagua When it reopened in the *Santo Mauro* hotel in 1992, this renowned eatery already had an elite *madrileño* following from its previous location in the *Sanvy* hotel. The same Basque-Navarrese fare that has long attracted locals is served in the sophisticated atmosphere of the restored library of a turn-of-the-century French palatial mansion, redecorated in glowing Art Deco. Traditional specialties include monkfish and spider crab stew; entrées with oxtail, pig's feet, lobster, or blood sausage; and exquisite desserts. Open daily; Sundays exclusively for hotel guests. Reservations advised. Major credit cards accepted. 36 Zurbano (phone: 319-6900).

Cabo Mayor The owner and chef both have won the National Gastronomy Award, and for good reason: Their fresh seafood from the province of Cantabria is imaginatively prepared, and the vegetable dishes are superlative. If it's on the menu, try the *cigalas y langostinos con verduras al jerez sibarita* (crayfish and prawns with green vegetables in sherry sauce). Closed Sundays, the last 2 weeks of August, *Christmas Week, New Year's Week,* and *Easter Week.* Reservations advised. American Express, Diners Club, and Visa accepted. 37 Calle Juan Ramón Jiménez (phone: 250-8776).

Café de Oriente Anything from *tapas* to French haute cuisine can be enjoyed here in a delightful *madrileño* atmosphere. It is an ideal place for afternoon tea or cocktails at a sidewalk table overlooking the square and the Royal Palace or inside the café (reservations unnecessary); for fine Castilian dining downstairs in the vaulted 17th-century Sala Capitular de San Gil (reservations advised); or for superb French-Basque cuisine in the adjacent restaurant (reservations advised) or one of the private dining rooms frequented by royalty and diplomats (reservations essential). Closed Mondays for lunch, Sundays, and August. Major credit cards accepted. 2 Plaza de Oriente (phone: 247-1564).

El Cenador del Prado Favored by aficionados of nouvelle cuisine, this place is artistically decorated in a style reminiscent of an elegant conservatory, allowing indoor dining under the stars. Try *patatas a la importancia con almejas* (potatoes with clams) or the *pato al vinagre de frambuesas* (duck with raspberry vinegar). Closed for lunch on Saturdays and all day Sundays. Reservations necessary. Major credit cards accepted. 4 Calle del Prado (phone: 429-1561).

La Dorada Fresh seafood of every imaginable variety is flown in daily from the Mediterranean to this mammoth establishment, which serves Andalusian fare. Particularly noteworthy is the fish baked in a crust of salt, an Andalusian practice that results, surprisingly, in a dish that's not salty. Closed Sundays and August. Reservations are essential, as this place is always crowded — and you'll enjoy the food even more if you reserve one of the private dining rooms. Major credit cards accepted. 64-66 Calle Orense (phone: 270-2002).

Gure-Etxea One of the best for Basque dishes in Madrid, serving specialties such as *porrusalda* (leek and potato soup with cod) and a variety of fish dishes. Both the atmosphere and the service are pleasant. Closed Sundays and August. Reservations advised. American Express and Visa accepted. 12 Plaza de la Paja (phone: 265-6149).

Lhardy A *madrileño* institution since 1839, and the decor, atmosphere, and table settings haven't changed much since then. One specialty in the upstairs dining rooms and private salons is *cocido madrileño*, the typical stew. At *merienda* time in the late afternoon, the street-entrance restaurant and stand-up bar fill with regulars who serve themselves the *caldo* (broth) of the *cocido* from a silver tureen, and also enjoy finger sandwiches, canapés, cold cuts, pastries, cocktails, or coffee. Closed Sunday and holiday evenings and the month of August. Reservations essential for the private dining rooms. Major credit cards accepted. Carrera de San Jerónimo (phone: 521-3385).

Paradís Madrid This branch of a well-known Barcelona eatery is in a turn-of-the-century mansion alongside Plaza de las Cortes. The menu is primarily Catalan-Mediterranean: mushrooms served in several delicious ways (one stuffed with duck liver), five variations of *bacalao* (cod), and a "catch of the day." A separate menu called "Homage to the Great Chefs" features original dishes of illustrious Basque and Catalan chefs. The *Bodiguilla* bar serves *tapas* and typical Catalan *pan con tomate* (bread spread with tomato) until 1:30 AM. Closed for Sunday dinner. Reservations advised. Major credit cards accepted. 14 Marqués de Cubas (phone: 429-7303).

Platerías Its intimate low-key elegance in the heart of Old Madrid creates a pleasant atmosphere for enjoying authentic Spanish dishes such as *callos a la madrileña* (succulent tripe, Madrid style), *chipirones* (cuttlefish in its own ink), and remarkable vegetable plates. Closed Sundays. Reservations advised. Major credit cards accepted. 11 Plaza Santa Ana (phone: 429-7048).

La Trainera Another favorite of seafood lovers. All the fish and shellfish is extremely fresh; try the grilled sole. Closed Sundays and August. Reservations advised. MasterCard and Visa accepted. 60 Calle Lagasca (phone: 276-8035).

Antigua Casa Sobrino de Botín Also known as *Casa Botín,* this is one of Madrid's oldest restaurants — founded in 1725 — and still an excellent value. It is famous for its Castilian-style roast suckling pig and baby lamb, one of which is usually featured on the *menú del día.* Lunch and dinner seem to fall into two "shifts," with the early-eating tourists first, followed by *madrileños,* whose normal dining hours are after 2 and 9 PM, respectively. Open daily. Reservations unnecessary. Major credit cards accepted. 17 Calle Cuchilleros (phone: 266-4217).

Café Gijón This 103-year-old Madrid institution is a traditional meeting and greeting place for intellectuals and artists. During the summer, the sidewalk café is one of the city's liveliest. Open daily. No reservations. Visa and MasterCard accepted. 21 Paseo de Recoletos (phone: 532-5425).

El Callejón A bust of Hemingway and walls chockablock with celebrity photos attest to those who have enjoyed the friendly atmosphere and home-cooked food here in the past. An informal Old Madrid place, it serves a different regional specialty each day of the week, but *callos a la madrileña* is always on the menu, and *tapas* abound. Open daily. Reservations unnecessary. Major credit cards accepted. 6 Calle Ternera (phone: 531-9195).

Casa Lucio This casual restaurant in Old Madrid has become an institution among the elite, who enjoy fine Spanish food — especially seafood. Closed Saturdays for lunch and during August. Reservations essential. American Express and Visa accepted. 35 Calle Cava Baja (phone: 265-3252).

Casa Paco The steaks served in this old tavern are excellent. Other specialties include typical *madrileño* dishes. Closed Sundays and August. No reservations. Visa accepted. 11 Calle Puerta Cerrada (phone: 266-3166).

La Chata This totally typical *mesón* bears the nickname of Madrid's adored Infanta Isabel (the youngest child of Queen Isabel II), who is depicted on the hand-painted tile façade by Eduardo Fernández. Delicious morsels are served at the *tapas* bar, and the small restaurant specializes in roast suckling pig and lamb dishes. Closed Sunday evenings and Wednesdays. No reservations or credit cards accepted. 25 Calle Cava Baja (phone: 266-1458).

El Cuchi The Spanish link of Mexico's famous *Carlos 'n' Charlie's* chain, with specialties of both worlds served by a gregarious staff. Open daily. Reservations unnecessary. Major credit cards accepted. 3 Calle Cuchilleros (phone: 255-4424).

Los Galayos A typical tavern serving fine Castilian roast suckling pig and lamb, with a *tapas* bar and an outdoor café right alongside the Plaza Mayor. Open daily. Reservations unnecessary. Major credit cards accepted. 1 Plaza Mayor (phone: 265-6222).

El Ingenio This unpretentious, family-run restaurant, decorated with Don Quixote and Sancho Panza memorabilia, serves impeccably fresh seafood and locally grown pork, lamb, and beef. Closed Sundays and holidays. Reservations unnecessary. Major credit cards accepted. Just off the Plaza de España at 10 Calle Leganitos (phone: 541-9133).

La Mesa Redonda A small eatery on one of Old Madrid's most charming little streets. Its American owners serve the best *Thanksgiving* dinner in town. Other specialties include beef bourguignon and stews. Dinner only; closed Sundays. Reservations unnecessary (except for *Thanksgiving*). No credit cards accepted. 17 Calle Nuncio (phone: 265-0289).

Posada de la Villa Although the 3-story building is relatively new, this authentic eatery dates back to 1642, when it was originally a *posada* (inn) for out-of-towners. It has retained its tradition of hospitality and still offers fine typical dishes such as *cocido madrileño* and roast pig and lamb. Closed Sunday evenings. Reservations unnecessary. Major credit cards accepted. 9 Calle Cava Baja (phone: 266-1860).

La Quinta del Sordo The façade of this award-winning restaurant is adorned with fine hand-painted tile mosaics. Its name means "house of the deaf man," referring to the place where Goya lived in Madrid. Reproductions of Goya art and memorabilia add to the decor. An array of fine Castilian dishes offers memorable dining in a pleasant atmosphere. Closed Sunday evenings. Reservations unnecessary. Major credit cards accepted. 10 Calle Sacramento (phone: 248-1852).

Riazor An unpretentious turn-of-the-century establishment with a cordial atmosphere, fine traditional fare, and a cornucopia of hot and cold *tapas* served at the bar. Open daily. Reservations unnecessary, except for groups. Visa accepted. Located 1 short block south of Plaza Mayor at 19 Calle Toledo (phone: 266-5466).

Taberna del Alabardero A Madrid classic, this was the tavern of the Royal Palace guards. There is a wonderful *tapas* bar, and succulent Spanish and Basque dishes are served in cozy dining rooms reminiscent of 19th-century Madrid. Open for lunch and dinner daily. Reservations unnecessary. Major credit cards accepted. 6 Calle Felipe V (phone: 541-5192).

INEXPENSIVE

Foster's Hollywood It's a *restaurante americano,* complete with a variety of hamburgers and barbecued spareribs. But far from being *yanqui* fast-food joints, this small chain of pleasant restaurants offers good service and atmosphere. Open daily at all locations. No reservations. Major credit cards accepted. Several locations: 1 Calle Magallanes (phone: 488-9165); 3 Calle Apolonio Morales (phone: 457-7911); 1 Calle Tamayo y Baus (phone: 231-5115); 16 Calle del Cristo (phone: 638-6791); 14-16 Av. de

Brasil (phone: 455-1688); 80 Calle Velázquez (phone: 435-6128); and 100 Calle Guzmán el Bueno (phone: 234-4923).

El Granero de Lavapiés Good vegetarian food in one of Old Madrid's most typical neighborhoods. Closed Saturdays during the month of August. No reservations or credit cards accepted. 10 Calle Argumosa (phone: 467-7611).

Mesón Museo del Jamón Any restaurant with 4,000 hams dangling from its ceiling and draping its walls deserves the name "Ham Museum," and there are four such pork paradises in central Madrid. Fine hams from the regions of Jabugo, Murcia, Salamanca, and Extremadura are served in various ways, including sandwiches, at the stand-up bars and at dining tables. Also featured are an array of cheeses, a great deli, and roast chicken. Any dish can also be prepared to take out. No reservations or credit cards accepted. 6 Carrera San Jerónimo (phone: 521-0340); 72 Gran Vía (phone: 541-2023); 44 Paseo del Prado (phone: 230-4385); and 54 Calle Atocha (phone: 227-0716).

La Salsería Befitting its name, this small bar with an outdoor café specializes in sauces — 15 kinds, served in the holes of an artist's palette, in the center of which are ruffled fried potatoes for dipping. Try *spaghetti a la siciliana* as well. Closed Mondays. No reservations or credit cards accepted. Across the traffic circle from the *Mercado Puerta de Toledo,* at 2 Ronda de Toledo (phone: 266-0890).

Taberna de Antonio Sánchez Genuinely typical of Old Madrid, it has been a venerated favorite ever since it was founded by a legendary bullfighter more than 150 years ago. The small, unpretentious dining rooms are charming, the wonderful food — seafood, Spanish cuisine, salads, and desserts — served with care. Closed Sunday evenings. No reservations. Visa accepted. 13 Calle Mesón de Paredes (phone: 239-7826).

TAPAS BARS

Tapas probably originated in Seville, but today *el tapeo* (enjoying *tapas*) is a way of life throughout Spain, especially in Madrid, where there are literally thousands of places to do so. Practically every bar (not to be confused with pubs or *bares americanos,* which are for drinks only), *taberna, mesón, tasca, cervecería,* and even *cafetería* serves *tapas* — everything from little plates of green olives to an array of cheeses, sausages, hams, seafood, eggs, and vegetables that have been sliced, diced, wrapped, filled, marinated, sauced, or sautéed for hot or cold consumption. Most establishments specializing in *tapas* also have a few tables or even dining rooms in addition to their stand-up bar. Toothpicks and fingers are the most common utensils; shrimp, langostine, mussel, and clam shells, olive pits, napkins, and almost everything else are dropped on the floor, which is swept and scoured after each surge (from 1 to 3 PM and 7 to 9 PM, more or less — usually more).

A *chato* (glass of wine) or *caña* (draft beer) customarily is served with a free *tapita*. If you're hungry for more and the vast array of *tapas* on display is overwhelming, just point to what you want. If you prefer a larger portion, ask for a *ración*, which can be a small meal in itself. Don't pay until you've completely finished; the bartender probably will remember everything you consumed, even if you don't. He'll deliver your change on a saucer; leave a few *duros* (5-peseta coins) as a tip, and always say *gracias* and *adiós* when you depart.

Tapas bar hopping is at its best in the central and old sections of Madrid. One of the city's best is *La Trucha* (with two locations, both just off Plaza Santa Ana: 3 Calle Manuel Fernández y González; phone: 259-1448; and 6 Calle Nuñez de Arce; phone: 532-0882). They're jammed at *tapas* time, and with good reason: Everything from bull tails to succulent red pimentos, as well as *trucha* (trout), is served with gusto (closed Sunday nights, and they alternate July and August vacations). Nearby, the *Cervecería Alemana* (6 Plaza Santa Ana; phone: 429-7033) is, despite its name ("German Beer Parlor"), thoroughly *madrileño*, which is why the ubiquitous Hemingway frequented it, and artists, intellectuals, and students continue to flock here. Among the *tapas* are good hams, sausages, and cheeses (closed Tuesdays and August). Around Puerta del Sol are *Casa Labra* (12 Calle Tetuán; phone: 532-1405), which was founded in 1860 and has been jam-packed ever since — among the specialties is fluff-fried *bacalao* (cod) that melts in the mouth — and *Mejillonería El Pasaje* (3 Pasaje de Matheu; phone: 521-5155), which deals in mussels exclusively, fresh from Galicia. *La Torre del Oro* (26 Plaza Mayor; phone: 266-5016) is a lively Andalusian bar appropriately decorated with stunning bullfight photos and memorabilia, with recorded *sevillanas* music adding to the ambience; the *tapas* include such delicacies as baby eels and fresh anchovies, fried or marinated. In the same vicinity are *Valle del Tiétar* (5 Calle Ciudad Rodrigo; phone: 248-0511), in the northwest arcade entrance to the plaza, which offers *tapas*, Avila-style, with suckling pig and kid specialties; *El Oso y el Madroño* (4 Calle de la Bolsa; phone: 532-1377), with an authentic atmosphere and jovial clientele; and the unpretentious *El Chotis* (11 Calle Cava Baja; phone: 265-3230; closed Mondays and August), south of Plaza Mayor. Elsewhere, there's *Monje Cervecería* (21 Calle del Arenal; phone: 248-3598), a showcase of fresh seafood as well as lamb sweetbreads, and *La Mi Venta* (7 Plaza Marina Española; phone: 248-5091), where a friendly neighborhood atmosphere prevails and fine hot and cold *tapas* and *raciones* are served, with select hams the specialty. At *Bocaíto* (6 Calle Libertad; phone: 532-1219), north of the Gran Vía and Calle de Alcalá, animated *tapas* makers behind the bar prepare a limitless selection of outstanding treats, and giant Talavera ceramic plates on the walls are painted with fine reproductions of Goya's *Wine Harvest*. Adjacent is a deli and small dining room with communal tables.

Pamplona

The ultimate expression of Pamplona's gusto is the renowned *Fiesta de San Fermín*, held annually in July to honor the city's native-born patron saint, who was martyred in 287. Without a doubt it is Spain's wildest event, highlighted by the famous *encierros*, or "running of the bulls" through the town streets, and by attendant nonstop revelry. The fiesta, also known as the *Festival de los Sanfermines*, originated in the 17th century and was immortalized by Ernest Hemingway in his first novel, *The Sun Also Rises* (known as *Fiesta* in Spain). The book's vivid descriptions have drawn millions to the city over the years, and in deference to his place in the fortunes of the city, there is a statue of the writer on Paseo Hemingway, next to the *Plaza de Toros*.

The capital of the ancient Pyrenean kingdom of Navarre, Pamplona got its name from the Roman general Pompey, who camped here with his troops on a hillside above the Arga River in the winter of 75–74 BC. Long known as the Gateway to Spain, it lies at the junction of two mountain passes through the Pyrenees from France. The city (with a population of 185,000) is now the capital of the region of Navarre, one of Spain's 17 autonomous communities, and has grown beyond the core of the Old Town and its fortress walls.

The city was occupied by the Visigoths in the 5th century, by the Franks in the 6th century, and by the Moors in the 8th century. The Basques, with the help of Charlemagne, drove the Moors out in 750. Charlemagne remained, however, and soon after he sacked the city and tore down its defensive walls. In an act of patriotic revenge, Basque forces annihilated the rear guard of Charlemagne's army, led by the legendary Roland, in the Roncesvalles Pass in 778, an event later romanticized in the epic poem *Song of Roland*. Sancho III of Navarre made the city the capital of his kingdom in the year 1000, and so it remained until 1512, when the forces of King Ferdinand and Queen Isabella destroyed a second set of walls and occupied the city in the process of annexing Navarre to Castile. In the same century, during a battle to recapture the city, a young army captain named Iñigo López de Loyola (who ultimately became known to the world as St. Ignatius of Loyola) was seriously wounded and endured a lengthy convalescence here. He began to study religion, and in the 1530s founded the Society of Jesus, the Catholic religious order whose members are called Jesuits. Still later in the century, Philip II began a third set of walls, turning Pamplona into the most heavily fortified city in northern Spain.

The old section of the city, still partly surrounded by the historic fortress walls, is filled with old noble mansions, convents, and churches. Pamplona's central point is the Plaza del Castillo, which offers an overview of the town's diverse architectural styles. Fascist classic, Art Nouveau, and chrome and glass mix; arcades only make it partway around the plaza, and streets enter at odd, irregular angles. The lack of architectural consistency carries over to the city's churches. The mostly Gothic cathedral bears an unusual classical Greco-Roman façade of the baroque era; the Church of San Saturnino, a former fortress, is a composite of Gothic and Romanesque; and the exterior of the Church of San Nicolás is that of a medieval castle with Gothic embellishments.

What is consistent, however, is the strong bond among the people of Pamplona, and their independent spirit. When Charlemagne came down from the north to drive out the Moors, the *pamplonicas* welcomed him with open arms as a liberator, but when his desire to be a conqueror revealed itself, they quickly changed their attitude toward him. It also was in Pamplona that the Fueros, a bill of rights similar to the Magna Carta, was signed in the 13th century. It guaranteed the people of Navarre independence from Castilian monarchs, and imposed a system of justice that is still practiced today.

Neighbors of the strongly separatist Basque Country, the *pamplonicas* nonetheless maintain a tolerance for political and cultural differences. Pamplona's cultural and intellectual life is enlivened by several institutions of higher education, including the University of Navarre run by the rightist Catholic movement, Opus Dei, and the government-run Public University of Navarre, which opened in 1991, as well as various other professional and private institutes and schools. The hardworking, industrious *pamplonicas* are nevertheless a generally warm, friendly people who make their historic city a hospitable place for visitors.

Pamplona At-a-Glance

SEEING THE CITY

The most spectacular view of this hilltop city is from the roads descending the Pyrenees over the Roncesvalles and Puerto de Velate passes from France. As you approach the city limits, the fortress walls rise dramatically over Pamplona, which is topped by the spires of the cathedral and the clustered Old Town. The wide green belt of parks, gardens, and tree-lined avenues that surrounds the Old Town makes the walls appear even more spectacular.

SPECIAL PLACES

Pamplona is composed of an Old Town surrounded by modern suburbs. Just about everything a visitor will want to see is located in the old section, a compact area of extremely narrow, picturesque streets, which can be traversed on foot in less than 15 minutes. Three new parking lots in or near the Old Town — at Plaza de Toros, Plaza Blanca de Navarra, and Plaza San Francisco — have greatly eased the parking problems in the city center, but it's still a better idea to park on one of the streets outside the Old Town. Pamplona's modern suburbs, more than mere residential areas, are centers of life complete with restaurants, shops, bars, nightclubs, and discotheques. The suburb of San Juan, west of the Old Town, is considered the most desirable place to live.

PLAZA DEL CASTILLO This elegant, arcaded square is shaded by the intertwining boughs of carefully pruned trees. At the southwest corner of the plaza is the Palacio de la Diputación Foral. Built in 1847 and enlarged in 1932, it is the seat of the regional government (open to the public at variable times; no admission charge). The tree-lined Paseo de Sarasate, Pamplona's main promenade, begins at the south end of the plaza and runs past the Monumento de los Fueros, commemorating the region's 13th-century bill of rights.

CATHEDRAL Pamplona's cathedral — closed until the end of this year for interior repairs — stands at the northern tip of the Old Town, hard against the ramparts. Built on the foundations of a 12th-century Romanesque church, it is basically 14th- and 15th-century Gothic, but its west façade is a baroque, Greco-Roman fantasy that was constructed over the original Gothic portals in the late 18th century. The effect of stepping through this baroque façade to find a soaring Gothic church on the inside is strange, to say the least. The major work in the otherwise bare cathedral is the 15th-century alabaster tomb of King Carlos III, the founder of the cathedral, and his wife, Queen Leonor of Castile. Besides various chapels and altarpieces, there is a beautiful Gothic cloister, with lacelike stonework over the arches and delicately carved doorways. It can be visited while the cathedral remains closed, as can the *Diocesan Museum,* which is housed in the former monks' kitchen and refectory, and contains polychrome sculptures of sacred figures and other religious relics. Both the cloister and the museum are open daily, May through October 15 only, from 10 AM to 1 PM; admission charge. Plaza de la Catedral (phone: 225679).

AYUNTAMIENTO (TOWN HALL) This stunningly ornate baroque building is noted for its 18th-century façade topped with allegorical statues. The interior is not open to the public. Plaza Consistorial.

SAN SATURNINO A block away from the Town Hall, this 12th-century Romanesque church (with 13th-century Gothic additions) was constructed within former city fortifications, and two of its bell towers were originally defensive towers. The beautiful main portal is decorated with Gothic arches supported by columns whose capitals are embellished with scenes from the childhood of Christ and the Passion. Inside, notice the dark stained glass windows and the dome. Open daily from 8:30 AM to 12:45 PM and from 6:30 to 8:15 PM. Calle Mayor.

SAN NICOLÁS At the edge of the Old Town, this 13th-century, partly Romanesque church looks more like a fortified castle, complete with tower and fortress walls. The tower now has a spire on one of its corners, and the fortress walls have Gothic flourishes. The interior resembles a castle throne room, with wooden floors and starkly bare walls, but a few altars are worthy of closer inspection. Open daily from 7:30 AM to 12:30 PM and from 6:30 to 8:15 PM. 10 Paseo de Sarasate.

SAN LORENZO Beside the Parque de la Taconera (Taconera Park), this church is home to the heart and soul of Pamplona — the Chapel of San Fermín, the town's patron saint. Unfortunately, the quarters for this soul are relatively soulless — the interiors of both the chapel and the church are rather bare and nondescript. The statue of the saint that is paraded through town on the first day of the *Fiesta de San Fermín* is in the chapel under a marble pavilion. Open daily from 8 AM to 1 PM and from 4 to 8 PM. Corner of Calle Mayor and Calle Taconera.

MUSEO DE NAVARRA The 16th-century Hospital de la Misericordia once occupied this site and its Plateresque portal remains. The building was reopened by Spain's Queen Sofía in May 1990, after extensive renovations. Among the region's artistic treasures housed here are Roman mosaics, capitals from Pamplona's long-gone 12th-century Romanesque cathedral, paintings from the Gothic through the Renaissance periods, murals, a Goya portrait of the *Marqués de San Adrián* that is considered one of the painter's finest works, and luxurious 19th-century furniture. Open Tuesdays through Saturdays, 10 AM to 2 PM and 5 to 7 PM; Sundays, 11 AM to 2 PM. Admission charge. Calle Santo Domingo (phone: 227831).

Sources and Resources

TOURIST INFORMATION

The tourist information office (3 Calle Duque de Ahumada; phone: 220741; fax: 212059) is just off Plaza del Castillo. English-speaking personnel can supply maps of the city and brochures, including one with some interesting regional history and folklore. The office can also help with hotel reservations; local train and bus schedules are posted. Open daily from July through September, 10 AM to 7 PM. The rest of the year, open Mondays through Fridays from 10 AM to 2 PM and from 4 to 7 PM, Saturdays from 10 AM to 1 PM; closed Sundays.

LOCAL COVERAGE The *Diario de Navarra* and *Navarra Hoy* cover local and regional events in Spanish.

TELEPHONE

The area code for Pamplona is 48. If calling from within Spain, but outside the Navarre region, dial "9" before the area code and local number.

GETTING AROUND

AIRPORT The Noaín Airport is 3 miles (5 km) south of town via the N121 highway toward Zaragoza. A taxi from the airport to virtually anywhere in Pamplona costs from $12 to $15. There is daily direct air service to Madrid and Barcelona. The airport (phone: 317512) will provide information.

BUS An excellent local bus system crosses the town and all areas of interest, including the out-of-the-way train station (take bus No. 9). Buses to Burguete and Estella depart from Estación de Autobuses de Pamplona (2 Calle Conde Oliveto; phone: 223854).

CAR RENTAL Major rental agencies include *Hertz* (in the *Tres Reyes Hotel,* Calle Jardines de la Taconera; phone: 223569) and *Avis* (29 Monasterio de la Oliva; phone: 170068).

TAXI Taxis are available on the street or by calling 232330, 230000, or 232100.

TRAIN Pamplona is on the main line connecting San Sebastián, Zaragoza, and Barcelona, with service twice daily in both directions; there is also daily direct service to Madrid. The train station (phone: 122211) is on Calle Rochapea, 1½ miles (2 km) from the center of town. To reach it, take bus No. 9, which runs every 7 minutes from Paseo de Sarasate. A taxi from the center of town will cost about $4.50. There is a *RENFE* ticket office at 8 Calle Estella (phone: 126981).

SPECIAL EVENTS

The annual *Fiesta de San Fermín* is Pamplona's claim to fame.

BEST FESTIVAL

Fiesta de San Fermín This annual event takes place from July 6 through 14 and is dominated by the running of the bulls through Pamplona's streets. The *encierros* (the runs) from the bull corral by the river to the bullring take place at 8 AM every morning from July 7 through July 14; every evening at 6:30 PM bullfights take place in the *Plaza de Toros* bullring. Hundreds of brave and/or crazy men run in front of the bulls each morning in the traditional costume of white shirt and pants, red beret, bandanna, sash, and a rolled-up newspaper. Women are traditionally discouraged from participation, but no one will stop them. Indeed, several women were among those injured during the 1990 and 1991 runnings.

The route from the bull corral to the bullring is 1.8 miles. At 8 AM, a *chupinazo,* or signal rocket, is launched as a warning to the participants, most of whom immediately start to run. Seconds later, another rocket signals the release of the bulls and the start of the *encierro*. If the bulls are not in a tight herd, a third rocket is fired to warn the runners of a separated or stray bull. The *encierro* lasts only a few minutes. Once the bulls reach the ring, they are quickly penned, although the festivities continue inside the ring as the runners and other amateur matadors (equipped with blankets, sheets, newspapers, and other homemade capes) do "battle" with assorted escort calves and steers. The side streets along this mad, run-for-your-life course are planked up, funneling both runners and bulls from the corral to the ring. Vantage points for spectators are hard to obtain after about 7 AM.

The six bulls that are run each morning appear in the ring for the bullfights. For many spectators, the real show is not the bullfights but the antics of the *peñas* in the stands — one of the rowdiest crowds in the country — who spend the entire time spraying each other with champagne, flour, powdered sugar, and *sangría*. Tickets for the bullfights are sold almost a year in advance, but 10% are held back and sold at the bullring each evening for the next day's fights. Get in line at about 5 PM if you hope to get one of these tickets; otherwise, deal with the dozens of scalpers who ring the arena each afternoon.

Though hotel space is tight during *San Fermín*, it is less of a problem than it used to be. In addition to standard accommodations, local families offer rooms for rent, and many of these are excellent bargains. For those interested in participating in the bull run, talk to a seasoned veteran and decide upon a strategy. Americans tend to congregate at the *Bar Txoco* in Plaza del Castillo (on the corner nearest the bullring) and at the *Windsor Pub* next to *La Perla* hotel (see *Checking In*). Local officials often discourage foreigners from participating in the *encierro*, and postcards and photos posted throughout the town showing gory scenes of bulls' horns sticking through runners usually serve as sufficient deterrence. Those who want to watch the festivities are encouraged to make arrangements to see them from the balcony of a pension or a private house, or to watch them on television (the runs are broadcast live throughout Spain).

Additional *San Fermín* festivities are focused in the Old Town, including parades of papier-mâché giants and bands from Pamplona and neighboring towns. Bars remain packed throughout the day and night. The only lull takes place between noon and 5 PM, when it's too hot to remain outdoors in the sun.

SHOPPING

With the exception of leather wineskins, which are sold in every shop in town, Pamplona is not noted for any local handicrafts. There is, however, a Pamplona food specialty — coffee-, vanilla-, and milk-flavored toffees called *pastilla,* which you can buy in any *pastelería* (bakery) in town. The anise-flavored Basque liqueur, *pacharán,* available in most liquor stores, is also worth a try. A top brand is Etxeko, which comes in a black bottle. Pamplona has only one department store, *Unzu,* located in the center of town (7 Calle Mercaderes), which is well stocked with goods at prices somewhat lower than those of the boutiques surrounding it. *Venta Berri* (56 Calle Zapatería; phone: 210024) carries a complete range of Navarre handicrafts and food products, including ceramics, crystal, tapestries, embroidery, chocolates, cheeses, and wines. The most fashionable, newest, and most spacious shops are in Pamplona's New Town, off Avenida Carlos III. The Old Town area just to the west of the Plaza del Castillo, on Calles San Nicolás, San Miguel, Comedias, and Zapatería, is another shopping district, but the shops are smaller and more pedestrian. Shopping hours are generally from 9:30 AM to 1:30 PM and from 4:30 to 7 PM, but may vary from shop to shop.

SPORTS AND FITNESS

Among the most popular sports is jai alai, a form of pelota, played in frontóns, or courts, throughout the region. Mountaineering is widely practiced in the area, and cycling is very popular. (Miguel Induraín, the 1991 and 1992 winner of the prestigious *Tour de France* bicycle race, is from Villalba, just 3 miles/5 km from Pamplona.)

FISHING The rivers around Pamplona and the outlying areas boast an abundance of salmon, trout, barbel, tench, carp, eels, and freshwater crabs. Be sure to check on any local or seasonal regulations with the Federación de Pesca (phone: 107853 or 107859) before casting.

GOLF The 9-hole *Club de Golf Ulzama* course is located in the town of Guerendian, in the Ulzama Valley, 13 miles (21 km) south of Pamplona. Call for information on tee times and greens fees (phone: 305162 or 305471).

JOGGING The best area for jogging in Pamplona is around the city walls in the vicinity of the cathedral.

SWIMMING Pamplona's most popular public swimming spot is the municipal pool at *Aranzadi,* just north of the city walls (phone: 223002). It's open daily, June through September, from 10:30 AM to 9 PM; admission charge. The *Tres Reyes* hotel (see *Checking In*) has a heated pool for the use of guests.

THEATER

Teatro Gayarre (Av. Carlos III; phone: 220139) offers performances throughout the year. The Escuela Navarra de Teatro (5 Calle San Agustín; phone: 229239) is a theater school that stages various performances and occasionally hosts visits by theater companies from Barcelona and Madrid. Almost all performances are in Spanish.

NIGHTCLUBS AND NIGHTLIFE

Pamplona has a very active nightlife. At about 7 PM, the citizenry empties into the streets for the evening *paseo* (stroll). Soon after, everyone converges on the bars for *tapas,* and children play around sidewalk café tables. This camaraderie continues until approximately 10 PM, when many head off for dinner, and then picks up again around midnight. Weeknights are quieter than weekends; on Saturday nights, bars, cafés, and discotheques stay packed until the wee hours.

The most popular discos are in the San Juan district, just outside the

Old Town walls. Try *Reverendos* (5 Calle Monasterio de Velate), a private club that will admit anyone dressed in the latest trend, or *Más y Más* (Av. Bayona), another favorite. *O.N.B.* and *Bye Bye* (outside San Juan on Calle Abejeras; phone: 235937 and 236100, respectively) are a dual disco; the latter attracts a trendier younger crowd, while *O.N.B.* caters to a slightly older group of single professionals. Another top San Juan district pub is *Opera* (1 Monasterio Ijarte; phone: 170211). For live music, try the *Boulevard Jazz Bar* (6 Plaza Reyes de Navarra; phone: 272759), around the corner from the *Ciudad de Pamplona* hotel.

Best in Town

CHECKING IN

The number of hotel rooms in Pamplona has increased in the past few years, to the relief of *San Fermín* visitors, but note that during the fiesta, hotels are allowed to double their normal high-season rates. Lodging with local families is another option at this time — people offering rooms to let congregate outside the tourist office. (The local tourist office does not rate any of these rooms.) During the non-fiesta high season (mid-May to mid-September), expect to pay $90 or more for a double room in a hotel listed as expensive, $60 to $90 in an establishment described as moderate, and $55 or less in an inexpensive place. The telephone numbers listed below do not include area codes. The area code for Pamplona is 48; if calling from another part of Spain, dial "9" first.

EXPENSIVE

Europa This luxurious, modern establishment is an extension of the better-known restaurant of the same name (see *Eating Out*), located just off the Plaza del Castillo. Its 25 rooms, all air conditioned, have TV sets and marble bathrooms. 11 Calle Espoz y Mina (phone: 221800; fax: 229235).

Iruña Park Large and modern, this hostelry has 225 rooms, complete with TV sets and private gardens, and caters to conventioneers. It boasts a wide range of facilities, including a hairdresser, a sauna, a restaurant, and several bars. Ronda de Ermitagaña (phone: 173200; fax: 172387).

Tres Reyes The best Pamplona has to offer, set in a park between the Old Town and the San Juan district. All 180 rooms are air conditioned and comfortable. There is also a heated swimming pool and a good restaurant, and the service is excellent. Perfect for shelter from the storm of *San Fermín,* but be prepared to pay dearly for it. Jardines de la Taconera (phone: 226600; fax: 222930).

MODERATE

Nuevo Maisonnave A traditional favorite, it's centrally located in the Old Town on a quiet street (which remains relatively quiet even during *San Fermín*).

There are 152 comfortable rooms, all air conditioned. This place is similar to the *Tres Reyes* but lacks a pool and some of its other amenities. Two parking garages can accommodate 140 cars. 20 Calle Nueva (phone: 222600; fax: 220166).

Orhi Located across from the Plaza de Toros, this refurbished 55-room hotel is a 5-minute walk from the Plaza del Castillo. It has a cafeteria and shares ownership of *Casa Mauleon* (see *Eating Out*), which is on the main floor of the same building. 7 Calle Leyre (phone: 228500; fax: 228318).

La Perla On the Plaza del Castillo, this 67-room hostelry is a favorite during *San Fermín* as it overlooks Calle Estafeta, the longest straightaway of the *encierro*. Unfortunately, it offers little else. The rooms are modern and functional; there is no restaurant or bar on the premises. 1 Plaza del Castillo (phone: 227706).

Yoldi The 48 rooms here are modern and comfortable. For years, this establishment has been the choice of visiting matadors, and it is the place where all the aficionados gather to discuss the bullfights during *San Fermín*. Located on a quiet street, a short walk from the bullring and the Plaza del Castillo. There's a cafeteria. 11 Av. San Ignacio (phone: 224800; fax: 212045).

INEXPENSIVE

Eslava A small, old, 28-room hotel in the Old Town. The rustic wood-beamed rooms all have private baths. Some offer beautiful views over the city walls and into the valley beyond. There's a cafeteria and a bar. Closed December 26 through January 6. 7 Plaza Virgen de la O (phone: 222270; fax: 225157).

EATING OUT

Pamplona is not a diner's paradise, but it does offer some interesting dishes that combine the heartiness of the mountains with the traditional fare of northern Spain. The local cuisine is Basque, which means plenty of grilled meats, stews, and fresh fish from nearby mountain streams and the Atlantic. Favorites include local *trucha a la navarra* — whole trout cooked with a slice of salty smoked ham; and *merluza* (hake). Lamb might be baked in a wood-fired oven, chopped up and smothered in a sauce, or served simply as chops. During *San Fermín,* the bulls killed in the previous day's fights are served in a wonderful stew. Dinner for two, including wine, will cost $65 or more in restaurants listed as expensive and $40 to $60 at places listed as moderate; inexpensive meals are available at a number of self-service, cafeteria-style restaurants around the city. The numbers below do not include area codes. The area code for Pamplona is 48; if calling from another part of Spain, dial "9" first.

EXPENSIVE

Casa Angel A favorite for lunches, the grill here is renowned for its excellent meat dishes, such as *solomillo a la parrilla* (grilled filet of beef) and *salchicha* (small sausages). Other specialties include fried peppers and traditional Basque fare. Closed Sundays, *Christmas,* and in August. Reservations advised. Major credit cards accepted. 43 Calle Abejeras (phone: 243962).

Casa Otano On the second floor over the bar of the same name, it has one of the best all-purpose menus in town, featuring traditional local dishes. Closed Sunday afternoons and for 4 days after *San Fermín.* Reservations advised. No credit cards accepted. 5 Calle San Nicolás (phone: 225095).

Don Pablo Across from the *Tres Reyes* hotel, this dining spot has a menu of both French and Spanish dishes and a modern atmosphere of smoked glass and chrome. Try the *merluza* (hake), and *lenguado con salsa mousseline* (sole with Dutch sauce of eggs, butter, lemon, and cream). Closed Sunday evenings and August. Reservations necessary. Major credit cards accepted. 19 Calle Navas de Tolosa (phone: 225299).

Europa An opulent dining room, considered the home of nouvelle cuisine in Pamplona, offers, among other things, excellent roquefort filet steaks. Closed Sundays, except in May and during *San Fermín.* Reservations necessary, especially during the festival. Major credit cards accepted. 11 Calle Espoz y Mina (phone: 221800).

Hartza One of two restaurants in Pamplona boasting a Michelin star. It offers traditional regional food, including fish, game, wild mushrooms, and fresh seasonal produce. Try the *merluza de la casa* or *besugo a la bermeana* (sea bream). Closed Sunday evenings and Mondays, late July to late August, and *Christmas* week. Reservations advised. American Express, Diners Club, and Visa accepted. 19 Calle Juan de Labrit (phone: 224568).

Josetxo Famous for more than 30 years for its Basque dishes, this is the other local eatery with a Michelin star. Specialties include *sopa crema de cangrejos* (cream of crab soup), delicious trout and rabbit dishes, *cordero al chilindrón* (Navarre-style lamb with peppers), and *lubina* (sea bass), grilled or in a white wine sauce. Closed Sundays, except in July; closed August. Reservations advised. Major credit cards accepted. 1 Plaza Príncipe de Viana (phone: 222097).

Las Pocholas Among the best Pamplona has to offer, this is the place for vegetable stew, bull's tail stew, lobster with garlic sauce, and other traditional fare. The restaurant's official name is *Hostal del Rey Noble,* but everyone in town knows it as *Las Pocholas.* Closed Sundays and August. Reservations necessary. Major credit cards accepted. 6 Paseo de Sarasate (phone: 222214).

MODERATE

Aralar Baby lamb and roast suckling pig cooked in an open, wood-fired oven are the specialties here, accompanied by a bottle from the excellent wine list.

Closed Wednesday afternoons. Reservations advised. Major credit cards accepted. 12 Calle San Nicolás (phone: 221116).

Casa Mauleon The main dining room resembles a wine cellar with giant barrels lining the walls, and if you're lucky, you may be serenaded by locals singing up a storm here during *San Fermín*. Excellent meals are served at lunch and dinner — try the stuffed peppers. Open daily. Reservations advised. Major credit cards accepted. 4 Calle Amaya (phone: 228474).

Erburu Tucked in one of the back streets of the Old Town, it's hard to find but worth the search. Try the *conejo asado con ajo* (roast rabbit with garlic) or any of the other local specialties. This is a crowded but friendly place. Closed Mondays, Sunday evenings, and for 3 weeks after *San Fermín*. Reservations advised. Major credit cards accepted. 19 Calle San Lorenzo (phone: 225169).

TAPAS BARS

They seems to be spaced every 50 feet throughout the Old Town, especially along Calle San Nicolás and Calle San Gregorio. *Cordovilla* (Calle Navarrería) is well known for its *pimientos fritos, calamares fritos,* and *tortillas,* while *Bar Noé* (9 Calle de las Comedias) has excellent *tapas* ranging from peppers and pâtés to fish salads. The bars around Plaza del Castillo also serve great *tapas.* One popular spot is the *Windsor Pub* (next to *La Perla* hotel), which features seafood *tapas* including small crabs, langoustines, shrimp, and squid in its own ink.

Salamanca

The golden glow of Salamanca lingers long after you have left this city. The splendid Plateresque, Renaissance, and baroque façades of the buildings in the historic section of town — made of soft, fine *piedra arenisca* (amber sandstone) — have, with age, acquired a warm distinctive patina that grows ever richer with the passing centuries and that makes the cityscape truly memorable.

Unlike other towns in Spain, Salamanca has remained reasonably free of the deleterious effects of modern architecture and mass tourism. The home of one of the world's most ancient universities, it has conducted itself through the ages with dignity — so much so that its magnificent monuments and academic structures can seem somewhat imposing to visitors. But Salamanca is really an intimate, lively place, with an army of students to nip any nascent pompousness in the bud.

While the Phoenicians were busy establishing Cádiz in the south, the area of Salamanca was inhabited by Iberian tribes who left their mark with the imposing carved stone bulls, or *verracos,* that are seen throughout the province. Beginning about 900 BC, the Celts from the north, mingling with the Iberians of the central plateau, created two Celtiberian tribes known as Vettons (primarily herdsmen) and Vacceos (primarily farmers).

Hannibal conquered the city in 220 BC during the Second Punic War, and soon after, under the Romans, it became an important communications and trade center. A long, peaceful, and prosperous Roman reign was brought to a contentious halt with the arrival of Germanic tribes in the 5th century. Under the Vandals and Visigoths, and then the Islamic Moors, Salamanca fell into relative obscurity. After its reconquest from the latter in 1085, the area was resettled by an ethnic mix of Franks, Castilians, Portuguese, Jews, Galicians, and some English.

The University of Salamanca was established in 1218, making it — with Paris, Bologna, and Oxford — one of Europe's oldest universities. It achieved great renown and garnered tremendous intellectual respect for its role in reintroducing the world to the works of the ancient Greek and Muslim philosophers, translated into Latin and Old Spanish by the university's Muslim, Jewish, and Christian scholars. Favored by kings and popes, the university reached its peak of prestige during Spain's golden age. Early in the 16th century, 8,000 of Salamanca's 20,000 residents were university students. Cervantes, St. John of the Cross, and others studied, taught, or spent time in Salamanca, the prime intellectual breeding ground of the period. Delicate and elaborately detailed, the Plateresque façade of the university in the Patio de Escuelas is a symbol of the spirit and wealth of those times.

With the waning of Spain's golden age during the 17th century, Salamanca shared in the decline of Castilian cities, a condition that lasted throughout the 18th century. At the turn of this century, the city had only 25,000 inhabitants; but despite the tremendous political upheavals of 20th-century Spain, Salamanca today boasts a population of over 159,000. The university also continues to attract a sizable foreign student body, which lends a cosmopolitan air to this otherwise staunchly Castilian town.

Present-day Salamanca society is clearly divided into students and non-students, who, for the most part, studiously avoid each other. The university — which is not what it used to be — has buildings throughout the city, and most after-class socializing takes place in the city's numerous bars. Meanwhile, the *salmantinos* go about their business largely indifferent to the cultural legacy handed down to them through the centuries. It is left to the legions of visitors, drawn here by the city's architectural and intellectual riches, to marvel at Salamanca's golden splendor.

Salamanca At-a-Glance

SEEING THE CITY

The best view of the city is from the *Parador de Salamanca* (see *Checking In*), located on a hill south of the city and across the Tormes River. On Saturdays, Sundays, and holidays, many of the monuments are illuminated for several hours after nightfall. The spires of the city's side-by-side cathedrals and the dome and towers of La Clerecía dominate the scene.

SPECIAL PLACES

Many of Salamanca's streets are narrow and winding, with numerous one-way thoroughfares, but the Centro Ciudad (City Center) signs lead those arriving by car right into the heart of the city. Once there, it is best to proceed on foot, as all the main sights are concentrated compactly in the *zona monumental* (monument zone), largely between the Plaza Mayor and the river. Visiting hours for the city's sights are erratic, so be sure to check with the main tourist information office (see below) for current hours, though even those may not turn out to be completely accurate.

CITY CENTER

ROMAN BRIDGE Spanning the Tormes River, this 26-arch bridge was constructed by the Romans in 217 BC. In the middle of the bridge stands an imposing carved stone bull, or *verraco,* the handiwork of the Iberian tribes who first lived in the area. Local historians say that the statue has always been in the vicinity of the bridge since its pre-Roman inception, but it has been in its present post since the mid 1800s. Once villified as a symbol of the pagan past, it was at one point thrown into the river on orders from a provincial governor; his successor had it fished out a few years later. The bridge, located below the *parador*, near the old walls of the town, is now open to pedestrian traffic only.

PLAZA MAYOR Deemed by many to be the most beautiful plaza in all of Spain, there can be no better place to sit down and enjoy a cup of coffee than this golden, ingot-shaped trapezoid. Foreign students sit on the cobblestones and practice their Spanish, while mothers sit on benches and try to keep their children from rolling on the ground. In the evening, bands of students uniformed in black and red breeches, leotards, and billowing sleeves wander through the plaza armed with violins, guitars, and mandolins. They are *la tuna,* occasionally coming to rest around a café table, singing local songs, attracting crowds, and drinking on the house. Like most places in Spain, this 18th-century square wasn't always quite so peaceful; it used to double as the city's bullring (and still does on rare occasions).

The square measures roughly 63,500 square feet, with arcades housing boutiques, souvenir stores, pastry shops, and assorted bars and eateries surrounding it at ground level. Above the arcades are 3 stories of balconies, interrupted only by the façade of the Town Hall, which juts out and up to break the uniformity. Begun in 1729 and completed 34 years later, the plaza was originally built as an enclosed market area and arena for public fiestas. It remains the heart of town and the focal point of the festivities of the *Feria de Salamanca,* celebrated every year during the second 2 weeks in September.

CATEDRAL VIEJA (OLD CATHEDRAL) AND CATEDRAL NUEVA (NEW CATHEDRAL)
These stand adjacent to one another, though they are 4 centuries apart in age. Visitors ordinarily enter the old structure through the new one. The Catedral Nueva was begun in 1513 and was in use by 1560, although it wasn't consecrated until 1733. Conceived in a Gothic vein, in actual construction it also drew from the Renaissance and baroque vernaculars. Outside, the church bristles with more than 400 Gothic spikes, and the main doorway, facing Calle Cardenal Playdeniel, is a prime example of the Plateresque stone carvers' art, with biblical scenes in high relief and ornamental borders so richly detailed they tax the eye. Inside, the New Cathedral is notable for the 18th-century baroque wooden choir stalls; for the two organs; for the Cristo de las Batallas, which is a famous 11th-century Romanesque crucifix said to have been carried into battle by El Cid; and for the Capilla Dorada, located near the entrance to the Old Cathedral, its walls plastered with small statues of saints, angels, and prophets.

The Catedral Vieja, down a flight of stairs off the south aisle of the new one, dates from the 12th century. Its plan, columns, capitals, and external arches are in Romanesque style, its internal arches and vaults are Gothic. Simpler and more fortress-like than its replacement, the church's monochromatic interior is enlivened by an extraordinary 15th-century main altarpiece made up of 53 panels depicting the lives of Christ and the Virgin Mary. Among the rooms around the adjoining cloister, be sure to note the

12th-century Talavera Chapel, used at one time for Mozarabic rite masses and topped with a distinctive Romanesque-Mudéjar dome; the 14th-century Santa Barbara Chapel, where university examinations once were held and where candidates for the degree customarily spent the night before finals praying; and the Santa Catalina Chapel and Salas Capitulares (Chapter Rooms), set up as a museum. Most of the exterior of the Old Cathedral is obscured by the new one, but before leaving the complex entirely, walk around back to the Patio Chico (Small Courtyard), from which the older church's strange-looking Torre del Gallo (Rooster Tower), covered with scale-like stones, is visible. Open daily from 10 AM to 2 PM and from 4 to 6 PM; closed Sunday afternoons in winter. There is an admission charge to the Old Cathedral (which includes the cloister chapels and museum). Plaza de Anaya (phone: 217476).

UNIVERSIDAD (UNIVERSITY) Built of golden stone during the Middle Ages, and now well into its golden years, Salamanca's university is pushing a perky 800 years of age. The university's facilities are dispersed through the city, but the core of its "campus" is just around the block from the cathedrals.

The university's original main building, erected during the reign of the Catholic Monarchs and bearing a famed Plateresque façade, is on the Patio de Escuelas and is one of Salamanca's enduring landmarks. The leafy curlicues, twisted gargoyles, imaginary birds, and heraldic animals seem to have been the work of an army of jewelers. Immediately inside is a courtyard ringed by classrooms, one of which (the Paraninfo Room) houses a portrait of King Carlos IV by Goya. Note the beautiful painted ceilings all around the courtyard, and especially the ceiling of the university foyer (opposite the visitors' entrance), with its lacy Moorish design of star shapes in dark wood. A beautiful staircase with carved balustrade leads to the upper level of the courtyard, topped by another fine coffered Mozarabic ceiling. The university's old library, a repository of over 40,000 volumes and 3,000 manuscripts, is located up here, but it is no longer open to visitors.

At the opposite end of the Patio de Escuelas is the Escuelas Menores (Minor Schools) building. It also has a Plateresque façade and a beautiful courtyard, on the far side of which is a room containing a fresco of the zodiac by Fernando Gallego known as *Cielo de Salamanca* (Salamancan Sky). Both the main university building and the Escuelas Menores are open from 9:30 AM to 1:30 PM and from 4:30 to 6 PM Mondays through Saturdays, and from 10 AM to 1 PM on Sundays. One admission charge for both buildings. Patio de Escuelas (phone: 294400, ext. 1150).

MUSEO DE BELLAS ARTES/MUSEO DE SALAMANCA (FINE ARTS MUSEUM/SALAMANCA MUSEUM) Through the door adjacent to the Escuelas Menores and under the 15th-century roof of the former house of Dr. Alvarez Abarca, Queen Isabella's physician, the museum has an eclectic display of paintings and sculptures, both Spanish and foreign, old and modern. Open Tuesdays through Saturdays from 10 AM to 2:00 PM and from 4:30 AM to 8 PM; Sundays from 10 AM to 2 PM. Closed Mondays and every other weekend. Call before you go. Admission charge. Patio de Escuelas (phone: 212235).

CONVENTO DE SAN ESTEBAN (CONVENT OF ST. STEPHEN) This 16th-century church, part of a Dominican convent, is just down Calle Tostado from Plaza de Anaya. It sports another of Salamanca's stunning Plateresque façades, this one depicting the martyrdom of San Esteban and the crucifixion of Christ. Inside is a sumptuous, late-17th-century golden altarpiece by José Benito de Churriguera, in the upper reaches of which is *Martirio de San Esteban* (Martydom of St. Stephen), painted by Claudio Coello. To the side of the church is the beautiful 2-story Claustro de los Reyes (Kings' Cloister), the only one of the convent's three cloisters that is open to the public. From its second story, a door opens into the church's *coro alto,* (high altar), from which the view of the altarpiece is breathtaking. Open daily from 9 AM to 1 PM and from 4 to 7 PM. Admission charge. Plaza Santo Domingo (phone: 215000).

CONVENTO DE LAS DUEÑAS (CONVENT OF THE NUNS) Nearly next door to San Esteban, the 15th-century Moorish-style structure here was a private home before it was donated to a group of *dueñas* (nuns, or pious women of high social standing living in community). Only the five-sided, 16th-century Renaissance cloister is open to visitors, but it's a real treat. Whereas most of the rich stone carving in Salamanca is too distant or too much in the dark to be easily seen, the elaborate capitals of the cloister's upper tier are only slightly above eye level, so their charming, amusing, and grotesque human and animal figures can be brought into sharp focus. The *dueñas* sell their homemade sweets at the *despacho* (shop) in a corner of the entry courtyard. Open daily from 10:30 AM to 1 PM and from 4 to 5:30 PM. Admission charge. The *despacho* is open from 10 AM to 1 PM and from 4 to 7 PM. Plaza del Concilio de Trento (phone: 215442).

CASA DE LAS CONCHAS (HOUSE OF SHELLS) One of the more famous buildings in Salamanca, it dates from the 15th century and incorporates Moorish, Gothic, and Renaissance elements. Unfortunately, it's not open to the public, but the façade, covered with the carved seashells that give the building its name, is noteworthy. The scallop shell is the emblem of St. James and, by extension, the international symbol for pilgrims. (Scallop shells mark the Pilgrims' Route to Santiago de Compostela.) The shell was also the badge of the Pimental family, one of whose members was the bride of the building's owner, a member of the Maldonado family. Their symbol, the fleur-de-lis, is on the coat of arms above the door. Corner of Rúa Antigua and Calle de la Compañía.

In addition to the Casa de las Conchas, there are a number of other noteworthy façades in Salamanca. Be sure to give a passing glance to the Clerecía (or Real Clerecía de San Marcos), a huge 17th-century collegiate church on the corner opposite the Casa de las Conchas, and to the Palacio de Monterrey, a characteristic Spanish Renaissance palace of the early 16th century at the Plaza de Monterrey end of Calle de la Compañía. The Palacio de Monterrey is privately owned and not open to the public; the church is open during church services, which are held approximately at 8:15 AM and 7:30 PM; Sunday mass is at 1 PM. Although the church holds no great treasures, visitors usually find the cloister charming and restful.

ENVIRONS

ALBA DE TORMES About 11 miles (18 km) southeast of Salamanca is the village of Alba de Tormes, just over a medieval bridge with 22 arches crossing the Tormes River. Turn left at the end of the bridge and park beside the unfinished Basílica de Santa Teresa. Then walk up between the basilica and the Iglesia de San Pedro (with the red brick bell tower) to the Plaza de Santa Teresa, where the Convento de Madres Carmelitas Descalzas and the Iglesia de Santa Teresa are the goal of a steady influx of faithful pilgrims. The church is primarily Renaissance, with Gothic and baroque flourishes. The marble vault above the altar bears the mortal remains of St. Teresa of Avila, who founded the convent and died here in 1582. To see the relics and the cell where she died illuminated, apply at the Centro Teresiano Información across the plaza, open Mondays through Fridays, from 10 AM to 1 PM and 4 to 8 PM. The center also houses a small museum exhibiting mementos of St. Teresa's life, and photos of Pope John Paul II's visit to Alba de Tormes in 1982, the 400th anniversary of the saint's death.

BÉJAR This old Moorish fortress town is set in the spectacular Sierra de Béjar, 45 miles (74 km) southeast of Salamanca (on CN-630). Ruins of the old Arab walls surrounding Béjar still remain, and the town's monuments span several hundred years from Moorish constructions in the 11th century to the baroque Plaza Mayor (Main Square). The nearby Sierra de Béjar and Sierra de Candelaria ranges are popular with Spanish mountaineers.

EXTRA SPECIAL	The *Casa-Museo Unamuno* (Unamuno House-Museum), the 18th-century house

where the renowned scholar, poet, and philosopher Miguel de Unamuno lived from 1900 to 1914 (while he was rector of the University of Salamanca), is now an intimate museum containing his notebooks, library, and many personal possessions, including drawings, paper birds, a large crucifix, a small deck of cards (he enjoyed playing solitaire), and his brass bed. Open weekdays from 11 AM to 1 PM and from 4 to 6 PM, weekends from 11 AM to 1 PM. Admission charge. 25 Calle de los Libreros (the hours tend to be somewhat erratic, so it's best to check beforehand; phone: 294400, ext. 1196). (Note — the museum is not to be confused with the house Unamuno moved into when he was no longer university rector, which is at 6 Calle Bordadores and is not open to the public.)

SALAMANCA SOURCES AND RESOURCES

Sources and Resources

TOURIST INFORMATION

The main tourist information office (39 Gran Vía; phone: 268571) is open weekdays from 9:30 AM to 2 PM and from 4:30 to 7 PM; Saturdays from 9:30 AM to 2 PM. Information is also available at the Oficina de Información kiosk (in the eastern wall of the Plaza Mayor; phone: 218342). It's open Mondays through Saturdays from 10 AM to 1:30 PM and from 5 to 7 PM; Sundays and holidays from 11 AM to 2 PM. Both outlets can provide current information regarding hours and admission fees, as well as maps, brochures, and detailed information on local accommodations in all price ranges. For a detailed city map, go to *Librería Cervantes* (11-13 Calle Azafranal; phone: 218602), one of Salamanca's top bookshops, and ask for a *callejero*.

LOCAL COVERAGE *El Adelanto* and *La Gaceta Regional* are local dailies in Spanish, covering local, provincial, national, and international news and events. The monthly *Lugares,* distributed free of charge and also in Spanish, is the best source for information on nightlife and entertainment in Salamanca.

TELEPHONE

The area code for Salamanca is 23. If calling from another part of Spain, dial "9" before the area code and local number.

GETTING AROUND

Salamanca is a small, compact city, and all the sights are within walking distance of one another. Sites are easy to find, too, at least in the *zona monumental,* which is a good thing, because the buildings of Salamanca were renumbered in 1989. For some time to come, brochures and other published materials probably will be full of wrong street numbers. In this chapter, every effort has been made to supply the correct number — but even when the visitor is armed with the correct address, it can be difficult to determine which number beside any given doorway is the correct one.

BUS The bus station (33 Calle Filiberto Villalobos; phone: 236717) is a short distance from the center of town. Schedules are printed in *El Adelanto* and *Lugares.* There is frequent daily service to Zamora, Madrid, Avila, Seville, Barcelona, and León, as well as to nearby Alba de Tormes.

CAR RENTAL Major rental companies include *Hertz* (131 Av. de Portugal; phone: 243134) and *Avis* (49 Paseo de Canalejas; phone: 269753). Local car rental firms include *Castilla* (49 Paseo de Canalejas; phone: 257430); *Prado Mar-*

tín (5 Plaza de Santo; phone: 242549); and *Sánchez González* (163 Av. de Portugal; phone: 220396).

TAXI There are two taxi stands by the Plaza Mayor, one on Calle del Corrillo, and the other on Plaza del Poeta Iglesias, in front of the *Gran* hotel. Taxis can be hailed throughout the city, or by radio service (phone: 250000).

TRAIN The Salamanca train station (Paseo de la Estación; phone: 220395) is a short cab ride from the city center. There is a *RENFE* office near the city center (10 Plaza de la Libertad; phone: 120202). There is frequent daily service to Madrid, Avila, Valladolid, Barcelona, and Porto, Portugal.

SPECIAL EVENTS

In mid-July, the city sponsors the *Verano Cultural de Salamanca,* a week-long series of silent movies, contemporary Spanish cinema, singers, and theater groups from Spain and abroad. The *Feria de Salamanca,* held annually during the second 2 weeks in September, features music, costumes, parades, various theatrical events, and almost daily bullfights.

MUSEUMS

In addition to those described in *Special Places,* Salamanca's *Museo de Historia de la Ciudad y Museo Diocesano* (Museum of City History and Diocesan Museum) is also worth a visit. Housed in city history museum are various stones of archaeological and architectural interest, plus items associated with local composer Tomás Bretón (1850–1923); in the *Diocesan Museum,* upstairs, are several late-15th-century paintings by Fernando and Francisco Gallego, and a triptych of St. Michael by Juan de Flandes. Open Tuesdays through Saturdays from 9 AM to 2 PM and from 5 to 8 PM. Admission charge. Plaza de Juan XXIII (phone: 213067).

SHOPPING

Most of the more interesting shops are in the Plaza Mayor and the surrounding streets to the north, although there is almost nothing sold in Salamanca that isn't also available almost anywhere else in Old Castile. Stores are generally open from 10 AM to 1:30 PM and from 5 to 7 or 8 PM.

FERES Lladró porcelain and Majórica pearls. 27 Plaza Mayor (phone: 215913).

HANDY-CRAFT Belts, ceramics, baskets, and assorted international handicrafts. 53 Rúa Mayor (phone: 263395).

OSCAR Mantillas, fans, flamenco paraphernalia, and other Spanish souvenirs. 15 Plaza Mayor (phone: 213636).

SEGURADO Traditional Spanish souvenirs and novelty items. 10 Plaza Mayor (phone: 212362).

SPORTS AND FITNESS

Salamanca's modern sports complex, *Pabellón Deportivo* (Parque de la Alamedilla; phone: 234069), has a swimming pool, ice skating rink, and basketball and handball courts. Call for availability information and fees. The city also has a variety of gymnasiums and fitness clubs that are open to the public for a fee. Contact the tourist office for further information.

FISHING Trout fishing in the Tormes, Francia, Mayas, Frío, Quilames, and Batuecas rivers requires a license (there's a fee), with the season usually running from March through October. There are no special restrictions or requirements for non-residents. For more information, contact the *Consejería Agricultura,* Ganadería y Montes (Sección de Montes), 28-30 Calle Alfonso de Castro (phone: 232600).

HUNTING Some hunting areas are restricted to Spaniards only, while others have very strict rules and regulations for all would-be hunters. There's small game (hare, rabbit, partridge, turtledove) and large (wild boar, mountain goat, deer). For more information, contact the *Consejería de Agricultura,* listed above.

SQUASH The *Kata Squash Club* (79 Av. de Alemania; phone: 259689) rents courts and also has a well-equipped gymnasium.

SWIMMING Besides the *Pabellón Deportivo* (see above), both the *Complejo Torres* (Carretera de Madrid; phone: 215754) and the Parque Sindical (Carretera de Fuentesanco) have swimming pools open to the public for an admission charge.

THEATER AND MUSIC

During the academic year, theatrical performances take place under the auspices of the university. Concerts are presented by the university, by the *Sociedad de Conciertos,* and by other organizations. The stage at the university's *Teatro Juan del Enzina* (phone: 214274) hosts many of the theatrical events, while the *Paraninfo Room* and the university chapel are used for concerts. The *Teatro Bretón* (Plaza Bretón; phone: 269844), one of several movie theaters in town, is also used for concerts. During the July and September festivals, events proliferate.

NIGHTCLUBS AND NIGHTLIFE

Although there is a disco scene, nightlife in Salamanca usually involves hanging out at a bar or, in good weather, people watching at an outdoor café in Plaza Mayor. At the northeast corner of the plaza, the Art Nouveau-style *Café Novelty,* Unamuno's former haunt, has been going strong since 1905. Two bars offer live jazz performances during the university year (October through May) — *Corrillo* (1 Cerrada del Corrillo, at the edge of Plaza Mayor; phone: 269111) and *Mezcal* (9 Cuesta del Carmen; phone: 213077). Discos come and go, but among those with staying power are *María* (36 Av. Mirat), *Limón y Menta* (18 Calle Bermejeros), and *Hindagala* (Plaza de la Reina).

Best in Town

CHECKING IN

Considering its rather modest size, Salamanca has an impressive array of lodgings, ranging from student pensions and *hostales* to large, full-service hotels. The tourist information office offers a listing of hotels it has inspected and graded, complete with prices and details on facilities. Expect to pay $70 to $100 for a double room with private bath at hotels classified as expensive and less than $40 at places described as inexpensive (there's really no choice in between). All telephone numbers are in the 23 area code unless otherwise indicated.

For an unforgettable experience, we begin with our favorite *parador*, followed by our recommendations of cost and quality choices of hotels, listed by price category.

A SPECIAL HAVEN

Parador de Salamanca This 108-room modern, multilevel *parador* overlooks Salamanca from its location just across the Tormes River. The rooms have glass-enclosed terraces with cushioned bamboo chairs — an excellent perch for watching the sunset, when Salamanca's buildings turn rich shades ranging from golden yellow to crimson. All the rooms have private baths, equipped with direct dial telephones. There is also a coffee shop, a dining room, an outdoor swimming pool, a garden, a convention hall, and ample parking. 2 Calle Teso de la Feria (phone: 268700; in the US, 212-686-9213; fax: 2154.

EXPENSIVE

Gran Just off the Plaza Mayor's southeastern corner, its lobby is a spacious local gathering place and its 100 rooms are decorated in a traditional style, with dark wood furnishings. The comfortable rooms have large, marble private baths, soundproofed windows, TV sets, and air conditioning; the hostelry has 2 bars and the *Feudal* restaurant, featuring regional dishes. 3-5 Plaza del Poeta Iglesias (phone: 213500; fax: 213501).

Monterrey Sister to the *Gran* hotel, it's not far from the Plaza Mayor, although it's located beyond the *zona monumental*. The wood and velvet lobby is attractive; the 85 rooms and 4 suites are not quite as nicely furnished as those of its sister, but are air conditioned. A pleasant café, spacious public rooms, and the fine *El Fogón* restaurant complete the picture. 21 Calle Azafranal (phone: 214400; fax: 903214).

Rector This small, elegant, and exclusive hostelry is ideally located next to the Old Cathedral. With only 13 rooms, all air conditioned and with private baths, this place exudes a calm, intimate atmosphere. No restaurant, but

breakfast is served daily in the guestrooms or in the breakfast room. 8
Rector Esperadé (phone: 218482).

Regio Located 2½ miles (4 km) south of town, on the N501 highway heading
toward Avila, its 121 rooms are centrally heated and air conditioned, with
private bath. Facilities include a cafeteria, a restaurant, an Olympic-size
pool and a children's pool, 2 bars, and gardens. Carretera de Salamanca-
Madrid, Km 4, Santa Marta (phone: 130888; fax: 130044).

Sol Salamanca The city's newest hotel is located in the center of town within easy
walking distance of major attractions. It offers 53 double rooms, 6 single
rooms, and 4 suites, all with air conditioning and mini-bars. There's a
cafeteria, and 24-hour room service is also available. 8-14 Alava (phone:
261111; fax: 262429).

INEXPENSIVE

Emperatriz Housed in a medieval building in the heart of town, this hostelry has
24 rooms with full, private baths, and 38 with showers only. The halls are
rather dark and forbidding, but the rooms are comfortable and clean, if
somewhat spartan. 44 Calle de la Compañía (phone: 219200).

El Zaguán This clean and pleasant 15-room hotel is located just off the Plaza
Mayor. Most doubles have full, private baths; singles have showers only.
7-9 Calle Ventura Ruiz Aguilera (phone: 214705).

EATING OUT

The traditional roast suckling pig and lamb of Castile are also the staples
of Salamanca's finest restaurants. Sausages such as *farinato* and *morcilla*
are local specialties, more typically served in *tapas* bars than in full-fledged
eateries. Another local dish is *chanfaina,* a hearty country stew made with
rice, spring lamb, chicken, and *chorizo* (spicy Spanish sausage). While
regional wines appear on most menus, they are generally considered inferior to the better riojas. Dinner for two with wine will cost $45 to $65 in
expensive restaurants, $25 to $40 in those listed as moderate, $20 or less
in inexpensive places. All telephone numbers are in the 23 city code unless
otherwise indicated.

EXPENSIVE

El Botón Charro Tucked away in a narrow alley off the Plaza del Mercado, this
place offers a nouvelle twist to traditional Castilian cuisine. Closed Sundays. Reservations unnecessary. Visa accepted. 6-8 Calle Hovohambre
(phone: 216462).

Châpeau This stylish Castilian establishment has gained fame for its old-fashioned style of cooking in wood ovens. Specialties include stuffed red peppers, scallops baked in light pastry, and the traditional roast suckling pig.

Closed Sundays and August. Reservations advised. Major credit cards accepted. 20 Calle Gran Vía (phone: 271833).

Chez Victor Owner-chef Victoriano spent 13 years perfecting his craft in France; thus, his innovative cuisine has a decidedly French accent — as well as Salamanca's only Michelin star. The fare changes with the seasons, but year-round standards include *raviolis rellenos de marisco* (ravioli stuffed with seafood), *ragú de salmón y alcachofas* (salmon and artichoke stew), and *tarta de cebolla* (savory onion tart). For dessert, there's homemade ice cream and sorbets in unusual flavors. Closed Sunday evenings, Mondays, and August. Reservations advised in June and July. Major credit cards accepted. 26 Calle Espoz y Mina (phone: 213123).

MODERATE

La Posada Located next to the Torre del Aire, it features such regional specialties as *alubias con codornices o con almejas* (beans with quail or clams) and assorted game in season; or try the chef's suggestions of the day. Open daily; closed for 3 weeks in August. Reservations unnecessary. Major credit cards accepted. Plaza Santo Domingo (phone: 204578).

Río de la Plata Small, charming, and usually very crowded, this eatery is a block from the Plaza Mayor. In addition to Castilian dishes, the kitchen excels at seafood; there are also good homemade desserts and fine wines. Closed Mondays and July. No reservations. No credit cards accepted. 1 Plaza del Peso (phone: 219005).

INEXPENSIVE

El Bardo The clientele here consists mainly of students. The menu could best be termed "national" rather than regional, and the set meals are particularly economical. Closed Mondays and October. Reservations unnecessary. No credit cards accepted. 8 Calle de la Compañía (phone: 219089).

El Dorado Near the Plaza del Mercado, with a reputation for marvelous service and solid home-style cooking. Closed Tuesdays. Reservations unnecessary. No credit cards accepted. 3 Calle del Clavel (phone: 217212).

TAPAS BARS

Calle Prado has a string of them, including *Gran Tasca* (3 Calle Prado), *Marín* (5 Calle Prado), and *Bar Mi Vaca y Yo* (11 Calle Prado). Outstanding among the many on Calle Ventura Ruiz Aguilera (better known to locals as *la calleja* — the alley) is *El Candil* (10 Calle Ventura Ruiz Aguilera). Also try *Plus-Ultra* (Calle del Concejo, off Plaza Mayor). There is often someone strumming a guitar in Salamanca *tapas* bars; sometimes there's a group of musicians from the university.

San Sebastián

Just 12 miles (19 km) from the French border, on Spain's North Atlantic Coast, San Sebastián is a world apart from the rest of the country. Its cafés serve the best croissants south of the Pyrenees, it's the only city in Spain without a bullring, and it has no real business area. Its avenues are broad and tree-lined, its shops luxurious and chic, and its climate is more Atlantic than Mediterranean. Set around one of Europe's finest natural bays, the Bahía de la Concha (Bay of the Shell), this most elegant turn-of-the-century Belle Epoque beach resort is protected from northerly winds by Mt. Urgull and Mt. Igueldo, which rise up on either side of the town. The wide, curved Playa de la Concha, one of the most beautiful beaches in Spain, is topped by an exquisite promenade of ornate railings and impressive buildings, and the walkways on either side of the Urumea River are another taste of 19th-century elegance in this otherwise modern, tidy, and pretty city. In the summer, San Sebastián is packed with visitors from France, Italy, and the rest of Spain, and is especially busy during the international jazz and film festivals in July and September. Yet even during peak season, when there isn't a spare hotel room to be had, this surprisingly small city (pop. 182,000) has the calm air of a small town.

The first recorded mention of San Sebastián was in 1014, when a donation was made by King Sancho el Mayor to a monastery here. In 1200, the new castle on Urgull fell to King Alfonso VIII of Castile. San Sebastián joined the Sea Brotherhood with other coastal towns in 1294 and established trade relations with England and Brittany. Harbor construction began in 1450; in the Middle Ages, the city's inhabitants were well known for the whaling and cod fishing that took them as far as the Newfoundland banks. San Sebastián became a large port, and from its wharves, oil and wine were shipped to the rest of Europe. By the 18th century, the city had a special cacao trading deal with Caracas, Venezuela. With the growth of Bilbao along the coast, however, the city's importance as a port declined, and today its seafaring activities are limited to a little anchovy, sardine, and tuna fishing.

In 1813, near the end of the Peninsular War, which was fought by Napoleon and France against Great Britain, Portugal, and the Spanish guerrillas on the Iberian Peninsula, the town was burned down. Local residents rebuilt; in 1814 they laid the four cornerstones of the Plaza de la Constitución in the center of the Parte Vieja (Old Town) adjacent to the old fishing port on the city's eastern promontory. By the 1840s, the Old Town was resurrected and San Sebastián had quietly reestablished itself as the major town on the Spanish coast between France and Bilbao.

It wasn't until 1845, however, when Queen Isabella II spent the summer in San Sebastián, that the city became a high class holiday resort. In 1863, the town was demilitarized and the city walls were demolished. This allowed urban expansion to boom in the 1860s, and the first buildings in the residential and shopping districts were raised as the glorious line of promenade buildings above La Concha began taking shape. By the 1870s, San Sebastián was the summer home for many European aristocrats; in 1887 La Concha was awarded the title of royal beach; and in 1902 a municipal company was established to promote the city and build a grand hotel. By this time, San Sebastián had been a Spanish pioneer in installing a tram system, electric street lighting, and telephone service.

On July 8, 1912, Queen María Cristina opened the grand hotel named after her. The hotel became King Alfonso XIII's winter residence, and members of many European royal families spent long periods there. Completely restored during the 1980s, it's still one of the best hotels in northern Spain and, with the majestic *Victoria Eugenia Theater* standing alongside, it is a marvelous example of the Belle Epoque architecture for which San Sebastián is renowned.

Located in the midst of Basque Country — known as the País Vasco to the Spanish, as Euskadi to the Basques themselves — San Sebastián is also a center of Basque culture and nationalist pride. The town is in the province of Guipúzcoa, the smallest province in Spain and — of the three that make up the Basque Country — the one that has best preserved its Basque customs. The town is known to its inhabitants by its Basque name, Donostia, and the complex Euskera language is spoken by at least 50% of the *donostiarras,* as the city folk are known, and by up to 90% of the people in neighboring towns.

Basque political upheaval has put San Sebastián on the front pages of Spanish newspapers for all the wrong reasons. Since Franco's reign ended in 1975, the Basque nationalist movement intensified, resulting in the death of more than 720 people. San Sebastián's Old Town and Alameda del Boulevard were, until recently, the scenes of frequent clashes between radical separatists and riot police. Most Basques are nationalists who are demanding greater political independence from Madrid; a small minority back the ETA (*Euskadita ta Askatasuna;* "Euskadi and Freedom") who advocate armed struggle, not unlike Ireland's IRA. The Old Town's walls still are splashed with graffiti extolling the justice of the Basque fight for self-determination and the violence of the ETA, but the 1990s have brought relative calm to the city.

The local sense of Basque national identity is also displayed during the many fiestas held throughout the year, when traditional Basque music is played on three-holed tin whistles known as *txistus,* and on small drums, and there's Basque folkloric dancing. Rural sports are also an integral part of Basque culture; pelota, or jai alai, is well known outside the Basque region.

San Sebastián is also renowned for excellent food. The city is acknowledged as the birthplace of the new Basque cooking, a culinary culture that emerged in earnest nearly 20 years ago. But the city's reputation as a culinary center goes back more than 100 years, when the first gastronomic societies were founded by local fishermen, who cooked their catches in quayside kitchens. Today, there are 1,000 all-male societies in the Basque Country, whose dining rooms are for members and guests only (the best-known ones in San Sebastián's Old Town now allow women to dine at certain hours). Visitors can inquire at the tourist office about the chances of being invited to a society dining room, but if it can't be arranged, San Sebastián's restaurants offer some of the best food in Spain, second only to the restaurants of Madrid.

To truly appreciate San Sebastián, take an early evening stroll along the Paseo de la Concha, walking along the charming streets surrounded by the deep, still bay and low, undulating hills. Then stop for the pre-dinner *poteo* (a glass of wine or two) and *tapas* in the Old Town, before feasting at one of the city's fine dining spots. You'll soon begin to understand why visitors fall in love with this beautiful, fascinating city.

San Sebastián At-a-Glance

SEEING THE CITY

San Sebastián is best surveyed from either Mt. Igueldo or Mt. Urgull. Urgull, the more accessible of the two, is crisscrossed by wooded and winding paths that can be joined where the Old Town meets the fishing port, or from the Paseo Nuevo, the promenade that begins beyond the aquarium and skirts the hill. Below is the tiny fishing port, brightly colored and more touristic than industrial. Then there's the splendid La Concha, backed by 2 miles of elegant hotels and apartment blocks (no building is higher than 7 stories). A rocky promontory separates the Playa de la Concha from the next beach, Playa de Ondarreta, and beyond it is the higher Mt. Igueldo.

Mt. Igueldo is best ascended by car, by the bus that leaves every few minutes from the Boulevard (marked Igueldo), or by the funicular that leaves from the end of Ondarreta Beach. The hill dominates the western end of the city, and it offers wonderful views of the Basque coast toward Zarauz and Guetaria. There is an amusement park and an extremely good camping site at the top of the hill, with excellent views inland. The view of the city is superb.

SPECIAL PLACES

La Concha Beach is the pearl in the San Sebastián oyster and, with its promenade, dominates the city (except at night, when the Old Town and the fishing port at La Concha's eastern end take over). South of the Old Town and La Concha is the charming shopping and residential area, bordered to the east by the Urumea River. This area (from the Alameda del Boulevard to Plaza de Guipúzcoa, on past Avenida de la Libertad to Plaza de Bilbao and the cathedral) is placid and pleasant, not much more than 100 years old. Indeed, because most of the city was built within the past 130 years — even the "Old Town" is 19th century — San Sebastián is short on historical monuments. Every single sight, monument, and museum can easily be exhausted in a day — even more reason for a calm and unhurried visit.

IN THE CITY

PLAYA DE LA CONCHA This superb beach is the symbol of San Sebastián and undoubtedly the most famous stretch of sand in Spain. When the tide is out, several acres of fine sand are exposed. In the winter, there are soccer tournaments. In the summer, it is a family beach, thankfully free of hordes of radio-blasting rowdies. The promenade above the beach — Paseo de la Concha — is equally delightful, with ornate balustrades and richly ornamental Belle Epoque lampposts. Extending westward beyond a small rocky outlet is Ondarreta Beach, also clean and excellent, but smaller than La Concha.

LA PARTE VIEJA (OLD TOWN) The Old Town is not architecturally significant, apart from a handful of buildings that survived the burning of the city in 1813, but it is the marketplace and social center of San Sebastián. Its narrow, bustling streets, bordered by the Alameda del Boulevard, the estuary of the Urumea River, Mt. Urgull, and the port, are packed with bars, taverns, specialty shops, restaurants, and gastronomic societies. The arcaded Plaza de la Constitución, with the former City Hall at one end, stands in the center. Bullfights used to be held in the square, and the numbered balconies where spectators once gathered still remain. The city's two most important churches are survivors of the 1813 fire — the Gothic Church of San Vicente (Calle Narrica), San Sebastián's oldest building, dating from 1570, and the graffiti-covered baroque Church of Santa María (Calle 31 de Agosto; phone: 423124), completed in 1764.

MUSEO DE SAN TELMO (MUSEUM OF SAN TELMO) The early-16th-century building opposite the Church of San Vicente began as a Dominican monastery (1544–1834), became an artillery barracks in 1836, and was converted into a beautiful museum in 1932. Of greatest interest is the section dedicated to Basque ethnography, with paintings, statues, farming utensils, fossilized skeletons, and spinning tools. Artist José María Sert painted a series of works on the subject of Basque mythology especially for the museum; there also are three paintings by El Greco. Open Mondays through Saturdays from 9:30 AM to 1:30 PM and from 3:30 to 7 PM, Sundays from 10 AM to 2 PM. No admission charge. Plaza de Zuluaga (phone: 424970).

AYUNTAMIENTO (CITY HALL) Originally a casino, this twin-towered building is now one of the most impressive city halls in Spain, with an exquisite decor and numerous marble staircases. Opened in 1887, the *Gran Casino* instantly became the center of business activity and progress in the city. Among other things, the casino financed the Alderdi-Eder Gardens, which brighten the area around City Hall with squat tamarind trees and a children's playground. A ban on gambling in 1924 closed the building until 1947, when the City Council moved in. City Hall is open to the public during office hours; no admission charge. Calle Ijentea.

PALACIO DEL MAR (AQUARIUM) Officially known as the *Oceanographical Museum,* the aquarium has many types of marine fauna on view; the first-floor museum boasts collections of shells, fish, seabirds, seaweed, crustacea, and coral. Open from 10 AM to 1:30 PM and 3:30 to 7:30 PM (summers until 8 PM); closed Mondays from mid-September through mid-May. Admission charge. 34 Paseo del Muelle (phone: 421905).

MUSEO NAVAL (NAVAL MUSEUM) Set in an 18th-century building on the wharf, near the aquarium, this charming museum opened in 1991. Hundreds of nautical instruments, models, and maps document the historical Basque connection to the sea. A library and a video room are open from mid-June to the end of September. Open Tuesdays through Saturdays, from 10 AM to 1:30 PM and from 5 to 8:30 PM; Sundays, from 11 AM to 2 PM. Closed Mondays. No admission charge. 24 Paseo del Muelle (phone: 430051).

MUSEO DIOCESANO (DIOCESAN MUSEUM) Religious artifacts adorn this 3-year-old church-run museum. Open Tuesdays through Saturdays, from 4:30 to 8 PM. Admission charge. Plaza Sagrada Familia (phone: 472362).

CASTLE OF SANTA CRUZ DE LA MOTA Around the ruins of the castle on top of Mt. Urgull are the remains of several rusting cannon left by Napoleon's troops when the Duke of Wellington stormed the town in 1813. Within the castle are three modern chapels topped by a nearly 100-foot statue of Christ, visible from anywhere in the city. Mass is held on Sundays in one of the chapels. Open daily, from 7 AM until dusk. Mt. Urgull.

URUMEA RIVER The real delight here consists of the walks along either side of the river as it flows into the Bay of Biscay. The Urumea is spanned by three Parisian-style bridges of great charm for lovers of the Belle Epoque ornate. The 1905 Puente María Cristina, which leads from the residential area at Plaza de Bilbao to the main France–Madrid railway station, is especially flamboyant, with tiered turrets at either end. The Puente Santa Catalina, nearer to the sea, takes traffic over to the unspectacular Gros district, where there is a third San Sebastián beach. A $20-million project to transform Gros beach into a larger, safer spot, with a breakwater and a promenade, is scheduled to be completed by 1995. The Puente Zurriola de Kursaal is just yards from the sea, near the historic *Victoria Eugenia Theater* and the *María Cristina* hotel. On either side of the river, along the

Paseo República Argentina or the Paseo de Francia, the 10-minute stroll offers a pleasant alternative to La Concha.

CATEDRAL BUEN PASTOR (GOOD SHEPHERD CATHEDRAL) San Sebastián's largest church, the 250-foot-high cathedral was inaugurated in 1897. A neo-Gothic structure with striking exterior flying buttresses and a belfry that opens to a central nave, it stands in a large square in the modern quarter. It made headlines on July 18, 1946, the 10th anniversary of the outbreak of the Spanish Civil War, when Basque nationalist Joseba Elósegui climbed to the top and raised the then-banned Basque flag. Open Mondays through Saturdays from 7:30 AM to 12:30 PM and from 5 to 8:30 PM; Sundays from 9AM to 2 PM and 5 to 7:30 PM. Plaza del Buen Pastor (phone: 464516).

PALACIO MIRAMAR The English-style Miramar Palace stands on a low hill overlooking La Concha and Ondarreta, with the residential district of Antiguo behind it. Built in 1893, it served as a royal residence until 1929, the year Queen María Cristina died. It was recently renovated but is still closed to the public. The expansive lawns, however, are open from 9 AM to 9 PM in summer and from 10 AM to 5 PM in winter. No admission charge.

PALACIO DE AYETE Built by the Duke of Bailen in 1878, the Ayete Palace was the summer residence of King Alfonso XII and Queen María Cristina until the Miramar Palace was constructed. Set back from the bay on the Ayete estate, amid more than 25,000 acres of beautiful parkland, the palace was also the summer residence of Generalísimo Francisco Franco from 1940 until his death in 1975, and the site of his cabinet meetings every summer. The palace is closed to the public, but the lush forest trails are worth a stroll. Open summers, from 10 AM to 8:30 PM; winters, from 10 AM to 5 PM. No admission charge.

ENVIRONS

MONTE IGUELDO A trip to the heart of Mt. Igueldo affords some idyllic panoramas of the dramatic coastline of the Bay of Biscay and the Guipúzcoan countryside, not to mention a chance to sample some traditional local cider, second in fame and quality only to that from Asturias. Take the steep road to the Igueldo campsite and turn right, down a narrow lane opposite the *Bar Gure-etxea*. After a mile, there is the *Bar Asador Nícolas,* a simple *sidrería* (cider house) that has stupendous views over the haystack-dotted countryside, with the sea visible beyond. A liter of the excellent local cider costs just $1.50; the best brewing months are February through April.

FUENTERRABÍA Known as Hondarribia in Euskera (the Basque language), this beautiful town lies 14½ miles (23 km) east of San Sebastián, and overlooks the French town of Hendaye, from which it is separated by the

Bidasoa River. Not surprisingly, Fuenterrabía was a fortress town for centuries, and historians have lost count of the number of sieges it suffered. So many Castilian kings honored it for fighting off French attacks that the town bears an official title meaning "very noble, very loyal, very courageous, and always very faithful." The town's Nagusi Kalea (Main Street) is straight out of the Middle Ages, and the nearby narrow streets are flanked by Renaissance and baroque mansions with huge carved eaves and wrought-iron balconies. Its many fine restaurants make it a popular destination on Sundays. The town is dominated by an 11th-century fortress that was restored by the Holy Roman Emperor Charles V in the 16th century and is now home to the *Parador el Emperador*, which is closed for repairs. Buses to Fuenterrabía ($1.15) leave every 15 minutes from Calle Oquendo, behind the *Hotel María Cristina*; the trip takes about 35 minutes.

EXTRA SPECIAL Stand anywhere on or near the beach from Mt. Urgull to Mt. Igueldo at 11 PM on any night during the *Aste Nagusia* (Great Week) fiestas, around August 15, for San Sebastián's renowned fireworks displays. The fiestas coincide with the *International Fireworks Competition*. San Sebastián's fireworks week is regarded by Spaniards as the best in Europe. Find a spot early — after 10:30 it's usually impossible to get a good vantage point.

Sources and Resources

TOURIST INFORMATION

There are two very helpful tourist offices a short walk from one another. The Centro de Atracción y Turismo (CAT) is run by the City Council (on Calle Reina Regente, next door to the *Victoria Eugenia Theater;* phone: 481167). The office is open Mondays through Fridays from 9 AM to 2 PM and 3:30 to 7 PM, Saturdays from 9 AM to 2 PM. This office is responsible for the promotion of San Sebastián and Guipúzcoa only, and has excellent information on local fiestas, rural sports, and so on. Nearby is the Oficina de Turismo del Gobierno Vasco (1 Paseo de los Fueros; phone: 426282), run by the Basque Autonomous Government. It is open Mondays through Fridays from 9 AM to 1:30 PM and 3:30 to 6:30 PM, Saturdays from 9 AM to 1 PM. English-language tourist brochures are available at both locations, although many are poorly translated.

LOCAL COVERAGE The best newspapers for local news (in Spanish) are the moderate *Diario Vasco,* the moderate nationalist *Deia,* and the radical nationalist *Egin* (half Spanish and half Basque). The best place to buy international newspapers is the kiosk in front of the Banco de Bilbao, near the La Concha end of Avenida de la Libertad.

TELEPHONE

The area code for San Sebastián is 43. If calling from within Spain, but outside Guipúzcoa province, dial 943 before the local number.

GETTING AROUND

Any point in San Sebastián is easily reached on foot, except for the top of Mt. Igueldo, which can be reached by taxi or the bus marked Igueldo from the Boulevard.

AIRPORT San Sebastián Airport is in nearby Fuenterrabía, but it handles only domestic flights (phone: 642240; flight information: 641267). The nearest international airport is Bilbao's Sondika Airport.

BICYCLE Bicycles can be rented from *Mini* (10 Calle Escolta Real; phone: 211758), for between $7.50 and $11.50 per day.

BUS City buses stop running at around midnight. It's best to buy a *bonobus,* a card allowing 10 trips for about $3; a single journey costs 90 pesetas (about 70¢). Several bus companies offer service within the Basque Country and beyond. Their offices are on or around the Plaza de Pío XII. Ask for details at either of the tourist offices.

CAR RENTAL The major car rental companies with offices in San Sebastián are *Atesa* (2 Bajo, Antón de Luzuriaga; phone: 272286); *Avis* (2 Calle Triunfo; phone: 461556); *Europcar* (60 Calle San Martín; phone: 461717); and *Hertz* (2 Calle Marina; phone: 461084). Parking in the city center, especially during the summer, can be a problem, but a new 1,000-vehicle underground car park at Plaza del Buen Pastor should help.

TAXI Cabs are not plentiful. The main stands are located on the Alameda del Boulevard by Calle Mayor and at 31 Avenida de la Libertad, or call 420340.

TRAIN All trains from the French border crossing of Hendaye-Irún, 12 miles (19 km) away, stop at San Sebastián's Estación Norte (phone: 283599), just over the María Cristina Bridge by the Paseo de Francia, on their way to Madrid. A second station, the Estación Amara (phone: 450131), of the narrow-gauge *FEVE* line linking San Sebastián with Bilbao, is by the Paseo de Errondo. For visitors with children, a miniature tourist train called the *Txu-Txu* (pronounced *Choo-Choo*) leaves City Hall and trundles around the Old Town and the promenade daily every half hour from 11 AM to 2 PM and 4 PM to 9 PM, with commentary in several languages.

SPECIAL EVENTS

One of Spain's great undiscovered festivals, the January 19 and 20 *Tamborrada* (Festival of Drums), takes place in San Sebastián. January 20 is *St. Sebastián's Day,* but the festivities start on the 19th, with a hearty feast in one of the gastronomic societies or restaurants. Then, for 24 hours beginning at midnight on the 19th, the Old Town is filled with people dressed as 19th-century soldiers, bakers, and chefs, all banging *tambores* (drums), in keeping with a tradition that began in the early 19th century — although nobody knows exactly how or why. There are over 40 *tamborrada* processions, but the two most important are the adults' procession at midnight on the 19th in the Plaza de la Constitución, and the children's procession — with 4,000 children — at midday on the 20th outside City Hall.

The next important event is the *International Jazz Festival,* or *Jazzaldia,* during the second half of July, followed by the *Aste Nagusia* (Great Week) of carnivals around August 15, which involves Basque sports, processions, folkloric displays, gastronomic competitions, and even pro-independence alternative events, in addition to incredible nightly fireworks displays. The last 2 weeks of August offer the *Classical Music Fortnight.* The *Basque Fiestas,* which promote and celebrate Euskera, the Basque language, begin on the first Sunday in September. The famous *Regatas de Traineras* (fishing-boat rowing races), which have been held on La Concha Bay since 1879, are held on the first two Sundays in September. Tens of thousands gather to watch and wager money on teams from every town and village along the Basque coast and, during the week between the races, to participate in Basque sports — tree chopping, rock lifting, pelota, oxen dragging rocks — as well as folkloric dancing, improvised poetry and theater performances in Euskera, and basket making. San Sebastián's most prestigious annual event is the *International Film Festival,* during the second half of September, now one of the premier events of its type in Europe.

SHOPPING

San Sebastián is one of the wealthiest cities in Spain, and its proximity to France gives it a certain snobbery when it comes to taste and style — not to mention price. San Sebastián does not have any department stores and has few supermarkets. Its two central food markets, very colorful and interesting, are *Mercado la Brecha* (at the river end of the Boulevard) and *Mercado San Martín* (on Calle Urbieta, 2 blocks from La Concha). Avenida de la Libertad is one of the best shopping streets. Calle San Marcial, Calle Loyola, and the square surrounding the Buen Pastor Cathedral are also prime venues. Shopping hours are generally from 9:30 AM to 1:30 PM and 3:30 to 8 PM. Most stores and shops are closed Sundays; some close Monday mornings as well. The following are some notable shops.

AUZMENDI Trendy clothes for both sexes by the best known local designer. 28 Av. de la Libertad (phone: 424060).

BILINTX LIBURUDENDA A great spot to browse, with a good sampling of Basque music — both traditional and modern — and books in English about the

Basque Country. Two Old Town locations: 30 Calle Fermín Calbetón (phone: 420930) and 10 Calle Esterlines (phone: 420224).

CASA BASARTE The best selection of *txapelas* (genuine Basque berets) in town. 18 Calle San Jerónimo (phone: 426096).

JUGUETERÍA ANTÓN Basically a toy shop, but with an amazing collection of Spanish jigsaw puzzles. Designs range from Goya paintings to Moorish tiles, containing up to 8,000 pieces. 23 Calle San Jerónimo (phone: 425017).

RAMÓN HERNÁNDEZ Exclusive men's and women's outfitters, with expensive imported and local styles. 23 Av. de la Libertad (phone: 426849).

SPORTS AND FITNESS

BICYCLING Cycling is an important sport in the Basque Country, and a number of premier cyclists hail from this region; local hero Miguel Induraín won both the *Giro d'Italia* and the *Tour de France* in 1992.

BOATING Rowing is a Basque passion, especially when the vessel is a large *trainera,* or fishing boat. The tradition dates from the days when fishermen used to row back into harbor, usually against a fierce cross wind. Don't miss the *Regatas de Traineras* (see *Special Events*).

FISHING Fishing from the rocks and even surf casting are popular. The tourist offices can provide details.

GOLF The 18-hole course at the *Real Club de Golf de San Sebastián* (phone: 616845) is 14½ miles (23 km) east of the city in Fuenterrabía. The 9-hole *Real Club de Golf de Zarauz* (phone: 830145) is 16 miles (26 km) to the west in Barrio de Mendilauta.

HORSE RACING San Sebastián's racetrack (in the town of Lasarte, about 4 miles/6 km south of the city) is the only one in Spain to hold summer races. For information, contact the *Sociedad Hipódromo de San Sebastián* (2 Plaza de Zaragoza; phone: 425465).

PELOTA A pelota court is called a frontón, and there are many in the city. The most popular is the *Frontón de Anoeta* (phone: 455917), in the excellent indoor sports complex of the same name; games take place at 10 PM on Fridays year-round, and on Wednesdays in August. Also highly recommended is the *Galarreta Jai-Alai* (phone: 551023) in the nearby town of Hernani, with games Thursdays, Saturdays, and Sundays at 4 PM.

SOCCER San Sebastián's *Real Sociedad* was one of the Spanish League's shock teams of the 1980s. After winning nothing since its formation in 1909, it won the coveted league title in 1981 and 1982 and the *Spanish Cup* in 1988, and was league runner-up on two other occasions. The team has fallen on hard times since the Barcelona team, which has more money, lured away four of *Real's* best players. The club plays its home games in *Anoeta Stadium.*

SWIMMING La Concha is obviously the first choice, for its beauty, fine sand, and safe waters. Even on rough days, Santa Clara Island, in the middle of the bay, tames the mightier waves, although they are often big enough for reasonable surfing. Ondarreta Beach is also very good, and popular among locals. Gros Beach, the smallest, is good for surfing and is in the midst of major physical improvements. There are indoor pools in the *Piscina de Bidebieta* (1 Calle Serapio Mugika; phone: 398091) and in the *Anoeta* sports complex in the Amarra neighborhood. All indoor facilities have an admission charge.

TENNIS Courts are available for rent at the *Real Club de Tenis* (Calle Peine de los Vientos; phone: 215161) just behind the beach.

THEATER AND MUSIC

The grand *Teatro Victoria Eugenia* (Calle Reina Regente; phone: 481150), with its richly decorated ceiling, dome, and spacious foyer, opened just 11 days after the neighboring *María Cristina* hotel in 1912. San Sebastián's home for theater, classical music, ballet, and opera, it also hosts the *International Film Festival* in September and the *Classical Music Fortnight* in late August. July's *International Jazz Festival* is held in the pavilion at the *Anoeta* sports complex (phone: 451201) and the open-air Plaza de Trinidad in the Old Town. *Anoeta* is also the venue for major rock concerts, since San Sebastián, together with Madrid and Barcelona, is a "must" on the European tours of many US and British groups.

NIGHTCLUBS AND NIGHTLIFE

A good night out in San Sebastián involves a hearty Basque meal followed by drinks in one of the numerous late-night bars in the Old Town or in one of the classier pubs on the streets close to La Concha. There are no nightclubs or shows as such, but the discotheques vary from wild and teenage to somewhat more sedate. The best known is *Discoteca Ku* (in Barrio de Igueldo, halfway toward the campsite; phone: 212051), open from midnight to dawn for the super-cool. There is a very lively discotheque along the Paseo de la Concha, virtually on the beach, called *La Rotonda* (phone: 428095). The *Piscina* disco (phone: 218136) is near Ondarreta Beach. The *Be Bop Bar* (3 Paseo de Salamanca) is a piano bar with occasional live jazz performances, not far from the *Victoria Eugenia Theater.* The city's hippest music bars are grouped on Calle San Bartolomé — the best are *Zacro* (17 San Bartolomé); *Kokolo* (No. 34); *Twickenham* (No. 36); and *El Cine* (No. 23; phone: 460783). The *Casino Gran Kursaal* (in the *Londres y de Inglaterra* hotel, but not affiliated with it; phone: 429214) is open Mondays through Fridays from 6 PM to 2 AM; Saturdays and Sundays from 6 PM to 3 AM. The entrance fee is about $5.25.

Best in Town

CHECKING IN

By Spanish standards, San Sebastián's hotels are expensive. Some of the "high-quality" hotels are either slightly tatty or characterless, but are saved by their proximity to the beach. There is also a shortage of accommodations — there are only about 3,000 hotel beds in the city and no more than 6,500 in the whole of Guipúzcoa province, making it difficult to find vacancies in July and August, and impossible during September's *International Film Festival*. There are a few new hotels: the 180-room *Ondarreta*, near the beach; the *Pío XII;* and the *Anoeta,* near the sports complex of the same name. Expect to pay more than $170 a night for a double room at a very expensive hotel, $115 to $170 at an expensive hotel, and $60 to $105 at a moderate one. All telephone numbers are in the 43 area code unless otherwise indicated.

VERY EXPENSIVE

María Cristina The queen of Spain's North Atlantic coast, this turn-of-the-century holiday residence for European royalty and aristocracy underwent a major refurbishing several years ago, in which all its Belle Epoque glory was restored. The 139 rooms and public areas are exquisitely appointed, and feature a wonderful view of the Urumea River estuary and the Bay of Biscay. The place is filled with actors and film directors during the *International Film Festival,* held next door at the *Victoria Eugenia Theater.* Its *Restaurante Easo* is excellent, and there are afternoon tea concerts in the *Gritti* piano bar. Paseo República Argentina (phone: 424900; in the US, 800-221-2340; fax: 423914).

EXPENSIVE

Costa Vasca A good uphill walk away from Ondarreta Beach, this recently refurbished establishment, San Sebastián's largest property, has 203 modern rooms. It has some style, however, and the service is very good. There is an attractive restaurant, a swimming pool, a tennis court, and a garage. 15 Av. Pío Baroja (phone: 211011; fax: 212428).

Londres y de Inglaterra Still glorious, though slightly faded, this elegant survivor of the 19th century lies in the coveted central section of the Paseo de la Concha, overlooking the beach. It offers unbeatable views of Mt. Urgull, Mt. Igueldo, and the bay. In addition to 145 recently refurbished rooms, there's a restaurant, and the street-level glass-fronted *Swing Bar* — a great place to sip a drink and watch the world stroll by. The *Casino Gran Kursaal,* though not affiliated with the hotel, is also located here. 2 Calle Zubieta (phone: 426989; fax: 420031).

Monte Igueldo A car is essential for guests here, because this 125-room hostelry is a good drive up Mt. Igueldo. Its rooms offer wonderful views; unfortunately, the atmosphere is less festive than at other hotels in the city. It has a restaurant and a swimming pool. Mt. Igueldo (phone: 210211; fax: 215028).

San Sebastián This place is on the main road to Bilbao and Madrid, so expect plenty of noise if your room faces the road. With 92 newly refurbished rooms, however, it shouldn't be too difficult to avoid this problem. There's a restaurant and a swimming pool; Ondarreta Beach is nearby. 20 Av. de Zumalacárregui (phone: 214400; fax: 217299).

MODERATE

Europa A charming 19th-century building converted into a hotel, it's just 60 yards from La Concha. Some of the 65 rooms have large balconies facing the beach. 52 Calle San Martín (phone: 471730; in the US, 800-528-1234; fax: 471739).

Niza Located on the La Concha promenade, this property's obvious strong point is the view of the bay. It's a pleasant, informal place, with 41 comfortable rooms and a good pizzeria. 56 Calle Zubieta (phone: 426663; fax: 426663).

EATING OUT

The gastronomic pleasures of San Sebastián can be broadly divided into traditional Basque fare and the more modern Basque cooking, which began in earnest in the mid-1970s, and owes much to the city's proximity to France. The Basque Country is still fairly agricultural, with rich soil split into small holdings — a true market economy where fresh produce (including several kinds of vegetables that can't be grown farther north in Europe) is available every day. Fresh seafood is available daily, too, and in San Sebastián itself, seafood reigns supreme. Among the delicacies peculiar to the area are *kokotxas,* gelatinous hake gills. Their distinctive taste and texture are perfect for the slow cultivation of the thick sauces essential to much of Basque cooking. *Kokotxas* are rarely eaten by themselves; a good combination is *merluza con kokotxas y almejas* — hake, hake gills, and clams in a lemon, oil, and parsley sauce. Most restaurants serve *cogote de merluza,* baked hake head. Another Basque favorite is *angulas,* tiny young eels, a must on special occasions. Another local specialty is *txangurro,* spider crab baked in its shell. Dinner for two, including wine, will cost upwards of $75 in an expensive restaurant, between $50 and $70 in a moderate restaurant, and less than $50 in an inexpensive one. All telephone numbers are in the 43 area code unless otherwise indicated.

For an unforgettable dining experience, we begin with our culinary favorites, followed by our recommendations of cost and quality choices listed by price category.

Akelarre This two-Michelin-star champion of new Basque cooking is picturesquely situated on the slopes of Mt. Igueldo, in a splendid building with memorable views of the city. National Gastronomy Award–winning owner-chef Pedro Subijana blends the traditional with the new in an always-changing menu. Always outstanding are his herb salads, leg of lamb with mushrooms, *lomos de rodaballo a la vinagreta aromática* (turbot in aromatic vinaigrette), and a fine array of homemade desserts and pastries. Other specialties, from time to time, include *morcilla envuelta en hoja de berza sobre puré de alubias rojas* (blood pudding wrapped in a cabbage leaf on a purée of red beans) and *lubina a la pimienta verde* (sea bass with green pepper). Closed Sunday nights, Mondays, and December. Reservations essential well in advance. Major credit cards accepted. Barrio de Igueldo (phone: 212052).

Arzak Truly an institution in the Basque Country, this restaurant is, with *Zalacaín* in Madrid, one of only two restaurants in Spain to have earned three Michelin stars. Housed in the large house just outside San Sebastián on the road to France where owner-chef Juan Mari Arzak was born, the restaurant won the National Gastronomy Award in 1974 and has been on the crest of the wave ever since. New Basque cuisine and *nueva cocina* (nouvelle cuisine) are the featured specialties, with an emphasis on seafood; try *krabarroka* (scorpion fish pâté), *merluza* (hake) in green sauce, *chipirones en su tinta* (squid in its own ink), oyster soup with green asparagus, *consumé de buey con cigalas y caviar a los aromas a perifollo y estragón* (ox consommé with Norway lobster and caviar in a chervil and tarragon sauce), or smoked salmon tartar with caviar. Non-seafood choices include salted baby lambs' brains seasoned with mint and lime. Closed Sunday nights, Mondays, 2 weeks in June, and November. Reservations essential well in advance. Major credit cards accepted. 21 Calle Alto de Miracruz (phone: 43-285593).

EXPENSIVE

Casa Nicolasa The most conservative and serious of San Sebastián's restaurants has an austerely elegant decor. But the traditional food is excellent, prepared by master chef José Juan Castillo and served by his wife, Ana María. Situated on the edge of the Old Town by the *Mercado la Brecha,* it is a haven of time-honored dishes where Basque ingredients dominate. Closed Sundays and Monday nights (except in August and September). Reservations essential. Major credit cards accepted. 4 Calle Aldamar (phone: 421762).

Juanito Kojua Thick, wooden beams help create a homey, warm atmosphere in this delightful Old Town establishment, and the service is efficient and discreet. The food is traditional, unpretentious, and very well prepared, especially the fish. Try *revuelto de Guibelurdiñas* (scrambled eggs with delicious locally picked wild mushrooms) and *cola de merluza rellena de txangurro* (hake tail stuffed with spicy spider crab). Closed Sunday nights. Reservations advised. Visa accepted. 14 Calle Puerto (phone: 420180).

Panier Fleuri Classic cuisine with a French Basque accent is served at this eatery, now in the hands of the third generation of the Fombedilla family, led by Tatús, a marvelous woman who has won the National Gastronomy Award. Try *becada asada* (roast woodcock). The wine cellar is legendary, with many rare and vintage samples. Closed Sunday nights, Wednesdays, the first 2 weeks in June, and mid-December to early January. Reservations necessary. Major credit cards accepted. 1 Paseo de Salamanca (phone: 424205).

Patxiku Kintana Owner Patxiku was a champion pelota player, and emblems of the sport enliven an otherwise stark decor. This place in the heart of the Old Town often rocks with the laughter of this huge, cheery Basque. His mother, Maritxu, and wife, Pepita Echevarría, help "Patxi" create a traditional menu with many innovations. Try *vieiras con salsa de algas al armagnac* (scallops with seaweed and brandy sauce). Closed Tuesday nights, Wednesdays (except in August), *Christmas,* and *Easter.* Reservations advised. Major credit cards accepted. 22 Calle San Jerónimo (phone: 426399).

MODERATE

Rekondo The grilled fish and meat here are works of art created by bullfighter-turned-restaurateur Txomin Rekondo. The wine cellar, which diners are encouraged to visit, is the largest of any restaurant in Spain — boasting over 200,000 bottles. Try the *mendreska de bonito* (grilled tuna steak). There is a wonderful open-air dining patio — but watch out for giant crickets and other flying insects in the summer! Closed Wednesdays (except during *Easter* week), 2 weeks in February, and November. Reservations advised. Major credit cards accepted. Paseo de Igueldo (phone: 212907).

Urepel Don't be put off by the drab exterior. It's friendly inside, and only the freshest food from that day's market is served. The impeccable menu features traditional Basque fare, as well as novelties from across the border, such as *pato de caserio filiteado a la naranja* (country-style duck with oranges). There is generally goose or duck on the menu, which is unusual in San Sebastián. Closed Sundays, Tuesday nights, late June to mid-July, *Christmas,* and *Easter.* Reservations essential. American Express, Diners Club, and Visa accepted. 3 Paseo de Salamanca (phone: 424040).

INEXPENSIVE

Alotza An intimate family atmosphere awaits diners in this Old Town bar-restaurant, where the food is on a par with many more highly rated establishments. The *pimientos rellenos de txangurro* (peppers stuffed with spider crab) and *cola de merluza a la donostiarra* (hake tail in rich green sauce) are delicious, as are the house pastries. Closed Wednesdays. Reservations unnecessary. Major credit cards accepted. 7 Calle Fermín Calbetón (phone: 420782).

Basarri Noisy and crowded, it is one of the many no-nonsense, value-for-money establishments in the Old Town. Join a table of singing Basques enjoying *merluza a la koskera* (baked hake). Closed Mondays, the first week of June, and the first week of November. No reservations. No credit cards accepted. 17 Calle Fermín Calbetón (phone: 425853).

TAPAS BARS

The best of San Sebastián's *tapas* bars include *La Espiga* (43 Calle San Marcial; phone: 290307); *Negresco* (5 Calle Zubieta; phone: 460968); *La Cepa* (7 Calle 31 de Agosto; phone: 426394); *Ganbara* (21 Calle San Jerónimo; phone: 422575); *Astelena* (1 Calle Iñigo; phone: 426275); *Haizea* (8 Calle Aldamar; phone: 425710); and *Portaletas* (8 Calle Puerto; phone: 426435).

Santiago de Compostela

During the Middle Ages, it is estimated that anywhere from 500,000 to 2,000,000 visitors a year poured into this city in northwestern Spain. They arrived from all over Europe — from as far away as Scandinavia and Britain, from Italy, Germany, and France. Many who came were guided en route by what is considered to be the world's first travel guidebook, written in 1130 by a French monk. Though they may have set out alone, they eventually became duos, trios, bands, and masses traveling together across the continent, and the exposure to other cultures fostered by this movement of peoples eventually had enormous influence on medieval thought, art, and architecture.

Santiago became an object of pilgrimage in 813, when the grave of St. James (Santiago in Spanish), one of the 12 apostles, was discovered by a peasant who is said to have been led to the spot by a bright shining star (Compostela means field of the star). A church was erected over the site to protect the remains. As its fame grew, Santiago became, along with Jerusalem and Rome, one of Christendom's three holiest cities.

The discovery of the relics of St. James served as a unifying force for all European Christians, and in particular for Christians in northern Spain, who, thus inspired, redoubled their efforts to throw out the Moors. Stories of the Reconquest are filled with accounts of Christian knights who claimed they were spurred on to victory by visions of St. James striking down the infidels with his lightning-fast sword. While scholars disagree as to whether or not James ever really went to Spain, the belief in his presence had a tremendous influence on Spanish history. With the discovery of the tomb, Christian Spain found its patron saint.

The famous Camino de Santiago (Way of St. James), the pilgrims' route to Santiago, is one of the world's oldest tour routes, marked by the churches, monasteries, hospitals, and hospices (the latter the hotels of the day) set up to accommodate them as they moved toward their destination. (For further details of the history of St. James and the pilgrimages, see *Pilgrims' Route,* DIRECTIONS.) The route remained heavily traveled until 1589, when Sir Francis Drake attacked La Coruña and the Bishop of Santiago de Compostela removed the relics from the church for safekeeping and they subsequently disappeared. The pilgrimages ceased until the relics were rediscovered in 1879. Today, pilgrims and the city still do the saint honor, and in *Jubilee* years — years when his holy day (July 25) falls on a Sunday (the next one is 1999) — the celebrations are especially intense.

Beyond the cathedral, the city's main attraction, Santiago's narrow streets offer an appealing collection of smaller churches, monasteries, and convents, as well as bars, shops, and old merchant houses. The city is also the site of one of Spain's earliest and most important universities, which gives it the flavor of a modern university town, with tiny pubs, Celtic music, and nonstop conversations on the affairs of the world. When its inhabitants empty into the streets to discuss the ramifications of life in Gallego, the local dialect, it seems that life in the Galician capital (pop. 106,000) hasn't changed much at all.

Santiago At-a-Glance

SEEING THE CITY

The walkway along the Coto de Santa Susana, a hill that rises across from the cathedral, offers a wonderful panoramic view of Santiago. For an evocative look at the city from the midst of its clustered buildings, head for the balcony off the cathedral cloister, which looks out over the roofs of the town and down the bustling Calle del Franco.

SPECIAL PLACES

The main commercial streets — Calle del Franco, Rúa del Villar, and Rúa Nueva — radiate from the right front of the cathedral and are exquisite examples of medieval thoroughfares, lined with opulent houses with elegantly sculpted façades and intricate ironwork. Behind the cathedral are the historic streets that for centuries led pilgrims — many of them on their knees — into Santiago at the completion of their long journey. A few blocks behind the cathedral, in the Plaza de Abastos, is the bustling town marketplace, packed with fish, meat, fruit, and vegetable stands, open every morning except Sundays.

CATEDRAL (CATHEDRAL) The culmination point of one of the world's primary pilgrimages, the cathedral was built on the site of a Roman graveyard and the foundations of a basilica built by Alfonso II in the 9th century to house the remains of St. James. All but St. James's tomb were destroyed by the Moors in 997. The present structure was begun around 1075, and was largely completed in the 13th century. The relics of St. James are buried under the high altar.

The cathedral is basically a baroque shell around a Romanesque interior. Its western side, known as the Obradoiro (Goldwork) façade, is considered among the most beautiful cathedral façades in Christendom. Facing the Plaza del Obradoiro and towering above a broad flight of steps, the Obradoiro façade, completed in 1750, is a baroque masterpiece of decorative flourishes and merging curves and lines.

Facing south onto Plaza de las Platerías is the cathedral's famous Puerta de las Platerías (Goldsmith's Door), a 12th-century Romanesque work. The Puerta Santa (Holy Door), also known as the Puerta del Perdón (Pardon Door), open only in *Jubilee* years, faces east onto Plaza de la Quintana and dates from 1611. The north façade, facing Plaza de la Azabachería or Plaza Inmaculada, contains the Puerta de la Azabachería.

Illuminated exclusively by candles and occasional shafts of sunlight, the cathedral's interior is a magnificent world of Romanesque opulence and hushed reverence. Just inside the Obradoiro entrance is the Pórtico de la Gloria (Gate of Glory), essentially an older, Romanesque façade within the baroque one. Carved by the renowned sculptor Master Mateo between 1168 and 1188, the Gate of Glory was part of the original Romanesque cathedral. A sculptural masterpiece, it has three arched doorways and more than 200 carved figures. The central column of the main doorway, carved as a Tree of Jesse, rises to a figure of the seated St. James. It is customary for pilgrims to touch the marble pillar upon their safe arrival, and after centuries, five smooth finger holes have been worn into the marble. At the base of the pillar, kneeling and facing the high altar, is a sculpted self-portrait of Master Mateo. Many pilgrims tap their head against his, hoping to receive some of his genius. Above, on the central arch, are the 24 old men of the Apocalypse surrounding Christ; they hold instruments, one of which (the central one) is a Galician *zanfona,* found only in Celtic regions of the world. The left arch bears a grouping of statues of the imprisoned ten tribes of Israel, and Adam and Eve on either side of Christ. The Last Judgment is depicted on the right arch.

The high altar is a dazzling creation in silver and gold backed by another statue of St. James. The altar is built atop the crypt of St. James, and the faithful can climb down the stairs to pay their respects. Many pilgrims also climb up behind the altar to embrace the statue and kiss the saint's mantle. The cathedral museum contains ecclesiastic items such as the *botafumeiro* (giant incense burner) used during important services, a collection of tapestries depicting everyday life in the Middle Ages, and archaeological artifacts. The portico off the museum offers excellent views of the town and of the Plaza del Obradoiro. The cathedral is open daily from 8 AM to 8 PM; museum hours are 10 AM to 1:30 PM and 4 to 7 PM. Admission charge to the museum. Plaza del Obradoiro.

PARADOR DE LOS REYES CATÓLICOS (HOSTAL OF THE CATHOLIC MONARCHS)

This magnificently decorated 15th-century former royal hospital and pilgrims' *hostal,* located in the Plaza del Obradoiro next to the cathedral, is now one of Spain's most memorable hotels (see *Checking In*). Built under the personal supervision of King Ferdinand and Queen Isabella, and completed in the 17th century, its highlights include an exquisite Plateresque entrance and four 16th- and 18th-century cloistered courtyards with lovely fountains. The complex should be toured with a personal guide; it's also normally included as part of wider group tours. No admission charge. Plaza del Obradoiro (phone: 582200).

MONASTERIO DE SAN PELAYO DE ANTE-ALTARES Located directly behind (east of) the cathedral, this colossal monastery originally was founded by Alfonso II. The present structure dates back to the late 17th century and contains a small church with a baroque altarpiece flanked by altars bearing the story of the life of the Virgin Mary. There is also a small museum. Open daily from 10 AM to 1 PM and 4 to 6:30 PM. Admission charge to the museum. Vía Sacra.

CASA DE LA PARRA Next to San Pelayo, and named for a bunch of grapes, this 17th-century baroque mansion is now an art gallery, featuring new exhibitions of contemporary works on a regular basis. Open from noon to 2 PM and 7 to 9:30 PM; closed Sundays. No admission charge. Vía Sacra.

MONASTERIO DE SAN MARTIÑO PINARIO Originally dating from 912, this multi-styled monastery features three majestic 17th- and 18th-century cloisters and a church with a wide central nave and an ornate baroque altarpiece by Casas y Novoa. Behind the equally ornate supporting altarpieces are some of the most beautiful choir stalls imaginable. Open daily from 10 AM to 1 PM and 4 to 7 PM. Admission charge. Plaza Inmaculada, with the church opening onto Plaza San Martiño.

SANTA MARÍA LA REAL DEL SAR This 12th-century Romanesque collegiate church is not large, but it has giant 18th-century flying buttresses supporting its walls. The need for them becomes apparent inside: The church was built on soft, sandy soil, and the columns began to slip as the weight of the ceiling bore down over the years. From an interior perspective, they appear to be falling outward — thus the buttresses to keep the church stable. About half a mile (1 km) south of the Old Town. Open daily from 10 AM to 1 PM and 4 to 6 PM; ring the bell marked *claustro* around the back of the church for admission. Admission charge. Calle de Castrón d'Ouro.

Sources and Resources

TOURIST INFORMATION

Santiago's Oficina de Turismo (43 Rúa del Villar; phone: 584081) can provide general information and an excellent glossy brochure on the city that includes a detailed map. During the annual *Feast of St. James,* the tourist office also distributes a guide to events. Open weekdays from 10 AM to 2 PM and 4 to 7 PM; Saturdays from 9 AM to 2 PM.

LOCAL COVERAGE The local newspapers are *El Correo Gallego,* a daily publication written in Spanish with the occasional article in the Galician dialect, and *La Voz de Galicia.*

TELEPHONE

The area code for Santiago is 81. If calling from another part of Spain, dial "9" before the area code and the local number.

GETTING AROUND

Most of Santiago's sights, pubs, restaurants, and shops are within a relatively small, walkable area.

AIRPORT The Santiago airport is in Labacolla, 7 miles (11 km) east of the city via the C547 highway. Buses to Santiago leave the airport eight times a day, coinciding with flight schedules. Buses to the airport leave from the old *Iberia Airlines* office (in the Old Town, 24 Calle General Pardiñas). For tickets and reservations, however, call or go to the new *Iberia Airlines* office in the New Town, 25 Calle Calvo Sotelo (phone: 597550). For additional airport information call 574200 or 572024; for *Iberia* reservations, call 574200.

BUS Santiago's city bus routes connect various points of the Old Town, but there is little cause to use them, as the town is so compact. The fare is about 50¢. The central bus station is located on Calle San Cayetano (phone: 573718). There is unpredictable daily service to Madrid, Barcelona, La Coruña, Vigo, Pontevedra, and San Sebastián.

CAR RENTAL Rental companies include *Autos Brea* (8 Calle Gómez Ulla; phone: 561336), *Avis* (10 Calle República de El Salvador; phone: 573718), *Budget/Autour* (3 Calle General Pardiñas; phone: 586496), and *Hertz* (145 Av. de Lugo; phone: 583466; and at the airport; phone: 598893).

TAXI Call one of the city cabstands for a taxi (your hotel will know the nearest one). There are two main, midtown taxi stands (Av. de Figueroa; phone: 585973; and Av. General Franco; phone: 561020). Late-night service is available from the Plaza Galicia stand (phone: 561028).

TRAIN The Santiago train station (phone: 596050) is about a 10-minute walk down Avenida General Franco from the Old Town — or take the No. 14 bus. There is frequent, daily train service to Madrid, La Coruña, San Sebastián, Irún, Pontevedra, Vigo, and Porto, Portugal.

SPECIAL EVENTS

Santiago's major annual celebration has its origins in the great medieval pilgrimages to the tomb of St. James the Apostle.

BEST FESTIVAL

Fiesta del Apóstol (Feast of St. James the Apostle) The actual feast day, July 25, is the climax of about 2 weeks of celebration. Festivities run from July 15 to the end of the month, with the main events occurring from July 23 through July 26. Galician folkloric shows, competitions, special theater presentations, and daily concerts are among the attractions. There is also a jazz festival, featuring performances by major international groups, in the Plaza del Toral during the days immediately preceding the feast day.

A spectacular fireworks display is held in front of the cathedral on the eve of the feast (July 24), and the day itself is marked by a high mass, street bands, special theater, and an orchestral presentation in the Plaza del Obradoiro. The mass, televised live throughout Spain, includes the swinging of the *botafumeiro* (giant incense burner) across the cathedral transepts. During *Jubilee* years (the next one is in 1999), established by papal bull in the 12th century, the cathedral's Puerta Santa is open and pilgrims who visit the shrine receive special grace.

MUSEUMS

Besides the attractions listed in *Special Places,* Santiago boasts a number of other churches, monasteries, and religious buildings, some housing small museums. Two worth visiting are the *Museo de Pobo Galego* and the *Museo Municipal,* both set up in the Convento de Santo Domingo and containing various ethnographic illustrations of rural Galician life. They're open Mondays through Saturdays from 10 AM to 1 PM and 4 to 7 PM. Admission charge. Calle de Santo Domingo (phone: 583620). The *Museo Galego de Arte Contemporáneo,* a modern-art museum, is planned for the site next to the convent. At press time, no opening date had been announced.

SHOPPING

Santiago's main shopping district is located in the New Town on Calles General Pardiñas, República de El Salvador, Alfredo Brañas, and Montero Ríos. The Old Town's most popular street for shopping is Calle Calderena, which runs parallel to Rúa Nueva. A wide variety of street vendors operate along Rúa Nueva, and there is a weekly Sunday market at Plaza de Abastos, next to the Convent of San Agustín. Shopping hours are generally Mondays through Fridays from 9:30 AM to 1:30 PM and 4:30 to 7 PM, Saturdays from 9:30 AM to 2 PM, but may vary.

ANTIGÜEDADES SAJONIA Featuring antiques, glassware, jewelry, and fine furniture. 22 Calle Gelmírez (phone: 582830).

CONFITERÍA MORA One of the best-known pastry shops in town, a good place to buy a *tarta de Santiago.* Rúa del Villar (phone: 581014).

FERNANDO MAYER Very good old European prints and paintings. 6 Plaza de las Platerías (phone: 582536).

RETABLO Fine antiques and artworks. 1 Plaza de la Quintana (phone: 582526).

SARGADELOS One of the best places to purchase Galicia's unique Sargadelos ceramics. Rúa Nueva (phone: 581905).

TENDA Another shop specializing in fine antiques, ceramics, and jewelry. 23 Calle Gelmírez (phone: 582520).

VIELRO Silver and jet jewelry in an unpretentious built-in booth. 5 Plaza Immaculada.

XANELA Creative local souvenirs, including tiny, hand-carved cathedrals, ceramic dolls, and religious medallions. 14 Rúa Nueva (phone: 584171).

SPORTS AND FITNESS

GOLF Though hardly a duffer's paradise, one course stands out.

TOP TEE-OFF SPOT

Golf La Toja, Isla de La Toja This 9-hole course lies on an island in the Ría de Arousa, 50 miles (80 km) south of Santiago de Compostela; a bridge links the island to the mainland. At first sight, the course seems rather easy. But looming pines, the adjacent sea, and a constant wind add unexpected pressure. *La Toja*'s club membership totals 250, but some 5,000 golfers tackle its narrow fairways and doglegs every summer. Since it is open year-round, it is possible to avoid the summertime crowds. Isla de La Toja, Pontevedra 36991 (phone: 86-730726 or 86-730818).

The private, 9-hole *Real Aero Club* golf course is located near the airport. Non-members and visitors are permitted to play on a space-available basis. Call for information (phone: 592400).

SWIMMING A public pool is available in the *Santa Isabel Sports Complex* (just south of the Old Town; phone: 586039). There is also a public swimming pool at the university (phone: 584216). Both facilities charge a small admission fee. The pools at the *Peregrino* and *Araguaney* hotels are also open to the public (see *Checking In*).

TENNIS The university has tennis courts. Call well in advance for information on availability and to book court time (phone: 584795).

THEATER AND MUSIC

There are no regularly scheduled theater or musical seasons in Santiago, but frequent cultural events are held at the *Auditorium of Galicia,* whose full name is the *Palacio de la Opera, Exposiciones y Congresos* (Avenida Burgo das Naciòns; phone: 573855). Like most Spanish university towns, there is a student *tuna* group, which performs in Plaza del Obradoiro and surrounding squares. Members of the *tuna* wear student capes, and when they are not serenading a woman, their songs tend to be indelicate.

NIGHTCLUBS AND NIGHTLIFE

Santiago is packed with pubs, bars, and discotheques. A night on the town might consist of *tapas* (see *Eating Out* and *Tapas Bars*) from 6 PM to 8 PM, dinner from 9 PM to midnight, and pub and disco hopping from 11 PM to 3 AM. Among the popular pubs in the Old Town, mostly found around the walls of the San Pelayo monastery, are *O'Galo d'Ouro* (14 Calle de Conga; phone: 582180), which offers a cozy atmosphere in two small rooms built into medieval horse stables, complemented by a diverse selection of music on the CD jukebox, and *Modus Vivendi* (1 Plazuela de Feixoo), small and also occupying old stables. A small pub with no advertised name at 22 Calle de San Pelayo de Antes-Altares is also worth testing. Farther around the monastery, at *Paradiso Perdido* (3 Calle San Pelayo), customers walk down a stairway where thousands of students have carved their names. *La Casa das Crechas* (3 Vía Sacra) is a Celtic music pub where the bartenders and waitresses speak only Gallego — at any moment both the upstairs and downstairs rooms may be filled with the sound of musicians playing an impromptu reel or two on fiddle, tin whistle, and guitar. Popular discotheques include *Discoteca Araguaney* at the *Araguaney* hotel; *Discoteca Kilate* in the *Peregrino* hotel; and *Ruta 66* (Calle Santiago de Guayaquil; phone: 566208).

Best in Town

CHECKING IN

Santiago boasts hundreds of places to stay, ranging from luxurious hotels to tiny pilgrim's *hostals,* although the options shrink when only those establishments with private bathrooms and locations within walking distance of the monumental area of town are considered. A double room will cost $100 or more in a hotel listed as expensive, from $60 to $95 in a moderate one, and $60 or less in an inexpensive one. Since the summer weather is generally mild, air conditioned rooms are pretty much nonexistent. All telephone numbers are in the 81 city code unless otherwise indicated.

For an unforgettable experience, we begin with our favorite *parador,* followed by our recommendations of cost and quality choices of hotels, listed by price category.

A SPECIAL HAVEN

Parador de Los Reyes Católicos This magnificently decorated 15th-century former royal hospital and pilgrims' *hostal,* located in the Plaza del Obradoiro next to the cathedral, is now one of Spain's most memorable *paradores.* The building itself is a tourist attraction (see *Special Places*). Designed by Enrique de Egas, a favorite architect of King Ferdinand and Queen Isabella, it so captured the interest of the Catholic Monarchs that they personally made decisions about its interior details, such as where to install fireplaces and what wood to select for the floors. The 157 elegant rooms, which feature canopied beds and antique desks, surround four splendid Renaissance courtyards and a chapel with a beamed ceiling and wrought-iron grill. The elegant dining room with its vaulted ceilings and its candlelit room offers Galician specialties. There are also shops, a garden, and concert, conference, and exhibition halls. 1 Plaza del Obradoiro (phone: 582200; in the US, 212-686-9213; fax: 563094).

EXPENSIVE

Araguaney A modern, luxurious, totally impersonal 64-room hotel in the heart of the New Town, it's a popular choice of visiting businesspeople. There's a heated swimming pool, a restaurant, a travel agency, a sauna, and a discotheque on the premises. 5 Calle Alfredo Brañas (phone: 595900; fax: 590287).

MODERATE

Compostela An old establishment in a great location, just across the street from one of the main entrances into the Old Town. The 99 rooms have all the amenities (telephones, TV sets, room service), although the hotel could use some sprucing up and a bit of brightness. Breakfast, lunch, and dinner are served in the restaurant on the premises. 1 Av. General Franco (phone: 585700; fax: 563269).

Peregrino This rather nondescript modern hotel is Santiago's largest. Some distance from the center of town, it has 148 plain rooms and a restaurant. But it does have two major advantages: good, quick service and an excellent, large, open-air pool. Av. Rosalía de Castro (phone: 521850; fax: 521777).

Rey Fernando A pleasant, modern place close to the train station, with a charming staff and a comfortable TV lounge. The 24 rooms are bright and functional, and the surrounding streets are lively — without being noisy — during the school year. There is a breakfast room for guests only. 30 Calle Fernando III El Santo (phone: 593550; fax: 590096).

Universal In an excellent location across the street from the Old Town and across the square from the *Compostela* hotel, it has 54 rooms with showers and direct-dial telephones. There is a *tapas* bar on the premises. 2 Plaza Galicia (phone: 585800).

Windsor Santiago's most popular *hostal,* this pleasant establishment remains full almost year-round, so book well in advance. The 70 rooms are spotless, the lobby glistening, and service is always rendered with a smile. 16 Calle República de El Salvador (phone: 592939).

INEXPENSIVE

Mapoula Another *hostal* in the Old Town, this is one a few steps from the Plaza Galicia. The 10 rooms are all nicely furnished and have private baths; the proprietor takes a personal interest in her guests. 10 Calle Entremurallas (phone: 580124).

EATING OUT

Galician cooking manifests the region's Celtic influences and its proximity to the sea. One specialty is the *empanada,* a flat potpie filled with anything from salami and mushrooms to squid and octopus or rabbit with hot peppers. Another favorite is *pulpo* (octopus), which might be served simply, with potatoes and onions, or chopped up, salted, and topped with a tangy pepper sauce to be enjoyed with beer or wine as a *tapa.* Still another specialty is *caldo gallego,* a hearty vegetable soup made with beef or ham broth. Shellfish is prepared with a variety of sauces. Fish is generally baked, broiled, or sautéed, and then combined with potatoes, onions, peppers, and asparagus. Dinner for two with wine will cost $60 or more in restaurants listed as expensive, $40 to $50 in moderate restaurants, and $35 or less in inexpensive eateries. With its large student population, Santiago can be one of the least expensive places to eat in Spain. Many restaurants regularly offer inexpensive student lunch and dinner specials, consisting of an appetizer, entrée, fruit, bread, and wine, all in generous portions. Another inexpensive way to dine is to find a restaurant serving *platos combinados* — set dinners such as salad, pork with peppers, and potato croquettes, or soup, veal, or steaks with potatoes — which cost $4 to $5.25 per plate. All telephone numbers are in the 81 city code unless otherwise indicated.

EXPENSIVE

Anexo Vilas Under the same management as *Vilas* (see below), this place serves similarly superb Galician dishes — the food here may even be a touch better. The menu is virtually identical to that of its sister restaurant, so expect to savor some of the best cooking northwestern Spain has to offer. Closed Mondays. Reservations necessary. Major credit cards accepted. 21 Av. Villagarcía (phone: 598387).

Don Gaiferos There's a rivalry of sorts between *Vilas* and *Don Gaiferos* for the best cooking in town, and diners are the winners. This has a beautiful Old Town location in three stone-arched rooms, a wonderful regional atmosphere, and excellent Galician food. Closed Sunday evenings and from *Christmas* through early January. Reservations advised. Major credit cards accepted. 23 Rúa Nueva (phone: 583894).

Retablo Featuring local and continental fare, superbly prepared and served in an elegant dining room lit by brass chandeliers. Closed Sundays. Reservations advised. Major credit cards accepted. 13 Rúa Nueva (phone: 565950).

Vilas One of Santiago's best restaurants, it's an unassuming place, with simple decor, but it has been turning out excellent food since early this century. A long bar with photographs of Spanish soccer heroes leads to dining rooms adorned with oil paintings, white tablecloths, barrels, and a bookshelf full of wine bottles. Try any of the fish dishes, including *sardinas "Mama Sueiro"* (sardines with sweet peppers and garlic; available April through June only). Closed Sundays. Reservations necessary. Major credit cards accepted. 88 Av. Rosalía de Castro (phone: 591000).

MODERATE

La Arzuana Normally packed with locals, this is one of Santiago's most popular restaurants. The dining room opens out to a vine-covered patio. Specialties include creations made with clams, mussels, and shrimp. For groups of 6 or more, the management will prepare a bowl of *queimada* — a regional "witch's brew" made from a local firewater called *orujo,* coffee, orange peel, and sugar — and then set it on fire right at the table. Open daily. No reservations or credit cards accepted. 40 Calle del Franco (phone: 581198).

INEXPENSIVE

Bodegón de Xulio An unassuming place with simple tables in the back. Big portions of seafood of all kinds are featured; *tapas* are served at the tables as well. Closed Sundays, *Christmas,* and February. No reservations. No credit cards accepted. 24 Calle del Franco (phone: 584639).

Casa Manolo This small spot tucked into a small street near the town market is a local institution. Galician specialties are served up as fast as you can order; the fixed-price menu has over a dozen appetizer and entrée choices; and the portions are enormous. Closed Sundays July through September, *Christmas,* and *Easter.* No reservations or credit cards accepted. 27 Rúa Traviesa (phone: 582950).

TAPAS BARS

Bar after bar along the Old Town's Calle del Franco and Rúa del Villar serves seafood *tapas* (small clams, sardines, and octopus with spicy peppers and salt) along with beer and wine. This is the place to try traditional country wine — something like a new wine, not fully fermented — served in small bowls called *tazas* (it can also be ordered in soup-bowl-size *cuncas*). The tiny *Bar Negreira* (75 Rúa del Villar; phone: 580740) is frequented by virtually everyone in town — stay long enough and you may meet the mayor. *Restaurante El 42* (42 Rúa de Franco; phone: 581009) serves superb *almejas* (clams) and *berberechos* (tiny sweet clams) at big tables and at the bar.

Segovia

Occupying a rocky perch high above two deep valleys, between the northern slopes of the Sierra de Guadarrama and the high, flat tableland of Castilla y León, Segovia has a city center that reaches an altitude of 3,280 feet. Many compare its overall silhouette to that of a ship, with the Alcázar rising high in the west like a prow above the confluence of the Eresma and Clamores rivers. Only 57 miles (91 km) northwest of Madrid, Segovia is a favorite retreat for both foreign travelers and Spaniards, who often make day trips from the capital to savor its scenic charm, historic sights, and outstanding food.

The Romans endowed the city with its greatest marvel: a 2,000-year-old aqueduct that used to deliver water to the upper reaches of the city and rises almost 100 feet above the Plaza del Azoguejo. City traffic once passed through the same slender arches that Roman chariots did; but the aqueduct is now closed to traffic as engineers study the extent of damage caused by the vibrations of cars, trucks, and buses rumbling underneath.

Two Roman roads also converged in Segovia, further attesting to its former stature as a strategic military town. With the incursion of the Visigoths in the 6th century, a gradual decline began, subsequently accelerated by 200 years of Muslim rule. Then, revitalized by the Reconquest, Segovia greatly enhanced its prestige in 1474 when Isabella the Catholic was proclaimed Queen of Castile in the Plaza Mayor. Decline set in again, however, after the Comuneros uprising of 1520–21, when the *comunidades* (autonomous cities) of Castile, led by Juan de Padilla of Toledo and Juan Bravo of Segovia, revolted unsuccessfully against the absolutism of the Holy Roman Emperor Charles V. The city was left badly damaged, and regained its prominence only after Philip V chose nearby La Granja as the site for his castle in the early 18th century.

At the turn of the 20th century, two artists — one painter and one poet — focused their creative attentions upon Segovia and Castile. The painter, Ignacio Zuloaga, was a master at capturing Segovia's special light and the earthy quality of its inhabitants. The poet, Antonio Machado, an Andalusian who lived for more than a decade in a house on Calle de los Desamparados that is now a small museum, proclaimed his enchantment with the region in a book of poems entitled *Campos de Castilla*.

Today, resting largely on its historic laurels, Segovia's population of 55,000 depends greatly on a steady stream of visitors from the capital for its continuing prosperity. And many return again and again — it is one of Spain's most beautiful cities, and the roast suckling pig is the city's greatest gastronomic lure. Most Sundays throughout the year, the Plaza Mayor bristles with exuberant throngs honing their appetites on aperitifs and *tapas* in anticipation of the succulent, sweet pork nestled beneath crisp, brown skin. Later, sated diners walk off their extravagance with a stroll through the narrow streets of the city center, making their way from the Alcázar to the cathedral to the Roman aqueduct, past Romanesque churches, buildings covered with the *esgrafiado* designs that are characteristic of Segovia, and numerous spots from which to admire panoramic views.

Segovia At-a-Glance

SEEING THE CITY

Approximately 1¼ miles (2 km) north of Segovia along the N601 highway leading to Valladolid, the *Parador de Segovia* offers a marvelous view of the entire city. On Saturday and Sunday nights, the aqueduct and cathedral are illuminated.

SPECIAL PLACES

The major monuments of Segovia are within the confines of the old walled city. Although the walls, which date from the time of the Reconquest, are barely in evidence today, three of the original seven gates — San Cebrián, Santiago, and San Andrés — still stand. The walls gave the old part of Segovia its ship shape, with Alcázar the bow and the Roman aqueduct the stern. The cathedral and Plaza Mayor are roughly amidships. Segovia is known for its remarkable collection of Romanesque churches. They, and numerous other monuments, are within the walls, but a number of remaining sights are beyond and below the walls on the starboard side, on both sides of the Eresma River. As with most medieval cities in Spain, driving in the old part of town is a tortuous affair. Come by car or a taxi to the Plaza Mayor, then explore the area within the walls on foot.

WITHIN THE WALLS

ALCÁZAR This Disneyesque castle-palace at the western end of town perches above the confluence of the Eresma and Clamores rivers. In fact, Walt Disney used it as a model for the castle in *Sleeping Beauty*. Built during the 12th and 13th centuries on top of an older fortress, it was enriched and enlarged in the 15th and 18th centuries with numerous magnificent chambers. In this castle the Princess Isabella first met Ferdinand, and in 1474, she set forth from the Alcázar to be crowned Queen of Castile in Segovia's Plaza Mayor; a painting commemorating that event today hangs in the castle's Sala de la Galera. The Alcázar was also the site of Philip II's fourth marriage — this one to Anne of Austria. In the 16th century, the Torre del Homenaje (Tower of Homage, also known as the Tower of Juan II), covered with the typically Segovian *esgrafiado* decoration suggestive of Moorish times, was used as a state prison. King Carlos III installed the Artillery Academy in the Alcázar in the 18th century, and in 1862, a fierce fire gutted the place. Rebuilt in a romantic vein, it has a simple charm that is still magical and elegant. Of special interest are the Mudéjar ceilings and tilework, and the authentic period furnishings. The 360° view of the Castilian countryside from the top of the Tower of Juan II is worth the 152 steps up, but you can get a good view of sights outside the city walls from the garden in front of the Alcázar. Open from 10 AM to 2 PM and from 4 to 6 PM; Sundays from 10 AM to 6 PM. Admission charge. Plaza del Alcázar (phone: 430176).

CATEDRAL (CATHEDRAL) Built in the late Gothic style at a time when Renaissance structures were in vogue (1515 to 1558), the cathedral was, by order of the Holy Roman Emperor Charles V, constructed on a higher and more secure site than the cathedral it replaced, which had been destroyed in the revolt of the Comuneros. Though it is known as the "Lady of the Spanish cathedrals" because of its elegance, slender lines, and restrained austerity, its treasures are not comparable to those of the cathedrals of León or Salamanca. Among them are the Flamboyant-style choir stalls and cloister, both brought from the old cathedral; the 16th-century carving of *La Piedad* by Juan de Juni in the Capilla del Santo Entierro (the first chapel to the right as you enter the church); and the altarpiece in the Capilla de Santiago (next to the museum entrance). Also note the chapels around the apse; painted in pale rococo colors, they are quite different in feeling from the rest. The museum contains an 18th-century gold carriage used in *Corpus Christi* processions. Open daily from 9 AM to 12:45 PM and from 3 to 6:45 PM April through October; from 9 AM to 12:45 PM and from 3 to 4:45 PM from November through March. Admission charge to the cloister, museum, and Sala Capitular. Plaza Mayor (phone: 435325).

PLAZA DE SAN MARTÍN This square, at the heart of the walled city, is bordered by old mansions, including the Casa del Siglo XV (House of the 15th Century), often mistakenly identified as the house of Juan Bravo, a 16th-century Segovian who was one of the leaders of the Comuneros uprising and whose statue presides over the lower level of the square. The tower off to one end is the 14th-century Torreón de Lozoya, and the portico running along a side belongs to the 11th-century Iglesia de San Martín, the most centrally located of numerous Romanesque churches in Segovia.

CASA DE LOS PICOS A late-15th-century Renaissance mansion, distinguished by the pyramidal stones adorning its façade, it is now home to the Escuela de Artes Aplicadas y Oficios Artísticos (School of Applied Arts and Artistic Pursuits). It often mounts student art exhibits and other somewhat unusual displays. Calle Juan Bravo (phone: 430711).

ROMAN AQUEDUCT This landmark is one of Europe's finest examples of Roman architecture, and the most complete Roman monument in Spain. A majestic row of double arches, made only of oiled granite blocks, the aqueduct was built some 2,000 years ago without the use of cranes, pumps, or even mortar, but with that sense of elegance that the Romans brought to even their most functional creations. They cut the granite to a perfect, jigsaw fit, then stacked the blocks into a remarkable feat of engineering to siphon spring water to the city from the Acebeda River. Stretching from the dusty orange hills above the dry Castilian plain to the city, the aqueduct is formed by 166 arches in 2 tiers (the lower level forming prized parking spaces), and is 21,500 feet long and 96 feet high. The most impressive frontal view is from Plaza del Azoguejo, where the aqueduct reaches its highest point. Climb the steps on the left side of the square for the best longitudinal view of the arches stretching into the distance and the sea of red tiles created by the city rooftops. At the very top, go through the wall, under an arch, and around to the lookout point. Plaza del Azoguejo.

BEYOND THE WALLS

IGLESIA DE LA VERA CRUZ Across the Eresma River just northwest of the city, this early-13th-century church was constructed by the Knights Templars in the late Romanesque style. Its shape, with 12 sides, is unusual in Spain, and was modeled after the Holy Sepulchre in Jerusalem. Inside is a 2-story circular room (a sort of church-within-a-church), a 13th-century carved wooden Christ above the central apse, and the Lignum Crucis chapel in the base of the tower. The church once housed a part of the True Cross, from which it takes its name. Open from 10:30 AM to 1:30 PM and from 3:30 to 7 PM in spring and summer (until 6 PM in fall and winter); closed Mondays. Admission charge. Carretera a Zamarramala (phone: 431475).

MONASTERIO DEL PARRAL Founded by Henry IV in the mid-15th century and given to the Spanish order of St. Hieronymus, this monastery is also located across the Eresma River, half a mile (1 km) north of the city. The church, a blend of Gothic, Renaissance, and Plateresque elements, was designed and begun by Juan Gallego at the end of the century, but its façade was left unfinished. The monastery was abandoned after the suppression of religious orders in 1835, but it has been restored and is once again occupied by the Hieronymus brothers/priests (Jerónimos in Spanish). Notable are the polychrome altarpiece carved by Juan Rodríguez and the alabaster tombs of the Marqués de Villena and his wife, also carved by Rodríguez. The monastery is open Mondays through Saturdays from 9 AM to 1 PM and from 3 to 6:30 PM; Sundays, 9 AM to 12 PM (admission by donation). Calle del Marqués de Villena (phone: 431298).

CONVENTO DE CARMELITAS DESCALZAS San Juan de la Cruz, the 16th-century Catholic poet and friend of St. Teresa (1542–91), is buried in this convent, where he was once the prior. The convent houses a collection of his belongings, including the original of his work *Cántico Espiritual.* There's also a good view of the Alcázar. Open daily from 10 AM to 1:30 PM and from 4 to 7 PM. No admission charge. San Juan de la Cruz (phone: 436049).

CONVENTO DE SAN ANTONIO EL REAL Built by Henry IV during the mid-15th century as a country house, it was later given to the Franciscans and the Poor Clares religious orders, who inhabit it today. In the church is a wonderful original Mudéjar ceiling over a huge, lavishly gilt main altarpiece, plus three smaller altarpieces, including one with a remarkable 15th-century Flemish rendering of Calvary in three-dimensional carved wood. A nun takes visitors around the cloister and adjoining rooms, where there are more original *artesonado* ceilings and, set in the walls, several small Flemish Calvary scenes in painted terra cotta. Open daily from 4 to 6 PM. Admission charge to the cloister. To reach the convent, follow the Roman aqueduct from behind the *Mesón de Cándido* side of Plaza del Azoguejo; when it ends, with arches about waist high, the convent is only a short distance away. Calle San Antonio el Real (phone: 420228).

IGLESIA DE SAN MILLÁN One of the most beautiful of Segovia's Romanesque churches, it stands in full view in an open square between the aqueduct and the bus station. It was built by Alfonso I during the 12th century and has four apses, three doorways, two 13th-century porches, and a remodeled 11th-century Mozarabic tower that dates from a previous structure on the spot. Open during services. Av. Fernández Ladreda.

ENVIRONS

PALACIO REAL DE LA GRANJA DE SAN ILDEFONSO Seven miles (11 km) along the N601 highway toward Madrid stands La Granja, a royal palace built by Philip V, the first Bourbon King of Spain, grandson of Louis XIV of France. Set in the foothills of the Guadarrama mountains, the palace is surrounded by meticulously manicured gardens. The palace, completed in 1739, was the most impressive example of 18th-century architecture in Spain, more European than Spanish in feeling, since the French-born king and his Italian wife, Isabella Farnese, employed architects schooled in the Hapsburg tradition. Unfortunately, a fire in 1918 destroyed the private quarters of the royal family and damaged much of the remaining structure. Extensive restoration has re-created the public and official areas, which remained in use through the days of Alfonso XIII (who reigned until 1931). Visitors see room after room with marble floors, painted ceilings, lace curtains, tapestries, and crystal chandeliers — most of the latter outstanding works produced by the nearby Fábrica de Cristal de La Granja. Tours include the throne room and Philip and Isabella's mausoleum, as well as a priceless collection of 16th-century tapestries. Visits to the palace are by guided tour only, usually conducted in Spanish (although an English- and French-speaking interpreter is available), but you can wander through the lovely Versailles-style gardens behind the palace, a wonderland of fountains, pools, statues, and tree-lined avenues. The gardens are open daily all year, from 10 AM to 8 PM in summer (until 6 PM in winter). The palace is open from 10 AM to 1:30 PM and from 3 to 5 PM; Sundays and holidays, from 10 AM to 2 PM; closed Mondays. The fountains, dependent on rainwater, are normally turned on only a few days a week (usually Thursdays, Saturdays, and Sundays at 5:30 PM, from late March through early July. Admission charge to the palace. San Ildefonso (phone: 470019).

PALACIO DE RIOFRÍO Heading back to Segovia from La Granja on N601, look for the sign and turnoff marked Riofrío. Follow the road 4 miles (6 km) and pass through the intersection following the second sign marked Palacio y Bosque de Riofrío. Continue another 4 miles (6 km) and turn left at the intersection for SG724. A guard signals the entrance to a protected parkland where an amazing multitude of friendly deer greets you along the road leading the last few miles to the palace. (Save your admission ticket to show to the guard on your way out.)

The rather plain exterior of this 18th-century peach-colored palace with lime-green shutters belies the elegance within. Built by Isabella Farnese, who feared that she might be ousted from La Granja by the new king, her stepson, after Philip V's death, and originally conceived as a hunting palace for her own son, it later served as a residence for Alfonso XII, grandfather of Juan Carlos, the present king. Notice the striking series of draped doorways; the chandeliers (mostly of Spanish construction); several tapestries by Goya and Bayeu; and the furnishings and decorations from the days of Alfonso XII. The northern wing of the palace has been given over to a *Museo de la Caza* (Museum of the Hunt), which features reproductions of hunting paraphernalia from the prehistoric to the modern era. Open from 10 AM to 1:30 PM and from 3 to 5 PM; 10 AM to 2 PM on Sundays and holidays; closed Tuesdays. All visits to the palace are by guided tour only (in Spanish usually, but an English- and French-speaking guide is available); admission charge (phone: 470019).

Sources and Resources

TOURIST INFORMATION

The tourist information office (10 Plaza Mayor; phone: 430328 or 436049) has a variety of helpful brochures, current information regarding hours and admission fees, and general information on accommodations. Open Mondays through Fridays from 9:30 AM to 2 PM and from 5 to 7 PM, Saturdays from 10 AM to 2 PM; during the summer it stays open until 4 or 5 PM. In addition, a *caseta* (trailer), usually parked at the aqueduct, serves as a mobile tourist office with flexible hours. It is generally open on Sundays and holidays when the other office is closed (phone: 430328).

LOCAL COVERAGE *El Adelantado de Segovia* is the city's daily Spanish-language newspaper. The *Guía Semanal de Segovia* and the related *Guía Provincial de Segovia,* available free in hotels and at the tourist office, provide up-to-the-minute information on what's happening in the city and province, respectively. Both *El Escaparate,* a biweekly newspaper covering the city and region, and the monthly *Guía Gastronómica de Segovia,* which provides listings and information on the city's restaurants, *tascas,* bars, nightlife, and historic sites, are written in Spanish, but most of the material is decipherable by non-Spanish-speaking readers. Also look for a copy of the English edition of *Segovia — Patrimonio de la Humanidad* (Segovia — Heritage of Mankind), complete with suggested itineraries and detailed historic, cultural, and artistic information.

TELEPHONE

The city code for Segovia is 11. If calling from another part of Spain, dial "9" before the area code and local number.

GETTING AROUND

Segovia is a small city, and most of its sights can be easily visited on foot. Seeing sights on the edge of town, however, will require a car or taxi.

BUS City buses ply the streets daily from 7 AM to 11 PM, stopping at most of the major attractions. The Estación de Autobuses (phone: 427725), Segovia's main bus station for long-distance buses, is located on Paseo de Ezequiel González, at the corner of Avenida Fernández Ladreda (reachable from Plaza Mayor by the No. 3 bus marked "Puente de Hierro"). There is daily service to and from Madrid, Avila, Valladolid, and other towns and villages throughout the province of Segovia. Buses for La Granja, 20 minutes away, also depart from here. Bus schedules can be found in the *Guía Provincial de Segovia.*

CAR RENTAL *Avis* has an office at 123 Calle Zorrilla (phone: 422584).

TAXI A taxi almost always can be found in the Plaza Mayor; another stand is in Plaza del Azoguejo. Radio-dispatched cabs also are available (phone: 436680 or 436681). If you are going to a site outside the city, be sure to arrange a pick-up time with the driver.

TRAIN Segovia's train station, Estación de Ferrocarril *RENFE* (phone: 420774), is located on Plaza Obispo Quesada, reachable by bus No. 3 from Plaza Mayor. There is frequent service to Madrid (Atocha and Chamartín stations), Medina del Campo, and Valladolid. Schedules of service to Madrid are in the *Guía Provincial de Segovia.*

MUSEUMS

In addition to those described in *Special Places,* the museum below may be of interest. Note that the *Zuloaga Museum,* dedicated to the famous local ceramist Daniel Zuloaga, and located in the former Iglesia de San Juan de los Caballeros, is closed for restoration until at least the middle of this year. Also at press time, the *Museo Provincial de Bellas Artes* (Provincial Fine Arts Museum), which houses a collection of local paintings from the 15th, 16th, and 17th centuries, was in the process of moving to a renovated old slaughterhouse near the Alcázar called the Casa del Sol. Check with the tourist office for more information on both museums.

CASA-MUSEO ANTONIO MACHADO (ANTONIO MACHADO HOUSE-MUSEUM) The simple old house that was the home of the poet from 1919 to 1932 is once again furnished with his possessions. Open Tuesdays through Sundays from 4 to 7 PM (to 6 PM in winter). No admission charge. 5 Calle de los Desamparados (phone: 436649).

SHOPPING

Because Segovia is popular with day-trippers from Madrid, its shopping opportunities tend to consist mostly of souvenirs and mementos. The usual assortment of wineskins, castanets, T-shirts, fans, and mantillas blossoms around all the major sights, and along Calle Marqués del Arco near the cathedral. There is a weekly market on Thursdays at Plaza de los Huertos that has some handicrafts. Ceramics are a good buy in Segovia, where prices are lower than they are in Madrid.

EL ALFAR Ceramics and souvenir items. 22 Calle del Roble (phone: 424215).

ARTESANÍA MONJAS DOMINICAS Reproductions of antique figures, such as those found in Renaissance altarpieces, made (of resin) and sold by nuns; prices range from $15 for a small angel, up to $1,500 for a large Nativity scene. Convento de Santo Domingo, Calle Capuchinos Alta (phone: 433876).

LA CASA DEL SIGLO XV Glassware, porcelain, leather goods, jewelry, records and tapes, and toys. 32 Calle Juan Bravo (phone: 434531).

MI PIEL High-quality leather goods — belts, handbags, suitcases. Centro Comercial Almuzara, 6 Calle Juan Bravo (phone: 426141).

LA SUIZA Lladró porcelain, crystal, silver, and other souvenirs. 14 Plaza Mayor (phone: 430334).

SPORTS AND FITNESS

There are two popular ski areas in the Guadarramas near Segovia. Both La Pinilla (35 miles/56 km to the northeast) and Navacerrada (17 miles/27 km south) offer a wide range of skiing opportunities and various accommodations. Consult the tourist information office for details.

THEATER AND MUSIC

Madrid is too close for Segovia to have become a theater- or concertgoer's dream. Nevertheless, the *Teatro Juan Bravo* (Plaza Mayor; phone: 431228) manages to maintain a fairly full schedule of drama, ballet, and orchestral, chamber, and popular music concerts.

NIGHTCLUBS AND NIGHTLIFE

Although there are no nightclubs of note, Segovia has an ebullient nightlife. Next to the aqueduct, *Oky* (1 and 3 Carmen; phone: 432128) is a popular disco where, as in other Spanish cities, ballroom dancing — tango, rumba, and even salsa — is back in style. Another popular dance in Segovia is a local version of the folkloric and energetic *jota*. On weekends *segovianos* enjoy the *verbena* (street fair) set up in the Plaza Mayor, where the "in place" is the *Ave Turita* bar. During summer months, Plaza San Martín with its three outdoor cafés — *El Gimnasio, El Ojo,* and *El Narizotas* — is especially lively.

Best in Town

CHECKING IN

Depending on the season, expect to pay $70 to $110 for a double room with private bath in hotels classified as expensive, $45 to $70 for a moderate one, and less than $40 for an inexpensive one. All telephone numbers are in the 11 area code unless otherwise indicated.

EXPENSIVE

Los Arcos Modern and cheerful, it's located outside the walls near the Church of San Millán and the Roman aqueduct, within walking distance of the rest of the prime sights. There are 59 rooms with bath or shower and air conditioning (some facing the city's steepled skyline); the *Cocina de Segovia* restaurant; and 2 bars. Parking is available. Affiliated with Best Western. 24 Paseo de Ezequiel González (phone: 437462; in the US, 800-528-1234; fax: 428161).

Infanta Isabel This luxury property occupies a thoroughly remodeled 19th-century mansion located alongside the main square, facing the cathedral. Its 29 heated and air conditioned rooms have satellite television, radios, direct-dial telephones, and mini-bars. The headboards and nightstands are all decorated by a local artist. There is a meeting room for up to 25 people, a *cafetería,* a breakfast room, and room service. 1 Isabel la Católica (phone: 443105; fax: 433240).

Los Linajes Within the walls of the Old City, this hotel — Segovia's best — retains an 11th-century façade that was part of a palace belonging to the Falconi family, and has charming public rooms arranged around a minuscule inner courtyard. The 55 rooms offer panoramic views, complete baths, color TV sets, and central heating. 9 Calle Dr. Velasco (phone: 431201; fax: 431712).

Parador de Segovia In a modern tile-roof brick building, this government-run *parador* with two lake-like outdoor pools and a spa-like indoor pool sprawls over a lush garden-forest setting called El Terminillo. Most of the spacious public areas and 80 guestroom balconies offer a spectacular panoramic view of the Guadarrama Mountains and the Segovia skyline. Amenities include air conditioning, central heating, a sauna, tennis courts, a bar, and a restaurant (see *Eating Out*). About 1 1/2 miles (2 km) along the road to Valladolid. Carretera de Valladolid (phone: 430462; in the US, 212-686-9213; fax: 437362).

MODERATE

Acueducto In a prime location near the aqueduct (but next to a noisy highway), this hostelry has 78 spacious rooms with all amenities including air conditioning and satellite television, as well as a good restaurant and convention facilities. 10 Padre Claret (phone: 424800; fax: 428446).

INEXPENSIVE

Plaza This very popular and very clean *hostal* has 28 rooms. All the doubles have complete private baths and telephones; some singles have only a sink, or a sink and shower. The *Mesón Don José María* restaurant (see *Eating Out*) is located next door. 11 Calle Cronista Lecea (phone: 431228).

EATING OUT

Segovia is a favorite spot for *madrileños* (residents of Madrid) to spend a Sunday and indulge in what is reported by many to be some of the finest *cochinillo* — roast suckling pig — in Castile. A *horno de asar* (roasting oven) sign outside announces a "roast" restaurant serving this specialty; so does the poor naked piglet on a platter that is usually displayed in the window. Expect such places to be crowded on weekends, even in low season. *Cochifrito,* a local variation of the pervasive suckling pig, is fried with garlic and parsley. Other local specialties include the hearty, flavorful *sopa castellana* (a soup of ham, paprika, bread, and poached eggs), *cordero asado* (roast lamb), and *ponche segoviano* (similar to a sweet pound cake). Dinner for two with wine will cost $45 to $70 in an expensive restaurant, $25 to $40 in a moderate one. All phone numbers are in the 11 area code unless otherwise indicated.

EXPENSIVE

Mesón de Cándido Located at the foot of the aqueduct, it's just as much an attraction for visitors, as evidenced by the photos of famous people who have dined here and the guestbooks with their autographs. This restaurant enjoys a well-deserved reputation throughout Spain for its good food and excellent service. The traditional dishes of Segovia, including *cochinillo,* are here, accompanied by a fine *Ribera del Duero* house wine. The building, with parts dating from the 15th century, has been classified as an official historic monument, and the restaurant, in operation since the 1860s, has walls adorned with hand-painted plates, copper pots, and other memorabilia. Open daily. Reservations advised on weekends. Major credit cards accepted. 5 Plaza del Azoguejo (phone: 425911).

Mesón Duque The sign outside still boasts of the Maestro Asador de Segovia (Segovia's Master Roaster) title won in 1895. Situated on a street running between the aqueduct and the Plaza Mayor, this is the *Mesón de Cándido*'s main competitor. Its ambience is classic Castilian, and it is noted for its *cochinillo, judiones de la Granja* (white bean stew), and various beef and veal dishes, although the quality of the food can be uneven. Open daily. Reservations advised on weekends. Major credit cards accepted. 12 Calle Cervantes (phone: 430537).

Parador de Segovia A cut above the quality of conventional *parador* cooking, this restaurant offers a fine view of Segovia to go along with the *sopa castellana,* sweetbreads, salmon, *merluza* (hake), *perdiz* (partridge), roast lamb, *cochinillo,* and fresh crayfish and trout from the Eresma River. Outside of town, 1¼ miles (2 km) along the road to Valladolid. Open daily. Reservations advised on weekends. Major credit cards accepted. Carretera de Valladolid (phone: 430462).

MODERATE

El Bernardino Another traditionally decorated place for sampling the Castilian mainstays, it has plates and paintings on the walls, a beamed ceiling, and a nice view over the city's rooftops. There are set menus in several reasonable price ranges. Open daily; closed in January. Reservations advised on weekends. No credit cards accepted. 2 Calle Cervantes (phone: 433225)

Casa Amado The decor is less elaborate than that of some other Segovia establishments, but the food surpasses the lackluster ambience. Besides the Castilian standards, specialties include many fine fish dishes and a memorable *cordero lechal al ajillo* (suckling lamb with garlic sauce). Good bread, fine flan (custard), and attentive service complete the picture. Closed Wednesdays and October. Reservations advised on weekends. No credit cards accepted. 9 Av. Fernández Ladreda (phone: 432077).

Mesón Don José María Segovia's most popular place for Sunday lunch and *tapas* throughout the week — with good reason: The food is extremely good, the service friendly, and the house wine a fine Ribera del Duero red. Besides *cochinillo* and *cochifrito,* specialties include *ancas de rana rebozadas* (breaded frogs' legs), homemade *morcilla* (blood sausage), and, for dessert, *pastel de frambuesa con nueces* (raspberry cream with walnuts). Open daily; closed November. Reservations advised for Sunday lunch, or go early. Major credit cards accepted. 11 Calle Cronista Lecea (phone: 434484).

Mesón Mayor This fine recent addition has become one of Segovia's best. Owner Fidel Diez González left *Mesón de Cándido* after 10 years, and created a cheerfully lit cellar restaurant (the dining room houses original Roman vaults) featuring first-rate local fare at reasonable prices. Open daily.

Reservations advised on weekends. Major credit cards accepted. 3 Plaza Mayor (phone: 428942).

La Oficina Serving fine, simple meat and fish dishes, this spot dates back to 1893, and is filled with paintings and memorabilia. Just off the Plaza Mayor, it's a good spot for lunch. Open daily. No reservations. Major credit cards accepted. 10 Cronista Lecea (phone: 431643).

Seville

Although Seville had no opera house until 1991, the city has been the stage for some of the world's most famous operatic heroes and heroines. Carmen, the barber of Seville, and Don Giovanni all played out their high drama in its winding alleys, secluded patios, jasmine-scented gardens, and fountain-filled plazas. And no one has ever taken down the set. Carmen's cigarette factory, Escamillo's bullring, the wrought-iron balconies where Don Juan trysted — even, some claim, the barbershop — are all still in place.

After Madrid, Barcelona, and Valencia, Seville, a university center with a population of 683,000, is Spain's fourth-largest city. Seville is also one of Spain's loveliest cities, and it works at preserving the fascinating Roman-Arabic-Judaic-Christian past that made it so. The city is the capital of the eight-province Autonomous Region of Andalusia, and Andalusian details are faithfully maintained on the traditional whitewashed buildings with gold trim. Golden sand (*alvero*) is trucked in 20 miles from the hills of Carmona to be used ornamentally in local gardens, and the famous Seville orange trees shade the town's tiled sidewalks. Restaurants, hotels, and shops lean to fanciful Moorish arabesque details, colored tiles, and white-walled beam-ceilinged interiors.

Beginning in spring, Seville (Sevilla in Spanish) lives in its streets. *Semana Santa* (Holy Week) fills them with 7 nights of religious pageantry. On its heels, the *Feria* (April Fair) is a week of nonstop revelry, and even after it's over, the fun goes on: Teenagers strum their guitars at café tables, the rattle of castanets sounds from around a corner, a group at the *tapas* bar breaks out in steady, syncopated flamenco clapping, and 10-year-old *señoritas* in brilliant polka-dot dresses dance the *sevillanas* in the plaza.

Yet much of the city sports a new look, thanks to the remarkably far-reaching changes wrought for *Expo '92,* the world's fair celebrating the 500th anniversary of Christopher Columbus's history-making voyage. The most extensive development is La Cartuja Island, which served as the site of the fair, and has been converted into a science theme park, and a business and technology complex. Seven new bridges cross the Guadalquivir River, linking the island to downtown Seville. Other improvements include several miles of a new, downtown riverfront esplanade, new railroad and bus stations, a new main terminal at Aeropuerto de San Pablo, and dramatically improved roads in and around the city and province. In addition to the *Maestranza Opera House,* Seville gained 22 new hotels, dozens of refurbished museums and other buildings, a vast new *Convention Center,* and cemented its status as a prime tourism destination.

Prized for its river, a 70-mile-long highway to the sea, Spain's only inland port city has been taken by the Romans, Phoenicians, Greeks, and Carthaginians. But the character of the city that is seen today dates largely from the 8th century, when the Moors crossed the Strait of Gibraltar to begin their fruitful 500-year reign. The city enjoyed a flourishing 100 years under the Almohads, Moorish conquerors who arrived in the mid-12th century and fostered an unprecedented climate of intellectual, artistic, and commercial cooperation among the resident communities of Christians, Arabs, and Jews. Expert engineers, they built up the port and repaired the city's fortifications; the outer walls of the Alcázar, the clean-lined Torre del Oro, and the lower portion of the Giralda Tower remain in testimony to their skill.

Though Seville fell to Ferdinand III in 1248, the Moorish influence continued for at least 2 centuries. It can be seen inside the Alcázar walls, in the ornate 14th-century palace of King Pedro el Cruel (Peter the Cruel), which was built by Mudéjar workmen (Moors who continued to live and work in Spain after the Christian conquest) using traditional Arab design.

Columbus's voyage to the New World was the beginning of Seville's most glorious period. The Catholic Monarchs, Ferdinand and Isabella, established their headquarters for New World exploration and trade in the Alcázar, and Columbus's return up the Guadalquivir inspired successful trips by Ferdinand Magellan and Amerigo Vespucci, who sailed out from the Torre del Oro. The golden age of Seville was under way — though not for the city's ill-fated Jews, who were forcibly converted, slain, or driven from their homes in the Judería (the present Barrio de Santa Cruz) by the Spanish Inquisition.

During the 16th and 17th centuries, Seville was the richest and most powerful city in Spain, filled with Renaissance palaces, churches, and monasteries decorated with frescoes and paintings by native sons Bartolomé Esteban Murillo and Juan de Valdés Leal and by adopted son Francisco de Zurbarán, who was born in a village nearby. (Seville-born Diego Velázquez left early for the court in Madrid, and his hometown is seriously deficient in his works.) Ironically, the river that earned the city its earlier acclaim was the same conduit that would turn its economic tides. With the gradual silting up of the Guadalquivir, and navigation from Córdoba impaired, the city's fortunes turned down sharply, and Cádiz, perched on the Atlantic, took over Seville's lucrative trade.

Today, with the river long since restored to its original course, Seville is again a major port, shipping minerals, manufactured goods, and agricultural products. In the wake of *Expo '92,* Seville is better than ever. Once you've been here, you'll agree, *"Quien no ha visto Sevilla no ha visto maravilla"* — He who has not seen Seville has never seen a wonder.

Seville At-a-Glance

SEEING THE CITY

The core of Seville sprawls along the east bank of the Guadalquivir River. The most breathtaking city view and best orientation point is from the top of the Giralda Tower, 307.8 feet high. Abutting the cathedral, La Giralda is as symbolic of Seville as the Eiffel Tower is of Paris. Enter at the Plaza Virgen de los Reyes.

SPECIAL PLACES

Visitors to Seville spend most of their time on the east bank of the river in the compact area of an Old Town that once huddled inside the city walls. Most touristic highlights are concentrated around or between the city's two most central bridges, the mid–19th-century Eiffel-esque Isabel II Bridge, commonly known as El Puente de Triana, and the San Telmo Bridge to the south. Closer to the former are the old *Maestranza* bullring, the *Maestranza Opera House,* downtown shopping streets, and the recently refurbished *Museo de Bellas Artes* (Museum of Fine Arts). Near the San Telmo Bridge are María Luisa Park, the university, and the Torre del Oro. Clustered in the middle, a few blocks inland, are Seville's four greatest treasures: the cathedral, the adjoining Giralda Tower, the Alcázar, and the winding streets of the Barrio de Santa Cruz.

Across the Guadalquivir, on the west bank, is the Barrio de Triana, a working class district with its own colorful personality. Once a Gypsy haven, it still resounds with flamenco music from *tabernas* (dance studios), even in special evening masses at the San Jacinto church. Countless *sevillanas* lyrics sing praise to Triana.

North of the Triana Bridge are motor-vehicle and pedestrian-only bridges crossing the river to La Cartuja Island.

Public attractions are open from 9:30 or 10 AM to 1:30 or 2 PM and from around 4 or 5 PM to 7 or 8 PM; some hours change with the seasons. Museums tend to be open mornings only; closing days tend to be Sundays or Mondays. Check with the tourist office (see *Tourist Information*) for the most up-to-date hours. Many places close during July and August.

WARNING In recent years, Seville has experienced a wave of pickpocketing and purse snatching, usually by gangs of youths from the suburbs. Women should keep money in an inside pocket, not a purse. Men should keep track of their wallets. Never put purses down in a café or on the seat of the car beside you, and never leave anything valuable in a parked car. Exercise caution around the Gypsies outside the cathedral. Many simply want to charge outrageous sums to tell your fortune, but others will distract you with chatter and jostling while an accomplice goes to work on your wallet. Crimes against foreigners here are usually for profit, however, not bodily harm.

CITY CENTER

REALES ALCÁZARES (ALCÁZAR, OR ROYAL PALACE) For all their furor against the Moors, the Spanish monarchs recognized the Moorish talent for palaces.

This delicate Mudéjar creation boasts the work of Moorish craftsmen left unexpelled after Seville was reconquered in the 13th century. A favorite of Spanish royalty, it was begun in the 14th century by King Peter the Cruel and later expanded by Ferdinand and Isabella and by the Holy Roman Emperor Charles V. The lavish interior, similar to Granada's Alhambra but on a smaller scale, is full of mosaics, patios, wrought-stucco windows, and finely tooled ceilings. However, unlike the Alhambra, which deteriorated during years of abandonment and has required massive restoration, the Alcázar compound was maintained by Spanish royalty, who used it as a residence into this century, adding upper stories and new wings.

The best way to see the palace is to wander through the clusters of courtyards and chambers, with their lacy plaster decoration, dazzling carved-wood ceilings, and graceful Arabic script of verses from the Koran. The colonnaded Patio de las Doncellas (Court of the Maidens), with its multi-lobed arches resting on sets of twin marble columns, is a good place to start. This was the center of official palace life and it leads to the great, square Salón de Embajadores (Ambassadors' Hall), where Charles V was wed to Isabella of Portugal. Not to be missed is the graceful Puerta de los Pavones (Peacock Arch), a surprising note, since Moorish designs rarely portrayed animals. Among the dozens of other splendid royal rooms, a universal favorite is the Patio de las Muñecas (Dolls' Court), which was the hub of the palace's living quarters; to ensure privacy, only blind musicians played here.

The Patio de la Montería, Queen Isabella's 15th-century addition, houses the Cuarto del Almirante (Admiral's Apartment), where she established the Casa de Contratación, headquarters for New World exploration and commerce. The austere rooms hold such New World mementos as a model of the *Santa María* and 15th-century navigators' maps. Another wing, added by Charles V, is accessible through Pedro's palace. Filled with an exceptional series of Flemish tapestries woven with silk, gold, and wool, chronicling the Holy Roman Emperor's triumphs in his Tunisian campaign of 1535, it's also the wing that leads to the overgrown palace gardens, a sight straight out of the Arabian Nights (see below). The Alcázar is open Tuesdays through Saturdays from 10:30 AM to 5:30 PM, Sundays and holidays from 10:30 AM to 1:30 PM. Admission charge. Plaza del Triunfo (phone: 421-4971).

JARDINES DEL ALCÁZAR (ALCÁZAR GARDENS) Moorish, Renaissance, and modern gardens are all part of the Alcázar complex. There's a choice of paths through flower-filled plots past the Charles V Pavilion and an orange tree supposed to have been in existence in Pedro's day, to a myrtlewood maze, palm groves, rose gardens, and a fountain where ducklings bathe. Hours are the same as for the Alcázar, above, and the admission charge to the Alcázar includes the gardens.

PLAZA DE TOROS DE LA REAL MAESTRANZA DE CABALLERÍA (BULLRING) The giant crimson door of Seville's bullring swings open on *Easter Sunday* to begin the bullfighting season, which runs until October. The Spanish spectacle of the corrida, or bullfight, is quintessentially Andalusian — modern bullfighting began in the Andalusian town of Ronda, near Seville, in the 18th century — and while the bullring in Madrid may be larger, Seville's *Maestranza*, built in the 1760s, is more beautiful. An appearance here is a must for all of the world's greatest matadors. The corridas are held sporadically on Sunday and holiday afternoons at 6:30 PM (daily during the *Feria*); check with the tourist office. In peak season, tickets range from about $25 in the sun to $150 in full shade (remember, the summer sun is still blazing at 7 PM in the south of Spain), and should be bought well in advance at the ring, at the *Agencia Teatral* (phone: 422-8229), or in bars along Calle Sierpes. Both the ring and its small museum are open Mondays through Saturdays from 10 AM to 1:30 PM; admission charge. 12 Calle Velázquez, Paseo de Colón (phone: 422-3506).

CATHEDRAL It is somehow symbolic of Spain's religious history that her largest cathedral should be squeezed between a Moorish Alcázar and a once Arab and Jewish neighborhood renamed for the Holy Cross, and that its bell tower should be a dressed-up minaret.

The cathedral was begun in 1402 as a grandiose symbol of Christian Seville at a time when Granada was still in Muslim hands (and would be for another 90 years). The Great Mosque of the Almohads, on the same site, was demolished, but its most exquisite minaret (the present Giralda Tower; see below) was saved to become the cathedral's spire. Built to be so large that "those who come after us will take us for madmen," Seville's cathedral is the third-largest Christian church in Europe after St. Peter's Basilica in Rome and St. Paul's Cathedral in London. Three hundred feet long, 250 feet wide, and 184 feet high, the building has three carved, arched portals — but not the soaring façade that might be expected. Go around to the Plaza del Triunfo visitors' entrance. There, at the south transept, stands the 19th-century tomb of Christopher Columbus (however, at least two other countries also claim to be the explorer's final resting place).

The enormous sweep of the cathedral is hard to appreciate because bulky choir stalls and a soaring Capilla Mayor (Main Chapel) block the center aisle, and the Flemish stained glass windows are set so high that their light barely penetrates the shadows. A magnificent three-sided gold *reja* (grille) encloses the chancel and its 70-foot-high carved wooden *retablo* (altarpiece), the largest in Spain. At the apse stands the domed 16th-century Capilla Royal (Royal Chapel) with a *reja* showing Ferdinand III, conqueror of Seville and later sainted, receiving the keys to the city. His well-preserved body, displayed to the public on the *Feast of San Fernando* (May 30) and on the anniversary of the day he reconquered the city from the Moors (November 23), lies in a silver tomb at the foot of the statue of the city's patron saint, the Virgen de los Reyes, or Virgin of the Kings. King Pedro and his mistress, María de Padilla, are in a crypt below the chapel.

Masterpieces by Murillo, Valdés Leal, Zurbarán, and Jacob Jordaens are in the badly lit St. Anthony Chapel. Two more Murillos are in the treasure rooms of the Sacristía Mayor (Vestry) along with the crown, studded with more than 1,000 colored stones, that is worn by the Virgen de los Reyes for her procession on August 15. Also in the vestry are a 650-pound silver monstrance, which is carried in the *Corpus Christi Day* procession, and a cross said to have been made from the first gold Columbus brought back from the New World. Murillo's *Holy Family* and works by Leal, Zurbarán, Titian, and Goya are in the Sacristía de los Calices (Chalice Vestry), and Murillo's *Immaculate Conception* is in the oval Sala Capitular (Chapter House). On the north side of the cathedral is the Patio de los Naranjos (Orange Tree Court) with remnants of the original fountain of ablutions and the bronze-sheathed Puerta del Perdón (Door of Forgiveness) from the Great Mosque. Open Mondays through Saturdays from 10 AM to 6 PM, Sundays from 2 to 4 PM. Admission charge. Plaza del Triunfo.

LA GIRALDA (GIRALDA TOWER) On a clear day, it's possible to see the olive groves around Seville in a 360-degree view from this 20-story bell tower, the same one from which the muezzin called the faithful to prayer when it was the minaret of the Great Mosque. Its ingenious *sebka* rhomboid brick patterning so pleased the Christians that they spared the tower and used it for their new cathedral. The four huge golden spheres, called the Apples of Yanmur, with which the Almohads had topped their tower in the 12th century, are no longer extant. Instead, the 307.8-foot tower is topped with a belfry, lantern, and an almost 12-foot-high revolving statue representing the Faith, all additions of the 16th century. The statue, known locally as the *Giraldillo,* serves as a weather vane (*giralda* in Spanish, hence the name of the tower). There's no elevator, but the climb is easy, via 35 inclined ramps and some stairs, designed to be ridden up easily on horseback. Windows along the way present gargoyle-framed previews of the full panorama. The towering Giralda is visible from all over Seville, and is brilliantly illuminated at night. Hours are the same as for the cathedral, above, and the admission charge to the cathedral includes La Giralda.

BARRIO DE SANTA CRUZ (SANTA CRUZ QUARTER) Hugging the walls of the Alcázar is the old Jewish quarter, or Judería, a medieval neighborhood of narrow, winding streets, handkerchief-size plazas dotted with café tables, whitewashed houses dressed with wrought-iron balconies and geraniums, and flower-filled patios behind fanciful gates. Seville's Jewish community flourished here for generations under the Moors but vanished in the 15th century after the Inquisition. Later the area became the playground of the aristocracy, and today it still attracts the Spanish well-to-do. One convenient way to begin a tour is by turning right upon leaving the Patio de Banderas at the exit of the Alcázar and walk up Romero Murube. Turn right again at the Plaza de la Alianza and head up Calle Rodrigo Caro into the lovely pebble-paved Plaza de Doña Elvira, where there are inviting benches under the orange trees. From here, any street will lead to one or another of the barrio's loveliest places.

CASA DE MURILLO (MURILLO'S HOUSE) Seville's favorite son lived his last years in this typical old Barrio de Santa Cruz house, now furnished with period pieces (not Murillo's own) and five of his lesser paintings. The visit is especially interesting if the caretaker has time to take you around. Open Mondays through Fridays from 10 AM to 2 PM; open later for special exhibitions. No admission charge. 8 Calle de Santa Teresa (phone: 421-7535).

HOSPITAL DE LA CARIDAD (CHARITY HOSPITAL) The man who founded this 17th-century baroque masterpiece was the model for Don Juan. Saddened by the death of his wife or repentant over past peccadilloes, the aristocratic Miguel de Mañara became a monk and used his wealth to build this hospital for the indigent. It's now a home for the elderly poor, and residents can still be seen taking their ease among the tropical plants in the ocher- and rose-walled patios. De Mañara also financed the adjoining church, San Jorge, worthy of a visit for its rich ornamentation, including great golden twisted columns before the altar, and for its trove of Murillos and Valdés Leals. Open Mondays through Saturdays from 10 AM to 1 PM and from 3:30 to 6 PM, Sundays and holidays from 10 AM to 12:30 PM. Admission charge. Near the Torre del Oro. 3 Calle Temprado (phone: 422-3232).

TORRE DEL ORO (TOWER OF GOLD) Seville's most romantic symbol, on the banks of the Guadalquivir, was once one of 64 defensive towers built along the city wall (remnants of the wall can be seen near the Basílica de la Macarena, in the northeast section of town). Dating from 1220, its clean lines are typical of the simple but forceful Almohad style that produced the Alcázar walls and the Giralda. The tower is 12-sided and was originally faced with ceramic tiles finished in gold, an Andalusian specialty. The tiles have disappeared, but when it's illuminated at night, the Torre del Oro still glows. The tower contains a small maritime museum and provides a nice view. Open Tuesdays through Fridays from 10 AM to 2 PM, weekends from 10 AM to 1 PM. Closed Mondays and holidays. Admission charge. Paseo de Colón (phone: 422-2419).

ARCHIVO GENERAL DE INDIAS (ARCHIVE OF THE INDIES) Juan de Herrera, the same architect who planned the 16th-century Escorial monastery near Madrid for Philip II, designed this building to house the old Lonja (Stock Exchange). In the 1660s, the building housed the Seville Academy, the art academy founded largely by Murillo. Today it's the repository of documents on Spain's role in New World exploration, conquest, and commerce. A majestic red marble stairway leads to a great gallery where there are 43,000 cardboard files filled with an estimated 80 million original documents. Some 400,000 priceless papers, which include correspondence between Columbus and Queen Isabella, are locked away in air conditioned storage. Only researchers with university credentials may examine the documents, but anyone will get the idea from the displays of drawings, charts, letters, account books, and royal decrees. Open Mondays through Fridays from 10 AM to 1 PM for visitors; 8 AM to 3 PM for researchers; closed weekends and holidays. Between the cathedral and the Alcázar. Av. de la Constitución (phone: 421-1234).

PLAZA NUEVA Seville's central city square is fronted by the block-long Renaissance Ayuntamiento (City Hall). A bronze statue of Ferdinand III on horseback stands at its center. North of the cathedral on Avenida de la Constitución.

LA MAESTRANZA OPERA HOUSE Over the years, Seville's winding alleys, romantic patios, graceful plazas, and gardens heady with the scent of jasmine have served as the inspiration for some of the world's best-loved operas — from Rossini's *Barber of Seville,* Verdi's *La Forza del Destino,* and Mozart's *Marriage of Figaro* and *Don Giovanni* to Beethoven's *Fidelio* and Bizet's *Carmen.* It was not until 1991 that Seville got an opera house of its own. Now considered one of the world's premier venues of its kind, it hosts world class operatic performances (with an emphasis on the obligatory Seville-inspired works), as well as quintessentially Spanish *zarzuelas* (light opera), classical music, and jazz. 5 Nuñes de Balboa (phone: 422-3344).

MUSEO DE BELLAS ARTES (FINE ARTS MUSEUM) Still farther north, near the Plaza de Armas, this recently renovated museum has a collection of international art from the 16th through the 20th centuries that is second in Spain only to that of the *Prado* in Madrid. There's an especially fine selection of paintings by Murillo, Zurbarán, Valdés Leal, and other Spanish artists. It is housed in the 17th-century baroque Convent of La Merced, whose patios, cloisters, and chapel are works of art in themselves. Open Tuesdays through Sundays from 9:30 AM to 3 PM. Admission charge. 9 Plaza del Museo (phone: 422-0790).

UNIVERSIDAD DE SEVILLA (UNIVERSITY OF SEVILLE) The monumental Royal Tobacco Factory that Bizet used as the setting for the first act of his opera *Carmen* has been part of the University of Seville since the 1950s. It's the largest building in Spain after the Escorial. Look for carved bas reliefs at the main entrances, and walk through some of the vast graffiti-covered halls and courtyards for a view of contemporary student life. Just south of the *Alfonso XIII* hotel. Calle San Fernando.

PARQUE DE MARÍA LUISA (MARÍA LUISA PARK) The San Telmo Palace, whose colorful baroque façade can be seen behind the *Alfonso XIII* hotel, was built as a naval college and now is used as a seminary. During the 19th century, however, it belonged to María Luisa, sister of Queen Isabella II, and the present María Luisa Park, the Bois de Boulogne of Seville, was the palace grounds. This swanky park and elegant plaza out of some fairy-tale colonial city were given to Seville in the early 1900s, and the extravagant buildings in it were built for the 1929 *Iberoamerican Exposition.* In summer, all Seville strolls the park's long, forested allées. Av. de la Constitución.

PLAZA DE ESPAÑA Practically at the entrance to María Luisa Park, along Avenida Isabel la Católica, is a grandiose, semicircular plaza surrounded by a Renaissance-style government office complex, originally built for the 1929 exposition. Twin baroque towers, ornate lampposts, and bridges with blue and white terra cotta balustrades make the Plaza de España look like a Mexican fantasy of Venice. The canal that follows the semicircle of the plaza is so long that rowboats can be rented for mini-excursions. Take time to walk over the canal's beautiful all-tile bridges and to browse the alcoves set into the curving plaza wall. Each highlights one of Spain's 50 provinces with a lively tiled mural.

PLAZA DE AMÉRICA At the far end of the park, in a beautifully laid-out area of palm-shaded terraces, rose gardens, lily ponds, and splashing fountains, stand three more stunning buildings left from the exposition. The one in the center houses Andalusia's government headquarters; the other two are the *Museo Arqueológico* (see below) and the *Museo de Arte y Costumbres Populares,* a folk museum with exhibits of regional life (open Tuesdays through Saturdays from 10 AM to 2:30 PM; closed Sundays and Mondays; admission charge; phone: 423-2576). Parque María Luisa.

MUSEO ARQUEOLÓGICO (ARCHAEOLOGICAL MUSEUM) This museum, in a Plateresque-style exposition building, contains a definitive collection of artifacts from excavations in western Andalusia. Don't miss the Roman section, which has statues, jewelry, and coins found in the ruins of the ancient city of Itálica (see below), just outside Seville. Open Tuesdays through Sundays from 10 AM to 2 PM. Admission charge. Plaza de América (phone: 423-2401).

CASA DE PILATOS (HOUSE OF PILATE) A trip to this 16th-century mansion, the last of the great private houses in Seville open to visitors, is an entrée to the splendid lifestyle of an Andalusian nobleman of days long past. The Marqués de Tarifa, who finished it in 1540, is supposed to have been inspired by the house of the Roman emperor in Jerusalem, but his architects didn't spare Mudéjar, Plateresque, and Gothic glories. The ceiling of the grand staircase has been compared to the Alcázar and the tiled walls and patios are sensational. There's also a collection of Roman sculpture. Open daily from 9 AM to 6 PM. Admission charge. In the ancient San Esteban eastern part of town. 1 Plaza de Pilatos (phone: 422-5298).

LA CARTUJA ISLAND

The site of *Expo '92,* Cartuja Island is now one of Seville's permanent attractions. Before the advent of the exposition, this barren island was inhabited only by the 15th-century Carthusian Monastery of Santa María de las Cuevas — where Christopher Columbus lived and prepared for his voyages — and the adjacent 19th-century ceramics factory. Both were impeccably restored to become the lavish Royal Pavilion of Spain, which is being turned into a museum. Two-thirds of the 98 pavilions and other buildings erected for *Expo '92* remain. Perhaps the island's biggest draw is an interactive science theme park, similar to Epcot Center at Florida's Walt Disney World. There are also high-tech industrial parks, which house multinational corporations, a monorail, and track and rowing facilities. Plans are being developed for a new soccer stadium on the northern end of the island.

Located in the Guadalquivir River, just "offshore" from northern downtown Seville, La Cartuja Island is easily accessible from downtown Seville via the Puente de la Cartuja pedestrian bridge at Plaza de Armas. A newer pedestrian bridge, La Barqueta, is farther up the river in the northern part of the city. Motor vehicles can cross on the Calatrava, the Chapina, and other bridges. For up-to-the-minute information on La Cartuja Island and the status of its attractions, inquire at the tourist office.

ENVIRONS

ITÁLICA The impressive ruins of this Roman city, founded at the end of the 3rd century BC by the Roman general Scipio Africanus, are about 5 miles (8 km) northwest of Seville, just outside the town of Santiponce. The birthplace of Hadrian and Trajan, its main attraction is the colossal amphitheater, said to have held 25,000 spectators. The site has been completely excavated, revealing largely intact mosaic floors, baths, and temple remains. There's a museum, although major finds are in Seville's *Museo Arqueológico.* The Roman amphitheater is used as a stage for dance festivals. When special events are not scheduled, the site is open Tuesdays through Saturdays from 9 AM to 6:30 PM, Sundays from 9 AM to 3 PM in April through September; Tuesdays through Saturdays from 9 AM to 5:30 PM, Sundays from 10 AM to 4 PM during the rest of the year. Admission charge. Buses leave every 30 minutes from the Plaza de Armas bus station.

Sources and Resources

TOURIST INFORMATION

The regional Oficina de Información de Turismo (Tourist Information Office; 21B Av. de la Constitución; phone: 422-1404), conveniently located near the cathedral and endowed with an enthusiastic, multilingual staff, is open Mondays through Fridays from 9:30 AM to 7:30 PM, until 8 PM on Saturdays, and from 10 AM to 8 PM on Sundays. Useful maps and informative brochures are available in English, free of charge. (Worth having is the easy-to-follow city map available free at *El Corte Inglés,* the big department store on Plaza del Duque; there's another branch on Calle Luis

Montoto, near the Santa Justa train station.) A get-acquainted bus tour of the city isn't a bad idea. Half-day motorcoach city tours, and excursions to surrounding sights, can be arranged through any of several travel agencies or your hotel concierge. For a licensed private guide, call *Guidetour de Sevilla* (phone: 422-2375) or ask at the tourist office.

The US Consulate is at 7 Paseo de las Delicias (phone: 423-1885).

LOCAL COVERAGE Daily newspapers widely read in Seville are *El Correo de Andalucía* and provincial editions of the daily *ABC* and *El País*. Visitors rely on *El Giraldillo,* a free monthly guide to upcoming events, available in several languages and distributed in shops and hotels, as well as at the tourist office. The weekly *Guía del Ocio* leisure magazine has information on art, entertainment, dining, and nightlife in Spanish, but the names and addresses are easy to understand.

TELEPHONE

The area code for Seville is 5. If calling from another part of Spain, dial "9" before the area code and local number. Note that all Seville phone numbers now have seven digits and begin with a "4". Many brochures and other printed materials still give old numbers with only six digits; to convert these to the new system, simply preface them with a "4".

GETTING AROUND

It's possible to walk almost anywhere in the city, but the summer heat and the duration of most tourist visits, too short for a leisurely pace, may make other modes of transportation desirable.

AIRPORT Seville's Aeropuerto de San Pablo (phone: 451-0677) is 8 miles (13 km) from town. There is frequent airport bus service; from downtown, buses leave for the airport from the Puerta de Jerez, next to the *Alfonso XIII* hotel, at 6:30, 7:30, and 8:30 AM and every half hour thereafter until 9:30 PM (phone: 442-0011). Cab fare for the 20-minute ride should be around $15.

BUS Bright orange buses go everywhere in the city. Pick up a route map at the tourist office or in front of the *Inglaterra* hotel in Plaza Nueva, where city routes begin. Fare is 100 pesetas (about $1 — exact change not required); discounted 10-trip tickets, which cost 450 pesetas (about $4.50), are available in Plaza Nueva and at kiosks elsewhere. The tourist office also has schedules of intercity buses, which leave from two stations (be sure to ask which you'll be using): the new Plaza de Armas station (on the river next to the Cahorro Bridge; phone: 490-8040), or Prado de San Sebastián station (1 Prado de San Sebastián; phone: 441-7111).

CAR RENTAL International rental companies represented include *Avis* (15 Av. de la Constitución; phone: 421-6549; and at the airport); *Europcar* (32 Calle

Recaredo; phone: 441-9506; and at the airport); and *Hertz* (3 Av. Repúb-lica Argentina; phone: 427-8887; and at the airport).

HORSE AND CARRIAGE A delightful way to see the city. During the *Feria,* even the locals do it. Rates, regulated by the city, run about $30 per hour, up to $60 during the *Feria.* Choose your *coche caballo* from the lineup around the cathedral square or at María Luisa Park.

TAXI Since distances are short, fares in town average under $6. Drivers legiti-mately charge extra for bigger pieces of luggage and for travel after 10 PM and on holidays. Hail cabs on the street or call *Radio-Taxi* (phone: 458-0000) or *Tele-Taxi* (phone: 462-2222).

TRAIN The state-of-the-art Santa Justa train station, designed for *Expo '92* and for the 21st century, is located on Avenida Kansas City (Seville's US sister city boasts a replica of La Giralda). A generally expanded and speedier rail network now radiates from Seville all across the peninsula. *RENFE*'s high-speed bullet trains now zoom between Seville and Madrid in 2½ hours. Seville's famous neo-Mudéjar Plaza de Armas building was the Córdoba train station until 1990. Although it's still called *Estación de Córdoba*, it now houses offices and an important art exhibition center. Schedules and tickets can be obtained from the *RENFE* office (29 Calle Zaragoza; phone: 441-4111), near Plaza Nueva, at the Santa Justa train station, and at some travel agencies.

SPECIAL EVENTS

Two world-famous festivals make springtime prime time in Seville. The city is mobbed for both events, with hotels booked a year in advance, restaurant tables at a premium, and rates for horse and carriage rides doubled.

BEST FESTIVALS

Semana Santa (Holy Week) Perhaps one of Seville's most popular fiestas is *Holy Week,* a 7-day celebration that begins on *Palm Sunday* and lasts through *Easter Sunday.* The week is highlighted by some of the most colorful floats around (guaranteed to dazzle even the most weary paradegoer), as well as rows and rows of masked paraders prancing through the streets.

Feria de Abril (April Fair) Two weeks after *Holy Week, Feria,* which began in the mid-19th century as a rural livestock market, dominates the city. Andalusia's high-stepping horses, in tassels and bells, go through their paces, and brightly costumed groups parade around town in flower-decked coaches. There are nightly corridas, fireworks, amusements, and danc-ing — mainly *sevillanas* — in the streets.

MUSEUMS

Most of the museums of interest to visitors are discussed in *Special Places*. In addition, Seville has the *Museo de Arte Contemporáneo* (5 Calle Santo Tomás; phone: 421-5830), a repository of Spanish art of the 20th century in an 18th-century building. It's open Tuesdays through Fridays from 10 PM to 7 PM, and Saturdays and Sundays from 10 AM to 2 PM. Admission charge.

SHOPPING

Anyone looking for the bargains of a few years back will do better shopping at home, but if you covet a gorgeous hand-embroidered, silk-fringed shawl, you've come to the right place. Seville has Andalusia's largest selection of mantillas, fans, hand-embroidered linen and shawls (if prices sound too low, make sure it's not machine embroidery), flamenco dresses, castanets, and guitars. Plenty of the above can be found in colorful shops around the cathedral and in the Barrio de Santa Cruz. For more, plus shoes and handbags, go downtown, and don't miss Calle Sierpes. Seville's favorite pedestrian street, tiled in rose and blue, winds downtown for about 5 blocks between Plaza de San Francisco, behind the Ayuntamiento, and Plaza la Campana, an intersection of several streets near Plaza del Duque (some maps give its full name, Plaza del Duque de la Victoria). Nearby are tiny Calle Rosario and Calle Muñoz Olive, lined with boutiques selling Italian and French fashions. Seville's two big downtown department stores, *El Corte Inglés* (two locations: Plaza del Duque, and Calle Luis Montoto, near the Santa Justa train station) and *Galerías Preciados* (Plaza de la Magdalena), are good fallback stops because they don't close for siesta — and they're good bets for a quick, inexpensive lunch.

Seville's antiques shops are among Spain's best. Plaza del Cabildo houses antiques shops such as *Antigüedades Lola Ortega* (Plaza del Cabildo; phone: 421-8771). Also try *Segundo Antigüedades* (89 Calle Sierpes; phone: 422-5652) and the shops along Calle Placentines. Every April, one of Spain's best antique fairs takes place in Seville. For information, call *Asociación de Anticuarios,* 7 Calle Rodrigo Caro (phone: 95-421-6558).

The city's biggest outdoor market sets up its stalls from 10 AM to 2 PM every Sunday along Alameda de Hércules. This is the place for crafts, costume jewelry, antiques, and novelty items. The Plaza del Cabildo (opposite the cathedral) hosts a coin and stamp mart every Sunday from about 10 AM to 2 PM.

In addition, a leather crafts and jewelry fair takes place daily except Sundays on Plaza del Duque opposite *El Corte Inglés*. The picturesque Triana food market occupies tumbledown stalls under the Triana Bridge across the river, and the indoor *El Arenal* food market is near the bullring at Calle Pastor y Landero (both markets are open mornings and closed Sundays). Other possibilities:

LA ALCAZABA Delicate hand-painted ceramic tiles and platters from Seville and other regions, including the lovely florals from Valencia. Near the Alcázar exit. 1A Calle Joaquín Romero Murube (phone: 421-8088).

ARTESANÍA TEXTIL Mantillas, silk shawls, embroidered linen, fans, and everyday leather coats and jackets for men and women, sold in a factory-to-customer atmosphere near Plaza del Cabildo. 33 Calle García de Vinuesa (phone: 422-1606). Also in the Barrio de Santa Cruz at 4 Plaza de Doña Elvira (phone: 421-4748).

ARTESPAÑA Part of the Spain-wide, government-sponsored chain, selling arts and crafts from all over the country — and they pack and ship. Near *El Corte Inglés*. 2 Plaza de la Gavidia (phone: 422-1865).

EL CABALLO Andalusian horsemen come to this shop near the bullring for the finest leather riding boots, saddles, traditional riding suits, and flat, wide-brimmed hats. 14 Calle Adriano (phone: 422-2047).

CASA RUBIO Exquisite lacy, hand-painted fans. 56 Calle Sierpes (phone: 422-6872).

CERÁMICA SANTA ANA A large selection of ceramics at good prices. In Triana. 31 Calle San Jorge (phone: 433-3990).

CERVANTES One of Spain's largest general bookstores. There is sure to be a title on one of its 7 floors for any who wish to spend an afternoon browsing. 5 Calle Azafranal (phone: 422-9328).

CONVENTO DE SAN LEANDRO Authentic *yemas* (dainty sweets of egg yolk and sugar) made by the resident nuns. Near the Casa de Pilatos. 1 Plaza de San Ildefonso (phone: 422-4195).

JUAN FERONDA Mantillas, shawls, flamenco dresses, linen; several stores, but the best selection is at the one near La Giralda. 18 Calle Argote de Molina (phone: 422-8467).

LOEWE The ultimate in luxury leather (women's handbags begin at around $350), wallets, attaché cases, luggage, and couture by a fifth-generation Madrid firm, with some items up to 30% less than at US branches. 12 Plaza Nueva (phone: 422-5253) and at the *Alfonso XIII* hotel (phone: 422-1371).

MARTIAN Hand-painted ceramics of the highest quality. 74 Calle Sierpes (phone: 421-3413).

EL POSTIGO ARTESANÍA A group of boutiques in a 3-story arcade; made-to-measure flamenco dresses, religious art, antiques, contemporary jewelry, ceramics, paintings, and leather goods are sold. Calle Arfe at Plaza del Cabildo (phone: 421-3976).

SPORTS AND FITNESS

Several sports facilities, including track and rowing centers, were built on La Cartuja Island for *Expo '92,* and are expected to be opened to the public. Check with the tourist office.

BOATING Clubs along the right bank of the Guadalquivir, including *El Náutico* (phone: 445-4777), offer facilities for sailing, rowing, and canoeing. Also look for the "Barcos" sign along the river in the vicinity of Plaza de Cuba.

BULLFIGHTING The *Maestranza* bullring is the setting for Seville's bullfights. The season opens on *Easter Sunday* and runs until mid-October. See *Special Places* for ticket information.

HORSE RACING Seville's racetrack is the *Hipódromo del Club Pineda* (Av. de Jerez; phone: 461-1400). The club offers horseback riding facilities and instruction, a 9-hole golf course, and a swimming pool. Races take place on Sundays from October through February or March.

JOGGING María Luisa Park in the cool of the morning is the place to run.

SOCCER The city's two teams are *El Betis,* based at the *Benito Villamarín* stadium (phone: 461-0340), and *Sevilla,* which plays at the *Sánchez Pizjuán* stadium (phone: 457-5750). The season runs from September to the beginning of May.

SWIMMING The *Alfonso XIII, Doña María,* and other hotels have pools; if yours doesn't, try the *Municipales Chapina* (Av. Cristo de la Expiración; phone: 433-3654), one of several municipal pools in town.

TENNIS Hotel concierges sometimes can arrange guest sessions at private tennis facilities such as the *Betis Tennis Club,* Calle San Salvador (phone: 423-1028).

THEATER AND MUSIC

The refurbished *Lope de Vega Theater* (Av. María Luisa Park; phone: 423-1835), originally built for the 1929 *Iberoamerican Exposition,* features international theatrical works. For opera buffs, the riverside *Teatro de la Maestranza* (5 Nuñes de Balboa; phone: 422-3344) is considered one of Europe's best opera houses. Among its offerings are a host of Seville-inspired works — Rossini's *The Barber of Seville,* Verdi's *La Forza del Destino,* Beethoven's *Fidelio,* Donizetti's *La Favorita,* Mozart's *Marriage of Figaro* and *Don Giovanni* — as well as quintessentially Spanish *zarzuelas,* classical music, and jazz.

NIGHTCLUBS AND NIGHTLIFE

Seville keeps the flamenco flame burning nightly in rousing song and dance cabarets called *tablaos,* even more authentic than those of Madrid, especially since flamenco is Andalusian. The *tablao's* handful of dancers, guitarists, and singers run through a repertoire of stylized songs and dances that express Gypsy sorrows, loves, and joys. Tickets, which can usually be reserved through hotels, cost around $35, one glass of wine included; depending on the season, there are two or three shows a night. *Los Gallos* (11 Plaza de Santa Cruz; phone: 421-6981), a romantic little theater in the Barrio de Santa Cruz, has a well-known troupe. *El Arenal* (7 Calle Rodo; phone: 421-6492), in a cobbled alley near the river, puts on an authentic *tablao* and also offers a dinner show for about $45. *El Patio Sevillano* (11 Paseo de Cristóbal Colón; phone: 421-4120) has a program that includes flamenco, folk dance, and classical guitar. Do-it-yourself flamenco can be sampled by joining the locals on the floor of one of the *sevillanas* discos called *salas rocieras* on the Barrio de los Remedios's earthy Calle Salado. (*Sevillanas* is the city's own folk dance, related to flamenco.) Go after 1 AM, when the young crowd begins warming up to dance at *Canela Pura,* a modest storefront pub (9 Calle Salado), or drop in at nearby *Tres Faroles* (8A Calle Salado), or at *La Garrocha* (11 Calle Salado).

For a change of pace, spend an evening in the little Euro-style bars, pubs, and outdoor cafés between Calle Virgen de Africa and Calle Virgen de las Montañas near *La Dorada* restaurant in Los Remedios. For international disco, the action is at *Holiday* (downtown at 73 Calle Jesús del Gran Poder, in the former red-light district; phone: 437-9655); *El Coto* (in the *Lebreros Hotel,* 118 Calle Luis Montoto; phone: 457-9400); or *Río* (Calle Betis; phone: 427-4194), a large club, on a block where there are numerous riverside clubs. Go late.

Best in Town

CHECKING IN

As the capital of Andalusia, Seville attracts business and government travelers as well as tourists, so there's a wide selection of hotels. Rates usually are lowest during the hot summer months, when Spaniards are taking their own vacations at the beach. Prices are much higher during *Semana Santa* and the *Feria;* however, prices have abated since *Expo '92,* and the abundance of hotels makes for competitive rates. Unless otherwise noted, all our choices are within reasonable walking distance of the central area including the cathedral, Alcázar, and the Barrio de Santa Cruz, and have some English-speaking personnel. Hotels have air conditioning unless otherwise noted, and breakfast is available even when there is no formal restaurant. Expect to pay more than $280 for a double room in hotels listed as very expensive, from $140 to $280 in those described as expensive, from $90 to $140 in those listed as moderate, and from $35 to $80 in places in the inexpensive category. All telephone numbers are in the 5 area code unless otherwise indicated.

For an unforgettable experience, we begin with our favorite *parador,* followed by our recommendations of cost and quality choices of hotels, listed by price category.

A SPECIAL HAVEN

Parador Alcázar Del Rey Don Pedro, Carmona This majestic *parador*, the former 14th-century retreat of King Pedro the Cruel, overlooks lush green countryside where cows graze and farmers plow, about 21 miles from Seville. The high-ceilinged dining room, with its coats of arms and huge paintings, is fit for a king. There is also a lovely Moorish garden full of colorful tiles and bright yellow seats, an excellent spot to sit and sip a drink of sherry, special to the region. There is a full-service restaurant as well as a bar on the premises. The 59 rooms are immaculate but otherwise routine. (phone: 55-141010).

VERY EXPENSIVE

Alfonso XIII Admittedly, this is a reproduction of a Spanish palace. It was built in 1929 for the *Iberoamerican Exposition* (and completely remodeled for *Expo '92*), but it has *azulejo*-lined hallways, 149 ultra-spacious guestrooms, a regal lobby, a white marble courtyard, and a Moroccan garden with a big swimming pool and poolside bar. Seville's grande dame (now part of the CIGA chain) is not only a hop, skip, and jump from the Alcázar, but within walking distance of downtown in one direction and María Luisa Park in the other. Its restaurant is the elegant continental *Itálica*. 2 Calle San Fernando (phone: 422-2850; in the US, 800-221-2340; fax: 421-6033).

Príncipe de Asturias Located on the north end of Cartuja Island, this state-of-the-art landmark was built for *Expo '92* and bears the title of the son of the present King Juan Carlos I, heir to the throne of Spain. Designed in three ultramodern circular modules, the luxurious establishment has 300 rooms and suites with all amenities (7 of them even have private swimming pools), plus tennis and squash courts, a swimming pool, a health and fitness center, conference and business facilities, and 2 restaurants. Isla de la Cartuja (phone: 446-2222; in the US, 800-333-3333; fax: 446-0428).

EXPENSIVE

Casas de la Judería Tucked in the historic heart of the Barrio de Santa Cruz, near Plaza Santa María la Blanca, these furnished luxury apartments occupy a group of refurbished 3-story buildings that once belonged to the Duke of Béjar, patron and benefactor of Cervantes. Each of the 31 one- to three-bedroom units has a fully equipped kitchen, direct-dial telephones, and satellite TV; some have terraces and private elevators, and some even have Andalusian-style patios with a fountain. 7 Plaza de Santa María la Blanca, Callejón de Dos Hermanas (phone: 441-5150; fax: 442-2170).

Husa Sevilla Facing a small square in the Triana district, this place is in a new building, but one that is true to traditional Sevillian style — pastel stucco façade, wood-beamed ceilings, potted plants, hand-painted tiles, and marble accents. It has 116 rooms and 16 suites (all soundproof), a bar, a café, and a restaurant. Only a few blocks back from the river, it's a 15-minute walk across the Triana Bridge to the core of the city. 90 Pagés del Corro (phone: 434-2412; fax: 434-2707).

Inglaterra Its very central location makes this sleek, remodeled old-timer a convenient place to stay. The big, comfortable, contemporary salon is an after-work gathering spot for downtown bankers and businesspeople. The 116 rooms have modern furnishings; some have terraces on the square. Service is efficient, and there is a sunny second-floor restaurant. 7 Plaza Nueva (phone: 422-4970; fax: 456-1336).

Macarena Sol Casablanca kitsch describes the decor of this 327-room property, with its mirror-trimmed Andalusian façade and rattan-furnished lobby-bar patio complete with fountain. The rooms are comfortable, there is a good restaurant, a busy cafeteria, shops, and an executive floor with special services and amenities. Across from the old Roman and Moorish walls and the Basílica de la Macarena, it's a taxi ride away from the center of town. 2 Calle San Juan de Ribera (phone: 437-5700; in the US, 800-336-3542; fax: 438-1803).

Tryp Colón A luxurious rival to the *Alfonso XIII,* this is an old hotel that's been completely redone, right down to the white sofas and the restored antique glass dome in the upstairs lobby. The property — with its 204 rooms and 14 suites — is handy to the bullring, and a bullfighting theme prevails in the fine *El Burladero* restaurant (see *Eating Out*). Located in the middle of downtown. 1 Calle Canalejas (phone: 422-2900; fax: 422-0938).

MODERATE

América An affordable, efficient, modern business traveler's hotel in the heart of the downtown shopping district, across from the *El Corte Inglés* department store. It has 100 rooms, motel decor, a cafeteria, good service, and it's close to Calle Sierpes, the *Museo de Bellas Artes,* and the Triana Bridge. 2 Calle Jesús del Gran Poder (phone: 422-0951; fax: 421-0626).

Bécquer On a lovely café-lined street 2 blocks from the Triana Bridge and a short walk to the *Maestranza* bullring, shopping, and the *Museo de Bellas Artes,* this property offers a wood-paneled lobby, big-hotel service, and 126 average rooms. No restaurant. 4 Calle Reyes Católicos (phone: 422-8900; fax: 421-4400).

Doña María The location (one door up from the cathedral square), the combination of period charm and up-to-date convenience, the romantic decor in the 61 rooms (all one-of-a-kind), and the little rooftop swimming pool in the shadow of La Giralda make this intimate, luxurious little place Seville's number one small hotel choice. No restaurant. 19 Calle Don Remondo (phone: 422-4990; fax: 421-9546).

Puerta de Triana Across the street from the *Bécquer* (above), this hostelry costs even less. There are 65 rooms, some with balconies on the avenue. Despite the postage-stamp lobby with the soft-drink machine and blaring TV set, it's an outstanding buy. 5 Calle Reyes Católicos (phone: 421-5401; fax: 421-5404).

Goya This *hostal* (inn) is in a narrow house with gaily striped awnings in the Barrio de Santa Cruz, 20 shipshape rooms, a charming upstairs garden — and budget-minded guests congratulating one another on finding it. No air conditioning; no restaurant. Write early for reservations. 31 Calle Mateos Gago (phone: 421-1170).

EATING OUT

The capital of Andalusia sets a fine table, although all of the city's dazzling *tapas* bars (see below) may keep you from sitting down to it. The star of restaurant menus haute or lowly is sweet Atlantic seafood from Huelva. Try *fritura* (baby fish and eels, batter-dipped and deep-fried to airy crispness), *urta a la roteña* (bass baked in a tomato casserole), *gambas al pil pil* (shrimp sautéed in olive oil and hot red peppers), or *merluza a la plancha* (hake simply pan-fried in a bit of olive oil). Delicious cured country ham is found everywhere in Spain, but the local mahogany-colored *jamón de Jabugo,* found in better *tapas* bars, is the best. Other dishes to try are Seville's favorite, *huevos a la flamenca* (baked eggs with asparagus and peas), in cold weather, *rabo de toro* (oxtail stew), or, in warm weather, gazpacho, the cold tomato and cucumber soup. Order wine from Jerez, or try a big pitcher of cooling sangria laden with orange and lemon slices.

Seville's restaurants observe the traditional long lunches, closing in late afternoon and opening again around 8 PM for early-bird diners. (If you crave a sandwich in between, drop by an American-style cafeteria or ask for a *bocadillo* — a sandwich on a hard roll — anywhere you see *tapas.*) Menus with English translations are the rule, and many economy restaurants compete for tourists by displaying photographs of their popular dishes. Expect to pay from $65 to $110 for an average three-course meal for two with house wine in a restaurant listed below as expensive (the *menú de la casa* could run less), from $25 to $65 in a moderate restaurant, and under $25 in an inexpensive one. Opening days and hours change from time to time and many places close for at least a month's summer vacation, so be sure to call before you go. All telephone numbers are in the 5 city code unless otherwise indicated.

EXPENSIVE

La Albahaca Gracious dining prevails in this stately old mansion that a famed Spanish architect built for himself in the Barrio de Santa Cruz. Dine late on such delicacies as *perdiz del coto en cacerola* (partridge casserole) or *lubina al hinojo* (a type of sea bass with fennel), then attend the midnight *tablao* at *Los Gallos* right next door. Closed Sundays. Reservations necessary. American Express, Diners Club, and Visa accepted. 12 Plaza de Santa Cruz (phone: 422-0714).

El Burladero The name refers to the bullfighter's protective barrier at the entrances to the arena, and the taurine theme here extends from photographs of past heroes on the walls to cattle-brand designs woven into the damask tablecloths. The menu, largely continental, includes regional specialties from all over Spain, among them the Andalusian *bacalao al horno con patatas* (baked salt cod with saffron and potatoes) and *pochas con almejas* (white kidney beans with clams). Open daily. Reservations necessary. American Express, Diners Club, and Visa accepted. 1 Calle Canalejas (phone: 422-2900).

La Dorada This big, bright, seafood restaurant was the model for branches in both Barcelona and Madrid. Order the specialty, *dorada a la sal* (sea bream baked in a crust of rock salt, which is cracked open at tableside to release the tender, sweet, steaming fish), or the *fritura malagueña* (tiny baby eels, baby squid, and red mullet dipped in batter and fried to a crunch). Closed Sundays and August. Reservations advised. Major credit cards accepted. 6 Calle Virgen de Aguas Santas (phone: 445-5100).

Egaña-Oriza A chic, Basque-owned bastion of nouvelle cuisine, it's *the* place to be seen in Seville. It enjoys a glamorous greenhouse setting against a wall of the Alcázar Gardens. Out front, café tables have a good view of the adjoining Murillo Gardens, the flashy fountain in Plaza San Juan de Austria, and promenading *sevillanos*. The menu runs to elegant innovations such as *gazpacho con langostinos de Sanlúcar* (gazpacho with Sanlúcar prawns) or *solomillo con mousse de foie a las uvas de Corinto* (steak with foie gras in a grape sauce). Closed Sundays and August. Reservations essential for lunch or dinner. Major credit cards accepted. 41 Calle San Fernando (phone: 422-7211).

Enrique Becerra This little gem is hidden away on a narrow street off the Plaza Nueva. Besides the cozy dining room on the main floor, there are private dining salons upstairs. Friendly waiters offer advice about the chef's highly personalized menu. Closed Sundays at lunch. Reservations advised. Major credit cards accepted. 2 Calle Gamazo (phone: 421-3049).

Figón del Cabildo The decor of heavy plaster, brick, and wood beams is the perfect setting for Sevillian specialties in this popular spot across Avenida de la Constitución from the cathedral. Try *berenjenas gratinadas con jamón* *y langostinos* (eggplant with ham and crayfish) or *sopa de picadillo* (consommé with egg yolk and ham). Closed Sunday evenings. Reservations advised. Major credit cards accepted. Plaza del Cabildo (phone: 422-0117).

La Isla Though locals are put off by its formality, the restaurant's high-backed, black-lacquer chairs and salmon tablecloths create a relaxing setting in which to enjoy extraordinarily fresh seafood flown in from Galicia. This is a comfortable place to spend the afternoon after a hard day in the nearby Alcázar. Closed August. Reservations advised. Major credit cards accepted. 25 Calle Arfe (phone: 421-5376).

El Rincón de Curro Anyone will tell you that this comfortable restaurant in Los Remedios is the best place in town for meat dishes, although there's a good seafood menu, too. Food critics have singled out the *cochinillo asado a la segoviana* (roast suckling pig) and the *chuletón de buey al plato caliente* (steak sizzling on a hot clay plate). Closed Sunday evenings and August. Reservations necessary. Major credit cards accepted. 45 Calle Virgen de Luján (phone: 445-0238).

MODERATE

Hostería del Laurel This place has a come-on that's better than its food — Don Juan supped here (or at least the man who inspired the legend did). Nevertheless, an acceptable menu of Andalusian standards, served in country dining rooms hung with bunches of garlic and dried laurel, makes it a pleasant lunch stop in the Barrio de Santa Cruz. Open daily. Reservations advised. American Express and Visa accepted. 5 Plaza de los Venerables (phone: 422-0295).

Mesón Don Raimundo If there's time for only one meal in Seville, have it in this restaurant, in a convent ruin in the Barrio de Santa Cruz. A long, dark alley overgrown with vines leads to capacious dining rooms decorated with massive Arab cooking vessels and farm utensils; a cozy barroom is patterned in tiles clear to the ceiling. Ask owner Raimundo Fernández for advice on the dishes he's adapted from old Arab-Spanish cookbooks: The baby lamb roasted over grape vines is especially good in the fall. Also try his *sopa de almejas con piñones* (clam soup with pine nuts) and the *pato mozárabe* (duck stuffed with apples, honey, nuts, and sultanas). Closed Sunday evenings. Reservations advised. American Express, Diners Club, and Visa accepted. 26 Calle Argote de Molina (phone: 422-3355).

Río Grande Located in Triana, the best time here is evening, when the Torre del Oro across the river is bathed in lights. There's a paella that's rich with goodies, perfect gazpacho, and *salteado de ternera a la sevillana* (diced veal with local green olives, carrots, and potatoes). Everyone should eat here once, or at least come for *tapas* at the long bar in the building across the patio. Open daily. Reservations necessary. American Express, Master-Card, and Diners Club accepted. 70 Calle Betis (phone: 427-3956).

Taberna Dorada Newer and snappier than most Seville seafood spots, this place attracts the young set. Closed Sundays and August. Reservations advised. Major credit cards accepted. 18 Calle José Luis de Casso (phone: 465-2720).

INEXPENSIVE

Bodega El Diamante A chain of *buffets libres* (all you can eat, self-service), not only a great buy, but also a way to eat quickly and without language problems. There's more than one, but this location generates so much traffic that the food is fresher and hotter. Load up on paella, *ensalada rusa* (potato salad with vegetables and mayonnaise), fried fishsticks, fish salads, hard-boiled eggs in mayonnaise, sliced tomatoes, fried eggplant, green and red peppers, and fresh fruit, but leave the *salchichas* (rubbery hot dogs) alone. Closed Sundays. No reservations. Visa and MasterCard accepted. 10 Av. de la Constitución (no phone).

Las Escobas It claims to be Seville's oldest restaurant, having fed the likes of Lope de Vega, Miguel de Cervantes, and Lord Byron, and the elaborately carved bar and oak-paneled ceiling are convincing, despite the remodeling it has undergone. Of all the little eateries lined up on the streets north of the cathedral, this is the most pleasant place for *platos combinados* (economy specials). Open daily. Reservations unnecessary. Visa accepted. 62 Calle Alvarez Quintero (phone: 421-4479).

TAPAS BARS

Tapas originated in Andalusia. In fact, it is said that they were invented in Seville when, in the old days, wine or sherry was served with a slice of ham covering the glass like a lid (*tapa*) in order to keep flies from diving into the wine. Another version holds that *tapas* were served free to drivers to dilute the effects of the wine and keep them sober on the road. Whatever the truth, the selection of *tascas* (*tapas* bars) in Seville is bountiful, and the camaraderie of *tasca* hopping is irresistible. A larger portion of a particular *tapa* is called a *ración* and can be a small meal in itself. Follow the crowd and you'll find it beating a path to the door of *Modesto* (5 Calle Cano y Queto, next to the Murillo Gardens), where the *acedías* (deep-fried baby sole) and *pimientos aliñados* (red and green peppers in a spicy marinade) are the talk of the town. *Sanlúcar-Mar* (in a tower at the far end of the Triana Bridge) has a cozy basement restaurant and small upper dining terraces, but the selection of *tapas* at the inviting U-shaped glass-and-brass bar on the main floor is so spectacular that you'll want to make a meal right there — or take *tapas* on a terrace that looks straight down the river with the city gleaming on both sides. Also at the end of the bridge, just down the steps from *Sanlúcar-Mar,* is a little sailors' bar, *Kiosko de las Flores,* where the young crowd consumes beer and plates of big green olives into the night. Not far away are *El Puerto* (on Calle Betis, next door to the *Río Grande* restaurant), with a multilevel terrace right on the river — you serve yourself from a cafeteria bar — and a sit-down restaurant indoors; and *La Albariza Bodega* (6 Calle Betis), where upended black wine barrels serve as tables. Order plates of dry *serrano* ham, aged *manchego* cheese, olives, and sausages from the counter in back and stand around a barrel with a *copa* (glass of wine). Back across the river, in the Barrio de Santa Cruz, is the venerable *Casa Román* (next to the *Hostería del Laurel* restaurant in Plaza de los Venerables), a *tasca* that looks like a rustic country store (there's a deli counter up front). It serves the finest Jabugo ham in town — at around $12.50 per 100-gram portion (just short of a quarter pound). You can also choose from among their selection of other excellent but much less expensive hams.

Toledo

Cervantes hailed Toledo as that "rocky gravity, glory of Spain and light of her cities." Indeed, throughout its history, the city has been a shining center of scholarship and spirituality. The Romans founded the city of Toletum in 193 BC on a site originally settled by a tribe of Celt-Iberians. The city was part of the Visigoth kingdom in the 6th and 7th centuries, then was invaded by the Arabs in 712. For centuries it flourished as a city of silk and steel where clergy, merchants, and the military peacefully coexisted under Moorish rule. At one time it had a population of 200,000, almost four times what it is today, and a prominent Jewish community thrived alongside the Moors and Mozarabic Christians.

Even when King Alfonso VI and El Cid recaptured the city for Christendom in 1085, a cosmopolitan tolerance endured. Before the full weight of the Catholic church pressed down to obliterate or banish the competition during the Spanish Inquisition, Christians, Muslims, and Jews cooperated in intellectual exchange and trade, and for nearly 5 centuries, Toledo enjoyed a reputation throughout the Mediterranean as a center of learning. Alfonso the Wise, King of Castile, grew up in this heady cultural mix and founded the influential School of Translators here during the 13th century. Under his rule, Castilian Spanish became the official language, replacing Latin. His court of Jewish scholars made esoteric Greek and Arabic science (as well as Islam and Judaism) accessible to the people of northern Europe. Alchemists studied and worked alongside mathematicians and philosophers. Prosperity brought commissions for exquisite Mudéjar craftsmanship, characterized by intricately ornamental plaster ceilings and sumptuously patterned tile and brick walls — much of which can still be seen in Toledo's chapels, synagogues, hospitals, and palaces.

However, an abrupt pogrom in 1355 and the 1391 massacre at the Santa María la Blanca Synagogue were early warnings that Toledo's tolerance would not last, regardless of local traditions. Jews who refused to be baptized were killed or banished, and in 1499, 4,000 Moors were baptized.

After Queen Isabella's death in 1504, aging King Ferdinand ruled from Toledo. When the new king, Carlos I of Spain, inherited the mantle of Holy Roman Emperor in 1519 and became Charles V, Toledo became an imperial city. In addition to Spain, Carlos commanded Naples, Sicily, Sardinia, Germany, Franche-Comté, and the Low Countries, as well as the American lands newly plundered by the conquistadores. Resentment quickly grew against the king and his court of foreigners. Between 1520 to 1521, Toledo's Juan de Padilla joined with Juan Bravo of Segovia in a local citizens' revolt, known as the Comuneros uprising, which was quickly crushed.

In 1556, just 5 years after he assumed the throne, Philip II, son of

Charles V, moved the capital to Madrid, but Toledo remained the spiritual center of Spain. Distancing himself from the established church, King Philip II decided to build a state palace north of Madrid that would overshadow the great cathedrals of Toledo. Eager artists from all over Europe competed for commissions at El Escorial, but one Cretan painter, Doménikos Theotokópoulos, soon fell from Philip's favor and was dismissed. He set up his studio in Toledo, where he became known simply as El Greco.

Today, it is El Greco's skewed vision of Toledo, with its roiling clouds over elongated figures and startling clashes of color in almost geometric composition, that most visitors come to see. Indeed, the skyline has not changed measurably since he completed his *View of Toledo.* The artist's adopted hometown has no shortage of his work. In fact, it's rare to find so many of a major artist's paintings still located near their place of creation.

Toledo's new status as a mere provincial capital and the fact that far more politically significant prizes were within striking distance spared this city from the worst of the battles that ravaged Spain in succeeding generations. But the Spanish Civil War was fought here with full fury. The huge restored Alcázar, which dominates the highest ground in Toledo and was once rebuilt by Charles V as a royal residence, was besieged for a grim 2 months in the summer of 1936. Franco's Nationalist forces held out against the Republicans despite blasts of dynamite that collapsed much of the fortress, formerly the most prestigious military academy in the nation.

Fortunately, today Toledo faces no more threatening an onslaught than the hordes of visitors who inevitably get lost in its tangle of narrow alleyways. City residents resolutely provide directions, respond to queries in countless languages, and rarely lose their graciousness. When the last tour bus pulls away at dusk, however, Toledo is returned to its residents, and, it seems, to its past. This is the best time to explore the twisting byways of this ancient city, finding the way back by remembering the coats of arms carved in stone on the buildings along your route.

Toledo At-a-Glance

SEEING THE CITY

For an overall perspective, drive along Carretera de Circunvalación, following the banks of the Tagus River, which surrounds Toledo like a moat. As the road climbs the hillsides, it passes close to a little hermitage called Virgen del Valle, and provides a sweeping view of the city. Close by is an outcropping called Cabeza del Moro (Moor's Head). Anywhere on the hillside offers a good view. Just to the left is the *Parador Conde de Orgaz* (see *Checking In*), the best place to watch the sunset, a drink in hand on the patio, with all of Toledo stretched out below. Just above the Alcántara

Bridge is the Castillo de San Servando, a monastery revamped as a school, which offers a panorama from a different angle. For a more intimate view over Toledo's tiled rooftops and spires, climb the cathedral's belfry. A door on Calle Hombre de Palo (Straw Man Street) opens onto stairs in the cloisters that ascend the tower. *Miradero* literally means "lookout," and from this area, not far above the Puerta del Sol on the Cuesta de las Armas, cafés offer a fine vantage point out over the river and beyond. From nearly any strategic spot along the old walls, there is a sentry's view of the surrounding countryside.

SPECIAL PLACES

Toledo has so many points of interest that tourists would be hard-pressed to view even the exteriors of all historically important monuments on a single visit. If time is especially limited, pick up the free brochure from the tourist office at the Puerto de la Bisagra and follow its "essential itinerary," which is arranged in a very convenient sequence. Visiting hours are erratic, so it's a good idea to call ahead.

ALCÁZAR Despite numerous sackings, torchings, and even bombings, this strategic building has been regirded, patched up, and continually put back into service. The Moors refashioned the Visigothic citadel, which was built over an old Roman fort, and El Cid reputedly served as the city's first governor here. The present structure dates from the time of Charles V, who converted it into a palace, though most of it is now a product of reconstruction. The north façade, with its Plateresque portal, was designed by Alonso de Covarrubias, as was the east façade, which is by far the oldest. Since the Imperial Court left the building almost 500 years ago, it has been wracked by misfortune. The palace became a state prison in 1643, and German, British, and Portuguese troops burned it in 1710, during the War of the Spanish Succession. After restoration by Cardinal Lorenzana, it stood only 35 years before French troops gutted it during the Peninsular War. It later reemerged as the national military academy, though it suffered another blaze at the hands of careless cadets and again had to be overhauled. Its worst days were during a Civil War siege in 1936, when a band of Nationalists, along with over 600 women and children, holed up inside for 2 months until Republican bombs again reduced it to ruins. Open Mondays through Saturdays from 9:30 AM to 1:30 PM and from 4 to 5:30 PM (6:30 PM in summer); Sundays from 10 AM to 1:30 PM and from 4 to 5:30 PM (6:30 PM in summer); closed Mondays. Admission charge. Calle Capuchinos (phone: 223038).

CATEDRAL PRIMADA DE TOLEDO (CATHEDRAL OF THE PRIMATES OF TOLEDO) For such an enormous building, the cathedral can be surprisingly difficult to locate. Boxed in by other buildings, on approach, it seems to disappear. In the main (or west) façade, between the tower and the dome, there are three lovely Gothic portals: the Puerta del Perdón (Gate of Pardon) in the middle, flanked by the Puerta del Juicio (Gate of Justice) on the right and the Puerta del Infierno (Gate of Hell) on the left. The 14th-century Puerta de Reloj (also called de la Chapinería, or Clock Gate), in the north wall, is the cathedral's oldest, and is lavishly adorned with Gothic pointed arches and ornaments. The Puerta de los Leones (Lions' Gate), on the south, is the most flamboyant, with its great bronze doors. The modern entrance is a plain doorway to the left of the Puerta de Mollete, just off Calle Hombre de Palo.

Inside, the architectural styles run the gamut from Gothic to Mudéjar to flagrant rococo. The wrought-iron screens are magnificent, and 800 stained glass windows from the 15th and 16th centuries help light the vast space. Yet even the glorious rose window looks ordinary next to the skylight that directs a single celestial beam onto the altar. The altar, known as the *Transparente*, is a bit of baroque heaven, a swirl of saints and chubby angels created by Narcisco Tomé in 1732. Some of the paintings have three-dimensional appendages, innovations that have remained controversial throughout the centuries. The polychrome retable above the altar is exquisitely carved, and the walnut choir stalls are also exceptional. The sacristy contains a wealth of paintings, including 28 by El Greco, as well as works by Velázquez, Titian, Van Dyck, and Goya. The Capilla Mozárabe, beneath a dome designed by El Greco's son, is the only place on earth where the ancient rituals of the Visigoths, dating from the 5th and 6th centuries, are still observed in Latin and Spanish at 9:30 AM; it is kept locked between masses. The treasury (*tesoro*) displays the gold and silver Arfe monstrance, which is carried through the streets on the *Feast of Corpus Christi*. Standing 10 feet high and weighing 450 pounds, this elaborate reliquary incorporates gold from Columbus's first shipload back from the New World. The cathedral is still in use, and visitors often encounter a mass or a lavish wedding in progress. Open daily from 10:30 AM to 1 PM and from 3:30 to 6 PM (7 PM in summer); Sundays from 10:30 AM to 6 PM (7 PM in summer). Admission charge to the sacristy, treasury, choir, chapterhouse, and King's Chapel. Plaza Mayor (phone: 222241).

IGLESIA DE SANTO TOMÉ (CHURCH OF ST. THOMAS) This unremarkable 14th-century Mudéjar church is crowded with visitors because of one painting, El Greco's *El Entierro del Conde de Orgaz* (Burial of the Count of Orgaz). The famous canvas was painted some 250 years after the funeral of the count, who had funded the church's first major reconstruction. The scene is split into heaven and earth, with a row of mourners marking the divide. Their faces are portraits of prominent citizens, all in 16th-century dress. El Greco's own face is supposedly just above that of the young St. Stephen, and the boy in the foreground is the painter's son, Jorge. The monogram on his pocket handkerchief is El Greco's signature. Open Tuesdays through Saturdays from 10 AM to 1:45 PM and from 3:30 to 5:45 PM (6:45

PM in summer); Sundays from 10 AM to 1:45 PM. Admission charge. 1 Plaza Conde (phone: 223456).

TALLER DEL MORO (MOOR'S WORKSHOP) This almost palatial 14th-century building was once used as a workshop by Moorish masons completing cathedral commissions. Displays are mostly of carpentry and tiles, and the Mudéjar style of the building, with its *artesonado* (artisanry) ceilings and plasterwork, is exemplary. Open Tuesdays through Saturdays from 10 AM to 2 PM and from 4 to 6:30 PM; Sundays from 10 AM to 2 PM. Admission charge. 4 Calle Taller del Moro (phone: 227115).

CASA Y MUSEO DEL GRECO (EL GRECO HOUSE AND MUSEUM) The name is a misnomer, for El Greco never lived here, but this was his old neighborhood, and this house did belong to his landlord. Admirably restored to its 16th-century state, the house is charming due to the small scale of the furnishings, especially the tiny kitchen, and its quaint, cobbled courtyard, surrounded by a wood-carved gallery, Renaissance porticos, and intricately carved Mudéjar friezes. Spectacular views of the surrounding hills, dotted with patrician villas that have changed little since El Greco's day, can be had from the south-facing balconies on the upper floor. The garden is very pleasant, and there's a fine collection of the painter's later works, particularly noteworthy for its bold portraits of the apostles. Open Tuesdays through Saturdays from 10 AM to 2 PM and from 4 to 6 PM (7 PM in summer); Sundays from 10 AM to 2 PM. Admission charge. 3 Calle Samuel Ha-Levi (phone: 224046).

SINAGOGA DEL TRÁNSITO (TRAVELER'S TEMPLE) This major synagogue, founded in 1366, was converted into a monastery, but many of the original trappings were preserved. Rich cedar carvings grace the 12-foot-high *artesonado* ceiling and lacy Mudéjar plasterwork is incised with Hebrew inscriptions and stars of David. Exhibits at the *Sephardic Museum* installed here include a marble pillar from the 1st or 2nd century, with carved Hebrew inscriptions, alongside silver manuscript cases, robes and wedding costumes, amulets, and elaborate objects used in Jewish festivals. Open Tuesdays through Saturdays from 10 AM to 2 PM and from 4 to 6 PM (7 PM in summer); Sundays from 10 AM to 2 PM. Admission charge. Calle Samuel Ha-Levi (phone: 223665).

SINAGOGA DE SANTA MARÍA LA BLANCA This architectural gem, built in 1180, was once the primary Jewish synagogue in Toledo, and was later converted into a church by the Knights of Calatrava. The façade is rather drab, but inside, white horseshoe arches and delicately carved white columns shimmer with light. The polychrome altarpiece was added in the 16th century. Demoted to a barracks in 1791 until a general commanded its make-over into a quartermaster's store and saved it from further abuse, the synagogue has been remarkably restored to its original Almohad-period splendor. Open daily from 10 AM to 2 PM and from 3:30 to 6 PM (7 PM in summer). Admission charge. 2 Cuesta de los Reyes Católicos (phone: 228429).

MONASTERIO DE SAN JUAN DE LOS REYES The outside walls of this grandiose monastery are hung with chains once worn by Christian slaves in Moorish Granada. The chains were brought here, after the slaves gained their freedom, in testament to a faith that fueled the final Christian victory of the Reconquest. Inside, the great church is done in soaring Isabeline style, and incorporates Mudéjar and Gothic touches with Renaissance art. Construction began in 1476 and wasn't completed until the early 17th century. An important center for the Franciscan order, the monastery was originally planned as the mausoleum of King Ferdinand and Queen Isabella (they were actually buried in Granada). The initials F&Y (for Fernando and Ysabel) appear repeatedly throughout the building, along with the shields of Castile, León, and Aragon; the pomegranate of Granada; and the royal yoke and arrows motif. The Flemish architect Juan Guas designed most of the interior, with its massive round columns and the great shields supported by haloed eagles. Open daily from 10 AM to 1:45 PM and from 3:30 to 5:45 PM (6:45 PM in summer); closed *Christmas* and *New Year's Day*. Admission charge. 21 Cuesta de los Reyes Católicos (phone: 223802).

HOSPITAL DE SANTA CRUZ Cardinal Pedro González de Mendoza initiated plans for this elaborate orphanage and hospital just off Plaza de Zocodover in the early 16th century, and the project was completed by Queen Isabella after his death. The building now houses the *Museum of Fine Arts,* the *Museum of Applied Arts,* and the *Provincial Museum of Archaeology,* showcasing swords and scimitars, ceramics, vestments, furniture, tapestries, and paintings, including 25 by El Greco. Off the lovely Plateresque patio is an archaeology exhibit of mostly Roman finds. A display of prehistoric items is in the basement. The intricate ceiling, lavish stairways, and spacious rooms are typical of 16th-century hospitals where pleasant surroundings were considered vital to the cure. Open Tuesdays through Saturdays, from 10 AM to 6:30 PM; Sundays from 10 AM to 2 PM. Admission charge includes entrance to the *San Román Visigothic Museum* (see below). 3 Calle Cervantes (phone: 221402).

MUSEO DE LOS CONCILIOS Y DE LA CULTURA VISIGÓTICA (MUSEUM OF THE COUNCILS AND VISIGOTHIC ART) It was here in the heights of the city that the Visigothic kings held several councils during the 5th and 6th centuries AD. The site is now occupied by a 13th-century Mudéjar church, the Iglesia de San Román, which has been turned into the only museum of Visigothic art and artifacts in Spain. The collection of votive crowns, bronze brooches, Maltese crosses, and funerary inscriptions from the period is rather paltry, but the church merits a close look for its architecture alone. Open Tuesdays through Saturdays from 10 AM to 2 PM and from 4 to 6:30 PM;

Sundays from 10 AM to 2 PM. Admission charge includes entrance to the Santa Cruz Hospital. Calle San Clemente (phone: 227872).

CRISTO DE LA LUZ (CHRIST OF THE LIGHT) Also known as the Mezquita, this minuscule "mosque," perhaps intended originally as a sepulchral chamber, was built in 980 AD, and is one of the most venerable Moorish buildings on the Iberian Peninsula. Near the Puerta del Sol, it was erected on top of Visigothic ruins and later became a Mudéjar church. Delicate horseshoe arches inside are supported by more ancient Visigothic capitals, and paintings in the Mudéjar annex, though worn, are rare surviving examples of Toledan Romanesque art. Cristo de la Luz is shrouded in legend; according to one, El Cid's charger fell to its knees here during a post-Reconquest victory parade and refused to rise until a Visigothic crucifix, with a votive candle still flickering, was miraculously uncovered in a bricked-up niche. Opening hours are erratic. No admission charge. Calle Cristo de la Luz.

HOSPITAL DE TAVERA This large 16th-century hospital located outside the city gates contains Cardinal Juan Pardo de Tavera's extensive collection of paintings and also features apartments furnished by the Duchess of Lerma in a lavish 17th-century style. The cardinal's magnificent tomb and the family crypt for the Dukes of Medinaceli are in the chapel off the double patio. Impressive portraits by Titian, including the huge *Portrait of Charles V*, hang in the vast dining hall, but José Ribera's odd *Bearded Woman* is stashed in a side room, camouflaged by bland cityscapes on either side. Upstairs are works by Tintoretto, Zurbarán, and, of course, El Greco, most notably, his enormous last canvas, the *Baptism of Christ by St. John*. Open daily from 10:30 AM to 1:30 PM and from 3:30 to 6 PM. Admission charge. Calle Baja (phone: 220451).

CIRCO ROMANO (ROMAN CIRCUS) Not much remains of the Roman arena, only a few mosaics and a reconstructed building outside the gates north of town. Still, this is a pleasant place to stroll after the cramped and twisting streets of the city, and its size (original capacity 20,000) hints at the strength of the Roman settlement, Toletum. Off Avenida de la Reconquista.

ENVIRONS

MONTES DE TOLEDO South and west of Toledo, along either the C401 road or the N401 highway and the local routes branching off of them, rise the harsh uplands that were long celebrated in troubadors' couplets. Streams interlace the scrubby bush cover of rock roses, heather, and cork oaks. The area is best explored by car. Picnickers should be aware of the wild variety of game, mostly in the heights: deer, wild boar, lynx, foxes, and even wolves. Much of the land is private hunting ground, particularly in the southern stretches near Los Yébenes, but there are prehistoric sites scattered throughout the area. Calancho, Los Navalucillos, and Hontanar all boast curious megalithic relics. Ciudad de Vascos, near Navalmoralejo, is an ancient Hispano-Moorish ghost town protected by a fortress. Odd stone boars or bulls — *verracos* — can be seen at the castles Castillo de Bayuela and Torecilla de la Jara. The town of Guadalerzas is spanned by an impressive late Roman aqueduct with 24 arches. One of the prettiest valleys, reached by heading west toward the higher sierra behind Guadalupe, is Robledo del Mazo, where the locals still wear traditional straw hats decorated with baubles and tiny mirrors.

ROUTE OF THE CASTLES The area surrounding Toledo is littered with castles, most constructed during the time of the Reconquest. About 8 miles (13 km) southwest of Toledo (local road 401) lies Guadamur, a small town dominated by a magnificent 15th-century castle that was restored in the 19th century. The rooms, occupied for a time by Queen Joan the Mad and her son, the future Emperor Charles V, are furnished with Spanish period furniture. Leaving Guadamur and continuing south, take the first right turn toward San Martín de Montalbán. Go past San Martín de Montalbán; the next right turn will bring you to the hamlet of Melque, which contains one of the most beautiful and least known castles in Spain, a jewel of Moorish-Christian (Mozárabe) architecture. The Melque castle, which also shows traces of Visigoth influence, boasts one of the largest pointed Gothic military arches ever built. Close to the castle lie the ruins of two Roman dams. Other noteworthy monuments on this southwest circular route are the Gothic-Renaissance chapel at Torrijos, the 15th-century Mudéjar castle at Maqueda, and the turreted edifice at Escalona on the banks of the Alberche River.

ILLESCAS El Greco lovers will want to head north 21 miles (34 km) on N401 to this village for a visit to the Convento del Hospital de la Caridad. The 16th-century convent contains five El Grecos, including a magnificent *Coronation of the Virgin.* Open Mondays through Saturdays from 9 AM to 1 PM and from 4 to 7 PM; Sundays from 9 AM to 1 PM. Admission charge. If the church is closed, knock on the door of the adjacent hospital, and one of the nuns will let you in. 2 Calle Cardinal Cisneros, Illescas (phone: 511625).

EXTRA SPECIAL Talavera de la Reina and Puente de Arzobispo are traditional ceramic centers and are an easy day's excursion from Toledo via C502. Talavera is the largest city in the province, so don't expect a quaint potter's village. On the fringes of the city, just past the main park, is the Hermitage de la Virgen del Prado, a showcase for the famous *azulejos,* distinctive blue and yellow glazed picture tiles, which date back to the 14th century and were the preferred decorations for the finest palaces and monasteries. Pottery from Talavera features multicolor designs; browse along the main street, where vendors sell shelf after shelf of platters, vases, and bowls.

To reach Puente de Arzobispo, popular for its more subdued, green-toned pottery, drive west on the N-V highway to Oropesa, then south for 9 miles (14 km) to a fortified bridge across the Tagus River. Shops and vendors in the village sell ceramics for less than the equivalent items would cost in Toledo, but since quality here is consistently high, there are no astonishingly inexpensive wares. Valdeverdeja, a smaller and prettier village, lies just 4½ miles (7 km) to the west and sells distinctive unglazed red earthenware. Farther west on the N-V highway, just past Oropesa, is a turnoff to Lagartera, the village where the best La Mancha embroidery originates. Every cottage has its own display of the free-form floral stitching, which decorates silk hangings, tablecloths, peasant bonnets, and full skirts. Return to Toledo through Talavera (the quickest route); for a more leisurely and scenic drive, loop down on local roads through the Montes de Toledo.

Sources and Resources

TOURIST INFORMATION

The Oficina de Turismo (just outside the Puerta de la Bisagra; phone: 220843 or 210900) provides brochures and an excellent foldout map — indispensable for negotiating the winding streets. Open Mondays through Fridays from 9 AM to 2 PM and from 4 to 6 PM; Saturdays from 9 AM to 1:30 PM.

LOCAL COVERAGE Understanding Spanish is a must for gleaning information from the local press. The local daily newspaper, *La Voz del Tajo*, has good entertainment and dining listings. Regional editions of the Catholic national daily, *Ya*, also cover local events. More esoteric topics are explored in *Toletum*, published sporadically by Toledo's Academy of Fine Arts and Historical Sciences. *Castilla–La Mancha* is the provincial monthly magazine.

TELEPHONE

The area code for Toledo is 25. If calling from within Spain, but outside the Toledo area, dial 925 before the local number.

GETTING AROUND

The visitor's own two feet are the best bet in a town full of dead ends, blind corners, twisting cobbled alleys, and very steep hills. If you're traveling by car, it's a good idea to park in one of the eight covered garages within the walled precinct, as far uphill as possible, and then wander.

BUS There is a bus station, Nueva Estación de Autobuses, on the ring road around Toledo (Carretera de Circunvalación; phone: 226307). Two companies — *Continental* (4 Calle Geraldo Lobo; phone: 227360) and *Galiano* (Paseo de Miradero; phone: 223641) — offer frequent daily service to Madrid and other towns in La Mancha. Buses depart for and return from Madrid every half hour from 6:30 AM to 10 PM on weekdays. On Sundays and public holidays, the half-hourly service commences at 8:30 AM and ends at 11:30 PM.

CAR RENTAL Like most medieval towns, Toledo is meant for pedestrians; car rental is not advisable. With the exception of *Avis* (Paseo de Miradero; phone: 214535), the international firms do not have offices in Toledo, but operate out of Madrid, an hour's drive away. One local agency is *Maroto Iglesia* (4 Calle Don Diego; phone: 224337).

TAXI Toledo's two taxi stands are located on Cuesta de Alcázar and Cuesta de la Vega. Roving taxis with an illuminated green light can be hailed as they pass or called (phone: 221968).

TRAIN The train trip to Madrid takes slightly longer than the bus journey. Trains depart for Madrid every 90 minutes from 6:15 AM to 9:50 PM. The return service runs from 8:45 AM to 8:55 PM. The train station is located across the Puente de Safont (on Paseo de la Rosa; phone: 221699).

SPECIAL EVENTS

Semana Santa, or *Holy Week,* has subdued beauty in Toledo; especially moving is the Procession of Silence, which winds through the streets on *Good Friday.* A more boisterous procession — the carrying of the Virgen del Valle around the hillsides near her hermitage on the far side of the river — occurs during the local *Romería,* on *May Day* (May 1) afternoon. Enormous excitement is unleashed for the *Feast of Corpus Christi,* when the town dresses up in folk costume and the precious Arfe monstrance from the cathedral treasury is carried through the city streets. This has been Toledo's ultimate celebration for 8 centuries; it takes place on the Thursday of the ninth week after *Holy Week.* Check with the tourist office for full details and the traditional parade route. Fireworks light the August skies during the *Fiesta de la Virgen del Sagrario,* held annually from August 14 through 20. This fiesta solicits the Virgin's protection for the coming year, and some of the festivities take place inside the cathedral cloisters.

MUSEUMS

Besides those mentioned in *Special Places,* Toledo has two other museums, listed below. In addition, there seven palaces and over 40 churches and convents in the city, many with impressive collections of sculpture and paintings. Amid such a surfeit of art and historic relics, a visitor often can stumble onto treasures merely by investigating what is behind a promising-looking doorway.

MUSEO DE ARMAS BLANCAS DE LA REAL FÁBRICA DE ARMAS (ROYAL ARMS FACTORY MUSEUM OF HAND WEAPONRY) The Royal Arms Factory itself, dating from 1783, is on the outskirts of town. It is now a military installation manufacturing modern weaponry and is closed to the public, but its comprehensive collection of traditional swords, shields, and lances, including the weapons of such personages as El Cid and Boabdil, is on display on the patio of the Alcázar. Open from 9:30 AM to 1:30 PM and from 4 to 5:30 PM (6:30 PM in summer); Sundays from 10 AM to 1:30 PM, and 4 to 5:30 PM (6:30 PM in summer); closed Mondays. Admission charge for the Alcázar includes entrance to the museum. Calle Capuchinos (phone: 221673).

MUSEO DE ARTE CONTEMPORÁNEO (MUSEUM OF CONTEMPORARY ART) Installed in the distinguished Casa de las Cadenas, the museum contains works by contemporary Spanish artists, including Alberto Sánchez, who lived and worked in exile in Moscow until his death in 1962. Prohibited throughout Generalísimo Francisco Franco's regime, his paintings now fill two rooms here. Open Tuesdays through Saturdays from 10 AM to 2 PM and from 4 to 6:30 PM; closed Sundays and Mondays. Admission charge. 15 Calle de Las Bulas (phone: 227871).

SHOPPING

The swordsmiths of Toledo were renowned in more swashbuckling days, and knives of all sorts and even suits of armor are sold here to this day. Damascene, the Moorish art of inlaying gold, copper, or silver threads on a matte black steel background, is also a thriving craft. Souvenir shops throughout the city offer an amazing range of items, some quite mysterious in their function, all decorated in the distinctive black-and-yellow inlaid patterns. Most traditional are the small sewing scissors that snap threads in the sharp beak of a gilded stork, but there is a vast choice of earrings, bangles, cuff links, tie tacks, letter openers, picture frames, and decorative platters. Good, handcrafted damascene is expensive; machine-made items cost less than half the handmade price. The pottery sold in shops and along the roadside is generally of high quality, although it's not strictly local. Still, unless a specific trip is planned to the neighboring ceramic centers of Puente de Arzobispo or Talavera de la Reina (see *Extra Special*), Toledo's shops offer a wide selection.

Marzipan, some of it prepared by nuns, is a local specialty. Small items made of sweet almond paste, a Moorish legacy, are a traditional *Christmas* treat, though available year-round. Popular sweet shops include *Barosso* (11 Calle Real del Arrabel); *Casa Telesforo* (17 Plaza de Zocodover; phone: 223379); and *Confitería Santo Tomé* (two locations: 5 Calle Santo Tomé; phone: 223763; and 11 Plaza de Zocodover; phone: 221168).

Toledo is a major supplier of furniture to the Spanish market, and has been for many years. Most of the antiques shops are on the Toledo–Madrid highway, within the area just outside the city. Try *Balaguer* (Pasadizo del Ayuntamiento and Calle Puerta Llana); *Linares* (Calle de los Reyes Católicos in front of the San Juan de los Reyes monastery); and the *Olrey* shopping complex (in Olías, about 10 miles/16 km from Toledo on the Toledo–Madrid highway).

One of Spain's largest regional crafts fairs, the *Feria de Artesanía Castilla-La Mancha*, takes place in Toledo during the first 2 weeks of October. Held outdoors at La Peraleda fairground, the annual event showcases the full gamut of local arts and crafts. For more information, contact *FARCAMA (Feria de Artesanía Castilla-La Mancha)*; 5 Plaza de España, 13600 Alcázar de San Juan, Ciudad Real (phone: 26-546558)

Bargaining is not unheard of in Toledo, but it is best to haggle only if seeking a discount when buying a number of items, and only if you're paying in cash. Bargaining ruthlessly and then pulling out a credit card is an invitation to ridicule. With the waves of day-trippers from Madrid, many merchants have little time for dickering over prices, although some in quieter shops view it as entertainment. Of the many stores and shops in Toledo, the following are of particular interest:

CASA BERMEJO A source of top-quality Toledo damascene, including that made by Santiago Sánchez Martín (see below). 5 Calle Airosas (phone: 220346).

CASA TELESFORO Some of the best marzipan in town. 17 Plaza de Zocodover (phone: 223379).

CONFITERÍA SANTO TOMÉ More marzipan — marginally less expensive than that of *Casa Telesforo* and a close match for quality. 5 Calle Santo Tomé (phone: 223763), with a branch at 11 Plaza de Zocodover (phone: 221168).

SANTIAGO SÁNCHEZ MARTÍN A damascene artisan who has been inlaying 24-carat gold by hand for 40-plus years. This is his workshop, featuring 40 different models of mirror frames, jewelry, decorative pitchers, and other items. 15 Calle Río Llano (phone: 227757).

SUÁREZ A wide range of damascene items; personalized shields with your own family crest can be specially prepared, if you supply the design. 19 Paseo de los Canónigos (phone: 225615).

SPORTS AND FITNESS

FISHING The best fishing in the Tagus River, which forms a natural moat around Toledo, is in the river basin, far from the city. Near Finisterre Dam, about 28 miles (45 km) southeast of the city, black bass have been introduced. In other reservoirs where fishing is encouraged, carp and large pike abound. Fishing permits are available from the Valencia office of *ICONA (Instituto Nacional para la Conservación de la Naturaleza)*; in Toledo, 6 Plaza San Vicente; phone: 222158); or call *Caza y Pesca* (phone: 213124).

FLYING Anything from a hang glider to a propeller plane is a possibility in the skies over Toledo, where unseen assets beckon pleasure pilots from all over Europe. Steady updrafts and less-predictable waves and slopes in the air occur when La Mancha's miles of broad plateau suddenly rear up as a range of mountains, producing almost a washboard effect. The *Royal Aero Club of Toledo* (20 miles/32 km from the city in Mora de Toledo; phone: 300194) specializes in gliding. The *Ocaña/Toledo Aerodrome,* regional headquarters for the Civil Aviation Authority, offers instruction in gliding, ultra-lights, ballooning, skydiving, and powered flight. Some courses include lodging (for more information, call 130700 or 130769). Pilots must have foreign licenses validated before taking off.

HUNTING The season for small game (partridge, rabbit, hare, quail, dove, and so on) runs from the third Sunday in October through the first Sunday in February. Stalking of larger game starts in September, and the waterfowl season continues through March. The most plentiful hunting grounds are on the highest slopes of the Montes de Toledo. Any area signposted *coto* is a hunting reserve in one of four categories: common use, local, private, or national. Hunters must have a license from their own country, as well as a seasonal permit and insurance. Obtain a customs permit for shotguns and rifles before entering Spain; a separate permit is required for leaving the country. For more information, contact *Caza y Pesca* (phone: 213124) or visit *ICONA*'s office (6 Plaza San Vicente; phone: 222158).

SWIMMING Swimmers can use several public pools in town, but the biggest and cleanest (aside from the guests-only facility at the *Parador Conde de Orgaz*) is at the Circo Romano campground (21 Calle Circo Romano; phone: 220442), just north of the old walls. There is an admission charge, plus a weekend surcharge.

TENNIS Arrangements can be made to use courts at the private *Club de Tenis de Toledo* (Calle Navalpino, Km 49; phone: 224278). There's an admission charge.

WINDSURFING The sport is forbidden in many of the manmade lakes, but when the Cazalegas Reservoir is full, sailing and windsurfing are popular. Contact the tourist office for details.

THEATER AND MUSIC

The *Teatro de Rojas* (4 Plaza Mayor; phone: 223970) has been carefully restored to its 19th-century grandeur. Details regarding any classical Spanish production to be staged here are available from the box office or through the tourist office. Usually, however, this lovely venue is used as a cinema for dubbed foreign movies. Sacred music is the norm in Holy Toledo, and can be heard at vespers at most of the 40-odd churches throughout the city.

NIGHTCLUBS AND NIGHTLIFE

The clue to nightlife in Toledo is to be part of *la movida,* the movement, or the action, and not to stay in any one place too long. Most people stop for a drink or two, then move on to another café or pub. The trendiest late-night drinking spot for *la movida* is *Otto Max* (6 Av. de America). In summer, the open-air terraces near the ramparts come alive. The youngest crowd gravitates to the sundry establishments along Calle Chapinería, Calle Sillería, and Callejón Barrio Rey, while a more sophisticated scene takes place beneath the arcades of the Plaza de Zocodover and the adjoining streets. *La Sal* (Calle de la Sal) attracts young professionals. Discos tend to be quite provincial and young. The brashest one in town is *Sithon's* (4 Calle Lucio). *Máscara* (in the *Galería del Miradero*) is the trendiest, while *Gris Disco* (Carretera Toledo–Avila, Km 2.5) is the most self-conscious. For live music, *Broadway* (Calle Alfonso XII) offers jazz on Friday and Saturday evenings, while yuppies frequent the posher *Catedral de la Música* (4 Calle Quintanar), where local bands play contemporary music.

Best in Town

CHECKING IN

Although the vast majority of visitors descend on Toledo just for the day, quite a few are enticed to stay the night, so good hotel rooms can be at a premium. Expect to pay $110 and up for a double room in a hotel listed as expensive; $60 to $80 at a moderate one; and less than $45 in one listed as inexpensive. All telephone numbers are in the 25 area code unless otherwise indicated.

EXPENSIVE

Parador Conde de Orgaz The stunning view of Toledo makes up for this property's location, far from the center of town. There are 77 well-equipped, air conditioned rooms with color TV sets, private baths, and views. Modern design incorporates traditional architectural styles of the region, and decorations include lovely provincial ceramics. The restaurant serves regional specialties, at a price, and there is an outdoor swimming pool. Reservations are recommended. Paseo de los Cigarrales (phone: 221850; in the US, 212-686-9213; fax: 225166).

MODERATE

Alfonso VI Comfortable lodgings directly in front of the Alcázar. All 88 air conditioned rooms have color TV sets and private baths, and the public areas are done up in austere Castilian style, which contrasts with the bright commercial gallery near the lobby. 2 Calle General Moscardó (phone: 222600; fax: 214458).

Almazara A particularly tranquil spot, with splendid views and friendly service. All 21 rooms have color TV sets and private baths. Well worth the 2-mile (3-km) detour outside town, though it is only open from mid-March through October. 47 Carretera Piedrabuena (phone: 223866).

Cardenal This 18th-century cardinal's palace in the shade of the city ramparts is now a *hostal,* evocative of a grand age. All 27 rooms are air conditioned, with private baths. The overall atmosphere is elegant and distinguished, but the service can be a bit desultory. The place is best known for the meals served in its 2-tiered garden (see *Eating Out*). 24 Paseo de Recaredo (phone: 224900; fax: 222991).

Carlos V This newly refurbished hotel, with its heraldic entrance and palatial exterior, is tucked in a tiny plaza directly west of the Alcázar. The east-facing rooms of the 66-room establishment are the most desirable because they offer views of the cathedral and are farthest away from the bar next door, which often blares loud music late into the night. 3 Plaza Horno de la Magdalena (phone: 222100 or 222104).

Los Cigarrales This pleasant 36-room country house on the far side of the Tagus River has excellent views of Toledo. Each room is air conditioned and decorated with wooden beams and glazed tiles. The management is friendly. 32 Carretera de Circunvalación (phone: 221672; fax: 215546).

El Greco An agreeable and cozy addition to Toledo, this 35-room bed and breakfast establishment is ideally located in the Jewish Quarter, a few steps from its namesake *Casa y Museo del Greco* and the adjacent *Sinagoga del Tránsito.* Some of the rooms facing south in the former mansion overlook the gardens of the Paseo del Tránsito and offer views of the handsome hillside estates, popularly known as "cigarrales," across the Tagus River. This tasteful inn also a features a pleasant indoor patio and attractive regional tile and pottery decorations. 13 Alamillos del Transito (phone: 214250; fax: 215819).

María Cristina Situated within the walls of the former Hospital de San Lázaro near the bullring, it offers 65 air conditioned rooms with private baths and all modern conveniences. A popular spot for business meetings and banquets. Honeymooners can book a special suite under the dome of the ancient chapel. The vast dining room of the restaurant *El Abside* resembles a Moorish tent (see *Eating Out*). 1 Calle Marqués de Mendigorría (phone: 213202).

INEXPENSIVE

Los Guerreros The 13 clean and comfortable rooms are air conditioned and have private baths, and the extremely friendly management and staff makes this *hostal* a favorite with students. Quite a distance from the city's principal sites. 8 Av. de la Reconquista (phone: 211807; fax: 228811).

Santa Isabel Centrally located and a few steps from the cathedral, this small 15th-century converted inn is an intimate, popular spot. Soberly decorated, it has 22 rooms, all with private bathrooms, but no air conditioning. An attraction is the spacious interior patio, where guests can while away the evenings with a cool drink. Most rooms provide an excellent view of surrounding historic buildings. 24 Calle Santa Isabel (phone and fax: 253136).

EATING OUT

La Manchan cuisine is not particularly distinguished, except for the basics: a good sharp cheese and a hearty red wine. Be prepared to eat *perdiz estofada* (marinated partridge) at room temperature; it won't be served piping hot. Toledan-style partridge, stewed in red wine, is less tart. Roast lamb is usually a good bet, and crisp grilled *chuletas* (lamb chops) can be exquisite. In season, venison, hare, and game birds are served with originality. Low-cost meals are scarce in this city, where restaurants raise prices for tourists too tired to look for something else. An à la carte, three-course dinner for two with wine will cost $60 or more in a restaurant listed as expensive, $30 to $50 in a moderate restaurant, and $25 or less in an inexpensive one. The *menú del día,* or daily special, is almost always the most reasonably priced option and usually includes wine and bread along with at least two courses. All telephone numbers are in the 25 area code unless otherwise indicated.

EXPENSIVE

El Abside Quite offbeat, by Toledan standards, with an adventurous crowd. The ancient Moorish tower adjacent to the *María Cristina* hotel has been revamped as a spacious and bright dining room; the bright blue decor and painted Moorish patterns are as festive as a nomad's party tent. The cuisine is imaginative, but the nouvelle touch can be a bit shaky. Try the almond soup and duck with honey-orange sauce. Various Arab-Sephardic dishes provide a choice for vegetarians. Closed Sundays. Reservations advised. Major credit cards accepted. 1 Calle Marqués de Mendigorría (phone: 213202).

Asador Adolfo The most elegant, best-run restaurant in town, with authentic Mudéjar trimmings and artistic cooking. Specialties include roast suckling pig served in a sizzling earthenware pot and tender venison in mushroom sauce. Desserts, especially the intricately designed marzipan, are hard to resist. Owner Adolfo Muños is a gracious, attentive host, who will proudly show off his 40,000-bottle wine cellar. Recommended house vintages include Priorato del Ucles. Closed Sunday evenings. Reservations advised. Major credit cards accepted. Located near the cathedral, this 14th-century building can be hard to find; it's hidden away on a corner shared by 7 Calle Hombre de Palo and 6 Calle la Granada (phone: 227321; fax: 216263).

Aurelio The flagship of Toledo's sole "chain" establishment has traditional rustic ambience with antique pottery on the walls, and serves time-honored Castilian dishes from the kitchen of Aurelio Montero, one of Toledo's classic chefs. Partridge and lamb are the house specialties, but save room for the *arroz con leche* (rice with milk), a far cry from ordinary rice pudding. Closed Tuesdays. Reservations advised. Major credit cards accepted. 8 Plaza del Ayuntamiento (phone: 227716).

La Botica Located in the heart of the city, this stylish place has a formal dining room upstairs, and a cafeteria and outdoor terrace for those who want to people watch. Cosmopolitan variations of Castilian standards and innovative dishes such as eggplant and shrimp gratin are served with flair. Fresh fruit sherbets provide a light finish. Open daily. Reservations unnecessary. Visa accepted. 13 Plaza de Zocodover (phone: 225557).

Cardenal Tucked up against the city walls, this elegant 18th-century palace offers alfresco dining in fine weather. Roast lamb and suckling pig, Castilian specialties, rival the partridge *a la toledana.* Fresh asparagus and strawberries are a must in the spring. Open daily. Reservations advised. Major credit cards accepted. 24 Paseo de Recaredo (phone: 220862).

MODERATE

Casa Aurelio Sister to *Aurelio* (see above), serving excellent cream of crab soup, partridge, quail, sirloin, and other traditional Castilian dishes in a somewhat less formal atmosphere. Closed Wednesdays. Reservations advised. Major credit cards accepted. 6 Calle Sinagoga (phone: 222097).

Chirón A comfortably air conditioned dining place that serves the Toledo standards: partridge, thick slabs of potato omelette, homemade crusty bread, and *manchego* cheese. Closed the first 2 weeks in August. Reservations advised. Major credit cards accepted. Paseo de Recaredo (phone: 220150).

La Cubana Cross the Tagus River at the Puente de Alcántara for filling local dishes that taste just that much better when eaten on the open-air terrace. There is also a wood-paneled dining room. Closed the first 2 weeks in September. Reservations unnecessary. Visa accepted. 2 Paseo de la Rosa (phone: 220088).

Hierbabuena A romantic spot where diners eat by candlelight beneath an intricate Mudéjar ceiling. Latecomers may be seated in a slightly musty side chamber, which is plainly a whitewashed cave. Service is elegant yet friendly. Game (in season) and duck in plum sauce are the house specialties. Closed Sunday evenings and Mondays. Reservations advised. Visa accepted. 9 Calle Cristo de la Luz (phone: 223463).

Marcial y Pablo This traditional Castilian restaurant near the city's main northern gate serves such specialties as *cuchifritos* (a potpourri of lamb, tomatoes, and eggs cooked in a saffron and white wine sauce) and partridge pie in an intimate wood-paneled dining room. Popular with politicians. Closed August. Major credit cards accepted. 11 Nuñez de Arce (phone: 220700).

Mesón Aurelio A sister to the formal *Aurelio* and the less formal *Casa Aurelio*, this casual place serves traditional Castilian dishes plus partridge, quail, and steaks. Closed Mondays. Reservations advised. Visa accepted. 1 Calle Sinagoga (phone: 221392).

Sinaí Although this spot is on a street in the Judería named for the Catholic Monarchs, the dishes here are kosher and Moroccan. The couscous and the tangerine steaks are recommended. The restaurant plays host to an annual *Passover* feast. Open daily, but closes at 6 PM. Reservations unnecessary. Visa accepted. 7 Cuesta de los Reyes Católicos (phone: 225623).

Venta de Aires An old and famous Toledo establishment, as many locals as tourists eat here for the typical Toledo fare: marinated partridge, *tortilla* (potato omelette), garlic soup, and the regional *manchego* cheese. The marzipan is made on the premises. A large tree-shaded terrace is wonderful for summer dining. Closed Sunday evenings and Mondays. Reservations unnecessary. Major credit cards accepted. 35 Calle Circo Romano (phone: 220545).

TAPAS BARS

Several *tapas* bars line the narrow streets just off the Plaza de Zocodover, particularly Callejón Barrio Rey. *Bar Ludeña* (in Plaza de la Magdalena, just below Barrio Rey) is a colorful place offering a wide variety of *tapas,* snacks, and inexpensive meals. *Los Cuatro Tiempos* (5-7 Calle Sixto Ramón Parro) has a downstairs *tapas* bar featuring a splendid ceramic decor. *La Tarrasca* (4 Callejón del Fraile) is actually a restaurant, but you can eat *tapas* at the bar.

Valencia

Valencia is known the world over as the home of paella, possibly the most international of all Spanish dishes. But this city, an agricultural capital that is Spain's third-largest, offers far more than fish, sausage, and rice. The city has, as its local cheerleaders say, *mucha marcha* — lots of life. Like nowhere else in Spain, the residents of Valencia took to the Arabs' love for flame and fireworks, still evidenced in the city's *fallas,* riotous celebrations that draw tens of thousands of visitors every March. The cafés of the old city bustle with people year-round, and the economy thrives.

But Valencia is a rose with thorns. The Old City, set along an elbow of the Turia River, is surrounded by a depressing sprawl of working class housing blocks, and many travelers bypass it in favor of the better-known sites to the north and south. However, it is in the Old City that you find the architecture, museums, and unusually rich historical heritage of what once was one of Spain's most powerful kingdoms.

Valencia lies at the heart of the *huerta,* a crescent of alluvial plain made fertile by a complex irrigation system that has been in use for some 2,100 years. Water has transformed the area into an agricultural paradise: a flat, rich plain covered with millions of orange trees, and numerous market gardens, flower nurseries, and nut tree orchards. Everything depends on the precious water of the Turia River, and the elected judges of Valencia's Water Tribunal have been meeting every Thursday since the Middle Ages outside the cathedral to settle disputes. The proceedings are open to the public and are held in Valencian, a dialect of the Catalan language.

The Romans founded Valentia in 137 BC, although Greeks, Phoenicians, and Carthaginians coasted this area and traded with the native Iberians long before. The city eventually fell into the hands of the Visigoths and, in the 8th century, the Arabs, who invaded the peninsula from northern Africa. It was the Arabs who gave the region some of its most lasting features — its orange groves, the palm trees that line its avenues, the glazing techniques that made its ceramics famous, tremendous improvements to the irrigation system still in use today, fireworks, silk, and rice, which is grown in paddies to the south. In succeeding centuries, Catholics razed all Moorish landmarks, leaving only an Arab bathhouse that is closed to the public today. The first of the Catholic "liberators" was El Cid, the legendary hero who took the town in 1094 and died here 5 years later. Following his death, his brave wife, Doña Jimena, was unable to hold the city, and it slipped back under Arab control for another 150 years.

Valencians regard King Jaime I of Aragon, known as the Conqueror, as their true liberator. Following a 5-month siege, the warrior-king marched into the city in triumph one September day in 1238, granting its Christian inhabitants special rights, or *costums,* in return for their allegiance to the crown of Aragon. During the Middle Ages, the Black Death ravaged the city twice, and a violent pogrom in Valencia's old Jewish quarter set off popular attacks on Jews and converted Moors. Vicente Ferrer, a brilliant but bigoted Valencian cleric who was later sainted and made patron of his native city, delivered virulent anti-Semitic diatribes and helped frame discriminatory laws aimed at religious minorities. When the Spanish Inquisition came to the city in 1482, at least 100 Valencians were burned at the stake for refusing to convert. This sad story of religious intolerance would be completed about 130 years later, with the expulsion from Spain of the last remaining 170,000 converted Moors in 1609.

The Bourbons came to rule Spain in the early 18th century via the War of the Spanish Succession — a war in which Valencia, along with Aragon and Catalonia, backed the defeated Hapsburgs. The city paid for its mistake with the Nueva Planta decree of 1707, which stripped it of its ancient rights and generated resentment that still exists today. The kingdom became a province; its viceroy, a captain general sent from Madrid.

For better or for worse, Valencia has since been involved in just about every war and rebellion in Spain, winning a gritty reputation for independence and liberal-mindedness. In 1808, led by one Father Rico, the populace stormed the city arsenal and rose bloodily against Napoleon's occupying troops; Marshal Louis Gabriel Suchet managed to restore French rule only 4 years later. Over the following decades, Valencia was a hothouse of conspiracies, plots, and failed uprisings, notably the Republican-inspired insurrections of 1856 and 1864. A rebellion during the Revolution of 1868 was settled only with an artillery bombardment of the city.

True to its liberal past, Valencia fought on the losing side during the Spanish Civil War. For most of 1937, with Madrid under seige, Valencia became the Republican capital. It was shelled and bombed until it finally fell to Generalísimo Francisco Franco's troops. In the decades of repression that followed, the local language was almost stamped out; but after Franco died, it made a strong comeback and is now widely spoken.

With a population of 750,000, the city today has the feel of an overgrown agricultural capital, despite its heavy industry and sprawling development. Although past its age of glory, Valencia boasts one exceptional and famous 20th-century writer: Vicente Blasco Ibáñez (1867–1928), best known to English speakers for *Blood and Sand,* possibly the finest novel ever written on bullfighting.

One of the great attractions of Valencia is precisely that it is not a major tourist attraction. With its furniture, ceramics, and many other industries, and the industrial port of El Grao, it can be off-putting to the casual passerby. But visitors soon find it to be a charming, particularly Spanish place. Valencians are less affected than most by the onslaught of coastal tourism in recent decades, so most have a genuine desire to show the visitor why their city deserves a second look.

Valencia At-a-Glance

SEEING THE CITY

For those who don't mind a grueling, 207-step climb, a perfect view of the city can be had from Valencia's most popular monument, El Miguelete, the cathedral's 14th-century octagonal bell tower on the Plaza de la Reina. Clustered around the tower are all the principal buildings of the Old City, and the visitor sees a vista of bridges over the Turia River bed, blue-domed churches, and the fertile *huerta* stretching beyond the ends of the city's streets. The tower is open daily from 10:30 AM to 12:30 PM and from 5 to 6 PM. Admission charge. Enter through the cathedral.

SPECIAL PLACES

Valencia's last set of city walls was torn down in 1865, but almost all of the city's main monuments and museums are within the relatively small area it once enclosed. The area is defined to the north by the bed of the Turia River (which has been rerouted farther away from the city to solve the chronic flooding that had long plagued the old section), and on the west, south, and east by Avenida de Guillem de Castro, Calle de Xàtiva, and Calle Colón, respectively. A major shopping, restaurant, and hotel district lies southeast of the old section, in the blocks just beyond Calle Colón. In the city's port of El Grao, 2½ miles (4 km) to the east, and on the Levante beach just north of it, there are dozens of popular seafood restaurants, as well as some interesting turn-of-the-century buildings in the Spanish Modern style, which is reminiscent of Art Deco.

CATEDRAL (CATHEDRAL) Angled oddly into a corner of the Plaza de la Reina, the Old City's main square, the cathedral is a mixture of styles, as reflected in its three portals, which are Romanesque, Gothic, and baroque. Construction was begun in 1262 on the site of a mosque razed by the Catholic conquerers. Although the basic structure of the cathedral was completed towards the end of the 13th century, the main chapel and some side chapels were not completed until the 18th century. Highlights include the tower (see *Seeing the City*), the Gothic dome, the chapter house, and the main altarpiece, which depicts the life of Christ on six panels. The main chapel contains the pulpit used by San Vicente Ferrer to give some of his apocalyptic orations, and one of the leading Spanish candidates for the "true" Holy Grail — a much-revered agate cup, set with emeralds and pearls on a base of pure gold. The church also boasts some fine paintings, including the *Baptism of Christ* by Juan de Juanes, but the real art treasures are housed in the *Museo de la Catedral,* which contains works by Zurbarán, Juan de Juanes, and others. Notice also the Goya paintings in the museum. The cathedral is open Mondays through Saturdays from 10:30 AM to 12:30 PM and from 5 to 6 PM; open Sundays for mass only. The museum is open Mondays through Saturdays from 10:30 AM to 2 PM; in the summer it is also open from 4:30 to 6 PM. Admission charges for the museum and tower. Plaza de la Reina (phone: 391-8127).

BASÍLICA DE LA VIRGEN DE LOS DESAMPARADOS (BASILICA OF THE VIRGIN OF THE FORSAKEN) An arcade connects the cathedral to this elliptical building, which was completed in 1667 and is said to have been the first mental asylum in the world. The structure contains fine frescoes by Antonio Palomino on the interior of the dome, and a sculpted image of the Virgin of the Forsaken, the patroness of Valencia, that was supposedly sculpted by angels. On the second Sunday in May (*Virgin's Day*), and during the *Feast of Corpus Christi,* the Virgin is carried through nearby streets in processions marked by showers of rose petals and other flowers. Plaza de la Virgen.

MUSEO PROVINCIAL DE BELLAS ARTES (PROVINCIAL FINE ARTS MUSEUM) Many people come to this first-rate art museum, one of Spain's best (but least-visited), just to see the small, brooding self-portrait painted by Velázquez in 1640. While this is its single unquestioned gem, the museum also houses an interesting collection of Valencian religious "primitives" of the 14th, 15th, and 16th centuries. These paintings are remarkable for their graphic, naïve vigor: Blood gushes from Christ's sword wound into a goblet in one painting; the Lactating Virgin spouts milk from her swollen breasts into the mouth of the infant Christ in another. Downstairs, there are early Iberian and Hispano-Roman artifacts. There is also a small treasure of works upstairs by Francisco Ribalta (who died in Valencia in 1628), Ribera, Murillo, El Greco (*St. John the Baptist*), Van Dyck, Hieronymus Bosch, and Goya, who once taught at the Fine Arts Academy that runs the museum. Open Tuesdays through Saturdays from 10 AM to 2 PM and from 4 to 6 PM; Sundays from 10 AM to 2 PM (closed afternoons in August). Admission charge. Located just across the Real Bridge. Calle de San Pío V (phone: 360-5793).

JARDINES DEL REAL (ROYAL GARDENS) Next door to the fine arts museum, this small paradise of rose gardens, bougainvillea, palms, mimosas, jacarandas, cypress, and myrtle trees also has a diminutive but pleasant zoo. The gardens and the zoo are open daily from 10 AM to sundown. Admission charge for the zoo. Calle de San Pío V (phone: 362-3512).

LA LONJA DE LA SEDA (SILK EXCHANGE) This structure in the heart of the Old City is the finest example of Gothic architecture in a city renowned for the genre. In addition to an array of gargoyles, the façade features a series of fantastic and often erotic small figures. The first room is the main Silk Exchange, a great vaulted hall supported by 24 twisting columns reminiscent of massive hanks of silk; on Fridays from 1 to 3 PM, fruit wholesalers hold auctions reminiscent of 16th-century silk fairs here. Next to this hall is the tower of La Lonja, said to have once served as a prison for bankrupt silk merchants. A remarkable circular stairway, with no central support, leads from a courtyard of orange trees to an upstairs hall noted for its elaborately gilded and carved wooden ceiling. Open Tuesdays through Thursdays from 10 AM to 2 PM; Fridays from 10 AM to 3 PM; Sundays from 10 AM to 1 PM. No admission charge. Plaza del Mercado (phone: 391-3608).

MERCADO CENTRAL (MAIN MARKET) One of the finest — and largest — market buildings in Spain is made even more delightful by the colors and smells of the products of the *huerta,* and the glazed *azulejo* tiles showing Valencian citrus fruits and vegetables. Built in 1928, the market is a fine example of Valencian modernism, and is visually similar to a turn-of-the-century railroad station, with glass skylights supported by an elaborate framework of iron girders. Open Mondays through Saturdays, the market offers a quick taste of modern Valencian life. Plaza del Mercado.

PALACIO DEL MARQUÉS DE DOS AQUAS The amazing façade of this 18th-century rococo palace was designed by the painter Hypólito Rovira, who died in a Valencian mental asylum in 1740. Its main entrance is a riotous alabaster fantasy of crocodiles, Cupids, a Virgin with Child, and two men spilling jugs of water — the "two waters" of the Marqués de Dos Aguas. The building now houses the *Museo Nacional de Cerámica,* Spain's leading ceramics museum. The gilded and tiled interior of the building, a kind of Hollywood version of a European palace, is a showcase of centuries of excellent pottery from the outlying towns of Paterna, Alcora, and Manises, beautifully glazed work that was widely sought across Europe in the late Middle Ages. In other rooms, there are works by Picasso, a Valencian tiled kitchen, and pottery from other regions of Spain and abroad. At press time, the museum was closed for restoration work; be sure to call ahead. Admission charge. 2 Calle Poeta Querol (phone: 351-6392).

MUSEO FALLERO This small museum is crammed with *ninots* — the satirical papier-mâché figures that are burned in effigy at midnight on *St. Joseph's Day* (March 19) as part of the *falla* celebrations for which Valencia is famous. Each year, the best *ninot* is saved from the flames and is preserved here. Open Mondays through Fridays from 10 AM to 2 PM and from 4 to 7 PM; Saturdays from 11 AM to 2 PM; and, in the winter, Sundays from 10 AM to 2 PM. Admission charge. 24 Calle Ninot (phone: 347-6585).

MUSEO TAURINO Almost hidden away in a covered concourse next to the bullring, one of Spain's leading taurine museums is filled with bullfighting memorabilia. The collection includes examples of 19th-century bullfighting garb; savage-looking lances, swords, and pics; suits of lights worn by some leading toreros when they were gored; and the stuffed heads of some of the bulls. Valencia was for many centuries a leading city for bullfighting, though its reputation has fallen off in recent decades. Open Mondays through Fridays from 10:30 AM to 1:30 PM. No admission charge. 18 Pasaje Doctor Serra (phone: 351-1850).

ESTACIÓN DEL NORTE (NORTH STATION) Many visitors, whether arriving by train or not, take the time to visit this charming railroad station, one of the most beautiful in Europe. Both the interior and exterior are decorated with *azulejo* tiles bearing such Valencian motifs as oranges, the *huerta,* and *barracas,* the region's traditional thatch-roofed houses. The ticket counters and the cafeteria are especially delightful. 24 Calle de Xàtiva (phone: 351-3612).

TORRES DE SERRANOS AND TORRES DE QUART The 14th-century gate next to the northern Puente Serranos (Serranos Bridge) was fully restored in 1930 and remains an imposing fortified arch. A second gate, another remnant of the medieval walls, is the 15th-century Torres de Quart, nearby on Avenida de Guillem de Castro. Like a proud old warrior, it still bears the scars of French cannonballs from the Peninsular War, the war waged by Napoleon against the British, the Portuguese, and the Spanish guerrillas. On the ground level of the Torres de Serranos is a small maritime museum. Although the towers are closed to the public, the museum is open to visitors Tuesdays through Fridays from 10 AM to 1:30 PM and from 4 to 6 PM; Saturdays from 10 AM to 1 PM (phone: 391-9070).

INSTITUTO VALENCIANO DE ARTE MODERNO/IVAM (VALENCIAN INSTITUTE OF MODERN ART) Hard by what remains of the Old City walls (in fact, a vestige of the medieval ramparts protrudes into one of the galleries), not far from the Torres de Quart, this is one of a recent crop of museums in Spain devoted exclusively to modern art. The collection is housed in two locations — an ultramodern stone-and-glass building called the Centre Julio González and, nearby (and in complete contrast), a restored 13th- to 16th-century Carmelite convent called the Centre del Carme. In addition to the permanent collection of some 1,400 pieces (paintings, drawings, and sculpture by Julio González, a lifelong friend of Picasso, form the nucleus), the Centre Julio González has an auditorium, a restaurant-bar, and a bookshop, and is host to a year-round schedule of changing exhibitions and special cultural events. Both buildings are open Tuesdays through Sundays from 10 AM to 8 PM; no admission charge Sundays. Centre Julio González, 118 Av. de Guillem de Castro; Centre del Carme, 2 Calle Museu (phone for both: 386-3000).

PALAU DE LA MÚSICA (MUSIC PALACE) Across the Aragón Bridge from the Old City, Valencia's concert hall, built in the now-dry bed of the Turia River in 1987, is a rather bizarre mix of reflecting pools, palm trees, small temple-like structures, and a main building that resembles an exceptionally swank greenhouse. It is known to locals as the "microwave" because of its initial lack of air conditioning, and its designers also failed to include a system to clean its vast glass surfaces — leading the city to hire mountaineers to do the job. 1 Plaza del Rey (phone: 360-3356 for information; 361-5212 for tickets).

ENVIRONS

MANISES The town of Manises was a major pottery center in the Middle Ages, when emissaries from the richest courts of Europe vied to buy its fine wares, characterized by distinctive blue-and-white patterns. While otherwise unattractive, the town today is packed with ceramics factories and retail shops, many of which sell good reproductions of pieces in Valencia's *Museo Nacional de Cerámica* at bargain prices. Manises is about 4½ miles (7 km) west of Valencia, and is well served by city buses.

SAGUNTO In 219 BC, the Iberians, the first inhabitants of this fortified rocky ridge, set their possessions and themselves afire rather than surrender to the Carthaginian general Hannibal. The Romans eventually rebuilt the town, and it was successively held by the Visigoths, the Arabs, and, in the 19th century, the French. Today, Sagunto has an impressive 8,000-seat amphitheater, as well as an ancient acropolis, and nearly half a mile of mostly Moorish medieval walls and ramparts. An old Roman forum is marked by a huge broken stone marked with the letters "FORV." The long ridge occupied by the fortifications provides a dramatic, 360-degree view of orange groves, the surrounding mountains, and the Mediterranean. The castle is open Tuesdays through Saturdays from 10 AM to 2 PM and from 4 to 6 PM (7 PM in summer); Sundays and holidays from 10 AM to 2 PM; closed Mondays. Admission charge (phone: 266-5581). The complex also includes the *Museo Arqueológico,* which contains Roman mosaics and other artifacts. At press time the museum and amphitheater were closed for restoration; call before visiting to see if these sites have reopened.

Modern Sagunto has a population of nearly 60,000, and boasts an old Jewish quarter, a supposed Temple of Diana, and other sites. For more information on the city, contact the Sagunto tourist office (Plaza de Cronista Chabret; phone: 266-2213). Sixteen miles (26 km) north of Valencia, the city is easily reached by car and has frequent bus and train service.

EXTRA SPECIAL   Just 9½ miles (15 km) south of Valencia lies one of Spain's largest and most beautiful lakes, La Albufera, in the center of the Albufera national park. This peaceful, lagoon-like lake, surrounded by rice paddies, is home to more than 250 species of fowl, including European flamingos and other unusual birds, as well as the baby eels and fish that have long attracted local fishermen. The lake is separated from the sea by a thin strand of sand and pine trees between the towns of El Saler and El Palmar. In either of these places, or along the highway connecting them, visitors can easily rent flat-bottom boats from local fishermen. The sunsets from this side of the lake are stupendous. In El Palmar, try the *alli al pebre* (baby eels fried in garlic sauce) at the *Racó de l'Olla,* near the lake (Carretera de El Saler; phone: 161-0072).

Sources and Resources

TOURIST INFORMATION

There is no shortage of tourist information offices in Valencia, with four run by the city and a large fifth one under the aegis of the regional government. This regional office, the Conselleria d'Industria Comerc y Turisme (48 Calle de la Paz; phone: 352-4000), near the Plaza Alfonso el Magnánimo, can provide information on both the city and the surrounding areas, and also has some good publications. The office is open Mondays through Fridays from 9 AM to 2 PM and from 5 to 7 PM; Saturdays from 9:30 AM to 2 PM. The main Municipal Tourism Office is located in Valencia's City Hall (1 Plaza del Ayuntamiento; phone: 351-0417), and is open Mondays through Fridays from 9:30 AM to 1:30 PM and from 4:30 to 7 PM; Saturdays from 9:30 AM to 2 PM. The other offices are located at the airport in Manises (phone: 153-0325) and near the city's northern limits (at 1 Av. de Cataluña; phone: 369-7932). These offices are open Mondays through Fridays from 9 AM to 2 PM and from 5 to 7 PM.

LOCAL COVERAGE Two small, locally oriented newspapers serve Valencia: *Las Provincias* and *Levante. Turia* is a weekly guide to local entertainment, including theater, music, and dining. *Geográfica Valenciana,* a paperback collection of excellent photographs of the region, is sold at the regional tourist office and in local shops. English-language newspapers are easily found in the Plaza del Ayuntamiento and other central squares in the Old City.

TELEPHONE

The area code for Valencia is 6. If calling from another part of Spain, dial "9" before the area code and local number.

GETTING AROUND

Downtown Valencia is perpetually packed with cars, and on-street parking is nearly impossible, so it's advisable to walk through the Old City, which is relatively small and easily seen on foot. Trips to outlying areas, including the port, can be made by train or bus, but taxis are quite inexpensive.

AIRPORT The surprisingly busy Valencia Manises Airport (phone: 370-9500), 4½ miles (7 km) northwest of Valencia, near the pottery center of Manises, has flights to most Spanish cities, as well as most major European capitals. Take bus No. 15, which departs the main bus station hourly.

BOAT From Valencia, it's a quick trip to the Balearic Islands of Majorca, Minorca, and Ibiza. *Trasmediterránea* (15 Calle Manuel Soto; phone: 367-6512/0704; and at the port; phone: 323-7580) offers year-round, daily ferry service Mondays through Saturdays from the port of El Grao to Majorca, and less frequent service to the other islands.

BUS Most of the city bus lines a visitor will want to use depart from the Plaza del Ayuntamiento. Ask for help at the Municipal Tourism Office in the same square or get a schedule at *EMT* (1 Calle Nuestra Señora de Gracia; phone: 352-8399). The long-distance bus station (13 Av. Menéndez Pidal; phone: 349-7222), which also serves the airport, is a 10-minute walk north of the Old City, across the Glorias Valencianas Bridge. There is frequent daily service to Madrid, Barcelona, Málaga, and other cities and towns.

CAR RENTAL The leading international and Spanish firms have offices at the airport and downtown. Agencies in the city include *Avis* (17 Calle Isabel la Católica; phone: 351-0734); *Hertz* (7 Calle Segorbe; phone: 341-5036); *Europcar* (7 Av. de Antic Regne de Valencia; phone: 374-1512); *Ital* (19 Calle Isabel la Católica; phone: 351-6818); *Flycar* (3 Calle San José de Calasanz; phone: 384-5879); and *Furgocar* (12 Calle Linares; phone: 384-5500).

SUBWAY A metro system serves the city's west side, but virtually no tourist sites. Fare depends on the distance traveled.

TAXI Taxis can be hailed on the street or called by telephone (phone: 370-3333 or 357-1313).

TRAIN Valencia's main railway station for long-distance trains is the Estación del Norte (Calle de Xàtiva; phone: 351-3612), a colorful iron-and-glass building at the foot of the Old City. Tickets also can be bought at the *RENFE* office (2 Plaza Alfonso el Magnánimo; phone: 352-0202). The creaky old narrow-gauge train that goes to the port of El Grao and northwest through the outlying *huerta* to Liria leaves from the Estación Puente de Madera (1 Calle Cronista Rivelles; phone: 347-3750), just across the Turia River bed from the Serranos Towers.

SPECIAL EVENTS

The *cremá,* or bonfire, is a popular means of celebration in the region of Valencia, and the one for St. Joseph is the *crème de la cremá.*

BEST FESTIVAL

Las Fallas de San José This fiesta in March dates back to the Middle Ages, when the carpenters' guild used to burn a year's worth of accumulated wood shavings on the feast day of St. Joseph, its patron saint. Now, the city's neighborhoods compete in building hundreds of elaborate *ninots* — giant, satirical floats made of colored papier-mâché and wood. A week-long rush of bullfights, concerts, parades, flower-bedecked processions, and all-out partying ends at midnight on the saint's day (March 19) to a thundering chant of *"Fuego"* — "Fire!" — and a burst of fireworks, as the *falleros* light a fantastic array of satirical effigies and the flames leap into the sky. The *fallas* draw huge crowds from Spain and abroad, so hotel reservations are essential.

Also in the early spring, *Holy Week* is marked by boats parading in maritime processions. The patroness of the city, the Virgin of the Forsaken, has her day on the second Sunday of May, followed by the *Feast of Corpus Christi,* when Valencian *rocas,* baroque holy images of great beauty, are rolled through the streets. The city fills up with tourists again during its *Feria de Julio,* a week-long fair in early July that includes topnotch bullfights, music, fireworks, and a paella contest. And in early October, Valencians — who love all manner of pops, fizzles, and flares — host the *International Pyrotechnic Festival,* a tournament of the world's finest makers of fireworks.

MUSEUMS

Noteworthy museums not mentioned in *Special Places* (above) include the following:

MUSEO HISTÓRICO MUNICIPAL A small but interesting museum containing a collection of paintings and mementos pertaining to the history of Valencia, ensconced in the Ayuntamiento (City Hall). Open Mondays through Fridays from 9 AM to 1:30 PM. No admission charge. Plaza del Ayuntamiento (phone: 352-5478).

MUSEO JOSÉ BENLLIURE The former home of one of the city's most famous painters now houses a museum of his work. Benlliure spent most of his life in Italy, but returned to Valencia in his later years and died here in 1937. Open Tuesdays through Fridays from 10 AM to 1 PM and from 4 to 6 PM. No admission charge. 23 Calle Blanquerías, near Portal Nuevo (phone: 391-1662).

MUSEO PALEONTOLÓGICO Skeletal remains and other artifacts are displayed in the Almudín, a 14th-to-16th-century granary decorated with *azulejos* and curious frescoes. Open Tuesdays through Fridays from 10 AM to 2 PM and from 4 to 6 PM; Saturdays and Sundays from 10 AM to 2 PM. No admission charge. Calle Arzobispo Mayoral (phone: 331-8562).

MUSEO DE LA PREHISTORIA In the former Bailía Palace, exhibits of cave paintings, Roman pots, Stone Age and Iberian ceramics, and other archaeological remains of the Valencian region. Open Tuesdays through Fridays from 10 AM to 2 PM and from 4 to 6 PM; weekends from 10 AM to 2 PM. No admission charge. 36 Calle Corona (phone: 331-7164).

SHOPPING

Valencia thinks of itself as a design center, and this is reflected in the scores of attractive and very upscale boutiques and designer shops found here. Some of the finer shopping streets — Calle de la Paz, Calle Poeta Querol, Calle de Colón, and Calle Sorni — compare favorably with anything found in Madrid or Barcelona. Valencia is also home to some of Spain's best pottery, Manises stoneware (see *Special Place*), and Lladró porcelain, and glassware is also blown and sold in the region. *Azulejos,* the brightly colored ceramic tiles so gloriously developed by the Arabs in Spain, are a local pride and joy. Another indigenous specialty is the painstakingly hand-sewn silk garments that make up traditional Valencian women's costumes — and sell at huge prices. Business hours are generally weekdays from 9:30 AM to 1:30 PM and 4:30 to 8 PM. Most of the best stores are found around the southeastern portions of the Old City.

ALTARRIBA A remarkable toy store with a wide selection of model trains from around the world, as well as a collection of peculiarly Spanish miniatures. 22 Calle Mar (phone: 332-3024).

ARTESPAÑA A state-run crafts shop featuring fine handmade ceramics, furniture, hand-blown glass, and leather goods at reasonable prices. 7 Calle de la Paz (phone: 391-6403).

CARLA Specializing in fine silk, including garments for women. 4 Calle Bordadores (phone: 391-8430).

EL CORTE INGLÉS Valencia has two branches of the popular national department store chain; they remain open during the lunch hour and on Saturday afternoons. 26 Calle Pintor Sorolla (phone: 351-2444) and in the *Nuevo Centro Shopping Mall,* 15 Av. Menéndez Pidal (phone: 347-4142).

LLADRÓ The internationally known maker of porcelain figurines; it also offers its own line of leather goods. Three locations: Calle Marqués de Sotelo (phone: 351-0937), Calle Poeta Querol (phone: 351-1625), and in the *Nuevo Centro Shopping Mall* (phone: 347-0086).

LOEWE One of Spain's most elegant — and expensive — purveyors of men's and women's clothing, leather goods, luggage, and accessories. Men's store at 7 Calle Poeta Querol (phone: 352-7372); women's store at 7 Calle Marqués de Dos Aguas (phone: 352-4253).

NERI An exclusive ceramics and kitchenware store, offering some of the finest traditional pottery in the city. 1 Calle Poeta Querol (phone: 351-8961).

SPORTS AND FITNESS

BOATING The *Real Club Náutico* (Royal Nautical Club; Camino Canal; phone: 367-9011) offers boat rentals, a sailing school, fishing, scuba diving and snorkeling, and full yacht service.

BULLFIGHTING One of the largest rings in Spain is located next to the train station (28 Calle de Xàtiva; phone: 351-9315). Corridas, or bullfights, are held for a week during the *fallas* and the July festival, otherwise irregularly.

GOLF There are four golf courses near Valencia. The 18-hole, par 72 *Campo de Golf El Saler* (phone: 161-1186) is at the *Parador Luis Vives,* sandwiched between the Mediterranean and the Albufera lagoon 11 miles (18 km) south of Valencia on a strand of pine trees and sand dunes. Also try the 18-hole *Club de Campo del Bosque* (Calle Chiva; phone: 251-1011), 2½ miles (4 km) from town; or the 18-hole *Club de Golf Escorpión* (phone: 160-1211) at Bétera, 12 miles (19 km) northwest along the road to Liria. There is also a 9-hole course 7½ miles (12 km) west of town in Manises (phone: 379-0850).

SOCCER Valencia's first-division team is a cause célèbre in the area, with victory liable to provoke flag waving, horn honking parades downtown. Valencia plays at the *Estadio Luis Casanova,* Av. de Suecia (phone: 360-0550).

SWIMMING The beaches just north and south of the port, Playa de Levante and Playa de la Punta, are too polluted to make swimming advisable. There are miles of popular beaches to the south, toward El Saler, that are cleaner.

TRINQUETE This is a peculiarly Valencian form of that great Spanish sport, pelota (best known to Americans in one of its many forms, jai alai). The crowd sits along one side of the frontón while players bat a calfskin ball over a net with their hands. Afternoon games are played daily except Tuesdays and Sundays at the *Trinquete Pelayo,* 6 Calle Pelayo (phone: 352-6845).

THEATER AND MUSIC

There are several theaters in Valencia, but only one has consistently interesting Spanish and European productions: the *Teatro Principal* at 15 Calle Barcas (phone: 351-0051). The 19th-century theater also holds an opera season, usually in the fall and winter, and hosts occasional jazz, dance, and other festivals. Valencia's futuristic *Palau de la Música* (see *Special Places*) hosts world class concerts of classical and other music during much of the year.

NIGHTCLUBS AND NIGHTLIFE

Valencia has a thriving bar scene, although it is unusually scattered. Younger and hipper bars tend to be concentrated around the Plaza del Carmen and Calle Caballeros in the Old City — *Café Lisboa* (35 Calle Caballeros; phone: 392-1764) doubles as a photo gallery. A truly charming Old City bar, the *Cervecería Madrid* (10 Calle Abadía de San Martín; phone: 352-9671), is owned by Constante Gil, who painted the hundreds of naïve canvases that decorate the place's 2 floors. Nearby, in the Plaza del Ayuntamiento, walk through the front door of the old *Cine Rialto* (phone: 351-5603), a theater that shows foreign films in their original language, into the *Cafetería Rialto* (phone: 351-5603), a perfect spot for a drink. Quite a trek northeast of the Old City is the Plaza Xuquer, which is surrounded by bars and fast-food joints popular with students from the nearby university. Bars aimed at an older crowd are on Gran Vía Marqués del Turia, east of the Estación del Norte, the main train station. Large, all-night discotheques are found on the highway to El Saler — the *Spook Factory* (Carretera del Saler, Pinedo; no phone) is one of the most popular. For those with a taste for the tables, *Hotel-Casino Monte Picayo* (phone: 142-1211), is a pricey luxury complex featuring every gaming, lodging, and sporting service imaginable. Casino hours are 7 PM to 5 AM nightly. Monte Picayo is 9½ miles (15 km) north of Valencia, on the N-340 highway to Barcelona.

Best in Town

CHECKING IN

Hotel space in Valencia isn't a problem, except during the March 12–19 *fallas* (see *Special Events*), when reservations are an absolute must. The city also hosts a number of business conventions throughout the year that can suddenly fill several hotels. Parking is a year-round nightmare anywhere close to the Old City, a fact that should be considered when choosing accommodations. Hotel rooms cost less on the whole than those in other large cities that are more firmly established on the tourist track. Expect to pay $110 and up for a double room at an establishment listed as very expensive, $65 to $110 at an expensive hotel, $40 to $65 at a moderate place, and $35 or less at an inexpensive one. All phone numbers are in the 6 area code unless otherwise indicated.

VERY EXPENSIVE

Astoria Palace When Spanish politicians, entertainers, and other celebrities visit Valencia, this is where they stay. Manuel Benítez, "El Cordobés," rode the shoulders of a crowd direct from the bullring into the lobby here. Sumptuously decorated and ideally located on a small square in the heart of the Old City, the hotel manages to retain an atmosphere of personal attention. All of its 208 rooms and 20 suites are air conditioned and have color TV sets, radios, and, on request, mini-bars. Other facilities include a restaurant, a convention center, private dining rooms, parking, and a discotheque. 5 Plaza Rodrigo Botet (phone: 352-6737; fax: 352-8078).

Melia Valencia R. D. Jaime A short taxi ride from the city center, near the *Palau de la Música,* stands this luxurious, spacious, and somewhat impersonal establishment. The lower lobby contains a concourse of shops, a hairdresser, and a sweeping marble staircase that leads up to a sitting room, an English-style bar, and convention and meeting rooms. The restaurant offers both international dishes and reasonable versions of Valencian specialties. Upstairs, the 314 air conditioned rooms are very large and well serviced; the bathrooms, huge. The hotel is primarily a businessperson's place, however, in a somewhat gloomy location outside the life of the Old

City. 2 Av. Baleares (phone: 360-7300; in the US, 800-336-3542; fax: 360-8921).

Dimar Functional is the operative word at this 95-room modern establishment a long walk from the central city. A pleasant lobby leads to clean and carpeted air conditioned rooms that offer color TV sets, mini-bars, and rambling bathrooms. The hotel is only a few steps from a district known for its upscale boutiques and fine restaurants. 80 Gran Vía Marqués del Turia (phone: 395-1030; fax: 395-1926).

Inglés This property, which overlooks the *Ceramics Museum* in the heart of the Old City, is the former palace of the Duke and Duchess of Cardona, and is a historical landmark. Old World charm characterizes the lobby and the connected restaurant, but the 62 rooms, although all equipped with TV sets, are a bit faded and old-fashioned. The sunlit restaurant is elegant, with classy if slightly stuffy service; it's an especially pleasant place for a lingering breakfast. 6 Calle Marqués de Dos Aguas (phone: 351-6426; fax: 394-0251).

Reina Victoria Luis Ferreres Soler, the designer of this centrally located 1910-vintage building, was clearly influenced by 19th-century French architecture, but threw in a splash of modernism. Glass encloses corner balconies, the dining room, and the lobby, giving the interior a light and airy feel. Many of the 97 air conditioned rooms offer striking views of the Old City. The bar is dark, woody, and very English; the restaurant and its marble-floored dining room are local favorites. The service here is excellent. Convention facilities are also available. 4 Calle Barcas (phone and fax: 352-0487).

MODERATE

Bristol Behind a turn-of-the-century brick, stone, and glass façade are 40 pleasant rooms in the center of the Old City. It's a short walk from the *Ceramics Museum* and other downtown monuments. The service is pleasant and helpful. 3 Calle Abadía de San Martín (phone: 352-1176).

Excelsior Comfortable and pleasant, with a wood-paneled lobby, it's just a few steps from the *Astoria Palace* and costs only half as much. All 65 rooms have color TV sets and clean, comfortable appointments and facilities. Downstairs, a white brick cafeteria-bar and an elegant little dining room are both enjoyable spots, and the service is good. 5 Calle Barcelonina (phone: 351-4612).

Llar Cheerful, helpful service, an ideal location for those who aren't set on staying smack-dab in the Old City, and unusually homey wood-and-plaster rooms are the highlights of this 50-room establishment. It's on the artery of a bustling and upscale shopping district, no more than a 10-minute walk to almost anywhere in the city. 46 Calle Colón (phone: 352-8460).

Alcázar Offering 18 quiet rooms just off the Plaza del Ayuntamiento, easily located by a huge and somewhat garish 4-story sign hanging out over the street. The rooms are small and a bit depressing, but it's hard to beat the price. The larger part of the establishment is a 2-story restaurant specializing in popular Valencian and Spanish dishes; the tavern downstairs, hung with hams, is charming. Try the *tapas* at the bar. 11 Calle Mosén Femades (phone: 352-9575).

Castelar At the foot of the Plaza del Ayuntamiento, this family-run property offers 17 clean, comfortable rooms for less than half the price of similar digs across the street at the much larger *Europa*. Each room has running water; the shared bathrooms are well maintained and clean. There is no restaurant on the premises. 1 Calle Ribera (phone: 351-3199).

EATING OUT

Valencia is home to Spain's most internationally famous dish of all — paella — and the city's restaurants compete vigorously with one another to concoct the most delightful version of this dish. Paella was originally peasant fare — rice with whatever happened to be at hand. In Valencia, unlike in other regions of Spain, the traditional *paella Valenciana* concentrates on the quality, texture, and flavor of the rice, and excludes additional ingredients. Those who want seafood included should order *paella marinera* (seafood paella) or *arroz con mariscos* (rice with shellfish). Other delicious rice dishes include *arroz a banda* (rice with fish, garlic, onion, tomato, and saffron); *arroz en bledes* (rice with stewed cabbage, tomato, red peppers, white beans, and garlic); and *arroz al forn* (rice cooked in an oven casserole with chickpeas, potatoes, garlic, paprika, and sometimes pork ribs). *Fideuà,* a paella in which vermicelli is used in place of saffron rice, is the rage among Valencia's contemporary master chefs. All vegetables and fruits in the region are likely to be excellent, as they come straight from the fertile *huerta.* Another local delight is *horchata,* a cold, refreshing summer drink made with *chufas* (earth almonds), water, and sugar; the best way to sample it is in the cafeterias and orchards of Alboraya, the village — about 4 miles (6 km) north of Valencia — where it's made. A local pastry is *mona de pascua,* a spongy *Easter* cake. The region's wines are many, with a tendency to the slightly sweet, but none has so far received much recognition elsewhere. Note that good restaurants in Valencia are not concentrated in the Old City, and several are in the port of El Grao. Expect to pay $60 or more for a meal for two with wine in restaurants listed as expensive, $40 to $60 in moderate restaurants, and $35 or less in inexpensive ones. All telephone numbers are in the 6 city code unless otherwise indicated.

Eladio Eladio, the Swiss-trained owner, is a master of fish — hake, sea bass, anglerfish, turbot, and sole — which he brings south from the stormy Atlantic waters off his native Galicia. The menu occasionally verges on nouvelle cuisine but generally sticks to European and Galician dishes. Try the *pulpo a la gallega* (Galician octopus), and don't miss the pastries prepared by Eladio's wife, Violette Fontaine. Closed Sundays and August. Reservations necessary. Major credit cards accepted. 40 Calle Chiva (phone: 384-2244).

L'Estimat Located in the port of El Grao, this eatery has several large dining rooms overlooking the beach. The specialities here are Valencian rice dishes, but the seafood — especially the prawns in garlic sauce and the baby squid sautéed in butter — is worth a try. Closed Tuesdays and mid-August through mid-September. Reservations advised. Visa accepted. 18 Av. del Neptuno (phone: 371-1018).

El Gourmet Consistently fine Spanish and continental food, coupled with excellent service, have made this place one of Valencia's most popular. Try some of chef Jaime Capilla's specialties: *revueltos de berenjenas con gambas* (scrambled eggs with eggplant and shrimp), *merluza con almejas* (hake with clams), and *perdiz moscovita al hojaldre* (muscovy partridge in pastry), among others. Closed Sundays, *Holy Week,* and August. Reservations advised. Major credit cards accepted. 3 Calle Taquígrafo Martí (phone: 395-2509).

La Hacienda A few steps outside the city's old east gate, it serves Spanish dishes and other selections in a room decorated with mirrored walls and elegant old furniture. The *rabo de toro a la cordobesa* (oxtail stew, Cordoban-style) is renowned, and game, in general, is very good. Closed Saturday afternoons, Sundays, and *Holy Week.* Reservations advised. Major credit cards accepted. 12 Av. Navarro Reverter (phone: 373-1859).

Lionel A dining room that is meant to reflect elegant French turn-of-the-century style, it is pleasant but perhaps a bit grandmotherly. Usually good are the homemade soup, croquettes, partridge, and rabbit. The kitchen emphasizes duck and turkey dishes, but tends to overcook both. Service is adequate. Closed Sundays and mid-August to mid-September. Reservations advised on weekends. Major credit cards accepted. 9 Calle Pizarro (phone: 351-6566).

Ma Cuina Very good Basque and Valencian cooking make this popular spot worth a visit. Closed Saturday afternoons and Sundays, *Holy Week,* and August. Reservations advised. Major credit cards accepted. 49 Gran Vía Germanias (phone: 341-7799).

Los Madriles A favorite of Valencia's bullfighting aficionados, this small Castilian restaurant serves such Madrid regional specialties as *cocido* (chickpea stew), *cordero al horno* (oven-baked lamb), and *ternera en su jugo* (veal in its own juices). Good rioja wines are served in a humble but charming atmosphere under walls of bullfight posters. Closed Sunday evenings (all day Sunday during summer), August, and *Holy Week*. No reservations or credit cards accepted. 50 Av. de Antic Regne de Valencia (phone: 374-2335).

La Marcelina In a row of several dozen restaurants lining the beach near the port of El Grao, this is one of the more famous of Valencia's old beach establishments. For more than a century, it has been offering great paellas and, in summer, music on an outdoor terrace. Closed Sunday evenings (all day Sunday during summer). Reservations unnecessary except Saturday evenings in summer. Major credit cards accepted. 8 Av. del Neptuno (phone: 371-2025).

Marisquería Civera Without a doubt, the best shellfish in the city — and that probably goes for the fish, too. There's a galaxy of seafood and vegetable *tapas* laid out on the counters, all absolutely fresh. Closed Mondays and during the month of August. This *marisquería,* or shellfishery, is always busy, so go early or make reservations. Major credit cards accepted. Across the Serranos Bridge, at 11 Calle Lérida (phone: 347-5917).

Nevada In 1979, this hidden treasure won the international prize for *fideuà,* and since then the dish has gotten even better. An excellent — and exceedingly fairly priced — place to sample Valencian rice dishes. Try *arroz al horno, arroz negro con chipirones* (black rice with squid), or *arroz con mariscos* (rice with shellfish). Closed Tuesdays and all day Sunday during the summer. No reservations. Major credit cards accepted. In a nondescript residential neighborhood. 53 Av. Fernando el Católico (phone: 325-5121).

La Pepica This grand old eatery is on the beach next to *La Marcelina* and is known as *the* lunchtime spot for paella and other Valencian rice dishes. Walk past the great open kitchen, hung with hundreds of black paella pans, and into a spacious dining room overlooking a white sand beach (there are outdoor tables in summer). Open daily; closed November. No reservations. Major credit cards accepted. 6 Av. del Neptuno (phone: 371-0366).

La Riuà *Arroz a banda* (rice with seafood) is Pilar Lozano's specialty. Two different rice dishes are served daily in this 3-level dining room lavishly decorated with glazed tiles and handicrafts and located in the heart of the Old City. Seafood dishes also are very good, and the *menú del día* (menu of the day) is a bargain. Closed Mondays and August. Reservations advised on weekends. Major credit cards accepted. 27 Calle Mar (phone: 391-7154).

La Montaraza Spanish fare, especially good roast meats and sausages, at a fair price. Closed holidays and Sunday evenings (all day Sunday during summer). No reservations. Major credit cards accepted. 47 Calle Olta (phone: 373-1653).

Rue de la Paix Decent, reasonably priced French cooking that's even less expensive if ordered from the *menú del día*. Closed Saturdays at lunch and all day Sundays. Reservations unnecessary. No credit cards accepted. 18 Calle de la Paz (phone: 351-2610).

TAPAS BARS

Valencia's leading *tapas* streets are Calle Mosén Femades, just off the Plaza del Ayuntamiento, and Calles Ribera and Convento Jerusalén. *Taberna Alcázar* (9 Calle Mosén Femades; phone: 352-9575) is a rustic and charming bar in the hotel and restaurant of the same name; its old wooden bar practically groans under the weight of the *tapas*. Mushroom *tapas* are especially good at *Amorós* (3 Calle Llop; phone: 351-7057), centrally located and sometimes thronged, while *Casa Mario* (3 Calle Roteros; phone: 331-7006), in the offbeat and increasingly interesting Barrio del Carmen near the Serranos Towers, does a terrific job with shellfish *tapas* and *raciones* (bigger than appetizer-sized *tapas*).

Diversions

Exceptional Experiences for the Mind and Body

Quintessential Spain

The Iberian Peninsula is like a hypothetical aisle marked "Experience" in a choice-laden supermarket — full of good things that come in a variety of enticing packages. So just as sherry comes in *fino, amontillado, manzanilla,* and *dulce,* flamenco can be either raucous side-street strumming, a tourist sideshow in Granada's Sacromonte Caves, or a whirl-perfect spectacle on a limelighted Madrid stage. Gazpacho can be eaten with a spoon or drunk with a straw, and there are endless varieties of seafood, from the hearty cod stews of the Basque Country to the elaborate mussel-and-shrimp paella of Valencia. Nor do all Spaniards speak Castilian. There is a language related to Portuguese spoken in the region of Galicia, a different form of Catalan on each Balearic Island, and the exotic language of the Basques, called Euskera, that apparently isn't related to anything else on this planet.

Iberia's range of flavors comes from its capacity for absorption. One of Spain's most characteristic painters was a Greek (El Greco), the Bourbon dynasty was French, and an American popularized Pamplona's *Fiesta de San Fermín* (in recognition of which the city named a square for him — Plaza Hemingway). The New World sent the old one tomatoes, potatoes, chocolate, coffee, and the gold that decorated Toledan swords and made Madrid one of the most powerful cities in Europe. Africa gave Spain an architectural heritage and the microtonal wail of Spanish flamenco. And Mother Nature gave the country an often crushing heat that spawned such relaxing institutions as the afternoon siesta, the evening *paseo,* the strategically placed café, and the evening gathering around the motor scooter in a small town square.

Still, there are several experiences that capture the special spirit of this singular peninsula, and provide a visitor with an insight into its irresistible personality.

BULLFIGHT IN PAMPLONA, Navarre This Sunday ritual, heralded by fanfare and pomp, is an assault on all the senses: the ocher turf glaring in the late afternoon sun; the band's tinny blare; the gaudy, spangled costumes of the procession; the *bandilleros'* ballet; the coarse, feverish crowd watering its passion with warm wine squirted from bulging skins; the bull's thundering fury; the graceful arrogance of the matador; the swirl of the fuschia and yellow *muleta;* the flash and plunge of the sword. This celebration of life and death and "grace under pressure," as Hemingway described it, is watched on television in living rooms and bars all over Spain. The president of the corrida (usually a local public official) sits in box seats high above the arena with a group of advisors, and decides when to begin each phase of the event. The matador's artistry and daring determine whether the president, like an emperor decreeing mercy or death for a gladiator with a flick of his thumb, will award him one or two ears. The crowd plays a major role by wildly waving white handkerchiefs at the president indicating their support for the matador. An extraordinary performance will bring two ears and a tail. Each morning during the *Fiesta de San Fermín* in July, the bulls for the day's corrida are sent galloping down narrow, barricaded streets on a 2-mile route to the *Plaza de Toros.* The animals receive a measure of revenge when they manage to gore a handful of the hundreds of brave (or crazy) men — and a few women — who, dressed in the red and white colors of the festival, race before the bulls.

LONELY ARAB CASTLES OF ANDALUSIA It takes a car, a sharp eye, a love of detours, and a well-stocked picnic hamper to find the romantic, weed-strewn ruins of castles that once guarded every hill and port in Arab Al-Andalus. Perched on crag-tops, these worn, but still stern, battlements formed a Maginot Line along the tense border between the Muslim and Christian worlds of long ago, where the names of towns still bear the epithet *de la frontera* ("on the border"). But this martial past acquires a latter-day peaceful haze if the scant remains are contemplated with the benefit of a bottle of wine, a hunk of *manchego* cheese, some smoky slices of *jamón serrano,* and a handful of Spanish olives. Because the road to the top can be nearly vertical, it's probably best to leave the car in the olive grove or by the cluster of whitewashed houses that invariably cower in the castle's shadow. Count on being alone at the top, except perhaps for a state employee who is likely to be as lonely as the ruins he guards and will be more than happy to point out the storerooms, the water drains, the narrow, L-shaped passageways meant to thwart a battering ram, the direction from which the Christians finally came, the best angle for a snapshot, and the precise plot in the distant cemetery where his grandfather is buried.

TAPAS AND PATIOS, Córdoba, Andalusia The glare of the southern sun and the heady odor of orange blossoms are everywhere in Córdoba, settling on the city, seeping from the cobblestones, sliding through the painted shutters, making everyone sleepy and sultry and hot. A *tapas* bar is the perfect refuge for sodden sightseers and lounging locals, who gather in the grudging breeze from a creaking electric fan, nursing chilled sangria and gazpacho. Beneath the glass counter are countless accompaniments to a glass of beer — marinated mushrooms, shrimp in garlic sauce, olives seasoned with thyme, fried squid, bits of sausage, roasted sweet peppers with olive oil, smoked ham, spicy meatballs — all available in the mouthful-size portions that make them *tapas* and not a meal. Throughout the day, the floor becomes littered with shrimp tails, toothpicks, and crumpled paper napkins (it's traditional for patrons to let them fall to the ground). For those who can bring themselves to step out into the sticky Andalusian summer, occasional cool gusts of comfort come from the patios not quite hidden behind wrought-iron grilles or wooden doors left ajar just enough for one to peer in and breathe deeply. Geraniums, jasmine, and lemon trees lovingly arranged against patterned, tiled walls offer sun-stroked visitors a fresh, perfumed caress. The lushest and most colorful patios win prizes in the city's 2-week *Fiesta de los Patios* in May.

FLAMENCO IN THE BARRIO DE TRIANA, Seville The impromptu stomp, strum, snap, clap, and growl gets going around 1 or 2 AM in the working class district of Triana. The patrons of the earthy bars along the Calle Betis bring their own guitars and tambourines — the dancing is unrefined and improvised, and the singing is soulful and throaty. Flamenco grew out of a mixture of *sevillanas,* liturgical chants, the call of the Moorish muezzin, and plaintive Gypsy folk tunes, catalyzed by the Inquisition into a music of guttural sounds lamenting the fate of the heathen in brutally Catholic Spain. Although the song and dance performances — *tablaos* — in the more gentrified Barrio de Santa Cruz (where foreigners pay pricey cover charges) are filled with high artistry, this, with its rough edges and drinking and picking of pockets, is the real thing.

ON HORSEBACK THROUGH EXTREMADURA The name means "beyond the Douro River," where the local specialties are black-bull steaks and cured hams made from snake-fed pigs. Ride here in the spring, before the heat has burned away the tapestry of flowers and turned the rich, red soil a cracked and sunbaked brown. At a leisurely canter, you can't help but savor the cork woods and chestnut groves that motorists mostly miss on their way to the hilltop monasteries of Guadalupe and Yuste. And in some parts, you and your mounts will be the only visitors — few cars ever make it up the stomach-churning curves through the forests of Las Hurdes, the northernmost part of Extremadura. There is some poetic justice in the stares you will attract as you ride into a dusty shepherd town, for it was Extremaduran peasants-turned-conquistadores who rode the first horses off Spanish galleons and into the New World — and were taken for half-equine gods.

THE ROYALTY TRAIL, Castile-León Like children romping in a playroom shin-deep in toys, the Kings and Queens of Spain scattered palaces, gardens, and summer retreats all over Castile. They all can be visited, but take it slow, because if you try to retrace the dainty steps of royalty in one whirlwind day, your tour will meld into a sumptuous haze of polished wood and tarnished mirrors and the very chair where Carlos the Some-thingth sat. Start at the *Prado,* once the storehouse for the king's art collection, to see court life through Diego Velázquez's keen, cruel eye for the pomposity, frills, and formalities of the 17th century. His portraits of the royal family and paintings such as *Las Meninas* (The Maids of Honor) seem like sociological studies of how the other half a handful lived. The itinerary then spirals out from King Juan Carlos's current throne room in Madrid's Palacio Real, swooping through extremes of opulence: the once-suburban, still-idyllic Parque del Retiro; the tapestried walls of El Pardo; the passionate austerity of the royal monastery of El Escorial, in the mountains above Madrid; the weave of graveled walks and marble stairways at Aranjuez; and the bursting geyser fountain at La Granja de San Ildefonso, outside Segovia.

Paradores

No visit to the Iberian Peninsula is complete without a visit or an overnight stay in a Spanish *parador*. Imagine sleeping where kings and queens slept, walking corridors and chambers where Franciscan monks walked, and dining in elegant rooms where nobles and aristocrats sat down to countless formal meals over the centuries. The Spanish people pride themselves on their rich sense of such traditions, and have impeccably restored and converted ancient landmark castles and monasteries into magnificent hotel accommodations, offering travelers a historic return to the past, complete with modern — and often luxurious — facilities.

Spain's first *parador* (an inn that offers food and shelter to travelers) was introduced west of Madrid in the Sierra de Gredos in 1928, when King Alfonso XIII opened a lodge to be used primarily as a base for hunting excursions. This concept of low-cost accommodation became so popular that it eventually expanded into the world's most successful transformation of long-abandoned national treasures. There are 85 *paradores* in the countrywide network today; the newest one is in the town of Cuenca.

Many of the *paradores* are restored convents, palaces, manor houses, monasteries, and castles, filled with original decorations and antiques. Other *paradores* are constructed of gleaming marble and boast the latest modern touches — including indoor and outdoor swimming pools, golf courses, and other sports facilities. All have good or even fine restaurants serving breakfast, lunch, and dinner, and featuring regional specialties and wines. All also carry the red, white, and rosé wines bottled under the *parador* label by a quality Rioja winery.

Not all *paradores* are for everyone. Most of the rooms are doubles furnished with twin beds. Travelers who want a double bed should request a room with a *cama de matrimonio,* but be advised that normally there are only a few per *parador*. Some *paradores* are remote, located on the outskirts of town (requiring a car to get to most sightseeing stops). Travelers unable to climb stairs should inquire about elevators, since some *paradores* do not have easy access to all rooms and public areas. *Parador* rooms are equipped with TV sets and mini-bars, though not all have radios.

Although it is possible to travel through Spain from *parador* to *parador* without reservations, this practice is not recommended. Ask the *parador* concierge to phone ahead to determine availability and to make reservations. Rates are seasonal in the majority of the *paradores,* but some have one price structure year-round. Low season runs from November through March, mid-season is from April through June, and high season is from July through October. Expect to pay between $85 and $225 for a double room (the average price is about $110). Breakfast buffet ($11) is extra, as is a tax for all charges (about 6%). For more information about the *paradores* of Spain, contact *Paradores de Turismo de España* (18 Calle Velázquez, Madrid 28001; phone: 1-435-9700), or the network's US representative, *Marketing Ahead* (433 Fifth Ave., New York, NY 10016; phone: 212-686-9213).

For information on recommended *paradores* in or near major cities, see the *Checking In* sections of the individual reports in THE CITIES. Below are our favorite *paradores* located in small towns or in the Spanish countryside.

PARADOR DE ALMAGRO, Almagro, Castile–La Mancha Don Quixote loved the region of La Mancha, and so will any guest staying in this former 16th-century Franciscan convent. The 55 air conditioned rooms are built around no fewer than 16 galleried inner patios, and the building abounds in decorative touches that recall its original function. It also features gardens, a wine cellar, a swimming pool, and a convention hall. The *parador*'s popularity often exceeds its room capacity, so make reservations well in advance. The restaurant is especially good, featuring imaginative variations worked up from regional raw materials, fabulous desserts, and an excellent selection of *reservas* — the *parador* takes the top pick from the 25 million liters produced annually at the wine cooperative of nearby Daimiel. From May through October, Almagro's main square becomes an open-air theater for classical works performed by topnotch national and international companies. The town is also famous for its lace. Information: *Parador de Almagro,* Ronda de San Francisco, Almagro 13270 (phone: 26-860100).

PARADOR DE CHINCHÓN, Chinchón, Castile–La Mancha This lovely village, a half-hour's drive southeast of Madrid, is primarily known for its anisette liqueur, its *Holy Week* re-creation of the Crucifixion and the Resurrection, and its summer amateur bullfights in the main square. Fourteen years ago, the town's 17th-century convent was transformed into a 38-room *parador,* replete with air conditioning, murals, wall tapestries, and other ornate furnishings. There's a wonderful glass-walled circular hallway overlooking a beautiful courtyard — a perfect spot for afternoon tea. The *parador* also boasts a chapel, a garden with winding paths and goldfish ponds, a swimming pool, and a convention hall. Information:

Parador de Chinchón, 1 Av. del Generalísimo, Chinchón 28370 (phone: 1-894-0836).

PARADOR ZURBARÁN, Guadalupe, Extremadura Adventurous travelers should take a ride south from Oropesa to the town of Guadalupe to visit the Monasterio de Nuestra Señora de Guadalupe. The unearthing in the late 13th century of a long-buried statue of the Virgin Mary was the reason for the construction of the monastery (the statue is now enshrined on the altar). The 40-room *parador,* where Queen Isabella stayed — in fact, the building was used for the signing of contracts with explorers setting out for the New World — offers magnificent sunset views of the town and monastery, which are nestled in the mountains. The rooms look out over a central courtyard with Moorish-style gardens. Information: *Parador Zurbarán,* 10 Calle Marqués de la Romana, Guadalupe 10140 (phone: 27-367075).

PARADOR SAN MARCOS, León, Castile-León One of the most impressive hostelries in the country, this converted 16th-century monastery hosted pilgrims on their way to Santiago de Compostela for centuries. Travelers making the trek from Madrid to northern Spain today find this *parador,* with its 16th-century coffered ceiling, Plateresque exterior, and grand staircases, a perfect stop. The 258 rooms make it the largest property in the *parador* network. Facilities include gardens, a nightclub, a hair salon, a child-care center, and a convention hall. Information: *Parador San Marcos,* 7 Plaza San Marcos, León 24001 (phone: 87-237300).

PARADOR VIRREY DE TOLEDO, Orepesa, Castile — La Mancha According to legend, this massive medieval stone castle was built by Hercules' army, and later housed powerful Spanish and Moorish lords and kings. Today it looms over a valley of squat olive trees and small farms, about 72 miles (117 km) from Toledo. A short walk from Oropesa's Plaza Mayor, this 44-room *parador* is just 2 miles (3 km) away from the small town of Lagartera, famous for its lacework. Local women still can be seen sitting outside their homes and practicing this centuries-old craft. Information: *Parador Virrey de Toledo,* 1 Plaza del Palacio, Oropesa 45560 (phone: 25-430000).

PARADOR GIL BLAS SANTILLANA DEL MAR, Santillana del Mar, Cantabria A graceful manor house and former home of the local Barreda-Bracho family, this *parador* helps visitors to envision what life was like in this region centuries ago. The building is made of heavy stone walls and arches, and the 56 rooms feature wood-beamed ceilings, tile floors, rustic furnishings, and all the amenities. Information: *Parador Santillana del Mar,* 11 Plaza de Ramón Pelayo, Santillana del Mar 39330 (phone: 42-818000).

PARADOR DEL GOLF, Torremolinos, Andalusia This 60-room *parador* is a golfer's paradise (see also *Great Golf*). The 18-hole course was designed by English architect Tom Simpson, and it has a resident professional and a well-stocked pro shop. It also boasts an oceanfront location, a circular swimming pool, tennis courts, a playground, a library, and gardens. Thanks to its non-golf facilities, this place is also popular with vacationing families. Information: *Parador del Golf,* Apartado 324, Torremolinos, Málaga 29620 (phone: 52-381255).

Shopping Spree

No matter where the dollar stands relative to the peseta, the temptation of shopping in Spain is irresistible. Colorful hand-painted tiles and lovingly sewn handicrafts are eye-catching, easily luring the visitor into one of the country's many stores and open-air marketplaces. Although there are no great bargains anymore, the quality is high and there's a wide array of leather goods, embroidered items, jewelry, fine porcelain, and fashion ranging from very basic handicraft sweaters and clothing to haute couture.

Spaniards are traditional strollers. They take to the streets as a pastime, particularly for browsing in the plethora of small specialty shops found in most cities. But the relaxed ambience and 3-hour lunchtime shop closings (except for major department stores) mean that visitors must make careful shopping plans. Standard shopping hours in Spain are Mondays through Fridays from 9:30 AM to 1:30 PM and from 4:30 to 8 PM, and Saturdays from 9:30 AM to 3 PM. Department stores are open Mondays through Saturdays from 10 AM to 8 PM. Many shops are closed in August, but department stores remain open year-round. Spanish shopkeepers tend to be helpful, warm people who take extra time to satisfy customers. Most, however, do not speak English.

BEST BUYS

Following is an item-by-item guide to what to buy in Spain. For listings of recommended shops in Spain's major metropolises, see the *Shopping* sections of the individual reports in THE CITIES.

ANTIQUES Spain is an excellent hunting ground for antiques, with a wide range of dealers, auction houses, and non-commercial institutions that offer many items at bargain prices. For additional details, see *Antiques and Auctions* in this section.

BOOKS AND MAPS Even if you're not be able to read Spain's treasured old books, it's still fun to browse. Many bookstores have dozens of booths and stalls filled with books from around the world, both old and new; some stores specialize in reduced-rate and secondhand books, old editions, and rare titles. Much of Spanish literature is printed in both Spanish and English; for students of Spanish, what better way to practice than reading one of the classics in its original language?

CERAMICS AND TILES The diversity of Spain's regions is highly evident in the country's wide range of ceramics. The 700-year Arab domination prevails in ceramic designs of the southern regions; wall plates are enameled and trimmed in 24-karat gold. Later, when the English settled in the area around Cádiz, florals and busy scenic designs became the preferred style.

DESIGNER CLOTHING Spain demonstrates a cosmopolitan flair for fashion, especially in the cities and towns close to the French border. The country's designers have emerged as strong rivals to French and Italian creators. Spanish fashion is provocatively alluring, yet it keeps a classical line. Whatever the latest trend, visitors can rest assured that Spain's designers are up-to-date.

EMBROIDERY AND LACE In Spain, embroidery prices are determined by the intricacy of the stitch, not by the size of the item. Look carefully: Stitches made by a human hand cannot duplicate themselves over and over, and will therefore lack consistency; the more perfect the stitch, the more likely that an item was machine-made.

Palma de Mallorca, on the island of Majorca, is known for its beautiful handmade embroidered items. Toledo and the nearby village of Lagartera are famous for their embroidery, lace, and needlework. In Lagartera, the place where the best La Mancha embroidery originates, every cottage has its own display of the free-form floral stitching, which decorates silk hangings, tablecloths, peasant bonnets, and full skirts.

FOOD AND WINE Food shopping in Spain is a pleasure, probably because local customers are so demanding. Everything is fresh — sometimes so fresh that food stores hang unskinned rabbits in their windows. Spain also is known for its wines, especially sherries and riojas.

GIFTWARE Spanish porcelain pieces, particularly the Lladró figurines, are collectors' items. The Lladró factory is located in Valencia, along the Mediterranean coastline. There is also a factory store that sells hard-to-distinguish seconds for one-third to one-half off retail (cash-and-carry only). Ceramic and porcelain tableware and giftware are well made and exported worldwide.

HANDICRAFTS Finely crafted carvings, pottery, glass, leather, and metalwork can be found throughout the country. Damascene, the Moorish art of inlaying gold, copper, or silver threads on a matte black steel background, is a thriving craft in Toledo. It's used on boxes, plates, and swords, as well as in jewelry.

JEWELRY There are excellent jewelry bargains in Spain. Look for the famous Majórica pearls, but watch out for imitations. There is only one authentic brand — *Perlas Majórica* — and "Majorca" or "Mallorca" pearls should not be confused with the real thing. Look for the official agency seal and for the unique 10-year International Certificate of Guarantee that comes with each piece. Sizes run from 4 to 14 millimeters in diameter, in hundreds of combinations. The pearls can be found throughout Spain, but the factory is in Manacor, on the island of Majorca, and the shop in Palma is at 11 Avenida Rey Jaime III. Cordoban silver filigree pieces are another favorite souvenir item. Pieces of bronze, gold, and silver in contemporary designs are also widely available. Fine gold jewelry, by law, is 18 karat.

LEATHER GOODS Spanish leather items are subtle, soft, and a good value. Most leather on the Iberian Peninsula comes from sheep and lambs; cows produce a heavier quality skin that's made into jackets and coats. There are thousands of stores selling leather jackets, coats, gloves, pocketbooks, wallets, and other items. Generally speaking, shoppers can tell the quality of the leather by the feel. The softer it is, the more expensive.

MUSICAL INSTRUMENTS Who can resist listening to the beautiful sounds of Spanish guitars? Those in Spain are primarily classical and flamenco.

SHOES Spain offers a wide variety of sleek footwear designs. The leathers used are soft and durable. Women's shoes rarely come in half sizes, but men's do. The Charles Jourdan brand is in many shops and is more reasonably priced than in French stores. Many shoe stores also carry leather accessories. When buying a pair of Spanish shoes, use the size only as a reference; the last of a Spanish shoe sold in Spain is different from the last of a Spanish shoe made for the American market. Also keep in mind that Spanish lasts don't always fit American feet.

Antiques and Auctions

Antiques bargains abound in Spain for the careful, tireless shopper. It is particularly notable for its antique jewelry, old books, and ceramics, especially the boldly designed 17th-century Talavera polychrome plates, modeled after the Italian works of Faenza and Urbino.

AUCTIONS

As any auction addict knows, this is a sport that combines the fanaticism of the stock market, gambling casino, and living theater. *Subastas* (the Spanish word for auctions) are held mainly in the two largest cities, Madrid and Barcelona, although antiques dealers may be able to tell visitors about some in other parts of the country. Unlike auctions in New York, which usually are quite specialized, Spanish *subastas* offer an assortment of many kinds of objects.

Auctions are the perfect answer to rainy day blues, although neophytes might want to keep in mind the following advice:

Don't expect to make a killing. Even Chinese peasant children are hip to the art market today, it seems. But chances of unearthing a real find are better for those who shop at smaller auctions.

Buy the catalogue before bidding. Catalogues often include a list of estimated prices. Those prices are not a contractual commitment, but they do act as a guide for prospective buyers. An elaborate stylistic code hints at the conviction the house may have about the age or authenticity of an item. The use of capital letters, of artists' full names, and of words like "fine," "rare," and "important" all carry positive connotations. The use of a last name only and of words like "style" and "attributed" should serve as warnings.

Visit the pre-sale exhibition carefully, thoroughly, and even repeatedly. There is the pleasure of browsing in a store without a hovering clerk. Even more important is the prospective buyer's chance to examine the offerings. *Caveat emptor* is the prevailing rule at any auction. Serious buyers should have paintings taken down from the wall and ask to handle objects under lock and key. Those who can't be at the sale can leave a commission bid with the auctioneer, or even place a bid by telephone, but if they can't be at the exhibition they should be wary of buying.

Decide on a top bid before the auction begins, and don't go beyond it. Bidding has its own rhythm and tension. The auctioneer becomes a Pied Piper, with buyers winking, blinking, and nodding in time to his or her music. This situation arouses unusual behavior in some people. Suddenly their self-worth is at stake, and they'll bid far beyond what the item is worth — or even what they can afford. A bid may be canceled by promptly calling out "Withdrawn." *Note:* In determining their top price, bidders should remember to add the house commission, which is generally 10% but can be more, and any Value Added Tax.

Following are major auction spots:

BARCELONA A wide assortment of antiques is auctioned periodically at *Balchi* (227 Carrer del Roselló; phone: 3-217-5607). Best known for quality of goods are the monthly *subastas* held at *Sotheby's* (2 Passeig Domingo; phone: 3-215-2149), *Brok* (167 Carrer de Pau Claris; phone: 3-215-5028), and *Prestige* (277 Carrer de Valencia; phone: 3-215-6847). Jewelry auctions are held periodically at *Subarna* (257 Carrer de Provença; phone: 3-215-6518).

MADRID In Madrid, two international auction houses have branches: *Sotheby's* (8 Plaza de la Independencia; phone: 1-522-2902) and *Christie's* (7 Calle Valenzuela; phone: 1-532-6627). Auctions are conducted at the *Ritz* hotel about five times a year, alternating between paintings and decorative objects. Works by such famous artists as Goya and El Greco may be sold at astronomical prices. Other places in Madrid for *subastas* include *Ansorena* (52 Calle Alcalá; phone: 1-532-8516), where jewelry and *platería* (silver) are auctioned off monthly; *Durán Subastas* (12 Calle Serrano; phone: 1-401-3400), which has about five sessions monthly, divided according to the type of selections; and *Fernando Durán* (11 Calle Conde de Aranda; phone: 1-431-3806), which conducts between six and ten events a year at the *Wellington* hotel. Commissions usually range from 12% to 15% above *el precio de adjudicación* (the sale price).

RULES OF THE ROAD FOR AN ODYSSEY OF THE OLD

The following rules apply to savvy shopping at auctions, antiques shops, and markets:

Buy for sheer pleasure and not for investment. Treasure seekers should forget about the supposed resale value that dealers habitually dangle in front of amateur clients. If you love an object, you'll never part with it. If you don't love it, let someone else adopt it.

Don't be timid about haggling. This is as true at a posh Madrid shop on Calle Serrano as at *El Rastro* flea market. You'll be surprised at how much is negotiable — and the higher the price, the more it has to fall.

Buy the finest example you can afford of any item, in as close to mint condition as possible. Chipped or tarnished "bargains" will haunt you later with their shabbiness.

Train your eye in museums. Museums that specialize in items you collect are the best of all. Take a close look at the famous paintings and sculptures in Madrid's *Prado* museum.

Peruse art books and periodicals — preferably before you go antiques hunting. Unfortunately, however, there is a lack of English-language reading material available.

Get advice from a specialist when contemplating a major acquisition. Major auction houses like *Sotheby's* have fleets of resident specialists available for consultation. The Tourist Office of Spain may also be able to offer some assistance.

For listings of recommended antiques shops in Spain's major metropolises, see the *Shopping* sections of the individual reports in THE CITIES.

Most Visitable Vineyards

Spain has a long-standing wine making tradition. Since the days of the Phoenicians and Greeks, sweet wine has been made in southern Spain. Under the Romans, wine production spread throughout the country and was eventually brought to the Americas along with the Spanish conquistadores. Today, Spain is the world's third-largest wine producer. Until recently, Spain had more acreage devoted to vines than any other European country, but due to an excess of wine in the 12-nation European Community, many Spanish vineyards have been uprooted or abandoned under an EC incentive plan. Much like Italy, production is fragmented and spread over a wide area, with 65% of it managed by 600 cooperatives comprising more than 100,000 members.

Running the full range from the aperitif and dessert wines of Andalusia to the brut *cavas* of the Penedès and a fine assortment of brandies, Spain's viniculture is a vast and varied adventure in good drinking. In addition to the famous rioja reds, Spain produces a large assortment of other red wines, the best hailing from the temperate northern climes. East of the Rioja region, Navarre makes full-bodied, fruity red wines from the same Rioja grape varieties; south of the Rioja along the Duero Valley, the Ribera del Duero appellation is gaining increasing cachet; and Catalonia's Penedès and Lleida areas produce some of the country's best red wines from native grapes, as well as from such acclimatized varieties as the cabernet sauvignon, merlot, and pinot noir. Less sophisticated, but still eminently drinkable, are the reds of the central La Mancha plateau and the regions around Valencia and Alicante.

Though white wines are produced throughout Spain, those of Rioja and Catalonia have earned international renown. The rioja whites, often made with the native viura grape, were formerly matured in oak, but are now mostly cold-fermented in stainless steel to retain the crisp freshness of the fruit. La Mancha now produces a flowery white from the airén grape, and the fast-rising Rueda appellation relies on verdejo or sauvignon blanc. In Galicia, the whites have a light, natural effervescence, while Jerez produces a small amount of table wine from the palomino sherry grape. For free maps, brochures, and other information on Spanish wines, contact *Wines of Spain* (Commercial Office of Spain, 405 Lexington Ave., 44th Floor, New York, NY 10174-0331; phone: 212-661-4959). Admission fees are rare at Spanish wineries, and the *bodegas* (wine cellars) mentioned below are accustomed to receiving visitors, although it is advisable to make arrangements in advance. Many wineries sell a selection of their products on the premises; if not, local wines can usually be obtained at nearby shops.

RIOJA Best known among the Spanish table wines, riojas — emanating from a hilly region on the western side of the Ebro Valley in northern Spain — have been around since Roman times. At the end of the 19th century, when French vineyards were devastated by disease, wine makers from Bordeaux moved here, giving an immense boost to the regional production, which leans more toward reds than whites. These wines are similar to a bordeaux or burgundy, but with a higher alcoholic content (between 10 and 12.5%) — which is generally true of most Spanish wines in comparison with those of other European countries. The rioja reds are made principally with the native tempranillo grape, but small quantities of the garnacha, mazuelo, or graciano grapes are typically blended in. The wine has a characteristic oak taste and vanilla aroma. Within the Rioja region are three sub-regions: Rioja Alta, Rioja Alavesa, and Rioja Baja. The wines of the first two, in the hilly west, are considered the best.

The younger wines are labeled either *crianza* or *sin crianza*, meaning with or without aging. The *crianza* wines are aged for no less than 2 years, of which at least 6 months must be spent in an oak cask. *Reservas* and *gran reservas* are the mellow old wines that have spent long years in cask and bottle. Red *reservas* are aged for at least a year in oak casks and 2 years in the bottle, leaving the winery no earlier than the 4th year after vintage. Red *gran reservas* spend no less than 2 years in casks and a minimum of 3 in the bottle, leaving the winery no sooner than the 6th year after vintage. The same production regulations apply throughout Spain, but in the Rioja, the hoary old *bodegas* steeped in tradition still age their reds considerably longer in oak to cultivate the vanilla bouquet and the velvety texture that are their trademarks. Rioja also produces saucy *claretes* (light reds or rosés) and dry whites. There are dozens of vineyards in the Rioja, with the most important ones found in Logroño (the region's capital), Haro, Cenicero, and Fuenmayor.

Bodegas Berceo Established in 1872, this winery in Haro, some 30 miles (48 km) from Logroño, makes fresh, fruity whites and rosés, fruity young reds with good color, and well-rounded *reserva* reds with body and acidity. Visits must be arranged in advance. Information: *Bodegas Berceo, 38-40 Calle Cuevas, Haro, La Rioja 26200 (phone: 48-670050).*

Bodegas Campo Viejo Visitors to the regional capital will enjoy wines from the cellars of this enormous *bodega.* The whites and rosés are young and fruity; the reds, mature, aromatic, and light on the palate. Visits must be arranged in advance. Information: *Bodegas Campo Viejo,* 3 Calle Gustavo Adolfo Bécquer, Logroño, La Rioja 26006 (phone: 41-238100).

Unión Vitivinícola (Bodegas Marqués de Cáceres) This Cenicero winery, located 14 miles (22 km) from Logroño, has made quite an international name for itself since opening in 1970. Its whites and rosés are fresh and fruity, and its reds are full-bodied, smooth, and long. Visits must be arranged in advance. Information: *Unión Vitivinícola,* Carretera Logroño, Cenicero, La Rioja 26350 (phone: 41-454000).

For further information on the region and its wineries, contact either of the following associations: *ARBOR-Agrupación de Artesanos Bodegueros de Rioja* (43 Gran Vía Juan Carlos I, Logroño 26002; phone: 41-225304), or *Grupo de Exportadores de Vinos de Rioja* (7 Gran Vía, Logroño 26002; phone: 41-257555).

CATALONIA This region in the northeast corner of Spain borders the Mediterranean and produces a great variety of wines, the best known among them are those of Ampordá (reds and rosés), Alella (dry or sweet whites), and the Penedès (whites and reds). But the pièces de résistance of the region are the champagne-like sparkling wines known as *cavas,* produced in brut, sec, and demi-sec varieties. Since 1872, when Spain produced its first bottle of *cava,* the country has become one of the largest producers of sparkling wines in the world. Although *cava* is made by the *méthode champenoise,* or Champagne method, it is not a budget substitute for champagne, since the native parellada, macabeo, and xarello grapes give it its own distinctive regional characteristics. About 95% of Spanish *cava* comes from the

Penedès, with the majority of producers grouped around the town of Sant Sadurní d'Anoia.

Tables wines are also produced in Penedès, which spreads across the south of Barcelona province and the northeast of Tarragona province. The careful harvesting and elaboration of base wines to create sparkling wines have given rise to high-quality whites that are fruity and fresh and have an alcoholic strength of between 9 and 13%. The rosés are similar to the whites, and the area also produces light, smooth reds. For additional information on the wines or the area contact *Consejo Regulador de Vinos Espumoso,* 24 Avenida de Tarragona, Vilafranca del Penedès, Barcelona 08720 (phone: 3-890-3104).

Bodegas Miguel Torres Founded in 1870, this winery makes premium wines from cabernet sauvignon and chardonnay grapes, as well as fine popularly priced red, whites, and rosés. A 30-seat tour bus transports visitors around the winery and through the vineyards. Visiting hours are weekdays from 9 AM to 1 PM and from 3 to 6 PM. Information: *Bodegas Miguel Torres,* 22 Comercio, Villafranca del Penedès 08720 (phone: 3-890-0100).

Codorníu Since 1551, the Codorníu family has been producing still wines. In 1872, it produced Spain's first *cava.* Now a national monument welcoming more than 200,000 visitors a year, the winery produces more than 45 million bottles of *cava* annually in its underground wine cellar network extending 15 miles on 5 levels. These pale yellow sparkling wines have a flowery aroma and lovely flavor. The winery is open Mondays through Thursdays, from 8 to about 11:30 AM and from 3 to about 5 PM; Fridays, from 8 AM to 11:30 AM. Closed weekends and August. Information: *Codorníu,* Calle Afueras, Sant Sadurní d'Anoia, Barcelona 08770 (phone: 3-891-0125).

Freixenet This winery has been producing light, fresh, and aromatic *cavas* since 1889. Open Mondays through Thursdays, with tours at 9 and 11:30 AM and 3:30 and 5 PM; on Fridays there are tours at 9, 10, and 11:30 AM. Open selected weekends in November and December (call to confirm). Information: *Freixenet,* c/o Mercedes Argany, 2 Joan Salas, Sant Sadurní d'Anoia, Barcelona 08770 (phone: 3-818-3200).

JEREZ DE LA FRONTERA Among the world's most popular aperitif wines, genuine sherry comes only from the region of Jerez de la Frontera at the southern tip of Spain. Produced in great cathedral-like *bodegas,* these wines are continuously blended, the younger and older wines mixing in a series of casks that constitute the *solera.* The result: virtually no vintage sherries and a quality that is absolutely consistent from year to year.

The predominant grape varieties are palomino *fino,* palomino jerez, Pedro Ximénez, and muscatel. The four standard styles of sherries are *finos* (pale, dry, and light, often with a hint of bitter almonds), *manzanillas finas* (very dry, with the tang of the sea air of their native Sanlúcar de Barrameda), *amontillados* (amber sherries with more depth and body, and a nutty flavor), and *olorosos* (dark and fragrant, dry in their natural state, but often sweetened with Pedro Ximénez wine to achieve the rich, raisiny creams that elegantly top off a meal). In addition, pale cream is a new style — a light, medium sherry with a touch of sweetness.

Before heading down to Jerez, contact Bartolomé Vergara, Director of Public Relations, *FEDEJEREZ (Federacion de Bodegas del Marco de Jerez)*, 2 Eguiluz, Jerez de la Frontera, Cádiz 11402 (phone: 56-341046).

González Byass Established in 1835, this winery produces a fine range of *finos, olorosos,* and sweet sherries. It also offers a unique ritual, featuring a mouse that climbs a miniature ladder to sip a daily dram of sherry from a glass set out expressly for it. Visits are on weekdays only, and must be arranged in advance through the public relations department. Information: *González Byass,* 12 Calle Manuel María González, Jerez de la Frontera, Cádiz 11408 (phone: 56-340000).

Pedro Domecq A maker of wines since 1730, Domecq produces the full range of sherries in its vast facilities. All visits must be arranged through the public relations department, and the winery is closed on weekends and during August. Information: *Pedro Domecq,* 3 Calle San Ildefonso, Jerez de la Frontera, Cádiz 11404 (phone: 56-331900).

Spas

The spas of Spain are a slightly different breed from those in the US. Unlike their American counterparts, which are predominantly exercise- and fitness-oriented, Spanish spas take more of a therapeutic approach. They are health resorts in a purer sense, and are monitored by Spain's National Health Association. In Spain, *balnearios* (spas) tend to focus on three specific approaches: thalassotherapy, in which ocean water, seaweed, and algae are used for therapeutic purposes; hydrotherapy, using mineral water drawn from natural springs; and mud therapy, which relies on rich volcanic or natural spring sources. Spain has 128 spa resorts spread throughout its various regions. Some are simple, concentrating solely on relaxation and cures, while others are more elaborate, offering the best in resort, spa, and sports facilities. The *Spanish National Association of Spas* (23 Calle Martín de los Heros, 4-D, Madrid; phone: 1-542-9775) provides detailed information about the country's *balnearios.*

BALNEARIO DEL GRAN HOTEL LA TOJA, Isla de la Toja, Pontevedra Built in 1907 and recently renovated, this is one of Spain's finest spa resorts. Tucked away on a small, secluded island in the Atlantic Ocean off the coast of the northwestern Galician province of Pontevedra, the spa rises in grand majesty from a lush forest. Surrounded by tranquil waters and romantic beaches, it specializes in cures for skin diseases, rheumatism, and respiratory disorders, reduction of stress and tension, and physical rehabilitation.

Facilities include thermal baths, vapor inhalation rooms, a thermal swimming pool, mud and bubble baths, a gymnasium, and a sauna. Physiotherapy and massages are also administered. In addition, the 200-room *Toja* hotel offers a wide range of leisure activities and facilities, including tennis, golf, swimming, elegant restaurants, entertainment, and a casino. A 10-day stay is recommended for best results. Information: *Gran Hotel la Toja,* Isla de la Toja, Pontevedra 36991 (phone: 86-730025).

BALNEARIO PRATS, Caldes de Malavella, Girona Situated in a 100-room Catalan-style hotel, this casual spa specializes in treating rheumatism, arthritis, and other circulatory and respiratory ailments. Aching joints are soothed through the use of hydrotherapy, bubble baths, Scottish showers, underwater massages, sauna, infrared lamp therapy, and paraffin, wax, and clay treatments. Information: *Hotel Balneario Prats,* 7 Plaza Sant Esteve, Caldes de Malavella, Girona 17455 (phone: 72-470051).

BALNEARIO VICHY CATALÁN, Caldes de Malavella, Girona Small, comfortable, and relatively undiscovered, this traditional spa resort north of Barcelona may be short on elegance, but it makes up for that with its commitment to health. Facilities include pressure baths with controlled jets, bubble baths, massage and pressure jet showers, paraffin mud baths, Finnish and steam saunas, vapor inhalation treatments, a gymnasium, tennis courts, a swimming pool, and a playground. Information: *Hotel Balneario Vichy Catalán,* 30 Av. Dr. Furest, Caldes de Malavella, Girona 17455 (phone: 72-470000).

HOTEL DE LAS TERMAS, Archena, Murcia This 19th-century hotel is simple: 69 rooms and 6 suites. Its claim to fame is its mineral water, which has chlorinated, iodized, brominated, and sulfurous properties said to have regenerative power. The spa specializes in treating rheumatism, respiratory ailments, and obesity. Thermal pools, a fitness center, massage, mud applications, and beauty treatments are also available. When this place is filled up, its proprietors will refer visitors to other modest lodgings that also offer mineral springs. Information: *Hotel de las Termas,* Carretera del Balneario, Balneario de Archena, Archena, Murcia 30600 (phone: 68-670100).

INCOSOL SPA AND RESORT, Marbella, Costa del Sol This 9-story, 200-room modern hotel, set along Spain's famous Costa de Sol, has everything. The spa facilities are so wide-ranging that guests could spend a week just sorting through the choices. Treatments include medical checkups and thorough case histories by a resident doctor, obesity treatments, massage, toning, laser therapy, acupuncture, mud baths, a variety of facial treatments, physiotherapy, hydrotherapy, electrotherapy, and more. The spa specializes in helping patients with weight problems, geriatric problems, and beauty care. There is also tennis, golf, squash, and water sports at the nearby beach. Information: *Incosol Spa & Resort Hotel,* Golf Río Real, Marbella,

Costa del Sol 29600 (phone: 52-773700; in the US, 800-R-WARNER; in Canada, 800-344-6535).

LOUISON BOBET'S THALASSOTHERAPY, Mijas, Costa del Sol Built in 1986, the *Byblos Andaluz* hotel is one of Spain's most modern and most efficient spa resorts. The Institute of Thalassotherapy's philosophy is based on the medicinal properties of warm sea water; there are up to 18 different treatments using water heated to 99F to penetrate the skin and tone up the body. The institute also specializes in treating rheumatic illness, body pampering, and overall physical fitness. Accommodations consist of deluxe suites and mini-suites overlooking rolling greens, mountains, and the whitewashed town of Mijas. The hotel was designed to resemble a Moorish palace, complete with patios and long white porticoes; rooms open onto small courtyards filled with fountains, flowers, and orange trees. Many guests come here to play golf on the 2 courses, or to bask in the pleasures of *salud y sol* — health and sun. The 135-room hotel also features 3 restaurants, 5 tennis courts, sightseeing tours, and evening entertainment. Information: *Hotel Byblos Andaluz,* Club de Golf de Mijas, Apartado 138, Fuengirola, Málaga 29650 (phone: 52-473050 or 52-460250). In the US, contact *Leading Hotels of the World,* 747 Third Ave., New York, NY 10017 (phone: in New York City, 212-838-3110; elsewhere in the US, 800-223-6800).

VITATOP, Loja, Granada This modern resort, built in 1986, is a sparkling Moorish wonder, neatly tucked amid a lush Mediterranean forest high up in the Sierra Nevada. Each of the 60 elegantly appointed rooms in *La Bobadilla* hotel offers maximum comfort — all have private terraces and gardens and huge bathtubs. The spa here is similar to a fitness club, featuring a modern gymnasium with full Nautilus equipment, a heated indoor swimming pool, a Jacuzzi, 2 Finnish saunas, 2 Turkish steambaths, a small chapel, and a solarium. Professional fitness counseling, personal programs, and massages are also available. There is also a beauty salon, 2 restaurants, an outdoor swimming pool, 2 tennis courts, horseback riding, and skiing nearby. Information: *Hotel La Bobadilla,* Finca La Bobadilla, 52 Apartado, Loja, Granada 18006 (phone: 58-321861). In the US, contact *Marketing Ahead,* 433 Fifth Ave., New York, NY 10016 (phone: 212-686-9213).

Best Festivals

In Spain, the calendar year is a kaleidoscope of celebration, a constant whirl of dancing, drinking, and devotion. There are festivals to honor saints, bulls, horses, flowers, grapes, and shellfish. There are symphony orchestras and blaring local bands, dancers in ballet slippers and on stilts, and evenings lit by chandeliers or fireworks. The festivals provide a chance for young Spanish men to show off their skills — and the original machismo — in climbing poles, wrestling bulls, or standing on each other's shoulders to form Catalonia's six-story *castellers,* or human towers. Each festival bears the trademark of its town, like the stomp, strum, clap, and yodel of Granada's *International Festival of Music and Dance,* or the flowers and frills of Seville's *Feria de Abril.* Most festivals fall on Catholic holidays — *Carnaval, Corpus Christi,* and *Holy Week* before *Easter* are celebrated everywhere — but many still show traces of their pagan roots — the *Bonfires of San Juan* (celebrated in Alicante) mark the summer solstice. For a complete listing of events, contact the *National Tourist Office of Spain,* 665 Fifth Ave., New York, NY 10022 (phone: 212-759-8822).

A word of caution to those planning to hurl themselves into the merriment at one of Spain's frothiest celebrations: Crowds are very much a part of most festivals, so be prepared for crowded hotels, crowded restaurants, crowded streets, and crowded auditoriums. Advance planning will mitigate much of the discomfort — so reserve rooms ahead of time — but it's still necessary to be prepared mentally for being jostled, for waiting in line, and for paying $2 or more for a can of warm cola — all part and parcel of festival-going.

For details on the most important festivals in Spain's major cities — Pamplona's *Fiesta de San Fermín; Semana Santa* (Holy Week) and *Feria de Abril* (April Fair) in Seville; Valencia's *Las Fallas de San José;* and the *Fiesta del Apóstol* (Feast of St. James the Apostle) in Santiago de Compostela — see the *Special Events* sections in the individual reports in THE CITIES. The following festivals, held in smaller Spanish towns, are worth a long detour.

THE BONFIRES OF SAN JUAN, Alicante After the sun sets on the longest day of the year, the light keeps burning through the short *nit de foc,* or "night of fire." From June 20 through 29, scavenged boards, blocks of wood, shoeboxes, and old upholstery are feverishly assembled into a gigantic tower resembling an oversize, highly flammable Erector Set. Then, on June 24, in the name of St. John the Baptist, it is burned: a sort of latter-day bonfire of vanities or auto-da-fé. The pyre symbolizes the sins of the town, and the cardboard human figures writhing in the flames look like heretics and witches sacrificed by the Spanish Inquisition. By dawn, the wind has dispersed the cinders and the sunshine has dissolved the lurid lights, but the festival continues with 5 more days of parades and nightly fireworks shows that make the thought of sleep a purely theological quibble. Information: *Oficina de Turismo,* 2 Explanada de España, Alicante 03002 (phone: 6-521-2285).

MOORS AND CHRISTIANS, Alcoy, Alicante The 7-century war of the Reconquest is shrunk every April into a tightly scripted, 2-day game of capture-the-flag. The town of Alcoy near Alicante is first duly conquered by Moors in blackface, wielding scimitars and wearing feathered turbans, embroidered cloaks, and shoes with 6-inch, turned-up points. On the second day, the Christians, firing harquebuses, storm the "castle" erected in the town square for the occasion. The routed infidels flee through the smoke and embers, still carrying their vicious-looking pikes but, in their baubled headgear, fringes, and feather boas, looking more like primitive witch doctors than Moorish warriors. The victors parade triumphantly with their protecting statue of the Virgin, amid the beating of drums and the dull thuds and crackling of fireworks. Information: *Oficina de Turismo*, 2 Explanada de España, Alicante 03002 (phone 6-521-2285).

THE MYSTERY OF ELCHE, Elche, Alicante The residents of Elche have been staging this religious drama — a celebration of the Assumption of the Virgin — for more than 6 centuries, making it the world's longest-running play. Performances take place in the 17th-century Church of Santa María. While the songs feature an ancient dialect similar to Catalan, the action is actually fairly easy to follow, especially with the added benefit of breathtaking special effects (the descent of the angels from the church's lofty blue dome is a definite emotional highlight). Admission is free — though competition for seats is keen — for the play's first (August 14, at 6 PM) and second (August 15, at 6 PM) acts. For compressed 1-day performances of the play — staged on August 11, 12, and 13 — seats can be secured in advance by writing before July 15 to the tourist office, and then confirming the reservations by telephone. Information: *Oficina de Turismo*, Parque Municipal, Elche, Alicante 03203 (phone: 6-545-2747).

FERIA DEL CABALLO, Jerez de la Frontera, Andalusia Jerez is famous for sherry and horses, and even has a museum devoted to both, but during the *May Horse Fair*, the steeds steal the show. Straight-backed riders in felt hats and embroidered uniforms canter through the streets, and carriage drivers guide harnessed teams through the myriad maneuvers of dressage. All around the city, horses jump, trot, whinny, rear, gallop, spar with bulls, or simply stand still to be admired. The preening white Cartujanos with cottony manes are the graceful stars, descended from the horses the Moors rode during their conquest of Spain, and bred through the centuries in Andalusia. The fair is still faithful to its 13th-century origins as a livestock market; you may have come for the costumes, parades, and bullfights that are part of any Spanish festival, but if in a Walter Mitty life you ever cast yourself as a cowboy, or if you have a weakness for gambling, you just might ride away on your own, newly purchased, horse. Information: *Oficina de Turismo*, 7 Alameda Cristina, Jerez de la Frontera 11400 (phone: 56-331150), or *Oficina de Turismo*, 1 Calle Calderón de la Barca, Cádiz 11003 (phone: 56-211313).

ROMERÍA DEL ROCÍO, Almonte, Andalusia Fifty days after *Easter*, pilgrims pour through the fields and olive groves of Andalusia in a slow stream of flower-festooned horses and beribboned oxen, converging on the rural sanctuary of El Rocío, 40 miles (64 km) from Seville. As in the grand finale of a Broadway musical, the white covered wagons and little surreys with a fringe on top trundle westward, flanked by extras in wide-brimmed hats and brightly colored, flouncy skirts, dancing to the music of flutes and tambourines. The festival mixes equal parts of fervor and fun. Pilgrims march silently at night over the candlelit marshes, then break out into foot-stomping, finger-snapping *seguidillas*. The climax comes with the parading of the statue of the *Virgen del Rocío,* hoisted on the shoulders of the faithful in a brilliant scene painted in sun, sweat, and tears. There are no accommodations in El Rocío or in Almonte, so stay in Seville, Cádiz, or Huelva, and try to hitch a ride on a wagon. Information: *Oficina de Turismo,* 14 Av. de Alemaña, Huelva 21001 (phone: 55-257403).

CARNAVAL, Santa Cruz de Tenerife, Canary Islands Rooted in an ancient pagan rite, and mixed with the apocalyptic Catholic bingeing before the severity of *Lent,* this *Carnaval* has the flavor of a Spanish *Halloween.* It is celebrated for 12 days in February throughout Spain, but nowhere more extravagantly than on the island of Tenerife, where tradition melds with a Greenwich Village sense of fashion to produce wild parades and costumes that would have made Liberace look staid. It is an orgy of purple makeup, leopard-skin leotards, sequined hats, masks, feathers, capes, and wigs. Ornate carts function as mobile bandstands, stages, and puppet theaters, and the air is filled with strums and songs and wheezing clarinets. Information: *Oficina de Turismo,* Bajos del Palacio Insular, Santa Cruz de Tenerife 38001 (phone: 22-605586 or 22-605590, ext. 238).

HOLY WEEK AND THE FESTIVAL OF RELIGIOUS MUSIC, Cuenca, Castile–La Mancha Cuenca froths over the sides of its cliff, leaving a frozen dribble of houses hanging in the gorge above the Huécar River. During *Holy Week,* trumpets echo between the sheer, rock walls — eerie calls from the Middle Ages to the modern world below. Above, austere processions, silent except for the solemn fanfares, wind slowly through the narrow alleys. Penitents carry sculpted and painted scenes from the Passion story, and members of religious brotherhoods march together in the forbidding robes and pointed hoods of the Spanish Inquisition. A rowdy procession of "the drunkards," accompanied by drum rolls, is well-attended by the local youth. Each evening, in the Church of San Miguel and other venues, orchestras and choirs from all over Europe perform recitals of religious music ranging from somber motets to Wagner's mystical *Tannhäuser.* Every year, a new work commissioned for the festival is played here for the first time. Information: *Oficina de Turismo,* 8 Calle Dalmacio García Izcara, Cuenca 16004 (phone: 66-222231).

A RAPA DAS BESTAS, San Lorenzo de Sabuceno, near Pontevedra, Galicia For most of the year, horses roam over Galicia's green hills, but on the first weekend of July, an age-old chore becomes a spectacle, as hundreds of horses are rounded up, pounded down the mountainside, and careened into *curros* (corrals). They spend 2 days of imprisonment, eating bales of hay and thinking of the greener grass on the wild side of the fence. The town's young men then wrestle them to the ground and crop their manes or mark their hides with a symbol to identify their owners, afterward releasing them as branded animals. Information: *Oficina de Turismo,* 2 Calle General Mola, Pontevedra 36001 (phone: 86-850814).

Sacred Spain

All over Spain, every invasion, migration, and wave of conversion left its signature in stone, much of which has been all but erased by time and the furor of the Reconquest. As generations of Catholics poked at the hegemony of the Moors, finally pushing them back into North Africa in 1492, they destroyed mosques and erected huge cathedrals in their place. And despite the recently named *calles de la Judería* that crop up in medieval quarters, the statues of Maimonides, and the Star of David pendants for sale in trinket stores, not many traces remain of the thousands of Jews who, until their expulsion or forcible conversion that began in 1492, lived in Spain for centuries alongside Phoenicians, Romans, Visigoths, Arabs, and Christians.

Spain's most famous metropolitan churches, cathedrals, and monasteries are described in detail in the *Special Places* sections of the individual reports in THE CITIES. In addition, don't miss the following sacred sites, which are located in smaller cities and towns:

MUSEU D'ISAAC EL CEC, Girona, Catalonia The steep, narrow streets of the Call Jueu (Jewish Quarter), climbing away from Girona's ocher reflection in the Onyar River, were home to a medieval Jewish community teeming with merchants and mystics. Located here is the *Museu d'Isaac el Cec,* named for a blind sage of the *cabala,* a sort of 12th-century teacher of the Jewish brand of mysticism that promised its disciples control over the universe through the mastery of a special force. Few buildings in Spain are unmistakably Jewish, but here a Star of David is laid in the floor of the patio, under the tables of the café that now shares the building with a center for Sephardic studies and an exhibition hall. Information: *Oficina d'Informació Turística,* 1 Rambla Llibertat, Girona 17004 (phone: 72-202679).

REAL MONASTERIO DE SANTA MARÍA DE GUADALUPE, Guadalupe, near Cáceres, Extremadura Within the grim fortress walls, standing guard over the rocky dry landscape, is a womb of luxury. In the center, on a golden throne, sits the *Virgen Negra de Guadalupe,* made of carved and painted wood. With her black face and silver hand, she rules over the Catholic Hispanic world. From this region, and in her name, tough sons of Extremadura left with stony faces and iron hands to ensure that America became part of that world. The Italian painter Luca Giordano produced the paintings of the life of the Virgin that cover the walls. Information: *Oficina de Turismo,* 36 Plaza Mayor, Cáceres 10003 (phone: 27-246347).

CATHEDRAL, León, Castile-León With sparer lines and fewer frills than those of Burgos or Seville, León's cathedral looks more French, softened by a Spanish, orangish hue. Step out of the León sun and into its cool interior, where the heavy walls seem like slender frames for the panoramic movie-screen-size windows, whose stained glass saints throw a bejeweled glimmer on the gray, stone floor. The windows are an illustrated catalogue of vices, virtues, and the wages of both, which taught, warned, and admonished illiterate medieval Spaniards — but modern visitors may need a catalogue and a pair of binoculars to understand them. Information: *Oficina de Turismo,* 3 Plaza de Regla, León 24003 (phone: 87-237082).

Great Golf

The British brought golf to the Iberian Peninsula around the turn of the century, but it was another 50 years before the game acquired any degree of popularity — and then it remained an activity of only the very social or the very rich. Today, an increasing number of foreign golfers have discovered that Spain's 100 or so courses offer the perfect formula for a golfing vacation: a beautiful natural setting, ideal climate almost year-round, and some rather challenging layouts. In Spain alone, the number of golf clubs has grown five-fold over the last 2 decades. American visitors will find little problem adjusting to Spanish course configurations; they tend to be designed in the American mold — target golf, with fairly narrow fairways leading to greens surrounded by bunkers and trees.

Most trips to Spain begin in the capital, and championship courses surround Madrid (for golfing details, see *Madrid* in THE CITIES). The most popular courses, however, are found in the south. There are 18 courses along the 85-mile stretch of highway between Málaga and Sotogrande on Spain's Costa del Sol, among them the oldest and best known in the land. Ten new golf courses have opened during the past 3 years in the Costa del Sol alone. But some courses have become so overrun that increasing numbers of golfers are turning to the less-crowded courses of northern Spain, where spectacular scenery is often an added attraction. Some of the best are listed below.

Golf fees vary at most resorts. For guests staying at a golf hotel, greens fees usually are included. The cost for 18 holes generally runs between $30 and $50 during the low season, and between $50 and $100 during peak months. Club rentals start at $10, handcarts at $5, gas or electric carts at $20. Lesson costs vary according to the reputation of the pro and the price level of the resort. Some courses require a valid US handicap certificate. Information: *Royal Spanish Golf Federation,* 9-5 Calle Capitán Haya, Madrid 28020 (phone: 1-555-2682 or 1-555-2757).

CLUB DE GOLF LAS PALMAS, Las Palmas, Grand Canary Island Spain's oldest golf club is located on a ravine at the edge of the Bandama Volcano, 9 miles

(14 km) south of Las Palmas. The meandering 18-hole course is both challenging and eye-catching. The clubhouse provides sweeping views of the volcano. Information: *Club de Golf Las Palmas,* Carretera de Bandama, Km 14, Las Palmas, Grand Canary 35300 (phone: 28-351050).

LA MANGA CAMPO DE GOLF, Los Belones The two 18-hole championship layouts, designed by Paul Putman, offer tantalizing views of the Mediterranean from nearly every tee, and the sights and scenery provide a sort of ancillary hazard. Gary Player has called it the "most superbly maintained course in the world." Information: *La Manga Campo de Golf,* Carretera Cabo de Palos, Los Belones, Cartagena, Murcia 30385 (phone: 68-564511).

CLUB DE CAMPO DE GOLF DE MÁLAGA, Málaga Just 6 miles (10 km) from Málaga and 4 miles (6 km) from Torremolinos, this 18-hole Costa del Sol seaside course is over half a century old. Studded with eucalyptus trees, it is completely flat; its greens are well defined by bunkers. Information: *Club de Campo de Golf de Málaga,* Apartado 324, Málaga 29088 (phone: 3-381120).

GOLF TORREQUEBRADA, Málaga A stunning 18-hole, par 72 mountainside course, 6,446 yards long. Numerous elevated tees offer fine views of the countryside and the sea. One especially challenging hole requires players to clear the top of a grove of trees. Alternative (though still tricky) routes are provided where the more obvious challenges may prove too much for less-talented players. There is plenty of other activity for non-golfers who have tagged along: The *Torrequebrada* hotel offers tennis, swimming, and a casino. Numerous villas and condominiums built in whitewashed elegance surround the course, giving it a Mediterranean charm unlike other such sites on the Costa del Sol. Information: *Golf Torrequebrada,* Apartado 67, Benalmádena Costa, Málaga 29630 (phone: 52-561102).

GOLF GUADALMINA, Marbella Part of a resort complex offering two 18-hole courses, tennis, horseback riding, water skiing, a private beach, and 3 swimming pools, this is an ideal destination for golfers with non-golfing family members or friends along. The southern course, along the sea, is largely flat with only an occasional dogleg. The northern course is hilly, with elevated greens, varied bunkers, and water hazards, making it the more challenging of the two. There is a golf pro, pro shop, club and gas cart rental, a driving range, and putting green. The complex offers superb views of the Rock of Gibraltar on the horizon. Information: *Golf Hotel Guadalmina,* San Pedro de Alcántara, Marbella, Málaga 29670 (phone: 52-883455 or 52-883375).

GOLF NUEVA ANDALUCÍA, Marbella Two 18-hole courses designed by Robert Trent Jones, Sr. undulate along a river valley below the Sierra Blanca just 5 miles (8 km) from Marbella. One course is called *Los Naranjos,* for the orange groves that dot the back 9; the other, *Las Brisas,* was the site of the *1983 Spanish Open.* Both courses are often tormented by wind, and they contain a full complement of water hazards and bunkers. Information: *Golf Nueva Andalucía,* Apartado 2, Marbella, Málaga 29080 (phone: 52-780300 or 52-815206).

HOTEL BYBLOS ANDALUZ, Mijas This Moorish hideaway offers two 18-hole Robert Trent Jones, Sr. courses. The first course, *Mijas,* a par 72, spreads out before the hotel, offering postcard views of whitewashed Andalusian villages and azure skies. The second course, *Los Olivos,* a par 71, is to the west of the hotel. This gently rolling track requires long shots and considerable technical skill to deal with the numerous water hazards and closely sheltered greens. The hotel organizes its own annual *Challenge Competition* during the first weeks of November. Facilities include 3 swimming pools, horseback riding, 5 tennis courts, a world class spa (see *Spas* in this section), and shopping excursions. Information: *Hotel Byblos Andaluz,* Urbanización Mijas Golf, Apartado 138, Fuengirola, Málaga 29650 (phone: 52-473050 or 52-460250).

CLUB DE GOLF DE PALS, Platja de Pals Twenty minutes up the coast from the Costa Brava course (see below), this club by the sea is studded with Mediterranean pines. It hosted the *Spanish Open* in 1972. Now and then, between the dunes, the Mediterranean is visible. Less alluring is the wind, which proves a year-round hazard and blows most defiantly during the *tramuntana,* Catalonia's version of the French mistral — a cold, dry wind that knows no particular season. The small club membership welcomes visitors year-round. Closed Tuesdays from mid-September through June. Information: *Club de Golf de Pals,* Platja de Pals, Pals 17256 (phone/fax: 72-637009).

REAL CLUB DE GOLF DE CERDANYA, Puigcerdá This 65-year-old club in the Pyrenees is often touted as Europe's finest mountain course. Located 19 miles (30 km) east of the principality of Andorra, the club is a 4-hour drive from Barcelona. Its 18 holes dot a valley, 4,000 feet above sea level, that extends into nearby France. Open year-round, it's primarily a summer and autumn course, but mild weather from January through March often allows for play during these months as well. The *Chalet del Golf* clubhouse offers simple, comfortable rooms and suites. Accommodations are also available at the nearby *Del Prado* and *Park* hotels. Information: *Real Club de Golf de Cerdanya,* Apartado 63, Puigcerdá, Girona 17520 (phone: 72-881338 or 72-880950).

CLUB DE GOLF COSTA BRAVA, Santa Cristina de Aro, Catalonia Pines and cork oaks line the fairways of this par 70 course set in a wooded valley a few miles from the Mediterranean, 19 miles (30 km) southeast of Girona, and about 70 miles (112 km) from Barcelona. Some holes are quite narrow and sharply doglegged. The front 9 has its ups and downs, and snakes through a forest of oaks; the back 9, down in the valley, is relatively flat. The 4th and 18th holes are among Catalonia's best. The Ridaura River, dry for much of the year, cuts across the former; a long par 4 uphill bedevils the latter. The clubhouse is a distinctive, well-preserved, 18th-century Catalan country manor. Closed Wednesdays. Nearby hotels include the *Costa Brava, Murla Park,* and the *Park Sant Jordi.* Information: *Club de Golf Costa Brava,* Santa Cristina de Aro, Girona 17246 (phone: 72-837150 or 72-837152; fax: 72-837152).

REAL GOLF DE PEDREÑA, Santander This course lies on a peninsula in the middle of a bay, some 15 miles (24 km) east of Santander. Pine, cypress, and eucalyptus trees adorn the challenging 6,277 yards, which require the use of virtually every club in the bag. Severiano Ballesteros, Spain's most famous golfer and international superstar, lives adjacent to the 7th hole. All guests must be accompanied by a member. Information: *Real Golf de Pedreña,* Apartado 233, Santander 39000 (phone: 42-500266).

PARADOR DEL GOLF, Torremolinos This 60-room *parador* near Málaga is a golfer's paradise. The 18-hole course — the oldest on the Costa del Sol — was designed in 1925 by English architect Tom Simpson and has a resident pro on the premises. The ocean, a swimming pool, tennis courts, and a playground are non-golf pluses. Information: *Parador del Golf,* Apartado 324, Carretera de Málaga, Km 3, Torremolinos, Málaga 29620 (phone: 52-381255).

REAL SOCIEDAD DE GOLF DE NEGURI, Vizcaya Dating from 1911, this par 72 course is one of Spain's oldest. Its front 9 abuts the sea, amid dwindling pines reminiscent of English links. The back 9 features narrow fairways and an occasional dogleg. There are various accommodations nearby. Information: *Real Sociedad de Golf de Neguri,* Apartado 9, Algorta, Vizcaya 48990 (phone: 44-690200 or 44-690208).

Tennis

In Spain, tennis usually takes a back seat to golf. But many hotels and resorts have tennis facilities, and beginners and experts alike will find an abundance of places to play. Racquets, balls, and courts are easily rented, and a single player can find a partner easily. The majority of tennis facilities are located along the Costa del Sol, which is in the midst of rapid expansion, with more and more emphasis being placed on residential developments — small communities of villas and townhouses clustered around sports facilities and the sea. So far, only the British have truly "discovered" this area, and thanks in part to their inroads, almost everyone speaks English. The Costa del Sol is considerably developed; many have labeled it the Miami of the Mediterranean. There are a number of exclusive areas where the tennis enthusiast can enjoy a vacation amid golden beaches, turquoise waters, and the uniquely Spanish atmosphere of Andalusia.

Most Spanish tennis courts have either an asphalt or clay surface, and traditional tennis whites are preferred — often required. Expect to pay about $10 per hour for court time. In most cases, court time must be reserved in advance. There also is an emphasis on the social aspects of tennis, and visitors will find that many hotels sponsor weekly tournaments and "get acquainted" parties where tennis enthusiasts can meet and mingle. In addition, there are a variety of members-only tennis clubs spread throughout Spain's major cities and resort areas where, for a small additional fee, guests are permitted to play. For details on courts in the major cities, see the *Tennis* entries in the individual reports in THE CITIES. The top tennis spots in Spain's resort areas are listed below.

Tennis as a spectator sport is also catching on in Spain — thanks in part to the stocky Spanish sensation, Aranxtha Sánchez-Vicario. Spain plays host to a series of championship events each year. For details on Spanish tennis tournaments, contact the *Royal Spanish Tennis Federation* (618 Av. Diagonal, Barcelona 08028; phone: 3-201-0844, 3-200-5355, or 3-201-5586) or the *ATP* (4 Sawgrass Village, Suite 240, Ponte Vedra Beach, FL 32082; phone: 904-285-5776).

CAMPO DE TENIS DE LEW HOAD, Mijas, Costa del Sol Australian Lewis Hoad, the 1956 and 1957 *Wimbledon* champion, first spotted this hilly enclave in 1966, and decided it was the perfect spot to build a tennis ranch. Twenty-five years later, the "ranch" is a favorite spot for both serious players and beginners serious about learning the game. This facility is not a resort but a full-service tennis center and club, where guests sharpen their skills and socialize with other tennis enthusiasts. The tennis school is run by Manrique Floreal, a professional who teaches the Aussie style, a gentle technique that emphasizes the reception of opponents' serves. Facilities include 8 hard courts (the Spanish refer to this surface as "quick"), which are surrounded by exotic and carefully landscaped gardens, and a well-stocked pro shop. There are weekly singles and doubles tournaments for advanced players. There is also a bar overlooking the courts, a restaurant, changing rooms, saunas, a swimming pool, massage facilities, a beauty salon, aerobics classes, art exhibits, and occasional concerts. Guests can rent one of the exclusive villas that surround the club, or find accommodations in nearby Fuengirola and Mijas. Information: *Campo de Tenis de Lew Hoad,* Apartado 111, Carretera de Mijas, Fuengirola, Málaga 29640 (phone: 52-474858).

DON CARLOS, Marbella, Costa del Sol The privacy and excellent facilities here have helped this 212-room resort, located in the heart of a 130-acre private estate of pine woods, exotic flowers, and subtropical gardens, achieve its standing as the official home of the European Women's Tennis Association. Martina Navratilova is among the many top-ranked professionals who have practiced and competed here. Throughout the year, visitors usually can catch a glimpse of a superstar or two either playing or relaxing at the restaurant overlooking the courts. Don't be overwhelmed by the abundance of talent; the mood here is casual and relaxed, and a beginner will feel as comfortable as a pro. There are 11 courts (6 clay, 5 hard; 4 courts are floodlit), between the swimming pool and the sea. In addition, the hotel offers windsurfing, sailing, water skiing, a driving range, horseback riding, a gymnasium, a sauna, and a Jacuzzi — all free to hotel guests. There's also an 18-hole golf course — the *Santa María*. Information: *Don Carlos Hotel*, Jardines de las Golondrinas, Marbella, Málaga 29600 (phone: 52-831140 or 52-831940); in the US, *Hotel Don Carlos USA Marketing Office*, 322 E. 39th St., New York, NY 10016 (phone: in New York City, 212-949-7145; elsewhere in the US, 800-338-4510).

MARBELLA CLUB, Marbella, Costa del Sol One of the most famous hotels on the coast, and the cornerstone of Marbella, this Relais & Châteaux resort is a fine place to mix tennis and beach life. Set in a subtropical garden by the sea, the club shares tennis facilities with the *Puente Romano* hotel (see below). Information: *Marbella Club Hotel*, Carretera de Cádiz, Km 178, Marbella, Málaga 29600 (phone: 52-771300); in the US, *Leading Hotels of the World*, 747 Third Ave., New York, NY 10017 (phone: in New York City, 212-838-3110; elsewhere in the US, 800-223-6800).

LOS MONTEROS, Marbella, Costa del Sol Also among the most prestigious hotels and sporting resorts on the coast, this is an ideal getaway spot that will keep guests as busy or as relaxed as they wish. Set among pine woods and tropical gardens are 10 hard courts, 2 of which are floodlit for night play, as well as 5 squash courts, a paddle tennis court, 2 swimming pools, a terrace bar, a pro shop, a gymnasium, saunas, massage facilities, a beautician, a nursery, a nightclub, and golf nearby. Guests are automatically considered tennis club members and may use the courts free of charge, subject to availability and club regulations. Information: *Los Monteros Hotel*, Marbella, Málaga 29600 (phone: 52-771700); in the US, *Distinguished Hotels*, c/o Robert F. Warner, Inc., 307 Fifth Ave., New York, NY 10016 (phone: 212-725-4500; in the US outside New York City and in Canada, 800-888-1199).

PUENTE ROMANO, Marbella, Costa del Sol This self-contained Moorish residence is a city in itself. For the tennis enthusiast, there are 11 courts — 4 hard, 5 clay, and 2 artificial surface (Astroturf) — on which to practice, as well as a large stadium that plays host to many national and international tournaments. Björn Borg was once the pro at the tennis center here; today, former *Wimbledon* champion Manolo Santana holds court. In addition to tennis, the resort offers surfing, water skiing, a fitness center, swimming pool, horseback riding, and polo; there's golf nearby. The 220 rooms and suites are built in pueblo-style Andalusian *casitas*, which overlook tropical gardens and waterfalls. Information: *Puente Romano Hotel*, Apartado 204, Marbella, Málaga 29600 (phone: 52-770100); in the US, *Utell International*, 500 Plaza Dr., Secaucus, NJ 07096 (phone: 201-902-7800 or 800-448-8355).

SOTOGRANDE, Estepona, Costa del Sol Guests have access to some of the best and most varied sports facilities on the coast in the enormous Sotogrande complex. The tennis center offers first-rate instruction, and the secluded hotel is peaceful and well looked after by a helpful and attentive staff. All rooms have separate sleeping and living areas, as well as private patios and fountains. Information: *Hotel Sotogrande,* Carretera 340N, Km 131, Sotogrande, Cádiz 11310 (phone: 56-795100).

Sensational Skiing

When most people think of skiing in Europe, they think of Switzerland, Austria, and France. Yet Spain, the second-most-mountainous country in Europe, has excellent skiing facilities that seem to be one of the country's best-kept secrets. In the north, there are the Pyrenees, which guard the border with France, and the Picos de Europa, between Cantabria and Asturias; in the south, the Sierra Nevada range, which rises 10,000 feet just southeast of Granada; and in the center of the country, the Guadarramas, north of Madrid. In addition, there are ski areas in the provinces of Burgos, Soria, La Rioja, and Teruel. Skiing is possible from January through May in the north, and from January through March in the south and lower elevations.

Spain offers novice through advanced skiers the thrills of a lifetime — and once experienced, these hills will not soon be forgotten. Spain is also one of Europe's bargain ski capitals; hotels, meals, drinks, equipment, and lift passes are available at prices far below those found in the Alps. Other benefits include an abundance of snow, relatively mild weather conditions, and plenty of sunshine. Some large international resorts, such as Tuca-Betrén, Baqueira-Beret, and Cerler — all in Catalonia — and Pals, in Andorra, have it all — a vast array of runs and lifts, troops of multilingual instructors, a selection of winter sporting opportunities such as ice skating and tobogganing, an abundance of shops, shimmering hotels, high-speed nightlife, and the glossy aura of Europe's leisure classes. But there also are numerous cozier, family-oriented villages, many of them linked to a constellation of neighbors by far-reaching networks of chair lifts and cable cars.

Throughout most of the resort regions, those who like their luxury rugged can hire a helicopter for a quick trip up a mountaintop blanketed with glittery virgin powder, and enjoy the subsequent opportunity to carve a solitary trail back down through miles of untracked mountainside. For those whose special pleasure is cross-country skiing, be aware that the sport is beginning to boom here; a wide choice of trails and excursions (and a good supply of the necessary equipment) is readily available. And no matter where you go, there's a very high standard of cooking in the restaurant dining rooms adjacent to the slopes.

Words of caution: If you need an English-speaking instructor from the area's ski school, say so when signing up, or risk having to learn to recognize "Bend your knees" enunciated in all-too-faultless Spanish. Know the local trail markings — green for novice, blue for intermediate, and red for expert. Be prepared for sometimes hair-raising traffic — both on the mountain roads and on the slopes. Since skiing as a mass activity is a Juan-come-lately in Spain, the average level of expertise is lower than is routinely found in Switzerland, France, or Austria, and the traditions of slope safety and etiquette are not always readily apparent. For those familiar with European skiing, be aware that the high and low skiing seasons in Spain are significantly different from those of the better-known Alpine regions. All weekends are designated as high season, with premium prices on hotels, lessons, and lifts. High season also applies to the period from *Christmas* through *New Year's,* and the first week of January. Prices rise again during February and the first 2 weeks of March.

CERLER, Huesca, Aragon Close to the French border, Cerler boasts 5,875 acres of spectacular skiable terrain for skiers of all abilities. The 23 trails, the highest slopes the Pyrenees have to offer, provide plenty of challenges; the majority of the trails are over 3 miles long and are served by 11 chair lifts. There is also an ice skating rink and a wide variety of other activities, including sledding and swimming. Information: *Oficina de Turismo de Huesca,* 23 Calle Coso Alto, Huesca 22022 (phone: 74-225778).

EL FORMIGAL, Huesca, Aragon A favorite stomping ground of the current King of Spain and his family, this is just one of five resorts in the area (Astún, Cerler, Panticosa, and Candanchú are the others). Together they constitute one of the most attractive and unspoiled regions in Spain, guaranteed to motivate even the most sedentary to hit the hills. As the westernmost resort in the Pyrenees, El Formigal lacks woodland, instead boasting great open spaces — perfect for beginners and intermediates. Only 2 of the 24 runs are designated for experts, but most are rated as difficult. The wide-open off-piste possibilities compensate, however — for those strong enough to handle heavy snow. A double chair lift rises out of the town, reaching the mid-station and the main mountain restaurant. From here, beginners can enjoy gentle slopes, intermediates can drop down to the lower gondola station, and experts can take a chair lift or T-bar to the summit and enjoy a 3,000-foot drop back into the village. There is also a slalom course, 6 hotels, and a wide variety of activities, including very lively nightlife. Information: *Oficina de Turismo,* Estación de Formigal, Sallent de Gallego, El Formigal, Huesca 22000 (phone: 74-488125), or *Oficina de Turismo de Huesca,* 23 Calle Coso Alto, Huesca 22022 (phone: 74-225778).

ALTO CAMPO, Santander, Cantabria This is one of those resorts where the skiing season lasts until late May. The resort lies in the Brana Vieja Valley, sheltered from harsh winds. On a clear day, the distant peak of Tres Mares, the Polaciones Valley, and the heights of the Picos de Europa are visible.

The slopes here vary from easy to extremely difficult, making skiing available for enthusiasts of all levels. Information: *Oficina de Turismo*, 1 Plaza de Velarde, Santander 39001 (phone: 42-310708).

LA MOLINA, Girona, Catalonia This is one of the oldest ski resorts in Spain, as well as the closest to Barcelona. For this reason, the resort attracts a weekend crowd that usually overwhelms the 17 chair lifts. During the week, however, there are rarely any lines. Only 3 of the 22 trails are listed as difficult, making the resort a favorite for skiers of all abilities. There is also a 3-mile cross-country course, and 3 ramps for ski jumping. The resort was created with skiers specifically in mind, and features modern, self-contained hotels, good restaurants, a smattering of shops, and a group of lively discos and bars. Nine *hostales* are located nearby. Information: *Oficina de Turismo*, Av. Supermolina, La Molina, Girona 17573 (phone: 72-892031; fax: 72-892204).

VAL D'ARAN, Lleida (Lérida), Catalonia Past the orchards and vineyards of Catalonia and up into the Pyrenees Mountains bordering France lies one of the most beautiful alpine valleys in the world — and the ski resorts of Tuca-Betrén and Baqueira-Beret. Tuca-Betrén, the lesser known of the two, offers a wide variety of slopes and trails that will challenge even the most experienced skier. In fact, all of the resort's 18 slopes and trails are marked either advanced or expert. The first trail starts at the 5,000-foot level; the highest peaks overhead top off at 9,000 feet. Eight miles (13 km) away is Baqueira-Beret, one of the most extensive ski resorts in Europe outside the Alps. It attracts a predominantly French clientele from north of the border, although King Juan Carlos also is a frequent visitor. The facilities and restaurants are more modern and sophisticated here than in Tuca-Betrén. Baqueira-Beret offers 43 slopes and trails, 22 lifts, 2 slalom courses, and helicopter service to the peaks for the thrills of fresh powder. Due to the terrain — steep slopes and wide courses — there is great skiing variety. The skiing on the Baqueira side is down tight trails with a dense lift network of T-bars and double chair lifts. The skiing above Beret is in a wide-open bowl served by three strategically placed triple chair lifts. Of special note is the descent from the peak of Cap de Baqueira, the highest point. Val d'Aran's two distinct segments are separated by a row of natural stone and mortar villages, scenery for which the word "charm" was coined. Much of this area looks the way it did in the 13th, 14th, 15th, and 16th centuries — give or take a few power lines and Seats (Spanish-built Fiats). This area has almost 5,000 rooms in hotels, inns, and quaint *pensiones*. Information: *Oficina d'Informació de Baqueira-Beret*, Vielha, Lleida 25530 (phone: 73-645050 or 73-645884), or *Oficina d'Informació Turística*, Calle Arc del Pont, Lleida 25000 (phone: 73-248120).

SOLYNIEVE, Sierra Nevada, Granada This resort is a cluster of concrete buildings huddled above the tree line in the far south of Spain, only 20 miles (32 km) from Granada and 60 miles (96 km) from the coast at Motril. Here, the perpetually snow-covered mountains rise to 11,420 feet. The scenery is inspiring and the snowfields are seemingly endless. Its status as a ski resort, however, is not all that high. The skiing here, though extensive, is tame and not particularly demanding, but it will keep advanced beginners and intermediates happy. With its wide, treeless slopes and patient Spanish instructors, Solynieve is perfect for beginning skiers. The resort boasts 19 lifts, which serve some 30 miles of trails. The village itself is rather soulless; even the southern Spanish personality can't seem to help fire up the nightlife. Granada, a short trek down the mountain, makes up for this. But in the spring, Solynieve does offer dependable snow and the opportunity to ski in the morning and then drive down to the Costa del Sol for an afternoon of sun on the beach or a round of golf — so be sure to pack sunscreen and sunglasses. Information: *Federación Andaluza de Esquí*, 78 Paseo de Ronda, Veleta, Granada 18000 (phone: 58-250706), or *Patronato Provincial de Turismo de Granada*, 2 Calle Libreros, Granada 18001 (phone: 58-227510).

ANDORRA One of Europe's last feudal protectorates, this tiny co-principality, governed nominally by Spain and France, has abundant snow from November through April. Combined with an excellent climate of dry air and sunny skies, this is truly a skiers' paradise. Some of Europe's best inexpensive skiing can be found at the resorts of Pas de la Casa–Grau Roig, Soldeu–El Tarter, Pals, Arinsal, and Ordino Arcalis. Pas de la Casa–Grau Roig, just within the French border, is the oldest resort, and has 18 trails for advanced skiers, a slalom course, and several tame slopes for beginners, as well as 25 lifts and 33 hotels. Soldeu–El Tarter is the largest complex, with 28 slopes (including 5 designed especially for children), a 7½-mile cross-country course, 22 lifts, 20 hotels, and 3 self-contained apartment blocks. Pals features 20 trails, a forest slalom course, 2 children's slopes, and 14 lifts. Arinsal, next to the village of the same name, has 23 slopes ranging from beginner to expert, all served by 15 lifts. Ordino Arcalis is the most dramatically beautiful of Andorra's resorts, offering 16 slopes, 11 lifts, and 4 modern hotels in nearby El Serrat. Information: *Sindicat d'Iniciativa de les Valls d'Andorra*, Carrer Dr. Vilanova, Andorra la Vella, Andorra (phone: 73-820214); in the US, *Tourist Office of Andorra*, 120 E. 55th St., New York, NY 10022 (phone: 212-688-8681).

Horsing Around

It almost goes without saying that Spain is the land of the horse. It was here that the Moorish invaders crossed the Bab steeds of their homeland with the native Iberian stock that had provided mounts for conquerors from Julius Caesar to Richard the Lion-Hearted. They came up with a noble breed renowned for its sturdy legs, strong back, and agility — the Andalusian.

Raising Andalusian thoroughbreds is still a tradition carried on at over

100 ranches in southwestern Spain. Visits can be arranged through the breeders' association, the *Real Sociedad Española del Fomento de la Cría Caballar,* located at the *Hipódromo de la Zarzuela* in Madrid (phone: 1-307-0140). The association also provides a free brochure listing the names and addresses of its members. In addition, there are some 50 other ranches dedicated to preserving the pure Arabian bloodline, reintroduced at the turn of the century. Information: *Asociación de Criadores de Caballos Arabes,* 20 Calle Hermosilla, Madrid 28009 (phone: 1-275-9065).

To witness with what grace Andalusian horses lend themselves to classical European and Spanish dressage, a visit to Jerez de la Frontera's *Escuela Andaluza del Arte Ecuestre* (Av. Duque de Abrantes; phone: 56-311111 or 56-311100) is a must. This school was founded in 1972 by Alvaro Domecq, of the local sherry dynasty, who has since retired after years as Spain's top-ranked *rejoneador,* a bullfighter on horseback. The 35 Spanish mounts are trotted out in their fancy dress gear every Thursday for a 2-hour show entitled "How the Andalusian Horses Dance." During the second week of May, the people of Jerez de la Frontera emerge blinking from their sherry vaults to welcome riding enthusiasts from all over the world for their annual week-long *Horse Fair.* Spanish equestrian specialties on display, along with much dancing, hand-clapping, and *fino* drinking, include the *acoso y derribo,* in which riders use long blunt poles to isolate one bull from a stampeding herd and overturn it. The colorfully dressed riders then try their hand at *doma vaquera,* or Spanish rustic dressage, performing a series of showy maneuvers that climax when the horses approach at full gallop, then come to a dead halt before the judges' stand. Some extremely flashy carriage driving rounds out the city's tribute to the animal that was originally bred with patient perfectionism by the Carthusian monks, who were based here until the last century.

HORSE TREKKING

The sport of horse trekking involves day-long trips on the back of a sturdy native horse or pony, and has participants traveling mainly at a walk — partly because most are inexperienced riders, partly because the riding is through dense forests and steep mountain terrain, along narrow trails and roads that don't lend themselves to a faster pace. Absolute novices may be provided with some instruction, but ordinarily it will be at a relatively elementary level. In recent years, a number of agencies specializing in horseback treks have rediscovered the old cattle trails and royal bridle paths of the Middle Ages — all to prove their point that Spain looks very different when observed up close from the back of a congenial quadruped. The following are some of the best Spanish horse trekking centers, which offer trips lasting anywhere from a day to a month. Backup vehicle, insurance, meals, and lodging, mainly in *paradores* are usually included.

Equestrian Tours Almansur: One of Spain's most popular trekking centers, it caters to the American market. Most of the clientele come back for a second look at Extremadura and the Sierra de Gredos. Information: *Equestrian Tours Almansur,* Deheser del Roble, Las Ventas de San Julián, Toledo 45568 (phone: 25-430488; fax: 25-430533); in the US, *FITS Equestrian,* 685 Lateen Rd., Solvang, CA 93463 (phone: 805-688-9494 or 800-666-3487; fax: 805-688-2943).

Equiberia: Provides programmed "à la carte" (you set your own agenda) tours in Andalusia as well as set tours in Seville and the Coto Doñana park. There is also a popular horse, bull, and sherry tour, which visits the royal equestrian school, the sherry *bodegas,* and equestrian and bull estates throughout Andalusia. The agency will assist in renting horses, carriages, and other equestrian paraphernalia, in the acquisition and transportation of Andalusian horses, and will provide information on the best stables and dressage courses. Information: *Equiberia,* 2 Calle Julio César, 1 Derecha, Seville 41001 (phone/fax: 5-421-1311).

Rutas a Caballo: More than 15 years' experience and numerous repeat clients from the US, Germany, and Switzerland make this a best bet for everyone from serious riders to the merely determined. Popular routes include trails through Segovia, Andalusia, and Coto Doñana. Information: *Rutas a Caballo,* 21 Calle Juan Bravo, Madrid 28006 (phone: 1-576-7629).

Viajes Geosud: Organizes outings to order for groups of 3 to 15 in Almería, the Sierra de las Alpujarras of Granada, and northern Navarre. Information: *Viajes Geosud,* 9 Calle Juan de Dios, Madrid 28015 (phone: 1-542-6194).

POST TREKKING/TRAIL RIDING

There's nothing quite as delightful as seeing the Spanish countryside from the back of a horse or sure-footed native pony, heading from ranch to ranch through narrow trails, along abandoned train beds, and down wide sandy beaches — and staying away from the trekking center for up to a week at a time. Post trekking, or trail riding, as this activity is called, is not generally recommended for riders without experience, as it usually involves good horses and a fast enough pace to cover about 25 miles (40 km) a day. Usually a warm camaraderie develops among riders en route, as they traverse the rural miles. Post trekking is also a practically worry-free holiday: There are guides to keep riders going at a reasonable pace, to make sure the group doesn't get lost, and to arrange for the rider's luggage to be transported from one hostelry to the next.

ALMERÍA Those who think they know the desert probably haven't seen or even imagined anything quite like the arid wastelands of Tabernas, a stretch of mind-boggling barrenness between the Sierra Nevada and Almería's still-undeveloped Mediterranean beach resorts. After 3 days riding through a scallop-edged sea of surreal sandstone, where the sun has bleached every color out of the landscape, it's a relief to return to the *cortijo,* or workday ranch, located on the Cabo de Gata Peninsula, and the greenery of its adjacent national park. People can also visit Yuka City, which has kept the corner saloon doors swinging even after the paella-Western boom of the 1970s went bust. Groups require a minimum of three riders; there are no fixed departure dates, and accommodations (an ad hoc combination of inland ranches alternating with hotels on the coast) and itineraries are available by specific arrangement only. Information: *Viajes Geosud* (see above).

ASTURIAS Misty, mountainous, gorgeous, and green, Spain's northern coast serves as a gateway to secluded inland valleys settled by a hard-boiled race of cider-swigging mountain men who spend their days tending their cattle and flocks of merino sheep. All this is within a few hours' riding time from Gijón, where excursions of 1 to 3 days lead up into the sierra to the sprawling Valle del Peón, the seven lakes of Saliencia, the Somiedo Wildlife Reserve (full of brown bears, wolves, wild boar, and imperial eagles), and other no-frills natural wonders. Information: *Compañía Asturiana de Rutas y Excursiones,* 8 Plaza Romualde Alvargonzález, Gijón 33202 (phone: 85-341968).

Near Oviedo, the capital of Asturias, *Trastur,* a cooperative of youthful trekking enthusiasts, has a setup aimed at a young, casual, and outdoorsy clientele: riding by day and partying determinedly through the night in the log cabin shelters of the *vaqueros,* the Asturian livestock drivers. Their trails lead from the crossroad towns of Tineo and Navelgas, where this rough-and-ready culture is best preserved, then north to the pretty fishing village of Luarca. Arrangements must be made by telephone from the enthusiasts' base in Tineo, and they will pick up guests in Oviedo. Information: *Trastur,* Tineo (phone: 85-806036), or in Madrid (phone: 1-477-9236) for outing schedules.

AVILA The Sierra de Gredos is where Madrid's horsey set heads for a taste of real wilderness. The mountains have a certain preeminence for trail riders and boast 7,500-foot peaks, as well as deep ravines clawed out of the landmass by glaciers. Many of the routes also overlap the adjoining Tiétar Valley. A week-long trek of this area is offered by *Gredos — Rutas a Caballo.* Information: *Gredos — Rutas a Caballo,* 13 Calle Guijuelos, Hoyos de Espino, Avila 05001 (phone: 21-384110). This trek and other short half-day outings also can be booked in Madrid (phone: 1-576-7629).

In August, when the plains of Extremadura are broiling, *Equestrian Tours Almansur* moves its horses to the northern side of the Gredos range to keep cool. Twice a month, week-long sallies take riders down to visit the walled city of Avila, as well as along the Piedrahita River for a look at the palace of the Dukes of Alba. Another group, *Turismo Ecuestre La Isla,* has

3-day rides from its ranch in Navaluenga to Avila, and week-long trips through the Gredos central highlands and to the remote Lagoons of Gredos. Departures are from May through September. Information: *Equestrian Tours Almansur* (see above) or *Turismo Ecuestre La Isla,* Madrid (phone: 1-633-3692).

CÁDIZ Dusty cattle trails head down the heartland of Andalusia's wild west, where the whitewashed towns all bear the tag *de la frontera* as a reminder that this was where Muslim and Christian Spain fought most furiously for control. The 260-mile (416-km) route starts in Arcos de la Frontera, with 5- to 7-hour stretches in the saddle, then breaks for an unhurried picnic lunch. The trail leads through bull breeding ranches and fields of cultivated sunflowers drooping on their 5-foot stalks, and it ends with a gallop through the Atlantic surf. Stopover specials include a day in Jerez de la Frontera, with a visit to that city's celebrated School of Equestrian Arts, and a canter along the beachside Roman ruins of Bolonia. Provision is made for an occasional afternoon on two legs for a peek at the pueblo or to bask on the beach. Accommodations at the *Arco* ranch, as well as the *hostales* along the way, are clean and comfortable, but not luxurious. Private baths are included — and will be needed. Bring a 10-gallon hat and a canteen of equivalent capacity, as the summer temperatures can hover around 100F.

Rutas a Caballo, which pioneered this trek, offers departures every third weekend from March through October, including accommodations and all meals — which are simple and good. A shorter 8-day version that heads to the sea, forsaking the return trek, is also available. In May, June, October, and November, *Rutas a Caballo* offers an inland tour of the *pueblos blancos,* the celebrated whitewashed towns of Andalusia, including Arcos de la Frontera, Grazalema, Zahara de la Sierra, and Ronda. It also offers a 1-week variant, the 140-mile (224 km) "Atlantic Sea Tour," allowing for 3 days inland riding and 4 days splashing along the beach as the breakers come rolling in from the Strait of Gibraltar, with Morocco's Atlas Mountains visible on the other side. Information: *Rutas a Caballo* (see above).

Equiberia offers a popular tour of the sherry, horse, and bull country around Seville. Information: *Equiberia* (see above).

COTO DOÑANA NATIONAL PARK, Huelva A unique chance to spend a week trotting through the salt marsh and scrub of one of Europe's largest and most ecologically vital wildlife sanctuaries. After picking up riders in Seville, the organizers get one and all saddled up in Arcos de la Frontera. From there, it's a 2-day ride via Jerez de la Frontera to where the land turns swampy and some of more than 150 different species of birds — including flamingos, imperial eagles, and many more birds of prey — can be observed roosting above the deer, lynx, and wild boar that inhabit the 50,000 acres of restricted parkland. Riders and mounts are ferried across the marshes in shallow-draft skiffs. A visit to the shrine of the Virgen del Rocío, which is inundated by pilgrims each May during one of Spain's most colorful outbursts of religious fervor, is also included. *Rutas a Caballo* offers departures in May, July, September, and November. Information: *Rutas a Caballo* (see above).

EXTREMADURA The rugged and still-backward land that toughened up Spanish conquistadores such as Cortés and Pizarro opens itself up for reciprocal exploration from the New World on treks ranging from 1 to 3 weeks. The wide-ranging "Route of the Conquistadores" leaves very little of the region unseen. Riders explore the Monfragüe National Park, a unique sanctuary for migratory birds; the poor but pretty pueblos of the Jerte Valley and La Vera; the Roman city of Mérida; the monasteries of Guadalupe and Yuste; and the historic towns of Cáceres, Trujillo, and Plasencia. Departures are scheduled in early September only, and include 22 days on the trail.

The Monastery of Guadalupe is a 14th-century sanctuary visited by pilgrims from all over the Spanish-speaking world. But its larger mountain setting is a treat seldom seen by anyone, although its deep valleys and dense oak forests make it well worth the 8-day outing, covering 105 miles (168 km). Departures are scheduled for April, May, September, and October.

All of the Extremadura excursions can be booked through *Equestrian Tours Almansur,* which offers an excellent selection of Hispano-Arab mounts and provides first class accommodations and meals at the various *paradores* in the region. It also offers a week-long close look at the Tiétar River Valley, on the fertile southern flanks of the Gredos mountain range. In the US, *FITS Equestrian* handles excursions. Departures are scheduled from May through November, except in August, when it's simply too hot to trot. Information: *Equestrian Tours Almansur* or *FITS Equestrian* (see above for details on both).

GRANADA No visit to the Andalusian hinterland would be complete without a side trip to the rugged and impressive Alpujarras Range, where experienced mounts negotiate the sharp precipices through chestnut woods, lavender scrubland, and steep pueblos. Tours of 1 to 10 days on the trail are available year-round; each includes approximately 5 hours of daily saddle time and lodging at village inns along the way. Non-riders can accompany the caravan in a covered jeep-type support vehicle. Information: *Rutas Alternativas,* Bubión, Granada 18412 (phone and fax: 58-763236), *Viajes Granatur,* Granada 18412 (phone: 58-223580), or *Viajes Geosud* (see above).

Arrangements can be made through any of the agencies above to take part in an excursion — offered annually during the first week of August — that heads from the outskirts of Granada, through the Sierra Nevada (the second-highest mountain range in Europe, after the Alps), and into the High Alpujarras, coming down onto the beaches of the Mediterranean around Almuñecar. Most of the riders taking part bring their own horses, but steeds supplied by the organizers are also available.

LEÓN Seldom visited — except by hunters out for pheasant or skiers on their way to the nearby ski resorts — the extensive facilities offered by *Campament-Finca "La Granja,"* a modern campsite complex 25 miles (40 km) north of the provincial capital, include access to up to ten horses and guides for 1- to 3-day sallies into the high sierra. Treks include visits to a saltwater lake island, the Valdecortero caverns, the hermitage of Valdorria, and more. This is also a good place for trout fishing. Information: *Campament-Finca "La Granja,"* La Vecilla, León 24840 (phone: 87-741222).

NAVARRE Riders (a minimum of three) can tour one of the farthest-off-the-beaten-track regions in all the Iberian Peninsula, the northern part of the province of Navarre. The route travels along hidden, willow-shrouded rivers, forests of oak and beechnut, hilly pastureland, and up into the foothills of the Pyrenees, where the Cima de San Martín, the world's second-deepest canyon, is located. One- and 2-week routes are offered. Accommodations consist of simple village inns, with the odd night spent in a hotel. Horses are 7- to 11-year-old mixed Spanish-English veterans. Information: *Viajes Geosud* (see above) or *Aralar-Zalditegia*, Caserio Artola, Baraibar 31879 (phone: 48-504214).

SEGOVIA The royal bridle paths laid down by the 14th-century Castilian sovereigns to tie their precarious kingdom together, along the trails of the *mesta* (medieval sheepherders guild), are the arteries leading straight into the heart of ancient Spain. *Rutas a Caballo* brings the highlands of Old Castile, with its castles, churches, hermitages, rivers, and forests, within easy reach of its home base, *Molino de Río Viejo,* a ranch set around a centuries-old water mill, 12 miles (19 km) northwest of the provincial capital.

A 2-week excursion leads through the Sierra de Guadarrama, along the Duratón River canyon, and past the royal summer palace of La Granja, stopping in Sepúlveda, Pedraza, Turegano, and other towns with emblazoned palaces gone to ruin after their medieval glory. Departures are scheduled twice monthly, May through August, and once each during March, April, September, and October. A shorter 8-day version of the same route can be booked any month of the year. One-day and weekend outings from the mill are also offered. Information: *Rutas a Caballo* (see above) or *Molino de Río Viejo,* N-110, Km 172, Collado Hermoso, Segovia 40170 (phone: 11-403063).

MORE HORSING AROUND

LA TRANSHUMANCIA This is the big chance for closet cowboys (and lovers of the movie *City Slickers*). Every year, around June, Spanish cowpunchers round up their stock from the warmer winter grasslands of Extremadura and move them to summer pastures around León, Avila, Salamanca, and Soria in a week-long cattle drive that is one of Europe's largest. Visitors can accompany the cowboys as they go off branding them dogies and fording the Tagus River, sampling a lifestyle that did not end when Clint

Eastwood left the rawhide range. But in between the long stretches of prairie, visitors will bed down at the luxury *paradores* of Trujillo and Oropesa, and at other stylish hotels. The roundup takes place around the second week of June, but the number of participants is limited. Information: *Equestrian Tours Almansur* (see above).

SPAIN FROM THE SADDLE For true equestrians who want to see all of Spain from the saddle, *Rutas a Caballo* offers a solid month in the stirrups — a trek from Segovia down the royal bridle paths running southeast to the Atlantic coast of Andalusia. The tour, available in June and October, also passes the foothills of the Sierra de Guadarrama into the barren 4,000-foot-high tableland of Avila province, followed by the evergreen oak forests of Extremadura to Guadalupe, Trujillo, Cáceres, and Mérida, up into the Sierra Morena and through the Guadalquivir River Valley to Seville and Arcos de la Frontera. Information: *Rutas a Caballo* (see above).

Best Beaches

Welded to Europe by a thin strip of land reinforced by the Pyrenees Mountains, the Iberian Peninsula seems to have been made to maximize its shoreline. The fantastically varied blends of sea, sand, and civilization range from the bathtub-like waters of the Mediterranean to the shivering shocks of the Atlantic surf, from the lonely and lush, mist-soaked greenery of northwest Spain to the teeming glitz of the Costa del Sol and the stardust of Ibiza.

One way to choose a beach is by its lack of name recognition. Since many of Spain's most popular beach resorts are now being reduced to functional blots encased in concrete, visiting them is as much of a return to nature as going to lunch at a salad bar. Many visitors, therefore, carefully take the time to seek out remote and undiscovered ocean paradises, far removed from the sands of mass tourism. Many others, however, head straight for the crowds. For those unable to avoid the large resorts, but wishing to escape the masses, try a visit in late August or September.

BALEARIC ISLANDS In an archipelago whose recent history is a catalogue of famous visitors, ranging from the Spanish royal family on Majorca to a generation's worth of hippies on Ibiza, the number of people who share these beaches is in inverse proportion to the time one invests in reaching them. Palma de Mallorca, seemingly everyone's first stop, is a busy port city complete with condos, a cathedral, and convention-size hotels. Miles of sandy beaches stretch to the east; those from Ca'n Pastilla to El Arenal are lined with high-rise hotels, restaurants, and discos, known collectively as the Playa de Palma. To the west lie a cluster of smaller beaches — Cala Mayor, Palma Nova, Magaluf, and, beyond the Bay of Palma, Paguera. The smaller island of Minorca has miles of solitary pine-ringed beaches, sloping countrysides, and historic ruins, making it a worthwhile trek from even the tiniest town. Its capital is Mahón, whose serried whitewashed houses were given distinguished Georgian make-overs during the island's British colonial days. Just outside town is the Stone Age village of Trepucó, one of the prehistoric mini-Stonehenges that dot the island (another reason 18th-century colonists thought that Minorca should belong to England). Information: *Oficina de Turismo,* 13 Plaza de la Esplanada, Mahón, Minorca 07701 (phone: 71-363790).

Ibiza, the third-largest island, lives up to its reputation as the jet set playground of Europe, and home away from home for famous artists and pseudo-artists, movie stars, rock performers, fashion designers, and all the other beautiful people. The city is atop a hill overlooking a natural harbor on the southeast corner of the island. The beaches here range from the tourist-filled resort-packed kind to unoccupied stretches of bleached sand and deserted coves, like the salt flats of Las Salinas to the south. Information: *Oficina de Turismo,* 13 Paseo Vara de Rey, Ibiza (phone: 71-301900).

EL CABO DE GATA, near Almería, Andalusia At the southeastern tip of Spain, on the edge of the Costa del Sol and squarely in the middle of nowhere, El Cabo de Gata ("the Cape of the Cat") is the place to go to get away from it all — including hotels, paved roads, and vegetation. The dusty, brush-covered desert that turns imperceptibly into beach looks as if it should be accompanied by the twang and whistled tune of a spaghetti (or paella) western. This is indeed where many a parched cowboy squinted into the pretend Texas sun before whipping out his Colt .45. San José is the cape's only (barely) burgeoning resort, but the city of Almería is only a short drive away, and the town of Mojácar (just up the coast, though a long way around by road) clambers quaintly up a hillside a mile or two back from the shore and has a *parador*. Accommodations here are scarce and by no means luxurious, but the food is good and there are some bargain prices to be enjoyed. Information: *Oficina de Turismo,* 4 Calle Hermanos Machado, Edificios Servicios Múltiples, Almería 04004 (phone: 51-230607 or 51-233549).

CANARY ISLANDS An hour's water skiing from the coast of the Western Sahara, the volcanic archipelago of the Canaries belongs technically to Spain, geographically to Africa, and physically to the moon. This is one of the main winter destinations for Europeans escaping the cold of the continent. Called the Fortunate Isles, the Canaries are bathed by the Gulf Stream and, with approximately the same latitude as Florida, enjoy a spring-like climate throughout most of the year, with temperatures around 70F. Although the islands have a sizable share of high-rise hotel resorts that crowd the beaches, there are also many stretches of unspoiled, sandy coastline, particularly on the islands of Lanzarote, Fuerteventura, and Grand Canary. Lanzarote's three tourist-created resorts, Costa Teguise (a jet set spot north of Arrecife), Puerto del Carmen (a popular vacation spot with the tour crowd south of Arrecife and the airport), and the less-developed, but more-picturesque Playa Blanca (on the southern tip where some of the best beaches can be found), are fairly uniform, controlled by strict building codes that dictate, among other things, the height of the buildings.

There are white sand beaches on the tiny island of La Graciosa, off the northwestern coast of Lanzarote, and on the island of Fuerteventura to the south; the southeast coastline around Jandia and the quaint northern resort of Corralejo are particularly lovely. The Playa del Inglés-Maspalomas area of the southern Grand Canary island has several miles of impressive dunes and whitewashed bungalow villages. Information: *Oficina de Turismo,* Parque Municipal, Arrecife 35500 (phone: 28-811860); *Grand Canary Oficina de Turismo,* Parque de Santa Catalina, Las Palmas (phone: 28-264623); *Oficina de Turismo,* Fuerteventura, 3 Av. 1 de Maio, Puerto del Rosario (phone: 28-851024).

COSTA BRAVA, Tossa del Mar, Catalonia The Costa Brava looks like a landscape painted by Cézanne — straight brushstrokes of ocher cliffs rising from the flat blue base to a daub of pine-tree green, the clean horizontals of Tossa's old port, and the vertical slice of a fishing boat's mast. The town lies in one of this weatherbeaten coast's many snug, sandy inlets; these once gave shelter to Phoenician sailors, but now provide exposure to Nordic bathers. Choose from Tossa's three beaches: La Playa Grande, Mar Menuda, and Es Codolar, each as spectacular as the next. If Tossa seems too tame after dark, or its medieval Villa Vella too old, head for Lloret de Mar, a casino-powered resort where young people sizzle till dawn. If even Tossa seems rowdy, the cliff-top *Parador de Aiguablava* (phone: 72-622162) in Bagur offers contemplative views of the see-through water 400 feet below and the sea-floor rocks 40 feet below that. Information: *Patronat de Turisme Costa Brava,* Palau de Putacio, 5 Pujada San Marti, Girona 17004 (phone: 72-208401) or *Oficina d'Informació Turística,* 4 Calle de l'Esglesia (at the bus terminal), Tossa 17320 (phone: 72-340100).

COSTA CANTÁBRICA, Santander, Cantabria This elegant city, almost as close to the powdery snow as it is to the powdery sand, is proud of the quality of its double life — its measured off-season pace and its summer pulsation of students, orchestras, and tourists, all drawn by Santander's spectacular beaches, its festivals of music and dance, and its summer university. Dense crowds and a rather rough Atlantic are the trademarks of the Playa del Sardinero, while the beaches on the bay are graced by those who prefer gentler surf. Comillas, some 40 miles (64 km) from Santander, is a quiet, still-aristocratic resort, where visitors are more likely to run across a marquis than a marquee. The wide Playa Comillas, where the titled sunbathe until they achieve the color of expensive leather, ends in a small pleasure port. The nearby Oyambre Beach is twice as long, with half the tourists. Information: *Oficina de Turismo,* 1 Plaza de Velarde, Santander 39001 (phone: 42-310708).

COSTA DEL SOL, Marbella, Andalusia The Costa del Sol is a glittering avenue of low-slung bathing suits and high-rise prices, and Marbella is the center of Europe's wealthy worshipers of sun and self. The tennis courts and golf courses are world class, but the primary sport here is people watching. The world's wet set finds shelter in the nearby yacht harbor at Puerto Banús, and the smoothness of Estepona's silky water is guarded from the rough and tumble of the Atlantic by the Rock of Gibraltar, visible from the town's wide beachfront. In the other direction, past Málaga (pass it quickly; it is the tourists' Ellis Island), is the town of Nerja, with a *parador,* a cliff-top boardwalk, and a set of spectacular caves scooped out by water flowing through the soft limestone. Information: in Marbella, *Oficina de Turismo,* 1 Av. Miguel Cano, Marbella 29600 (phone: 52-771442); the rest of the Costa del Sol, *Oficina de Turismo,* 4 Pasaje de Chinitas, Málaga 29015 (phone: 3-221-3445 or 3-222-8948).

RÍAS BAJAS, La Toja, Galicia The Celts once came to green Galicia and gave it their bagpipes, heaths, and a wet Gaelic fog. But when the mist slides off the fjords of the Rías Bajas, it reveals some of the peninsula's most voluptuous coastline, where meadow lanes link small stone churches to shingle-roofed villages, and the people speak Galician, a language of their own. Reachable by bridge from the town of O Grove, La Toja is a dressed-up island complete with large, expensive hotels, swimming pools, golf courses, a spa, and a casino. Although the island has been overdeveloped, its beaches are still alluring. In a region where the specialty is squid cooked in its own ink, O Grove is religious about its seafood. On the second Sunday in October, the town celebrates the *Feast of the Exaltation of Shellfish.* Information: *Oficina de Turismo,* 2 Calle General Mola, Pontevedra 36001 (phone: 86-850814).

SAN SEBASTIÁN This pearl of a city on an oyster shell–shaped bay situated between two emerald mountains is one of the most popular resorts in northern Spain. It's in the heart of Euskadi (the Basque Country), where jai alai takes precedence over tennis, and residents test their machismo in log chopping competitions and run with the bulls in neighboring Pamplona every July. Believed to be descendants of the original Stone Age residents of the Iberian Peninsula, the Basques speak a language unrelated to Latin or Gaelic, or to any known language in the history of the world. Fortunately, almost all of them also speak Castilian (Spanish), especially when dealing with tourists. Although the weather can be unreliable in this part of Spain, during most summer months this slice of coast is thickly spread with oiled bodies. At sunset the crowds flow into the streets of San Sebastián's Old Quarter, drifting between *tapas* bars and stand-up counters, and dining on mini-courses of fresh shrimp, dried cod in tomato sauce, and squid in its own ink. Information: *Oficina de Turismo,* 1 Paseo de los Fueros, San Sebastián 20004 (phone: 43-426282) and *Centro de Atracción y Turismo* (*CAT*), Calle Reina Regente, San Sebastián 20004 (phone: 43-481167).

Gone Fishing

With countless miles of sun-soaked Atlantic and Mediterranean coastline, unpolluted waters, and over 200 varieties of fish, Spain is truly an angler's paradise. Deep-sea enthusiasts can wrestle year-round with swordfish, ray, tuna, shark, trout, and snapper, while freshwater anglers can cast for tench, salmon, carp, trout, pike, bass, barbel, and chub. Although there are numerous lakes and rivers for fishing, it is not a wide-open free-for-all. In order to protect and maintain their fish populations, Spain places numerous restrictions on both local and visiting fisherfolk. The country has limits on where and when fishing is permitted, as well as various catch limits. These laws are often so dizzying that the effort to obtain permits and satisfy restrictions may not be worth the day spent at sea. A lottery-style drawing is held each fishing season, and permits are issued to the winners. If the maximum number of seasonal permits has been distributed before a visitor's arrival, he or she may be out of luck.

Nearly all game fishing waters in Spain are tightly controlled by the country's various local and regional governments. Some regions do not allow foreigners to fish in their waters, period! Those that do require the appropriate licenses and permits, but bear in mind that these documents do not grant fishermen the right to clean out the ocean, lakes, rivers, or streams. Spain also has strongly enforced catch limits, as well as strict rules regulating minimum sizes, bait and tackle, and Sunday fishing. Sea angling is discouraged, and is considered illegal in some regions; the seas along the Costa del Sol and the Costa Brava are rare exceptions.

Three types of fishing are possible in Spain: deep-sea, river and lake, and underwater. Permits are available from the *Instituto Nacional para la Conservación de la Naturaleza* (*ICONA*) through each of its offices in the various autonomous communities. In Madrid, *ICONA* is located at 4 Gran Vía de San Francisco (phone: 1-347-6000); its Barcelona office is at 5 Plaça Dr. Letamendi (phone: 3-330-6451). The permits vary according to the type of fishing to be practiced. Be warned: Most federations have strange hours; some don't open until after 6 PM, and some are open only from 9 AM to noon. Also, many *ICONA* staff members throughout Spain do not speak English. Permits cost about $10 per day, and a passport is required. Salmon and trout permits cost about $5; a license, which is separate, costs about $10. It is advisable to check with a travel agent or the National Tourist Office of Spain in the US before going. The tourist office provides a fishing map called *Pesca* (fishing), which outlines the best available areas. For the particulars once there, check with the *Spanish Fishing Federation* (3 Calle Navas de Tolosa, Madrid 28013; phone: 1-532-8352; fax: 1-532-6538). Other good sources include the *Promoción de Caza y Pesca* (41 Duque de Sexto, Madrid 28010; phone: 1-276-3661); and the *Consejería de Agricultura y Cooperación de la Comunidad Autónoma de Madrid* (60 Calle Orense, Madrid 28020; phone: 1-455-7703). The most-rewarding months for angling are March through August.

ANDALUSIA Outside the cities of Granada and Jaén are some of the country's best spots for catching trout, crab, pike, and cyprinids. Maximum catches allowed range from 10 to 80. The season is best from March 1 through August 15, except along the Guadalquivir, Jándula, Rumblar, and Guadalén rivers in the fishing reserves of Estación, Andújar, San Juan, San Julián, and Rumblar, where people can fish (mostly for cyprinids) year-round. Surrounded by the ranges of the Sierra Morena and the Segura, this is one of the most scenic and enjoyable fishing regions in the country. Information: *Oficina de Turismo,* 1 Calle Arquitecto Bergés, Jaén 23007 (phone: 53-222737).

CANTABRIAN COAST Wedged between the Basque Country to the east and Galicia to the west, this area is one of Spain's most unspoiled. Choose a base in Santander, Oviedo, Pontevedra, or Lugo, and experience the pleasures of medieval living. This natural paradise remains virtually untouched, and visitors will relish its history, artistry, modesty, and gorgeous beaches. On top of all that, the fish are never far away. This is the place for catching salmon and enjoying a meal while overlooking the twinkling waters. Information: *Oficina de Turismo,* 1 Plaza de Velarde, Santander 39001 (phone: 42-310708) or *Consejería de Ganadería, Agricultura y Pesca de la Diputación Regional de Cantabria,* 1 Pasaje de la Puntida, Santander 39071 (phone: 42-312969).

CASTILE-LEÓN Head to Avila, Burgos, or Seville for some of the best angling central Spain has to offer. Restrictions apply a bit more heavily here, to the point where people have to check their days for fishing. Usually, Fridays and Saturdays are all right. Catches are restricted as well; the take-home limit ranges from 6 to 10. Best bets are trout and cyprinids. Information: *Oficina de Turismo,* 4 Plaza de la Catedral, Avila 05001 (phone: 21-211387), or *Oficina de Turismo,* 7 Plaza de Alonso Martínez, Burgos 09003 (phone: 47-203125; fax: 47-276529).

CATALONIA Most avid fishermen know the areas around Barcelona, Girona, and Lleida as some of the most prolific year-round spots for catching trout, black bass, and cyprinids. Like other areas, strict restrictions apply. Also check out the areas along the Costa Brava. These rough waters are perfect for underwater fishing. Check with *ICONA* (phone: in Barcelona, 3-330-6451) or the local tourist office for details. The Catalan Pyrenees are also good for trout and salmon. About half of the 250 lakes in the Pyrenees National Park are stocked with various kinds of trout, and there is at least one good fishing stream in each valley. Information: *Oficina de Informació de la Generalitat de Catalunya,* 658 Gran Via de les Corts Catalanes, Barcelona 08010 (phone: 3-301-7443 or 3-317-2246; El Prat Airport, phone: 3-478-4704), or *Consejería de Agricultura, Ganadería y Pesca de la Generalitat de Catalunya,* 329 Carrer Còrsega, Barcelona 08037 (phone: 3-237-8024).

CANARY ISLANDS Unpolluted waters and continual spring-like weather, created in part by the mild Gulf Stream, make this archipelago a fisherman's paradise. Some 1,500 species of fish, including swordfish, stingray, tunny, grouper, eel, and giant ray, thrive in these waters, and craft and equipment rentals are numerous (available at most harbors). *Nautisport* (phone: 22-791459) runs shark fishing trips from Los Cristianos quay on Tenerife, as well as daily fishing excursions organized from Los Gigantes harbor, Santiago de Teide, in southeast Tenerife. Deep-sea fishing from Corralejo on Fuerteventura can be organized through *Escudo in Jandia* (phone: 28-852293), or *Pez Velero* (phone: 28-866173). Information: *Dirección General de Medio Ambiente*, 35 Av. de Anaga, Santa Cruz de Tenerife 38080 (phone: 22-286400).

Freewheeling by Two-Wheeler

Because of the mild climate in Spain, touring by bicycle is easy and the itinerary possibilities are nearly inexhaustible. Visitors who pedal through the Spanish countryside will get to know parts of the country that most vacationers never see. These are the real sights, the hidden enclaves still untouched by tourism. Leisurely bicycle rides pass through tiny fishing villages and medieval towns dotted with Moorish ruins. In Spain, a bike ride can cover a variety of terrain, from the hilly land of olive groves to flat vineyards and lush countryside overflowing with orange and lemon trees.

Those who have traveled around Europe by bicycle before will find that a cycling vacation in Spain is slightly more primitive than in most other Western European countries. There is hardly an abundance of sophisticated repair shops, nor even the guarantee of well-surfaced secondary roads (though the situation is improving). Bicycle rentals are available in Spain, but not omnipresent. Intermediate and diehard cyclists will want to bring their own bicycles and gear. Airlines will generally transport bikes as part of passengers' personal baggage, but they may insist that the entire bike be crated; check with the airline before departure. Also be sure to confirm insurance coverage. And note that when traveling by train in Spain, a bike (like luggage) must be placed in the last car, so make sure that it is properly labeled with name, address, and the stations of origin and destination. A sturdy lock is another sensible precaution.

Some cyclists choose to travel alone through Spain. Others, however, team up with fellow cyclists and soon become fast friends. The natives are so friendly they will practically apologize if they cannot accompany a rider to his or her destination (many riders often wind up staying in one place longer than they had planned). It does help, however, to have a rudimentary understanding of Spanish, especially when touring the rural routes, as most people in the countryside do not speak English. A pocket dictionary is heartily recommended. As usual, taking along a basic set of tools and spares, including a tire pump, puncture repair kit, tire levers, spoke key, oil can, batteries and bulbs, rag, extra spokes, inner tubes and tires, pliers, and odd nuts and bolts, is also a good idea. Traveling with a minimal amount of cash and a credit card is also advised. In addition, take along a good map; Michelin generally has the best. In Madrid, check out the maps and books at *La Tienda Verde* (The Green Shop; 38 Calle Maudes; phone: 1-533-0791), which stocks the best assortment on naturalist tours; books are available in both Spanish and English. In Barcelona, try *Lliberia Quera* (2 Carrer Petritxol; phone: 3-318-0743) for good maps of and guides to Catalonia.

If the thought of biking alone is less than a satisfactory vacation idea, there are numerous organized bicycle tours in both countries. Companies offering bicycling and other package tours are listed in GETTING READY TO GO.

When cycling in Spain, always remember that it is more relaxing and enjoyable to take it slowly and enjoy the country's sights and sounds. After choosing a region, consult the local tourist literature. Then plot out the tour on a large-scale highway map of the country. Base daily mileage on what usually is covered on the road at home, but be sure to allot time for en route dawdling — chats with the natives, walks through ruined castles, wine and *tapas* at the local bar.

The Spanish cycling federation can also provide a roster of competitive biking events. Information: *Federacion de Ciclismo,* 16 Calle Ferraz, Madrid 28008 (phone: 1-542-0421).

ANDALUSIA This region's warm year-round climate, well-marked and well-paved roads, and scenery rank it as one of the best places to go biking in Spain. Home to feisty flamenco dancers and sun-splashed villages, Andalusia also boasts three of the country's most fascinating cities: Granada, Córdoba, and Seville. Begin the tour in Granada, with a steep ride up to the Alhambra, a complex of palaces, fortresses, and gardens built during the 13th and 14th centuries. Then meander in Columbus's historic footsteps to Santa Fe, the city where King Ferdinand and Queen Isabella signed the famous agreement sponsoring the explorer's famous voyage. Next, head to Córdoba, one of Spain's oldest cities. Along the way, the route skirts past two rivers, the Marbella and the Guadajoz. The terrain along the route is fairly easy, consisting mostly of gentle downhill slopes and flat land. The road begins to climb just beyond the small village of Torres Cabrera. At the top of the next stretch, the slope of Lobatón (best climbed with a 20–24 gear ratio), awaits a picture-postcard view of Córdoba, which is reached by an easy descent. The city's roads are narrow and cobbled, but soon after leaving the city limits, following the Avenida de Medina Azahara, they get better. Heading south toward Seville, the route passes through alternating views of extensive fields and barren wastelands. Occasionally, a fortress pokes up its revered head in the distance. Seville is one of the most romantic cities in Spain and one of its most touristic. The roads, most of

DIVERSIONS BICYCLING

347

which were dramatically improved in preparation for *Expo '92*, are well marked, the scenery full of history and beauty. Always be careful to lock up the bike and take off one of its wheels; unfortunately, caution is necessary here (as in most major Spanish cities), as crime has become an all-too-frequent problem. After Seville, it's a 1-hour ride northeast to Carmona, once a thriving Arab stronghold, to view its famous 14th-century mansions. Stop for lunch at Carmona's *Parador Alcázar del Rey Don Pedro* (phone: 54-141010), the former palace of King Pedro el Cruel (Peter the Cruel). Information: *Oficina de Turismo*, 2 Calle Libreros, Granada 18001 (phone: 58-227510); *Oficina de Turismo*, 10 Calle Torrijos, Córdoba 14003 (phone: 57-471235); and *Oficina de Turismo*, 21B Av. de la Constitución, Seville 41004 (phone: 5-422-1404).

BASQUE COUNTRY The hilly Basque Country is best known for the town of Guernica, made famous by Pablo Picasso's painting of the same name, depicting the horrors of the Spanish Civil War. It is an interesting area to explore because its culture and its people — even its language — are quite different from the rest of Spain. The area will appeal to cyclists who enjoy diverse geography. The tour rolls past rugged mountains and stony undulations to soft, sloping, wide sandy shores and steep, pine-covered hillsides. In San Sebastián, the road along the *puerto*'s edge travels past some of the best seafood restaurants serving fresh food caught that day. Cycle along the Bilbao coast for some of the finest and most surprising scenery along the North Atlantic coast. Information: *Oficina de Turismo*, 1 Paseo de los Fueros, San Sebastián 20004 (phone: 43-426282).

CASTILE-LEÓN This is a land of fairy-tale images, including that of El Escorial, King Philip II's somber yet lavish palace-monastery near Madrid; the near-perfect 11th-century walled city of Avila, framed by the snow-capped ridge of the Sierra de Gredos; and Segovia, home to an ancient Roman aqueduct and the Alcázar, a medieval castle. This trip pedals past the royal palace and gardens of La Granja de San Ildefonso, often referred to as the Versailles of Spain, and the romantic spiraling cathedrals of Burgos and the handsome square at Valladolid. Start either in Madrid or at El Escorial, and plan enough time for a visit to the *Valle de los Caídos* (Valley of the Fallen), a spectacular memorial to those who died in the Spanish Civil War. Information: *Oficina de Turismo*, 10 Calle de Floridablanca, San Lorenzo de El Escorial, Madrid 28036 (phone: 1-890-1554); *Oficina de Turismo*, 4 Plaza de la Catedral, Avila 05001 (phone: 21-211387); and *Oficina de Turismo*, 10 Plaza Mayor, Segovia 40002 (phone: 11-430328).

CATALAN PYRENEES Intermediate pedalers will enjoy the challenge of this region, as it is filled with a number of ups and downs, but the views here are so spectacular that even beginners should give it a try. The area is the home of many of Spain's better ski resorts, including Baqueira-Beret and Tuca-Betrén, and during spring and summer, rich green and yellow fields crisscross the wide valleys and small undiscovered villages. Because of the proximity to France, the French influence on the food and the people here is very obvious. Ask the staff at the tourist office for the map *Valles Superiores del Segre/Ariege,* which covers the High Urgell, Cerdanya, and the Ribes Valley. A favorite tour is through the Aigües Tortes National Park, with the Sant Maurici Lake, just south of Val d'Aran. This national park is a wonderland of crashing waterfalls and serene lakes, which makes for very pleasant bicycling. Information: *Oficina d'Informació Turística,* Av. Valira, La Seu d'Urgell, Lleida 25700 (phone: 73-351511).

COSTA BLANCA The "White Coast," which extends from the fortress town of Denia down to Torrevieja, is another resort rich in natural beauty that is perfect for the cyclist. Like the Costa del Sol, it has its share of unspoiled spots. Venture to Alicante, inlaid with festive red tiles and graced with the famous Castillo de Santa Bárbara, full of secret passageways and tunnels. Nearby, Elche is known for its half-million palm trees, which supply all of Spain with fronds for *Palm Sunday.* Information: *Oficina de Turismo,* 2 Explanada de España, Alicante 03002 (phone: 6-521-2285).

COSTA BRAVA The "wild coast" is rougher and rockier than its sister resort areas, but just as magnificent. Most people flock here during the summer, so try to visit during the off-season, when it is more tranquil and easier to explore. Be careful, though, as many hotels and restaurants close at the end of the high season. The roads here are well paved, but the terrain is often steep, physically challenging, and, in some spots, even dangerous. This tour is not recommended for novice cyclists. Information: *Oficina de Turismo,* Centra de Lloret, Tossa de Mar, Girona 17320 (phone: 72-340108).

COSTA DEL SOL Although this area along Spain's southern coast falls under the jurisdiction of the region of Andalusia, it warrants a special mention. This tour passes through hills that drop off into the gentle surf of the Mediterranean and along roads that coil around the crashing waves. The Costa del Sol officially extends from Sotogrande del Guadiaro east of Gibraltar, in the Spanish southwest, to the town of Nerjis, east of Málaga. Those seeking the action and international flavor of some of Europe's most popular and lively beach resorts should pedal into the crowded resorts of Málaga, Marbella, and Torremolinos. Farther inland, the frenetic tourism of the resorts subsides, replaced with quiet small towns of whitewashed houses where the essence of Old Spain still thrives. One of the best places to enjoy a fiery Andalusian sunset is from the Puente Nuevo in Ronda, where the cliffs glow a soothing orange and red, reflecting the strong Spanish sun. In general, the roads along the Costa del Sol are in fairly good condition and easy to follow. Cyclists traveling in the off-season should prepare to ride west to east, thus avoiding the strong easterly winds. Also not to be missed is the great Rock of Gibraltar. The view is breathtaking along the Strait of Gibraltar all the way to the Moroccan coast. Although the area itself is British rather than Spanish (Gibraltar is a British Crown Colony), a visit here offers a chance to view one of the Iberian Peninsula's most famous sights. Information: *Oficina de Turismo,* 4 Pasaje de Chinitas, Málaga 29015 (phone: 3-221-3445 or 3-222-8948).

COSTA DE LA LUZ This coast, which runs from the Tarifa on the southern tip of Spain overlooking the majestic straits of Gibraltar to the town of Ayamonte on the Portuguese border, is less congested and more ruggedly scenic than the Costa del Sol. Relatively flat, it makes for a scenic bike route. Of particular interest are the picturesque town of Vejer de la Frontera, perched on a limestone headland near Cabo de Trafalgar, where Lord Nelson's navy crippled a Napoleonic fleet; the flamenco, horse, and sherry town of Jerez de la Frontera; Sanlucar de Barrameda, with its revered *manzanilla* wine and spectacular sunsets over the Guadalquivir River; and the white, sandy beaches at Matalascanas and Castilla. If you happen to be traveling in May, stop at the shrine of El Rocío, inside Coto Doñana National Park, where one of Europe's most picturesque and lively *romerías* (pilgrimages) takes place complete with costumes and music. Information: *Jefatura Provincial de Turismo*, 5 Av. de Viya, Cadiz 11007 (phone: 56-256056) or the *Delegación Provincial de la Junta de Andalucía*, Plaza de la Constitución, Cádiz 11007 (phone: 56-227505).

NAVARRESE PYRENEES There is probably no area in Spain quite as suited for quiet pedaling as this region along the valleys of the Arga and Aragon rivers, where mountain valleys swoop down to the dusty red desert. Begin this itinerary in Sangüesa, an ancient town on the Aragon River, and travel northeast, past the large and austere Cistercian monastery of Leyre, whose ancient church with its 12th-century crypt was the final resting place of the Kings of Navarre. Continue west into the sleepy town of Roncal, with its cobbled streets and stone houses, and the more upbeat town of Isaba, just to the north. Ahead lies Roncesvalles, historically known for the *Song of Roland,* an epic poem that romanticized the defeat of Charlemagne's rear guard during its retreat from Spain. The monastery here marked the beginning of the famous Pilgrims' Route as it entered Spain from France en route to Santiago de Compostela in the northwestern corner of the country. Don't be surprised by the sign warning of cattle on the loose in the valley of Valcarlos, a few miles from the French border, which marks the end of this tour. Information: *Oficina de Turismo,* 2 Calle Mercado, Sangüesa, Navarre 31400 (phone: 48-870329).

Great Walks and Mountain Rambles

Almost any walker will say that it is the footpaths of a country — not its roadways — that show off the local landscape to best advantage. Closer to earth than when driving or even biking, those on foot notice details that might not otherwise come to their attention: Valleys perfumed with edelweiss, hillsides dotted with medieval villages, sheep gamboling in the shade of fig and cork oak trees, and the friendly company of the sun makes the leaves shine and the mountaintops glisten.

The geographic diversity of the Iberian Peninsula makes walking here a wonderful journey full of surprises. Many paths were literally walked into existence by generations of people traveling to work, market, or church, or were carved by medieval pilgrims and advancing or retreating soldiers. Today, there is terrain for walkers and hikers of all abilities — from picnic stroller to fearless alpinist. The high mountain ranges of Spain's Picos de Europa and the Pyrenees and the green valleys of the Basque Country all make for peaceful, pleasant strolls or climbs. Spain also boasts a number of national parks to explore, while visitors less attracted to wilderness will find villages perched on high, with cobblestone streets, mansions, churches, ruins, and shops that are guaranteed to hold their interest and challenge their feet. Add to this a climate that is generally benign (Spain's southern coast is a Mediterranean paradise year-round), friendly natives, and good food, and you have all the ingredients necessary for a perfect expedition.

Before choosing a specific area of the country for hiking, look at a general road map of Spain that shows physical characteristics, so as not to opt for terrain that is too demanding for your level of fitness. For those who are sedentary, the choice of a mountainous region would be fool-hardy. To make the outing safe and pleasant, it is imperative for hikers to know their own limits. Unless they are very experienced, hikers always should stick to the defined areas — and *always* let someone know the planned destination and time of expected return (leave a note on the car if hiking alone). Those who prefer going as part of an organized tour should contact a local hiking club, a travel agent, or one of the tour packagers offering hiking tours (see GETTING READY TO GO).

Since hot weather is not necessarily a welcome companion on a walk, it's best to avoid the southern regions in midsummer. And since it can get warm almost anywhere in Spain between May and September, the wise walker will get most of a day's journey done before midday. Basic hiking essentials include a sturdy pair of shoes and socks, long pants if headed into heavily wooded areas, a canteen, a hat, sunblock, rainwear, and something warm, just in case. It is always best to dress in layers. Also make sure to wear clothes with pockets, or bring along a pack so that both hands can remain free. Some useful but often overlooked tools include a jack-knife, waterproof matches, a map, a compass, a Spanish *bota* or water pouch, and snacks. In the more remote areas, a backpack, sleeping bag and pad, cookstove, food, and other gear are required.

Spain is consistent only in its diversity. There are the extreme peaks of the highlands, the Pyrenees, and the Picos de Europa, and the lowlands of the Basque Country. The best times of year to hike these areas are late spring and early autumn, when the flora and fauna are at their most vibrant and the temperatures are at their most delightful. Always check the weather in advance. Like the topography, the temperature varies enormously from region to region; the high plains of the center suffer from fierce extremes — stiflingly hot in summer and bitterly cold in winter. The Atlantic Coast, in contrast, has a permanent tendency to dampness and a relatively brief summer. Much of the Mediterranean is warm virtually the entire year, and the archipelago of the Canary Islands off the northwest coast of Africa has permanent spring-like weather.

BASQUE COUNTRY, San Sebastián The Basque Country is a land of contrasts. Just steps away from its industrial centers sit isolated hamlets, submerged in the silent surroundings of valleys and forests. The most spectacular sight here is the city of San Sebastián, and the green mountains and thundering ocean that surround it. Climb to the top of Mt. Igueldo, at the far side of the bay, for the best view of the countryside and the Atlantic. Information: *Club Vasco de Acampado,* 19 Calle San Marcial Bajo, San Sebastián 20008 (phone: 43-428479) or *Club de Montaña Kresala,* 9 Calle Euskal Erria, San Sebastián 20003 (phone: 43-420905).

AIGÜES TORTES NATIONAL PARK AND SANT MAURICI LAKE, Catalan Pyrenees This is for the hiker who rejoices in waterfalls and serene lakes. Some 20,000 years ago, a glacier blasted its way through what is now northern Lleida province, leaving behind a panoramic wonderland. The park is reached either from the village of Bohi to the west or from Espot, on its eastern edge. The park's tourist office provides numerous hiking suggestions. Of special interest is a 16-mile (26-km) walk that passes the mountain lakes surrounding Estany de la Llosa and enters the valley of Estany de Sant Maurici. Wild goats roaming the area are a frequent sight. Less traveled but equally rewarding is the path leading up to Aigües Tortes. Along the way, the trail passes through the Vall d'Bohi,one of the best places to view Romanesque architecture in the world. The land is predominantly rural and dotted with churches dating from the 12th and 13th centuries. The park is best viewed in late spring, summer, and autumn. Information: *Oficina d'Informació del Parc Nacional,* Sant Maurici, Espot 25597 (phone: 73-246650).

CATALAN PYRENEES Good, fairly gentle trails, coupled with plenty of historic sights and a hospitable nature, make this northeast corner of Spain a sensible choice for the less-ambitious walker in need of wayside distractions. By virtue of its location (just across the French border), hikers can experience a variety of cultures, languages, and foods. In La Seu d'Urgell, nature buffs will have a field day roaming quiet peaks, scouting for wild mushrooms. Other expeditions lie in the valley of Nuria, where wildflowers and waterfalls dot the landscape. Also popular is the majestic Puigmal peak, rising over 9,500 feet, and the nearby Queranca Lakes. Information: *Oficina d'Informació Turística,* Av. Valira, La Seu d'Urgell, Lleida 25700 (phone: 73-351511).

COVADONGA MOUNTAIN NATIONAL PARK, near Oviedo This national park lays claim to the western region of the Picos de Europa and boasts some of the most beautiful scenery in the country, as well as the largest number of annual visitors. It was here, according to legend, that the Virgin Mary interceded with God on behalf of the king, Don Pelayo, ensuring his warriors of victory against the Moors. Today, the park caters to both naturists and religious entourages. The Santa Cueva (Sacred Cave) is where Don Pelayo supposedly prayed to the Virgin. For those seeking solitude, it's best to avoid the park on and around September 8, when the area celebrates the *Day of the Virgin* with numerous festivities. During this period, head instead for the hills and enjoy the wildlife that inhabits it. The higher you hike, the more likely you are to encounter a fleeting glimpse of a bear, wolf, wildcat, or fox. At the mountain's base are two lakes of glacial origin: El Enol and La Ercina. Both swimming and camping are permitted here. The best times to visit are summer and autumn. The area gets a lot of rain, so be sure to bring the appropriate clothing. Information: *Federación Asturiana de Montañismo*, 16 Calle Melquíades Alvarez, Oviedo 33002 (phone: 85-211099).

NAVARRESE PYRENEES, east of Pamplona It takes a dedicated hiker to navigate his or her way through this rugged profile of the mountains and the valleys along the Arga and Aragon rivers. In return for the effort, however, the intrepid will get a close glimpse of some vital bits of history. The 24-mile (40-km) route from the Pyrenees through Navarre's mountain passes bisects the river valleys and is the same route used by thousands of 11th- and 12th-century pilgrims on their journey from France to Santiago de Compostela and the shrine of St. James. In Yesa, the route leads past a weathered stone monastery, once a center of power and wealth and the favorite charity and residence of the Kings of Navarre during the Middle Ages. Other remnants of medieval life worth exploring include nearby Tierman, an abandoned town on the shore of Yesa Lake, and Javier Castle, once a fortress and now a Jesuit college. Upon moving west through the mountains, each valley becomes a bit more green and moist. Noteworthy towns along the way include Roncal, Isaba, and Ochagava. Of special note is the town of Roncesvalles, historically known for the *Song of Roland*, the epic poem about Charlemagne's retreat from Spain, and the starting point for many medieval pilgrims. Information: *Oficina de Turismo*, 3 Calle Duque de Ahumada, Pamplona 31002 (phone: 48-220741).

ORDESA AND MONTE PERDIDO NATIONAL PARK, near Jaca, Aragonese Pyrenees Here, in Spain's northeast, is terrain that will please hikers of all abilities. This is one of the country's most beautiful areas. Its jewel-like gorges and waterfalls, steep mountains flowered with edelweiss, and dazzling forests of pine and beech are enough to encourage even the most sedentary of hikers. The park's finest scenic assets lie near the magnificent Escuain Gorge and the Yago River. There are also four distinct valleys to explore; the visitors' center provides a guided itinerary with recommended routes. The Ordesa area is a walker's paradise, with many routes available. The red *Cartographic Guide to Ordesa, Vignemale, and Monte Perdido* (about $5 in local bookstores) is a helpful guide. Although it's written in Spanish, its maps are easy to follow.

Recommended itineraries include Torla-Ordesa, an easy 8-mile (13-km) hike that winds through beautiful valleys and forests. Cross the bridge below Torla (Puente de la Glera) and follow the trail marked Camino de Turieto. More ambitious hikers may want to undertake the Torla-Gavarnie tour, a 24-mile (38-km) walk to the French town of Gavarnie. Following the valley, turn left at the river fork and continue along the Ara River for about 6 miles (10 km) before reaching the hamlet of San Nicolás de Bujaruelo. The trail goes directly into the mountains, crosses through the 828-foot-high Puerto de Bujaruelo, and descends straight into Gavarnie. For an even more scenic view of the Pyrenees, experienced hikers should take the Valle de Ordesa–Sierra Custodia–Valle de Vio triangle, which winds past thundering waterfalls, pine forests, and alpine valleys. Another challenging adventure is the 44-mile (71-km) Ordesa–Gavarnie trail, which starts near the Ordesa information hut and shoots straight up the steep gorge of the Circo de Salarons.

The Soasa Circle is a more realistic and relatively easy walk through the natural wonders of the Aragonese Pyrenees. Take a hearty lunch, as this walk covers a good 28 miles (45 km). Begin by following the gently sloping Arazas River eastward to the surging Cascada del Abanico. Here, the river roars over the rocks at lightning speeds. For a close view, cross the bridge a few minutes upstream and come back down to the observation point, situated on a huge rock. Continue toward Soasa, past more thundering falls, until the path leaves the forest. Once beyond the Gradas de Soasa (stepped waterfalls), the valley broadens and flattens. The fan-shaped Cascada de Soasa at the far end of the valley jets forth from between two cliffs, and is a welcome resting point. This marks the approximate halfway point of the climb; it is also a perfect vantage point for surveying the sweeping panorama of snow-capped peaks: Monte Arruebo, Monte Perdido, and Pico de Anisclo. Cross the river and follow the semi-hidden path that hems the tree line into mountain goat territory. The mountaintops and meadows blanketed with woolly-leafed edelweiss and multicolored butterflies are inspiring. But don't get too light-footed. The last leg of the excursion is a challenging climb, as the path clambers near jutting rocks and abrupt edges. It tumbles down, down, down, with views of the parking lot below teasing the mind until it is reached in about an hour.

The best areas of the park can usually be covered in 2 to 4 days. Accommodations can be found in the nearby towns of Huesca and Jaca. There is also the *Parador Monte Perdido* in Bielsa, in the province of Huesca (inside the park, at the head of the Pineta Valley; phone: 74-501011). The best time of year to visit the park is from mid-July through late August. Information: *Oficina de Turismo*, 2 Av. Regimiento de Galicia, Jaca 22700 (phone: 74-360098), or *Oficina de Turismo*, 23 Calle Coso Alto, Huesca 22022 (phone: 74-225778).

PICOS DE EUROPA, near Potes This stretch of remote territory is especially popular with backpackers and experienced hikers, who take advantage of its numerous trails that transcend the range's jagged profile, valleys, and lower slopes. Always be sure to check weather forecasts before setting off on a hike in this region, as the area is prone to sudden drops in temperature and surprise rainstorms. Note that only well-equipped and very advanced alpinists should attempt to scale the peaks themselves. Accommodations are few and far between here, and most hikers use the nearby town of Potes, along the Deva River, as a base. Quiet and snowbound in winter, Potes becomes a cosmopolitan climber's town in summer. Detailed maps, including those published by the Instituto Geográfico Nacional and the Federación Española de Montañismo, are available at *Bustamante,* a photo shop in Potes's main square; each costs about $3. Information: *Federación Asturiana de Montañismo,* 16 Calle Melquíades Alvarez, Oviedo 33002 (phone: 85-211099).

SIERRA DE GUADARRAMA, near Madrid This pine-covered mountain range, halfway between Madrid and Segovia, is one of the most beautiful in central Spain. Particularly noteworthy are the alpine village of Cercedilla and the breathtaking mountain pass of Puerto de Navacerrada, the geographic border between Old and New Castile. Cercedilla is a town of picturesque alpine chalets and cow pastures. Its *piscinas* (pools), set below cascading waterfalls, are a popular summer attraction. The peaks of Puerto de Navacerrada reach 6,102 feet and offer excellent views of the surrounding Castilian plains. Nearby, in the town of Rascafría, take a swim in La Laguna de Peñalara, a beautiful lagoon situated in a valley below the commanding mountain peak. Use either Madrid or Segovia as a base, but be forewarned: The weather here is wild, so dress warmly, even in summer. Information: *Oficina de Turismo,* 2 Duque de Medinaceli, Madrid 28014 (phone: 1-429-4951), or *Oficina de Turismo,* 10 Plaza Mayor, Segovia 40002 (phone: 11-430328).

SIERRA MORENA, near Córdoba Few travelers know of the Sierra Morena, and even most Andalusians have trouble placing it. Though not one of Spain's more dramatic mountain ranges (its highest peak rises to just over 4,300 feet), it is nonetheless an enjoyable and very relaxing climb. The best time to visit is in March and April, when the flowers are in full bloom. Expect to be given a private performance by armies of frogs and turtles that live along the stream. Most often, they are a hiker's only companions. The Moorish towns of Córdoba and Jaén make the best bases and starting points. Information: *Oficina de Turismo,* 10 Calle Torrijos, Córdoba 14003 (phone: 57-471235), or *Oficina de Turismo,* 1 Calle Arquitecto Bergés, Jaén 23007 (phone: 53-222737).

SIERRA NEVADA, near Granada The tallest range in all of Spain is also the most challenging. Even in summer the weather is severe, with whipping winds and temperatures that drop considerably at night. The peaks of these mountains, Mulhacén (11,407 feet) and Veleta (11,128 feet), are best tackled as a day trip, using Granada as a base. Particularly rewarding is the 25-mile (40-km) route surrounding Las Alpujarras, the small white villages that line the range's base. Capileira is the closest thing to a tourist center in the area, offering good accommodations and a few other adventurous activities; the area's best lodgings are at *Villa Touristica de Poqueira,* also known as *Villa de Bubión* (phone: 58-763111), a delightful village hotel about 10 minutes from Capileira. Those who decide to climb farther than Las Alpujarras should be no less than intermediate climbers, able to handle sudden wind changes and a fair amount of rough terrain. The region is best tackled in the summer, long after all the snow has melted. The highest peak on peninsular Spain — and the country's ultimate vantage point — is Mulhacén, often most accessible after May. The area is noticeably secluded; wild goats and birds are often the only company. Nearby are the town of Trévelez, Spain's highest community, renowned for its ham, and the cozy hamlet of Pitres. An alternative route is a hike up Mt. Veleta. Buses run year-round and climb as high as they can; from mid-June on, they can usually make it clear up the road to a point from which it's a treacherous 3-hour hike to the peak. Under clear skies, the view extends all the way to the Rif Mountains of Morocco. The most detailed map of the region is published by the *Federación Española de Montañismo* ($3), available in both English and Spanish in most of Granada's bookstores. Information: *Oficina de Turismo,* 2 Calle Libreros, Granada 18001 (phone: 58-227510).

TORCAL MOUNTAINS, near Antequera Some 30 miles (48 km) north of Málaga, and just south of the tidy agricultural-industrial town of Antequera, await two circular trails that will enthrall adventurous hikers who delight in exploring desolate rock gardens. The path marked with yellow arrows is about 8 miles (13 km); the red-arrowed tour covers about 12 miles (19 km). Both feature spectacular vistas of curious rock formations and begin and end in Antequera, at the *refugio* (refuge hut) at the base of the mountain. Information: *Oficina de Turismo,* Palacio de Nájera, Antequera 29200 (phone: 52-841827).

PICO DEL TEIDE, Tenerife Rising from the Cañadas plateau, surrounded by the 47-mile (75-km) Parque Nacional de la Cañadas del Teide, is Pico del Teide, a massive dormant volcano and Spain's highest peak at 12,200 feet. Hikes here offer panoramic views of the Canaries and the coast of Africa. Information: *Parque Nacional de las Cañadas del Teide,* Tenerife (phone: 22-330701).

Directions

Introduction

The Iberian Peninsula is a land that long has been irresistible to travelers and explorers. As far back as 650 BC, foreigners (mostly in the form of invaders back then) were arriving in Spain and discovering its diversity and individuality. During the Age of Discovery beginning in the 15th century, numerous explorers, sailing under the flag of Spain, went in search of other lands to call their own. Spaniards take enormous pride in their country, and today travelers from all over the world come to enjoy (not conquer) Spain's glorious beaches, challenging mountains, and breathtaking countryside.

Until the 1960s, Spain was considered the perfect destination for adventurous travelers, since public transportation was limited and primitive at best, and accommodations for visitors were far below other Western European standards. If hitchhiking and sleeping on the beach were your cup of tea, then this was the place to come. But with expanded air travel, improved train and bus services, and increased interest in European travel among young and old alike, Spain became an inexpensive and popular choice for travelers. As interest grew, facilities for the traveler improved (although visitors today will no longer find prices to be much lower than those in other Western European countries). At present, work is continuing on a tunnel beneath the Pyrenees that should make travel between France and Spain much easier. The tunnel is part of a European project aimed at establishing a modern road system among all of the continent's major cities by the year 2000.

Spain's diversity of culture — a direct result of numerous invasions by other countries — and its varied topography provide today's traveler with a colorful journey, filled with limitless options for side trips far off beaten paths. From Algeciras to Zaragoza, this land still offers plenty of places to tilt at your own windmills.

In the following pages, we have outlined 13 driving routes that we think best represent — and cover — every corner of this fascinating country. Roads are generally in good repair in Spain, unless otherwise noted, and with few exceptions each route is designed to take between 3 and 5 days. We have even included several delightful day trips from the capital city of Madrid. And if at any point you tire at the wheel, it's possible to break up your drive with an occasional ride on a rural railway. Each route includes numerous sightseeing highlights, suggested activities, and places to eat and stay. The *Checking In* and *Eating Out* sections at the end of each tour offer suggestions for the best hotels, inns, small *hostales, paradores,* and restaurants along the way.

Our routes cover this exciting land from the Pyrenees to the Strait of

Gibraltar; we also offer detailed descriptions and information about the Canary and Balearic islands. It's possible for each traveler to mix and match, or combine routes according to his or her timetable and interests. But if you are pressed for time, you will find that by following a single itinerary, you will get the best taste of what each region of Spain has to offer.

Galicia

Despite Eliza Doolittle's assertion, the rain in Spain does *not* fall mainly on the plain: It falls on Galicia. Cut off both geographically and culturally from mainstream Spain, Galicia contradicts the country's arid image. Its annual 64 inches of rain produce green mountain slopes, a network of blue-green rivers, pine and eucalyptus forests, palm trees, and lush terraces of vines. *Gallegos* rarely go out without umbrellas — even if a natural immunity to a few splashes means they often forget to use them. And in the fishing villages scattered along the coast and beside the *rías* (estuaries, or inlets), where the riverbeds are regularly raked for mussels and clams, the local costume includes an oilskin, over-the-knee galoshes, a pair of rubber gloves, and a resigned grin.

Galicia is also one of Spain's poorest regions. There are few Porsches here, mostly small domestic vehicles and shaky mopeds. There are also relatively few tractors, compared with the number of bullocks to be seen pulling carts of corn and other produce. And since there are also relatively few foreign visitors, the sight of a tourist car is often enough to stop a local resident in his or her tracks. The *gallegos* stare, and if you stare back and smile, so will they.

Historically, Galicians carved their land into hundreds of small holdings, each consisting of little more than a terra cotta–roofed shack, a few vines, a field of corn, and a donkey. By the turn of this century, those who could scrape together the pesetas left these difficult circumstances behind and emigrated to Central and South America. Argentina, in particular, was such a popular destination that, today, there are more *gallegos* in Buenos Aires than in Galicia. And emigration to Cuba has led to an unlikely affinity between Fidel Castro's nation and traditionally conservative Galicia.

The region was not always left out of the mainstream. During the Middle Ages, this distant corner of Europe became one of Christendom's three holiest places, when a peasant discovered what was thought to be the long-forgotten tomb of St. James, one of the 12 apostles, in the city of Santiago de Compostela. Over the years, the saint's remains became the object of a pilgrimage ranking second in importance only to one to Jerusalem or Rome, and the chapel built to house the bones grew to be the magnificent Cathedral of Santiago de Compostela, the final jewel in a chain of churches, monasteries, and hospices strung across northern Spain along the Camino de Santiago — the famous Way of St. James. (For additional details, see *Pilgrims' Route* in DIRECTIONS.)

Buildings in Galicia are either monumental or monumentally ugly. The historic centers of towns such as Santiago de Compostela, La Coruña, Lugo, Pontevedra, and Bayona are archetypical Spain, but beyond these oases of aestheticism, grim and granite ugliness prevails. Suburbs in the larger towns consist of characterless and often unfinished apartment blocks; the smaller, one-street towns are strung out in shades of gray; and even vast stretches of otherwise stunning coastline have been marred by tasteless, prefabricated holiday bungalows. There are exceptions, of course, including the *pazos* — the former homes of noble Spanish families, standing aloof in the countryside — and, attached to most small holdings, the *hórreos* — distinctive wooden and granite huts, perched on stilts, traditionally used for storing grain.

Galicia consists of four provinces — La Coruña and Lugo to the north, Pontevedra and landlocked Orense to the south — and its deeply indented coastline is divided into two sections. The wild, more exposed Rías Altas (Upper Estuaries) run westward along the coast of the provinces of Lugo and La Coruña, from Ribadeo roughly to the city of La Coruña; the gentler coves, wooded hills, and fishing villages of the Rías Bajas (Lower Estuaries) run south along the coast of the provinces of La Coruña and Pontevedra, from Muros down to Bayona.

The still and quiet estuaries closely resemble Norwegian fjords or Scottish lochs, with long stretches of palm-fringed sand that have yet to experience the commercialization that has altered the shore along much of the Mediterranean. From the Eo River, which borders Asturias, around to the Miño River on the Portuguese frontier, the shoreline is rugged and beautiful, as yet uncluttered by vacation homes and attendant businesses. But between the Rías Altas and the Rías Bajas is a stretch of coast called the Costa de la Muerte (Coast of Death), treacherous to sailors through the ages. It begins at Malpica and comes to an abrupt end at Cabo Finisterre, literally the "end of the land" for medieval man.

Galician cuisine revolves around seafood. Along the coast, entire communities are engaged in milking the sea and rushing the day's (or night's) catch to restaurant tables. Even the smallest restaurant has at least one fish tank full of crabs and lobsters. *Gallegos* tired of the sight of fish will probably opt for a plate of *lacón con grelos,* a potage of salted pork and turnip tops, usually accompanied by local wine drunk from a white porcelain cup.

Galicia is a wonderful region in which to drive, especially since the A9 highway, linking the region's two biggest cities and industrial areas — La Coruña and Vigo, 97½ miles (156 km) apart — was recently completed. A well-planned network of freeways, fast and scenic, delves into the remotest corners, backed up by numerous and fairly well maintained country roads. Road signs are excellent, even though several Castilian place-names have been altered by Galician separatists.

The route outlined below is a circular one, encompassing significant stretches of both coastline and countryside. It begins in Santiago de Compostela and hugs the coastline from the vicinity of Padrón, southwest of Santiago, to Pontevedra, before continuing due south through Vigo to

Bayona. From here it follows the seashore again, at times only yards from the water, before turning east along the Miño River, which forms the border with Portugal (and is known as the Minho in Portuguese), to the frontier town of Túy (where it is possible to walk or drive to Portugal across the bridge spanning the river.) The itinerary then cuts inland, following the Miño to Orense, then passing through the Ribeiro vineyard country around Ribadavia. From Orense, the route heads north via the old walled town of Lugo to Ribadeo on Galicia's north coast. Except for an excursion inland to Mondoñedo, the route now stays on the coast, exploring the Rías Altas around the northwest corner of Galicia to El Ferrol and La Coruña.

Because Galicia is not a hotbed of tourism, the choice of accommodations is limited. The region's nine *paradores,* particularly the two in Santiago de Compostela and Bayona, are the notable exceptions. The *paradores,* with their reliably high standards, represent the best value for the money in this region.

Expect to pay $90 or more for a double room in a hotel or *parador* described as expensive, $60 to $80 in one listed as moderate, and under $60 in one listed as inexpensive. Prices generally do not include breakfast, but eating out in Galicia is rarely a costly experience. Restaurants listed as expensive charge around $60 for a dinner for two, including wine; a moderate establishment, $40 to $60; and an inexpensive one, under $40. Telephone numbers listed below include local area codes; when calling from another area in Spain, dial 9 before the number.

> **NOTE** In this chapter, when two spellings are given (usually at the first reference to a place), the first one is in Spanish, and the second is in Galician, the local language.

SANTIAGO DE COMPOSTELA For full details on sights, hotels, and restaurants in this historic city, see *Santiago de Compostela* in THE CITIES.)

En Route from Santiago de Compostela Leave the outskirts of Santiago and head 12½ miles (20 km) south to Padrón on N550, an easy, fast main road that cuts through green fields and passes several *pazos* nearly hidden behind iron gateways. The majority of these stately manor houses were built along the rivers leading into the Rías Bajas by families who made their fortunes across the Atlantic. Beyond Padrón, at Ponte Cesures, leave N550 and take the coast road off to the right, signposted Villagarcía de Arousa. As the road hugs the woody southern shores of the Ulla River, leading into the Ría de Arousa, there are fine views across the water — unless it's raining, in which case mist rolls up the valley and settles in a low, dense layer. Lucky travelers will arrive in Villagarcía, 15½ miles (25 km) from Padrón, in time to see the townspeople up to their knees in the estuary, plucking shellfish from the sand flats. The *ría,* like the land in Galicia, has been sectioned off into "plots," and the scene is one of organized chaos as gulls scream, dogs bark excitedly, men chug around in boats, and women scour the beds for fish.

Continue on the coast road south. A short detour to the right, following the signposts to El Grove (O Grove), leads across a bridge to the island of La Toja (A Toxa), one of the region's few tourist developments — site of large expensive hotels, swimming pools, a spa, and a casino. The island itself is beautiful, but it has been developed to the point of saturation. Stop at the town of Cambados to see the beautiful houses, the Fefiñanes square with its handsome 17th-century palace, and the remarkable ruins of the Church of Santa Mariña. Signs to Praia da Lanzada lead to the most beautiful beach in Galicia, with long swaths of pale sands, palm trees, and shallow waters. A few miles farther is Combarro, a fishing village with a line of waterfront *hórreos* (granaries) that has been declared an artistic monument by the locals. Return to the coast road and continue south, curving around the peninsula to Pontevedra, 34½ miles (55 km) from Villagarcía.

PONTEVEDRA The streets of this old, charming town are lined with characteristic Galician glazed balconies called *solanas,* built to catch all the available sun but keep out the rain and wind. The town sits above the Pontevedra River, which at its wider points resembles a peaceful lake. There was a time when Pontevedra was a thriving hub for fishermen, merchants, and traders; but by the 18th century the delta had silted up, and sea traffic was forced to use the port at nearby Marín. (Ironically, the closest good beach is also at Marín.)

Concentrate on the Old Quarter, sitting on the doorstep of the *parador.* It's a peaceful mishmash of streets that rarely plays host to visitors. The town's main museum, the *Provincial Museum* (10 Calle Pasantería) is a solid granite building on the lovely Plaza de Leña, which looks like a stage set. The museum (open Mondays through Saturdays, 11 AM to 1:30 PM and 5 to 8 PM; Sundays and holidays, 11 AM to 1:30 PM) contains maritime exhibits, artifacts from Galician history through the 19th century, and a valuable collection of jewelry. Other sights include Plaza de la Herrería, an arcaded square presided over by the Convento de San Francisco, and the Church of La Peregrina, which is shaped like a scallop shell — the sign of the Pilgrim.

CHECKING IN

Parador Casa del Barón Believed to stand on the site of an old Roman villa, like many *paradores* it is a former *pazo;* but during its checkered past it has also been a school, a granary, a masonic lodge, and an 18th-century residence owned by the Barons of Casa Goda, who restored it. It has 47 rooms and flower-filled gardens. Plaza de Maceda, Pontevedra (phone: 86-855800; in the US, 212-686-9213; fax: 86-852195). Moderate.

EATING OUT

Casa Solla A top-rate Galician eatery. The shellfish dishes never disappoint, but the chef's strengths are in the traditional stew, meat, and fish dishes. Closed Thursday and Sunday evenings and *Christmas*. Reservations advised. Major credit cards accepted. Km 2 on the Pontevedra–El Grove road, Pontevedra (phone: 86-852678). Moderate.

En Route from Pontevedra Take the A9 freeway southwest 17 miles (27 km) to Vigo. Apart from Santiago de Compostela, it is here, in the Rías Bajas areas around Pontevedra, Vigo, and Bayona (Baiona), that Galicia welcomes most of its holiday visitors. With a milder and sunnier climate than their northern counterparts, the Rías Bajas are backed by thick pine forests, and the hidden coves and gently shelving beaches make this the only strip of coastline where swimming is a viable (though not very warm) option.

VIGO On the southern shore of the Ría de Vigo, Spain's largest fishing port is a lively, modern city, as well as a good example of how the deepwater anchorages and shelter of Galicia's coastline have been commercially exploited. Vigo is a remarkably clean and manicured place, perhaps because hulking transatlantic liners no longer berth at the city's harbor terminal. During the day, visitors can shop for the city's famous *angulas* (eels) at the morning fish auction down near the waterfront, or climb to the heights of Parque del Castro. This superb public park is built around the Castillo de San Sebastián, a 10th-century fortress. The views overlook the estuary and its narrow neck, where Sir Francis Drake sank gold-laden Spanish galleons. For lively nighttime bars, head for the old fishermen's quarter.

The entrance to the Ría de Vigo is sheltered by the Islas Cíes, a cluster of steep, abrupt rock islands with magnificent beaches, rich flora and fauna, spectacular cliff paths, and turquoise water. Passenger boats cross regularly to the islands from the port. Other beaches line the southern shores of the estuary in a practically unbroken strip.

CHECKING IN

Bahía de Vigo A comfortable, 110-room hotel, strategically placed opposite the old transatlantic terminal, it has a nautical decor throughout. 5 Calle Cánovas del Castillo, Vigo (phone: 86-226700; fax: 86-437487). Expensive to moderate.

Ciudad de Vigo Functional and impersonal, this 126-room hotel, in a pretty part of town, primarily serves local businessmen. 4 Calle Concepción Arenal, Vigo (phone: 86-227820; fax: 86-439871). Expensive to moderate.

EATING OUT

El Timón Playa With the Islas Cíes and the sea as a backdrop, you'll want to be sure to reserve a table by the window here. The food is simple yet delicious — try the cockle empanada. Closed Sundays. Reservations advised. Visa and American Express accepted. 12 Calle Carrasquería (phone: 86-490815). Expensive.

BAYONA (BAIONA) A lively tourist town 13 miles (21 km) south of Vigo via C550, Bayona sweeps along the shore at the entrance to the Ría de Vigo. It's a pretty town, as well as a historic one — Bayona welcomed Columbus's return on the *Pinta* in 1493 after his discovery of the Americas — and it has retained many of its medieval features. Much of the long harbor road is lined with nautically themed clothing shops and restaurants; stores on the maze of streets behind the harbor (try *Náutic Mare* on Calle Ramón y Cajal, a clothes shop with branches in Marbella and other chic points south) echo the maritime theme.

The town is dominated by Monte Real, a fortified peninsula across the bay; besides a defensive wall, the peninsula is the site of a 16th-century castle that pokes into the river and is now the town's *parador* (see below). When the winds get up, and the rain sweeps across the bay (which it frequently does), the waters turn gray and choppy — and the reason for the shipwreck lying on a group of treacherous rocks suddenly becomes clear. A huge statue of the Virgin Mary (known as the Virgen de la Roca) stands on the shoreline to the south of town, looking out to the Islas Cíes.

CHECKING IN

Parador Conde de Gondomar Widely ranked as the most beautifully located *parador* in northern Spain, it commands a privileged position atop Monte Real. In a turreted castle with its own fortress gate, the *parador*'s 124 rooms exude somber, monastic characteristics — even the staff moves silently along the corridors. Stay on a hot summer's day and make use of the outdoor swimming pool, sauna, and tennis courts, or enjoy dining at the excellent seafood restaurant. Carretera de Bayona, Bayona (phone: 86-355000; in the US, 212-686-9213; fax: 86-355076). Expensive.

Tres Carabelas Tucked down the back streets where ancient buildings echo to the sounds of noisy, adolescent-filled bars, this place is homey and comfortable though basic, with TV sets in all 10 rooms. 61 Calle Ventura Misa, Bayona (phone: 86-355133; fax: 86-355921). Inexpensive.

EATING OUT

O Moscón Don't let the name (The Big Fly) put you off — this eatery is cozy and smart, and features good local dishes. A lobster tank is on view from the promenade outside, and there is a display of gigantic crabs, an indication of the extensive range of seafood served here. The menu has

English translations. Open daily. Reservations advised. Major credit cards accepted. 2 Calle Alférez Barreiro, Bayona (phone: 86-355008). Moderate.

Jaqueyvi The name is made up of the beginnings of the words *jamón, queso y vino* (ham, cheese, and wine), and that is what this place serves, tapas-style. Open daily. Reservations advised. No credit cards accepted. Two locations: 45 Ventura Misa (phone: 86-356386) and 4 José Antonio, Bayona (phone: 86-356773). Inexpensive.

En Route from Bayona The 19 miles (30 km) along C550 heading south to La Guardia (A Garda) are bleak, but this is where the route is at its most intimate with the white foaming seas, the waves breaking dramatically against giant rocks — sometimes spraying the car windshield. A sharp turn inland at La Guardia brings an equally sharp change in landscape — the gentle Miño River, which forms the frontier with Portugal, replacing the waves and the coastal stone walls and springy turf giving way to woods, scruffy villages, the occasional oxen, and fields of green maize and graceful bamboo. At La Guardia you'll find Monte Santa Tecla, which offers spectacular views of the surrounding countryside, the Miño, and Portugal. Halfway up the mountain is a restored 2,000-year-old Celtic settlement. Follow C550 as it twists eastward along the river 17 miles (28 km) to the frontier town of Túy (Tui). Túy is a border town, with an attractive historic center leading up to a 12th-to-13th-century fortress-like cathedral. It's worth a stop to stroll across the river to Valença do Minho, Portugal, via the Ponte Internacional, the 19th-century suspension bridge designed by Alexandre-Gustave Eiffel, of Paris tower fame.

From Túy, take the N550 9 miles (14 km) north to Porriño (signposted Redondela and Vigo), then turn east along N120 and continue 34 miles (55 km) to Ribadavia, a scruffy but lively market town that heralds the entrance to Ribeiro vineyard country. Thick vines suddenly cover the slopes to the left and right as the road crosses the green waters of the Miño and connects to the rougher N202, which runs along the river's southern bank for 14 miles (22 km) to Orense (Ourense).

ORENSE (OURENSE) The approach to town, thick with dull apartment and office blocks, is suddenly relieved by a beautiful, seven-arched Roman bridge crossing the Miño into the town center. The bridge — the Puente Viejo — was reconstructed during the 13th century to ease the heavy traffic of pilgrims on their journey to Santiago. Orense is primarily an industrial town today, but it has been famous since ancient times for Las Burgas — springs of hot (149°F) medicinal drinking water that rise in the center of the Old Town. The 12th-century cathedral is the last of the great western Romanesque churches; its nave, aisles, and east end are grandiose, and the sculptures of the Pórtico del Paraíso (Paradise Doorway) are excelled only by the Gate of Glory in the cathedral in Santiago de Compostela. Otherwise, there is little to see here.

CHECKING IN

San Martín Smack in the Old Town; its 90 rooms are modern and functional. 1 Calle Curros Enríquez, Orense (phone: 88-235690; fax: 88-236585). Moderate.

Padre Feíjoo Close to the Old Town, this 71-room establishment is surrounded by a variety of fine restaurants. 1 Plaza Eugenio Montes, Orense (phone: 88-223100; fax: 88-223100). Inexpensive.

EATING OUT

San Miguel Sample excellent shellfish and Galician dishes on the summer terrace or in the tastefully decorated dining room. Closed Tuesdays. Reservations necessary. Major credit cards accepted. 12 Calle San Miguel, Orense (phone: 88-220795). Expensive.

En Route from Orense Leaving town, cross the Miño River and head north on N525 to the N540 intersection, 7 miles (11 km) from Orense. Take N540 north 16 miles (26 km) to Chantada, a charming little town known for its Monastery of San Salvador de Asma, an 11th-century Romanesque creation just outside town to the east; recently restored, the monastery's highlight is a collection of old Galician frescoes. Continue north on N540 another 24½ miles (39 km) to Guntín de Pallares, where N540 becomes N640 and continues another 11 miles (18 km) north to Lugo.

LUGO The center of this provincial capital, one of Galicia's quintessentially Spanish towns, is wholly surrounded by a mile-long, 30-to-45- foot-high, 15-foot-thick Roman wall, the best-preserved one of its kind in Spain. Join the handful of citizens walking their dogs along the ramparts. There are some 10 gates, but the most interesting one is the Santiago Gate, which opens before the Romanesque-Gothic Cathedral de Santa María overlooking Plaza Mayor. Arrive on a sunny Sunday morning and the entire town will be out taking a slow *paseo* (walk) in this tree-lined plaza. The outdoor tables of the cafés down one side of the square are packed, and toward lunchtime the Lugo band begins to play on the turn-of-the-century bandstand at the center of the square. The town's gracious 18th-century Town Hall is also located here.

CHECKING IN

Gran Hotel Lugo This big, modern, and very comfortable hotel with a swimming pool is a 5-minute walk outside the town walls. 21 Av. Ramón Ferreiro, Lugo (phone: 82-224152; fax: 82-241660). Expensive.

Parador Condes de Villalba About 20 miles (32 km) north of Lugo, this 6-room hostelry occupies an octagonal tower that used to be part of a medieval castle. Once the home of the powerful Galician Andrade clan, the castle still evokes feudal-era Spain, from its main entrance — the old drawbridge — to its simply appointed and somewhat somber rooms. There's a restaurant on the premises. Valeriano Valdesuso, Villalba (phone: 82-510011; in the US, 212-686-9213; fax: 82-510090). Expensive.

Méndez Núñez An upscale but friendly establishment with 100 comfortable rooms, just around the corner from the main plaza. 1 Calle Reina, Lugo (phone: 82-230711; fax: 82-229738). Moderate.

En Route from Lugo There's not much sign of civilization along N640 as it heads 56 miles (90 km) north to Ribadeo. It rides high, at first, over the green open plain, an occasional cattle farm camouflaged behind huge granite walls. As the road begins to follow the contours of the Eo River, it narrows to a single lane, its regular bends cutting through towering, pine-forested gorges. During the last few miles, watch the picturesque river — which here forms the boundary between the regions of Asturias and Galicia — unfold toward the coast at Ribadeo.

RIBADEO The sights of this palm-fringed resort town on the Ría de Ribadeo, where the Eo River meets the sea, include the Art Nouveau buildings of the Plaza de España in the town center, as well as a pretty beach. There is a pleasant walk out to the lighthouse on the Eo estuary, where fishermen take in their catch and children clamber down the cliffs. The town is dominated by the Torre de los Moreno, a tower built in 1905, whose copper dome is supported by four draped female figures. The Santa Cruz hill and hermitage, 1¼ miles (2 km) out of town, offers a marvelous view of the coastline. This is the site of the *Xira a Santa Cruz* pilgrimage, held annually on the first Sunday in August, with much traditional dancing and bagpipe music. Notice the bagpiper monument on the hill. Ribadeo's fishermen's quarter is full of *pulperías,* bars dedicated to the eating of octopus and the drinking of fine Galician wine from cups that resemble Chinese tea bowls.

MONDOÑEDO From Ribadeo, a worthwhile excursion can be made inland to the old Galician town of Mondoñedo, 24 miles (39 km) southwest on N634. Mondoñedo's twin-towered 12th-century cathedral is a treasure, and the entire straggling, sleepy farming town is delightfully nestled in a broad-bottomed valley. The cathedral has a carved and painted 15th-century wooden statue, La Virgen Inglesa (English Virgin), rescued from St. Paul's Cathedral in London during the Reformation and brought to Spain, where it was acquired by a Mondoñedo aristocrat. The church also contains a superb, though cluttered and unkempt, museum filled with 12th- and 13th-century objects such as Arab boards, candle holders, sand clocks, and marble images of Christ. Mondoñedo is famous for its sweet, sticky baked goods made from sponge cakes, vermicelli, and almonds.

CHECKING IN

Parador de Ribadeo The local link in the government-run chain, a modern, 47-room hostelry, inspires mixed reviews. Critics note that it's a could-be-anywhere *parador* of endless, shabbily carpeted corridors, bearable in summer but depressing under gray skies. Fans point out its wonderful views across the broad Eo estuary into Asturias. The breakfast display is impressive, but it's worth finding a more atmospheric restaurant in town in the evening. Popular despite the difference of opinion, so reserve rooms well in advance. Calle Amador Fernández, Ribadeo (phone: 82-110825; in the US, 212-686-9213; fax: 82-110346). Moderate.

EATING OUT

O Xardin A 5-minute walk into town from the *parador,* it's the nearest Galicia comes to a bistro-style restaurant-bar. It has a comprehensive menu of fish and meat dishes and a large selection of wines. Closed February. Reservations advised. Diners Club accepted. 20 Calle Reinante, Ribadeo (phone: 82-110222). Moderate to inexpensive.

En Route from Ribadeo West of town, the route explores the Rías Altas portion of the Galician coastline, hopping from one long, indented inlet to the next as far as La Coruña (A Coruña). Take N634 out of Ribadeo and follow it 15 miles (24 km) west to Foz, a fishing village and beach resort on the far side of the Ría de Foz. From Foz, C642 continues westward 12 miles (19 km) to Cervo, where a left turn and subsequent signs lead visitors the extra mile or so to the Royal Ceramics factory at Sargadelos. It's a large, futuristic-looking building; the factory makes and sells distinctive plates, jewelry, pots, and figurines (closed during early afternoon siesta).

Return to C642 and head west for 12 miles (19 km) to Vivero (Viveiro), where the scenery improves dramatically. Here, steep cliffs drop down to spectacular panoramas of flat sands and shallow seas, unmarred by hotels, restaurants, boats, or even people. The province of Lugo ends at the Sor River and the Ría de Barqueiro, just beyond Vivero, but C642 continues west to Ortigueira, a fishing town on the Ría de Santa Marta de Ortigueira 22 miles (35 km) west of Vivero, and then to Campo de Hospital. At this point, C642 bends south, while C646 continues west to the most beautiful of the Rías Altas, the Ría de Cedeira. Cedeira itself, 17 miles (27 km) from Ortigueira, is a sleepy, pretty little sardine fishing town built along the banks of the Condeminas River.

El Ferrol (O Ferrol) is a pleasant 24-mile (38-km) drive south of Cedeira on C646. It's set directly across the water from La Coruña and notable mainly as the birthplace of Generalísimo Francisco Franco (1892-

1975). It certainly doesn't score on looks but thrives today as Spain's principal naval base and dockyard. The main shopping area, lined with clothing, footwear, and pastry shops, leads down to a square in front of the Town Hall, and makes for lively *paseos* in the early evening. Also of interest is the 18th-century church of El Socorro, which houses a famous statue of Christ walking on water.

CHECKING IN

Parador el Ferrol A 39-room *parador* in an unlikely position overlooking the docks. Visitors are quite likely to be awakened at 8 AM to the sounds of a prerecorded trumpet fanfare as sailors perform their ritual flag hoisting ceremony in the mini-square outside the hotel. Calle Almirante Vierna, El Ferrol (phone: 81-356720; in the US, 212-686-9213; fax: 81-356720). Moderate.

LA CORUÑA (A CORUÑA) A 38-mile (61-km) drive around three of the Rías Altas from El Ferrol leads to Galicia's largest city and business center. An important trading post on the ancient tin route, La Coruña is today one of Galicia's largest coastal developments and an active commercial port, its main trade the curing, salting, and tinning of fish. Philip II's Invincible Armada was launched from here in 1588; its defeat resulted in 15,000 deaths and the loss of half the fleet.

The town, which sits on a peninsula jutting out into the Ría de la Coruña, is divided roughly into three sectors: the Old Quarter (around the neck of the peninsula), with its two 12th-century Romanesque-Gothic churches, Santiago and Santa María del Campo; the modern shopping quarter; and the busy port, bordering the beaches of Orzan and Riazor. The town is noted for its typically Galician 19th-century balconied buildings on the waterfront, but the most important single monument is the 2nd-century Tower of Hercules, the last remaining Roman lighthouse in operation (although in 1791 its original crumbling masonry was encased in brickwork).

CHECKING IN

Finisterre On La Coruña's seafront, it has 3 swimming pools, tennis courts, and 127 small but comfortable rooms, the best of which overlook the harbor. 22 Paseo del Parrote, La Coruña (phone: 81-205400; fax: 81-208462). Expensive to moderate.

EATING OUT

El Rápido Excellent grilled shellfish and other seafood dishes have been specialties here for over 40 years. Closed Monday evenings. Reservations necessary. Major credit cards accepted. 7 Calle Estrella, La Coruña (phone: 81-224221). Expensive.

Castile-León (Old Castile)

The Castilian *meseta* (plateau) is the historical and spiritual heartland that eventually gathered a united Spain around it. After the country's protracted Reconquest was born in the early 8th century in Asturias — a remnant of the old Visigothic, and therefore Christian, Spain, and the only part the Moors had failed to conquer — the movement spread southward across León and into the vast, elevated plateau of Castile, where it gained its greatest foothold. A shared commitment to driving the Moors out of Spain forged a firm bond between the kingdoms of Castile and León, and early in the 13th century the two kingdoms were united. In 1469 the region began a rapid rise to prominence when Isabella of Castile married Ferdinand of Aragon. By 1479, the couple ruled over a joint kingdom of Aragon and Castile that was the basis of modern Spain. Their union also set in motion the centuries-long and notoriously cruel quest for religious uniformity known as the Spanish Inquisition, first instituted by Isabella in Castile in 1478 and not abolished until the early 19th century.

At the dawn of the 16th century, with Spain at the height of its power, Castile occupied more than half of the Iberian Peninsula, extending from the Pyrenees to Gibraltar. But with the decline of Spain that took place after the defeat of its "Invincible Armada" came the decline of Castile, and the 18th century saw a steady emigration deplete the populations of its most prosperous cities and towns by as much as one-half.

Today's autonomous community of Castile-León comprises nine provinces: Zamora, León, and Salamanca, which correspond to the former kingdom of León, plus Palencia, Valladolid, Avila, Burgos, Segovia, and Soria, which correspond to the northern half of the former kingdom of Castile, and also to the historic region that was know as Castilla la Vieja (Old Castile). Virtually ringed by high mountain ranges, the immense Castilian plateau, which has an average altitude of 2,600 feet, occupies about one-fifth of modern-day Spain, yet its population barely tops 2,500,000. Here, vast fields stretch long, flat, and often uninterrupted to a dusty horizon. Exposed to everything from scorching hot summers to blustery, bone-chilling winters, it remains largely a region of wheat and corn fields, vegetable patches, and dairy and sheep farms, although it is not immune to changes mandated by Common Market membership and the subsequent progress that is sweeping through the peninsula.

Although there are occasional regional and chauvinistic rifts and rivalries between the provinces of Castile and the provinces of León, in general a common culture binds the nine provinces of Castile-León. This is particularly true in the culinary realm. The region is known as *la tierra de asados,* the land of roasts, and lamb and pork are favored here. Though its far from the sea, the region's rivers provide fine tench, trout, and *ancas de rana* (frogs' legs). Chickpeas, lentils, and assorted varieties of broad beans are the prime ingredients of some tasty, rib-sticking regional stews. A prime hunting ground, this region is also noted for its *liebre* (hare), *codorniz* (quail), *pichón* (pigeon), and *perdiz* (partridge). Among the favored desserts are *leche frita* (fried milk), *almendrados* (almond paste), and *yemas de Santa Teresa* (candied egg yolks).

Castile-León also produces one of the widest ranges of wines in all of Spain — from the robust reds of Toro to the delicate whites of Rueda. With more than 50,000 acres devoted to the grape, the region is third within Spain in terms of area planted in vines. Among the 13 noteworthy wine growing areas in the region, Ribera del Duero, Rueda, and Toro have achieved "Denomination of Origin" status (the equivalent of the French *appelation*).

Architecturally, Castile-León is primarily fluent in the Romanesque, Gothic, and Mudéjar vernaculars, which achieve their finest expressions in a profusion of cathedrals, castles, and palaces. Castile derives its name from the abundance of castles that guarded its numerous feudal interests during the Middle Ages. Given the ravages of time and man, however, these structures are notably scarce along the 500-mile (800-km) route described below. The itinerary stays mainly along the plain of what was Old Castile.

Throughout Castile-León, hotels charging $60 and more for a double room with private bath are classified as expensive, $35 to $60 as moderate, and less than $30, inexpensive. Dinner for two with wine will cost $50 and up in an expensive restaurant, $35 to $50 in a moderate restaurant, and under $30 in an inexpensive one. The telephone numbers listed below include local area codes; when calling from another area in Spain, dial "9" first.

The following journey into the Spanish heartland begins in Madrid, which is geographically separated from Castile-León by the Sierra de Guadarrama. For a full report on Madrid, its sights, hotels, and restaurants, see *Madrid,* THE CITIES.

En Route from Madrid Begin at the Plaza de Cibeles in the heart of Madrid and follow the Gran Vía and its extension, Calle Princesa, out past Moncloa until it becomes the N-VI highway at the edge of the city.

From Madrid to Avila, via N-VI and C505, is a distance of 69 miles (110 km). Take C505, which branches off from N-VI about 10 miles (16 km) northwest of Plaza de Cibeles. At this point, the city has been left behind, and after crossing a big bridge over the very small Río Guadarrama, the road becomes more rural and curvaceous. After another 11 miles

(18 km), just before the bridge crossing the Embalse de Valmayor (Valmayor Reservoir), there is a glimpse of Philip II's palace-monastery of El Escorial straight ahead. For the next few miles, the imposing monument ducks in and out of sight, until the turnoff 4½ miles (7 km) beyond the reservoir, when the road splits, veering right for San Lorenzo de El Escorial, the village that abuts the palace-monastery, and left for Avila and El Escorial itself (follow signs for "Monasterio de El Escorial," not just for "El Escorial"). About half a mile (1 km) farther on, C505 turns left to Avila, while C600 goes straight for a little over a mile (2 km) to the parking lot. For details on El Escorial, see the *Madrid Region* route in DIRECTIONS.

Head back to C505, en route to Avila. (Although well marked approaching El Escorial, the way out of town is not clearly signposted.) The road offers a good view of the towering monastery to the right, then continues to Avila amid mountains that were only a hazy mirage from Madrid. Ahead, a large sign marks the border of Castile-León, and in particular, the province of Avila; then the road gradually ascends the Castilian plateau to Spain's highest provincial capital (3,600 feet), which appears after the crest of a hill. Follow the Centro Urbano or Centro Ciudad signs into the city.

AVILA Built on the banks of the Adaja River, Avila is a city whose historical center is surrounded by remarkably well preserved rectangular walls that are most dramatic when viewed in silhouette against the surrounding Castilian plain. To the southwest, the wall, begun in 1090, divides Avila from an expanse of undeveloped land, but to the northeast, it has failed to contain the city, which has grown beyond its medieval boundaries and now has a population of nearly 50,000.

Avila's ramparts look like a row of sharpened teeth amid the dry stubble of the battlefield-brown plain. The 11th-century walls seem unweathered and brand-new. Construction of the wall began in 1090; it took 10 years and more than 2,000 workers to complete 88 semicircular towers, 9 gates, several posterns, and innumerable battlements along an 8,200-foot perimeter. It may feel as if the only way to get into the city is with a battering ram, but only a walk through a gate in the walls is necessary to see banks and cafés and hear the televised sounds of soccer games blaring through open windows. From the gardens of the *Parador Raimundo de Borgoña,* it's an easy climb up to the battlements for a squint into the distance for an approaching army of Moors.

As the birthplace and religious training ground of the famous Santa Teresa de Jesús de Avila, commonly known as St. Teresa of Avila, a Carmelite nun who founded a reformed order of Carmelites, the Barefoot (Descalzas) Carmelites, Avila has played a strong spiritual role in the evolution of both Castile and Spain. Born in 1515 in what is now the Convento de Santa Teresa (Plaza de la Santa; open daily from 9:30 AM to 1:30 PM and 3:30 to 9 PM; no admission charge), St. Teresa took her vows and had the spiritual experiences that paved the way for her canonization in the Monasterio de la Encarnación (Plaza de la Encarnación; open daily from 9:30 AM to 1 PM and 4 to 6 PM; admission charge). St. Teresa first put her religious principles into practice in the first Convent of the Barefoot Carmelite order, the Convento de San José, or Convento de las Madres, which is nearby (Calle del Duque de Alba; open daily from 10 AM to 1:30 PM and 4 to 7 PM; admission charge).

Avila's other noted sights are also religious in nature. Just inside the Puerta de los Leales is the starkly rectilinear, 12th-century stone cathedral (on Calle Alemaña), a plain structure, except for the ornately carved frieze above the multi-arched Gothic entrance. Inside the cathedral are three aisles and a central choir. The museum, housed in the 15th-century Capilla del Cardenal, contains hymnal tomes from the 15th century; silk-embroidered, gold- and lace-adorned garments of the 18th century; a 5-foot tall, 16th-century silver Custodia del Corpus that is paraded through the streets every *Corpus Christi Day* and looks like an overgrown, 6-tiered wedding cake ornament; a carved wooden coffin containing the remains of San Segundo, Avila's first archbishop; and a 16th-century Ecce Homo, a painting depicting Christ wearing His crown of thorns. Just inside the cathedral entrance, the bronze statue of San Pedro is kept shiny at the knees, nose, and hands by the faithful hoping that good fortune will rub off on them. The cathedral is open daily from 8 AM to 1 PM and 3 to 7 PM in May through September; from 10 AM to 1:30 PM and 3 to 7 PM in October through April. The museum is open daily except Mondays from 10 AM to 1:30 PM and 3 to 7 PM in May through September; from 10 AM to 1:30 PM and 3 to 5 PM in October through April; admission charge to the museum. Across the square from the cathedral is the town's tourist office, 4 Plaza de la Catedral (phone: 20-211387).

Avila's Romanesque Church of San Vicente (Plaza de San Vicente; open daily 10 AM to 1 PM and 4 to 6 PM; admission charge) is just outside the walls on the northeast, through the Puerta de San Vicente. Built between the 12th and 14th centuries, it has an arched loggia of gray stone that clashes in tone and tenor with the amber blocks of the main structure. The main attraction inside is the Sepulcro de los Niños Mártires, recalling the church's founding legend, which holds that three young siblings were martyred on this spot. Of a more welcoming nature is the Church of San Pedro (Plaza de Santa Teresa; open to visitors daily before and after religious services; hours vary), begun in 1100 as a Romanesque structure and later fitted with Gothic flourishes. Situated outside the walls opposite the Puerta del Alcázar at the far end of the Plaza de Santa Teresa, it contains — since Pope John Paul II's 1983 visit — a mounted "chapel" honoring the "Virgin of Czestochowa, Queen of Poland." The Monasterio de Santo Tomás, on Plaza de Granada, once isolated from the city proper, now stands at the very edge of Avila's urban expansion. Its checkered past includes use as the headquarters of the Inquisition (Tomás de Torquemada, the inquisitor general, lived here), a turn as the summer palace of Ferdinand and Isabella, and an interlude as the seat of a university. The final resting place of Ferdinand and Isabella's son, Prince Juan, today it is a Dominican monastery complete with church, cloisters, and choir, as well as an Oriental art gallery in the former royal apartments. The complex is open daily from 10 AM to 1 PM and 4 to 7 PM. Admission charge to the cloister, through which the complex is entered; additional charge for the art gallery.

CHECKING IN

Palacio de Valderrábanos Built as a palatial home late in the 14th century, it offers 73 rooms, all with private baths, and 3 suites, one of which is romantically situated in the tower. The restaurant, *El Fogón de Santa Teresa,* serves traditional Castilian dishes. Diagonally across from the cathedral, 9 Plaza de la Catedral, Avila (phone: 20-211023; in the US, 800-528-1234; fax: 20-251691). Expensive.

Parador Raimundo de Borgoña One of the state-run *paradores,* it incorporates the Palacio de Benavides, also known as the Palacio de Piedras Albas, built during the late 15th century. Abutting the northern city walls, its 62 rooms (12 of which are of palace vintage) all have private baths. The hostelry's gardens are next to walkways on top of the city walls that offer choice views of Avila and the *meseta* beyond. Local delicacies such as roast suckling pig, as well as more generic Spanish dishes (gazpacho, *truchas fritas con jamón serrano* — fried trout with smoked ham), are served in the dining room. 12 Calle Marqués de Canales y Chozas, Avila (phone: 20-211340; in the US, 212-686-9213; fax: 20-226166). Expensive.

Rey Niño Built in 1340 as a hotel, it is near the cathedral and has has 24 rooms that are structurally romantic and clean, but spare of furnishings. 1 Plaza de José Tomé, Avila (phone: 20-211404). Inexpensive.

EATING OUT

Mesón del Rastro Castilian cuisine featuring *truchas del Tormes* (trout from the Tormes River) and *mollejas de ternera* (veal sweetbreads), served in a rustic decor. Open daily. Reservations unnecessary. Major credit cards accepted. 1 Plaza del Rastro, Avila (phone: 20-211218). Moderate.

En Route from Avila Leaving town by the western gate, cross over the Adaja River and follow the signs for N501 and Salamanca. A half mile (1 km) on, there is a fine panoramic view of Avila at Cuatro Postes, a spot marked by four concrete posts with a cross in the center. The N501 highway covers the entire 61-mile (98-km) distance to Salamanca, passing broad fields marked by rock walls, sporadic outcroppings, occasional outbursts of trees and scrub, wheat fields, grazing sheep, and stands of sunflowers. Here and there, the *meseta* slopes down on either side of the road, giving the impression that the world drops off beyond the dust-hazy horizon. Suddenly, Salamanca materializes in spired splendor to the right.

SALAMANCA For a complete report on the city and its sights, hotels, and restaurants, see *Salamanca,* THE CITIES.

En Route from Salamanca The N630 highway from Salamanca to Zamora stretches north for 39 rather unscenic miles (62 km), crossing the border into the province of Zamora about halfway along the route. On the outskirts of town, avoid following the signposts to Zamora Este; continue straight on N630, bear right, and follow the signs for Centro Ciudad.

ZAMORA A 13th-century Romanesque bridge over the Duero River marks the historic center of Zamora, which rises steeply some 100 feet on the river's right bank. This is the city where El Cid spent part of his youth and was reportedly knighted. Its most outstanding feature is the cathedral (Plaza del Castillo); built during the 12th century with a few later additions, it has a great dome decorated in a curious Byzantine scalloped pattern. The cathedral museum contains an unsurpassed collection of tapestries, yet another example of the numerous hidden treasures Spain offers to those willing to stray off the beaten track. The museum is open daily from 11 AM to 2 PM and 4 to 8 PM, but closed Sunday afternoons; the hours tend to be unpredictable. (Out of season, the museum door is closed while the cashier-guide shows small groups around, so wait for the tour to end.) There's an admission charge. A fine view of the Duero River and the Romanesque bridge that spans it can be appreciated from the Puerta del Obispo, an arched gateway in the city wall behind the cathedral.

A favorite excursion from Zamora is to Pereruela, a small village with a few hundred inhabitants 10 miles (16 km) southwest of town via C527. A handful of families here still make fine ceramic cookware by hand; visitors can see the clay being sculpted and ovens being fired out back by the family barns. Although there are no shops, the goods can be purchased from the source, or from family members displaying their wares along the road.

CHECKING IN

Parador Condes de Alba y Aliste Installed in the former 15th-century palace of the Count of Alba y Aliste in the city's historic core, this beautiful *parador* offers 27 double rooms with private bath on the second floor of a Renaissance cloister. The property is endowed with a bar, a restaurant, gardens, and a swimming pool. 5 Plaza Viriato, Zamora (phone: 88-514497; in the US, 212-686-9213; fax: 88-530063). Expensive.

Dos Infantas Very pleasant, comfortable, and central, this place has 68 rooms, 5 of which are a tub shy of a complete bath. 3 Cortinas de San Miguel,

Zamora (phone: 88-532875; in the US, 800-528-1234; fax: 88-533548). Moderate.

Hostería Real de Zamora Located under the medieval city walls, this reconstructed 16th-century nobleman's mansion is within easy walking distance of the historic quarter. It was built over an old Jewish house, whose ritual bath still survives — as a goldfish pond. There are 15 comfortable rooms and 2 dining rooms. 7 Cuesta de Pizarro, Zamora (phone: 88-534545; fax: 88-534522). Moderate.

EATING OUT

París An elegant and intimate continental atmosphere accompanies a menu featuring the traditional Castilian *ancas de rana* (frogs' legs) and roast lamb, along with offbeat entries such as fresh vegetable pie and *rodaballo* (turbot) with spinach sauce. Open daily. Reservations advised. Major credit cards accepted. 14 Av. Portugal, Zamora (phone: 88-514325). Expensive.

Serafín Seafood is the specialty here, along with traditional Castilian and Zamoran fare. Open daily. Reservations advised. Major credit cards accepted. 10 Plaza Maestro Haedo, Zamora (phone: 88-531422). Expensive.

La Posada Quiet and refined, with local specialties including *mollejas a la zamorana* (sweetbreads in a spicy red sauce) and *lentejas* (lentil soup with garlic-spiced sausage and potato). Closed July 1–15. Reservations advised. Major credit cards accepted. 2 Calle Benavente, Zamora (phone: 88-516474). Moderate.

En Route from Zamora There are two ways to reach Benavente. If time is short, take N630 about 37 miles (60 km) north, then follow the Benavente signs to the N-VI highway, which leads to the turnoff for the center of town, another 5 miles (8 km) away from N630.

If time permits, however, take the longer route (a total of 69 miles/110 km), via the town of Toro, which is 20½ miles (33 km) due east of Zamora. Leave Zamora on N122, a road that parallels the Duero River. About halfway to Toro, the *meseta* stretches expansively into the distance on the right, with the Duero marking the boundary between the Tierra del Pan (Land of Bread) to the north and the Tierra del Vino (Land of Wine) to the south. Besides recently having its wine accorded *denominación* (appellation) status, Toro enjoys some historic and artistic distinctions. During the Second Punic War, Hannibal passed through the town; and during the early centuries of the Reconquest, Toro was a frequent battleground between Christian and Muslim forces. The peripatetic St. Teresa also established a convent here; and the Inquisition, one of its cruel tribunals. Follow the signs for Centro Ciudad, and the service road into town. The center is reached through either of two arched gateways. The first is the Puerta de Corredera (Sliding Gate), which leads straight beneath the arch of the 18th-century Torre del Reloj (Clock Tower), past the Plaza de España, and on to the town's main sight, the Church of Santa María la Mayor. The second gateway, Puerta Santa Catalina, is near the tourist information kiosk and a stone statue of an Iberian pig in the center of a small traffic circle. Passing through this gate, follow the street into the Plaza de España and turn left to the church.

The Colegiata de Santa María la Mayor, Toro's highlight, is a 12th-century Romanesque collegiate church (open daily from 10:30 AM to 1:30 PM and 5 to 7 PM in May through August; from noon to 1 PM and 7 to 8 PM in September through April — but hours are erratic, and if a guide is not on duty, ask for the priest in charge, who will gladly open the church). The western door, the Puerta de la Majestad, where guided tours begin, is crowned by seven pointed arches and compares favorably with the famed Pórtico de Gloria in Santiago de Compostela's cathedral. The sacristy contains several treasures, among them the well-known painting of the Virgen de la Mosca (Virgin of the Fly) — so named because of the fly on her knee.

The 12th-to-13th-century Romanesque-Mudéjar Church of San Lorenzo (Plaza de España) is another church worth visiting. Sweet and simple, it has a wonderful altar by Fernando Gallego, Plateresque tombs, and a beautiful polychrome mezzanine sagging with the weight of centuries. If the church is locked, ask someone at the tourist information kiosk to open it, but bear in mind that the presence of the tourist board staff is unpredictable.

Leaving Toro through the Puerta Santa Catalina, take N122 west, back toward Zamora, but turn right almost immediately at the sign indicating the road to Pozoantiguo and Castronuevo. After crossing the Valderaduey River and exiting Castronuevo, turn left onto ZA702 toward Villarrín de Campos, some 7½ miles (12 km) away. This entire route crosses the flat wheat fields that earned the area the epithet Tierra del Pan (Land of Bread). Pass Villarrín de Campos and head toward Estación de la Tabla, a mere scattering of warehouses and a granary, then continue on ZA701 toward Granja de Moreruela. This will lead to the right turn back onto N630 toward Benavente.

EATING OUT

Catayo A typical village tavern just off the Plaza de España, serving home-style meals at home-style prices and offering a selection of regional wines from the newly established *denominación* Toro. Open daily. No reservations or credit cards accepted. 7 Calle José María Cid, Toro (phone: 88-690060). Inexpensive.

BENAVENTE Situated on a promontory near the confluence of the Orbigo and Esla rivers, this town of 14,000 inhabitants offers a stunning view of the Castilian plain to the south and west. Santa María del Azoque, a 12th-century church of very irregular construction, is one of two special sights in town — be sure to walk around it to appreciate the kaleidoscopic effect of its diverse architectural elements. Most striking in its interior are three slender Gothic naves with precisely pointed arches. Open for mass at 9 AM and 7 PM daily, and more frequently on Sundays, the church is best visited just before or after the service.

The town's other special sight is the *Parador Fernando II de León,* on Paseo Ramón y Cajal (see below), which incorporates a well-preserved, 16th-century Gothic-Renaissance tower that was an addition to a 12th-century castle-palace. Installed in the vestigial tower are a lovely salon and, below that, an impressive bar (open 5 to 11:30 PM). Watching the sun set though the bar's oversized windows is a rare treat.

CHECKING IN/EATING OUT

Parador Fernando II de León This lovely *parador* offers 28 double rooms and 2 singles, all with private bath, and many with terraces offering splendid views. The dining room menu features such provincial dishes as *arroz a la zamorana* (rice Zamora-style — a kind of peasant paella with tripe, pig's ear, pig's knuckles, and chorizo in a red sauce) and sweetbreads with prawns. There's also a panoramic view. Major credit cards accepted. Paseo Ramón y Cajal, Benavente (phone: 88-630300; in the US, 212-686-9213; fax: 88-630303). Expensive.

En Route from Benavente León lies 44½ miles (71 km) north of Benavente via N630. Coming into town, follow the Centro Ciudad signs, cross over the Bernesga River, then turn left and follow the tree-lined boulevard that parallels the river all the way to the *Parador San Marcos.*

LEÓN This provincial capital traces its origins back to the mid-1st century, when the Romans built a fortification at the confluence of the Bernesga and Torió rivers. Its most remarkable structure is the beautiful cathedral (Plaza de Regla), built during the 13th and 14th centuries. Modeled after the cathedrals at Reims and Amiens in France, it is an exquisite example of Spanish Gothic architecture. Its glory lies in its more than 13,000 square feet of stained glass, the most dazzling display in Spain. The cathedral museum stands out for its commendable collections of Roman bronze figures and weapons, Neolithic artifacts, and Romanesque statues. The cathedral is open daily from 8:30 AM to 1:30 PM and 4 to 6:30 PM. The museum is open from 10 AM to 1:30 PM and 4 to 6:30 PM in May through August; from 10 AM to 1:30 PM and 4 to 7:30 PM in September through April; closed Saturday afternoons, Sundays, and holidays. There's an admission charge for the museum. (For additional details on the cathedral, see *Sacred Spain* in DIVERSIONS.)

About a 10-minute walk from the cathedral is another important León sight, the Romanesque Basilica of San Isidoro (Plaza de San

Isidoro), built in the 11th century, adorned and cloistered during the 12th, and partially reconstructed and enlarged during the 16th. Regrettably, the later remodeling obliterated much of the original Romanesque, but the basilica's pantheon remains one of the earliest examples of the Romanesque architectural genre in Spain. Here, 22 kings and queens of the old kingdom of León are buried beneath 12th-century frescoes that have prompted many to refer to this as the "Sistine Chapel" of Romanesque art; the pantheon also boasts capitals and a portal carved with scenes from the gospel, the earliest in Spain to be so decorated. A separate room houses the treasury, complete with illuminated Bibles and other fine relics. The church is open from 7 AM to midnight; closed Sundays, Mondays, and holiday afternoons. The pantheon is open daily from 9 AM to 2 PM and 3:30 to 8 PM in May through August; from 10 AM to 1:30 PM and 4 to 6:30 PM in September through April. There is an admission charge to the pantheon and treasury, which are seen on tours conducted by multilingual guides.

A third important monument in León, the *Parador San Marcos* (see *Checking In*), is located along the river and built in the Renaissance style. One of León's liveliest and loveliest landmarks, this was formerly the Monasterio de San Marcos, which was donated to the Order of Santiago by the Catholic Monarchs in appreciation of services rendered during the Reconquest. The monastery then became a hospital for pilgrims en route to Santiago de Compostela. During the Renaissance, it blossomed to its present sumptuousness; the *parador* now shares the grounds of the original monastery with the *Museo Arqueológico Provincial* (Provincial Archaeological Museum), which contains items from the Stone Age to the Renaissance. The adjacent Gothic church with its ornately carved choir stalls was a 16th-century addition. The museum is open from 10 AM to 2 PM and 4 to 6 PM; closed Sundays, Mondays, and holiday afternoons; admission charge.

All of the above sights of León are in the Old Town, which has been substantially rebuilt, although its streets still follow the old twists and turns, and which is surrounded by a modern city of high-rises. The tourist office (3 Plaza de Regla; phone: 87-237082) is just across from the cathedral. Not far away is the Plaza Mayor, surrounded by porticoes and, on most days, alive with a farmers' market.

CHECKING IN

Parador San Marcos This former monastery has 258 majestic double rooms and 7 suites. For additional details, see *Paradores* in DIVERSIONS. 7 Plaza San Marcos, León (phone: 87-237300; in the US, 212-686-9213; fax: 87-233458). Expensive.

Riosol Functional and comfortable, it has 141 rooms with private baths, direct-dial telephones, and color TV sets. This place is across the river from the other hotels. 3 Av. de Palencia, León (phone: 87-216650; fax: 87-216997). Expensive to moderate.

Quindós This very comfortable hotel has 96 rooms, each with private bath, direct-dial telephone, and a color TV set. There's also a public video salon and a restaurant. Centrally located, only 2 blocks from the *parador*. 24 Av. José Antonio, León (phone: 87-236200; fax: 87-242201). Moderate.

Don Suero On the street that runs from San Isidoro to the *parador,* it has 106 rooms with varying in-room bath facilities; all very clean. There is a cafeteria on the premises. 15 Calle Suero de Quiñones, León (phone: 87-230600). Inexpensive.

EATING OUT

Adonías The decor features a distinguished collection of Spanish ceramics, and the same emphasis on quality is present in both the food and the service. Closed Sundays and 3 weeks in July. Reservations advised. Major credit cards accepted. 16 Calle Santa Nonia, León (phone: 87-252665 or 87-206768). Expensive.

Casa Pozo From the coarse peasant bread to the homemade desserts, the food here is excellent, as is the service. There's also an extensive selection of rioja wines. Closed Sundays, the first half of July, and December 23 through January 7. Reservations unnecessary. Major credit cards accepted. 15 Arco de Animas, León (phone: 87-223039). Expensive to moderate.

Mesón Leonés del Racimo de Oro Just off the Plaza San Martín in a 17th-century mansion, this restaurant serves dishes made from local produce. Walk past the bar and upstairs to the beautiful rustic dining room. Closed Sunday evenings and Tuesdays. No reservations. Major credit cards accepted. 2 Calle Caño Vadillo, León (phone: 87-257575). Moderate.

El Palomo This centrally located no-nonsense restaurant is a favorite with local gourmets. Specialties include potatoes stewed with prawns and clams, and the acclaimed red peppers from Bierzo cooked in a variety of styles. There is also an impressive wine cellar containing 150 different labels. Closed Sunday evenings and Wednesdays. Reservations necessary. No credit cards accepted. 8 Calle Escalerilla, León (phone: 87-254225). Moderate.

En Route from León It is 80 miles (128 km) from León southeast to Palencia. Take N601, then N610, which veers off to the left about 42 miles (67 km) into the route at Becilla de Valderaduey.

PALENCIA Located on the left bank of the Carrión River, Palencia was once a capital city of the *vacceos,* a Celtic tribe. Construction of its cathedral spanned 2 centuries (14th to 16th) and took place on the site of a 7th-century Visigothic basilica. This earlier basilica, marked by three arches and a single rectangular Romanesque nave, has become the crypt of the present church. The cathedral museum contains a painting of *San Sebastián* by El Greco, a small sampling of Romanesque statues, and some 15th-century tapestries. The church and the museum are open Tuesdays through Saturdays 10:30 AM to 1 PM and 4 to 5:50 PM; Sundays and holidays from 9 AM to 2 PM. Plaza Antolín (phone: 88-701347).

Stop in at the Palencia Tourist Office (105 Calle Mayor; phone: 88-740068) for information on other sights in town, which include the Church of San Miguel, where, according to legend, El Cid married Doña Jimena.

CHECKING IN

Castilla la Vieja Not far from the Plaza Mayor, this place offers all the usual facilities in its 87 rooms, plus a restaurant. 26 Av. Casado del Alisal, Palencia (phone: 88-749044; fax: 88-747577). Expensive.

Monclus Smaller (40 rooms) and with fewer amenities than the *Castilla la Vieja*, this place is nonetheless clean and comfortable. Near the Plaza Mayor, 3 Calle Menéndez Pelayo, Palencia (phone: 88-744300). Moderate.

EATING OUT

Casa Damián Featuring Castilian classics and fine duero wines. Closed Mondays and July 22 through August 22. Reservations necessary. Major credit cards accepted. 9 Calle Martínez de Azcoitia, Palencia (phone: 88-744628). Expensive.

Mesón del Concejo Traditional Castilian fare is served; *chuleta de cervera* (veal cutlet from free-range calves) is a specialty. Closed Thursdays and for the month of November. Reservations unnecessary. MasterCard and Visa accepted. 5 Calle Martínez de Azcoitia, Palencia (phone: 88-743239). Expensive to moderate.

En Route from Palencia Valladolid is 29½ miles (47 km) south via N611 and N620. Here the dry, dusty, and monotonous Castilian *meseta* is at its harshest and most alienating. Along the way, 9 miles (14 km) south of Palencia, at Baños de Cerrato — near the railway junction of Venta de Baños — is what is reputed to be the oldest church in Spain, the Basílica de San Juan Bautista, built in 661 by the Visigoths.

VALLADOLID A former capital of Spain, this is where the Catholic Monarchs were married in 1469, where Columbus died in 1506, where Philip II was born in 1527, and where Miguel de Cervantes lived for 3 years. Napoleon used the city as a headquarters for his army in the early 19th century during the Peninsular War; unfortunately, they looted or destroyed many of Valladolid's ancient art treasures and monuments. For those willing to fight the traffic and battle the lack of coherent signs in this rather unattractive and fairly large (330,000 inhabitants) city, several sights worthy of attention do still remain. The late-15th-century Colegio de San Gregorio (Cadenas de San Gregorio) is noted for its façade, a masterpiece of the Isabeline style, and for its courtyard, wonderfully Plateresque, but above all for being the home of one of Spain's most important museums, the *Museo Nacional de Escultura Policromada* (phone: 83-250375). A repository of the types of polychrome wooden sculptures seen in churches all over the country, the museum includes works from the 13th through the 17th centuries and is particularly strong in sculptures by Castilian masters of the Renaissance (open Tuesdays through Saturdays from 9 AM to 2 PM and 4 to 6 PM; admission charge). The adjacent 15th-century Church of San Pablo (Plaza de San Pablo; open only during church services) is also worthy of note, above all for the ornate façade, its lower level a Gothic design carved by Simon of Cologne, its upper reaches Plateresque. Valladolid's cathedral was designed in the late 16th century by Juan de Herrera, of El Escorial fame, but it was finished much later, according to plans by Alberto Churriguera — note that the upper part of the façade is baroque. The *Museo Oriental*, located in the basement of the Real Colegio Padres Agustinos Filipinos (7 Paseo Filipinos; phone: 83-306900), houses the best collection of Asian art in Spain, consisting mainly of works from the Philippines and China (open Mondays through Saturdays from 4 to 7 PM; Sundays from 10 AM to 1 PM; admission charge). The 16th-century house where *Don Quixote* creator Cervantes lived beginning in 1603 stands on Calle Rastro, near the Plaza Zorilla. It can be visited Tuesdays through Saturdays from 9:30 AM to 3:30 PM and Sundays from 10 AM to 3 PM; admission charge (phone: 83-308810). Valladolid's Tourist Office is at 3 Plaza de Zorrilla (phone: 83-351801).

En Route from Valladolid The itinerary continues southeast on N601 via Cuellar, to Segovia and back to Madrid. For those not in a hurry, however, a detour of 37½ miles (60 km) round-trip southwest from Valladolid will lead to the small town of Tordesillas, perched some 2,280 feet above the Duero River. A typical Castilian *pueblo* and the place where Juana la Loca, mother of Charles I of Spain and grandmother of Philip II, was imprisoned until her death, Tordesillas was also the spot where the Spanish and Portuguese met in 1494 to sign the Treaty of Tordesillas, which divided the New World in two, giving all lands west of a line to Spain and all lands east to Portugal, a decision that ultimately resulted in Spanish-speaking Latin America and Portuguese-speaking Brazil. Besides a somewhat austerely attractive Plaza Mayor, the Church of San Antolín is worth a visit if only for the vista of the Duero and the medieval bridge that leads into town. The church museum houses the *Inmaculada* by Pedro de Mena, and an almost life-size sculpture of the Holy Family attributed to Gregorio Fernández. The palace-cum-monastery known as Santa Clara is a fine example of Mudéjar architecture, with a beautiful Arabic patio — a rarity in these parts. Both are closed Mondays. Hours are often unpredictable, but generally the museum is open 10AM to 2 PM and 4 to 6 PM.

Return to Valladolid and pick up the N601 highway south to Segovia. Along the 31-mile (50-km) stretch from Valladolid to the town of Cuellar, the terrain begins to roll a bit, and welcome hills appear near Santiago del Arroyo. Just before Cuellar, the route passes into the province of Segovia.

CHECKING IN/EATING OUT

Parador de Tordesillas Half a mile (1 km) from the center of town, this modern hostelry has 73 rooms, a bar, a garden, and a swimming pool. Its dependable restaurant offers a mixture of regional and national dishes and wines. Major credit cards accepted. Carretera Salamanca, Km 5, Tordesillas (phone: 83-770051; in the US, 212-686-9213; fax: 83-771013). Expensive.

CUELLAR From the crown of a hill, Cuellar commands an ample panorama, especially from just outside the walls of its 15th-century castle; now home to a school, the castle courtyard can be visited only if it happens to be open (there is no posted schedule).

EATING OUT

El Rincón Castellano Tucked away in a corner of the Plaza Mayor, this cozy restaurant specializes in fine home-style cooking, featuring the typical Castilian roast baby lamb, tasty *mollejas lechazo* (lamb sweetbreads sautéed with garlic and oil), and an ample *ensalada mesonero* (mixed salad with tuna, eggs, and olives). Open daily. No reservations. Major credit cards accepted. 13 Plaza Mayor, Cuellar (phone: 11-141031). Moderate.

En Route from Cuellar Stands of trees become more frequent along N601 south toward Segovia, 37½ miles (60 km) away. A little more than halfway there, the vague silhouette of the Sierra de Guadarrama appears in the distance. The entrance into Segovia is dramatic — the cathedral dominates the crest of a hill and the fairy-tale Alcázar perches at the extreme right (western) edge of town.

SEGOVIA For a detailed report on Segovia and its sights, hotels, and restaurants, see *Segovia,* THE CITIES.

En Route from Segovia The 55-mile (88-km) stretch of road between Segovia and Madrid via N601 (sometimes posted as CL601) winds through the pines of the scenic Sierra de Guadarrama, where many *madrileños* spend their weekends. Several miles beyond the mountain-ringed Embalse de Navacerrada at Villalba, the A6 highway veers off to the left for Madrid, becoming the N-VI highway about 5 miles (8 km) before reaching the capital.

North Atlantic Coast

The Romans could never fully conquer the area, the Visigoths were plagued by perpetual uprisings, the Moors suffered their first setback here as they tried to sweep across the Iberian Peninsula in the 8th century — and the most fearsome invaders of them all, 20th-century tourists, have so far managed to establish only a handful of beachheads. While the rest of Spain fell under the influence of one marauder after another, the country's northern coast, along the Atlantic Ocean, remained determinedly independent.

A Spanish saying has it that "in summer, the rich go south and the wise go north." For south, read constant and often blistering sun, packed beaches, and nonstop flamenco-flavored discotheques. The northern coast, on the other hand, offers thickly forested mountainsides, intensely green hills, and lush valleys and meadows to offset the stormy sea and the wave-battered cliffs. The entire coast from San Sebastián, just 12 miles (19 km) from the French border, to Ribadeo, 272 miles (435 km) to the west, is prone to dampness — mist, fog, a fine drizzle called *sirimiri* by the Basques, and just plain rain. But when the sun shines, the numerous beaches equal the best of the south. Many of these beaches are isolated and remote, protected by rugged cliffs, just as this area and its peoples have been throughout history.

Spain's Atlantic coastline edges four traditional regions that have become, in the post-Franco era, four *comunidades autónomas,* or autonomous communities, and are practically distinct countries. Our route covers three of them, ending just inside the fourth. It starts out at San Sebastián, the queen of northern Spain's beach resorts, in the thick of Basque Country. Westward beyond the bustling industrial port of Bilbao, the route leaves behind the Costa Vasca (Basque Coast) and enters Cantabria, the most Spanish of the northern regions, with its attractive coastal capital of Santander. Still farther west, it reaches Asturias, a beautiful, little-visited, emerald-colored region with a coast known, appropriately, as the Costa Verde (Green Coast). It then ends just inside Galicia, another region steeped in history and rich in folklore.

If the Basques are a mystery to most Spaniards today, they completely stump anthropologists, as well as philologists trying to ascertain the origin of the Basque language, Euskera. It has no apparent linguistic connection with any other language, and nobody knows where the extremely complex tongue came from, but it certainly predates the arrival in Europe of the Indo-European languages some 3,000 years ago. Recent research has tried, with little success, to link Euskera to pre-Indo-European languages such as those still spoken in the Caucasus and among the Berbers of North Africa.

Indeed, there is considerable evidence that the Basques are the last surviving representatives of Europe's aboriginal population. Although the Romans did occupy parts of the Basque region, they had a difficult time of it. Plutarch and others described a poor, warlike people with strong tribal features. The Basque Country was the last area of southern and western Europe to be converted to Christianity, and one of the last corners of Europe to be civilized.

Many Basques still live in isolated homesteads of fewer than 30 people. The Basque homesteads are flat-roofed, Alpine-style farmhouses known as *caserios,* where occupants sleep upstairs but share the downstairs with their animals. The Basques always had a highly individual lifestyle — they were renowned as North Sea whalers until the 18th century — and they had little use for central control, especially from outside the region. Not only did this attitude cause potential invaders to leave them alone, but it also meant that they enjoyed a long tradition of great personal liberties at a time when most of Europe lived in serfdom. By the 15th century, these liberties were enshrined in the *fueros,* a body of ancient laws and privileges that the Basques in Spain did not lose until well into the 19th century. The region's mysterious language, immunity from invasion, life in remote settlements with little or no central government, and the freedoms of the *fueros* all help to explain the current political turmoil, in which the Basques are seeking independence from Spain.

The Basques are the most indomitable of all the Spanish peoples as well as the most fun-loving of those in the north. They enjoy a reputation for being the biggest drinkers and the heartiest eaters in Spain, and for having the best cuisine, whether it's traditional fare or the new Basque cuisine that is all the rage. Basque specialties include such distinctive dishes as *cogote de merluza* (baked hake's head), *kokotxas y almejas* (hake gills and clams in a lemon, oil, and parsley sauce), *angulas* (tiny silvery elvers, or young eels), *bacalao al pil pil* (cod in a Bilbao-style green sauce), *porrusalda* (leek, cod, and potato stew), *marmitako* (fresh tuna, tomato, and potato stew), and *alubias* (beans).

Equally distinctive is the folklore of the region. Rural sports are an integral part of the Basque culture. The only Basque sport widely known outside the region is pelota (related to jai alai), but others include wood chopping, grass scything, rock dragging by bulls, and ram butting. Any fiesta will include traditional dances such as the *aurreska* — which honors the Basque flag, or *ikurriña* — and the *espatadanza,* or sword dance. They are accompanied by the simple music of the *txistu,* or three-holed tin whistle, and a small drum.

Cantabria is the name of the piece of Spain that separates the Basque Country from Asturias. The earliest evidence of human settlement in Spain, about 25,000 to 30,000 years ago, has been found around Santander, the capital of Cantabria. The culture of these early settlers, who crossed the Pyrenees from southern France, peaked around 15,000 BC, which is approximately the date of several caves with prehistoric paintings located at Altamira, near Santander. This region also has numerous Roman remains.

Westward, and only 25 miles (40 km) inland, are some of Spain's most remarkable mountains, the Picos de Europa. Mighty, craggy peaks, they rise giddily from the Bay of Biscay to form a buttress that divides Cantabria from Asturias. On the western fringe of the Picos is the National Park of Covadonga. The Battle of Covadonga in AD 718 marked the beginning of what the Spanish called the "Reconquest" — even though the Moors wouldn't be completely driven out of Spain until 1492. After the battle, the tough Asturians, who earlier had fiercely resisted the Romans and were subdued only after a 10-year war (29–19 BC), turned their attention to building churches and hermitages, while the rest of Spain skirmished with the Moorish armies. Many of these early Asturian or pre-Romanesque buildings still stand today, constituting the best and most complete series of 9th-century edifices in Europe.

The Reconquest pushed the Moors southward, and by 914 Asturias had gained control of León, most of Galicia, and the north of Portugal. This power was ceded only when the Asturian kings moved their court south from Oviedo and made León the capital of a combined Asturias-León. In 1388, Asturias became a principality. Much of Asturias today consists of red-roofed villages with their characteristic *hórreos,* granaries built on stone supports several feet high, scattered over the green carpets of the valleys and meadows. But the storm-ridden sea is the real spectacle here, and the uneven coastline exposes increasingly dramatic wave-battered cliffs as the route moves toward Galicia. Local food matches the local character: strong blue cabrales cheese, and a hearty stew of broad beans, pork, and sausages called *fabada,* are downed with cider, *the* drink of Asturias. Such a meal is often accompanied by the music of the region's best-known instrument, the *gaita,* a small bagpipe.

Anyone driving the entire route, including the two or three inland excursions, should allow several weeks to do it justice. Most of it features fine scenery — sea, fishing villages, beaches, and mountains — but there is also the bustle and shopping of Bilbao, Santander, Oviedo, or Gijón. From Bilbao westward into Galicia, the route is paralleled by a narrow-gauge railway line — *FEVE* — that is a travelers' dream. The *FEVE* line is slow and cumbersome (the state-owned *RENFE* rail network has long since taken over as the region's primary means of ground transportation), but it skirts beaches, runs across estuaries and through limestone gorges, and is often surrounded by forest and hills. For a more comfortable ride, catch the Santiago de Compostela–Bilbao *El Transcantábrico* luxury train (phone: 85-84096), which takes a leisurely 8 days to travel the North Atlantic Coast. A bus leaves from Santiago for El Ferrol, where passengers board the train, complete with a full-service restaurant. The excursion includes guided tours of Ribeados, Cangas de Onis, Covadonga, Santillana del Mar, Comillas, Oviedo, Santander, and Bilbao. The main road joining San Sebastián and Galicia has recently been improved, but construction continues, and an occasional rough stretch can slow down part of your trip. Maps can barely keep up with improvements (don't be surprised if your car rental map is out of date), so ask questions before you get under way.

The disadvantage of getting away from it all is the generally poor tourist infrastructure in the north of Spain. There are few top class hotels or restaurants outside the main cities, and even in town, accommodations are very hard to find in July and August. A double room with bath will cost $120 or more in a hotel listed as expensive, $70 to $110 in a moderate one, and below $65 in an inexpensive one. Dinner for two with wine costs $60 or more at restaurants listed as expensive, $45 to $60 at moderate restaurants, and $35 or less at inexpensive places. It is not difficult to find superb cooking at moderately priced restaurants, sometimes right next door to a dining spot that charges three times the price. The phone numbers listed below include local area codes; when dialing from another area in Spain, add a "9." Note that phone numbers can have either 6 or 7 digits.

> **NOTE** Most place-names in the Basque Country have two spellings. In this chapter, when two spellings are given (usually at the first reference to a place), the first one is Spanish, and the second — often vital for following signs along the route — is Basque.

SAN SEBASTIÁN (DONOSTIA) For full details on this charming beach resort just 12 miles (19 km) from the French border, see *San Sebastián,* THE CITIES.

En Route from San Sebastián The chief Basque city and port of Bilbao, 62½ miles (100 km) to the west, can be reached in an hour on the excellent A8 highway, which skirts undulating deep green Basque hills. But it would be an enormous shame to miss some of the pretty Basque fishing villages, not to mention a chance to sample some fine cuisine, along the way. Take A8 out of San Sebastián to reach the first stop, Zarauz (Zarautz), 14 miles (22 km) away. The turnoff, 2 miles (3 km) past the tiny fishing port of Orio, leads right into the town. Zarauz is a booming resort that hugs a magnificent 1½-mile beach. A vacation home for thousands of Basques from inland industrial towns, there are approximately 18,000 year-round residents, but the population quadruples in summer. During the Middle Ages, Zarauz was the site of much factional warring, and defensive structures typical of the period sprang up. One of the few surviving is the 15th-century, 3-story Luzea Tower, on Kale Nagusia, the central street. The 16th-century Palacio de Narros stands at the western end of town, with its back facing the sea. The 9-hole *Real Club de Golf de Zarauz* (Barrio de Mendilauta; phone: 43-830145), at the eastern end of town by the beach, is one of the Basque Country's best.

The beautiful fishing village of Guetaria (Getaria), with rocky promontories and great vistas, is 2 miles (3 km) from Zarauz. It had Roman origins but was subsequently founded as a country estate by Alfonso VIII in 1209. The impressive San Salvador church stands amid a remarkable group of medieval houses. Make sure to see its dramatically raked floor (look *up* to the altar) and the arched alleyway over the crypt, which leads to the sea. Today, the village (pop. 2,000) is nationally famous for seafood — local dishes include *cogote de merluza a la Getaria* (hake head grilled over charcoal in wire holders) and *txangurro al horno* (baked spider crab prepared in its own shell) — and as the home of *txakolí* wine, white and slightly sour, a perfect accompaniment to the seafood. Often compared to a good moselle, the Rolls-Royce of the *txakolís* is the locally produced Txomin Etxániz. Guetaria is also known for El Ratón (The Mouse), the rodent-shaped islet of San Antón that juts out from the harbor and can be seen for miles from either side of the village.

Six miles (10 km) along N634 is Zumaya (Zumaia), a less-attractive version of Zarauz that nonetheless enjoys the best surfing waves in the region. It's also home to the *Museo Zuloaga* (on N634, phone: 43-861015), a collection of paintings in an exquisite stone house incorporating the ruins of a 12th-century monastery. The small selection includes some Goyas and El Grecos. It's open mid-January to mid-October, Wednesdays through Sundays from 4 to 6 PM. Take the C6317 turnoff southward, 1¼ miles (2 km) beyond Zumaya, for a worthwhile excursion to the Belle Epoque spa resort of Cestona (Zestoa), 6 miles (10 km) inland, and to the Sanctuary of Loyola, between Azkoitia and Azpeitia, another 6 miles (10 km) farther on. The imposing shrine here was built on the site of the home of St. Ignatius of Loyola, the 16th-century founder of the Society of Jesus — the religious order whose members are called Jesuits.

Return through Cestona and join the A8 highway for the 3 miles (5 km) to the turnoff for Deva (Deba). Then, instead of taking N634, which turns inland at Deva, exit at the coastal C6212, a truly scenic road atop a cliff. Past the unattractive port of Motrico (Mutriku), the road leaves the province of Guipúzcoa (Gipuzkoa), one of three provinces making up the Basque Country, and enters Vizcaya (Biskaia), another Basque province (landlocked Alava, or Araba, is the third). The Vizcayan coast is a world of rocks and cliffs, small ports and coves, sheltered beaches, and small industries merging with the sea. Ondárroa is the largest Basque fishing port, but the real treasure of Vizcayan fishing villages is Lequeitio (Lekeitio), 8 miles (13 km) farther along a winding road with breathtaking views.

Lequeitio has a beautiful bay and two beaches, and is a typical Basque fishing port. Its vessels are a riot of color, mainly the red, green, and white of the Basque flag, and the wooden balconies and tall, narrow façades of its houses rest on the harbor itself. The 16th-century Santa María church is an impressive example of Vizcaya Gothic. The town is notorious for its September fiesta, which includes a boat race during which competitors pull off the heads of live geese tied to a rope across the bay.

Continue 15 miles (24 km) inland along C6212 to Guernica (Gernika), immortalized by Pablo Picasso's *Guernica,* a nightmarish painting of the world's first major aerial bombing of civilians. German bombers, assisting Generalísimo Francisco Franco in the 1936–39 Civil War, flattened the town in 1937 because of its symbolic value to the Basques, who were fighting on the Republican side. Thousands died, and the town has suffered from unimaginative postwar rebuilding, but it remains the traditional heart of Basque nationalism. It was here, under the Tree of Guernica, that the Basque parliament met throughout the Middle Ages. From the 15th century through most of the 19th century, successive Spanish monarchs were obliged to visit the same oak tree, which still stands outside the Casa de Juntas parliament building, to acknowledge their acceptance of the *fueros* system of privilege. Three miles (5 km) away, just off C6212 at Kortezubi, are the Santimamiñe caves, containing 13,000-year-old paintings.

Take C6315 south from Guernica to the junction with the A8 highway at Amorebieta, then follow the signs for Bilbao, 22½ miles (36 km) from Guernica.

CHECKING IN

Karlos Arguiñano In the same building as a well-known restaurant of the same name (see *Eating Out*) are 12 elegant and well-appointed guestrooms with all amenities. Closed *Christmas.* 13 Calle Mendilauta, Zarauz (phone: 43-130000; fax: 43-133450). Expensive.

Gran Hotel Balneario de Cestona A grand Belle Epoque spa, built in 1900, with 118 rooms. Facilities include hot thermal baths, meeting rooms, a period conference hall, 4 restaurants, tennis courts, a chapel, and gardens. Closed mid-December through April. Paseo de San Juan, Cestona (phone: 43-147140). Expensive to moderate.

Zarauz The largest hotel along the Basque coast outside San Sebastián offers 82 rooms, 100 yards from the beach. Facilities include a TV lounge, lovely gardens, and a restaurant. Closed *Christmas* through the second week in January. 26 Av. de Nafarroa, Zarauz (phone: 43-830200; fax: 43-830193). Moderate.

EATING OUT

Elkano Locals say it serves the best grilled fish in Guipúzcoa province, and the most succulent *rodaballo* (turbot) in the Basque Country. Also renowned for its *salpicón de bogavante* (lobster cocktail), *rape entero a la brasa* (whole braised anglerfish), and any northern fish in season. Closed Sunday evenings and for the first 2 weeks of November. Reservations advised. Major credit cards accepted. 2 Calle Herrerieta, Guetaria (phone: 43-831614). Expensive.

Kaia y Kaipe The name of this eatery means Upstairs and Downstairs in Basque, and it offers dining with a view as well as seafood prepared to perfection.

Try *txangurro al horno* (spider crab prepared in its shell) and the regional favorite, *cogote de merluza a la Getaria* (charcoal-grilled hake head). Wash it all down with the local *txakoli* white wine. Closed October. Reservations necessary. Major credit cards accepted. 10 Calle General Arnao, Guetaria (phone: 43-832414). Expensive.

Karlos Arguiñano One of the bright lights of the new Basque cuisine. The food here is vigorously Basque yet surprisingly original. Specialties include *liebre con rabo de ternera* (hare with calf's tail) and *sesos de ternera con hongos* (veal brains with mushrooms). Closed Sunday nights, Wednesdays, and *Christmas*. Reservations advised. Visa, Diners Club, and American Express accepted. 13 Calle Mendilauta, Zarauz (phone: 43-130000; fax: 43-133450). Expensive.

Masoparri Another good fish house, in an old country manor with a terrace facing the sea high above the harbor. Try *bonito a la parrilla* (grilled tuna) or *kokotxas en su gelatina* (hake's gill muscles in gelatin). Closed mid-December through late January. Reservations unnecessary. American Express, Diners Club, and Visa accepted. 1 Calle Sagartzaga, Guetaria (phone: 43-835707). Moderate.

BILBAO (BILBO) The green hills that are visible from any part of Bilbao make it hard to believe that this is Spain's sixth-largest city and the country's main port, with approximately 500,000 inhabitants (1.4 million in greater Bilbao). Standing on the central Arenal Bridge that spans the Nervión River and looking at the glorious City Hall and its utterly rural backdrop, you'd think you were in some middling river town. But look again. The Gran Vía, Bilbao's chief avenue, boasts gleaming skyscrapers, huge department stores, and elegant clothing shops. And a train ride along the banks of the Nervión estuary to the Bay of Biscay passes scores of dockyard cranes, shipyards, warehouses, factories, wharves, and iron and steel foundries. Bilbao's smokestack industries are in decline, and the air of industrial decay and political tension, along with the drab apartment blocks and frequent rain, make the city less than a touristic glamour spot. But Bilbao residents are renowned for their friendliness, and the city is packed with good places to eat and drink.

Founded in 1300, Bilbao didn't flourish until the Industrial Revolution, when Britain became its main trading partner. Even today the city reflects a strong British influence, seen in dress, architecture, and even in the long list of English managers in charge of the local soccer team, *Athletic Bilbao,* traditionally one of Spain's top three. Touristic interest centers on the Casco Viejo, or Old Quarter, which combines numerous fine clothing outfitters, specialty stores, traditional Basque restaurants, and bars. It is here that locals indulge in two Bilbao customs. One is the *chiquiteo,* the drinking in rapid succession of small wines or beers — no more than a mouthful each — at several bars in double-quick time. The other is *copa y puro,* the sipping of a liqueur, usually brandy or an anise-based brew called *patxarán,* and the smoking of a cigar after a hearty lunch (women as well as men follow both customs). To give either tradition a try, visit any of the bars on the Plaza Nueva.

The grandiose Santiago Cathedral, in the heart of the Old Quarter, has a cloister built in 1404, although the church was largely rebuilt in the 16th century after a fire. Nearby is the Plaza Nueva; built in 1830 and enclosed by 64 arches, it houses a flea market on Sunday mornings. *Gorostiaga* (9 Calle Victor; phone: 4-416-1276) is a curious Old Quarter shop where seven generations of the same family have been making hats since 1857; the specialty is the famous Basque beret, or *txapela,* although trilbys and Panama hats are also made. The *Teatro Arriaga* (in the Plaza Arriaga next to the Arenal Bridge just before the Old Quarter; phone: 4-463244) was built in 1890. Recently renovated, its jolly imitation French architecture provides a contrast to Bilbao's neo-classical style. Two museums are worth a visit. The *Museum of Basque Archaeology, Ethnology, and History* (4 Calle Cruz; phone: 4-455423; open Tuesdays through Saturdays from 10:30 AM to 1:30 PM and from 4 to 7 PM; Sundays, from 10:30 AM to 1:30 PM; no admission charge) has a special room devoted to the commercial life of Bilbao since 1500. The ivy-covered *Museum of Fine Arts* (in the English-style Doña Casilda Iturrízar Park; phone: 4-441-9536; open Tuesdays through Saturdays from 10 AM to 1:30 PM and from 4 to 7:30 PM; Sundays from 11 AM to 2 PM; no admission charge) features an extensive collection of Spanish and foreign paintings and sculpture from the Romanesque period to the early 20th century. El Greco, Velázquez, Ribera, Ribalta, Zurbarán, and Goya are represented, as are modern artists from Gauguin to Sorolla.

Two city center coffeehouses are worthy haunts for an early evening break. The *Café Iruña* (13 Calle Colón de Larreátegui; phone: 4-423-7021), built in 1903, has a tiled arabesque decor; the *Café la Granja* (Plaza Circular; phone: 44-230813), opposite the statue to Bilbao's founder, Don Diego López de Haro, has a genteel atmosphere. *Semana Grande* (Aste Nagusia in Basque, Big Week in English), Bilbao's week-long fiesta, runs from August 15 to 22. Ask at the tourist office (Alameda de Mazarredo; phone: 44-244819) for information — bullfights, rural sports, male-only open-air gastronomy contests, and folk dancing are all part of the festivities.

CHECKING IN

Ercilla Nearly always full, so book well in advance. All 347 rooms have air conditioning and private baths. The *Bermeo* restaurant (see *Eating Out*) is one of the city's best. 37 Calle Ercilla, Bilbao (phone: 4-443-8800; fax: 4-443-9335). Expensive.

Indautxu Conveniently located downtown, this 185-room luxury property was completely rebuilt within what had been an early–20th-century maternity hospital. There is a bar and a restaurant. Plaza Bombero Etxaniz, Bilbao (phone: 4-421-1198; fax: 4-422-1331). Expensive.

López de Haro A luxury establishment in the city center, this 6-story property was built in the quasi-English classic style of Bilbao, and the 53 rooms have a full range of amenities. On the premises is the *Club Náutico* restaurant. 2 Calle Obispo Orueta, Bilbao (phone: 4-423-5500; fax: 4-423-4500). Expensive.

Villa de Bilbao Modern and luxurious, there are 142 large air conditioned rooms, tennis courts, a heated swimming pool, a discotheque, hair salons, and a restaurant. 87 Gran Vía, Bilbao (phone: 4-441-6000; fax: 4-441-6529). Expensive.

Roquefer A delightful, family-run establishment in the Old Quarter. The 18 rooms are simple but clean. 2 Calle Lotería, Bilbao (phone: 4-415-0755). Inexpensive.

EATING OUT

Bermeo At the *Ercilla* hotel, and rated as one of Spain's best hotel-restaurants, it is the culinary gathering spot before and after all social, political, sporting, and cultural events. A Basque-Navarrese menu offers mushrooms, woodcock and partridge with turnip, steamed hake, and oxtail (the latter during the August bullfight week). Closed Sunday nights, Saturday for lunch, and weekends from June through August. Reservations necessary. Major credit cards accepted. 37 Calle Ercilla, Bilbao (phone: 4-443-8800). Expensive.

Guria Codfish is *the* Bilbao specialty, and it is never better than when prepared by Chef Génaro Pildain in his own restaurant. *Bacalao al pil pil* (cod baked in green sauce with peppers) is just one of the succulent dishes served. The menu is traditionally Basque. Closed Sundays and the first 2 weeks of August. Reservations advised. Major credit cards accepted. 66 Gran Vía, Bilbao (phone: 4-441-0543). Expensive.

Zortziko The choice for new Basque cuisine in Bilbao. The menu is pure poetry: *tartar de salmón en flor al aroma de eneldo* (salmon tartar in a flower shape with dilled mint sauce), *rodaballo asado a la vinagreta tibia y al aroma de genjibre natural* (baked turbot in a vinaigrette sauce with a hint of ginger), and *mousse de polen a la miel de encina* (honey mousse). Closed Sundays. Reservations advised. Major credit cards accepted. 17 Calle Alameda de Mazarredo, Bilbao (phone: 4-423-9743). Expensive.

Aitxiar A modest but atmospheric spot in the Old Quarter, this charming dining room behind a bar serves Basque favorites including *chipirones en su tinta* (squid in its own ink) and *porrusalda* (leek, onion, and cod stew). Closed Mondays and September. No reservations. No credit cards accepted. 8 Calle María Muñoz, Bilbao (phone: 4-415-0917). Inexpensive.

En Route from Bilbao The newly improved N634 (sometimes signposted as E-70) leads through 8 miles (13 km) of heavily industrial Greater Bilbao towns — Barakaldo, Sestao, Portugalete, and Santurce (Santurtzi) — on the left bank of the Nervión before it hits the countryside and, suddenly, Cantabria. For a last glimpse of the Basque Country and a view of the amazing Puente Colgante (Hanging Bridge), turn into the steep roads leading down to Portugalete.

Just a mile (1.6 km) farther on is Santurtzi, famous for its sardines, grilled in the open air by fisherwomen. Beyond is Castro-Urdiales, a surprisingly unspoiled fishing town. From the broad promenade and gardens on the seafront, the scene often includes the brightly colored sails of windsurfers and little boys fishing for crabs from the harbor steps. The Castro-Urdiales harbor is dominated by the dauntingly buttressed 13th-century Gothic Church of Santa María and the nearby ruined Knights Templars Castle, complete with lighthouse; in 1814, locals escaped from Napoleon's troops through secret castle passages to waiting British ships. Cave paintings in the vicinity are evidence of human presence 12,000 years ago.

Another 16 miles (26 km) along N634, past the lush green valley of Guriezo and after a spectacular descent into the town of Liendo, is Laredo. Undoubtedly it once had all the charm of Castro-Urdiales, but a 1960s building boom, and a parallel influx of European tourism, has disfigured the promenade facing the otherwise wonderful La Salvé beach. There is also a marvelous 13th-century Gothic church, Santa María; its exterior is not imposing, but its Bethlehem altarpiece is reckoned to be one of the finest jewels of Flemish sculpture in Spain. The church stands atop the Old Town, whose narrow cobbled streets wind down to the harbor. Laredo's *Battle of the Flowers,* when flower-bedecked carnival floats parade through town, takes place annually on the last Friday in August.

Toward Santander, the road passes through unattractive Colindres and over a steel bridge that spans the Asón estuary, to Solares. Here, just after the pink house with a Sala de Fiestas neon sign, the road divides. Take the N635 turnoff to Santander and follow the signs to the city center.

CHECKING IN

El Ancla An ideal place for families who want to spend time on Laredo's crowded beaches, this 25-room hostelry has a pleasant garden and offers excellent service. Although close to the beach, it is in the only residential zone away from tall concrete blocks. 10 Calle González Gallego, Laredo (phone: 42-605500; fax: 42-611602). Moderate.

EATING OUT

Risco Famed for its splendid sea views and traditional Cantabrian cooking, including perfect *pimientos rellenos de cangrejo* (peppers stuffed with crab) and a great selection of Cantabrian cheeses. Closed Mondays. Reservations advised. American Express, Diners Club, and Visa accepted. 2 Calle la Arenosa, Laredo (phone: 42-605030). Moderate.

SANTANDER A kind of staid San Sebastián, Santander has tried without real success since the early 1900s to rival the Basque resort. Although it was the royal summer residence from 1913 to 1930, the town (pop. 185,000) never quite knocked San Sebastián off the throne as the queen of northern Spanish resorts, perhaps due to its greater distance from France, to the fact that its beach and bay are not quite as stunning as La Concha, or to the terrible fire that destroyed much of it in 1941. The fire left the town essentially modern and dull — albeit with a large number of gardens (by Spanish city standards), as well as some very pleasant beaches.

The first surprise, for those entering the city from the east, is the bronze statue of Francisco Franco on horseback in the aptly named Plaza del Generalísimo, opposite City Hall. Activity in the city center revolves around the porticoed Plaza Porticada, or Plaza de Velarde, where the tourist office (phone: 42-310708) is found. One block toward the bay from the plaza is the very unattractive cathedral, largely rebuilt after the 1941 fire. It does, however, contain a beautiful high altar and the tiny 13th-century Crypt of Christ, the city's oldest monument

The Paseo de Pereda, which begins at the seaward end of the Plaza Porticada, is a broad, elegant promenade with palm trees and the huge, red arum flowers that dot the city. Notice the *Palacete del Embarcadero,* a small art gallery (admission charge), and the dock from which the only ferry between Spain and Great Britain sails (twice a week, Santander to Plymouth, *Brittany Ferries;* phone: 42-214500 or 42-214272). Farther along, past lines of 5-story glass-balconied houses that escaped the 1941 fire, is Puerto Chico, where dockland Santander ends (the town was a booming port from the 12th to the 16th centuries) and pleasure Santander begins. The first building here is the *Royal Maritime Club,* which rises out of the sea on concrete columns in the shape of a ship's upper decks. Beyond it, the road turns away from the sea for a while, then steps lead down to the first great local beach, the Magdalena. Clean and placid, it has a 100-foot backdrop of cliffs and trees (the ivy-covered structure above belongs to the Royal Tennis Society). At the end of the beach and up the hill is the English-style Magdalena Palace, a gift from the town to Alfonso XIII, which was turned into the International Menéndez Pelayo University after the king abdicated in 1931.

On the other side of the Magdalena promontory is the mile-long El Sardinero beach, dominated by the lavish 1914 Belle Epoque *Gran Casino* at Plaza Italia. One of only two casinos on the coast (the other is at San Sebastián), it is open from 7 PM to 4 AM (5 AM on weekends). Across the bay are the villages of Pedreña and Somo, both with huge, sand-duned beaches. Pedreña is the birthplace of golf pro Severiano Ballesteros and home to the golf course where he developed his skills, the *Royal Pedreña Golf Club* (phone: 42-500266).

Santander's beauty lies in its beaches, gardens, and promenades and, therefore, in bad weather, there's little to do here. There are two museums: the *Fine Arts Museum* (6 Calle Rubio; phone: 42-239485), which can claim a Goya, and the *Museum of Prehistory* (4 Casimiro Sainz; phone: 42-215050), which has important collections from the Upper Paleolithic period. The best restaurants are located along Calle Hernán Cortés, in the vicinity of Puerto Chico, but for an inexpensive meal and an authentic experience, go to the Barrio Pesquero (Fishing Quarter) — where the Santander working class eats — and choose any one of several fish restaurants with their huge dining rooms, simple decor, and unfussy, yet friendly, service.

The annual *International Festival of Dance and Music,* one of Spain's most prestigious, is held in Santander each August at the *Palace of Festivals*, a large, multi-purpose indoor arena near the center of town.

CHECKING IN

Real Opened in 1917 during Santander's heyday, when Alfonso XIII spent his summers in the city, this 124-room luxurious hostelry, set amid terraces and gardens, retains its early–20th-century architecture and atmosphere. There is also a restuarant on the premises. 28 Paseo de Pérez Galdós, Santander (phone: 42-272550; fax: 42-274573). Expensive.

Santemar A large, modern, and functional building next door to the *Gran Casino* and 50 yards from El Sardinero Beach, this 350-room hotel boasts conference rooms, a restaurant, a tennis court, a disco, and a cocktail lounge. 28 Calle Joaquín Costa, Santander (phone: 42-272900; fax: 42-278604). Expensive to moderate.

Central This bright blue, newly redecorated 40-room hotel, complete with a restaurant and a bar, is smack in the middle of town. 5 General Mola, Santander (phone: 42-222400; fax: 42-363829). Moderate.

EATING OUT

Bar del Puerto Not just a bar, nor a fishermen's tavern as it once was, but a restaurant of great renown, especially for its seafood. The upstairs dining room overlooks Puerto Chico. Open daily. Reservations necessary. Major credit cards accepted. 63 Calle Hernán Cortés, Santander (phone: 42-213001). Expensive.

Zacarías Featuring such specialties as *jibiones de huerta* (small peppers stuffed with shellfish) and *maganos encebollados* (squid fried in onions). Open daily. Reservations advised. Major credit cards accepted. 38 Calle Hernán Cortés, Santander (phone: 42-210688). Moderate.

Los Peñucos One of many excellent homespun fish restaurants in the Barrio Pesquero. Noisy, friendly, and full of locals. Try the *marmita* (tuna stew) and *besugo al horno* (baked sea bream). Open daily. No reservations. No credit cards accepted. 2 Calle Mocejón, Santander (phone: 42-229445). Inexpensive.

En Route from Santander Santillana del Mar and the Altamira Caves are 19 miles (31 km) to the west. Take N611 out of Santander, through the villages of Peña Castillo and Igollo and into the gently undulating country-side. Eight miles (13 km) down the road is Puente Arce, where a Roman bridge spans the creek-size Pas River. It's another 8 miles (13 km) to the C6316 turnoff for Santillana del Mar.

EATING OUT

El Molino Delightfully situated in gardens beside a creek, with an ancient coat of arms above the entrance, and two low wood-beamed dining rooms. The restaurant, set in a converted 17th-century farmhouse, was made famous by the late, award-winning chef Victor Merino, and is now in the capable hands of his son, Antonio. Try the Cantabrian fish and clam salad or the sea bream stew with thyme. Closed Mondays and Sunday evenings. Reservations advised. Visa, American Express, and Diners Club accepted. Carretera N611, Km 12, Puente Arce (phone: 42-574052). Moderate.

SANTILLANA DEL MAR/ALTAMIRA CAVES Santillana del Mar, which despite its name is nearly 3 miles (5 km) from the sea, is a unique collection of perfectly preserved medieval mansions and palaces strung out along two streets. Jean-Paul Sartre described it as "the prettiest village in Spain." The town's name is derived from Sancta Iuliana (St. Juliana), the name of a 3rd-century martyr whose remains were said to have been brought here during the 8th century by monks.

The spirit of Cantabria laces this delightful 6-block town. The imposing Romanesque houses and mansions lining the dark, ironstone streets are a chunk of the Middle Ages lifted into the 20th century. The village, with a population just short of 4,000, is a rural community that does not rely solely on tourism to survive. The locals sell cheese, sponge cake, and fresh milk from their stable doors, and despite the dozens of tourist buses that pour in every day, a medieval air pervades the town. The original monastery is now the 12th-century Collegiate Church of St. Juliana, with a wonderful façade and high altar complemented by sculptures and carvings added through the centuries. At the other end of the main street is the *Diocesan Museum,* formerly the 16th-century Convent of Regina Coeli, which houses an exceptional collection of painted wooden saints and other religious figures. There are several 16th- to 18th-century mansions to admire, each boasting an impressive coat of arms. Even the relatively humble rural homes, with their solid walls, eaves, balconies, and elegant doorways, are a joy to wander past. One-half mile (1 km) south of the village is a zoo, which is open year-round. In addition to the usual animals, there are some European bison, descendants of those depicted in the Altamira Cave paintings.

Often described as the Sistine Chapel of Prehistoric Art, the Altamira Caves — Cuevas de Altamira — contain the best Upper Paleolithic cave paintings in Europe. They are only a short walk southwest of Santillana, along a well-marked road, tucked beneath the soft green cow pastures that roll down to the cloudy Cantabrian beaches. Discovered by a hunter in 1879, the paintings, which were created from 15,000 to 9500 BC, consist of running, hunted, wounded bison, bulls, boars, and horses etched in red or yellow ocher and delineated in black. They range from 4 to 8 feet high and cover the walls and ceilings. Although in perfect condition when they were discovered, they have suffered serious deterioration — caused mainly by moisture from the breath of thousands of visitors during recent decades.

Unfortunately, it is now extremely difficult to get permission to enter the caves; only those with legitimate academic interests are permitted, although there may be exceptions. No more than about 20 people a day may take the 20-minute guided tour, and all tour requests must be made in writing at least 6 sometimes 12 months in advance, specifying group size and a range of possible dates for a visit. Send requests to: *Director, Centro de Investigación de Altamira,* Santillana del Mar, Cantabria 39330 (phone: 42-818005).

If you can't get permission to see the paintings, you can view the 'hombre de Morin,' a human fossil, located near the caves, and the museum, which contains some prehistoric remains, photographs of the caves, and information about prehistoric times. The museum next to the caves is open Tuesdays through Saturdays from 9:30 AM to 2:30 PM and from 4 to 8 PM; Sundays from 10 AM to 1 PM. Admission charge. For information on the other sights of Santillana, visit the tourist office in the town's main square (Plaza de Ramón Pelayo; phone: 42-818251).

CHECKING IN/EATING OUT

Parador Gil Blas One of Spain's most exciting *paradores,* this graceful 17th-century converted mansion offers 56 rooms and a fine restaurant. For additional details see also *Paradores,* in DIVERSIONS 11 Plaza de Ramón Pelayo, Santillana del Mar (phone: 42-818000; in the US, 212-686-9213; fax: 42-818391). Expensive.

Hotel Altamira There are 30 comfortable rooms in this charming 17th-century mansion, as well as a garden and a good restaurant. 1 Calle Cantón, Santillana del Mar (phone: 42-818025; fax: 42-840136). Inexpensive.

En Route from Santillana del Mar/Altamira Caves Continue west on C6316 to Comillas, 11 miles (18 km) away. The drive is a beautiful one past unspoiled villages, green meadows, the occasional Romanesque church, and the first sight of the hills that roll away toward the Picos de Europa. Comillas is a curious town, fascinatingly gloomy and leafy, with a lopsided town square that hosts a daily outdoor market. The town is dominated by three buildings designed by Barcelona architects in the late 19th century. The huge neo-Gothic Pontifical University, the work of Lluís Domènech i Montaner (who designed Barcelona's Palau de la Música Catalana), can be seen high up on a hill from any spot in the village. The private modernist-style palace of the Marqués de Comillas, designed by Juan Martorell, is on another hill nearer the village's two fine beaches. But the jewel of the trio is *El Capricho* (The Whim), on a still lower slope, the only building in Cantabria designed by the inimitable Antoni Gaudí. Built between 1883 and 1885, *El Capricho* is actually a Moorish-style optical illusion, a bizarre villa whose huge cylindrical tower, topped by a dome half-suspended in the air and supported by squat columns, makes the building look smaller than it is. Closed for some 20 years, it has been restored and converted into a luxury restaurant (see *Eating Out* below). A nice touch: A bell rings when any window is opened.

Leaving Comillas, follow the signposts 5 miles (8 km) to La Revilla, where C6316 rejoins N634. Two miles (3 km) on, across the La Maza bridge, which has been modernized since it first spanned the broad estuary during the 15th century, is San Vicente de la Barquera; its 13th-century Church of Santa María is a national monument because it is a perfect amalgam of Romanesque and Gothic architectural styles. Six miles (10 km) farther is Unquera, marking the end of Cantabria and the beginning of the Principality of Asturias. Unquera is a good place to stop and sample *corbatas,* a local puff pastry and almond sweet, and a good starting point for a drive into the Picos de Europa — N621 leads through spectacular scenery alongside the Deva River to the town of Potes, 24 miles (39 km) inland. Alternatively, stay on N634 through Unquera and drive 12 miles (19 km) to La Arquera and the AS263 turnoff to the beach resort of Llanes, the first sizable town in Asturias.

EATING OUT

El Capricho de Gaudí This modernist folly has been restored and put into service as a deluxe restaurant specializing in Basque and international cooking. There is a bar lounge on the top floor open only for private parties and a gift shop on the main floor. Open daily. Reservations advised. American Express, Diners Club, and Visa accepted. Barrio de Sobrellano, Comillas (phone: 42-720365). Expensive.

Fonda Colasa A favorite, humble eating house of the old style — it's been in the same family since 1890. Down-home, hearty fare is served in abundant portions; the meat stews and fish are excellent, and all the desserts are made on the premises. Closed October through April. No reservations. No credit cards accepted. 9 Calle Antonio López, Comillas (phone: 42-720001). Inexpensive.

LLANES The capital of eastern Asturias, Llanes is often written off as dull. In fact, the town has a delightful Old Quarter, much of which is being restored; the gentle feel of a typical Asturian fishing port; and about 30 remote and very clean beaches, including Poo, Celorio, and Barros, within a few miles to either side (ask for directions at the tourist office; 1 Calle Nemesio Sobrino; phone: 85-400164). In the past decade or so, Llanes has become the preferred vacation spot for several Spanish government ministers. The town is also famous for its August 16 *Fiesta de San Roque,* a day-long binge of folkloric dancing in traditional costumes. Llanes spreads upward from the tiny sheltered harbor at the foot of picturesque green hills and still retains chunks of its 13th-century ramparts. One segment girds the beer garden of the *El Antiguo* restaurant in Posada Herrera — a wonderful setting in which to enjoy a cold drink on a warm afternoon. Llanes is yet another coastal town with a magnificent church dedicated to Santa María, this one part 14th- and part 15th-century, part Romanesque and part Gothic. It also has a selection of interesting 15th- to 17th-century mansions, boasting their heraldic coats of arms.

CHECKING IN

Don Paco Fairly atmospheric, it has 42 rooms within the walls of a 17th-century palace adjacent to the old ramparts, with a lovely view of the harbor. Closed October through May. Parque de Posada Herrera, Llanes (phone: 85-400150; fax: 85-402681). Moderate to inexpensive.

EATING OUT

La Bolera This small upstairs dining room overlooks the quayside; the food is simple but of the highest quality. Seafood predominates — try *colas de langosta* (lobster tails) or *salmón a la ribereña* (local riverside salmon). Closed Wednesdays in winter. Reservations advised. American Express, MasterCard, and Visa accepted. El Muella, Llanes (phone: 85-401336). Moderate.

En Route from Llanes For a scenic drive to Ribadesella, take AS263 to Celorio for 3 miles (5 km) past dramatic mist-shrouded mountains to N634 to Llovio; just past the town, take the turnoff, then take N632; Ribadesella is just after the turnoff.

RIBADESELLA A good base for Picos de Europa excursions, Ribadesella offers a magnificent beach, great hotels, rustic eateries, a fabulous cave with prehistoric paintings, and *sidrerías* (Asturian cider bars). It is also home to the world's premier canoe festival, the *International Descent of the Sella River,* held annually since 1930 on the first Saturday of August. It attracts 800 participants from many countries and over 200,000 festive spectators, who join in all-night revelry after following the canoeists 11 miles down the river from Arriondas. However, the whole town shuts down during the winter months.

The town straddles the broad Sella estuary, crossed by a long, narrow bridge that is actually the N632 highway, from which the locals can be seen fishing for bass, sargo, and red mullet. The "port" side of town brims with bars, restaurants, and shops. The other side is residential, but includes the beach, flanked by two headlands, and the best promenade hotels and mansions, glorious with their creeping purple bougainvillea. At the beach end of the bridge is an odd-looking tourist office (phone: 85-860038; closed in winter), occupying a converted *hórreo,* one of the ancient granaries that dot the Asturian countryside.

A few hundred yards from the tourist office is the Cave of Tito Bustillo, named for the man who discovered it in 1968. Inside are 15,000- to 20,000-year-old cave paintings that have been pronounced the equal of those at Altamira and France's Lascaux. A vaulted niche in one gallery has shield-shaped red marks, believed to represent female vulva in an invocation to fertility. In another gallery are a large red horse, deer, reindeer, and a purple and black horse, many over 6 feet tall. A maximum of 400 visitors per day is permitted, so it's best to go in the morning. Open from 10 AM to 1 PM and from 3:30 to 5:15 PM, April 1 through September 30 (closed Mondays in April, May, June, and September; Sundays in July and August). Admission charge, except on Tuesdays.

Ribadesella is also a good place from which to ride on the *FEVE* railway. Take this classic rural train, which offers good glimpses of the sea, four stops east to the hamlet of Villahormes, and walk a mile past cornfields and a tiny chapel to the deserted beach. A half-hour stroll along AS263 and you'll find the station, at Nueva, from which to catch the train back to Ribadesella. Another pleasant excursion is to drive west of Ribadesella along N632 about 14 miles (22 km) to Colunga. Turn down AS256 and drive 2 miles (3 km) to the delightful fishing village of Lastres, whose steep, cobbled streets rise dizzyingly above the old harbor. A final treat before leaving Ribadesella is a taste of the local cider. In any of the quayside *sidrerías,* the waiter will pour the first glass from a bottle raised as high as the right arm can reach, while the left hand holds the glass low at an acute angle so the fine spray splashes on the inside of the glass — "aerating" the drink.

CHECKING IN

Gran Hotel del Sella The view from this hotel is an open panorama of the town's beautiful surroundings. All 82 rooms have private baths. Facilities include a restaurant, a swimming pool, and a tennis court. Closed mid-October through March. Calle La Playa, Ribadesella (phone: 85-860150; fax: 85-857449). Expensive.

Ribadesella Playa A simple but very comfortable 17-room mansion overlooking the beach. The murmur of breakers lulls guests to sleep. Closed *Christmas.*

The restaurant that is on the premises is open only between March and October. 34 Calle la Playa, Ribadesella (phone: 85-860715; fax: 85-860220). Moderate.

EATING OUT

Bohemia This eating house oozes atmosphere and specializes in traditional Asturian fare. Try the *ensalada templada de bocartes y langostinos* (warm salad with barnacles and prawns), *pixín relleno de centollo* (local white fish stuffed with spider crab), *entrecot al cabrales* (entrecôte with cabrales blue cheese), and *leche frita con arándanos* (fried milk rice with bilberries). Open daily. Reservations advised. Major credit cards accepted. 53 Gran Vía, Ribadesella (phone: 85-857649). Moderate.

El Repollu Small, basic, and family-run, this place serves the finest fish in town. The house cabrales cheese is a powerful experience. Closed October. No reservations. Major credit cards accepted. 2 Calle Santa Marina, Ribadesella (phone: 85-860734). Moderate to inexpensive.

Mesón Tinín This old-style cider-tavern restaurant is down to earth and lively. Try the Asturian *fabada* (bean, sausage, and bacon stew). Closed Sundays. No reservations. Visa accepted. 20 Calle Caso de la Villa, Ribadesella (phone: 85-860839). Inexpensive.

En Route from Ribadesella Western Europe's wildest mountains, the Picos de Europa, are only 16 miles (26 km) inland, and for anyone traveling westward along the coast, Ribadesella is the last logical point from which to detour for a visit. Now is also the time to visit the national shrine of Covadonga, marking the spot where Pelayo defeated the Moors in AD 718, thus beginning the Reconquest. The shrine is set at the edge of the National Park of Covadonga, which occupies the western part of the Picos de Europa and contains 8,000-foot-high mountains surrounded by magnificent scenery. Leave Ribadesella along Oviedo-bound N634 for Arriondas, 11 miles (18 km) away, and from there take the N634 turnoff for Cangas de Onis, which was the first Christian capital of Spain and Pelayo's home after he founded the kingdom of Asturias. Cangas is beautifully positioned: Its famous ivy-covered Roman bridge over the Sella River offers some of the best salmon fishing in Spain. The Covadonga shrine is 5 miles (8 km) ahead; it consists of a small cave with the image of the Virgin Mary, the tombs of Pelayo and King Alfonso I, a large, late–19th-century pink stone basilica, and a museum. The basilica and cave are open daily year-round from 9 AM to 7:30 PM; the museum is open from 10:30 AM to 2 PM and from 4 to 7:30 PM; admission charge to the museum. Another 7 miles (11 km) beyond are the two lakes at the center of the national park.

Drive back to Arriondas, and turn west onto N634 toward Oviedo. A mile (1.6 km) after Infiesto, take AS255 to Villaviciosa, near the coast. The cider capital of Spain, Villaviciosa has a beautiful Old Quarter and is famous for its jet stone handicrafts. For a different route back to N634, follow AS113 out of town and, after about 6 miles (10 km), take the turnoff signposted to San Salvador de Valdediós, down a steep lane. The monastery here, better known as El Conventín (Little Convent), is one of a remarkable series of 8th- and 9th-century buildings in the Asturian pre-Romanesque style. The site includes a separate stone chapel deep inside a verdant valley, built during the reign of King Alfonso III (866–911), at the time when Mozarabic influences had been introduced. Note the Cross of Victory, a symbol of Pelayo's feat (the original of which is in Oviedo Cathedral), in the small twin windows of the main façade. Afterward, return up the steep, unpaved road to AS113, rejoin N634 at Pola, and drive the remaining 5 miles (8 km) to Oviedo.

EATING OUT

Pelayo Nestled in a wild setting, a step from the National Park of Covadonga, the restaurant offers typical Asturian cuisine. Reservations advised. Major credit cards accepted. Covadonga (phone: 8-584-6000). Moderate.

OVIEDO The capital of Asturias, 17½ miles (28 km) from the coast, Oviedo forms a geographic triangle with Gijón and Avilés. Driving into Oviedo, surrounded by heavy industry, can be depressing; but the city is the least grim and industrial of the three, has the most interesting Old Town, and claims genuine historical significance. Early in the 9th century, the city became the capital of the tiny kingdom of Asturias, the Christian outpost of otherwise Muslim Spain. A millennium of history, from the 8th to the 18th centuries, is represented by dozens of buildings in the Old Town, including a handful of remarkable pre-Romanesque structures whose styles were 200 years before their time. Otherwise, Oviedo (pop. 195,000) is fairly nondescript.

The Old Town spreads around the 15th- to 16th-century cathedral, which has a marvelous Gothic tower, one of Spain's best altarpieces, and a fine museum that houses, among other things, an ivory cross and reliquary said to contain a piece of the True Cross. But the real treasure is the tiny Cámara Santa (Holy Chamber), built by Alfonso II to house relics rescued from Toledo when it fell to the Moors. The chamber, which was incorporated into the later cathedral (and which was damaged by an explosion in 1934 and was rebuilt after the Civil War), contains a startling array of priceless objects, including the gold-covered oak cross carried by Pelayo in the battle of Covadonga. Open Mondays through Saturdays from 10 AM to 1 PM and from 4 to 7 PM; admission charge. Behind the cathedral is the *Provincial Archaeological Museum* (3 Calle San Vicente), one of the most important in Spain, with collections from the Paleolithic period onward (open Tuesdays through Saturdays from 10 AM to 1:30 PM and from 4 to 6 PM, Sundays from 11 AM to 1 PM; closed Mondays;

admission charge). The tourist office is in front of the cathedral at 6 Plaza de la Catedral (phone: 8-521-3385). A visit to the 9th-century church of San Julián de los Prados ("*Santullano*" to the locals) in the northeast corner of town offers a look at what's left of the murals there.

Two miles (3 km) from the city, within 250 yards of each other on Naranco Hill, are two churches that are probably the finest examples of Asturian pre-Romanesque art. Santa María del Naranco and San Miguel de Lillo were both built by Ramiro I during his short 9th-century reign, and the former in particular is regarded as exemplary. Originally built as a palace, it included baths and attached living quarters until it was converted to a church during the 12th century. A rectangular, 2-floor building, it has a complex structure of barrel vaulting with reinforced arches resting on a system of blind arches. From the upper floor, huge open windows offer wide views. Other interesting features include the intricately chiseled stonework depicting hunting scenes, the Byzantine-style capitals, and the open porticoes at both ends, a revolutionary concept at the time. San Miguel de Lillo, just up the road, is a narrow, elevated building — its height is three times the width of its central nave. Both churches are open Mondays through Saturdays from 10 AM to 1 PM and from 3 to 7 PM May to October 15; from 10 AM to 1 PM and from 3 to 5 PM October 15 through April; admission charge.

Two minutes from Oviedo's Old Town is the beautiful San Francisco Park, a huge square of gardens, trees, and fountains — a pleasant refuge from the urban sprawl, right in the city center. The third week of September is fiesta time in Oviedo, with processions, folkloric dancing, and music in honor of Latin America on the 19th of the month, and celebrations for San Mateo, the local patron saint, on the 21st.

CHECKING IN

La Reconquista A converted 17th-century orphanage, sumptuously decorated and boasting a baroque façade, it is *the* elite social center of Oviedo. All 142 rooms are air conditioned and have private baths. The bar is a former cloister; there is a good restaurant, conference and banquet rooms, and a concert hall. 16 Calle Gil de Jaz, Oviedo (phone: 8-524-1100; in the US, 800-221-2340; fax: 8-524-1166). Expensive.

Gran Hotel España Stylish yet modern, with impeccable service, this place is geared especially to the business traveler. There are 89 rooms. 2 Calle Jovellanos, Oviedo (phone and fax: 8-522-0596). Expensive to moderate.

Clarín A 47-room hostelry, it's charmless, but spotless, modern, and well located. 23 Caveda, Oviedo (phone: 8-522-7272; fax: 8-522-8018). Moderate.

EATING OUT

Casa Fermín Chef Luis Gil has developed a super Asturian cuisine, using cider, apples, and local *fabes* beans. Try the *sopa de puerros y almejas* (leek and clam soup) and *merluza a la sidra* (hake in cider). Closed Sundays except in May and September. Reservations advised. Major credit cards accepted. 8 Calle San Francisco, Oviedo (phone: 8-521-6452). Expensive.

Trascorrales A beautiful wooden building set in a delightful medieval square in the heart of the Old Town, with main, back, and private dining rooms. Try the *perdiz con lombarda y castañas* (partridge with red cabbage and chestnuts) and *crema de manzanas gratinadas* (grated apple cream). Closed Sundays and *Christmas*. Reservations necessary. Major credit cards accepted. Plaza Trascorrales, Oviedo (phone: 8-522-2441). Expensive.

La Mar del Medio A popular, fishing boat–motif restaurant, it serves superb seafood in the heart of the Old Town. Open daily. Reservations advised. Major credit cards accepted. 18 Calle Mon, Oviedo (phone: 8-522-5575). Expensive to moderate.

En Route from Oviedo Follow the A66 highway 11 miles (18 km) due north, then join A8 for the remaining 7 miles (11 km) into Gijón.

GIJÓN Asturias's largest city, Gijón (pronounced Hee-*hon*) has a population of 260,000 and manages to be an active industrial center, a busy port, and a booming summer beach resort, all while remaining relatively unattractive. The city dates back to the 13th century, but few historical traces remain. Of chief interest to visitors is the seafaring Cimadevilla district on the Santa Catalina hill, which forms a headland at the western end of the 1½-mile-long San Lorenzo Beach. The 15th-century Palacio de Revillagigedo, the *Jovellanos Museum,* the City Hall, and the remains of some Roman baths are the noteworthy structures, found at the entrance to Cimadevilla. Also here is the tourist office (1 Calle Marqués de San Esteban; phone: 8-534-6046), and an impressive statue of Pelayo. On the right bank of the River Piles is the interesting and recently refurbished *Museo de las Gaitas* (Bagpipe Museum; in the Pueblo de Asturias; phone: 8-537-3335), with a collection of bagpipes from all over the world and a workshop. It's open weekdays from 10 AM to 7 PM; admission charge. August is the big month here: The *Day of Asturias* is celebrated on the first Sunday with a procession and music, and the *Semana Grande* carnival begins on August 15. The annual *International Trade Fair,* a 2-week exposition of the latest technology, also is held in August.

CHECKING IN

Hernán Cortés Dignified and graceful, in the city center, its 109 rooms feature all the usual comforts. There is a restaurant on the premises. 5 Calle Fernández Vallín, Gijón (phone: 8-534-6000 or 8-535-5645). Expensive to moderate.

Parador Molino Viejo The only *parador* in Asturias, this is a delightful old mill, with 40 rooms and a restaurant, located in a large park close to San

Lorenzo Beach. Parque de Isabel la Católica, Gijón (phone: 8-537-0511; in the US, 212-686-9213; fax: 8-537-0233). Expensive to moderate.

EATING OUT

Casa Victor Regarded as the town's best restaurant for fish, served in tavern-style ambience. Closed Thursdays, Sunday evenings, and November. Reservations advised. Major credit cards accepted. 11 Calle Carmen, Gijón (phone: 8-535-0093; fax: 8-537-0233). Expensive to moderate.

En Route from Gijón Avilés is 15 miles (24 km) to the west. To drive through rolling green Asturian hills rather than soulless industrial suburbs and housing estates on the way, take the A8 highway instead of N362.

AVILÉS Dominated by heavy industry, Avilés is a major iron and steel producing center. The few historical landmarks it possesses are swamped by housing estates or smokestack scenarios, and the sea, only 2½ miles (4 km) away, is one of Spain's pollution blackspots. But the city does have an Old Quarter (around Galiana, La Ferrería, and Rivero Streets) with a few 12th-century churches and several medieval mansions. The Church of San Nicolás has three 14th- and 15th-century chapels, and in front of the Church of San Francisco there is an ornate 17th-century fountain. On *Easter Sunday* and *Monday,* the city celebrates the *Fiesta del Bollu,* when everybody dons folk costume to eat *Easter* buns, drink white wine, and dance to traditional music.

En Route from Avilés The western Asturian coast is thankfully undeveloped, so there are picturesque villages en route; but good hotels and restaurants are hard to find. Industrial pollution is already left behind less than 3 miles (5 km) west of Avilés, at the small town of Salinas, which has a splendid, long, horseshoe-shaped beach with a pinewood backdrop. Continue on A8, take the turnoff marked N632 to Avilés traveling toward Soto del Barco, which runs through rolling countryside and crosses the Ría de Pravia estuary. Two miles (3 km) after the estuary is a worthwhile turnoff to Cudillero, a typical Asturian fishing village whose steep cliffside is wedged around the harbor, which features picturesque bars and restaurants. Return to N632 and proceed to Soto de Luiña, a tiny village from which a narrow lane leads to the Cabo Vidio headland, with magnificent coastal views. Then N632 continues past arable farmland, away from the sea, through numerous pretty villages, and into Cadavedo, where a large creaking road sign boasts "Voted prettiest town in Asturias — 1954." Cadavedo hasn't changed much since then, and its large sandy beach appears as clean and fine as ever. Soon after Cadavedo, the N632 rejoins the N634 on the way to Luarca, 45 miles (72 km) from Avilés.

LUARCA Tucked into an S-shaped cove with a delightful bay and fishing port, unrushed and unpretentious, Luarca is a maze of cobbled streets, stone stairways, and beautiful walks. The simple, colorful flowerpots that decorate the whitewashed harbor walls are as near as the place gets to ostentation, except for the stupendously ornate cemetery, with marble burial niches and grand family tombs, which is worth some attention. It's located just before the lighthouse and Atalaya chapel, 20 minutes' walk above the town. Another excellent stroll begins by the bridge that crosses the town's small river, where a stone stairway leads up to the Ermita (Hermitage). Walk 10 minutes beyond the Hermitage and you'll come to an old village crammed with ancient *hórreos* (granaries).

Luarca has a fine beach, and it offers one of the last chances before Ribadeo to enjoy an evening of cider with the locals in a traditional Asturian tavern. Three local celebrations are worth noting. On the last Sunday in July, representatives of a nomadic tribe of Asturian shepherds, the Vaqueiros, participate in the *Vaqueirada,* wearing traditional costumes and playing unusual instruments such as the *paye tsa,* a pan with a long handle struck with an iron key. A colorful sea procession takes place on August 15, and August 22 is the *Day of San Timoteo,* Luarca's patron saint. The tourist office (Plaza Alfonso X el Sabio; phone: 85-640083) is open from June through September.

CHECKING IN

Gayoso Old and atmospheric, with wooden balconies and 52 rooms of varying quality; its restaurant, a few doors away, is very good. The hotel is now open all year, though the restaurant still closes at lunchtime during the summer months. Paseo de Gómez, Luarca (phone: 85-640054; fax: 85-470271). Moderate.

EATING OUT

Leones Three huge metal chandeliers and rural antiques and cowbells lining the walls evoke medieval images. Try *revuelto de gambas, ajo, y espinaca* (scrambled eggs with shrimp, garlic, and spinach) and *sorbete de manzana* (apple sherbet). Open daily. Reservations advised. Major credit cards accepted. El Parque, Luarca (phone: 85-640995). Moderate.

En Route from Luarca To reach N634, follow the signposts for La Coruña. Ribadeo is 30 miles (48 km) away, past undistinguished Navia and Tapia de Casariago, which has a spacious bay, a picturesque beach, and good surfing. A bridge over the Eo River leads out of Asturias and into Galicia and, a mile away (1.6 km), Ribadeo. (For a complete description of Ribadeo, see *Galicia* in DIRECTIONS). Before leaving Asturias, take a detour inland; continue on N634 to Vegadeo and turn onto the rural AS-21, into the mountains, through breathtaking scenery, to Taramundi. In this ancient town, accommodations and food are first-rate, and the local pottery, cutlery, and cheese are worth buying.

CHECKING IN

La Rectoral The regional government of Asturias has renovated an 18th-century rectory, which as a hotel now offers 12 double rooms and 5 apartments complete with kitchen, bath, and wood burning fireplaces. The first floor rooms have terraces, the others have panoramic windows. Taramundi (phone: 85-634060). Expensive to moderate.

Pilgrims' Route

The discovery of what were believed to be the remains of St. James (Santiago in Spanish) in 813 made the town of Santiago de Compostela the third most important pilgrimage site in Christendom, after Jerusalem and Rome. During the first half of the 12th century, Amerique Picaud, a French priest, wrote five volumes of stories connected with St. James, including a detailed guide for pilgrims on the journey to Santiago. This *Pilgrims' Guide* is considered to be the first travel guidebook ever written. It provided information on hospices, churches, difficult portions of the journey, meals and lodging, local customs, where good water could be found and bad water avoided, and the character of the people in each area. Though the Picaud itinerary was not the only one followed, it became known over the centuries as the primary Camino de Santiago (Way of St. James), or the Pilgrims' Route.

The pilgrims, identified by the scallop shell (the emblem of St. James) pinned to their cloaks and by their floppy felt hats, believed that completion of the long and arduous journey excused them from half of their allotted time in purgatory. They came from all over Europe, and represented a wide spectrum of languages and cultures. The Pilgrims' Route, as it developed over the centuries, provides one of the most concentrated collections of Romanesque churches and Gothic cathedrals in the world, and the art decorating these religious monuments is a brilliant merging of Moorish, French, Italian, and Spanish influences.

The main Pilgrims' Route runs some 506 miles (810 km) through Spain, crossing the French border near Roncesvalles in the region of Navarre, and passing through Pamplona, Logroño in La Rioja, and Burgos and León in the region of Castile-León, on its way to the Galician capital, Santiago de Compostela. Marked by crucifixes during medieval days, it is designated today by modern signs showing the scallop shell of St. James stylized in the form of a star. It crosses the extremes of Spanish geography and climate, beginning high in the Pyrenees, then dropping into the fertile foothills and crossing the wide open, dry plains, before rising again over the mountains separating León and Galicia and winding through the hilly, lush green landscape of the Spanish northwest.

Although 3,000 to 4,000 pilgrims still arrive on foot each year (those who travel on foot, horseback, or by bicycle receive 3 days' free food and lodging in Santiago), for most visitors the journey can be made more comfortable. In addition to cars and buses, two luxury trains now travel to and from Santiago. The *Al-Andulus Expreso* moves north from Andalusia in August to cover the Pilgrims' Way from Barcelona, Pamplona, and Burgos, with guided tours in English in each of these cities. The *El Transcantábrico,* somewhat less luxurious, but still splendid, covers the North Atlantic coast from Santiago to San Sebastián via El Ferrol,

Luarca, Oviedo, Covadonga, Santillana del Mar, and Santander, traversing the first and last stages by bus. Modern pilgrims still come primarily to view the massive cathedral and its shrine. Indeed, to round the last corner and come face-to-face with the cathedral's golden granite baroque face and two soaring towers is, as travel writer Jan Morris maintains, "one of the great moments of travel."

A room for two in a hotel listed below as expensive will cost $80 and up; in a hotel described as moderate, between $60 and $80; and in an inexpensive place, $50 or less. A meal for two will run $65 or more in an expensive restaurant, $40 to $65 in the moderate range (the majority of the restaurants), and under $40 in an inexpensive place (also plentiful). The telephone numbers listed below include local area codes; when dialing from another area in Spain, dial "9" first.

RONCESVALLES The valley and pass through the Pyrenees here enjoy a certain historical renown because of the *Song of Roland,* an epic poem that romanticized the defeat of Charlemagne's rear guard during its retreat from Spain in 778. Later, the pass became the prime conduit for travelers along the Pilgrims' Route as it entered Spain from France, and in the 12th century King Sancho VII of Navarre (Sancho el Fuerte, the Strong) added an Augustinian monastery to the hospital that had been built to serve pilgrims on the Spanish side of the pass. Legend has it that a monk constantly rang a bell to guide pilgrims through the pass. Still in use, the monastery buildings are open to the public. A cloister leads to the entrance of the Colegiata Real (Royal Collegiate Church), one of the first Gothic churches built in Spain, consecrated in 1219, with a nave and two aisles that are beautiful examples of the Romanesque-to-Gothic transition. The church houses the famous *Madonna de Roncesvalles,* a 13th-century cedar figure of the Virgin Mary, clad in silver and adorned with jewels. Also off the cloister is the chapter house, containing the tombs of the monastery's founder, King Sancho, and his wife, Doña Clemencia, and a massive stained glass window depicting the king's victories. The monastery is open daily from 8:30 AM to 7 PM, depending on when masses are scheduled. An adjoining monastery building houses the small *Roncesvalles Museum,* with artifacts from the Camino de Santiago or related to it, including letters pilgrims wrote to people back home. The museum is open daily from 11 AM to 1:30 PM and from 4 to 6 PM in June through September (in winter it opens on Saturdays and Sundays for groups only); admission charge.

Down a road from the monastery is the Chapel of Sancti Spiritus, the oldest building in Roncesvalles, dating from the early 12th century.

CHECKING IN/EATING OUT

La Posada A small, quaint, 22-room hotel, beautiful and quiet, it is just steps away from the monastery. The restaurant offers high-quality fare. Closed November. Visa accepted. Roncesvalles (phone: 48-760225). Moderate.

En Route from Roncesvalles Take C135 south about 2 miles (3 km) to Burguete, a picturesque Basque town, where Ernest Hemingway stayed and went trout fishing. The town has the small Romanesque Church of San Nicolás, and a number of charming hotels and restaurants. Continuing southwest, stay on C135 as it winds along the Arga River to Pamplona. The sights from the road, as it passes over hills and around sharp bends, are spectacular. Ahead are the walls of Pamplona, 29½ miles (47 km) from Roncesvalles; its cathedral and fortifications resemble a glowing postcard photo when approached at sunset.

CHECKING IN

Burguete A *hostal* of 22 rooms with bath, across from the ancient church. If you arrive on a day when trout are plentiful in the stream, you're in for a treat in the dining room. Closed December through February. 51 Calle Unica, Burguete (phone: 48-760005). Inexpensive.

Loizu This 27-room *hostal* with private baths is kept spotless by the owner, who rules over the establishment with an iron hand. Closed December through mid-March. 3 Calle Unica, Burguete (phone: 48-760008). Inexpensive.

EATING OUT

Marichu A grill restaurant serving mainly meat dishes. Open daily June through September and during the *Easter* season; open weekends only the rest of the year. Closed January and February. No reservations or credit cards accepted. 2 Calle Roncesvalles, Burguete (phone: 48-760086). Inexpensive.

Txiki Polit The area's most picturesque eatery. Dine in either the small, elegant, wood-paneled room with the giant wooden chandelier, or in the long, traditional Basque dining room in the rear. Specialties include mountain trout with smoked ham, and *jarreta de cordero* (hock of lamb in onion sauce). Open daily except Mondays from July through mid-September; open only Saturdays and Sundays the rest of the year. Reservations advised. Visa and MasterCard accepted. 42 Calle Unica, Burguete (phone: 48-760019). Inexpensive.

PAMPLONA For a detailed report on the city, its sights, hotels, and restaurants, see *Pamplona* in THE CITIES.

En Route from Pamplona Follow N111 southwest for 27 miles (43 km) to Estella. Along the way, the topography changes from relatively mountainous terrain to a rolling plateau that gradually declines in altitude as it nears the central Spanish plains. For the most part, the road runs parallel to the original Camino de Santiago, passing through wide open fields that erupt into brilliant carpets of sunflowers in the summer. Ruins of old pilgrim hospitals can be found in the town of Cizur Menor, just outside Pamplona, and a stretch of the original route has been preserved in the small village of Zarquiegui. Both are obscure and hard to find, however, even with residents' directions. The first monument of note concerning the pilgrims' progress is the bronze statue of a pilgrim just outside the town of Puente la Reina, 15 miles (24 km) from Pamplona. The statue depicts a pilgrim in the traditional flowing cape and wide-brimmed hat, carrying a staff and a gourd for water — an image that is seen repeatedly along the route, particularly in statues of St. James dressed as a pilgrim.

It was in Puente la Reina that a less-traveled pilgrims' road — one that came from Arles, France, and crossed the Pyrenees via the Somfort Pass — joined the main route, which originated in Paris and descended via Vézelay and Le Puy to the Pyrenees and crossed into Spain via the Roncesvalles Pass. The two trails most likely joined here to take advantage of the bridge that gave the town its name, built across the Arga River in the 11th century. The bridge, with its six arches and peaked central span, stands as strong as ever, one of the best examples of medieval engineering still in existence. The Church of the Crucifix, a 12th-century Romanesque church that was part of a pilgrims' hospice, was rebuilt in the 15th century and is famous for a Y-shaped crucifix carved with an expressionistic Christ, which is believed to have been brought from Germany by a 14th-century pilgrim.

Continue along N111 to the next significant town, Cirauqui, which clings to the top of a hill overlooking the Salado River and is noted for the San Román church, with an excellent portal. The roads leading to town and the streets in town are very steep. In medieval days, the outskirts of Cirauqui were considered a danger spot for pilgrims; the *Pilgrims' Guide* warned of "evil doers" who would encourage pilgrims to water their horses in a nearby stream with bad water. When the horses became ill, the schemers drove off the pilgrims and skinned their steeds.

Back on N111, Estella, 12 miles (19 km) from Puente la Reina, becomes visible after a few more bends in the road.

CHECKING IN

Mesón del Peregrino Located at the junction of the two pilgrims' routes, the 15 rooms here all have private baths. There is a swimming pool, and the restaurant receives rave reviews for its substantial meals. Try the *pastel de bacalao* (salt cod pie). Hotel closed December; restaurant closed Sunday evenings and Mondays. American Express and Visa accepted. Carretera Pamplona–Logroño (N111), Km 23, Puente la Reina (phone: 48-340075; fax: 48-341090). Inexpensive.

EATING OUT

Fonda Restaurante Lorca This small, family-run eatery is in the center of Cirauqui, where its upstairs dining room overlooks the town square. The menu is a simple one, featuring chicken and veal entrées. There are some small rooms, but they are recommended only in an emergency. No reservations or credit cards accepted. 54 Calle Mayor, Cirauqui (no phone). Inexpensive.

ESTELLA Once the seat of the Kings of Navarre, this major stopping point on the Pilgrims' Route is packed with churches. The Church of San Pedro de la Rúa (St. Peter of the Way) dominates the entire town. Built during the 12th century, it is Estella's oldest church. It has a massive portal, and its interior features a mixture of Romanesque and Gothic influences. But its real gem is the small cloister tucked between the church and the towering cliff; its two remaining rows of columns are topped by some of the most intricately carved capitals in Europe, some depicting the life of Christ, but others portraying mythological subjects, with scenes of couples kissing — virtually unheard of in Catholic settings.

The exteriors of Estella's other churches are generally more impressive than their interiors. Santo Sepulcro (Holy Sepulcher) church, also in a transitional Romanesque-Gothic style, boasts a elaborately carved Gothic portal. The Church of San Miguel's portal also features magnificent carvings. The Estella Tourist Office (phone: 48-554011) is in the 12th-century Palacio de los Reyes de Navarra (Palace of the Kings of Navarre), one of the oldest secular buildings in Spain, located directly across from the monumental staircase that rises up to San Pedro.

CHECKING IN

Irache Estella's only *hostal* is modern, with 74 clean rooms and private baths. The restaurant is uninspiring and closed Sunday evenings, but there are plenty of good dining spots nearby. Carretera Pamplona–Logroño (N111), Km 43, Estella (phone: 48-551150; fax: 48-554754). Moderate.

EATING OUT

La Cepa An elegant establishment with a classic wood-carved bar overlooking the main square, serving classic Navarre regional cuisine. The wine list offers extensive selections from the Rioja and Navarre regions. Closed Mondays and 2 weeks in February. Reservations advised. Major credit cards accepted. 19 Plaza de los Fueros, Estella (phone: 48-550032). Expensive to moderate.

Maracaibo Across the square from *La Cepa,* it serves excellent regional specialties. Closed Tuesdays and during the first 2 weeks of October. Reservations advised. Major credit cards accepted. 22 Plaza de los Fueros, Estella (phone: 48-550483). Expensive to moderate.

En Route from Estella The Monastery of Irache, just 2 miles (3 km) south of Estella along N111, was built in the 12th and 13th centuries and is a particularly beautiful example of the transitional Romanesque-to-Gothic style (open Tuesday mornings and Wednesdays through Fridays from 10 AM to 2 PM and from 5 to 7 PM, Saturdays and Sundays from 9 AM to 2 PM and from 4 to 7 PM; admission charge). Continue southwest on N111 to the town of Los Arcos, 13 miles (21 km) from Estella, where the Iglesia Parroquial de la Asunción (Church of the Assumption) in Plaza Mayor offers a perfect example of baroque excesses. Virtually every inch of the interior walls and domes is covered with gilted decoration. Continuing another 4½ miles (7 km), N111 leads to Torres del Río, a town that is beautifully perched on a hillside dropping down to the river. Founded by the Knights of the Holy Sepulcher, it has an interesting octagonal church with a Moorish decor, including Mudéjar art in the vaulting of the main dome. The route continues another 13 miles (21 km) to Logroño, the only major town in the region of La Rioja.

LOGROÑO This is the capital of one of Spain's main wine producing regions. Rioja wines have long been considered among the best in Europe. The Rioja region also grows over 90% of Spain's asparagus. The modern town of Logroño is uninteresting, but the small Old Town at its core holds several religious treasures associated with the Pilgrims' Route. Everything is within easy walking distance of the massive main square. The Rúa Vieja and Calle Mayor, the two main arteries of the Old Town, have been traced by countless pilgrims over the centuries. The 15th-century Cathedral of Santa María la Redonda is austerely Gothic, set off by twin baroque towers and a baroque façade added in 1742. The Church of Santa María del Palacio, built on the site of the palace of the Kings of Castile, is famous for its eight-sided, pyramid-shaped steeple, constructed during the 13th century (the rest of the church was built in the 16th to 18th centuries). The portal of the smaller Church of St. Bartholomew, seemingly designed for a grand cathedral, is a fine example of Gothic sculpture; it depicts the life of the saint.

CHECKING IN

Murrieta There are more modern and more luxurious hotels elsewhere, but this 113-room hostelry is a good choice for older elegance. Located in the center of town, with a restaurant on the premises, it's only steps away from the *tapas* bars and monuments of the Old Town. 1 Calle Marqués de Murrieta, Logroño (phone: 41-224150; fax: 41-223213). Moderate.

La Numantina Near the main square in the Old Town, this *hostal* offers 17 clean rooms. Closed from *Christmas* through *Epiphany* (January 6). 4 Calle Sagasta, Logroño (phone: 41-251411). Moderate to inexpensive.

EATING OUT

La Chata This place serves Logroño's best roast baby goat and baby lamb. Closed Sunday evenings and Mondays, the first half of July, and 2 weeks in January. Reservations advised. Major credit cards accepted. 3 Calle Carnicerías, Logroño (phone: 41-251296). Moderate.

Mesón Charro The best *chuletas de cordero a la brasa* (lamb chops) in town are found here, in an informal, picnic-table setting. Open daily. Reservations advised. No credit cards accepted. 12 Calle Laurel, Logroño (phone: 41-224663). Moderate.

En Route from Logroño Take N232 out of Logroño to N120. From here, the road is very well marked as the Camino de Santiago; the landscape becomes drier, the fertile green of Navarre changing to a dusty brown. Follow N120 west toward Burgos, 70½ miles (113 km) from Logroño. Along the way, three small towns of the Rioja region offer important pilgrim sights. The first is Navarrete, a small town with a large 16th-century church. The next is Nájera, which was at one time the capital of the kingdom of Navarre and which became a main stop on the route when a large bridge was built over the Najerilla River. Nájera is the site of the Monastery of Santa María la Real, which was founded by a Navarrese king in the 11th century. Its 15th-century church is notable as a pantheon of 11th- and 12th-century royalty (the 12th-century tomb of Blanca de Navarra is outstanding), and for the particularly intricate Flamboyant Gothic carving of the choir stalls, completed around 1500; the cloister is also a fine example of Flamboyant Gothic design. The monastery and church are open daily except Mondays from 9:30 AM to 12:30 PM and from 4 to 7:30 PM in June through September; from 10 AM to noon and 4 to 7 PM in the winter; no admission charge.

Continue to Santo Domingo de la Calzada, the third significant town between Logroño and Burgos, and one of the major stops on the Pilgrims' Route during the 11th and 12th centuries. The town was named for an 11th-century monk who spent his life helping pilgrims. The Romanesque cathedral and bridge in town probably predate the 12th century. After this stop, continue west on N120 into the region of Castile-León, driving the remaining 42½ miles (68 km) to Burgos, capital of the province of the same name.

CHECKING IN/EATING OUT

Parador Santo Domingo de la Calzada This beautiful *parador,* situated in an old pilgrims' hostel that dates back to the 11th century, just underwent an extensive restoration. All 60 rooms have private baths and there's a restaurant on the premises. There are often concerts at the small church next door. 3 Plaza del Santo, Santo Domingo de la Calzada (phone: 41-340300; in the US, 212-686-9213; fax: 41-340325). Moderate.

BURGOS For a detailed report on the city, its sights, hotels, and restaurants, see *Burgos* in THE CITIES.)

En Route from Burgos Follow N120 westward for 19 miles (30 km) to the town of Olmillos de Sasamón, recognizable by the massive castle along the highway, then turn left down the road toward Castellanos de Castro and Castrojeriz. At this point, the Pilgrims' Route temporarily stops running parallel to the national highways and becomes quite convoluted, but the signs for the Camino de Santiago are easy to follow. About a mile (1.6 km) after the left turn, make a right turn at the sign for Castellanos de Castro. The road winds through fields and between densely planted trees, and actually passes through the ruins of the Convent of San Antonio, under the Gothic arches and past the ornate portal. Soon after, the Castle of Castrojeriz appears in the distance, 11 miles (18 km) from Olmillos.

CASTROJERIZ A poor pueblo of a place, Castrojeriz has three massive churches. Santa María del Manzano, a 13th-century collegiate church, is just to the left as the Pilgrims' Route enters the village. Now a veritable art museum, it was one of the most important churches along the route until the cathedral in Burgos was completed. The church features a 16th-century stained glass window, four ornate wooden altarpieces carved by Italian craftsmen, and a polychromatic sculpture of the Virgin of the Apple Tree. The town's three other churches, San Juan, Santa Clara, and Santo Domingo, are impressive from the outside, simple inside. The parish priest or one of his assistants usually will open them for visitors daily year-round, from 10 AM to 2 PM and from 4 to 8 PM (phone: 47-377036).

En Route from Castrojeriz Heading west out of town, be prepared to share the road with herds of sheep that graze in the area. Follow the local road (marked Melgar) for 16 miles (26 km) to Frómista, an agricultural center boasting perhaps the most beautiful Romanesque church along the route. Built early in the 11th century, San Martín has three perfectly formed naves, ribbed arches, and sculpted capitals on the columns. The exterior has two round towers, small arched windows, and an octagonal cupola, all fashioned to breathtaking excellence. Open daily from 10 AM to 2 PM and 4 to 8 PM.

The narrow country roads, still well marked as the Camino de Santiago, continue for about 12 miles (20 km) to Carrión de los Condes, another important stop on the Pilgrims' Route. The Church of Santa María has crumbling carvings of the Old Men of the Apocalypse and the Three Kings. The Church of St. James, tucked just off the main town square, has a beautiful façade with statues of the Apostles and an even more impressive portal with carvings depicting men at everyday work.

At Carrión de los Condes, the Pilgrims' Route returns to N120; follow it about 27 miles (43 km) west to Sahagún. Here, the churches of San Tirso and San Lorenzo are fine examples of early Romanesque brick construction, with interiors bearing extensive Mudéjar decorations. Continue to León, a 42-mile (67-km) drive from Sahagún, reached by heading west along N120 to the N601 intersection, and then taking N601 north into the provincial capital.

LEÓN For details on León, see *Castile-León (Old Castile)* in DIRECTIONS.

En Route from León Take N120 heading west from León 18 miles (29 km) to the village of Hospital de Orbigo, where a famous bridge crosses the Orbigo River. The bridge was the site of a celebrated series of jousts by the love-struck knight Suero de Quiñones, who, to prove his valor to the object of his devotion, challenged anyone who tried to cross the bridge for 30 days. Together with nine companions whose names are inscribed on the bridge, he took on all comers, breaking over 300 lances. His fame spread throughout medieval Europe, and the bridge crossing became known as the Passage of Honor. Another 10 miles (16 km) west of Hospital de Orbigo along N120 is the town of Astorga, with its medieval city walls, an impressive cathedral, and a palace designed by Antoni Gaudí.

EATING OUT

Il Suero de Quiñones Enjoy a drink and the view on the deck overlooking the Passage of Honor, then try one of the dining room's massive mixed salads or highly recommended lamb chops. Open daily. No reservations. Visa accepted. Located directly at the end of the bridge, Hospital de Orbigo (phone: 87-388238). Inexpensive.

ASTORGA Beautifully situated on a mountain spur 2,850 feet above sea level, Astorga served as a staging point for the final third of the Pilgrims' Route to Santiago. The Romans knew the city as Asturica Augusta, and Pliny the Elder described it as "magnificent." The Cathedral of Santa María, built during the 13th century on the site of an 11th-century church, has bell towers similar to those of León's cathedral, as well as similar massive stained glass windows. Its museum houses noteworthy works of medieval religious art. The cannonballs on the staircase are remnants of the Peninsular War against Napoleon. The four-panel painting of the life of San Antonio Abab is worth a close look. The museum is open daily from 10 AM to 2 PM and from 4 to 8 PM; admission charge.

Also visit the Episcopal Palace on the Plaza de la Catedral. It's a fanciful 19th-to-20th-century mock medieval creation of soaring towers, circular staircases, and a light-filled interior. The work of Antoni Gaudí — his most imaginative, spectacular creation outside Barcelona — it was commissioned by the bishop, a fellow Catalonian, after a fire destroyed its predecessor in 1886, but wasn't finished until 1909. The first two floors now house the *Museo de los Caminos,* a museum dedicated to the Pilgrims' Route, with an extensive collection of statues, paintings, notebooks, and journals from the heyday of the pilgrimage. It's open from 10 AM to 2 PM and from 4 to 8 PM, closed Sundays; admission charge.

CHECKING IN/EATING OUT

Gaudí Astorga's top choice, with a traditional Spanish decor of light walls and dark furnishings. Most of the 35 rooms overlook the whimsical Episcopal

Palace, and the restaurant downstairs is excellent. Major credit cards accepted. 6 Plaza Eduardo de Castro, Astorga (phone: 87-615654; fax: 87-615040). Moderate.

En Route from Astorga Continue westward on N-VI, the often excellent highway that links Madrid with La Coruña. As the road begins to climb, the views on both sides clearly show how arduous this part of the pilgrimage must have been. Though the highway here doesn't exactly follow the Pilgrims' Route, the smaller C120 does, winding through the Valley of El Silencio, bordered by rugged mountains, and passing the Cross of Iron. The cross is set into a pile of stones; the tradition was that each passing pilgrim add his own stone. The mountains that line N-VI are marked by giant coal deposits, evidence of the importance of mining in this region of Spain.

After 38 miles (61 km), N-VI drops to the town of Ponferrada, where an 11th-century iron bridge carried pilgrims over the Sil River. The massive Castillo Templario (Templar Castle), overlooking the river, appears spectacular from a distance, but it is little more than a standing outer wall (open from 10 AM to 1 PM and from 4 to 7 PM; closed Sunday evenings and Mondays). Ponferrada does have an excellent example of Mozarabic architecture in the tiny 10th-century Church of Santo Tomás de las Ollas, in which a ring of horseshoe-shaped arches surrounds the altar. The church is up a side road — there's a sign just as the main road enters the town (knock on the door of the adjacent house, where the caretaker lives). Ponferrada marks the beginning of the last stretch of the Pilgrims' Route before it enters the region of Galicia. Follow N-VI 12½ miles (20 km) to the town of Villafranca del Bierzo, with its outstanding *parador*.

VILLAFRANCA DEL BIERZO The town owes its founding to French pilgrims, who used the area as a stopover during the 11th century. The medieval buildings here include manor houses that line the famous Calle del Agua, which was known to pilgrims as one of the route's most beautiful streets. The Church of St. James, a typical example of 12th-century Romanesque architecture, boasts an excellent Portal of Forgiveness opening onto the route. Exhausted pilgrims, unable to reach Santiago, could pass through it into the church and receive the same indulgences as those given in Santiago. The town's other churches — all worth a visit — include San Juan en San Fiz, a well-preserved Romanesque building; Santa María de Cluniaco, laid out in the form of a Latin cross; and San Nicolás, a 17th-century church that was part of a Jesuit college.

CHECKING IN

Parador Villafranca del Bierzo A modern, 40-room hostelry, it's at the edge of town, a short walk from most of the ancient buildings. Closed mid-December to mid-January. Av. Calvo Sotelo, Villafranca del Bierzo (phone: 87-540175; in the US, 212-686-9213; fax: 87-540010). Moderate.

EATING OUT

La Charola For centuries, pilgrims have stopped here before beginning the most difficult part of the pilgrimage. Today, it also attracts truck drivers. Order the *cocido*, the typical stewed meat platter, and a huge tureen of noodle soup will appear, followed by a platter of vegetables, one of garbanzo beans and one of stewed meat and squid with potatoes. Wash it down with a bottle of wine and *gaseosa* (soda water), and finish with some of the local firewater — *orujo* — in your coffee. Open daily. Reservations advised. Major credit cards accepted. 19 Calle Doctor Aren, Villafranca del Bierzo (phone: 87-540200). Inexpensive.

En Route from Villafranca del Bierzo Leave town via N-VI, and the valley immediately narrows. The road zigs and zags as it climbs to enter the region of Galicia through the Puerto de Pedrafita do Cebreiro, 18 miles (29 km) from Villafranca. This is the last major pass to be negotiated before Santiago, and it is at this point that the main highway and the Pilgrims' Route once again part company, as N-VI takes a more northwesterly course for Lugo and the Pilgrims' Route turns into tiny mountain roads on a more southwesterly course to Santiago. As the road skirts the ridge rising to the summit, the views to the north are breathtaking, with bright yellow flowers punctuating the green mountains that stretch as far as the eye can see.

O CEBREIRO The ancient village of O Cebreiro (in Galician — its Castilian spelling is El Cebrero), not far from the Pedrafita do Cebreiro pass as you head west on the Pilgrim's Route, has a church and a pilgrims' hospice that were constructed as early as the 9th century, as well as some old reconstructed dry stone huts of Celtic origin. The church became famous following a miracle that was reported around 1300: A priest of little faith was saying mass in the presence of a peasant who had climbed through deep snow and wind to get there. Suddenly, as the priest was musing that it was silly for anyone to brave such weather for only a bit of wine and bread, the Host turned into flesh and the wine into blood. Word of this miracle of the Holy Eucharist spread throughout Europe, and the chalice in which it is said to have occurred is still kept in the church.

CHECKING IN/EATING OUT

San Giraldo de Aurillac Simple accommodations in one of Europe's most mystical locations. The 6 rooms of this *hostal* were built into the original, centuries-old hospice. The restaurant features simple but filling fare. Try the *caldo gallego* (Galician soup), *cocido* (stew), *almejas de San Giraldo* (clams in a special house sauce), and locally produced cebreiro cheese. No credit cards accepted. O Cebreiro (phone: 82-369025). Inexpensive.

En Route from O Cebreiro The narrow Pilgrims' Route road (or C535) continues westward. After Linares, there is a wonderful view to the left of mountain after mountain, eventually fading into the mist. Low stone walls appear, the sun glistens off slate roofs, and lush ferns line the road. As cattle graze in small roadside pastures, hay wagons, tractors, ox carts, and cows share the road with cars. In the winter, the vista is of stark, windswept fields of snow punctuated by naked trees. The tiny towns along these winding roads all have pilgrims in their past, and they have inherited an architecture that is more reminiscent of Ireland than Spain. The village of Triacastela has a pilgrims' jail with interesting graffiti on its walls; farther along, after passing through narrow gorges, the road turns around the massive Monastery of Samos (phone: 82-546046), which dates back to the Middle Ages, although little of its early structure remains. The monastery has a small Gothic cloister and a larger neo-classical one, the latter with modern frescoes on its upper level. The church, built in the 18th century, is purely classical in design. Tours of the monastery take place daily, every half hour from 10:30 AM to 1 PM and from 4:30 to 7 PM; no admission charge.

After Sarria, which is 32 miles (51 km) beyond O Cebreiro, the road, C535, continues westward; about 15 miles (24 km) past Sarria, it crosses the Miño River (Portugal's Minho), which has been turned into a massive lake by a dam. The old village of Portomarín has been lost forever, covered in water, but before it was flooded, the tower-like Church of the Knights of St. John of Jerusalem was dismantled and rebuilt on a hill behind the new town of Portomarín. It still has a beautiful rose window, and the decoration of its portal, resembling the *Gate of Glory* in Santiago de Compostela, is believed to be the work of Master Mateo.

About 7½ miles (12 km) west of Portomarín, C535 joins N540/N640, the main Orense–Lugo highway. Turn north toward Lugo, but drive only 5 miles (8 km) to the turnoff for C547, which leads to Santiago. Continue about 6 miles (10 km) to the sign marking Vilar de Doñas (just off the main road), a final church of significance along the Pilgrims' Route. The church was a chapter house of the Knights of St. James and a burial place for Galician knights killed fighting the Moors. After seeing the church, return to C547 and continue to Santiago de Compostela, which is another 59 miles (94 km) west. (For a detailed report on the city, its sights, its hotels, and its restaurants, see *Santiago de Compostela* in THE CITIES.)

Catalonia and Andorra

Every year, the beaches of the Costa Brava attract millions of tourists lured by the promise of inexpensive, fun-filled vacations. Most fly to Barcelona or Gerona and head straight for the coast, unaware of the traditional Catalan life that continues in villages, on farms, and in small towns throughout the region. A few miles from the high-rise hotels of the best-known resorts are glorious rocky coves, with beautiful beaches and little fishing villages. Inland, the countryside ranges from snow-capped mountains to plains baked red by a fierce sun. The rewards for the visitor include grandiose castles and cathedrals, creepy medieval passages, a 900-year-old convent, and a surrealistic art museum.

Catalonia, which has long considered itself separate from the rest of Spain, was the site of Greek trading posts as early as 500 BC, and was a Roman province by 200 BC. Later under Visigoth, then Moorish control, it was conquered by Charlemagne in AD 801, and, with the demise of the Carolingian Empire, was encompassed by the House of Barcelona at the end of the 9th century. The first usages of "Catalunya" and "Catalan" date from the 11th century, when Barcelona was a center of shipbuilding and trade. In the 13th century, under James the Conqueror, Catalonia became a major Mediterranean force, eventually expanding into Sicily, Minorca, Athens, Sardinia, and Naples. Catalan power did not last, however. Less than 50 years after its peak, the conquest of Naples in 1423, the marriage of Queen Isabella of Castile and King Ferdinand of Aragon began the unification of Spain, and by the end of the 15th century, Catalonia had lost control of its own affairs and was excluded from the lucrative trade with the newly discovered Americas. Over the centuries, several revolts were suppressed. In the 18th century, after the War of the Spanish Succession in which Catalonia backed Archduke Charles of Austria (who had promised Catalonian independence), the victorious Philip V stringently repressed the would-be nation, banning the use of the Catalan language.

By the end of the 19th century, however, the region was thriving, thanks to the burgeoning Industrial Revolution, centered in Barcelona. By 1900, the city symbolized the resurgence of a strong and confident Catalonia when it hosted an international *Universal Exhibition*. As the arts flourished anew, so did interest in Catalan as a written language, and poems and novels wound the web of solidarity ever more tightly. At the turn of the century, Barcelona, like Paris, was a hotbed of revolutionary creativity. Pablo Picasso was here, having arrived from his native Málaga at the age of 14; he would spend almost 10 years in the Catalan capital. Architects such as Antoni Gaudí were in the vanguard, adorning new city quarters with buildings of astonishing design — the local version of Art Nouveau, called Modernisme. Later, Joan Miró, Salvador Dalí, Antoni Tàpies, and other artists came to the fore. Barcelona was even the capital of a short-lived Catalan government, set up in 1932.

Unfortunately, the potential of Catalan power posed a threat to centralist forces in Madrid, and during the Spanish Civil War Catalonia made the mistake of backing the "wrong" side. When Generalísimo Francisco Franco took power, Catalonia again was subjugated; expressions of nationalism — such as the teaching of the staccato native language — were suppressed. The only place that Catalans could gather in great numbers was at the local soccer club, *F.C. Barcelona.* Boys were (and still are) signed up at birth to become members of the club that today epitomizes the Catalan spirit, regularly attracting more than 125,000 aficionados to its games.

Following Franco's death in 1975, Catalonia became one of Spain's 17 autonomous communities, enjoying the equivalent of US statehood. At long last, Catalans had their own government. With the revival of their language, street signs were changed from Spanish to Catalan, and the red-and-yellow Catalan flag was raised above public and private buildings alike. Throughout the area, roads and public utilities were improved and ancient buildings were restored as signs of Catalan pride.

Catalan cooking is part of the resurgence of Catalan culture. Traditional recipes are being revived: rabbit with almonds, partridge with grapes, chicken with lobster, and sea bass with thyme and baked squash. Not surprisingly, the cuisine features fish, fresh from the Mediterranean. The catch may be cooked *a la planxa* (grilled) or simmered with peas, tomatoes, and peppers in a *sarsuela;* trout from Pyrenean lakes and rivers is delicious *a l'agredolç,* with vinegar and honey. Confusingly, *truita* means both trout and omelette, so look under the heading *peix* (fish) on the menu, if you want to order seafood. The most famous Catalan specialty, however, is also the simplest: *Pà amb tomàquet* is a slice of bread rubbed with raw tomato and enlivened with olive oil, salt, and pepper.

Catalonia today spans some 12,370 square miles and is divided into four provinces — Tarragona, Barcelona, Lérida (Lleida in Catalan), and Gerona (Girona in Catalan). The 703-mile (1,125-km) route outlined below begins in Barcelona and heads north for some 41 flat miles (65 km) past the Costa Brava (Wild Coast) shoreline that is the playground of Europe, with some 15 million visitors per year. High-rises and crowded beaches have thoroughly domesticated the wilderness here, and ads push British-style pubs, fish-and-chips, and even cups of tea. At Lloret de Mar, the real Costa Brava begins, and the farther north the route goes, the more nature defeats the developers. Pinkish-red rock tumbles down to lime-green water, sandy inlets and bays are shaded by dense umbrella pines and cork oaks, and fishing boats can still be found among the yachts. It is an area that has attracted artists to picture-postcard villages, such as Cadaqués, still charming despite being "discovered."

The northern limits of Catalonia today are the Pyrenees, ancient green-gray mountains that provided little to sustain villages in the past, but now offer the golden rewards of skiing. Here, the route crosses the border into the tiny principality of Andorra, with its dramatic mountains, picturesque villages, scenic landscapes, and duty-free shopping. Beyond, the agricultural hinterland beckons, locked between mountain and sea and dotted by walled towns and villages. Dark with shadows from turrets and towers, arches and cloisters, they conjure up an illusion of medieval life that is broken only by sound of a motorbike or the sight of rooftop television antennas. The principality recently voted to become an independent republic, breaking its feudal links with Spain and France. Eventually, this could mean representation at the U. N. (it would be the third smallest country), a foreign embassy, and maybe an international dialing code.

Roads vary from four-lane highways to small but well-paved country roads. Catalonia's equivalent of an interstate highway, the *autopista* (toll highway), are designated with the letter *A*. All other roads and highways are free. Along the route, a double room can cost $225 or more at a hotel listed as very expensive; $75 or more at an expensive hotel; and $40 to $70 at a moderate hotel. Expect to pay $40 or more for a meal for two with wine at restaurants categorized as expensive, $15 to $35 at a moderate restaurant, and $15 or less at an inexpensive one. The telephone numbers listed below include local area codes; when calling from another area in Spain, dial "9" first.

> **NOTE** Many place-names in Catalonia have both a Catalan and a Castilian spelling. In this chapter, where two forms exist, the first one given (usually at the first, or most conspicuous, mention of a town) is the Catalan version and the version in parentheses that follows it is Castilian.

BARCELONA For full details on sights, hotels, and restaurants, see *Barcelona* in THE CITIES.

En Route from Barcelona Take the A7 highway (a toll road) north for 60½ miles (97 km) to Girona. After the industrial suburbs of Barcelona, it's a relief to see open countryside; across the fields, small villages sit on hilltops, always with a solid ocher church, sometimes a castle as well. The Tordera River marks the boundary between the province of Barcelona and the province of Girona, and soon the provincial capital looms up on the right. Take the Girona Sur exit and follow signs through the suburbs to the Centre Ciutat (City Center).

GIRONA (GERONA) The ancient part of the city has always been attractive, and renovations have enhanced its appeal. The best views of Girona are from the ancient stone footbridges across the Onyar River, but the city's main attraction, the cathedral, is located amid the steep, narrow alleys of the Old Town and is reached by an impressive 17th-century flight of 90 steps. Dating from 1316, the cathedral is of Gothic design, with a baroque façade, and it reflects the Catalan love of honest, simple lines. Awesomely vast inside, it has the world's widest Gothic nave (75 feet wide, as well as 200 feet long and 110 feet high), plus splendid 14th-century stained glass windows high in the gray stone walls. The museum contains invaluable illuminated manuscripts, including a *Commentary on the Apocalypse* dated 975; a Bible that belonged to King Charles V of France; and the unusual 12th-century *Tapestry of the Creation.* The cathedral and museum are open daily from 10 AM to 1 PM and from 4 to 7 PM in March through June; from 10 AM to 7 PM in July through September; from 10 AM to 1 PM and 3 to 6 PM in October through December; and from 10 AM to 1 PM during January and February; admission charge to the museum (phone: 72-214426).

Another fine example of local architecture is the nearby Sant Pere de Galligants (Plaça Sant Pere), a Romanesque monastery with a 12th-century octagonal tower; the monastery houses Girona's *Museo Arqueológico* (Archaeological Museum; open Tuesdays through Saturdays from 10 AM to 1 PM and from 4:30 to 7 PM; open mornings only on Sundays and holidays; closed Mondays; admission charge; phone: 72-202632). Close by, the 12th-century Banys Arabs (Arab Baths) are an unexpected reminder that Girona was a Moorish stronghold for some 300 years.

The Call Jueu (Jewish Quarter), a haunting maze of alleys and medieval buildings, is one of the best-preserved Jewish quarters in Spain. The synagogue in the *Museu d'Isaac el Cec* hosts Sephardic song recitals on Friday evenings in summer. The building is open from 10 AM to 2 PM during the winter; from 10 AM to 7 PM June through September; admission charge (phone: 72-216761). For additional details on the museum, see *Sacred Spain* in DIVERSIONS. The nearby *Museu d'Art,* in the former bishop's palace, houses an exemplary selection of medieval and 19th- and 20th-century Catalan paintings, and a 15th-century Catalogue of Martyrs. Open Tuesdays through Saturdays from 10 AM to 6 PM; mornings only on Sundays and holidays; closed Mondays; admission charge (phone: 72-209536).

CHECKING IN

Novotel Girona Modern, air conditioned, and comfortable, this place has 81 rooms, a swimming pool, and tennis courts. Located near the airport, 7½ miles (12 km) from town, just off A17 at Exit 8. Riudellots de la Selva (phone: 72-477100; in the US, 800-221-4542; fax: 72-477296). Expensive.

EATING OUT

La Roca Petita This family-run country eatery near the airport features local Catalan specialties and *canalones* stuffed with foie gras. Closed Tuesdays.

Reservations unnecessary. No credit cards accepted. Riudellots de la Selva (phone: 72-477132). Inexpensive.

En Route from Girona Follow C255 and the signs for Palamós. Pass Flaça and Corça, where signs advertising ceramics reveal the primary local industry. Continue another 2½ miles (4 km) to La Bisbal, a town well known for its pottery, where shops and factories — piled high with platters, umbrella stands, garden ornaments, hand-painted murals, and tiles — line the main street. From La Bisbal, continue on C255 about 5 miles (8 km), following signs for Begur, Palafrugell, and Palamós. Beyond the rise in the road, the Mediterranean appears to the left, dotted by islands — the Islas Medes. Turn left at the sign for Torrent, Pals, and Begur. Pals, a lovely old medieval town, is straight ahead, but follow the signs to Begur.

BEGUR (BAGUR) A small inland town surrounded by beautiful beaches and coves, Begur is at the heart of the Costa Brava. Begur has narrow streets, whitewashed houses, and, at the top, an imposing castle dating back to the 11th century and commanding wonderful views of the countryside. South of town, Aiguablava, or Blue Water, is an appropriately named *cala* (cove) and beach; neighboring Fornells rivals it; just north of town are Sa Tuna, Aiguafreda, and Sa Riera. The area is a good base for local excursions and diversions, which include taking a boat to explore the little coves, circumnavigating the Medes Islands' nature reserves by glass-bottom boat, or strolling the spectacular *Jardines Botanicos de Cap Roig* (Botanical Gardens). Many of the medieval villages inland, such as Peretallada and Ullastret, are worth a visit. The former, 900 years old, has only 500 inhabitants now, but hides behind impressive sandstone walls (its name means "cut rock"). Ullastret features an 11th-century church and a double wall, much of which has been restored.

CHECKING IN/EATING OUT

Hostal de la Gavina This sumptuous oceanfront hotel (a member of the Relais & Châteaux group) boasts a saltwater pool, 2 tennis courts, a sauna, a Jacuzzi, a gym, and proximity to the 18-hole *Club de Golf Costa Brava,* in Santa Cristina de Aro. There are 58 rooms and 16 suites — all elegantly appointed — plus a sophisticated restaurant. Closed mid-October through March. About 12 miles (30 km) southwest of Begur, in S'Agaro (phone: 72-321100; in the US, 800-677-3524; fax: 72-321573). Very expensive.

Mas de Torrent Another Relais & Châteaux property, this restored 18th century *mas* (an estate typical of southern France) offers 27 guestrooms and 5 suites. On the premises are private gardens, a restaurant, a pool, tennis, and horseback riding; there's also a golf course nearby, in Pals. About 5 miles (8 km) west of Begur. Torrent (phone: 72-303292; in the US, 800-677-3524; fax: 72-303293). Expensive.

Parador Nacional Costa Brava A low, white building, shaded by pine trees, overlooking a beautiful beach, this modern *parador* (the only one on the Costa Brava) has 87 air conditioned rooms, a bar, a restaurant, a gymnasium, a sauna, a swimming pool, and a convention hall. It's located across the bay from the *Aiguablava* hotel, about 3 miles (5 km) southeast of Begur. Platja de Aiguablava (phone: 72-622162; in the US, 212-686-9213; fax: 72-622166). Expensive.

Aiguablava Xiquet Sabater, one of the Costa Brava's great characters, has been running this charming seaside place since the late 1940s. All 86 rooms are air conditioned, with private baths, and many have a wonderful view of the sea. Facilities include a swimming pool, tennis courts, a nightclub, and 2 bars. The main dining room offers an international menu with Spanish overtones, but there is also a more intimate room serving à la carte Spanish selections. English is spoken. Major credit cards accepted. Located a bit over 2 miles (3 km) southeast of Begur. Platja de Fornells (phone: 72-622058; fax: 72-622112). Moderate.

En Route from Begur Backtrack westward in the direction of Girona and Figueres. Turn off to Pals, go through Regenços, follow signs for Pals and Figueres, then for Pals itself, 4½ miles (7 km) from Begur. Follow signs to the Recinte Gòtic.

PALS What was once a farming community is now a tourist attraction, thanks in part to restoration that has brought this 14th-century village back to life and earned it two national awards for its efforts. The village church, originally Romanesque but with some Gothic features as a result of later rebuilding, has an 18th-century façade. Climb the Torre de les Hores (Tower of the Hours) — so named because it once had a clock — in the 9th-century castle of Monteáspero, for lovely views of the coast. The Casa Pruna contains some important archaeological finds from the nearby beach, where there is also an 18-hole championship golf course at the *Club de Golf de Pals* (Platja de Pals; phone: 72-637009), and a worthy restaurant (see *Eating Out* below).

EATING OUT

Sa Punta Well known for its simple treatment of fresh seafood, an excellent wine list, and interesting desserts, it enjoys the distinction of a Michelin star. Open daily, but closed from mid-January to mid-February. Reservations advised. Major credit cards accepted. Platja de Pals, Pals (phone: 72-636410). Expensive.

En Route from Pals Continue north along the main road for 6 miles (9 km) to Toroella de Montgrí, where the square block of the 13th-century castle of Montgrí sits on a bare bump of a hill. Head 9 miles (14 km) for the coastal village of L'Escala, passing through Bellcaire d'Emporda and miles of flat fields where old men still scythe the grass by hand, and on to Empúries. A sign to the Ruines d'Empúries is off to the right.

EMPÚRIES (AMPURIAS) The archaeological site here consists of 8 acres of Greek and Roman ruins undergoing continuing excavation (which yielded a notable statue of Aesculapius, among other treasures) and reconstruction. The Greeks built the lower town during the 6th century BC, and Julius Caesar later constructed a "new" town for retired soldiers higher on the hill. It's worth the effort to climb up to the former Roman town to inspect the forum and the two houses, with courtyards and rooms paved with black-and-white mosaics (open daily from 10 AM to 2 PM and 3 to 7 PM in June through September; 10 AM to 1 PM and 3 to 5 PM in October through May; admission charge; phone: 72-770208).

CHECKING IN/EATING OUT

Nieves-Mar An old but comfortable family-run establishment of 80 rooms just south of Empúries. The beachfront location offers ideal views across the Golf de Roses (Bay of Roses); a swimming pool and tennis courts are on the premises. The restaurant offers a variety of fresh fish, simply prepared, as well as homemade fish soup. Closed December and January. Major credit cards accepted. 8 Passeig Marítim, L'Escala (phone: 72-770300). Moderate.

En Route from Empúries Take the main road north toward Roses (Rosas), skirting the old fishing village of Sant Pere Pescador and then Castelló d'Empúries, a small town with a magnificent 13th- to 15th-century Gothic church. Continue northeast toward Roses, a popular resort town on low hills 6 miles (10 km) around the bay from Castelló, but after the angular, modern development of Ampuriabrava rears up into view and the turnoff for Roses appears, go straight, following signs inland toward Cadaqués and turning left at the Campsa gas station. For the next 10 miles (16 km), the road crosses an open, rock-strewn Wuthering Heights–like moor flecked with rosemary and thyme.

CADAQUÉS This picture-postcard fishing village, made famous by Salvador Dalí and once the haunt of artists and intellectuals, has remained peacefully quaint, with a harbor, whitewashed houses, narrow lanes, and, in summer, art exhibitions and a music festival. The 18th-century parish church houses a valuable baroque high altar, carved by Pau Costa. A mile away, the cove of Port Lligat boasts Dalí's split-level house — surmounted by what appears to be a giant boiled egg.

CHECKING IN

Playa Sol Standard and modern, it offers 50 rooms overlooking the sea. Facilities include a swimming pool, tennis courts, and a cafeteria. Major credit cards accepted. 3 Carrer Platja Planch, Cadaqués (phone: 72-258100; fax: 72-258054). Expensive.

Rocamar This establishment has 70 comfortable, spacious rooms, all with TV sets. Right on the beach, it features a sauna, a gym, a heated swimming pool, and tennis courts. Open March through mid-January. Virgen del Carmen, Cadaqués (phone: 72-258150; fax: 72-258650). Expensive.

Port-Lligat Right next to Dalí's house, this simple but comfortable hostelry offers 30 rooms, a pool, a restaurant, and a bar. Open daily April through October; weekends only November through March. On the beach, in Cadaqués (phone: 72-258162). Moderate.

EATING OUT

La Galiota This small place is by far the best in town, boasting a Michelin star. It caters to an "artsy" clientele, and serves local seafood dishes and outstanding soufflés. It's very crowded in summer. Closed weekdays from September through May. Reservations advised. Major credit cards accepted. 9 Carrer Narcis Monturiol, Cadaqués (phone: 72-258187). Moderate.

En Route from Cadaqués Backtrack across the moor and make a right turn onto the local road north toward the village of Vilajuiga. At the entrance to the village, make a sharp right turn at the sign for Monestir de Sant Pere de Rodes. The road swoops up alongside olives and vines to open, rugged countryside, and after approximately 6 miles (10 km), there's a small parking lot. Park here and walk along the path to the majestic, brooding castle-cum-monastery, built by the Benedictines 1,000 years ago. On an overcast day, the two 90-foot-high towers loom out of the mist, while on a clear day the attractive former fishing village of El Port de la Selva, some 2,000 feet below, and the entire peninsula are visible, as are the town of Cerbère across the French border, the snow-capped Mt. Canigou inland, and the Golf de Roses to the south. The monastery buildings have been restored to reflect the wealth and power of Catalonia in the 10th and 11th centuries. Open daily from 9 AM to 1:45 PM and from 3 to 6:45 PM; admission charge.

Return to the main road at Vilajuiga and follow it for 8 miles (13 km) to Figueres, passing the old town of Perelada, which lends its name to the popular, often sparkling, local wines. The town has a luxury casino, the *Casino Castell de Perelada,* housed in the old castle. It has a good restaurant that serves local dishes (phone: 72-538125).

FIGUERES (FIGUERAS) Set in the heart of the Ampurdán plain, Figueres is a small town, best known as the birthplace in 1904 of the late Surrealist artist Salvador Dalí and the home of the *Teatre-Museu Dalí* (Dalí Museum and Theater). His sculptures feature a lobster basking on the receiver of a telephone, and a giant woman standing on the hood of a Cadillac. His paintings offer much of the same: A dog collar doubles as a viaduct, locks of hair curl into fruit, and a chest of drawers with huge, bare human feet ascends into heaven. Dalí worked here until 1982, and lived bedridden in the building's Galatea Tower until his death in 1989. The artist is buried in the museum's inner court, beneath the building's great glass dome. Over 300,000 visitors each year make the museum Spain's second most popular (Madrid's *Prado* ranks number one). To avoid the crowds, visit during lunchtime hours. Open daily from 11:30 AM to 5:30 PM in October through June; from 9 AM to 8:30 PM in July through September; admission charge (phone: 72-505697). The Figueres Tourist Office is at Plaça del Sol (phone: 72-503155).

CHECKING IN/EATING OUT

Ampurdán Adequate and comfortable, it offers 42 rooms in motel-style simplicity on the outskirts of town. The restaurant is the real prize here, rated one of Spain's best (it has a Michelin star). It specializes in real Catalan dishes, often pairing meat with fruit. Try the rabbit and prune terrine, or braised venison with quince sauce. Fish is also a good choice, and the local wines are excellent. Reservations essential for the restaurant. Major credit cards accepted. Antigua Carretera de Francia, Km 763, Figueres (phone: 72-500562; fax: 72-509358). Expensive.

Mas Pau Set in a quiet garden, this pretty, old, beamed, converted farmhouse offers 7 guestrooms, a swimming pool, and an award-winning (including a Michelin star) restaurant. Delicious saffron-flavored chicken and lobster, hearty venison, and subtle lambs' brains ravioli are a few of the menu favorites. Restaurant open April 3 to January 10. Reservations advised. Major credit cards accepted. Carretera de Olot, 3 miles (5 km) southwest of Figueres (phone: 72-546154). Expensive.

Durán In the heart of the Old Town, this is a real family-style establishment dating from 1870, with 65 modernized rooms. Like the *Ampurdán,* it is famous for food — delicate fresh salmon in lemon-butter sauce, hearty stuffed squash, *sarsuela* (fish stew), and eggplant mousse with fresh tuna. Reservations essential for the restaurant. Major credit cards accepted. 5 Carrer Lasauca, Figueres (phone: 72-501250; fax: 72-502609). Moderate.

En Route from Figueres As you head west along C260 toward Olot and Ripoll, the Pyrenees rear to the north as the road curves through pine forests and, in spring, acres of wildflowers. The village of Besalú, 15 miles (24 km) from Figueres, is worth a stroll-through. Follow signs to the Centre Vila and park in the large square, El Prat de Sant Pere. Careful renovation has beautified this mostly forgotten village. The church, Curia Reial (Law Courts), Town Hall, and covered marketplace are still in use;

in fact, the Curia Reial houses a traditional Catalan restaurant. The Casa dels Cornellà is believed to have been a merchant's house, judging by its courtyard, arches, and cloistered second floor. Cross the irregular arches of the fortified medieval bridge and observe, on the far side of the Fluvià River, the old Jewish quarter, complete with a *mikvah* (ritual bath), one of only a handful still existing in Europe. As a souvenir, purchase a floppy red Catalan cap (*barretina*), made in the town.

Proceed on C150 into a district known as La Gárrotxa, which means "torn earth," a reminder that the newly improved road to Olot, 13 miles (21 km) away, goes through volcanic countryside, though the 40 extinct cones are now overgrown. On the left, a sheer basalt cliff supports the dusty old village of Castellfollit de la Roca (Mad Castle on the Rock), some 200 feet above the abyss.

OLOT Although this town has succumbed to dreary industrial development and local workshops churn out seemingly endless religious souvenirs, Olot has managed to keep its folkloric traditions alive. Annually, on the second Sunday of July, some 5,000 dancers arrive to weave magical *sardanas*, traditional Catalan folk dances. On September 8, *gegants, nans*, and *cavallets* (papier-mâché giants, dwarves, and horses) perform dances, and on October 18, the *cena de duro*, "2-cent dinner," instituted in honor of Sant Lluc (St. Luke) in 1314, still includes wine, bread, and rice for a few pesetas. The *Museo des Artes Contemporaneo* (Museum of Modern Art), housed in a 19th-century palace (Carrer Hospici), displays a collection of works from the Olot School of Art, which was founded in the 19th century and became the workplace of many Catalan artists (open Mondays through Saturdays from 11 AM to 2 PM and from 4 to 7 PM; Sundays and holidays from 11 AM to 2 PM; admission charge; phone: 72-266457). Also admire the elegant Modernist façade of the Sola Morales house (38 Carrer Mulleres). The tourist office (Edifici Plaça del Mercat, Carrer Mulleres; phone: 72-260141) is nearby on the same street.

En Route from Olot Continue west along C150; after about 7½ miles (12 km), the road forks, with a right turn leading to Sant Joan de les Abadesses. The road sign says it's only 8 miles (11 km) to this remote village, but the drive is a tortuous one. However, the tranquillity of the village's convent of Benedictine nuns, founded in the 9th century (what is visible today is no earlier than the 11th century), may make up for the stress and strain. Otherwise, bear left at the fork and head on to Ripoll, 12 miles (19 km) away.

RIPOLL This town deserves greater recognition of its past role as a torchbearer for civilization. Wilfred the Shaggy, founder of more than one monastery in Catalonia, established the Benedictine monastery of Santa María here in the 9th century. By the 11th century its 246-book library was one of the richest in Christendom, famed throughout Europe as a center of learning and a meeting place for Christian and Arab philosophers. The town is pretty dreary now, except for the wonderful (but worn) 12th-century carved stone portal of the monastery church, which depicts seven biblical and allegorical scenes. During the summer, classical music recitals often take place in the cloisters. The monastery is open weekdays from 10 AM to 2 PM and from 4 to 7 PM, and weekends and holidays from 10 AM to 7 PM in summer; winter hours are 11 AM to 2:30 PM weekdays, 11 AM to 2 PM and 4 to 6 PM Saturdays and Sundays; admission charge (phone: 72-720013). For further information, contact the tourist office in Ripoll, Plaça de l'Abat Oliba (phone: 72-701109).

En Route from Ripoll Take N152 due north into the Pyrenees, following the twisting, rocky bed of the Freser River. Tiny, seemingly inaccessible dark-stone villages blend into the high cliffs above. Beyond Ribes de Freser, 9 miles (14 km) from Ripoll, the road climbs 15½ miles (25 km) to Tosas, a village 6,000 feet up, where snow-capped peaks are visible even in summer. A sleepy gas station provides welcome refueling for car and body, after which, instead of taking the main road to Puigcerdá, make a sharp left turn down to La Molina, a popular ski resort, and follow the valley road to Puigcerdá. Compared with other towns along the route, Puigcerdá is visually unremarkable, but it does have a dozen ski resorts within 30 miles to keep it busy.

Rather than enter Puigcerdá, turn left at the outskirts, taking C1313 southwest in the direction of Bellver de Cerdanya and La Seu d'Urgell. The road leads past the delightful mountain golf course of the *Real Club de Golf de Cerdanya* (phone: 72-880950 or 72-881338), goes on through a wide valley dotted with little hill villages, and crosses into the province of Lleida (Lérida). After Bellver, it runs alongside the Segre River, where fishermen stand waist-deep casting for trout, and goes through Martinet, a trout-fishing and hiking center; 20 miles (32 km) beyond Bellver is La Seu d'Urgell.

CHECKING IN/EATING OUT

Boix This comfortable, 35-room hotel by the Segre River is known for its breakfasts — a rarity in Spain — of homemade bread, jam, and local honey and butter. The restaurant is a splendid one (with a Michelin star), serving a French/Catalan menu: crayfish with mushrooms, trout with thyme, chicken in pastry, and duck with truffles, plus an excellent selection of Spanish and French wines. Reservations essential for the restaurant, which is closed Tuesdays off season and for 3 weeks in January. Major credit cards accepted. Carretera Lleida–Puigcerdá, Km 204, Martinet de Cerdanya (phone: 73-515050; fax: 73-515268). Expensive.

Chalet del Golf The timber clubhouse of the *Real Club de Golf de Cerdanya* has 16 rooms, plus a swimming pool, tennis courts, and a restaurant. Located

3 miles (5 km) southwest of Puigcerdá. Devesa del Golf, Puigcerdá (phone: 72-880962). Expensive.

Can Borell A farmhouse in a small village up a mountain road between Puigcerdá and Bellver de Cerdanya, this place offers 8 comfortable, rustic rooms and magnificent mountain views. *Conill amb peras i naps* (rabbit with pears and turnips), pigs' trotters with apple sauce, leek tart, and pears poached in the thick black wines of Tarragona are among the dining room's specialties. The establishment also serves as a cooking school. Reservations essential for the restaurant, which is closed Sunday nights (except in July, August, and September); both hotel and restaurant are closed 1 month during the winter. Call ahead to reserve a room and to check opening times. 3 Carrer Regreso, Meranges (phone: 72-880033). Moderate.

LA SEU D'URGELL (SEO DE URGEL) This ancient town flourished at the conjunction of two rivers, the Valira from the north and the Segre from the east. All around are rolling orchards and farmlands — the foothills of the Pyrenees. Boasting a bishop since 527, a cathedral since 839, and two saints (Just and Ermengol), La Seu is both historically rich and more conventionally affluent, but its main claim to fame is the status of its bishop, who, since 1278, has been the joint ruler — or co-prince — of the co-principality of Andorra. The Cathedral of Santa María, rebuilt during the 12th century and again during the 18th century, features the uncluttered openness that appeals to Catalans, and is noted for its façade and its 13th-century cloister. The church museum, *Museu Diocesà d'Urgell,* in a chapel of the cloister, possesses a prized 11th-century illuminated manuscript of the *Apocalypse of St. John the Divine,* written during the 8th century by the priest Beatus of Liébana. Open weekdays from 10 AM to 1 PM and from 4 to 7 PM in April through September; from 9:30 AM to 1:30 PM and from 3:30 PM to 8 PM in October through March; and Saturdays and Sundays year-round from 10 AM to 1 PM; admission charge (phone: 73-351177). Across from the church is the Carrer Major, with its medieval equivalent of a shopping mall, the great *porxos,* or arcades, that have sheltered vendors for centuries. The market, held on Tuesdays and Fridays, is worth a visit.

CHECKING IN/EATING OUT

El Castell Built into the hillside underneath the ruins of a 13th-century fortress about half a mile (1 km) southwest of town, this luxury hotel offers lovely views over the town and the valley and across to the Sierra del Cadí. A member of the Relais & Châteaux group, it has 40 rooms and suites with (rare in Spain) king-size beds, as well as a swimming pool. Eat on the terrace or dine magnificently in the *Celler Grill,* which serves regional and national dishes; the wine cellar has a priceless collection of French and Spanish vintages dating back to the 19th century. Reservations essential for the restaurant, which is closed Mondays; both hotel and restaurant closed from mid-January to mid-February. Major credit cards accepted. Carretera Lleida, Km 129, La Seu d'Urgell (phone: 73-350704; in the US, 800-677-3524; fax: 73-351574). Expensive.

Parador de Seu d'Urgell This modern, comfortable *parador* in town offers 84 spacious, air conditioned rooms, a swimming pool, and a restaurant serving French and Catalan specialties. Tapestries are part of the decor, and a 12th-century cloister from a former nearby church has been incorporated into the lobby and reception lounge. Reservations advised for the restaurant. Major credit cards accepted. Carrer Sant Doménec, La Seu d'Urgell (phone: 73-352000; in the US, 212-686-9213; fax: 73-352309). Expensive.

En Route from La Seu d'Urgell Driving north on C145, it's a quick 6 miles (10 km) to the border of one of the world's smallest countries, the autonomous principality of Andorra.

ANDORRA A co-principality governed nominally by Spain and France, Andorra is an independent country of approximately 50,000 inhabitants (only 8,000 natives, the rest mainly Spanish and French immigrants) and a duty-free haven set high in the Pyrenees. Recently, Andorrans voted to officially sever its feudal associations with both France and Spain and become an independent republic. This could mean a seat at the United Nations and maybe even an international dialing code. But as of press time, nothing has happened.

Andorra's mere 175 square miles contain a dramatic landscape of scenic lakes, racing rivers, verdant meadows, quaint mountain villages, good ski slopes, and the nation's capital city, Andorra la Vella, the highest in Europe (3,000 feet), where modern, high-rise buildings almost block out the view of the surrounding peaks. According to tradition, the founding of Andorra dates back to the 9th century, when Louis I, the son of Charlemagne, granted a tract of land to the Bishop of Urgell; dual allegiance dates to the 13th century, when later bishops, feeling their rule challenged by French noblemen, agreed to joint control. The country's blue, red, and yellow flag first waved in 1298, at which time Andorrans also accepted an agreement whereby, in even-numbered years, the Spanish bishop would receive the equivalent of $12 as tribute, in addition to six hams, six chickens, and six cheeses. In odd-numbered years, the French prince (originally the Count of Foix) would be presented with a cash tribute of 960 pesetas.

Because the same rules pertain today, Andorra is Europe's last feudal protectorate. French and Spanish authorities oversee the justice and postal systems (all mail is delivered free within Andorra, and peseta or franc denominations of stamps are issued for mail outside the country). But since 1419, the Andorrans also have elected a 24-member Council General and are, therefore, proud to have one of the oldest parliaments in Europe. The semi-independent state suits most Andorrans just fine. The past few decades have seen the country jump from medieval feudalism to 20th-century prosperity — Andorra is a major banking center — and from a strictly agricultural country to a model of modernization and growth.

One main, winding road cuts diagonally through Andorra, southwest to northeast, and along it traffic creeps in both directions, especially on weekends and during Spanish and French national holidays. At the borders, traffic jams of cars lined up to return to Spain and France can be monumental, caused by conscientious Spanish and French customs agents assessing the value of the duty-free purchases.

The Pyrenees may not be as dramatic or even as high as the Alps, but they are wider and far more rugged (which explains why Andorra remained a mostly medieval community until this century). Since the country is perched atop the mountains facing south, it has an excellent climate of dry air, brisk in winter and fresh in summer. Most of its villages are deep in the low valley, but in winter, some of Europe's best inexpensive skiing can be found at the resorts of Pas de la Casa, Grau Roig, Soldeu, Tarter, Pals, Arinsal, and Arcalis. In June, the high valleys, as yet untainted by developers, unveil some of the rarest, yet most abundant, wildflowers in Europe; carpets of narcissi, orchids, and iris stretching for hundreds of yards are a common sight.

In terms of historic sights, there are some attractive bridges arching across rushing streams, as well as a few tall, square bell towers on Romanesque churches. In Andorra la Vella, the 16th-century Casa de la Vall, which houses the governing Council General, is worth a visit (open Mondays through Fridays from 10 AM to 1 PM and from 3 to 7 PM; Saturdays from 10 AM to 1 PM; no admission charge). Outside of the capital, in Encamp, is the *Museu Nacional de l'Automòbil d'Andorra* (64 Av. Príncep Episcopal; phone: 32266), displaying a collection of antique cars, motorcycles, and bicycles from 1898 through 1950 (open from 10 AM to 1 PM and from 4 PM to 8 PM, with a lunchtime closing; closed Mondays; no admission charge).

However, shopping is the main attraction here, although in many cases the prices are only attractive to the French and the Spanish, thousands of whom cross the border daily to stock up on cigarettes, liquor, electronic equipment, leather goods, and fashions. The best stores are found in Andorra la Vella, whose main streets bustle like the aisles of *Bloomingdale's*. To recommend one store over another is futile, since most shops have standard prices and stock only the most marketable merchandise.

Spanish currency is accepted throughout the tiny principality. While there are no customs or passport formalities for entering Andorra (visitors have to beg officials to mark passports with their flowery stamp), remember that lines for re-entering Spain are often very long, especially in late afternoon. So are the lines at the service stations just within the Andorran border — a mandatory last stop for motorists, since gasoline prices are often one-third less than those of Spain or France. The country's tourist office, Sindicat d'Iniciativa, is located in Andorra la Vella on Carrer Dr. Vilanova (phone: 20214).

NOTE When calling Andorra from Spain, first dial 9-738; from the US, dial 011-33-628 and then the local number.

CHECKING IN

Andorra Palace The principality's best, offering 140 rooms with excellent mountain views. Modern and comfortable, it has a swimming pool, tennis courts, and a garage (parking in Andorra is a nightmare). Prat de la Creu, Andorra la Vella (phone: 21072). Expensive.

Mercure Andorra Part of the popular French chain and under the same management as the *Andorra Palace,* it's modern, efficient and comfortable, with 70 rooms, an indoor swimming pool, a sauna, and a garage. 58 Av. Meritxell, Andorra la Vella (phone: 20773). Moderate.

EATING OUT

1900 The French fare here has made many of Iberia's "top 30" listings, thanks to nouvelle dishes such as scallops with wild mushrooms, *magret de canard* (sliced breast of duck) with raspberry vinegar and beans, woodcock with wild garlic, and chocolate *millefeuilles* (pastry with whipped cream). Open daily; closed during July. Reservations essential. Major credit cards accepted. In a spa about a half mile (1 km) east of the capital. Plaça de la Unió, Les Escaldes (phone: 26716). Expensive.

En Route from Andorra The route now enters territory not often visited by tourists. Backtrack south on C145 to La Seu d'Urgell and continue south on C1313, following the Segre River and snaking through the gray, rugged gorge of Organyà, past Organyà itself (the proud possessor of the oldest document written in Catalan), and past the dammed valley at Oliana, with its reservoir, beehives, and orchards of almonds and apricots. The river, lined with poplars and streaked with shoals of boulders that have tumbled from the heights of the Pyrenees, broadens here.

Just beyond Oliana, at Bassella, 32 miles (51 km) south of La Seu d'Urgell, is the intersection with C1410. For those wishing to return to Barcelona, about 90 miles (144 km) from Bassella, this road (via Solsona, Cardona, and Manresa) is a shortcut. Along the way, the *Parador Nacional Duques de Cardona* (in an old castle in Cardona; phone: 3-869-1275; in the US, 212-686-9213) has 60 expensive rooms for guests. Otherwise, continue south along C1313 for about 11 miles (18 km) to Ponts, a logging town, and turn left onto the local road to Calaf. After a few minutes, turn right onto the road to Cervera, 21 miles (34 km) from Ponts, driving through rolling wheat fields and past hilltop hamlets, and crossing the main Barcelona-to-Zaragoza railroad tracks.

CERVERA The town was originally built around a 13th-century castle. Aim for the ancient main street, Carrer Major, which runs along the top of the ridge, with old houses on both sides. Halfway down, a sign points to the Carreró de les Bruixes Segle XIII (Passage of the 13th-Century Witches). The passage, which runs some 400 yards parallel to Carrer Major and underneath the old houses, is decorated with black cats, moons, witches' brooms, owls, and cobwebs, but is a spooky-enough experience even without these embellishments. Back into the daylight of the Plaça Major, which is a small square with a row of gargoyle-like faces holding up the balconies of the 18th-century Town Hall, wander to the Carrer Major to see the house where the Generalitat de Catalunya was established in 1359, and where, about a century later, King Ferdinand and Queen Isabella's marriage contract was signed. Cervera literally has been bypassed by the 20th century (the main road between Barcelona and Zaragoza tunnels under the Old Town), but it was still in the mainstream in the 18th and 19th centuries, when it was the site of a Castilian/Bourbon university. Cervera is also known for its annual *Crist Misteri de Passió* (Passion Play), some 500 years old. A special theater was built for the crowds that flock to see the play, enacted by over 500 local citizens in March and April. The town's tourist office is at 4 Passeig Balmes (phone: 73-531350).

En Route from Cervera The main road (N11) to Tàrrega, 7½ miles (12 km) away, is fast and straight, but Tàrrega itself can be a bottleneck. In the center of town, take the turn for C240 south toward Montblanch (Montblanc) and Tarragona and follow it through fields and vineyards, with intriguing villages off to either side, some with castles, some with churches. Just beyond Belltall, there is a sharp rise and the land drops away, revealing a lovely panoramic view across the plains of Conça de Barberà. Look for the sign down the hill, off to the right, for Vallbona de les Monges.

VALLBONA DE LES MONGES Catalonia boasts three great Cistercian abbeys: Vallbona de les Monges (for nuns), and Poblet and Santes Creus (for monks). Vallbona de les Monges is the least known, yet nuns have lived here without interruption since 1157. Fairly cut off from the rest of the world until a new road was pushed through in 1988, the convent is wedged into the middle of a village (pop. 275) and held up by tons of cement that are being poured into the foundations to keep it from falling down. Nuns conduct guided tours that include the church, whose soaring nave and belfry in a transitional Gothic style (12th to 13th century) are worthy of admiration. Open for guided tours daily, call for hours (phone: 73-330266); admission by donation.

En Route from Vallbona de les Monges Return to the main road (C240) and continue through Solivella to Montblanch (Montblanc), a photogenic town with 34 towers along its castellated walls, medieval streets, and handsome squares. Another 4 miles (6 km) west is the uninspiring town of L'Espluga de Francolí, 3 miles (5 km) above which is the thoroughly inspiring Monastery of Poblet.

POBLET The celebrated Monastery of Santa María de Poblet — a combined monastery, castle, and palace — was founded in 1151 by Ramón Berenguer IV, Count of Barcelona, in thanks to God for the recapture of Catalonia from the Moors. Although the monastery was abandoned when religious orders were suppressed in 1835, it was reestablished in 1940. Following 50 years of careful restoration and rebuilding, Poblet is now perhaps the finest monastic complex in Europe, surrounded by more than a mile of walls and guarded by a dozen turrets. Visits can include guided tours (conducted in Spanish, Catalan, and French only), which progress through a series of courtyards and gatehouses to the church, the huge cloister with its beautifully carved capitals, the Royal Pantheon with its alabaster tombs, and the 14th-century Gothic palace. The complex is open daily from 10 AM to 12:30 PM and from 3 to 6 PM; admission charge (phone: 77-870089).

En Route from Poblet Return to Montblanch and take the main Tarragona road (N240) as far as Valls, famous for its strange tradition of building *castells dels xiquets* (human towers). On June 23, 24, and 25, and on the Sunday following October 21, teams of men and boys, standing on one another's shoulders, compete to see who can build the highest tower. After Valls, follow signs to the left turn for C246 and Vendrell. Beyond Alío, follow the signs for the third great Cistercian institution, Santes Creus, which appears suddenly over the brow of a hill, about 21 miles (34 km) from Montblanch.

EATING OUT

Masía Bou Huge pottery wine jars mark this eatery, where specialties include grilled meat dishes and *calçotada,* a local dish of chops, sausages, broiled onions, and gravy. Weekends are especially busy between October and April. Reservations advised. Major credit cards accepted. Carretera de Lleida, Km 21, Valls (phone: 77-600427). Moderate.

SANTES CREUS Like the Poblet Monastery, the Monastery of Santes Creus was founded for the Cistercians by the Berenguer dynasty in the 12th century. The Kings of Aragon and Catalonia were among its patrons, and the monastery's abbot served as the royal chaplain. The complex includes medieval servants' quarters, a 12th-century church with a beautiful rose window, and 14th-century cloisters. Monks no longer live here, so the buildings are now used for exhibitions, conferences, and concerts. Open daily from 10 AM to 1 PM and from 3:30 to 7 PM (to 6 PM from April through September); admission charge (phone: 77-638329).

En Route from Santes Creus Backtrack south to C246, then west toward Valls to pick up N240, which leads south 12½ miles (20 km) to Tarragona.

TARRAGONA There are very few "undiscovered" cities in Europe, but Tarragona may well be one of them. A combination of excavation and restoration has revealed just how important the ancient city of Tarraco was to the Roman Empire for over 600 years. Julius Caesar, Augustus, and Hadrian lived here for a time; legend has it that Pontius Pilate was born here. The streets of the Old Town still run where the Roman streets once lay; yet on top of all this, there is a pleasant, large hill city with medieval areas, long avenues, and views out over the ocean. The Passeig Arqueològic (Archaeological Promenade) is a walk of about half a mile through the history of Tarragona, around the ancient walls enclosing the highest part of the town. At the base of the walls are the huge Cyclopean boulders laid down by Iberian tribes in the 6th century BC; above these are the Roman walls built in the 3rd century BC, topped by a later Roman stone layer, then a medieval layer, and then English-built ramparts added during the War of the Spanish Succession. To interpret all this, a personal multilingual guide is a good investment, as pieces of Roman history crop up in the shadows of medieval houses and modern apartment blocks. The *Museu Arqueològic* (Archaeological Museum; on Plaça del Rei; phone: 77-236211 or 77-236206) exhibits mosaics, capitals, statues, ancient household utensils, and other local finds. It's open Mondays through Saturdays from 10 AM to 1:30 PM and from 4:30 to 8 PM (4 to 7 PM in winter); Sundays and holidays from 10 AM to 2 PM; admission charge.

Next to the museum is the Pretori Romà (Roman Pretorium), a 2,000-year-old fortress, presumed to have been Pilate's birthplace. Just below, built into the hillside by the beach, is the Roman amphitheater, where excavations have unearthed the remains of what is believed to be a 2nd- or 3rd-century Christian church. Just above the ruins is the Balcón del Mediterráneo (Balcony of the Mediterranean), a cliffside promenade offering excellent views of the sea. A flight of Roman steps leads up to the fortress-like cathedral in the heart of the Old City, built on the site of the former Temple of Jupiter, which became a mosque under Moorish rule. Built in the 12th, 13th, and 14th centuries, with later additions, the cathedral is a mix of Romanesque, Gothic, Plateresque, and Churrigueresque architecture. Open daily from 10 AM to 1 PM from 4 to 7 PM.

There are two splendid Roman remains on the outskirts of town. The Pont de les Ferreres aqueduct (or Pont del Diable — the "Devil's Bridge"), some 200 feet long and located 2½ miles (4 km) from the center via N240, is a 2-tiered example of Roman engineering from Emperor Trajan's day.

The Roda de Barà (Bara's Arch), a 2nd-century triumphal arch, is located 12½ miles (20 km) north of Tarragona via A7. For more information, consult the tourist office in Tarragona (4 Fortuny; phone: 77-233415).

CHECKING IN

Imperial Tarraco Tarragona's best, with 170 spacious, modern rooms. Set high atop a cliff, it has spectacular views of the ocean and the ancient Roman amphitheater below. 2 Rambla Vella, Tarragona (phone: 77-233040; fax: 77-216566). Expensive.

EATING OUT

Sol Ric Dine in a terrace under the trees. The fish dishes are outstanding, and the house wines from Priorato are excellent. Closed Sunday evenings, Mondays, and mid-December to mid-January. Reservations essential. Major credit cards accepted. About a half mile (1 km) from town, 227 Vía Augusta, Tarragona (phone: 77-232032). Moderate.

En Route from Tarragona For a seaside break from sightseeing, follow N340, then C246, north along the coast 33 miles (53 km) to Sitges, the prettiest resort on the Costa Dorada (Gold Coast). An alternative route to the same destination would be the faster A7, turning east at Vilafranca del Penedès.

SITGES A typical Mediterranean seaside resort town, it is popular and classy, lively and cultured, pretty and, occasionally, tacky. The 1½-mile-long sandy beach of La Ribera is backed by a promenade lined with flowers and palm trees, cafés and restaurants, with a church at the north end. The Old Town is made up of little lanes and some magnificent old villas, homes of "Americanos" — Spaniards who made their fortune a century ago in Central and South America and retired here. Although the town has expanded over the years, there are few apartment blocks and no towering hotels. To the north, beyond La Punta, a 450-berth yacht harbor at Aiguadolç attracts the nautical fraternity. Summer weekends are very crowded, especially in late July and August, but a stay during the week or out of season can be very pleasant.

Sitges has three surprisingly good museums. *Museu Cau-Ferrat* (Carrer Fonollar; phone: 3-894-0364) has one of Europe's finest collections of artistic ironwork along with tiled walls and paintings by El Greco, Utrillo, and Santiago Rusiñol, the 19th-century romantic writer-artist (the museum is housed in his former studio). Next door, and functioning as an annex, is the *Museu Maricel de Mar* (phone: 3-894-4751), with sculptures, glass, mosaics, and drawings from the Middle Ages through the baroque period. The *Museu Romàntic* (Carrer Sant Gaudenci; phone: 3-894-2969), also known as *Casa Llopis,* is an 18th-century mansion sumptuously furnished with neo-classical antiques and paintings; there's a doll collection on the upper floor. Opening hours for all three museums are Mondays through Saturdays from 10 AM to 1 PM and from 5 to 7 PM (4 to 6 PM from October through May); Sundays and holidays from 10 AM to 2 PM. There are admission charges to all three museums.

During the town's *Feast of Corpus Christi* celebration in early June, intricately patterned floral carpets made of over 600,000 carnations cover the cobbled streets. A splendid car rally, featuring vintage automobiles, is held on the first weekend of March.

CHECKING IN

Calipolis Facing the waterfront, this modern establishment is somewhat frayed at the edges, but the 170 rooms are air conditioned and have private baths, and most have terraces overlooking the beach. *La Brasa* restaurant serves international and regional fare. Major credit cards accepted. Passeig Marítim, Sitges (phone: 3-894-1500; fax: 3-894-0764). Expensive.

Llicorella With 13 rooms, this Relais & Châteaux oceanfront property is modestly pleasant — the gardens even boast a modern art collection. A pool and a restaurant are on the premises; opportunities for tennis and golf are nearby. Open year-round. Major credit cards accepted. About 5 miles (8 km) south of Sitges. Sant Antonio, Cubelles (phone: 3-895-0044; in the US, 800-677-3524; fax: 3-895-2417). Expensive.

Terramar Isolated at the southern end of town, it offers 209 comfortable rooms and plenty of sports facilities, including tennis courts, a golf course, and riding stables. Major credit cards accepted. Passeig Marítim, Sitges (phone: 3-894-0050; fax: 3-894-5604). Moderate.

EATING OUT

Fregata Various fish dishes (served in large portions) and a thick fish soup are on the menu, supplemented by fabulous views over the water from a clifftop site. Closed Thursdays. Reservations advised. Major credit cards accepted. 1 Passeig de la Ribera, Sitges (phone: 3-894-1086). Moderate.

Mare Nostrum Know for its excellent local fish dishes, superbly prepared, plus a good wine cellar. Closed Wednesdays and from January 15 to February 15. Reservations advised. Major credit cards accepted. 60 Passeig de la Ribera (phone: 3-894-3393). Moderate.

La Masía Traditional Catalan cooking, with an emphasis on grilled meats, served in an old, rustic *masía,* or farmhouse. Open daily. Reservations advised. Major credit cards accepted. 164 Passeig Vilanova, Sitges (phone: 3-894-1076). Moderate.

En Route from Sitges For a final side trip before returning to Barcelona, head north through Sant Pere de Ribes into the Penedès wine region. After crossing the main Tarragona–Barcelona freeway, on the very edge of Vilafranca del Penedès, 14 miles (22 km) from Sitges, turn right for the Bodega Miguel Torres (22 Comercio; phone: 3-890-0100). This family wine business (Spain's largest independent one) dates back to 1870, but it is only in the last decade or so that Torres wines have gained international recognition. Visiting hours, by guided tour, are Mondays through Fridays from 9 AM to 1 PM and from 3 to 5 PM. The *Museu del Vi* (Plaça Jaume I; phone: 3-890-0582), in the center of town, is dedicated to the history of wine making in the region (open daily from 10 AM to 2 PM and from 4 to 6 PM; admission charge). Another wine-related excursion is to Sant Sadurní d'Anoia, the center of the sparkling wine — *cava* — industry in Spain, 7½ miles (12 km) north of Vilafranca. Here Cavas Codorníu, on the edge of town (phone: 3-891-0125), has been making sparkling wine by the champagne method since the 1870s. Open for tours Mondays through Thursdays from 8 to about 11:30 AM and from 3 to about 5 PM; Fridays from 8 to 11:30 AM; closed weekends and August; no admission charge.

CHECKING IN/EATING OUT

Els Sumidors This rustic, mountain *hostal* just outside of Sant Pere de Ribes has 7 traditionally furnished, stone-walled suites with beamed ceilings, tiled floors, and wooden doors. Facilities include a TV salon, a swimming pool, a sauna, and a solarium. The *Carnivor* restaurant, as its name suggests, specializes in grilled meat served in large portions. Open daily. Reservations advised. Major credit cards accepted. Sant Pere de Ribes (phone: 3-896-2061). Expensive.

Aragon

Since there is no coast in Aragon, many visitors — Spaniards included — dismiss this region as a place to be passed through quickly on the way to the mountains or the sea. At one time, however, Aragon was a kingdom that could not be ignored. From the time it was founded in 1035, it systematically enlarged both its territory and its sphere of influence. The kingdom of Navarre was an early ally, and astute matchmaking forged alliances with the powerful Berenguer family, bringing in the potent House of Barcelona and the region of Catalonia. The biggest matchmaking coup of all was the marriage of King Ferdinand II of Aragon to Queen Isabella of Castile and León. Under their rule, a united Spain extended its reach to the New World.

Aragon enjoys the dubious distinction of having Spain's worst climate. Summers are unbearably hot and winters can be extremely bitter. But visitors in late spring or early autumn will have few complaints about the weather, and lots to see and do. There are vineyards and wineries southeast of Zaragoza that welcome visitors and encourage wine tasting, and local fiestas offer a glimpse at the distinctive traditions of the region. Local women don their traditional embroidered aprons and pretty ankle-laced slippers for the festivities, and folks dance the odd, jig-like *jota*. In September, especially in the southernmost stretches, bull fever hits. *Encierros,* or the running of bulls through the streets into an enclosure, are certainly not unique to Pamplona. Small local variations occur near harvesttime as part of the observance of patron saints' feast days in the villages close to Teruel.

The route outlined below begins in Pamplona and enters the old kingdom of Aragon at the base of the Pyrenees, then goes south through a dreamscape of strange mounds and past a strategic castle on its way to Huesca. As it continues south, fields give way to wide flats near Zaragoza, the only sizable city in this sparsely populated region. Still farther to the southwest, past Calatayud, stark badlands hold such surprises as the Piedra Monastery, which looks like some colorful mirage in these raw, red hills. Once past a valley of orchards and vineyards, brick towers in geometric Mudéjar patterns rise above the arid scrub near Daroca and Teruel, at Aragon's southern extreme. From here, the traveler can opt to head for Valencia, on the coast, or turn inland, toward Cuenca and Madrid. Either way, a detour to the medieval town of Albarracín, guarding the heights to the west, is recommended.

Accommodations in Aragon described as very expensive will cost $130 and up a night for a double, expensive accommodations run $70 to $130, moderate hotels charge between $40 and $70, and at inexpensive inns, a room for two costs $35 or less. Weekend rates are almost always higher, even during low season. Dinner for two with wine will cost $70 or more in restaurants listed as expensive, $40 to $70 in moderate restaurants, and under $40 in inexpensive ones. The telephone numbers listed below include local area codes; when calling from another area in Spain, dial "9" first.

PAMPLONA For a detailed report on the city and its sights, hotels, and restaurants, see *Pamplona,* THE CITIES.

En Route from Pamplona Take the N240 highway southeast. If there's plenty of daylight and more than a couple of hours to spare for the initial leg of the trip, turn right onto C127 after about 25 miles (40 km) and detour through Sangüesa to the historic town of Sos del Rey Católico, where King Ferdinand was born in 1452. This solemn medieval town is the largest of the Cinco Villas de Aragón (Five Towns of Aragon), which were singled out for honor because of their loyalty to King Philip V during the 18th-century War of the Spanish Succession. King Ferdinand spent his childhood in the Palacio de Sada here, and the building, which contains his nursery, is open to visitors by guided tour in summers only; no admission charge. For hours, check at the tourist office in the *Parador Fernando de Aragón* (see *Checking In/Eating Out*). San Esteban, a 14th-century Romanesque church with fine 13th-century frescoes, carved capitals and columns, and the wooden Virgen del Perdón, is also worth a visit. The town is small and beautiful, and a stroll through its narrow cobbled streets leads past intricate grillwork and carved coats of arms on the mansions of aristocratic families.

From Sos del Rey Católico, loop back to N240, and turn right onto the highway. (Those coming directly from Pamplona will already be on N240.) At Puente la Reina de Jaca, a signpost indicates the turnoff to Jaca, another 12½ miles (20 km) east along C134.

CHECKING IN/EATING OUT

Parador Fernando de Aragón Perched on a hill near some remains of the town's ramparts, this *parador* has 65 rooms, all air conditioned. The outdoor terrace is a pleasant spot for a long lunch. If it's in season, order the plump white asparagus served with two sauces, the quintessential appetizer of north Aragon. Other typical regional dishes, such as *conejo con caracoles* (rabbit with snails) or *pochas con oreja de cerdo* (white beans garnished with pig's ear), may not appeal to squeamish types, but are quite delicious. Simpler dishes are also available. Closed December and January. Room reservations should be made well in advance. Major credit cards accepted. Sáinz de Vicuña, Sos del Rey Católico (phone: 48-888011; in the US, 212-686-9213). Expensive to moderate.

JACA Medieval pilgrims en route to Santiago de Compostela recuperated from their arduous trek over the Pyrenees at this ancient garrison town, on a hill above the left bank of the Aragon River. Today, however, this is a principal base for exploring the Aragonese Pyrenees, so most visitors head *toward* the mountains. During the summer, the University of Zaragoza holds courses for foreign students; during the winter, the town bustles with skiers. The tourist office (2 Regimiento de Galicia, Local 1; phone: 74-360098) has detailed maps for exploring the distant peaks and high valleys, such as Hecho and Anso. In town, Jaca's primary sight is its Romanesque cathedral, completed in 1076. The first important Romanesque building in Spain, the cathedral influenced every artist, architect, and craftsman who entered the country to work on churches during the 11th century. Though partially restored in Gothic and later decorated in Plateresque styles, much of the original Romanesque remains. The cathedral is open daily from 9 AM to 1:30 PM and from 4 to 8 PM; its museum (*Museo Diocesano*) is open Tuesdays through Sundays from 11 AM to 2 PM and from 4 to 7 PM, in July and August; Tuesdays through Sundays from 11 AM to 1:30 PM and from 4 to 6:30 PM, September through June. Admission charge (Plaza San Pedro; phone: 74-360348 or 74-361017). Buy some local cream cakes in the *Pastelería Echeta* (Plaza Catedrales; phone: 74-360343), or try the local candies made from pine nuts, known as *besitos* — or "little kisses." The *Festival Folklórico de los Pironeos* (Folkoric Festival of the Pyrenees) is held here in odd-numbered years on the first Friday in May; the next festival will be in 1995.

CHECKING IN

Conde Aznar This small, cozy, family-run establishment has 23 rooms, pleasant gardens, and an especially good restaurant, *La Cocina Aragonesa* (see below). 3 Espacio de la Constitución, Jaca (phone: 74-361050; fax: 74-360797). Moderate.

Gran The most prestigious hotel in town, it has 166 rooms, a bright garden, tennis courts, and a swimming pool that's open in the summer. Advance booking is recommended during the winter. 1 Paseo General Franco, Jaca (phone: 74-360900; fax: 74-364061). Moderate.

EATING OUT

La Cocina Aragonesa Regional cooking is done with panache here. During the fall, order exquisite game dishes such as *rollitos de jabalí* (wild boar in puff pastry). Closed Tuesdays, except during high season. Reservations advised. American Express and Visa accepted. At the *Conde Aznar Hotel,* 5 Calle Cervantes, Jaca (phone: 74-361050). Moderate.

La Fragua This converted blacksmith's shop now fires up the flames beneath appetizing pork chops, lamb, and beef. Open daily during high season (closed mid-April to mid-June). Reservations unnecessary. No credit cards accepted. 4 Calle Gil Berges, Jaca (phone: 74-360618). Moderate to inexpensive.

Gastón The hearty fare at this charming place, with a small upstairs terrace, includes stuffed peppers and pigs' trotters. Closed Wednesdays, except in high season, and September 20–30. Reservations unnecessary. Major credit cards accepted. 14 Av. Primo de Rivera, Jaca (phone: 74-362909). Inexpensive.

En Route from Jaca Proceed south on C125, following the twisting road past the green Lake Peña. The ruddy formations that loom like sculptures are called Los Malos (The Evil Ones). Take the N240 turnoff to Ayerbe, then follow the rough local road to the village of Loarre and its Castillo de Loarre (Carretera Forestal, Km 5.5; phone: 74-380049). Regarded as one of Spain's most important Romanesque fortresses, this 11th-century castle, built as a stronghold against the Moors, commands a sweeping view over a broad plain. Pay particular attention to its three magnificently restored towers and its Romanesque chapel (open Wednesdays through Sundays from 10 AM to 1:30 PM and from 4 to 7 PM from mid-March through mid-September; from 11 AM to 2:30 PM in the winter; phone: 74-382627; admission charge). Backtrack to N240 and drive east toward Huesca.

EATING OUT

Venta del Sotón One of Aragon's best restaurants, this is 9 miles (14 km) west of Huesca. Grilled chorizo (seasoned sausage) is a good starter, and the menu offers a fine selection of Spanish nouvelle cuisine. There is also a good wine cellar. Closed Tuesdays. Reservations advised. Major credit cards accepted. Carretera N240, Km 227, Esquedas (phone: 74-270241 or 74-270012). Expensive to moderate.

HUESCA This marks the start of the rich Ebro plain. A venerable town, Huesca was, in the first century BC, an independent state founded by the Roman Quintus Sertorius, who even established a school of Latin and Greek here, Spain's first university. The town was swept up in ensuing invasions by the Romans and the Moors, until Peter I of Aragon liberated it from the Moors in 1096 and made it the residence of the Aragonese kings until 1118. During the Spanish Civil War, it was a Franco stronghold and, as such, suffered considerable damage. Subsequent restoration and recent prosperity have made the town sprawl, but there is a medieval core to explore. The Gothic cathedral, built from the 13th to the 16th centuries, has a lovely, famous 16th-century alabaster altarpiece by Damián Forment, a sculptor who worked extensively in Aragon in both the Renaissance and Gothic styles (open daily from 8:30 AM to 1 PM and from 4 to 6 PM; no admission charge; phone: 74-220676).

However, Huesca renown is most often linked with the bloody Legenda de la Campana (Legend of the Bell), a 12th-century atrocity that is depicted across the street from the cathedral in a painting at the Town Hall.

On the pretext of wanting advice from rebellious nobles about how to cast a bell big enough to be heard through the entire kingdom, King Ramiro II lured his rivals into his council room and beheaded them as they filed in one by one. The chamber can be visited in the *Museo Arqueológico Provincial* (Plaza de la Universidad; phone: 74-220586), which incorporates part of the 12th-century palace of the Aragonese kings. The museum has been undergoing renovations, so check with the tourist office (phone: 48-888011) before visiting. Also tour San Pedro el Viejo, the 12th-century Romanesque church (Calle Cuarto Reyes; phone: 74-222387); King Ramiro spent the last years of his life as a monk here and is now buried in the church's San Bartolomé chapel (open Mondays through Saturdays from 9 AM to 1 PM and from 6 to 8:30 PM; Sundays from 9:30 AM to 1 PM; admission charge).

CHECKING IN

Montearagón This unpretentious place has views of the Pyrenees that make the 2-mile (3-km) drive to the outskirts of Huesca worthwhile. There are 27 rooms, a swimming pool, and a restaurant. Carretera Tarragona–San Sebastián (N240), Km 206, Huesca (phone: 74-222350). Moderate.

Sancho Abarca Here are 32 comfortable rooms near the center of town, close to the principal sites, in a very pretty setting. Management is friendly. There's also a restaurant on the premises. 15 Plaza de Lizana, Huesca (phone: 74-220650). Moderate.

EATING OUT

Bigarren Run by the same people who run *Navas* (see below), this dining spot specializes in seafood and meat. Reservations advised. Major credit cards accepted. 15 Av. Pirineos, Huesca (phone: 74-229560). Moderate.

Navas This comfortable, clubby place offers shellfish and beef specialties. After coffee and liqueur, they pass out Havana cigars. Reservations advised. Major credit cards accepted. 15 Calle San Lorenzo, Huesca (phone: 74-224738). Moderate.

En Route from Huesca The drive from Huesca is a quick, flat, 45-mile (72-km) run south along N123/N330 to Zaragoza, Aragon's regional capital, with more than 570,000 inhabitants.

ZARAGOZA Seen from the road, the slender towers and imposing domes of Zaragoza's two cathedrals are the only grace notes in a huddle of ugly warehouses, factories, and high-rise apartments. The Ebro River shines through the dusty heart of the city like a great ribbon, and there are some elegant fountains and tree-lined avenues. Once a Roman colony, it was ruled by the Moors for 400 years, although only the Palacio Aljafaría (Plaza del Portillo; phone: 76-435618), constructed in 1030, remains from that period. Built as a pleasure palace for Moorish kings, its original

Arabian Nights architecture was tampered with first by the Aragonese kings; then by Ferdinand and Isabella, who claimed it as their throne room; and later by the zealots of the Inquisition, who used it as a headquarters (today, part of the building houses government offices). Though it also endured an ignoble stint in the 19th century as an army barracks and most of its interior fixtures have been removed, it has noteworthy *artesonado* ceilings and other Moorish and Gothic ornamentation, as well as a splendid tiny mosque (open Tuesdays through Saturdays from 11:30 AM to 1:30 PM and from 4:30 to 6 PM; Sundays from 11:30 AM to 1:30 PM; admission charge).

By the time the Reconquest proclaimed the city as the capital of Aragon, Zaragoza was already a rich agricultural center. The local nobility, wary of any sovereign, managed to secure guarantees of autonomy known as *fueros,* and under these conditions, commerce in this crossroads city boomed. The impressive 16th-century La Lonja, or commercial exchange building, has a lovely Gothic vaulted ceiling, with cherubs dancing around the tops of the supporting columns; the building today houses temporary exhibits of local artists (Plaza Catedrales; no phone; open only during exhibitions, from 9 AM to 2 PM).

On either side of La Lonja are Zaragoza's two cathedrals. The 16th- to 18th-century Basilica of Nuestra Señora del Pilar (Our Lady of Pilar) has nearly a dozen *azulejo*-covered domes and four towers surrounding a larger, central dome. On the interior of the domes are frescoes, some by Goya. Also inside is the Capilla de Nuestra Señora del Pilar, a chapel that houses a Gothic statue of the Virgin del Pilar and a jaspar pillar upon which the Virgin Mary is said to have appeared to St. James in AD 40. The chapel draws devout pilgrims, and on the *Fiesta de la Virgen del Pilar* (October 13) fervent followers parade the bejeweled statue through the city streets by the light of 350 carriage-borne lamps. The cathedral's *Museo del Pilar* (19 Plaza de Nuestra Señora; phone: 76-223334) contains the jewelry and vestments used to adorn the statue, as well as some Goya sketches for the ceiling frescoes. Open daily from 8 AM to 2 PM and from 4 to 6 PM in April through October; from 9 AM to 2 PM and from 4 to 6 PM in winter; admission charge. The Old Quarter south of the basilica called "El Tubo" contains an interesting warren of narrow streets with traditional shops and restaurants.

Zaragoza's older cathedral is the 14th-century Gothic Cathedral of Seo (Plaza de la Seo; contact the tourist office for hours; phone: 76-393537). Also noteworthy is the Mudéjar architecture of the Church of Santa María Magdalena (Plaza de la Magdalena), which is elaborately decorated in brick and tile and topped by a large square tower. It's open Mondays through Saturdays from 9:15 to 9:45 AM and from 8 to 8:30 PM; Sundays from 9:30 AM to 1 PM and from 8 to 8:30 PM.

Zaragoza's *Museo de Bellas Artes* (Museum of Fine Arts; 6 Plaza de los Sitios; phone: 76-222181) contains a worthwhile collection of Roman mosaics and artifacts, as well as paintings and etchings by Goya. It's open Tuesdays through Saturdays from 9 AM to 2 PM; Sundays from 10 AM to 2 PM; closed Mondays; admission charge. Located in what was once the Palacio Pardo, the *Museo de Camón Aznar* (23 Calle Espoz y Mina; phone: 76-397328) houses the former collection of the scholar for whom the museum is named; included are works by Goya, Velázquez, and Zurburán. It's open Tuesdays through Sundays from 10 AM to 2 PM; closed Mondays; admission charge.

CHECKING IN

Gran This stately old hotel, with 138 air conditioned rooms, is considered to be Zaragoza's best. 5 Calle Joaquín Costa, Zaragoza (phone: 76-221901; fax: 76-236713). Very expensive.

Melia Zaragoza Corona The city's largest hotel has 249 comfortable rooms, all with mini-bars and color TV sets. There's a swimming pool and a disco on the premises. 13 Av. César Augusto, Zaragoza (phone: 76-430100; in the US, 800-336-3542; fax: 76-440734). Very expensive.

Don Yo Complete luxury without a stuffy staff, and with 180 beautifully appointed rooms — there is usually space on short notice. The *Doña Taberna* restaurant next door is associated with the hotel, but is not exceptional. 4-6 Calle Bruil, Zaragoza (phone: 76-226741; fax: 76-219956). Expensive.

Conde Blanco An efficient 83-room hostelry in one of the prettier sections of the city. No dining room, but a cafeteria provides quick snacks. 84 Calle Predicadores, Zaragoza (phone: 76-441411). Moderate.

EATING OUT

Los Borrachos The name translates as "The Drunkards," but it merely celebrates a favorite Velázquez canvas. Despite its ostentatious decor, this is a Zaragoza institution. Fresh game is the specialty, with boar, venison, and game birds on the menu in season. The asparagus soufflé is outstanding; only the homemade ice creams and sherbets surpass it. Service is attentive and the wine cellar is well stocked. Closed Mondays and August. Reservations advised. Major credit cards accepted. 64 Paseo de Sagasta, Zaragoza (phone: 76-275036). Expensive to moderate.

Costa Vasca This place boasts Zaragoza's only Michelin star. Enjoy a customary *tapa* and champagne appetizer before sampling one of the various Basque fish specialties that are served in the very proper dining room. Closed Sundays and *Christmas*. Reservations advised. Major credit cards accepted. 13 Calle Teniente Coronel Valenzuela, Zaragoza (phone: 76-217339). Expensive to moderate.

La Matilde The cooking at this family-run restaurant is adventurous: deep-fried camembert with homemade tomato chutney, exquisite monkfish steamed with clams, and for the brave, the celebrated *mollejas con trufas,* a delicacy made from young bird gizzards and black truffles. The wine cellar is extensive. Closed Sundays and holidays, *Holy Week,* August, and *Christmas.* Reservations advised. Major credit cards accepted. 10 Calle Casta Alvarez, Zaragoza (phone: 76-441008). Expensive to moderate.

Asador Goyesco This casual dining spot features regional specialties — the *setas de cardo con almejas* (forest mushrooms with clams) is a standout. Closed Sundays and in August. Reservations unnecessary. Major credit cards accepted. 44 Calle Manuel Lasala, Zaragoza (phone: 76-356870). Moderate.

En Route from Zaragoza Leave Zaragoza heading southwest on the N-II highway, now a speedy, though busy, four-lane highway. The distant mountains edge in and soon after, the scenery becomes stark. After 54 1/2 miles (87 km), the highway enters Calatayud, the second-largest city in the province of Zaragoza. A dismal cluster of traffic jams and neon signs gives way to tawny brick Mudéjar towers. The striking octagonal belfry on the collegiate Church of Santa María la Mayor (Calle de Obispo Arrué), which also has a notable Plateresque façade, is the best example — it once was the minaret of a mosque and it soars above the rooftops of the houses. There is another notable tower on the 12th-century Church of San Andrés (Calle Dato).

Proceed 9 miles (14 km) west along N-II and, just past Ateca, turn off at the sign for Nuévalos and the Monasterio de Piedra. The road goes through folds of scrubby plateau, then twists along the mountainside above the startlingly blue-green Tranquera reservoir.

NUÉVALOS The town itself is extremely small, with just one main street and few facilities. Its main attraction is the Monastery of Piedra south of town, and the public park that surrounds it. The overriding sounds on the approach are the trickles of cascades and a 174-foot waterfall thundering into the green stillness of old woods. This handsome monastery was founded by Cistercian monks from the all-powerful Poblet Abbey in Tarragona in 1194, as a retreat from the court intrigues that royal visitors inflicted on Poblet. Abandoned in 1835, the monastery itself is now a hotel (see *Checking In/Eating Out*), but the grounds — laced with paths, stairs, and tunnels, and filled with lush garden plots, bubbling streams, waterfalls, and grottoes — are open to the public. They are extremely crowded in the summer, when the mists from the cascades are the only antidote to the blazing heat of southern Aragon. The park and monastery are open daily from 9 AM until dusk; admission charge.

CHECKING IN/EATING OUT

Monasterio de Piedra This former monastery has 60 modern, air conditioned rooms, a swimming pool, and tennis courts. The restaurant is formal and serves tasty fare. Make reservations well in advance. Major credit cards accepted. Monasterio de Piedra, Nuévalos (phone: 76-849011; fax: 76-849054). Moderate.

Las Truchas Don't despair if the monastery is booked; this friendly *hostal,* with a busy (though undistinguished) restaurant and outdoor terrace, has 38 comfortable (though unstylish) rooms. There's also a playground, a miniature golf course, a swimming pool, tennis courts, and a convention room. Major credit cards accepted. Carretera de Cillas-Alhama (C202), Km 37, Nuévalos (phone: 76-849040; fax: 76-849137). Inexpensive.

En Route from Nuévalos The direct road to Daroca is so narrow that drivers are likely to get stuck behind frustratingly slow tractors with no place to pass, so take the valley road (C202) 16 miles (26 km) *back* to Calatayud. At Calatayud, turn right onto N234 for the final 22 miles (35 km) to Daroca. The town is hidden in a hollow, surrounded by 2 miles of crumbling walls that once boasted 114 fortified towers, many of which still stand. On the banks of the Jiloca River, Daroca was once a Roman military settlement, then saw heavy fighting under the Moors — mainly for control of the province by rival Moorish factions. King Alfonso I of Aragon liberated the town in 1122. Today, Daroca has few visitors, and not much sightseeing to offer aside from the impressive city gates and a few Mudéjar churches, which are currently undergoing restoration. Not much is left of the craft tradition that distinguished the medieval town; what remains is on display in the *Museo del Santísimo Misterio* (Museum of the Most Holy Mystery; Plaza de España; phone: 76-800761), which has distinguished woodcarvings, as well as an interesting alabaster altarpiece showing Flemish influence (open daily 10 AM to noon and from 4 to PM; admission charge). Most of the pottery on sale in town comes from Teruel and Zaragoza, but the best comes from Muel.

Drive south along N234 to Teruel, 62 miles (100 km) away, past cultivated fields that stretch to either side, with stark mountains on the distant horizon.

EATING OUT

El Ruejo In the heart of town, this pension is a favorite of young couples and young bullfight fans. The spacious dining room is very pleasant. Stick to the most popular regional foods, which are the freshest. Pork or lamb is the best bet, accompanied by a glass of the heavy and potent *vino de la tierra.* Reservations unnecessary. No credit cards accepted. 112 Calle Mayor, Daroca (phone: 76-800335). Inexpensive.

TERUEL The barren, flat-topped hills that surround this old-fashioned town, capital of the province of Teruel, are echoed in the ocher brick of its five Mudéjar towers. Teruel is considered to have the best examples of Mudéjar architecture in Spain. The most noteworthy are the Torre de San Martín, at the San Martín Church on Plaza de Pérez Prado, and the Torre del Salvador, at the church of the same name on Calle Salvador; both towers date from the 13th century and both are adorned with fancy brick-work and porcelain plaques and tiles. The cathedral tower, first built in the 13th century, was rebuilt in the 16th and 17th centuries and again in the 20th century following Civil War damage; it has a notable Mudéjar ceiling. A particularly grim winter during the Civil War in 1937 saw Teruel devastated as the Republicans — aided by American and British volunteers — gained control, only to lose it a fortnight later to the Nationalists. Los Arcos, the 16th-century aqueduct north of town, remained intact despite the heavy shelling and machine gun fire.

Teruel's main square is the Plaza de Torico, which is marked by an unusual fountain. In its center is a statue of a baby bull with a star between his horns, which has become the town's official symbol. Throughout Spain, however, Teruel is best known as the scene of the tragic love affair between Diego de Marcilla and Isabel de Segura, the star-crossed, 13th-century "Lovers of Teruel," whose story is reminiscent of *Romeo and Juliet.* A double grave, unearthed in the 16th century, was presumed to be theirs, and their embracing skeletons now rest in a macabre transparent crypt in a funerary chapel by another of the city's Mudéjar towers (San Pedro; open Tuesdays through Saturdays from 10 AM to 2 PM and from 5 to 7:30 PM; Sundays from 10:30 AM to 2 PM; admission charge). Over the centuries, many Spanish poets, dramatists, and artists have been inspired by the story, which has made Teruel a favorite destination for honeymoon couples. (For a detailed version of this tragic tale, visit the tourist office at 1 Tomás Nogués; phone: 74-602279.)

CHECKING IN

Reina Cristina The only comfortable establishment in town, it's near the Salvador church and tower and has 62 rooms equipped with the most modern conveniences. The dining room serves satisfactory regional specialties. 1 Paseo del Ovalo, Teruel (phone: 74-606860). Expensive.

EATING OUT

El Milagro Good home cooking that makes the most of local products. Roasts and mountain-cured ham, or *jamón serrano,* go well with the hearty cariñena wine. Open daily. Reservations unnecessary. Major credit cards accepted. It also has some modest rooms with showers available. Carretera Teruel–Zaragoza (N234), Km 2, Teruel (phone: 74-603095). Moderate.

En Route from Teruel To the southeast, N234 leads to Valencia; to the southwest, N420 leads to Cuenca and ultimately back to Madrid. But Albarracín, a village practically plastered against a steep slope 24 miles (38 km) west of Teruel, is worth a detour even for those planning to backtrack to Valencia rather than continue over the mountains to Cuenca. Leave Teruel heading north on N234, following the signs to the airport, and after about 6 miles (10 km), turn off where signposted to Albarracín. The road climbs steadily until it reaches the Guadalaviar River, which threads past a handful of modern apartments on the outskirts of the town.

ALBARRACÍN This small medieval village rises in a breathtaking vertical sweep to the snaggletoothed battlements that guard its rear, with the Guadalaviar River encircling it like a natural moat. The town fortifications date from the late 10th century and the 11th century, and exemplify the military style of that time. The village has retained its medieval character and as a result has been declared a national monument. Tall, half-timbered houses are daubed in rosy plaster, with balconies made of wrought iron or carved wood. Escutcheons mark the nobler houses, and around each corner is a view on a new level. The museum in the chapterhouse of the 13th-century Cathedral of El Salvador contains a collection of rather worn 16th-century Flemish tapestries, but the life-size trout carved from rock crystal is more treasured by the villagers (open daily from 11 AM to 1 PM and from 5 to 8 PM; admission charge). Despite its isolation, Albarracín has been discovered by intrepid summer crowds.

CHECKING IN

Albarracín This old house stands out from the rest of the village because it's the only building with a satellite dish. With 45 rooms, it is the most comfortable — if not the most authentic — place to stay, and it also has a passable restaurant. Calle Azagra, Albarracín (phone: 74-710011). Expensive to moderate.

EATING OUT

El Portal Right in the middle of the village, this welcoming bar serves hot snacks and hearty meals; the set menu is filling. Reservations unnecessary. Major credit cards accepted. 14 Portal de Molina, Albarracín (phone: 74-710290). Moderate to inexpensive.

En Route from Albarracín If the pass over the Montes Universales is open, take the spectacular winding drive through Tragacete and on to the strange formations of the Ciudad Encantada outside Cuenca (see *Castile–La Mancha (New Castile)*, DIRECTIONS). Otherwise, return to Teruel via the southern loop, past the three protected caves containing prehistoric petroglyphs of bulls stenciled on the rocks near Abrigos del Callejón. The caves are well marked and are hard to miss (huge arrows posted on trees and painted on cliffs mark the trails). From Teruel, head toward Valencia on the N234 and E26 highways, both clearly marked. The road passes through a wild area of the southeast corner of Teruel province called the Maestrazgo and soon flattens into the fertile Valencian *huerta*.

Madrid Region

It's not necessary to go as far as Toledo or Segovia to escape the bustle of Madrid or see a bit of Castile. Within an hour's drive of the capital, traffic permitting, it's possible to sample huge fresh strawberries at a green oasis in the dusty plains, visit the house where Cervantes was born, or take in the cool peaks of the Sierra de Guadarrama.

Madrid is often blisteringly hot in summer, and *madrileños* who don't go to the coast head for the hills of the Sierra de Guadarrama. The mountain towns aren't especially beautiful, but they serve as weekend retreats and bases for hiking (in winter, the higher villages attract about 300,000 skiers each year). There are also some beautiful scenic views, especially where the mountains overlook a river or a reservoir.

To the south, where the dusty plains of Castile–La Mancha begin, the countryside is far from exciting, but there are at least two spots in this area worth visiting. One is the delightful little medieval village of Chinchón, today famous for its widely consumed *anís de Chinchón* liqueur. The other is Aranjuez, a former royal residence that is still an oasis of luxuriant gardens and abundant vegetation. To the east, Alcalá de Henares is best known as the birthplace of the man who wrote *Don Quixote*. And the greatest cultural attraction in the immediate Madrid region is the monumental monastery and palace of El Escorial. A few miles away is the controversial monument called the Valley of the Fallen, the burial site of Generalísimo Francisco Franco.

This chapter has been designed so that, with one exception, these locations can be enjoyed in easily managed day trips (the Sierra de Guadarrama excursion is best done in 2 days). Apart from two establishments, no hotels have been recommended in this chapter, as it is assumed that the traveler will be based in Madrid. Both hostelries are categorized as expensive, which means a double room ranges from $110 to $130 a night. Along the way, lunch or dinner for two with wine will cost $75 and above in an expensive restaurant and between $55 and $70 in a moderate one. Note that the Province of Madrid Tourist Office (2 Calle Duque de Medinaceli; phone: 1-429-4951 or 1-429-3177) can be very helpful in furnishing information regarding the sightseeing attractions in the Madrid region. The numbers listed here include local area codes; when calling from another area in Spain, dial "9" first.

Day Trip 1: Chinchón and Aranjuez

These two towns are the most beautiful in the southern Madrid region. Chinchón, little more than a village, has hardly changed since the Middle Ages. Aranjuez is a green, spacious oasis in the dusty La Mancha plain, adorned with luxurious gardens surrounding royal palaces and regal retreats.

_____

En Route from Madrid Leave town at the main Atocha railway station in southern Madrid, following the A3 (which becomes the N-III) signs to Valencia. Fourteen miles (22 km) along a well-paved highway, the Arganda Bridge crosses the Jarama River; immediately afterward is the C300 turnoff to Chinchón, 28 miles (45 km) from Madrid.

CHINCHÓN To say there is nothing much to Chinchón (pop. 4,100) would be an understatement. Founded in 1085, the village's centerpiece today is the 16th-century Plaza Mayor, an oddly shaped "square" of rickety 3-story arcaded buildings topped with 224 wooden balconies. The village was immortalized in the film *Around the World in 80 Days,* and draws as many as 15,000 visitors per weekend, many of whom arrive in cars and park in and around the square. An underground garage some 275 yards from the plaza is scheduled to be completed this year, leaving the square traffic-free and even more attractive. Since 1502, the square has been the site of bullfights, and it is still occasionally cordoned off for them. They are usually held during fiesta week, August 13 through 18, but be warned — it is usually scorching hot at that time of the year.

Try to visit Chinchón during spring or early summer. Sit at one of the many open-air cafés in the Plaza Mayor and enjoy a small glass of the drink for which the village is nationally famous. The *anís* of Chinchón is made with the oily seeds of locally grown anise, a member of the parsley family, and alcohol. Those who haven't eaten yet should ask for the *dulce,* or sweet, variety — the *seco,* or dry, is potent stuff!

Chinchón is also famous for its garlic, and for bread baked in the shapes of fish, horses, owls, eagles, and other animals. The loaves can be bought varnished for decoration or unvarnished to eat. There are several bakeries on the Plaza Mayor — the widest assortment of strange breads is found at *Luis Ontalva* (25 Plaza Mayor). Looming over one side of the square is the parish church, the Church of the Asunción, built between 1534 and 1626, with an *Assumption of the Virgin* by Goya, who often stayed in Chinchón. Just behind the opposite corner is the *Parador de Chinchón* (see below), from which there is a good view of the well-preserved 15th-century castle, with its circular fortified towers; it was sacked, along with the rest of the town, by Napoleon's troops in 1808.

CHECKING IN

Parador de Chinchón A former 17th-century Augustinian convent, this 38-room *parador* is extremely tranquil and boasts terraced gardens, an open-air swimming pool, a bar, and a good restaurant. For additional details see *Paradors* in DIVERSIONS. 1 Av. del Generalísimo, Chinchón (phone: 1-894-0836; in the US, 212-686-9213; fax: 1-894-0908). Expensive.

EATING OUT

Mesón Cuevas del Vino An informal eating place located in converted wine and oil stores. In the basement, notice the 400-year-old caves between huge, centuries-old wine vats. Try *alubias de Chinchón* (local green beans in a meaty stock) and *cochinillo asado* (roast suckling pig). Reservations advised. American Express accepted. 13 Calle Benito Hortelano, Chinchón (phone: 1-894-0206). Moderate.

Plaza Mayor This delightful narrow building has 3 floors of small dining rooms, with a lovely balcony on the third. Fresh fish arrives daily and is well prepared; the roast lamb is succulent. Closed Wednesdays and the last week of August and the first week of September. Reservations unnecessary, except for lunch on Sundays. American Express, Diners Club, and Visa accepted. 10 Plaza Mayor, Chinchón (phone: 1-894-0929). Moderate.

En Route from Chinchón The pleasant country road to Aranjuez, 14 miles (22 km) away, is clearly marked; it passes through the village of Villaconejos.

ARANJUEZ This town (pronounced Ah-rahn-*hwayth*) enjoys a pleasant climate that provides a respite from the blistering summer heat. This fact wasn't lost on Spanish monarchs, whose efforts at creating a Spanish version of Versailles here attract many visitors today. The informal Jardín de la Isla, on an island in the river next to the Royal Palace, dates from Philip II's time in the 16th century. Philip V, whose rule spanned the first half of the 18th century, chose Aranjuez as a royal residence. His successors, Ferdinand VI and Carlos III, embellished the Royal Palace — a fire destroyed much of the original building in 1712, and the present building was constructed in 1744 — and built a huge square in front of it and the large, French-modeled Parterre gardens around it. From 1792 to 1803, Carlos IV built a second "palace," the Casa del Labrador, in some ways as beautiful as the first though much smaller, and added the vast landscaped park — Jardín del Príncipe (Prince's Garden) — that surrounds it.

The spacious leafy gardens and long, tree-shaded avenues of Aranjuez are the perfect place for an unhurried stroll. The Royal Palace and the Casa del Labrador are both richly decorated with ornaments, including priceless gifts from royalty around the world. The palace has hundreds of rooms; the best known is the Porcelain Salon, the former reception hall, whose walls and ceilings are covered with white porcelain by the Italian artist Gricci. The Casa del Labrador (or Peasant's House, so named because a farmworker's home used to stand on the site), in the nearby Jardín del Príncipe, contains an abundance of marble, gold, semi-precious stone, crystal, silk hangings, Roman mosaics, huge chandeliers, and 27 elaborate clocks. The gardens are open daily from 10 AM to dusk. The Royal Palace and the Casa del Labrador are open from 10 AM to 6:30 PM, April through

September; 10 AM to 5:30 PM, October through March; closed Mondays. A combined ticket allows entry to the palace (the visit here is by guided tour) and the Casa del Labrador; no admission charge to the gardens.

The town is nationally famous for its delicious crops, asparagus and strawberries in particular, and from March through May the roadsides are crammed with stalls selling produce. A meal isn't complete here without a first course of green asparagus and a dessert of strawberries and cream. A popular excursion for *madrileños* is the wonderful *Tren de la Fresa* (Strawberry Train), a 19th-century–style steam train that runs to Aranjuez from Atocha Station in Madrid every Saturday, Sunday, and public holiday from May through mid-October. The ticket (currently about $23) includes visits to the palace and the gardens — and free strawberries on the train. The Aranjuez Tourist Office (Plaza Puente de Barcas; phone:1-891-0427) is open Mondays through Fridays from 10 to 2 PM and from 3 to 4:30 PM; alternate Saturdays from 10 AM to 2 PM.

EATING OUT

Casa Pablo Pablo Guzmán offers an extensive menu of Castilian specialties, including fresh fish and game. The walls of the bar and the 2 dining rooms are covered with bullfighting posters and photos of writers, painters, and musicians who've eaten here. Closed August. Reservations unnecessary. Visa accepted. 42 Calle Almíbar, Aranjuez (phone: 1-891-1451). Expensive.

La Rana Verde The *Green Frog* is indeed green — the waiters' jackets, the menu covers, the decor, and even the Tagus River, which flows by numerous windows. Get here early for a riverside table. The place is touristy and large, but with good food — try *espárragos verdes naturales* (fresh green asparagus), *pavo en salsa de almendra* (turkey in almond sauce), and the inevitable *fresones con nata* (strawberries and cream). Open daily. Reservations advised. Visa and MasterCard accepted. 1 Calle Reina, Aranjuez (phone: 1-891-1325). Moderate.

En Route to Madrid For a quick drive 30 miles (48 km) back to Madrid, take the N-IV Madrid–Andalusia highway heading north.

En Route to Toledo Just south of Aranjuez on N-IV is the N400 turnoff to Toledo, 27 miles (43 km) away along a straight road that follows the Tagus River.

Day Trip 2: Alcalá de Henares and Nuevo Baztán

A person needs a strong interest in history to profit from a journey to Alcalá de Henares, formerly an ancient university center but now little more than a bustling bedroom community for Madrid, 19 miles (31 km) away; its streets, though lined with medieval buildings, are choked by permanent traffic jams. The only other place in this region east of Madrid worth visiting is the village of Nuevo Baztán, which has some curiosity value.

En Route from Madrid Take the A2 highway (it later becomes the N-II) out of northeast Madrid, easily found because it is the route to the well-marked Barajas Airport. This is also the main highway to Barcelona, so the traffic is often brutal. A few miles before Alcalá de Henares, the highway passes the US air base of Torrejón de Ardoz. The 16th-century Casa Grande at the entrance to Torrejón on 2 Calle Madrid is an interesting complex of farm buildings and wine cellars that have been converted into restaurants and an unusual museum of Russian and Nordic icons (phone: 1-675-3900) The museum is open Tuesdays through Saturdays from 11 AM to 2 PM and from 3:30 to 6 PM; from 3:30 to 6 PM on Sundays; admission charge. At Torrejón, travelers might want to take a 7½-mile (12-km) detour south along N206 to the sleepy village of Loeches (pop. 2,100), which was a Moorish fortress and still has a 16th-century church and two convents.

ALCALÁ DE HENARES The greatest writer in the Spanish language, Miguel de Cervantes, author of *Don Quixote,* was born here in 1547, but the town's history goes back much further. The area around Alcalá de Henares (pop. 155,000) includes several prehistoric, Roman, and Visigothic sites, but unfortunately none is open to the public. A 3,600-square-foot Roman site from the 4th century was discovered in 1988, and it includes an important multicolored mosaic from a villa in the Roman settlement of Complutum, in the Henares River valley. The nearest anyone can get to the remains is the *Museo Tear* (Camino de Juncal; phone: 1-881-3250), an archaeological museum and workshop where students piece together the remains (usually open Saturdays and Sundays from 10 AM to 2 PM; no admission charge). Greater access to such historic remains should come with the new *Museo Arqueológico Comarcal,* scheduled to open this year in the former Convento de la Madre de Dios in the Plaza de las Bernardas.

Alcalá's golden age began in 1498, when Cardinal Cisneros founded the famous Complutensian University. For many years the most important in Spain, it published Europe's first polyglot Bible, a six-volume work printed from 1514 to 1517, with side-by-side texts in Hebrew, Greek, Latin, Chaldee, and Syriac. Many colleges and convents were built in the next 2 centuries, but the historic university was moved to Madrid in 1836, and the city has declined in importance ever since. The original university complex, the Colegio de San Ildefonso, in the Plaza San Diego (near the main Plaza Cervantes), is now the site of the much newer Alcalá University, which has become an important center of North American studies. Its 16th-century Plateresque façade is interesting; the doorway leads into the arcaded Patio de Santo Tomás and the Paraninfo, or auditorium, and on to the adjacent Patio Trilingüe (Courtyard of Three Languages), so named because Greek, Latin, and Hebrew were taught here. The university can be visited daily except Mondays, but the hours vary; there's no admission charge.

Other monuments of note in Alcalá include the Iglesia Magistral de San Justo, an imposing 17th-century church with a Gothic portal; the 13th-through 16th-century Archbishop's Palace, badly damaged by fire in 1939 (most of the town's churches suffered damage during the 1931–39 Second Republic and Spanish Civil War); and the Chapel of San Ildefonso (2 Calle Pedro Gumiel), where Cardinal Cisneros's 16th-century marble tomb is on display. The *Salón Cervantes* (Calle Santiago), the town's only theater, was built in 1888 and is now open after many years of restoration. The unusual *Museo del Perfume,* opened at the end of 1991, is located at Gal, the soap-and-perfume factory, 1½ miles (3 km) from the town center, at Km 31 on N-II.

Local authorities are "75% certain" that Cervantes was born on the site of the *Casa de Cervantes* (48 Calle Mayor), where a well-reproduced period house and museum now stand. Built in 1956, the present building contains period furniture, an arcaded interior patio with eight granite columns holding up wooden balconies, and many old manuscripts and copies of *Don Quixote.* The house is open Tuesdays through Fridays from 10 AM to 2 PM and from 4 to 7 PM; weekends from 10 AM to 2 PM; no admission charge. The tourist office nearby (Callejón de Santa María; phone: 1-889-2694) is open Tuesdays through Saturdays from 9:30 AM to 1:30 PM and from 4:30 to 6:30 PM; Sundays from 9:30 AM to 1:30 PM.

EATING OUT

Hostería del Estudiante This early-16th-century eatery is part of the original university complex, adjacent to the Patio Trilingüe. The food is typically Castilian. Try *sopa castellana* (bread and garlic soup) and, in mid-afternoon, *chocolate con migas* (hot chocolate with fried bread crumbs). Open daily; during July and August, only lunch is served. Reservations advised during school terms (from October through June, approximately). Major credit cards accepted. 3 Calle Los Colegios, Alcalá de Henares (phone: 1-888-0330). Expensive.

San Diego A pleasant upstairs dining room, it faces the 16th-century university façade. Try the *churrasco de ternera* (thick steaks served on a grill over hot coals in a metal bowl, so that it slowly cooks on the table while diners are finishing the first course). Reservations unnecessary. Visa and MasterCard accepted. 5 Plaza San Diego, Alcalá de Henares (phone: 1-888-3097). Moderate.

En Route from Alcalá de Henares Take N230 south to Nuevo Baztán, 12½ miles (20 km) away, past the villages of El Gurugu and Valverde de Alcalá.

NUEVO BAZTÁN This semi-derelict village of barely 500 people is undergoing much-needed repairs. Its interest lies in the fact that it was designed during the early 18th century by the leading baroque architect, José de Churriguera, and is the only example of his work in the Madrid region. The parish Church of San Francisco Javier and the palace here are noteworthy, but are not expected to regain their full churrigueresque charm until restoration is completed. There are plans to eventually convert the palace into the International School of Music.

En Route to Madrid Madrid is 32 miles (51 km) from Nuevo Baztán, via Alcalá de Henares.

En Route to Guadalajara Another 15½ miles (25 km) along the N-II highway from Alcalá de Henares toward Barcelona is Guadalajara, a historic town; see *Castile–La Mancha (New Castile),* DIRECTIONS.

Day Trip 3: El Pardo, El Escorial, and the Valley of the Fallen

This trip takes in the foothills of the Sierra de Guadarrama and includes some of the prettier villages — as well as the most popular weekend and summer resorts — in the Madrid region. The main attraction is the Real Monasterio de El Escorial, one of the most famous monasteries in the world.

En Route from Madrid Take the A6 Madrid–La Coruña highway out of northwest Madrid; while still in the city's outskirts at Puerto de Hierro, take the C601 turnoff to El Pardo, a few miles ahead through some lovely woods.

EL PARDO The highlight of the quiet village, 9 miles (14 km) from Madrid, is the delightful El Pardo Palace, a royal residence built in the 16th century on the foundations of a former hunting lodge, partly destroyed by fire in 1604 and enlarged in 1772. Generalísimo Francisco Franco lived here until his death in 1975, and the palace now serves as home to visiting heads of state; when not occupied, it is open to the public. Inside are paintings, frescoes (including some showing the palace's original furnishings), period furniture, and an extensive, fine collection of wall tapestries. Other charming buildings nearby include the Casita del Príncipe (Prince's Cottage), also built in 1772, and the Quinta del Pardo (phone: 1-450-6775), with a collection of 19th-century wallpapers. These two and the palace (when not pressed into service as guest quarters for VIPs) are open Mondays through Saturdays from 10 AM to 12:15 PM and from 3 to 5:30 PM; 10 AM to 1:40 PM on Sundays in the winter; the complex opens at 9:30 AM in the summer; a single admission charge covers all three (phone: 1-376-0329). The Convento de los Capuchinos, on the outskirts of town, contains a magnificent early 17th-century wooden carving of the *Recumbent Christ* by Gregorio Fernández. The royal park preceding El Pardo houses the smaller Palacio de la Zarzuela, also a former hunting lodge, dating from the 17th century and rebuilt during the 18th century. Badly damaged during the Spanish Civil War, it was rebuilt in the 1960s and is now the principal residence of King Juan Carlos and Queen Sofía and closed to the public.

En Route from El Pardo Back on A6, the turnoff to El Escorial — C505 — is clearly marked at Las Rozas, which is 10 miles (16 km) from Madrid. The road leads to the small town of San Lorenzo de El Escorial, 29 miles (46 km) from Madrid, but way before reaching it, travelers see the enormous rectangular monastery looming in the distance.

EL ESCORIAL Philip II, the man who sent the "invincible" Spanish Armada to conquer Queen Elizabeth I's England and transferred the Spanish capital from Toledo to Madrid, was a deeply religious ruler who reigned during the zenith of Spain's Catholic Empire. In 1557, after Philip's army defeated the French in the battle of Saint-Quentin on St. Lawrence's Day, Philip decided to establish a monastery in the saint's honor. The building was also to serve as a mausoleum for his parents, Charles V and Queen Isabel, and as a royal summer residence.

Built over the course of 21 years (1563 to 1584) by some 3,000 people, El Escorial comprises not only a monastery, a mausoleum, and a royal residence, but also a church, two palaces, a school, and one of the most important libraries in Spain. An ambiguous structure, it manages to be both a grand repository of riches and a monument of grim, monastic austerity.

The severe exterior of the church, for example, gives way to the grandeur of the interior with its elaborate high altar, painted ceilings, and richly decorated side chapels. All the paintings are by Italian artists and show events in the life of Christ — except for one that portrays St. Lawrence being martyred on a grill. There are statues here of Philip and three of his four wives; England's Mary Tudor is missing simply because she never visited Spain. One of the chapels contains a beautiful statue of *Christ on the Cross,* created by Benvenuto Cellini in 1562 from one piece of marble. Directly below the main altar is the Panteón de los Reyes (or Royal Pantheon), reached by a marble and jasper stairway. Here, in black and brown gilded marble tombs, lies every Spanish monarch since the Holy Roman Emperor Charles V (King Charles I of Spain), except Philip V and Ferdinand VI. Also entombed are some of the country's queens, but only those who gave birth to a future king. Next door is the Panteón de los Infantes, where several princes and princesses are buried.

Many sections of El Escorial were added by later monarchs, which explains the varied styles in the Palacios (Royal Apartments). The centerpiece of the 16th-century Hapsburg Palace is a long room with a single

180-foot fresco depicting a glorious Catholic victory over the Moors. Philip's cell-like bedroom, where he died at age 71 from gout, says everything about the man. It is virtually undecorated, simple and austere, and in it hangs a single portrait of his pallid face, painted when he was 70. The 18th-century Bourbon Palace is considerably less somber. There are dozens of fine tapestries made at the Royal Factory in Madrid, many showing scenes designed by Goya. Elsewhere, the Biblioteca (Library), above the monastery entrance, has a marvelous Renaissance vaulted ceiling; among its treasures are the personal collection of Philip II, unique Arab and Hebrew manuscripts, the 10th-century Codex Albedensis, St. Teresa of Avila's personal diary, and a Bible lettered entirely in gold. The *Nuevos Museos* (New Museums) contain works of art by Bosch, El Greco, Ribera, Veronese, Velázquez, Zurbarán, Titian, and many others. The Escorial complex (phone: 1-890-5904) is open Tuesdays through Sundays from 10 AM to 7 PM (last entry at 6 PM), April through September; from 10 AM to 6 PM (last entry at 5 PM), October through March; admission charge. The tourist office in San Lorenzo de El Escorial is at 10 Calle Floridablanca (phone: 1-890-1554).

EATING OUT

Charolés Traditional Castilian food in what is traditionally the best place in "monastery town," although recently the menu has shifted its focus more and more to international fare. Try *cocido madrileño* (a mixture of chickpeas, boiled vegetables, and boiled meats) and *berenjenas rellenas con langostinos frescos* (eggplant stuffed with fresh prawns). In summer, dine on the charming open-air terrace. Reservations advised. Major credit cards accepted. 24 Calle Floridablanca, San Lorenzo de El Escorial (phone: 1-890-5975). Expensive.

Renacimiento This elegant restaurant, located in the plush *Victoria Palace* hotel, exudes the charm of a fancy British tea shop. Meat specialities, such as *churrasco* (T-bone steaks) dominate the menu. Reservations necessary in the summer. Major credit cards accepted. 4 Calle Juan de Toledo, San Lorenzo de El Escorial (phone: 1-890-1511). Expensive.

Mesón La Cueva A charming eatery in a former 18th-century inn, The Cave (in English — and that's what it feels like) serves the usual Castilian specialties and roast meats. Try *judías con chorizo* (broad beans with salami-style fried sausage). Closed Mondays. Reservations advised. No credit cards accepted. 4 Calle San Antón, San Lorenzo de El Escorial (phone: 1-890-1516). Moderate.

En Route from El Escorial Take C600 north for 6 miles (10 km) to the turnoff for *El Valle de los Caídos* (Valley of the Fallen). The huge cross is visible a few miles in the distance.

VALLEY OF THE FALLEN This stark place not only pays homage to the estimated 1 million dead of Spain's 1936–39 Civil War, but also to the thousands of men on the losing side who died while building the monument. The *Valle de los Caídos* (phone: 1-890-5611) is a huge basilica carved deep into a granite mountain in the forbidding Cuelgamuros Valley. It is topped by an enormous granite cross that stands 495 feet high — as tall as a 33-floor building — on the hill above it.

Generalísimo Francisco Franco ordered the place built as a final resting place for himself and for José Antonio Primo de Rivera, founder of the Spanish Falange, and in honor of the war dead. The crypt contains the coffins of 40,000 soldiers of both sides who were killed in the Civil War, but only prisoners of war from the losing Republican side worked on the monument. The basilica took 10 years (1940 to 1950) to construct, and the cross another 9 years — 19 years and thousands of lives in all. Everything was designed to have religious significance — the sculpture of Pity over the entrance is of the Virgin Mary holding Christ. Franco himself chose the tree from which a wooden cross inside the basilica was cut. The dome of the altar under the cross is a mosaic with 5 million pieces, one of the rare examples of gaiety in this dank underground tunnel (open Tuesdays through Sundays from dawn to dusk; admission charge).

En Route to Madrid Drive back to San Lorenzo de El Escorial and then proceed along C505 to Las Rozas for the final stretch along A6 to Madrid.

En Route to Avila Thirty-six miles (58 km) west of El Escorial along C505 is the walled city of Avila, the highest provincial capital in Spain. For details on Avila, see *Castile-León (Old Castile)*, DIRECTIONS.

Day Trip 4: Sierra de Guadarrama

This is a 2-day trip, with an overnight stop at the converted 14th-century monastery high up in the Sierra de Guadarrama range. The range, which peaks at close to 6,560 feet, runs along a line about 44 miles (70 km) northwest of Madrid. There are several small towns in these mountains, and recently expanded and improved skiing facilities. Although the towns are ordinary and the views are easily surpassed in northern Spain, the mountains offer an easy and pleasant escape from Madrid's summer heat.

En Route from Madrid Leave Madrid through the Arch of Triumph at Moncloa in the west of the city and drive past university buildings onto the A6 highway. Twenty-four miles (38 km) away, straddling A6, is Collado-

Villalba (at an altitude of 3,000 feet); cross the bridge spanning A6 and get on the old N-VI highway. Six miles (10 km) along is the village of Guadarrama (pop. 6,000), mentioned in Cervantes's classic, *Don Quixote*. It's a busy little place, founded by Alfonso X in 1268, with a handful of 18th-century buildings and an ornate fountain.

The M710 turnoff for Cercedilla is 200 yards beyond the village, and the old road climbs as it follows the Guadarrama River. At 3,900 feet, Cercedilla is a very popular hiking center. *Madrileños* drive out the 37 miles (59 km) on weekends, go for a 6-hour trek in the hills, and return in the evening. In winter, it is also an important base for skiing at Puerto de Navacerrada, just 8 miles (13 km) away.

Take C607 east out of town to N601, which leads to the village of Navacerrada, 3,945 feet above sea level and surrounded by lovely countryside. From Navacerrada, the 2-day trip can be continued along two possible routes. Five miles (8 km) north on C601 is the ski resort of Puerto de Navacerrada, which stands at 6,100 feet at the beginning of the most rugged part of the Sierra de Guadarrama. Stop here to admire the view from the highest point in the region accessible by road; there's little point in lingering unless you've come to ski. (The hotels and restaurants are standard fare for a middling ski resort.) From Puerto de Navacerrada, C604 starts and leads northeast into the mountains, toward El Paular, while N601 begins to descend as it continues northwest.

En Route to Segovia The N601 highway from Puerto de Navacerrada continues directly northwest to Segovia. For complete details on the city and its sights, hotels, and restaurants, see *Segovia* in THE CITIES.

En Route to El Paular Take C604 north from Puerto de Navacerrada, signposted to Rascafría. The road is very twisting and the mountains on either side are thickly wooded, with some very pretty sights. The hotel-monastery of *Santa María del Paular* is 14 miles (22 km) away, over the 6,000-foot-high Puerto de los Cotos pass.

A gentler alternative to El Paular is the long way around from Navacerrada, taking C607 eastward toward Cerceda, 5½ miles (9 km) away, then M611 another 4½ miles (7 km) to Manzanares el Real (pop. 1,800; altitude 2,980 feet). Manzanares el Real is famous for the charming and well-restored 15th-century castle of the Dukes of Infantado, one of Spain's best examples of Castilian military architecture. The castle, with its three cyclindrical towers, is a mixture of Mudéjar and Renaissance-Gothic styles, and it houses a small museum (phone: 1-853-00080) displaying models and documents relating to various Spanish castles. The adjacent Santillana reservoir enhances the castle's beauty (open Tuesdays through Saturdays from 10 AM to 2 PM and from 3 to 6 PM in the summer; from 10 AM to 5 PM in the winter; admission charge).

From Manzanares, take M612 for 5 miles (8 km) to Soto del Real, and then M614 another 5 miles (8 km) north to the pretty town of Miraflores de la Sierra (pop. 2,600). Despite recent expansion as a holiday center, the oldest part around the Plaza España retains a mountain village charm. The 16th-century parish church is of several different architectural styles.

EATING OUT

Asador La Fuente This traditional roast house has a 2-story dining room tastefully decorated with tiles, wood, and rustic bricks. There is also a terrace for summer dining. Try *morcilla de Burgos* (Burgos blood pudding) and *buey gallego en parrilla de carbón* (Galician beefsteak grilled over hot coals). Closed Mondays and mid-October to mid-November. Reservations necessary on weekends. Major credit cards accepted. 12 Calle Mayor, Miraflores de la Sierra (phone: 1-844-4216). Expensive.

Maito A comfortable and solid mountain house. Down-home cooking is featured, with many of the fruits and vegetables from the restaurant's own garden. Try *sopa pastora* (garlic and bread soup) and *cochinillo asado* (roast suckling pig). Open daily. Reservations advised. Major credit cards accepted. 5 Calle Calvo Sotelo, Miraflores de la Sierra (phone: 1-844-3567). Moderate.

En Route from Miraflores de la Sierra Take M6141 16 miles (26 km) away over the twisting, 5,890-foot-high Puerto de la Morcuera pass to the village of Rascafría (pop. 1,300). Less than a mile (1.6 km) away is the hotel-monastery of *Santa María del Paular* (see below), which is really all there is in El Paular. Both villages lie on C604.

CHECKING IN/EATING OUT

Santa María del Paular A quiet, converted 14th-century monastery, with 58 luxurious air conditioned rooms overlooking an arcaded patio, a fountain, and the surrounding pine forests. Facilities include a heated swimming pool, tennis courts, and gardens; there are bicycles for rent. The *Don Lope* restaurant is extremely good — try *sopa de cebolla gratinada* (onion soup with grated cheese topping) and *chuletón de Lozoya* (grilled local steaks). Visa, American Express, and Diners Club accepted. El Paular (phone: 1-869-1011; in the US, 800-221-2340; fax: 1-869-1006). Expensive.

En Route from El Paular and Rascafría Continue north on C604 past the village of Lozoya, where the road skirts the beautiful La Pinilla reservoir, to the main N-I highway. Before taking the highway south to Madrid, drive 4 miles (6 km) north to the walled village of Buitrago del Lozoya (pop. 1,300; altitude 3,200 feet), which is actually on a jut of land surrounded on three sides by the Lozoya River. There are some remains of the 10th-century Arab wall, and ruins of a 14th-century castle. The village had been a Roman settlement and later a fortress.

En Route to Madrid The Spanish capital is 48 miles (77 km) directly south on N-I, which is in excellent condition.

Castile–La Mancha
(New Castile)

Scattered across a landscape of arid mountains, thick-forested river valleys, and endless flat, stultifying plains, the communities of the Castile–La Mancha region appear as though they've been left behind by the modern world. Villages, though charming, seem cloaked in a sense of doom; little jewels of Renaissance religious architecture are boarded up and abandoned; and John Deere service signs — the only evidence of contemporary culture — line the main drags of dusty prairie crossroad towns. Tilled grain fields, vineyards, and shepherds who maneuver their flocks across the highway are reminders that hardscrabble agriculture provides over a third of this vast region's million and a half inhabitants with their only livelihood. Never a center of tourism, Castile–La Mancha, an autonomous community composed of the provinces of Guadalajara, Cuenca, Albacete, Ciudad Real, and Toledo, tends to be seen only by travelers on their way to somewhere else. But even if you omit the city of Toledo from the itinerary, the region's claim on the visitor's attention span is justified by three first-rate towns — Sigüenza, Cuenca, and Almagro — plus some unique swaths of landscape that stand out amid all the empty space that in some curious way manages to bind a vast, diverse region together.

The region was historically known as New Castile and, until 1977, it included Madrid and excluded Albacete. Originally part of the kingdom of Castile, its nucleus consisted of the southern lands that fell under Christian domination just after the reconquest of Toledo in 1085; the region was later expanded to include the harsh-contoured eastern plateau. New Castile was originally ruled by fighting religious brotherhoods (the Knights of Santiago, the Knights Templars, and the Knights of Calatrava) who received land and feudal privileges as rewards for their service in the Reconquest. While the Catholic church long wielded power from Toledo, secular control of the region later passed to noble dynasties. For centuries New Castile was the breadbasket of central Spain. But the land was never able to sustain a booming economy, especially after agriculturally more productive lands were incorporated into the greater nation unified by King Ferdinand and Queen Isabella in the 15th century. Miguel de Cervantes chose carefully when he had his fictitious Don Quixote seek out knightly adventures in tiny, dreary farm towns of La Mancha's flatlands.

For centuries the residents of the region managed a meager existence through farming and, for a time, small industry. Then, after years of neglect and relative isolation from the rest of Spain, the region's fortunes began to shift. In 1977 — 2 years after the death of Generalísimo Francisco Franco — the Spanish map was drastically overhauled, and the new autonomous community of Castile–La Mancha — which excludes Madrid and includes the adjacent province of Albacete — was formed. When the new regional authorities began to take inventory of their territory, they happily found that it had a lot more going for it than anyone had given it credit for: a varied and almost entirely untouched landscape, with winding rivers and inland lakes stretching from the arid, rust-colored foothills of Guadalajara to the lush green pine forests, towering granite cliffs, and deep-cut canyons of Cuenca. Even the vast, flat stretches of pokey old La Mancha turned out to possess towns of considerable charm, with extraordinary architectural flourishes in no way inferior to the castles, churches, and convents found in the rest of the region.

Unlike other parts of Spain, where visitors must pick their way through ugly industrial zones and high-rise apartment blocks to locate the "Old Quarter," this region has not only its monumental jewels fairly intact, but their settings as well. The market towns and villages have not changed much from former times, although they've paid a heavy social and economic price. Many villages have been abandoned altogether, and nearly all the towns along the way seem to be given over to elderly, beret-clad men. Women, strangely enough, remain unseen, and such adolescents as there are hang around listlessly on the street corners or in the rock 'n' roll bars, waiting for their chance to escape to the cities.

As might be expected, given the distinct provinces that make up this region, variety is the keynote in the culinary department. In northern Guadalajara, the Castilian taste for tender roast meat — suckling pig, lamb, and baby kid — predominates. In Cuenca, the visitor will come across a few dishes unheard-of elsewhere, such as *ajo arriero,* a creamy paste of mashed codfish and garlic, delicious when spread on Cuenca's excellent bread. In both areas, however, pride of place goes to small-game dishes — partridge, rabbit, and wild boar — and the trout, now mostly fattened in fish farms, but not too inferior to its riverbed cousin, and available year-round. La Mancha, where wine and cheese are first and foremost, is an altogether different story. But it, too, has a very tasty and unique menu, which shows its Moorish origins in unusual combinations of flavors: for instance, *migas del pastor* (croutons fried in olive oil, with garlic, ham, fatback, sausage, and grapes), stewed lamb seasoned with nutmeg, saffron, and white wine, and *pisto manchego* (a thick vegetable stew with beef or rabbit). The ubiquitous cheese, *queso manchego,* from ewe's milk, can be fresh from the farm or aged to bring out its strong flavor.

In laying out the following week-long drive through Castile–La Mancha, the entire province of Albacete and the provincial capital of Ciudad Real have been omitted; the former because its features are too similar to those covered elsewhere, and the latter because it's just not worth going out of your way to see. Autumn, when the leaves of the birch trees change color, is by far the best time to visit this region. At night, at these altitudes of 800 to 1,200 feet, the temperature can drop drastically — even in summer — so be prepared. And don't come in the winter; even local residents don't like it here during that severe season.

Expect to pay $60 or more for a double room with private bath in hotels classified as expensive, $40 to $60 in moderate hotels, and less than $35 in inexpensive ones. Dinner for two with wine will cost $45 or more in an expensive restaurant, $30 to $45 in a moderate restaurant, and below $25 in an inexpensive one. The telephone numbers listed below include local area codes; when calling from another area in Spain, dial "9" first.

En Route from Madrid Leave the city on the N-II highway heading northeast in the direction of the airport and Zaragoza. Be prepared for hideous traffic and endless factories, warehouses, and the automobile plants of Alacalá de Henares. Continue following the Zaragoza signs, giving Guadalajara a wide berth some 35 miles (56 km) along. Then, after about 11 miles (18 km) of what begins to look like real country, and after the 13th-century Templar castle of Torija (the Templars were a religious and military order) is visible on the right, take the turnoff for Brihuega (C201) immediately before the next overpass. Brihuega is a lovely, run-down old town, perched above a dried-up river gorge. It's worth a stop for a cup of coffee, some leg-stretching, and a look at the much-restored 13th-century Romanesque and Gothic Church of Santa María de la Peña and the ruins of the Old City walls, of which two city gates remain. Up the hill, the structure resembling a gigantic bandstand pavilion once served as the Royal Cloth Factory, established by the enlightened King Carlos III during the 18th century. It later became a marvelous French garden, but it has been left unattended for years, growing surrealistically wild. On the way out of Brihuega, a signpost indicates the old road to Sigüenza, forking to the right; take this, to avoid backtracking to the N-II, and follow it through fields that, in season, are a mass of sunflowers. After 11 miles (18 km), turn briefly north onto C204 to rejoin N-II heading for Zaragoza. Almost immediately afterward, exit N-II via the ramp for Sigüenza, and again join C204 north for 16 miles (26 km) into town.

SIGÜENZA By themselves, a castle and a cathedral do not a medieval town make, but when both dominate the skyline from surrounding hills, they seem equal to the task. The fairly prosperous farmers and artisans who live here, in what once was a major medieval archdiocese, confer a pleasant rural bustle. The town is set at an altitude of 3,360 feet, overlooking the Henares River, and inevitably all of the climbing streets lead to the 12th-century cathedral (Plaza de Don Bernardo; open Mondays through Saturdays from 10 AM to 1 PM and from 4 to 6 PM). A true beauty, the cathedral is the result of centuries of changing architectural and decorative styles, from the Mudéjar — the star-studded chapter house ceiling — to the Plateresque, all blending together with unusual harmony. Seek out and pay one of the ushers 5 or 10 *duros* (a 25- or 50-peseta coin) to unlock and illuminate the side chapel for a look at the town's main attraction, the tomb of the Doncel (Page Boy), who is represented in alabaster as a young man in knightly battle dress, with a sweetly innocent, melancholy expression, reclining on his side and reading from what might as well be a book of love sonnets. Beneath this captivating but mislabeled anonymous sepulchral statue are the remains of Don Martín Vázquez de Arce, who was, in fact, not a page boy but a 25-year-old married man and a full knight in Queen Isabella's service when he died in battle in 1486 during the Granada campaigns.

Other sites in town include an Ursuline convent, a baroque seminary, and the Romanesque Church of San Vicente. The *Diocesan Museum* (opposite the cathedral; no phone; open daily from 10 AM to 2 PM and from 4 to 7 PM; admission charge) has a vigorous late El Greco *Annunciation,* as well as Zurbarán's extraordinary *Immaculate Conception,* showing a preteen Virgin Mary floating over the city of Seville. A pleasant short walk — through the medieval arch between the cathedral and the Renaissance Plaza Mayor, keeping to the right where the modern bungalows begin, and on up the hill to the cemetery — leads to a great view of the cathedral and Sigüenza's castle, which has been turned into a *parador* (see *Checking In/Eating Out*); both are well lit after dark. The streets leading up to the *parador* are lined with crafts shops where hooked rugs, wrought-ironware, and decorative mirrors in hammered-copper and hardwood frames are sold. Jesús Blasco's workshop (Calle Cruz Dorada; phone: 11-390486) is the place for hand-sewn goatskin fishermen's boots and wineskins. Sigüenza's tourist office is located at 2 Cardenal Mendoza (phone: 11-391262).

CHECKING IN/EATING OUT

Parador Castillo de Sigüenza Commanding the crest of the town, this old Moorish fortress, later occupied and neglected by Sigüenza's bishops, now offers 77 rooms within its admirably reconstructed medieval battlements. Ask for one of the rooms with a balcony overlooking the Patio de Armas, available at a slight surcharge. The building has both air conditioning and central heating, and its huge interior halls make it a favorite place for business conventions. The restaurant offers a fine selection of regional specialties — game in season, fresh river crayfish, and roasts — in a pleasant atmosphere, though it's a bit overpriced. Major credit cards accepted. Plaza del Castillo, Sigüenza (phone: 11-390100; in the US, 212-686-9213; fax: 11-391364). Expensive.

El Doncel A comfortable, clean, 20-room *hostal* facing the town's elm-lined promenade. The restaurant specializes in roast kid. Major credit cards accepted. 1 Calle General Mola, Sigüenza (phone: 11-391090). Inexpensive.

El Motor This *hostal* on the town's farthest outskirts has 10 rooms and a restaurant that does a reliable if unexciting job with its mostly international menu, especially steaks. The restaurant is closed Mondays, the last 2 weeks in April, and the first 2 weeks in November. Visa accepted. Carretera Madrid, Sigüenza (phone: 11-390827). Inexpensive.

En Route from Sigüenza It's well worth an extra night in Sigüenza to allow for an excursion into the surrounding mountain towns. All told, the suggested loop that follows entails a detour of 172 miles (275 km), but it can be cut short at more than one point for the return to Sigüenza. From Paseo de la Alameda, head northwest on C114, following signs for Atienza, 19½ miles (31 km) away. Atienza's lordly 12th-century castle will be visible long before the rest of the town comes into view; a closer look reveals four Romanesque churches, red-tiled and half-timbered townhouses, the Plaza del Trigo (Plaza of Wheat) supported by lovely stone columns, and the 11th-to-13th-century arches of the town walls. At the fork in the road outside of town, make a left onto C101 going south toward Guadalajara. Jadraque lies 20½ miles (33 km) ahead, with its castle on a conical hill towering over lavender-studded fields that feed the bees that make the honey that is the province's main cash crop. Another 12 miles (19 km) ahead on C101 lies the walled town of Hita, home of the Archpriest of Hita, a renowned 14th-century poet. Early in July, this town comes to life for a medieval festival, complete with jousting tourneys, colorful folk dancing, and open-air theater performances. Continue south along C101 for 14 miles (22 km) until it rejoins N-II 4 miles (6 km) north of Guadalajara, the provincial capital. Leveled during the Spanish Civil War, Guadalajara does not pretend to be anything other than a high-rise bedroom community of Madrid, not worth the bother except to see the 15th-century Palacio de las Infantadas on the Plaza de los Caídos with its diamond-studded façade (open Tuesdays through Fridays from 10:15 AM to 2 PM and from 4 to 7 PM; Saturdays from 10 AM to 2 PM and from 4 to 7 PM; Sundays from 10 AM to 2 PM; admission charge). Afterward, if not returning to Sigüenza directly, take N320 east toward Sacedón and Cuenca, but turn onto C200 about 14 miles (22 km) down the road. Soon after, the town of Pastrana rises up on a geologic hump over the surrounding patchwork plains. A pleasant place for a stroll is the steep quarter that once housed Moors from Granada who worked on silk tapestries commissioned by the Dukes of Pastrana. Some of the tapestries are on display at the *Museo Parroquial* in the collegiate church, which is open sporadically, usually from 10 AM to 2PM and from 4 to 6 PM. At lunchtime on weekends and holidays, the nuns who live in the Convento de las Monjas de Abajo serve inexpensive home-cooked meals in the annex of their 16th-century convent on Calle de las Monjas. Return to Sigüenza by backtracking (the easiest route) on C200 to N320 west and around the Guadalajara bypass to N-II, then head north.

To continue the route from Sigüenza, proceed south on C204 to N-II, taking it 1½ miles (2 km) in the direction of Guadalajara until it meets C204 going south again. Pass Cifuentes and the nuclear power plant at Trillo, to the left. The reactor is cooled by the waters of the Tajo River, which the road does not cross until it is well up into the bluffs overlooking the Embalse de Entrepeñas (Entrepeñas Reservoir). Just outside the town of Sacedón, C204 intersects with N320, which forks sharply left toward Cuenca. For a coffee break, however, bear right for cottage-lined Sacedón, strategically placed on the so-called Sea of Castile, a manmade lake formed by the Entrepeñas Reservoir and the Buendía Reservoir just south of it. (The turnoff to a well-groomed garden and picnic area overlooking the dam is just before the first tunnel.) Then double back along N320, cross over the Guadiela River into Cuenca province, and drive the remaining straight, fast, level road to the intersection with N400 and, a little farther on, the provincial capital, some 59 miles (94 km) from Sacedón and 119 miles (191 km) from Sigüenza.

EATING OUT

El Castillo The reputation of this roadside *hostal* just outside Jadraque is based on the roast kid that comes sizzling from the wood-fired brick oven located around back. Open daily. Reservations necessary. MasterCard and Visa accepted. Carretera Guadalajara–Soria, Km 46, Jadraque (phone: 11-890254). Moderate.

El Ventorrero This *mesón* boasts rustic Castilian decor and has been run by the same family since the 1880s. The menu is traditional Castilian, which means excellent roast meats and game. Open daily. No reservations. Major credit cards accepted. 4 Calle López de Haro, Guadalajara (phone: 11-212563). Moderate.

CUENCA A spectacular setting, picturesquely and precariously located "hanging houses," natural wonders, elegant monuments, modern art, and good local food — it's almost impossible to be disappointed by Cuenca. The city's medieval Old Town is perched atop a steep escarpment where the Huécar River, a narrow trickle of a stream, intersects with the meandering Júcar River, graced by a bower of birch trees angled like crossed swords over its banks. The town's medieval streets cascade down the escarpment, so exploring it entails just two directions, up or down, and is best done on foot. (For those short of wind, there is a bus that runs every 20 minutes from the new quarter up to the Old Town's main square, the Plaza Mayor de Pío XII, or simply Plaza Mayor.) A view of the city from an outside vantage point is recommended first, however. Walk behind the cathedral, which edges the Plaza Mayor, past the Casas Colgadas (Hanging Houses), and over the steel footbridge that leads to the opposite side of the Huécar gorge; this site offers a great perspective on the most photogenic side of the Old Town.

The Casas Colgadas are 14th-century houses that, for want of space, were built several stories high and right at the edge of the escarpment, with wooden balconies cantilevered out over the gorge itself. Two have had their lath-and-timber innards wonderfully restored and transformed into the *Museum of Spanish Abstract Art* (3 Canónigos), displaying works by modern masters who settled in Cuenca in the 1950s and 1960s, such as Fernando Zóbel, Luis Feito, Antonio Tàpies, Eduardo Chillida, and Antonio Saura (open Tuesdays through Fridays from 11 AM to 2 PM and from 4 to 6 PM; Saturdays from 11 AM to 2 PM and from 4 to 8 PM; Sundays from 11 AM to 2 PM; admission charge). Across the street, the *Museum of Archaeology* (6 Obispo Valero) displays imperial busts and artifacts from the Roman settlements of Segóbriga and Valeria, as well as remains from the province's Bronze Age (open Tuesdays through Saturdays from 10 AM to 2 PM and from 4 to 7 PM; Sundays from 10 AM to 2 PM; admission charge).

Cuenca's cathedral (Plaza Mayor), built in the 12th and 13th centuries with a later façade, is notable for its design, an amalgam of French Gothic and Anglo-Norman styles unique to Spain, and for the mix of baroque and neo-classical details on the 18th-century altarpiece and side chapels, as well as a profusion of iron grillwork. The cathedral's *Diocesan Museum* (open Tuesdays through Fridays from 11 AM to 2 PM and from 4 to 6 PM; until 8 PM on Saturdays; Sundays from 11 AM to 2 PM; closed Mondays; admission charge) contains two El Greco canvases, the 12th-century statue of the Virgen del Sagrario, and some interesting Flemish tapestries.

For more spectacular views, over both river gorges and the granite cliffs opposite, take any of the streets going left — uphill — from the Plaza Mayor to the highest part of the rock plinth on which old Cuenca sits. A town map identifying the profusion of ruined convents, churches, and noble palaces along the way is available from the tourist office down in the New City (8 Calle Dalmacio García Izcara; phone: 66-222231). There are three ceramic shops on the Plaza Mayor, but these are stocked with far too much bargain merchandise imported from Andalusia. The workshop of master ceramist Alejandro Fernández Cruz on the Carretera de Madrid almost a mile (1.6 km) outside town is a good place to pick up decorated plates, water jugs, pitchers, and other ceramic knickknacks for reasonable prices. Segundo Santos's small shop (in town on the Plaza Mayor; phone: 66-214038), open only on weekends, is the place to buy lampshades, desk organizers, and notebooks made from delicate hand-laid paper, a decorative-textured white fashioned from wool scraps and *esparto* grass and stippled with colored threads.

Cuenca is known for its annual *Semana de Música Religiosa,* held the week before *Easter,* with performances packing the Church of San Miguel and other venues. Orchestral and polyphonic choral groups from all of Europe take part in the festival, notable for reviving the works of lesser-known Renaissance composers. An auditorium built into the Huécar cliffside was being finished at press time, and is expected to become the festival's new home (see *Best Festivals* in DIVERSIONS).

CHECKING IN

Parador de Turismo de Cuenca Spain's newest *parador,* the 85th in the government-run chain of lodgings, is in front of the famous hanging houses in the center of town. The converted 16th-century Convent of San Pablo has 61 fully air conditioned rooms and features private gardens, a restaurant, a pool, and tennis courts. Cuenca (phone: in Madrid, 1-435-9700/9744/9768/9814; local number unavailable at press time; in New York, 212-686-9213). Expensive.

Torremangana Conveniently located in the humdrum modern town that sprawls at the foot of the Old City, this hostelry is comfortable and efficient, with excellent service and parking facilities. All 120 modern rooms are air conditioned. 9 Calle San Ignacio de Loyola, Cuenca (phone: 66-223351; fax: 66-229671). Expensive.

La Cueva del Fraile A 16th-century manor house 5 miles (8 km) northwest of town. Built in the corral-style common to La Mancha, it has been so expertly reconstructed that it looks completely fake. Although sometimes noisy — the combination of thin walls, barking dogs, and noisy Spanish families on bus tours is somewhat of a drawback — the 63 rooms are always comfortable. The restaurant offers a tasting menu of regional specialties. Closed January and February. Carretera de Buenache, Cuenca (phone: 66-211571; fax: 66-211573). Expensive to moderate.

Posada de San José This 17th-century house, projecting ever so slightly over the Huécar gorge in the Old Town, was built by a son-in-law of the painter Velázquez and was later put to use as a convent. Subjected to a major restoration in the 1950s, which respected even the uncomfortably low ceiling beams, this is now a 25-room *hostal* (not all with private baths). It is invariably full on weekends, so make reservations well in advance. 4 Calle Julián Romero, Cuenca (phone: 66-211300). Moderate.

EATING OUT

Figón de Pedro Owner Pedro Torres put Cuenca on the culinary map with this atmospheric place, located in the heart of the new city. The extensive menu highlights trout, for which Cuenca is deservedly famous, as well as stewed lamb, partridge, and other regional specialties. Closed Sunday evenings. Reservations necessary. Major credit cards accepted. 13 Calle Cervantes, Cuenca (phone: 66-226821). Expensive.

Mesón Casas Colgadas In a hanging house next door to the *Museum of Spanish Abstract Art,* with a balcony out over the gorge, this restaurant is under the ownership of Pedro Torres of *Figón de Pedro* fame. It features a menu very similar to its famous sister, and also boasts a good selection of reasonably priced rioja wines. Closed Monday evenings. Reservations advised. Major credit cards accepted. Calle Canónigos, Cuenca (phone: 66-223509). Expensive.

El Espolón Devoid of decorative charm and on an unattractive street, it nevertheless serves excellent food. Try fixed-price menu standards such as garlic and egg soup, followed by trout or chicken in garlic sauce; wine and dessert are included. Open daily. No reservations or credit cards accepted. 10 Calle 18 de Julio, Cuenca (phone: 66-211872). Inexpensive.

San Nicolás Another place to sample a fixed-price menu of regional specialties. Try *morturelo,* a lumpy, purple-gray concoction of seasoned partridge, rabbit, and lamb's liver — traditional shepherd's food. Open daily; closed mid-November through mid-December. No reservations. No credit cards accepted. 15 Calle San Pedro, Cuenca (phone: 66-212205 or 66-214539). Inexpensive.

———————

En Route from Cuenca The itinerary continues southwest from Cuenca, but those with the time to spend an extra day in the area and a desire for a change of scenery may wish to pack a picnic lunch and make a detour to the northeast, into the surrounding Serranía de Cuenca mountain range, with its trout streams and spectacular birch and pine trees. To make the 94-mile (150-km) detour, take CU920/921, which begins at the small bridge where the Huécar and Júcar rivers converge, and head north along the Júcar for 13 miles (21 km) to the village of Villalba de la Sierra. Bear sharply right at the sign for Tragacete–Ciudad Encantada. Approximately 200 yards ahead, bear left, remaining on CU921. Climb up the mountain for 2½ miles (4 km), park at the souvenir stand, and walk up to the Ventano del Diablo, a natural balcony carved by wind and water erosion, which commands a striking view down the 10-mile-long canyon that the Júcar River has gouged out of its limestone bed. Return to the car, continue upward, and take the well-marked road to the right (CU913) to the Ciudad Encantada (Enchanted City). Here the sights are almost as Disneyesque as the name suggests. Centuries of erosion have sculpted the rock into fanciful shapes that resemble everything from balancing seals to gigantic mushrooms. It takes about 40 minutes to walk from end to end (admission charge).

Continuing along CU921 over the Júcar gorge toward Tragacete, the road is narrow but well graded (there are guard rails only on the sharpest curves, but two-way traffic, thankfully, is almost nonexistent). Pass the reservoir and the trout hatcheries of Uña, and follow the road inland, now some 4,600 feet above sea level. At Tragacete, a popular hunting village, turn left at the sign for Nacimiento del Río Cuervo and continue another 8 miles (13 km) on the rough road to the rest area and picnic grounds. At the Cuervo's source, streams come trickling in a crystal curtain out of the rock face and down a mossy, juniper-framed cliffside. Hiking paths abound.

After viewing the valley at Vega del Coronado, continue along the same road, which now curves back on itself and leads down the other side of the sierra, even more thickly forested with Scotch pine and holm oak. Follow the signs to Las Majadas. Along the way, the El Hosquillo Game Reserve allows a maximum of 45 visitors per weekend from mid-October through June. Reservations must be made at least 1 week in advance through the National Conservation Agency (ICONA) office in Cuenca (phone: 66-228022). Tours, consisting of a guided excursion in a Land Rover, turn up wild mountain sheep, ibex, wild boar, mouflon, roe deer, fallow deer, and some of the last brown bears in Europe — a must for wildlife lovers. Returning to the main road, proceed down the mountain about 6 miles (10 km) to the entrance to Las Majadas, a few acres of parkland where erosion has once again produced natural sculptures that rival those of the Ciudad Encantada. From here, the road emerges from the shadows of the pine and holm oaks and circles back to Villalba de la Sierra, then onto CU921 back to Cuenca.

To resume the itinerary, begin at the intersection in front of the tourist office in Cuenca and follow the signs to N400 for Tarancón and Madrid. After 32 miles (51 km), get off the N400 at the Carracosa del Campo exit, and take the poorly paved road to the monastery of Uclés, which becomes visible after 8 miles (13 km). From the outside, this rectangular, 16th-to-18th-century monastery-fortress, once the headquarters of the Order of Santiago, doesn't quite live up to its billing as the "junior Escorial," though it was in fact designed in part by the same architect who designed Philip II's gloomy retreat. Today, the Uclés monastery serves as a church-run boarding school for boys. While class is in session, the women who cook and clean for their charges permit visitors to look at the interesting baroque fountain in the courtyard (incongruously converted into a basket-ball court) and at the breathtaking Mudéjar refectory ceiling.

Continue along C720/C700 to the N-III Madrid–Valencia highway heading southeast; get off at the Saelices exit, but stay clear of the town and remain on the same road (CU304) for about 4 more miles (6 km). At this point, a turnoff leads to the low-lying mounds that are the remains of the Roman colony of Segóbriga, which flourished briefly but handsomely under the Claudian emperors. The inhabitants did well enough raising cattle and working the extensive selenite deposits nearby to build a consid-erable amphitheater and a theater for their leisure-time pursuits. Both are substantially intact and still bear ocher traces of Latin graffiti. A small museum (closed Mondays) displays archaeological finds, but the best pieces excavated here have long since been removed to Cuenca. Still, the Roman thermal baths and the Visigothic cemetery are worth a look.

Return to Saelices and the N-III highway, heading southeast in the direction of Valencia for 30½ miles (49 km) to the town of La Almarcha and the turnoff for N420 south. Here, the hills begin to flatten out and give way to the plains of La Mancha. Just ahead (22½ miles/36 km) is Belmonte, and the must-see castle of the Marqués de Villena, attached to the remnants of the Old City walls. This late-15th-century structure, complete with a drawbridge and dungeon, is of a variety uncommon in Spain, built with Renaissance flair as a fortified palace rather than a simply functional military outpost. The caretaker escorts visitors through the curious triangular precincts of this national monument. The contemporary collegiate Church of San Bartolomé in the center of town combines Renaissance architectural severity with the ornamental lavishness of the Gothic interior.

Back on N420, the landscape is now flat — fields of grapevines, grain, and melons, or vast horizons of empty plains under endless blue skies. The town of Mota del Cuervo, 10 miles (16 km) beyond Belmonte and aptly called "the balcony of La Mancha," provides a handy base from which to sally forth into Don Quixote's stomping grounds. At the town's crossroads, take N301 north toward Quintanar de la Orden and proceed 10 miles (16 km) to the tile-encrusted *Venta de Don Quijote,* purported to be the inn where the earnest daydreamer was jocularly dubbed a knight by the locals. Make a left at the intersection here, and proceed 3 miles (5 km) to El Toboso, which has cashed in on its fame as the home of Don Quixote's slatternly sweetheart.

CHECKING IN/EATING OUT

Mesón Don Quijote A modern, comfortable Best Western affiliate, 10 miles (16 km) from Belmonte, with 36 air conditioned rooms, a swimming pool, beautiful gardens, and 2 restaurants where regional cuisine is in its glory. Specialties include the famous *pisto manchego,* a sort of ratatouille; *chuletas con salsa diabla* (lamb chops with hot sauce); and partridge and quail in spicy casseroles. Major credit cards accepted. 2 Calle Francisco Costi, Mota del Cuervo (phone: 67-180200; in the US, 800-528-1234; fax: 67-180711). Expensive.

EL TOBOSO This neat little town has been embellished with plaques citing phrases from the Miguel de Cervantes classic to help visitors retrace the steps of Don Quixote, the fictional knight, and his squire, and remind all of his praise of its civic virtues. The House of Dulcinea (Calle José Antonio; phone: 25-197288), once the home of a local lady of loose morals who supposedly was the inspiration for the Cervantes character (she was known to her customers as *la dulce Ana,* or sweet Annie), has been converted into the so-called *Museo de Amor*. On display are an assortment of regional ethnological relics that could have been associated with the region's most famous personage — that is, if he had ever really existed (open Tuesdays through Saturdays from 10 AM to 2 PM and from 4 to 6:30 PM; Sunday mornings; admission charge). The scallop shell over the entrance to the town's 15th-century late Gothic church, which Don Quixote himself commended, indicates that El Toboso once was under the control of the Knights of Santiago.

En Route from El Toboso Take the local road south to N420 and head west (if setting out after an overnight in Mota del Cuervo, get on N420 directly). Just ahead are the windmills that in the novel unseated the loony Knight of La Mancha, beginning with the eight stalwart structures standing on the ridge above Campo de Criptana. Follow the pictographic signs pointing the way up through the one-way streets for a closer look. On three of the windmills, the gears and milling mechanisms have been maintained, though there is no schedule to indicate when the sailcloth arms will be revolving. Leaflets available at a tiny tourist office around the corner explain the history and function of these devices — which were, in fact, high-tech innovations imported from the Low Countries at the time Cervantes was writing.

Alcázar de San Juan, 7 miles (11 km) from Campo de Criptana, is a crossroads town totally dependent on an enormous oil refinery, and of more interest to the stomach than to the eye (see *Eating Out*). Turn south on C400 to Tomelloso, 19½ miles (31 km) away, a town floating on a sea of wine — it's said to be the world's number one alcohol-producing municipality. At Tomelloso, take a sharp right onto the local road to Argamasilla del Alba. Stop here at the church, and if you're lucky enough to find someone to open it up, he or she will point out the portrait of Rodrigo Pacheco, a gentleman of the vicinity whose loss of wits and subsequent odd behavior are said to have inspired Cervantes. Ring the bell at 8 Calle Cervantes, the unmarked street at the rear left corner of the church, and a caretaker will come out to unlock the Cueva del Medrano, where Cervantes was tossed into jail in 1597, accused of embezzlement during a disastrous stint as a government tax collector. It was apparently in this subterranean small-town hoosegow that Cervantes penned the literary masterpiece of Spain's golden age.

Continue along the local road to Manzanares, 24½ miles (39 km) from Tomelloso. Trucks carrying sugar beets and poultry feed make the going very slow, but the situation improves after the road skirts the silos and melon sheds of Manzanares. Follow the signs for Ciudad Real to reach N430 west, which intersects with N420. Follow the latter for for 2 miles (3 km), passing through the center of the wine-producing town of Daimiel, then take the turnoff for C417, which leads to Almagro, some 15½ miles (25 km) to the south.

EATING OUT

Caso Paco A lunch stop favored by truckers making the all-day haul between Andalusia and central Spain. In addition to regional dishes that will be new to most travelers, there are a few properly prepared fish choices on the menu. Closed Mondays. No reservations. MasterCard and Visa accepted. 5 Av. Alvarez Guerra, Alcázar de San Juan (phone: 26-540606). Moderate.

ALMAGRO The landscape is pure Kansas, but visitors will not find a Renaissance jewel of a town like this one anywhere within wishing distance of Wichita. The Order of Calatrava, the oldest and most important Spanish knightly order, established its headquarters here after winning the battle of Las Navas de Tolosa in 1212; the order's squiggly cross emblem can be seen on nearly every one of the historic buildings in town. The 16th-century Monastery of the Assumption of Calatrava, now commonly called the Convento de los Padres Dominicanos, located on the main street, Ejido de Calatrava, should not be missed. The friars in residence happily escort visitors around the extraordinary Renaissance cloister, which surrounds pillars of solid Carrara marble, and the attached Gothic church (open from 10 AM to 2 PM and from 4 to 7 PM; closed Sunday afternoons; phone: 26-860230).

The unusual green, glassed-in balconies propped up by the stone pillars of the elongated 14th-century Plaza Mayor reflect the southern German influence of the Fugger dynasty of banker-princes, who made Almagro their Iberian branch office during the 16th-century New World gold boom that helped keep Holy Roman Emperor Charles V solvent. Their palace, the Palacio de los Fúcares, has a stone staircase and assembly hall worth seeing (Arzobispo Cañizares; open daily except Sundays from 10 AM to 2 PM and from 4 to 8 PM).

Midway along the Plaza Mayor's south portico is the entrance to Almagro's unique *Corral de Comedias,* a theater dating back to the 16th century's golden age of Spanish drama. Its survival is due to the fact that it was bricked up and forgotten until 1954. If no one's on duty to show off the 2-tiered, half-timbered stage, the linteled galleries, and the pit for the groundlings, the tourist office (5 Mayor de Carnicerías; phone: 26-860717) will provide a guide. During the annual *Festival de Teatro Clásico,* held during the first 2 weeks of September, theater companies from all over the Spanish-speaking world muster forces on its creaky stage and perform classics by Calderón de la Barca, Lope de Vega, and their foreign contemporaries such as Shakespeare and Molière. Tickets go on sale in mid-August and sell out quickly. (They also can be reserved through the tourist office.)

A stroll around the heraldic mansions and palaces of the town's oldest quarter offers strong evidence that the women of Almagro continue to practice the local tradition of lace making. It's not uncommon to find practitioners sitting in doorways, wooden bobbins flying and clacking in their hands. There are also a few lace shops in the Plaza Mayor, where the markup is negligible. For fine table linen, handkerchiefs, and towels at bargain prices, call at the home/shop of María Carmen Manzano (24 Calle Dominicas; phone: 26-860908). Families from all over Spain also travel to Almagro to stock up on pickled baby eggplants, a regional delicacy packed in the earthenware jugs that are displayed in front of every shop in town.

CHECKING IN

Parador de Almagro Formerly a 16th-century convent, this is one of the most charming restoration efforts in the entire *parador* network. There are 55 air conditioned rooms, a swimming pool, and a good restaurant. Reserve well in advance. For additional details see *Paradores* in DIVERSIONS. Ronda de San Francisco, Almagro (phone: 26-860100; in the US, 212-686-9213). Expensive.

EATING OUT

Calatrava A dining alternative to the *parador,* featuring good, home-cooked Castilian dishes, and specializing in the traditional roast lamb and kid. Closed Monday evenings. Reservations unnecessary. Visa accepted. 7 Calle Bolaños, Almagro (phone: 26-860185 or 26-861353). Moderate.

En Route from Almagro Backtrack north on C417. Upon reaching Daimiel, take the turnoff on the left for the Tablas de Daimiel Nature Reserve. This road crosses the 4-lane N420, then follows a bumpy 7-mile (11-km) path out into the marshlands. After seeing so much of flat and dry old La Mancha, the vast shallow lagoons formed by the confluence of the Guadiana and Gigüela rivers come as a surprise. Equally surprising is the abundance of migratory waterfowl, notably herons, kingfishers, mallards, terns, cranes, and gulls. Unrestricted hunting and clandestine drainage to irrigate the surrounding farmland almost destroyed the lagoons and their nesting nomads until the area was declared a protected reserve in 1973. Four hiking trails have been laid out, allowing for walks that range from 1 to 3 hours. Camouflaged observation posts along the way serve as resting points and allow for close inspection of the winged residents. A free map and helpful English-language brochure are available at the reserve's entrance lodge.

Head back toward Daimiel on the old bumpy road and pick up N420 north to Madrid on the outskirts of town. (Those wanting to stock up on Castillo de Daimiel wine at giveaway prices, however, should stop in at the co-op outlet in town, on Paseo del Carmen.) Puerto Lápice, another crossroads town, lies 21 miles (34 km) ahead; it has possibly made a bit too much of its mention in *Don Quixote* — as the countless signs and statues attest. Follow the N-IV highway from here on into Madrid, with a couple of brief detours along the way. Ten and a half miles (17 km) north of Puerto Lápice, the highway slices through Madridejos, where a sharp left onto C400 toward Toledo leads to Consuegra, another 4½ miles (7 km) down the road.

EATING OUT

Venta del Quijote Situated in a former farmhouse complete with wooden beams, cartwheels, and huge earthenware wine tuns, this restaurant offers an extensive menu of exceptionally prepared Manchegan dishes and choice wines. A nice patio makes outdoor dining a possibility, weather permitting. Open daily. Reservations unnecessary. Major credit cards accepted. Carretera Madrid–Cádiz (N-IV), 4 Calle el Molino, Puerto Lápice (phone: 26-576110). Moderate.

CONSUEGRA The seven windmills lined up here are hollow shells, unlike those in Campo de Criptana, but they are in a far more dramatic — and photogenic — setting, high on a cliffside overlooking the entire town and next to the ruins of a windswept 14th-century castle. Consuegra is famous for its production of saffron, those expensive and irreplaceable reddish threads that are essential for a good paella. To get just 1 pound, it is necessary to pull the stigmas from over 100,000 crocuses. The *Saffron Festival* falls on the last Sunday in October, complete with folk dancing, wine tasting, and bullfighting, and provides the locals with a chance to whoop it up a bit after the pickers — almost all of whom are women — have finished their laborious task. Unfortunately, visitors can't buy saffron here — it's all sold to out-of-town dealers who toast and package the finished product elsewhere.

En Route from Consuegra Head back to Madridejos and, once again, take the N-IV highway going north. Make a quick stop in Tembleque, 16 miles (26 km) north of Madridejos, for a glance at the remarkable Plaza Mayor, a graceful, 2-tiered arcade of old beams and plaster, its one entrance crowned by the most un-Spanish-looking 3-story, peaked, gable-like structure. The N-IV highway leads next to Ocaña, 19½ miles (31 km) from Tembleque, and then to Aranjuez, another 10 miles (16 km) along (see *Madrid Region,* DIRECTIONS, for more on this town, a favored residence of the Catholic Monarchs and later Spanish royalty). From here, traffic jams are a reminder that Madrid is only 29½ miles (47 km) away.

Levante: Valencia to Murcia

Almond blossoms and white beaches, verdant orchards and stern mountain ranges, palm trees and sparkling blue water, and at least 300 days of sunshine a year — is it any wonder that the Mediterranean coast south of Valencia has become one of Europe's most popular vacation areas?

Spain's Levante region is the coastal fringe bridging the gap between Catalonia and Andalusia. It includes three provinces (Castellón, Valencia, and Alicante) and the single-province autonomous community of Murcia. Striking scenery, lively fiestas, unusual historical sights, and distinctive food are highlights of the region.

The middle section of this region, the Costa Blanca (White Coast), which lies in the province of Alicante, is the most popular. Every summer, hundreds of thousands of Spaniards and other Europeans flock here to bask in the sunshine and enjoy a wide range of sporting and entertainment activities. Resorts have mushroomed where there were only fishing villages and deserted beaches barely 35 years ago. The region caters to all tastes, and although it's easy to escape the crowds, it's not advisable to plan a vacation here during July and August. Spring and autumn are fine times to visit, and rainy winter days are usually followed by weeks of dazzling sunshine.

The Levante's lushness is due not only to the sunshine, but also to the Moors, who converted the arid but fertile plain between the treeless mountains and the sea into lush *huertas* (orchards and vegetable farms) by introducing an ingenious irrigation system. Remains of *norias*, giant Moorish water-raising wheels, can still be found on the *huertas*, where citrus fruits (thousands of tons of oranges and lemons are exported annually), dates, tomatoes, and a wealth of other fruits and vegetables still flourish.

The Moorish kingdom of Valencia, which dominated a vast slice of the coast, was added to James I of Aragon's Christian lands in 1238, and became part of the kingdom of Castile in the late 15th century. Murcia, which at one time acted as an intermediary between the Moors and Christians, was also conquered by Aragon, but remained a separately administered kingdom for another 2 centuries.

Although Castilian Spanish is the language of Murcia, the language commonly spoken in the region of Valencia is a local version of Catalan, known as *valenciano* in Valencia and as *alicantino* in Alicante. Anyone who speaks Castilian, French, or any other Latin language will not find this too difficult to understand, and those who attempt to master a few spoken phrases will certainly please the local residents. "Good morning" is *bon dia,* and "please" is *per favor.* Place-names often appear in both languages — for example, Alicante is Alacant in the local language; Elche is Elx. But everybody speaks Castilian, too, and since the Costa Blanca is such a popular vacation spot for British tourists, it is easier in some areas to find a speaker of English than of any other tongue.

Rice, which grows here in abundance, forms the basis for scores of regional dishes, including *paella valenciana* (rice with meat and seafood, including octopus and mussels), *paella marinera* (rice and fish), and *arroz con costra* (rice with pork and sausage, topped off with a half-dozen eggs). Squid and octopus are also popular local delicacies. Moorish influence is evident in such sticky desserts as *turrón* (nougat) and glazed walnuts. *Horchata de chufa,* a chilled mixture of *chufas* (earth almonds), cinnamon, sugar, and water, is a favorite drink. Some good wines are produced in the region, particularly the hearty jumilla and yecla reds in Murcia.

Many travelers time their visits to the region to coincide with one of the many reenactments of the epic struggles between Moors and Christians, some of which are among the most colorful, exuberant fiestas to be found anywhere. All along the coast, towns and villages spend the entire year preparing for their annual *Moros y Cristianos* battles. The towns of Alcoy (April 22), Elda (first week in June), and Villajoyosa (July 25), all in the province of Alicante, stage particularly spectacular make-believe battles. (See *Best Festivals* in DIVERSIONS.)

The route outlined below begins in Valencia and heads south to the gracious seaport city of Alicante and on to the inland city of Murcia, with a spur to Cartagena back on the coast before veering southwest toward Granada. Those who can't wait to see the glories of the Alhambra can do the Valencia–Granada run in 1 day, but there are abundant reasons to spend at least 4 to 5 days on the journey.

Along the way, expect to pay $100 or more for a double room in a hotel listed as expensive, and $60 to $100 in one described as moderate. A restaurant listed as expensive charges around $60 or more for a dinner for two, including wine; a moderate establishment, $40 to $60; and an inexpensive one, under $40. The telephone numbers listed below include local area codes; when calling from another part of Spain, dial "9" first. Note that phone numbers can have either 6 or 7 digits.

VALENCIA For a complete report on this city and its sights, hotels, and restaurants, see *Valencia* in THE CITIES.

En Route from Valencia The most interesting route out of Valencia follows the coast, past long sandy beaches, orange groves, and large rice fields. Head south on the A-V15 highway, and follow the signs to El Saler, 6 miles (10 km) south of Valencia. Just past it is La Albufera, Spain's largest lake, renowned for its wildlife and freshwater fish. Follow the local road on the right for 2 miles (3 km) to El Palmar, a village of thatch-roofed cottages on the lake edge, where rustic eateries serve *all i pebre,* a local specialty of eels fried in garlic. Return to A-V15 and proceed to Cullera, 25 miles (40 km) from Valencia; the town is hard to miss, since giant white letters spell out its name on the rocky hill rising above it. A small port town on the Júcar River, Cullera has been dwarfed by dozens of modern apartment blocks on the beaches toward the lighthouse, but it offers magnificent views from its castle ruins. Continue south, via N332 or A7, some 18 miles (29 km) to Gandía.

EATING OUT

Les Mouettes Enjoy French delicacies such as oyster ragout with leeks and truffles, as well as wines from Bordeaux and the Loire, on a pleasant terrace overlooking the beach (and high-rises). This place is famous among *valencianos* and has earned a Michelin star. Closed Sunday evenings, Mondays, and December 15 through February 15. Reservations advised. Major credit cards accepted. Subida al Santuario del Castillo, Cullera (phone: 6-172-0010). Moderate.

GANDÍA A modern town with some fine buildings, Gandía is set inland, surrounded by rice fields and groves of oranges — which are shipped from the harbor formed by the mouth of the Serpis River. It once was the capital of a duchy given by King Ferdinand to the Borgia family (known in Spain as the Borjas) in 1485. Alexander VI, the infamous Borgia pope, father of the equally infamous Cesare and Lucrezia Borgia, was born in Játiva, 25 miles inland. A later member of the family, who restored the family's good name by becoming a Jesuit, founding Jesuit missions in the New World, and eventually being named a saint — St. Francis Borgia — was born here in the family mansion. This, the 16th-century Palacio Ducal (Calle Santo Duque; phone: 6-287-1203), offers a fine patio and staircase, as well as beautifully decorated apartments. The building can be visited only on guided tours (conducted in Spanish only), which begin daily at 11 AM and noon and at 6 and 7 PM in May through October (in winter they begin at 5 and 6 PM); admission charge. Gandía's main tourist office is on the Avenida Marqués de Campo (phone: 6-287-7788); another, less useful tourist office is at 2-1 Purísima (phone: 6-287-4544). Three miles (5 km) from the town lies its port, El Grau, and a vast sandy beach that has succumbed to extensive tourist development. It comes to life at *Easter* and in summer, and most of the hotels are located here.

CHECKING IN

Bayren I Like most others in the area, this comfortable beachfront establishment caters primarily to Spanish vacationers. All 164 rooms are air conditioned, and there is a swimming pool, tennis courts, and live music and dancing in the gardens in summer. Closed for a month from late November to early December. 62 Paseo de Neptuno, Playa de Gandía (phone: 6-284-0300; fax: 6-284-0653). Expensive.

EATING OUT

As de Oros On the lengthy Gandía beachfront, this eatery is a shrine to fresh seafood. Sit back and enjoy everything from juicy prawns to succulent squid and grilled mullet, washed down by some of the country's best wines. Closed Mondays and 2 weeks in January. Reservations unnecessary. Major credit cards accepted. Edificio Bonaire, Paseo de Neptuno, Playa de Gandía (phone: 6-284-0239). Expensive.

En Route from Gandía It's a run of about 20 minutes down the A7 into the province of Alicante and the pleasant old port town of Denia (take exit 62 at Ondara). Travelers in the mood for an excursion or seeking a diversion for young children should detour to the *Vergel Safari Park* by taking N332 north at Ondara and proceeding 4 miles (6 km) before turning left (west) onto C3311 toward Pego. The park is home to elephants, tigers, zebras, and lions, as well as "singing" dolphins and roller-skating parrots (open daily from 10 AM to 5:30 PM; phone: 6-575-0285; admission charge). To reach Denia from Ondara, take C3311 east.

DENIA Thanks to its mild climate and excellent beach, Denia has prospered from tourism, yet it has retained its charm. Founded by Phoenicians, the town takes its name from a Roman Temple of Diana. The Visigoths made it an episcopal seat, and it later served as the capital of a Moorish kingdom. The *Museo Arqueológico* (phone: 6-578-0100, ext. 64), set in the 18th-century citadel perched above the town, contains some noteworthy Roman and Arabic relics unearthed in the area (open daily except Thursdays from 10 AM to 1 PM and from 3 to 6 PM in June through September; from 10 AM to 1:30 PM and from 5 to 8 PM in October through May; admission charge). There are also some interesting 18th-century buildings in the Plaza de los Caídos, including the Church of Santa María and the Town Hall.

Denia is a good base for excursions. There is year-round service to the island of Ibiza via a passenger and vehicle ferry, which departs every evening at 10 o'clock and takes 5 hours; from *Easter* through summer, a passengers-only ferry departs at 7:30 AM and takes 3½ hours. For those in a rush, afternoon hydrofoils make the journey in 90 minutes; contact *Flebasa* (at the port; phone: 6-578-4011) for details on ferries and hydrofoils. Note that the hydrofoils only operate during the summer months. Another pleasant way to see the Costa Blanca is on the narrow-gauge railroad that runs from Denia to Alicante. The trip takes 2 hours and 20 minutes and trains leave from the station on Calle Manuel Lattur in Denia. For more information, contact the Denia Tourist Office (9 Plaza de Oculista Buigues; phone: 6-578-0957).

CHECKING IN

Los Angeles Located in a tranquil setting on an excellent sandy beach, 3 miles (5 km) north of town, this place has 60 air conditioned rooms. Facilities include tennis courts. Closed November through mid-March. 649 Playa de las Marinas, Denia (phone: 6-578-0458; fax: 6-642-0906). Moderate.

EATING OUT

El Pegolí A favorite with seafood lovers. Gaze out from the spick-and-span dining room or the outdoor terrace at the blue Mediterranean and the rocky coastline below while enjoying one of two set menus, which usually include a salad, a plate full of shellfish, a well-grilled fish, wine, bread, and dessert. Closed Sunday evenings and from mid-December to mid-January. Reservations advised. American Express and Visa accepted. Playa de Les Rotes, Denia (phone: 6-578-1035). Moderate.

En Route from Denia Head south, following the coast road, which offers magnificent views. As the route corkscrews up from Denia over the San Antonio headland and winds down through almond trees to Jávea (Xabia in *valenciano*), look for the old windmills that once ground wheat.

JÁVEA Situated on one of the Costa Blanca's finer bays, between two capes — Cabo de San Antonio and the Cabo San Martín (the latter just around the coast from Cabo de la Nao) — this resort town's Old Quarter stands on a rise inland from the fishing and pleasure port. Narrow streets, watchtowers, stone houses, surviving city walls and gateways, and an old castle contribute to its medieval look. Worth a visit is the *Museo Municipal* (Municipal Museum) (1 Calle Primicias; phone: 6-579-1098), built by King Philip III during the early 17th century. It contains Roman and Punic remains, ceramics, and traditional crafts (open Tuesdays through Sundays from 10 AM to 1 PM; also open from 5 to 8 PM from June through September; admission charge). The great bulk of Montgó (2,465 feet) shelters Jávea from winter blasts, and the surrounding area has experienced a development boom; thousands of villas have been built along the attractive coast of rocky headlands and bays. Jávea's Tourist Office is in the port area (24 Plaza Almirante Bastarreche; phone: 6-579-0736).

CHECKING IN

Bahía Vista A secluded setting on a pine-covered headland 5 miles (8 km) southeast of Jávea proper, with beautiful views over the sea. It has 17 rooms, a swimming pool, and a bowling green, plus a restaurant serving international food. Portichol, Cabo la Nao, Jávea (phone: 6-577-0461). Moderate.

Parador Costa Blanca On Jávea's beautiful bay, 2½ miles (4 km) southeast of the town proper, this is an ideal base from which to explore the area. All 65 rooms are air conditioned; each has a mini-bar and a balcony overlooking the beach. Other facilities include a swimming pool, gardens, and a nearby boat dock. The restaurant features regional food. 2 Playa del Arenal, Jávea (phone: 6-579-0200; in the US, 212-686-9213; fax: 6-579-0308). Moderate.

EATING OUT

Chez Angel The emphasis here is on French cooking, served in a friendly atmosphere, although it is located in a rather drab shopping center (just under 2 miles/3 km southeast of the Old Quarter.) Try the onion soup and *tournedos calvados,* or Provençal-style lamb. Closed Tuesdays and December 20 through January 20. Reservations unnecessary. No credit cards accepted. Carretera Cabo la Nao, Centro Comercial Jávea Park, Jávea (phone: 6-579-2723 or 6-579-1300). Moderate.

Turpins Just opposite the *parador,* the menu here features international cooking; stuffed peppers and Dijon chicken are especially recommended. Closed Sundays and from December 20 through January. Reservations unnecessary. No credit cards accepted. 4 Playa del Arenal, Jávea (phone: 6-579-0713). Inexpensive.

En Route from Jávea The A134 runs inland to join N332 near Gata de Gorgos, which bills itself as the "Bazaar of the Costa Blanca." The shops along its main street offer baskets, mats, and bags of bamboo, willow, palm leaf, and esparto, some of them made locally. In the nearby hills are the picturesque vineyards of the *Maserof Wine Club* (11 La Mar, Denia), whose members own individual vines and each year receive the wine made from their own grapes. Peter Pateman, the bearded, Falstaffian Englishman who founded the club, loves to talk wine and welcomes visitors to his bodega on Sundays. To reach it from Gata, turn off N332 onto the road to Lliber and Jalón. In Jalón, turn left onto the road signposted Bernia; Maserof is 3 miles (5 km) along on the left. It's best to call the club's Denia office (phone: 6-578-1887) first or write to them at the address above.

Back on N332, the route continues south past eroded ocher hills, the azure sea, and countless almond trees, a breathtaking sight when they are in bloom in February. Just ahead, huge apartment blocks have blossomed on the beaches in the vicinity of Calpe. Fortunately, however, developers have been pushed back from the foot of Peñón de Ifach, now a natural park. Resembling the Rock of Gibraltar, the Peñón soars to a height of over 1,000 feet; a hike up to the top takes about an hour, but no one suffering from vertigo should try it — somebody topples off just about every year. Take a sweater, as it can be breezy up there.

Continue on N332 to Altea, a charming hillside town perched below the rugged Sierra de Bernia, 20 miles (32 km) from Gata.

ALTEA The name comes from the Moorish "Altaya," meaning "health for all," and many visitors proclaim this the Costa Blanca's prettiest town. Modern buildings now line the waterfront, but the Old Quarter remains. Steep, narrow streets climb up to the parish church with its blue tile dome, characteristic of churches in the Levante region. In recent years, a number of artists of various nationalities have made their homes here. The church square (Plaza de Calvo Sotelo) is a pleasant place to site and watch the passersby and the stallholders selling their crafts. If you're here on a Sunday afternoon, watch for local men playing *pilota de carrer,* a fiercely competitive game in which players whack a small hard ball at one another with their bare hands. Altea's Tourist Office is on the seafront, Paseo Marítimo (phone: 65-842301).

EATING OUT

La Costera Swiss specialties are served with a unique flair in this bizarre Old Quarter eatery. Rodolfo, the owner, puts on a hilarious, uninhibited musical show nightly, featuring everything from cossack dancing to flamenco. Open for dinner only. Closed Wednesdays. Reservations advised. Master-Card and Visa accepted. 8 Costera del Mestre de Música, Altea (phone: 65-840230). Moderate.

Bahía This family-run establishment, situated between the highway and the sea, is a popular lunchtime favorite. Specialties include a variety of tasty rice dishes and excellent *zarzuela* (fish stew). Closed January, *Christmas,* and winter Saturdays and evenings. Reservations advised on weekends. Visa accepted. Carretera Alicante, Altea (phone: 65-840011). Moderate to inexpensive.

En Route from Altea Follow N332 south toward Benidorm, 7 miles (11 km) away. For a pleasant, half-day excursion before entering the city limits, make a right turn onto C3318 and drive 7 miles (11 km) to the village of Polop. Once there, turn left onto the small local road that swoops 9 miles (14 km) over the mountains to Guadalest, a medieval village that is one of Spain's most spectacular — and impregnable — fortresses. Built by the Moors, it perches on a crag, accessible only through a 50-foot tunnel cut through the rock. Inside are old women who sit knitting, souvenir shops, and magnificent views of the surrounding countryside. Returning toward the coast, stop in Callosa, locally renowned for its honey. Just off C3318, to the north, are the spectacular Algar waterfalls, a good place to cool off on a hot day. Sit in one of the rock pools under a cascade of water, which spills down some 50 feet from the rocks above. Several of the nearby restaurants have pools, too.

BENIDORM This is the place for anyone who wants to take a day off from Spain. Formerly a simple fishing village, it has become an international resort town (almost everyone speaks English), cluttered with high-rise buildings and catering mainly to those on inexpensive package tours. Pensioners from all over Europe flock here in winter, and teenagers of all ages take over the place during the summer. There are two fine beaches (topless), and the town is immaculately maintained. Jousting tournaments, dog races, discotheques, and bars (the nightlife tends to get a bit wild) are some of the attractions. The huge *Benidorm Palace* nightclub (Calle Diputación; phone: 6-585-1661 or 6-585-1660) is the Costa Blanca's answer to the *Folies-Bergères,* complete with bare-breasted dancers and flamenco, while the *Casino Costa Blanca* (on the main highway between Benidorm and Villajoyosa, N332, Km 115, Villajoyosa; phone: 6-589-0700) packs in gamblers by the busload. A passport is required for entry; there's also an admission charge. Benidorm's Tourist Office is at 16 Avenida Martínez Alejos (phone: 6-585-3224).

CHECKING IN

Gran Delfín This first-rate establishment on the quieter, southern beach, is often busy, but there's never the crowded mayhem found at some of Benidorm's other hotels. The 87 spacious and comfortable rooms are air conditioned; there also is a swimming pool, tennis courts, lovely tropical gardens, and a good restaurant. Closed October to *Easter.* Playa de Poniente, La Cala, Benidorm (phone/fax: 6-585-3400). Expensive.

Don Pancho Right in town, the 251 rooms in this popular high-rise are air conditioned, comfortably furnished, and have individual balconies. There also is a swimming pool, lighted tennis courts, and gardens. Open all year. 39 Av. del Mediterráneo, Benidorm (phone: 6-585-2950; fax: 6-586-7779). Moderate.

EATING OUT

I Fratelli Elegant candlelit dining, intimate alcoves, an outdoor patio, and an Italian atmosphere — this is an unexpected find in Benidorm. The pasta is homemade; try the veal marsala with *tagliatelle,* or the duck *à l'orange.* Closed November. Reservations necessary. Major credit cards accepted. 21 Calle Orts Llorca, Benidorm (phone: 6-585-3979). Expensive.

La Pérgola The view of Benidorm Bay from the terrace of this restaurant slotted into a cliff is dazzling. The international menu includes Basque and French dishes and delicious desserts. Closed December through February. Reservations advised. MasterCard and Visa accepted. Edificio Coblanca, 10 Calle Hamburgo, Barrio Rincón de Loix, Benidorm (phone: 6-585-3800). Expensive.

En Route from Benidorm Once again, pick up N332 and continue 6 miles (10 km) south to Villajoyosa, a fishing town surrounded by fruit trees and olive groves. The narrow streets of the Old Town lead down to a pleasant palm-decked promenade lined with houses that have colorful, sun-bleached façades. Continue toward Alicante, which is 27½ miles (44 km) from Benidorm; 5 miles (8 km) short of the city, at the small village of San Juan, is the turnoff for the Canelobre Caves, which can be explored in a half day. If you have time for the side trip, turn right onto N340, and follow the signs for A183, which leads to the village of Busot. The caves are 4½ miles (7 km) beyond, in the stark Cabeco d'Or Mountains. Well-lit walkways lead through vast caverns filled with giant stalagmites and sta-lactites. The caves (phone: 6-569-9250) are open daily from 10 AM to 8 PM in April through September; from 10 AM to 6 PM in October through March. On the return trip head toward Busot, but take the first right on the local road to Jijona, noted for its production of *turrón* (nougat), eaten by the ton throughout Spain during the *Christmas* season. *El Lobo* factory (62 Calle Alcoy; phone: 6-561-0125) has a visitors' area, where the tooth-wrenching but delicious product can be sampled (open Mondays through Fridays from 9:30 AM to 1:30 PM and 4 to 8 PM). From Jijona, proceed back to San Juan on N340 south and pick up N332 for the drive to Alicante.

CHECKING IN/EATING OUT

El Montíboli Located about 2 miles (3 km) south of Villajoyosa, this is an ideal rest stop, safely away from the hubbub found farther north along the coast. It sits on a headland, with magnificent views over the sea, a swim-ming pool, a private beach, tennis courts, and a well-regarded restaurant (reservations advised). All of the 52 spacious rooms are air conditioned and have mini-bars. Major credit cards accepted. Carretera Benidorm-Alicante (N332), Km 108, Villajoyosa (phone: 6-589-0250; fax: 6-589-3857). Expensive.

ALICANTE This provincial capital (pop. 265,000), the heart of the Costa Blanca resort area, is a gracious Mediterranean city dominated by the Castillo Santa Bárbara, which glowers down from a hilltop. Long before the pre-sent tourist boom, Alicante was a fashionable wintering place, thanks to its mild climate. Around 200 BC, the Romans had a settlement here known as Lucentum. The same settlement, during 500 years of Moorish rule, was known as Al-Akant. In more recent times, Alicante has been an important port, exporting wine, raisins, and other agricultural products. Palm trees and arid surrounding hills give a hint of Africa to the city, an impression that is strengthened around the port area by the sight of Algerian women in caftans and Senegalese peddlers offering their wares. The Explanada de España, the promenade that fronts the harbor, is the place to stroll, sip a drink, and listen to the city band on Sunday mornings.

Alicante is a modern city of wide boulevards and numerous shops, but it does have an Old Quarter, a labyrinth of narrow streets lying on the lower slope of the Santa Bárbara hill. And despite the hordes of tourists who alight here to soak up the sun along the local beaches, Alicante remains surprisingly Spanish in character.

The Castillo Santa Bárbara, whose foundations date back 2,200 years, is Alicante's main attraction. To reach the castle, walk along Paseo de Gómiz, which continues northeast along the beach from the Explanada, to the 660-foot tunnel penetrating the rock; an elevator (admission charge) takes visitors up to see the dungeons, moats, and battlements, which offer splendid views over the city and coast. The castle is open daily from 10 AM to 7 PM in mid-June through September; from 10 AM to 6 PM in October through mid-June; no admission charge.

In the Old Quarter, the *Museo de Arte Siglo XX* (Museum of 20th-Century Art; 3 Plaza de Santa María; phone: 6-521-4578 or 6-521-0022), also known as the *Museo de la Asegurada*, contains sculptures, paintings, and etchings by such artists as Picasso, Dalí, and Tàpies (open Tuesdays through Saturdays from 10 AM to 1 PM and from 5 to 7 PM; no admission charge). The Church of Santa María, almost opposite the museum, has a wonderful 18th-century baroque façade, although it dates back to a much earlier period and was built on the site of a mosque.

Head toward the center of town along Calle Jorge Juan to the Ayuntamiento (City Hall), a 17th-to-18th-century palace with a magnificently ornate façade. The rococo chapel and some of the baroque rooms are open to visitors in the mornings (ask the caretaker to open them). Note the brass plaque on the pillar of the main stairway; it's the sea level benchmark from which all of Spain's altitude measurements are calculated. Between the Ayuntamiento and the modern Rambla de Méndez Núñez — which is at the edge of the Old Quarter and is the city's main throughfare — is Alicante's cathedral, San Nicolás (Calle Peñalva), built during the 17th century on the site of a mosque and dedicated to the city's patron saint, Nicholas of Bari. A national monument open only during services, it has a severe Renaissance style, with beautifully carved gilded altars. The pedestrians-only Calle Mayor, which runs behind the Ayuntamiento to the Rambla, and the side streets off it, are full of small shops selling typically Spanish gifts, leatherwear, pottery, and antiques.

On Tuesday and Saturday mornings, the *Mercadillo,* a lively open-air market, is held along the Paseo de Campoamor, beyond the Old Quarter to the north of the Plaza de España and the bullring. The *Teatro Principal* (Plaza de Ruperto Chapi, 2 blocks west of the Rambla; phone: 6-520-2380) has concerts and musicals during the winter season. In summer, nightlife centers on the disco-pubs of the Playa de San Juan, the long beach north of town. Alicante's own local beach, El Postiguet, is even more crowded, but the tiny island of Tabarca, a former haunt of pirates, lies a pleasant boat ride away. It is a good spot for snorkeling, with outdoor restaurants but no accommodations. Trips leave from the harbor along the Explanada, or from Santa Pola (a much shorter sea trip), a fishing port 12½ miles (20 km) to the south. Alicante's Tourist Office (2 Explanada de España; phone: 6-521-2285) can provide schedules.

During the week of June 24, the city goes wild with the unforgettable *Hogueres de San Juan* (Bonfires of St. John). The fiesta includes processions, bullfights, and fireworks, but the climax comes with the burning of colossal images, sometimes at considerable risk to life and limb, a legacy of pagan midsummer rites. (See *Best Festivals* in DIVERSIONS.)

CHECKING IN

Sidi San Juan Sol Modern and luxurious with a private beach, it's located 4½ miles (7 km) from the center of town, but close to the area with all the summer action. The 176 air conditioned rooms offer every comfort. Facilities include a restaurant, 2 swimming pools (1 heated), a gymnasium, a sauna, a discotheque, and a shopping arcade. Playa de San Juan, Alicante (phone: 6-516-1300; in the US, 800-528-1234; fax: 6-516-3346). Expensive.

Palas This pleasant establishment, which caters to a mature clientele, offers old-style charm on the seafront. Chandeliers and antiques add a gracious note to the decor. All 48 rooms are air conditioned and quite comfortable. There is a restaurant. Near the Ayuntamiento (City Hall). 5 Calle Cervantes, Alicante (phone: 6-520-9310). Moderate.

EATING OUT

El Delfín This Michelin one-star establishment is known for elegant snacking and dining. There is a broad range of traditional regional and French dishes to choose from (at moderate prices if you stick to the *menú alicantino*). Try the seafood pancake and the *salteado de foie gras, mollejas, y pato* (sauté of foie gras, sweetbreads, and duck). Open daily. Reservations necessary. American Express, Diners Club, and MasterCard accepted. 12 Explanada de España, Alicante (phone: 6-521-4911). Expensive to moderate.

Dársena An ideal lunch spot overlooking the harbor. More than 20 rice dishes, typical of the region, are served with style. Begin with *bisque de cangrejos al armagnac* (crab soup), and move on to *pastel de atún y espinacas* (tuna and spinach tart). Closed Sunday evenings and Mondays. Reservations advised. American Express, Diners Club, and Visa accepted. Muelle del Puerto, Alicante (phone: 6-520-7399). Moderate.

Nou Manolín At the justly renowned downstairs bar, order anything from oysters to "grandmother's stew," while trying some of the fine wines smartly racked above the counter. Upstairs, amid beams and tiles, sample a variety of regional and national dishes, including some of the region's most superb paellas. Closed *Christmas Eve*. Reservations advised. Major credit cards accepted. 4 Calle Villegas, Alicante (phone: 6-520-0368). Moderate.

En Route from Alicante Take N340 and proceed 15 miles (24 km) inland (southwest) to Elche, city of palms, the Lady of Elche, and the Mystery of Elche.

ELCHE Some 600,000 date palms, originally planted by the Phoenicians, grow around Elche (Elx in the local dialect). The dates are harvested from December to March. View the trees up close at the Huerto del Cura (Priest's Grove), a palm garden that also features an impressive collection of cacti and tropical flowers (open daily from 9 AM to 8 PM mid-June to mid-September; to 6 PM the rest of the year; admission charge; phone: 65-451782). Also within the grove is a replica of the *Dama de Elche* (Lady of Elche), a remarkable bust dating back to 500 BC, the original of which is on display in the *Museo Arqueólogico Nacional* (National Archaeological Museum) in Madrid. It was discovered in 1897 about a mile (1.6 km) south of Elche in the ruins at La Alcudia, where there now is a museum of Iberian and Roman relics (*El Museo Monográfico de la Alcudia;* open Tuesdays through Sundays from 10 AM to 1 PM and from 4 to 8 PM; admission charge; phone: 65-459667).

For a spectacular experience, visit Elche in August, when the world's longest-running play is staged in the blue-domed, 17th-century Church of Santa María. The *Misteri d'Elx* (Mystery of Elche), celebrating the Assumption of the Virgin Mary, has been performed by local townspeople for 6 centuries. Although the songs are performed in an ancient form of Catalan, the action is not hard to grasp, and the special effects, including the descent of angels from the lofty dome, are breathtaking. Entry is free (but competition for seats is keen) for the play's first (August 14, 6 PM) and second (August 15, 6 PM) acts. Alternatively, seats can be booked for condensed 1-day performances, staged on August 11, 12, and 13, by writing before July 15 to the Oficina de Turismo (Parque Municipal, Elche, Alicante; phone: 65-452747). Telephone after that date to confirm the reservation. A special performance is staged on November 1 in even-numbered years. (See *Best Festivals* in DIVERSIONS.)

CHECKING IN/EATING OUT

Huerto del Cura It would be worth a detour to stay in this tranquil hostelry, which is set amid beautiful gardens in its own palm grove and is linked to the *parador* network, although it's not actually a *parador*. There's a swimming pool and tennis courts; the 70 rooms have TV sets, mini-bars, and air conditioning (important in August). The restaurant, *Els Capellans,* offers regional food and international dishes, and is especially pleasant in summer when tables are set out on the swimming pool terrace. Reservations unnecessary. Major credit cards accepted. Av. Federico García Sánchez, Elche (phone: 65-458040; in the US, 212-686-9213; fax: 65-421910). Hotel, moderate; restaurant, expensive to moderate.

En Route from Elche Continue along N340, through the town of Crevillente to Orihuela, 21 miles (34 km) southwest of Elche in the Segura River Valley. The center of a rich agricultural area, Orihuela has a Gothic cathedral in which a famous Velázquez canvas, the *Temptation of St. Thomas Aquinas,* is kept under lock and key in the *Museo Diocesano* (Diocesan Museum); open Mondays through Fridays from 10:30 AM to 1:30 PM and from 4 to 6 PM; admission charge; phone: 65-300638). Velázquez painted the work at the request of Dominican friars, whose 17th-century Monastery of Santo Domingo, later a university and currently a high school, has fine baroque cloisters. Orihuela is the birthplace of Miguel Hernández, a goatherd who became one of Spain's finest poets before dying tragically in Alicante's jail in 1942. His house on Calle Miguel Hernández can be visited Mondays through Fridays from 10 AM to 1 PM and from 4 to 6 PM (no phone). If you don't find anyone there, contact the tourist office (25 Calle Francisco Diez; phone: 65-302747).

Still on N340, the road crosses into the province and autonomous community of Murcia; at Monteagudo, it passes a white statue of Christ atop a rocky pinnacle commanding the *huerta,* a jigsaw of tomato, pepper, citrus fruit, and cereal fields. From here, it's only a few miles to the capital.

MURCIA Most tourists pass through this pleasant and unhurried city of over 305,000 inhabitants on the Segura River on their way to Cartagena or the coast, so this is a good place for a short respite from summer crowds. The most important sights are in the older part of town on the north bank of the river. There, on Plaza Cardenal Belluga, is the mainly Gothic cathedral, begun in the 14th century, but with a magnificent baroque façade that was added in the 18th century. Inside, the Virgen de la Fuensanta, Murcia's patroness, presides over the altar. The church's Renaissance-baroque bell tower can be climbed for a stirring view of the city and the surrounding *huerta.* The *Museo Diocesano* (phone: 68-216344) contains La Fuensanta's gold crown, as well as one of Spain's finest polychrome woodcarvings, depicting in amazingly lifelike detail the penitent St. Hieronymus by the local sculptor Francisco Salzillo. The museum is open daily from 9 AM to 1 PM and from 5 to 8 PM in June through September; from 10 AM to 1 PM and from 3 to 5 PM in October through May; admission charge. More examples of the sculptor's work can be seen some distance away in the *Museo Salzillo* (1 Calle San Andrés; phone: 68-291893), which houses some of the woodcarvings that are carried in Murcia's *Holy Week* processions (see below), as well as a large number of terra cotta figurines depicting episodes from the Gospels and the daily life of Murcian peasants (June through September open Tuesdays through Saturdays from 9:30 AM to 1 PM and from 4 to 7 PM; Sundays from 11 AM to 1 PM; October through May open Tuesdays through Saturdays from 9:30 to 1 PM and from 3 to 6 PM; Sundays from 11 AM to 1 PM; admission charge).

Just north of the cathedral, on traffic-free Calle de la Trapería, stands the casino (phone: 68-212255), a 19th-century building that is another of the city's landmarks. Once a sumptuous private club for wealthier citizens, it is now a cultural center hosting a changing program of lectures, meetings, and other events. Marble, molded plaster, carved wood, and crystal chandeliers lend it an august air — visitors are welcome to look inside (open daily from 9 AM to 11 PM; closed July and August; no admission charge). Farther north, the street broadens into Avenida Alfonso X el Sabio, a boulevard with many sidewalk cafés and a favorite spot for people watching. Many small shops can be found in the network of narrow pedestrian streets between Calle de la Trapería and its parallel to the west, the Gran Vía. The local tourist office is on a parallel to the east, however, at 4 Calle Alejandro Séiquer (phone: 68-213716).

In Alcantarilla, 6 miles (10 km) outside of town on the road to Granada, is the *Museo de la Huerta* (Carretera de Andalucía; phone: 68-800340), which contains traditional crafts, costumes, and implements of the region. A huge *noria* (waterwheel), an iron replica of the wooden one used by the Moors to raise water, stands outside (open Tuesdays through Saturdays from 10:30 AM to 5:30 PM; Sundays from 11 AM to 5:30 PM; admission charge).

Murcia celebrates *Holy Week* with great solemnity and pomp in processions of stunning scope. More than 3,000 people take in a *Holy Wednesday* procession, which stretches for nearly a mile. Several of Salzillo's sculptures are borne through the streets on *Good Friday.* On *Easter Sunday,* a burst of gaiety sweeps the city with the start of the *Spring Fiesta.* Folk dancing, a jazz festival, and street festivals fill a week that ends with fireworks and a bizarre pageant known as the *Entierro de la Sardina* (Burial of the Sardine).

CHECKING IN

Siete Coronas Melia This large, modern establishment is situated opposite the gardens bordering the Segura River. It has an elegant lobby, and 108 well-appointed rooms with air conditioning and color TV sets. There is also a garage — important in Murcia, where parking is a problem. 5 Paseo de Garay, Murcia (phone: 68-217771; in the US, 800-336-3542; fax: 68-221294). Expensive.

Hispano II Close to the cathedral, this modern, family-run establishment has 35 air conditioned rooms with color TV sets. The restaurant serves good *tapas* and excellent regional food. Parking available. 3-5 Calle Lucas, Murcia (phone: 68-216152; fax: 68-216859). Expensive to moderate.

Rincón de Pepe Comfortable, tastefully decorated, and located in the city center, this property has 117 air conditioned rooms with private baths and minibars, as well as a justifiably renowned restaurant (see below). 34 Calle Apóstoles, Murcia (phone: 68-212239; fax: 68-221744). Expensive to moderate.

EATING OUT

Rincón de Pepe Its imaginative offerings of typical Murcian dishes have won it a Michelin star. Try the succulent *cordero lechal asado al estilo de Murcia* (roast lamb Murcia style, cooked with apples, pine nuts, and wine), wild partridge in jumilla wine, or the shellfish and truffle salad. Closed Sunday evenings and July 15 through August 15. Reservations necessary. Major credit cards accepted. 34 Calle Apóstoles, Murcia (phone: 68-212239). Expensive.

CARTAGENA Just 30½ miles (49 km) down the highway (N301) from Murcia is this ancient port city, which encapsulates the Mediterranean coast's turbulent past. Founded by the Carthaginians during the 3rd century BC, called Carthago Nova in its flourishing Roman epoch, pillaged by the Visigoths, independent under the Moors, and sacked by Sir Francis Drake in 1588, Cartagena was the port from which King Alfonso XIII sailed into exile after his 1931 abdication. Because of its deep, sheltered harbor, Cartagena is Spain's most important naval base. Ancient ramparts lend a fortress-like air to the city, which is dominated by four hills. The best overall view is from the Castillo de la Concepción, now more a park or garden than a fortress, where an Arab-built lighthouse stands. To the west lie the ruins of the 13th-century cathedral, destroyed in the 1936–39 Spanish Civil War. At the port, opposite a monument to sailors who died in the Spanish-American War, is one of the world's first submarines. The 72-foot-long, 85-ton brown-and-gray cigar-shaped craft was built by a local inventor, Isaac Peral, in 1888. The impressive City Hall lies close by and at one corner is the tourist office (Plaza del Ayuntamiento; phone: 68-506483). Calle Mayor, the pedestrian mall leading from the plaza, is lined with cafés.

Don't miss the *Museo Nacional de Arqueológia Marítima* (2 miles/3 km from the center of town, at Faro de Navidad, Puerto de Cartagena; phone: 68-508415 or 68-101166); take the Mazarrón road and look for the sign. It is a treasure house of exhibits related to Mediterranean shipping, including ancient amphoras, anchors, jewelry, and a full-size model of a Roman galley (open Tuesdays through Sundays from 10 AM to 3 PM; admission charge).

Easter Week attracts many visitors to Cartagena. Particularly impressive are the early-morning processions on *Good Friday*. During the procession from the fishing quarter of Santa Lucía, singers compete to show their mastery of the *saeta,* a spine-tingling flamenco lament. Around dawn, three processions blend together and continue as one.

CHECKING IN

La Manga Club A luxurious, British-run, sports-oriented resort located 15 miles (24 km) east of Cartagena on N332. The 47 air conditioned rooms overlook a verdant, carefully landscaped complex, which includes 2 championship golf courses, 13 tennis courts, 2 swimming pools, and a cricket field. There is also horseback riding, scuba diving, and windsurfing. Apartments and bungalows are available. Los Belones, Cartagena (phone: 68-564511). Expensive.

Cartagonova On a quiet street near the center of town. All 127 rooms are air conditioned and have color TV sets. Other facilities include a garage and a restaurant specializing in regional and international dishes. 3 Calle Marcos Redondo, Cartagena (phone: 68-504200; fax: 68-500502). Moderate.

EATING OUT

Los Habaneros Probably Cartagena's best restaurant, with an extensive wine cellar. Try the *paletilla de cabrita al horno* (roast kid) or *pollo con langosta* (chicken with prawns). Open daily. Reservations unnecessary. American Express, Diners Club, and Visa accepted. 60 Calle San Diego, Cartagena (phone: 68-505250). Expensive.

En Route from Cartagena If returning to Madrid (277 miles/444 km from Cartagena and 247 miles/395 km from Murcia), it's N301 nearly all the way (backtrack through Murcia). If proceeding to Granada, take N332, which weaves southwest over irrigated fields and barren ocher hills for 20½ miles (33 km) to Puerto de Mazarrón, on Murcia's Costa Cálida (Warm Coast), where adjacent beaches have attracted considerable tourist development. From Puerto de Mazarrón, it's a quick 4½ miles (7 km) inland to the town of Mazarrón, from which N332 continues south toward Aguilas, through scenery that becomes increasingly desert-like. Aguilas, an unhurried fishing port dominated by a 16th-century castle, has good beaches but limited accommodations and restaurant facilities. From Aguilas, return inland on the Lorca road, but turn left after 5 miles (8 km) toward Puerto Lumbreras, where an overnight stop can be made. The next morning, head west on N342 to Granada, 127 miles (203 km) from Puerto Lumbreras.

CHECKING IN/EATING OUT

Parador de Puerto Lumbreras A quiet, comfortable, modern *parador* with 60 air conditioned rooms, a swimming pool, and a garage. The restaurant, overlooking a pretty garden, serves local specialties, such as *costillos de cabrito en ajo cabañil* (kid cutlets cooked with garlic, paprika, and wine vinegar) and *berenjenas a la crema con gambas y jamón* (eggplant in a white sauce with prawns and ham). Major credit cards accepted. Carretera N340, Km 77, Puerto Lumbreras (phone: 68-402025; in the US, 212-686-9213; fax: 68-402836). Moderate.

Andalusia
and Gibraltar

The sunny southern region of Andalusia — eight provinces in an area about the size of Indiana — has come to symbolize Spain for much of the world. The home of flamenco also boasts three of the country's greatest architectural treasures: the fairy-tale Alhambra palace in Granada, Córdoba's Great Mosque, and the massive Gothic cathedral and evocative Santa Cruz quarter of Seville. Beyond these three "queen cities" are provincial capitals such as wind-whipped Cádiz, where every street leads to the sea, and Jaén, spreading like a white fan at the foot of an awesome fortress. With coastlines on both the Mediterranean Sea and the Atlantic Ocean, this fabled land claims some of Europe's most popular beach resorts. Overbuilding in these areas has become a real problem, but devotees maintain that the coast is still a little piece of earthly paradise.

Andalusia bears evidence of many great civilizations that settled along its shores. Phoenicians founded Malaca (Málaga) and Gadir (Cádiz), and Romans built major cities along the Guadalquivir Valley and the coast. The center of the centuries-long Moorish occupation that began in 711, Granada was its last stronghold until it fell to the Reconquest in 1492. All this history has left its mark, turning Andalusian cities and towns into vast museums of art and architecture. But there are plenty of dull towns and villages, too, as well as dirty beaches, barren and ugly stretches of countryside, and urban purse snatchers. However, the selective traveler will discover a seemingly endless variety of delights.

The driving route outlined below begins at Córdoba, gateway to Andalusia, and continues southwest through the Guadalquivir River valley — farmland for the most part and brutally hot in summer — to Seville, which is the capital of the region. It then traverses horse-and-sherry country around Jerez de la Frontera and makes its way to Cádiz, on the Atlantic coast, from which it heads southeast, skirting white villages and the Mediterranean coast before arriving at the Rock of Gibraltar, one of the world's great natural landmarks, and one of the last remaining British colonies. After turning inland to visit the gorge-split town of Ronda, it drops down to the coast again to pass through the touristic Costa del Sol. The route leaves the coast for good near the village of Salobreña, climbing rugged mountains en route to magical Granada, and finally heads north to the lesser-known towns of Jaén and Ubeda, almost untouched by tourism and well worth a visit.

Total highway driving for the route is approximately 612 miles (980 km). Fortunately, major highway improvements were made prior to *Expo*

'92 in Seville, vastly improving driving conditions. Including 2 nights each at the three major cities (Córdoba, Seville, and Granada), the minimum time to allow for the full tour is 15 days.

Accommodations include a few sinfully sumptuous abodes, starting at more than $150 a night for a double room in the very expensive category and $100 a night in the expensive category. However, there are plenty of perfectly acceptable, even exceptional, hotels (mostly government *paradores*) in the moderate range, from $60 to $100, and even the occasional inexpensive choice for under $55. (Hotel rates in and around Seville remain fairly high following the astronomical prices charged during *Expo '92*, but due to overcapacity hotels often offer special rates.) Most Andalusian hotels with fewer than three stars (by the government's official classification system) tend to be of the semi-fleabag variety suitable for determined budgeteers only. Expect to pay $70 or more for a meal for two at restaurants rated as expensive; $40 to $70 at places in the moderate category; and less than $35 at dining spots described as inexpensive. Prices include a bottle of house wine, dessert, and coffee. Note that local area codes are included in the telephone numbers listed below; when calling from another area in Spain, dial "9" first.

CÓRDOBA The first stop is Córdoba, once Europe's greatest city. It takes at least a day to see Córdoba's Mezquita (Great Mosque), to wander the alleyways twisting through the old Jewish Quarter, and to take in the atmosphere of a city that was once a great center of Arab and Jewish scholarship. For full details on the city's sights, hotels, and restaurants, see *Córdoba,* THE CITIES.

En Route from Córdoba Take N-IV toward Seville to Carmona, 65½ miles (105 km) southwest across gently rolling countryside known as "the frying pan of Andalusia" because of scorching summer temperatures. Suddenly in the distance loom a series of bluffs, where the town of Carmona has sat since antiquity, commanding the river plain of the Guadalquivir.

CARMONA Still partially surrounded by ancient Roman walls, this town has one of the richest histories in Andalusia. Known as Carmo to the Romans, the town straddled the famous Via Augusta, the Roman road that stretched from Cádiz to the north of Spain. In 206 BC, the Roman general Scipio crushed a Carthaginian army nearby. The road into town passes beneath the remnants of a 14th-century fortress — the Alcázar — cleverly transformed into an excellent *parador* (see *Checking In/Eating Out*), and through the 17th-century Puerta de Córdoba (Córdoba Gate), built into the Old Town walls. Once inside, go left up the hill to the *parador* (follow the signs) or follow Calle Santa María de Gracia to the center.

A town of about 23,000 residents, Carmona is just the right size for strolling — alone through quiet, white-walled streets or with everyone else out for the evening *paseo* in the circular Plaza de San Fernando, the town's nucleus. The plaza is lined with wrought-iron lampposts and centuries-old buildings, including the present and former town halls. Within walking distance is the double-arched Puerta de Sevilla from Moorish times; outside stands the Church of San Pedro (on Calle San Pedro), with a 17th-century bell tower modeled after the famous Giralda in Seville. The Gothic Church of Santa María (on Calle Martín López) contains the oldest calendar in Spain (6th century), carved on an arch in the Patio de los Naranjos.

The Roman necropolis about half a mile (1 km) outside town (off the Seville road) shelters several hundred tombs from 2,000 years ago. The Elephant Tomb, named for a statue at its entrance, features dining rooms and a kitchen that once had running water; historians believe that priests must have held some kind of banquet in honor of the deceased here. The Servilia Tomb is the size of a villa and has its own pool. The necropolis, which also contains a museum filled with Roman pottery, mosaics, busts, and glass vials, is open from 10 AM to 2 PM and from 4 to 6 PM; closed Sunday afternoons and Mondays; admission charge. For further details, contact Carmona's Tourist Information Office, Plaza de las Descalzas (phone: 54-142200).

CHECKING IN/EATING OUT

Parador Alcázar del Rey Don Pedro A Moorish fortress turned luxurious palace, it has 59 air conditioned rooms with spectacular views. There is also a huge outdoor pool, as well as an impressive vaulted dining hall serving classic Andalusian food. For additional details, see *Paradores* in DIVERSIONS. Major credit cards accepted. Carmona (phone: 54-141010; in the US, 212-686-9213; fax: 54-141712). Expensive.

En Route from Carmona Continue on N-IV and drive 24 miles (38 km) into Seville.

SEVILLE When Madrid became the capital of Spain in the 16th century, it was hardly the richest, the most powerful, or even the best known of Spanish cities. All those superlatives belonged to Seville. For a detailed report on the city's sights, hotels, and restaurants, see *Seville* in THE CITIES.

En Route from Seville From the center, take the A-4, a new four-lane highway south in the direction of Jerez de la Frontera and Cádiz. Drive 34 miles (54 km) to the junction with C343 at Las Cabezas de San Juan, turning off toward Espera and Arcos de la Frontera, 22 miles (35 km) away. Rather than go directly into Arcos, take the turnoff to Embalse de Arcos, a lake northeast of town along the road to El Bosque (C344). From this vantage point, Arcos looks like a white pyramid rising from the surrounding plain.

ARCOS DE LA FRONTERA Arcos (*de la frontera* is tacked onto the names of many towns that once stood along the Christian-Moorish boundary) sits on a lofty hill hemmed in on three sides by the Guadalete River. One of its attractions for visitors is its spectacularly situated government *parador,* perched along the edge of a cliff (see *Checking In/Eating Out*). Arcos is also among the most picturesque of a dozen or so whitewashed Andalusian hill towns known as the *pueblos blancos* (white villages) and is included on the Ruta de los Pueblos Blancos (Route of the White Villages), a popular driving route in the region. (A brochure with maps is available from Spanish tourist authorities in the US or in Spain.) The town has impressive *Easter Week* processions, including the singing of piercing melodies called *saetas* — a kind of *Easter* flamenco — and the running of a lone bull on *Easter Sunday.*

Legend has it that Arcos was founded by King Brigo, a grandson of Noah. Known as Medina Arkosh in Moorish times, this seemingly impregnable site was captured by Alfonso X in 1250. The Plaza de Cabildo (also known as Plaza de España), is the town's main square and the site of both the *parador* and a hair-raising terrace overlooking a valley of neat green fields and orchards. Also on the square is the old Town Hall and the Church of Santa María. Climb the 386 feet to the top of the bell tower, but try not to arrive at the stroke of 12. The views from on high are spectacular: Look for the 18th-century tower of the Church of San Pedro (Plaza de Cabildo) at the other side of the hilltop and for the former castle of the Dukes of Arcos, below and to the right, now occupied by an English aristocrat.

CHECKING IN/EATING OUT

Parador Casa del Corregidor This former vicar's home is a pleasing medley of tiles and antiques with 24 air conditioned rooms and a good restaurant that serves local specialties. Major credit cards accepted. Plaza de España, Arcos de la Frontera (phone: 56-700500; in the US, 212-686-9213; fax: 56-701116). Expensive.

En Route from Arcos de la Frontera Take N342 west 19 miles (30 km) to Jerez, a town steeped in all things Andalusian: bulls, horses, fiestas, and, of course, fine sherry.

JEREZ DE LA FRONTERA Jerez is the home of Spain's distinctive fortified wine — "sherry," in fact, is an English corruption of the name of the town, from which English, Scottish, and Irish shippers began buying wine as early as the 16th century. Although Jerez, the main production center and a fairly large town of about 200,000 people, does have other points of interest, most visitors get into the spirit of things by touring one of the sherry wineries, or bodegas, that are the prime local attraction.

Jerez has some 100 bodegas; the tourist office (7 Alameda Cristina; phone: 56-331150) has details on those that welcome visitors. Among them are the Harvey, González Byass, and Sandeman bodegas, but perhaps the best of the bunch belongs to the Domecq family (3 Calle San Ildefonso; phone: 56-331900), where visits can be arranged through the public relations department; closed weekends during August; no admission charge. Here visitors see the fermentation rooms, mixing tanks, warehouses for aging, and bottling lines, then sample one of the four main sherry varieties — *fino* (extra dry), *amontillado* (dry with fuller body), *oloroso* (medium dry with golden color), and *dulce* (sweet). For additional details, see *Most Visitable Vineyards* in DIVERSIONS.

The outstanding Real Escuela Andaluza del Arte Ecuestre (Royal Andalusian School of Equestrian Art), a rival to Vienna's renowned Spanish Riding School, is Jerez's second major attraction. Although the school has only been open since 1973, horse breeding and training has been an Andalusian enterprise since Moorish times, and it was the ancestors of the Hispano-Arab stallions strutting their stuff in Jerez that sired the famous Lippizaners. The "Dancing Horses of Andalusia" perform every Thursday at noon at the school's 1,450-seat arena (Av. Duque de Abrantes; phone: 56-311111 or 56-311100); admission charge. Practice sessions are held at the area on other days of the week (except Sundays) between 11 AM and 1 PM, and visitors may watch free of charge.

In early September, Jerez hosts the *Fiesta de la Vendimia,* an annual wine harvest festival. An even better time of the year to be in town is during the week-long *Feria del Caballo* (Horse Fair) in May, when aloof aristocrats, the *señoritos,* gather to show off their steeds and horsemanship. Each day begins with a promenade of riders, followed by a procession of ornate carriages. There are dressage and jumping competitions, a horse auction, and special *rejoneo* bullfights, when a man or woman on horseback faces the bull. Visitors can test their stamina at scores of *casetas* — open booths overflowing with wine and the seductive rhythms of improvised flamenco.

Jerez has its fair share of historical monuments and churches. Among the best are the 11th-century Alcázar, with Arab baths, located off a large square called the Alameda Vieja. It's open daily from 11 AM to 1 PM and from 5 to 8 PM; 6 to 9 PM in summer; although parts of the building may be off limits to visitors due to ongoing renovation; admission charge. Nearby, on the Plaza de Arroyo, is the 18th-century baroque Cathedral of San Salvador (La Colegiata), built above an old mosque. Other notable churches include the late Gothic San Miguel and the Santiago, each with finely carved portals. Better known are the city's secular monuments. The Domecq mansion on Alameda Cristina (across from the tourist office) was the home of the Ponce de León family, built by the explorer in 1557. To arrange a visit, call the Visitor's Department (phone: 56-331900) between 9 AM and 2:30 PM. The Renaissance-style Casa del Cabildo, the old Town Hall on the Plaza de la Asunción, today houses a library and an archaeological museum. It's closed weekends; admission charge.

CHECKING IN

Sherry Park An ultramodern establishment, it's on an elegant, tree-lined avenue — the town's main drag — near the riding school. It has 300 air conditioned rooms, a restaurant, and a swimming pool to help beat the summer heat. 11 Av. Alvaro Domecq, Jerez de la Frontera (phone: 56-303011; fax: 56-311300). Expensive.

Avenida Jerez Less sumptuous than its neighbor across the street, this modern high-rise offers comfort and a good location, if not a lot of atmosphere. There are 95 air conditioned rooms and a snack bar on the premises. 10 Av. Alvaro Domecq, Jerez de la Frontera (phone: 56-347411; fax: 56-337296). Moderate.

EATING OUT

El Bosque On the main avenue near the hotel selections, it's said to cater to the local sherry aristocracy. Andalusian dishes on the menu include such unusual items as a shellfish-and-salmon salad. Closed Sundays. Reservations advised. Major credit cards accepted. 28 Av. Alvaro Domecq, Jerez de la Frontera (phone: 56-303333). Moderate.

Gaitán Conveniently located near the tourist office, this small place features rustic decor and a menu of Basque and traditional Spanish specialties. Closed Sunday nights and Mondays. Reservations unnecessary. Major credit cards accepted. 3 Calle Gaitán, Jerez de la Frontera (phone: 56-345859). Moderate.

En Route from Jerez de la Frontera Leave town on N-IV bound for Cádiz, 22 miles (35 km) away. After 14 miles (22 km), the road to Cádiz veers to the right, while the main highway continues toward Algeciras as N340. Continue through prosaic, resort-style suburbs to the 18th-century Puerta de la Tierra, gateway to the Old Town of Cádiz.

CÁDIZ For the travel-weary coming from the sunbaked interior, the salty breeze of Cádiz (pronounced *Cah*-deeth) is a soothing tonic. It's said to be impossible to get lost here, because every street leads to water: Old Cádiz occupies a club-shaped peninsula that juts out into the Atlantic like the prow of an ocean liner, with the Bay of Cádiz to its back. A narrow isthmus connects it to the mainland. The setting is dramatic, but Cádiz is a bit rough around the edges, with the kind of seedy charm found in such places as Marseilles and Naples.

A deep, sheltered harbor inspired the Phoenicians to found the city around 1100 BC, and every subsequent Mediterranean power made it an important port. Cádiz's role in the discovery and colonization of the New World — and above all as a conduit for trade with the new Spanish possessions — made it wealthy, and it became a favorite of raiding Barbary pirates and English sea dogs such as Sir Francis Drake. When the Guadalquivir River silted up, effectively removing Seville as a competitor, Cádiz became the headquarters of Spain's American fleet, only to slide into obscurity when the country lost its overseas colonies. Today, the port is booming once again.

The best way to get an overview of the town is to drive the loop road that circles the perimeter, skirting a lovely seaside promenade. In fact, travelers will probably want to limit driving to this route alone, because while Cádiz — with almost 160,000 inhabitants — is only a bit smaller than Jerez in terms of population, it has none of that city's sprawl, and negotiating the cramped and confusing streets is extremely difficult. Directly in front of the port on the peninsula's east side is the bustling Plaza San Juan de Dios, site of the imposing City Hall and a dozen or so seafood restaurants with outdoor tables for people watching. (*Gaditanos* — the locals — appear to live on fish, shellfish, and wine, and the number of standup eateries in town, especially in the dank streets around this plaza, is astounding.) Not far away, but on the west side of town, sits the ultra-ornate, golden-domed Catedral Nueva (New Cathedral; in the Plaza de la Catedral), an architectural peacock begun in the early 18th century and finished 116 years later, but still wholly baroque. Outstanding features inside include the choir stalls and, in the museum, the Custodia del Millón, a 17th-century silver monstrance studded with thousands of jewels; in the crypt is the tomb of the Spanish composer Manuel de Falla (who was born in Cádiz). The old cathedral, the Church of Santa Cruz (Calle Fray Félix), a 17th-century rebuilding of a church with 13th-century origins, is near the new one.

The city's tourist office (1 Calle Calderón de la Barca, on a corner of the Plaza de Mina; phone: 56-211313) can direct you to the remaining sights in the city. The *Cádiz Museum*, also known as the *Museo de Bellas Artes y Arqueológico* (phone: 56-212281), on the same square, has respectable collections of art, including paintings by Zurbarán and Murillo, and archaeology, especially Phoenician and Carthaginian artifacts. It's open Tuesdays through Sundays from 9:30 AM to 2 PM; admission charge. Another stop might be the 17th-century Oratorio de San Felipe Neri, several blocks away on Calle Santa Inés. The small church is famous as the place where Spain's first liberal constitution was hammered out in 1812; a painting by Murillo hangs above the altar. Next door is the *Museo Histórico Municipal* (Municipal History Museum; Calle Santa Inés; phone: 56-221788), which has a fascinating ivory-and-mahogany scale model of Cádiz as it looked in the 18th century. It's open Tuesdays through Fridays from 9 AM to 1 PM and from 4 to 7 PM; weekends, mornings only; no admission charge. The Oratorio de Santa Cueva (Calle Rosario) contains religious frescoes by Goya.

Strolling through Cádiz is a delight, especially along the seaside promenade with its enormous banyan trees and verdant oases such as the Parque de Genovés, which offers summer concerts and a palm garden. Within the loop of the promenade, the streets and alleys of the Old Town twist and turn like tunnels in a rabbit warren. Just when they become too claustrophobic, however, or a bit too grimy, a sunny, palm-lined square appears. The same streets witness the town's uproarious *Carnavales*, well known throughout Spain. The week before *Lent*, residents go for days without sleep — singing, dancing in the streets, playing odd musical instruments, and rattling nerve-racking noisemakers. A fireworks display signals the end of the carnival celebrations, and the next morning all that remains are several tons of confetti and empty wine bottles.

CHECKING IN

Atlántico This modern, 6-story hotel is a member of the government *parador* chain, although it doesn't have the traditional character of the others. Overlooking the ocean, it boasts a beautiful pool. Its 173 rooms are air conditioned and have balconies; the dining room serves Andalusian food. 9 Parque de Genovés, Cádiz (phone: 56-226905; in the US, 212-686-9213; fax: 56-214582). Moderate.

EATING OUT

El Anteojo An excellent location and solid seafood dishes make this place a winner. Reservations advised. Major credit cards accepted. 22 Alameda de Apodaca, Cádiz (phone: 56-221320). Moderate.

El Sardinero This simple spot is the best of the many seafood restaurants on a square known for good fish. It offers a Basque kitchen — with specialties such as *merluza a la vasca* (hake, Basque-style) — and outstanding *tapas* at the bar. Closed Mondays. No reservations. Major credit cards accepted. Plaza San Juan de Dios, Cádiz (phone: 56-282505). Inexpensive.

En Route from Cádiz Head south toward Algeciras. The road, flanked by the Bay of Cádiz and the Atlantic, follows a narrow isthmus dotted with saltworks. After 10 miles (16 km), turn off to the main highway (N340), which travels along — a few miles inland, however — the southern half of the Costa de la Luz. This lesser-known Spanish *costa* stretches along the Atlantic all the way from Huelva near the Portuguese border to wind-pummeled Tarifa, where it meets the Mediterranean. The coastline is relatively unscathed by resort developments, and because of the extra effort necessary to reach it from the main highway, it's still possible to find isolated beaches of golden sand and mobs of seagulls.

VEJER DE LA FRONTERA This picturesque village is another of Andalusia's "white villages." It lords over the landscape 32½ miles (52 km) from Cádiz, just a mile (1.6 km) off the main road. The site is another exceptional one, used as a defensive bastion ever since the days when Romans were fighting Iberians. The Moors couldn't pass up a chance to plunk down a hilltop castle, and some of its old walls have been restored. Nearby, the Church of San Salvador (Calle Rosario) is a blending of Gothic and Mudéjar styles, built on the foundations of a mosque. The tiny streets here are no place to drive; if you'd like to explore, park in the lot at the entrance to the village.

CHECKING IN/EATING OUT

Convento de San Francisco This former monastery has been impeccably restored and contains Vejer's best restaurant. None of the 25 rooms is air conditioned, but summers are moderate here. Diners Club, MasterCard, and Visa accepted. Vejer de la Frontera (phone: 56-451001; fax: 56-451004). Moderate.

En Route from Vejer de la Frontera The N340 highway south to Tarifa passes a wild and windy landscape, with huge limestone outcroppings and a smattering of whitewashed farmhouses. One of the largest hunks of rock marks Punta Paloma, where the highway turns seaward. The E5 turnoff for Tarifa comes 28 miles (45 km) from Vejer, and it's another mile (1.6 km) into town.

TARIFA The town sits at Spain's southernmost point, looking out on the Strait of Gibraltar and, on a clear day, as far as Morocco. Head for the Old Quarter through an ancient portal. Within are the 16th-century Gothic Church of San Mateo and the 13th-century (reconstructed) Castillo de Guzmán el Bueno, still used as an army barracks. The castle is usually open from 11 AM to 2 PM and from 4 to 6 PM daily during the summer months, on weekends only the rest of the year; admission charge. (However, ongoing renovations have closed the castle periodically, so it's best to check with the tourist office before visiting: Avenida de Andalucia; phone: 56-684186.) Most people who come to Tarifa don't come for the sightseeing, but to take the hydrofoil that makes a daily run across the water to Tangier in Morocco. Windsurfing is another big draw.

En Route from Tarifa Return to N340 and head east toward Algeciras. This part of Andalusia, known as the Campo de Gibraltar, is mainly an industrial and shipping center, of little interest to tourists. Several miles east of Tarifa, however, the famous Rock of Gibraltar — a little piece of the British Empire isolated in the Mediterranean — comes into view, thrusting up from across the Bay of Algeciras.

ALGECIRAS This growing port city has little to offer visitors except wonderful views of the Rock. More than 3 million passengers a year use the ferries and hydrofoils that ply the Strait of Gibraltar between Algeciras and both Tangier and the Spanish enclave of Ceuta in North Africa. The city also has a grand old landmark hotel, the *Reina Cristina* (see below), the brainchild of a turn-of-the-century English lord who constructed a railroad across Andalusia. During World War II, the harborside hotel's guests were joined by a number of German spies, who watched ship traffic through the strait from their second-story rooms.

Reina Cristina The pink lady with green shutters, turrets, and a tiled roof manages to blend Victorian and arabesque into a nostalgic hideaway. Built about a hundred years ago and named for Spain's queen regent, the hotel sits apart from the rest of Algeciras, with its own terraced gardens, English library, and aging British clientele, who come for the service and the inspiring views of "Gib." It has 135 air conditioned rooms and a traditional, moderately priced restaurant. Major credit cards accepted. Paseo de la Conferencia, Algeciras (phone: 56-602622; fax: 56-603323). Expensive.

En Route from Algeciras If headed for Gibraltar, take N340 northeast 8 miles (13 km) to San Roque, then turn off to La Línea de la Concepción, from which the border lies 5 miles (8 km) away. If not visiting Gibraltar, turn off N340 onto C3331 just before San Roque and proceed directly to Ronda.

GIBRALTAR The self-governing British colony of Gibraltar is only 3 miles long and three-quarters of a mile wide, with approximately 30,000 inhabitants settled mainly in Gibraltar Town, on the Rock's west side. Tiny as it is, the colony is an immense source of bitterness among the Spanish, who consider themselves its rightful owners; their attempts to reclaim it led to the closing of the frontier between Spain and Gibraltar in 1969. For years, the Rock was accessible only by air or sea from the United Kingdom or North Africa. But the steel mesh gates swung open again in February 1985, and the border is now open round the clock. Visitors need only a passport, not a visa, to cross.

> **NOTE** The phone numbers listed below do *not* include area codes. If you are calling Gibraltar from within the Andalusian province (of which Spain considers Gibraltar to be a part, so calls are domestic) dial 9567 before the local number. If you are calling from elsewhere in Spain, dial 956 before the local number. If you are calling from La Línea de la Concepción, just across the border, dial only 7 before the local Gibraltar number. If calling from the US, dial the country code (350) before the local number.

The *Gibraltar Museum* (off Main St. on Bomb House La.; phone: 74289) tells the whole fascinating story of the Rock, which Spain lost to the Moors, and later to the British in 1713. It's open Mondays through Fridays from 10 AM to 6 PM; Saturdays from 10 AM to 2 PM; admission charge.

Although Gibraltarians are really more Mediterranean than British, both in temperament and language (a strange variety of Spanish with an abundance of English expressions), the British presence is unmistakable, from fluttering Union Jacks and friendly bobbies to photos of the queen and gin-and-tonic urbanity at the yacht club. If you want to see a changing-of-the-guard ceremony at the Governor's Residence on Main Street, inquire at the tourist office (in Cathedral Square; phone: 76400); it used to be a weekly event, but the ceremony now takes place about 5 times a year. Main Street, the Rock's backbone, is a throbbing half mile of discount shops (there's no VAT here), British retail institutions such as *Marks & Spencer,* and pubs such as the *Angry Friar* and *Old Vic's.* Unfortunately, Gibraltar has taken on an increasingly seedy appearance, and traditional hospitality has suffered from the onslaught of visitors since 1985.

Willis's Road, to the east of Main Street, leads past the Moorish Castle, with its square Tower of Homage, built in 1333 (admission charge). From here, Queen's Road climbs to the Upper Galleries, huge tunnels for housing artillery that were carved out by hand during the Great Siege (1779–83), when the Spanish tried to retake the island. They are open daily from 10 AM to 6 PM; admission charge. Farther up lies the Apes' Den, home of perhaps the world's most famous simians. Gibraltar's official mascots, they are so revered that Churchill vowed to protect them when their numbers dwindled. Daily feedings take place at 8 AM and 4 PM; no admission charge. Another way to reach the den is via a spectacular cable car ride that goes to the top of the Rock from just below the *Rock* hotel. More information on the sights can be obtained at the Gibraltar Tourist Office in Cathedral Square.

CHECKING IN

Rock This hotel is a classic of the British colonial genre, with 160 comfortable rooms, good service, and spectacular views. Other amenities are a restaurant with roast beef and Yorkshire pudding on the menu, a saltwater pool, miniature golf, and a nearby casino. 3 Europa Road, Gibraltar (phone: 73000). Expensive.

EATING OUT

Da Paolo Located at an attractive yacht harbor between the airport and town, it offers an imaginative menu in Art Deco surroundings. Closed Sundays and all of February. Reservations advised. Major credit cards accepted. Marina Bay, Gibraltar (phone: 76799 and 76288). Moderate.

Spinning Wheel The convenient location and the recommendation of a loyal following make this a top traditional choice. Lamb dishes are the specialty. Closed Sundays. Reservations unnecessary. Major credit cards accepted. 9 Horsebarrack Lane, Gibraltar (phone: 76091). Moderate.

En Route from Gibraltar Return to San Roque and take C3331 toward Ronda, spearing through farmland along the Guadarranque River and into the hills. Several of the towns passed before reaching the classic old

Andalusian town of Ronda are included on the Ruta de los Pueblos Blancos, among them picturesque Jimena de la Frontera, draped like a sheepskin on the side of a hill 22 miles (35 km) from San Roque and crowned by a castle. From Jimena, take C341; the road passes golden hills dotted with olive trees, citrus orchards, and clusters of white houses. After a stretch that soars high above a spectacular valley, the village of Gaucín appears, then tiny Algatocín and Benadalid. The final approach to Ronda, 37½ miles (60 km) from Jimena, provides inspiring scenery, with huge bare slabs of stone thrusting up from the landscape. This is the heart of the Serranía de Ronda range, a traditional retreat for bandits.

RONDA Its fame rests chiefly on El Tajo, a 360-foot gorge cut by the Guadalevín River that literally splits the town in two. Incredible cliff-hanging houses perch right along the edge of the precipice and look as if they might slide into the abyss at any moment. The 5-foot-high iron grilles on the 18th-century Puente Nuevo, one of three bridges that span the gorge, are all that separate visitors from a horrifying drop. The bridge links two towns and two eras. To the north lies the "new" town, called El Mercadillo, begun around 1500, after Ronda fell to the Christians. Here, a pedestrian street, the Carrera de Espinel, is lined with scores of shops, becoming a vibrant sea of shoppers and strollers each afternoon. At the head of the street is the Plaza de Toros, Ronda's famous bullring. Although bullfights are held only about once a month from May through October, visitors may inspect Spain's most beautiful bullring and its oldest (1785) daily from 10 AM to 6 PM; the nation's top bullfighting museum is also located here, in the cradle of modern bullfighting (phone: 52-877977; admission charge). The local Romero family developed most of the rules and techniques used today, including the introduction of the cape, the killing sword, and the group of assistants to the matador called the *cuadrilla*. Each September, at the *Corrida Goyesca* (Goya Bullfight) aficionados pay homage to a 19th-century family member, Pedro Romero, who killed 5,600 bulls during his career and fought until the age of 90. (Goya immortalized the epoch in several sketches and engravings.) End a tour of the New Town by strolling north from the bullring through the Alameda Gardens (Calle Virgen de la Paz), supposedly paid for with fines levied on anyone using foul language in public.

The Old Town, called La Ciudad, is a labyrinth of cramped streets and wrought-iron balconies brimming with potted geraniums. Here are some of Andalusia's finest aristocratic mansions, such as the twin-turreted 16th-century Renaissance Casa de Mondragón (off the Plaza del Campillo), which is now a crafts school that is closed to the public. A short walk away is the circular Plaza de la Ciudad, the coolest spot in town on a summer day. Fronting it is a 15th-century church, Santa María la Mayor, with a baroque altar dripping with gilt and a former Muslim mihrab (a niche indicating the direction of Mecca); the church's tower was once a minaret.

On the other side of the Old Town (near the bridge off Calle del Comandante Alejandro) are more mansions, including the Casa del Rey Moro, which is the restored home of King Badis, a Moorish ruler who drank wine from the jewel-encrusted skulls of his victims. (Today it's a private home that can't be visited.) Farther down the same street is the 18th-century Palacio del Marqués de Salvatierra (Calle Santo Domingo), the home of a Spanish aristocrat complete with Plateresque portal, marble staircase, and Alhambra-style gardens. The house is open daily except Thursdays from 11 AM to 2 PM and from 4 to 6 PM; no admission charge. At the bottom of the same hill, the Arab baths, which were recently renovated, are among the finest in Spain. They're open Tuesdays through Saturdays from 9 AM to 2 PM and from 4 to 6 PM; Sundays from 10:30 AM to 1 PM; admission charge.

CHECKING IN

Reina Victoria The grand old dowager of Ronda in the Mercadillo section has a gabled roof, English gardens, chandeliers, and dark wood furniture. Its 89 air conditioned rooms are often crowded with tour groups, but it's still a treat in a town with few hotels. 25 Av. Dr. Fleming, Ronda (phone: 52-871240; fax: 52-871075). Moderate.

EATING OUT

Don Miguel Clinging to one side of El Tajo next to the bridge, this spot offers a stunning outdoor terrace as well as good food. Rabbit in sherry sauce and devilfish with green peppers are on the inventive menu. Closed Mondays. Reservations unnecessary. Major credit cards accepted. 4 Calle Villanueva, Ronda (phone: 52-871090). Moderate.

Pedro Romero Bullfighting memorabilia give it atmosphere, and the traditional Spanish food is good. Try the *rabo de toro* (oxtail stew). Closed Sunday evenings. Reservations unnecessary. Major credit cards accepted. 18 Calle Virgen de la Paz, Ronda (phone: 52-871110). Moderate.

En Route from Ronda This route through Andalusia proceeds from Ronda to the Costa del Sol. Those on a tight schedule (as well as those who eschew the ravages of mass tourism), may want to head directly to Granada. If done in 1 day, this trip involves a fairly strenuous drive of 120 miles (192 km) along routes C341 and N342 via Antequera, a pleasant, medium-size town with dozens of historic churches and a Moorish castle. If traveling at a leisurely pace, stop in Antequera or farther along for a meal or an overnight stay.

To continue the complete Andalusia route, proceed from Ronda south to the Costa del Sol via C339, which drops from about 2,300 feet to sea level in a distance of 30 miles. The landscape along the way is a harsh blending of volcanic rock and red clay, studded with rare *pinsapo* firs, black cork oaks, wild olives, and mauve rock roses.

CHECKING IN/EATING OUT

La Bobadilla Set in the middle of isolated countryside, this hotel within the sumptuous resort, Vitatop, near Loja, about 20 miles (32 km) east of Antequera, is designed in authentic Andalusian style — tiled roofs, arches, and wrought-iron grilles. For more details, see *Spas* in DIVERSIONS. In addition to 60 luxurious rooms (all with their own patio or garden), there are extensive fitness facilities, a stable of horses for riding, and two highly rated restaurants. Major credit cards accepted. Finca La Bobadilla, Loja (phone: 58-321861; in New York City, 212-838-3110; elsewhere in the US, 800-223-6800; fax: 58-321810). Very expensive.

Parador de Antequera Another option for those en route to Granada. It features a pool and 55 air conditioned rooms, plus a popular restaurant serving regional specialties. Major credit cards accepted. Paseo García del Olmo, Antequera (phone: 52-840261; in the US, 212-686-9213; fax: 52-841312). Moderate.

PUERTO BANÚS AND MARBELLA The first town on the coast for those who arrive from Ronda is an insignificant resort, San Pedro de Alcántara. Only 2 miles (3 km) east of it, however, is the crown jewel of local tourism, Puerto José Banús, a yacht harbor filled with dozens of pleasant places to stop for a drink or a meal. The Port, as it's known to residents, is home to hundreds of craft of all sizes and pedigrees; Rolls-Royces and Mercedeses wait quayside, as their impeccably groomed owners join the evening parade of strollers who come to see and be seen on the promenade. Behind is a modern, quasi-Andalusian fishing village filled with luxury apartments and looking like a giant cardboard cutout.

Puerto Banús is technically part of San Pedro, but in spirit it belongs to Marbella, 5 miles (8 km) east, the fabled resort where the "beautiful people" play — or at least used to play, before package tourism began to drive them away. The golf is great at several local courses; so is the tennis, and the windsurfing and other water sports. Even sunbathing is better here than at other spots on the coast, thanks to a superb climate created by a backdrop of coastal mountains. The Old Town is a traffic-free oasis of cool, cobbled alleys and half-hidden squares brimming with aromatic flowers and fruit trees. Among them, the Plaza de los Naranjos, a truly idyllic spot with orange trees, gurgling fountains, and outdoor cafés, is the best. Also on the square are a statue of King Juan Carlos (where one of Franco once loomed), and the 16th-century Town Hall. The *Museo Arqueológico* (Archeological Museum) has been closed for renovations, but is due to reopen this year in the Hospital Bazán, on the Calle Viento. Call the tourist office (1 Av. Miguel Cano; phone: 52-771442) for the latest information.

Other sights in the Old Town are the parish Church of La Encarnación and its clock tower on the Plaza Caridad, and the adjacent Calle Gloria, a tiny street that has become a floral showcase. Nearby Calle Alamo leads to a nice upstairs bar called *The Townhouse*. Just across Avenida Ricardo Soriano from the Old Town lies the Alameda del Parque, a park and promenade with an abundance of vegetation and beautifully tiled benches. Two blocks away is the Mediterranean in all its glory, framed nicely with a promenade, the Paseo Marítimo, and a much smaller, humbler version of Puerto Banús, the Puerto Deportivo. The tourist office (see above) can supply further information.

CHECKING IN

Los Monteros One of Spain's most elegant hotels, set in a complete resort complex with few rivals. It caters to the affluent and famous, with prices to match, but it offers superb golf, tennis, horseback riding, 5 swimming pools plus the beachfront, water sports, a health clinic, and the acclaimed *El Corzo* restaurant, boasting one of Andalusia's few Michelin stars. The location, however, a few miles east of Marbella, is a drawback. Urbanización Los Monteros, Marbella (phone: 52-771700; fax: 52-825846). Very expensive.

El Fuerte Back down on earth, this older hotel enjoys a wonderful location amid manicured gardens between Marbella's beach and the Old Town. There are 262 rooms, 2 swimming pools, an illuminated tennis court, and 2 restaurants; ask for an air conditioned room in the new wing. Llano de San Luis, Marbella (phone: 52-771500; fax: 52-824411). Expensive.

EATING OUT

Don Leone For years the best dining spot at Puerto Banús, it offers solid Italian cooking and an ideal situation for people watching. Open daily; closed from November 20 through December 20. Reservations necessary. American Express accepted. Muelle Ribera, Puerto Banús (phone: 52-811716). Expensive.

La Hacienda Clearly the best dining experience in this area, this beautiful restaurant is located in a villa overlooking the sea, with a breathtaking view of the African coast. Belgian-born owner-chef Paul Schiff won a National Gastronomy Award and has developed an excellent reputation for his interpretations of favorite French dishes. The menu features lemon swordfish, guinea fowl, red mullet, duck's liver with figs, and lamb. Situated just outside the city in the Urbanización Las Chapas. Closed Mondays and Tuesdays. Reservations necessary. Major credit cards accepted. Carretera Cádiz–Málaga, Km 193, Marbella (phone: 52-831267). Expensive.

Mesón de Pasaje This friendly, impeccably managed little restaurant occupies an old house just off the Plaza de los Naranjos. Continental cooking at reasonable prices means it is often crowded. Closed Thursdays and from mid-November through mid-December. Reservations necessary. American Express and Visa accepted. 5 Calle Pasaje, Marbella (phone: 52-771261). Moderate.

En Route from Puerto Banús and Marbella The 16-mile (27-km) stretch of coast between Marbella and Fuengirola, once among the nicest on the Costa del Sol, now bristles with new developments. Avoid Fuengirola by taking the bypass (left toward Málaga) just west of town; 2 miles (3 km) farther along, another road heads 4 miles (6 km) into the hills to the pretty little village of Mijas, probably Spain's most photographed white *pueblo*.

MIJAS Despite being mobbed by busloads of sightseers and armies of souvenir hawkers, Mijas retains a good deal of its original charm. Much of the appeal derives from its spectacular site, welded to the side of a mountain and looking like a stack of sugar cubes against a pine-draped backdrop. From stunning lookout points, a gaze takes in much of the coast and the luminous Mediterranean as far as Morocco's foreboding Rif Mountains.

The road splits at the entrance to Mijas; take the left fork to a wide parking area, then walk up the hill to an early Christian shrine, the Santuario de la Virgen de la Pena (after passing the "burro taxi" service — corny but fun). Walk toward the center of town to the Plaza de la Constitución, a shady spot for watching village life. From here, a path leads up past the ultramodern bullring (where seats go for more than $40 a head; phone: 52-485548) to a terraced lookout area called the *cuesta de la villa* (literally, "slope of the town"), where visitors can enjoy that famous view.

CHECKING IN

Mijas The only real hotel in town offers 97 rooms, swimming, tennis, and a hairdresser (but no air conditioning), at slightly inflated prices. Guests pay for the view, which is spectacular. Urbanización Tamisa, Mijas (phone: 52-485800; fax: 52-485825). Expensive.

EATING OUT

Mirlo Blanco The excellent location and tasty Basque cuisine such as *txangurro* (spider crab baked in the shell) make this an ideal choice. Closed Sundays. Reservations necessary. Major credit cards accepted. Plaza de la Constitución, Mijas (phone: 52-485700). Moderate.

En Route from Mijas To avoid the congested coast, take the turnoff for Benalmádena just below Mijas (on the road to Fuengirola). After 7 miles (11 km), this narrow road, large sections of which have recently been repaired, cuts down to Arroyo de la Miel and the fringes of Torremolinos, a depressing high-rise package-tour complex. Another 2 miles (3 km) east of Arroyo, the road joins the Torremolinos bypass road (N340); from here, the destination is Málaga, 7 miles (11 km) away.

MÁLAGA The center of the Costa del Sol offers more shopping, cultural events, museums — more of everything — than any other place along the coast, but it also has more crime, traffic, noise, and pollution. Because of its busy international airport, the city's name is stamped in millions of passports every year, but most of the visitors who land here go elsewhere to stay. Málaga has been around since the Phoenicians, who founded a settlement to trade in salted fish; the hill overlooking the sinewy harbor was later fortified by every power to rule the Mediterranean. The sweet málaga wine has been famous since antiquity and is still served from 500-liter barrels at murky little bodegas. (One of the best is the *Antigua Casa Guardia* on the Alameda.)

The town's center is dominated by the refreshing Paseo del Parque, which begins at the Plaza de la Marina (where there is underground parking) and extends eastward. This pedestrian promenade and park, lined with palms and banana trees, features fountains, ponds with geese and ducks, and 3,000 species of luxuriant plants bathed in Málaga's intense light. Fronting it are the lemon-colored Ayuntamiento (Town Hall) and other government buildings. Beyond, to the east, are the bullring (Paseo de Reding; phone: 52-219482); the Paseo Marítimo promenade along La Malagueta Beach; and a nostalgia-tinged district of aging buildings known as El Limonar. Better beaches lie to the east at Baños de Carmen and El Palo.

The Alcazaba, an 11th-century Moorish fortress-palace, is perched directly above the park and reached via Calle Alcazabilla. The winding approach passes ruins of a Roman amphitheater, horseshoe arches, and walls draped in bougainvillea and wisteria. Peer down the murky hole where Christian prisoners were kept and, in the *Museo Arqueológico* (Archaeological Museum) in the main building, peruse the collection of artifacts. The Alcazaba is open weekdays and Saturdays from 10 AM to 1 PM and from 4 to 7 PM in the winter; and from 11 AM to 2 PM and from 5 to 8 PM in summer; Sundays from 10 AM to 2 PM year-round. Admission charge. Rearing up to the east is another Moorish fortress, the 14th-century Castillo de Gibralfaro, built on the site of an ancient Greek lighthouse. (It can be reached by a strenuous walk up from the Alcazaba, or by driving a mile east from the Paseo del Parque and then another mile up the hill.) Wander at will around the extensive ramparts and towers, which held off many an attack before the city fell to Christian armies in 1487. Open from 9 AM until dusk; no admission charge.

Málaga's Renaissance cathedral (Calle de Molina Larios in the center of town) has only one of the two towers originally planned because, so the story goes, money was diverted to help the colonials fight the American Revolution. It's quite dark inside, but look for the Corinthian columns as big as giant redwoods and the 17th-century choir stalls, with 100 seats and dozens of saints carved by the famous artisan Pedro de Mena. A small museum with religious artifacts is open daily, but has irregular hours; there's an admission charge. From the cathedral's north side, follow the signs to the *Museo de Bellas Artes* (6 Calle San Agustín). The eclectic collection — 20 rooms full, much of it on permanent loan from the *Prado* — includes paintings by Murillo and Ribera, as well as a small room devoted to the boyhood works of Málaga's most famous son, Pablo Picasso. The museum is open from 10 AM to 1:30 PM and from 5 to 8 PM; from 4 to 7 PM in the winter; closed Mondays and Sunday afternoons; admission charge. The house where Picasso was born, in 1881, is 2 blocks away (take a right on Calle Granada) in Plaza de la Merced, whose 19th-century buildings — with green shutters, tile roofs, and peeling yellow paint — retain some of the charm of the epoch. A plaque commemorates the event.

Not far from the museum (take Calle Granada toward the Plaza de la Constitución) is the Pasaje de Chinitas, where the *malagueña* style of flamenco evolved in the mid-19th century. Stroll along this car-free stretch of wrought-iron lamps and cobblestones, then stop for a drink at the *Bodega la Campana.* Or stop for *tapas;* some of the best *tapas* bars are a short hop from the Pasaje de Chinitas. Among them is *Bar Orellana* (3 Calle Moreno Monroy), famous for its *lomo mechado* (loin of pork, veal, or other meat, stuffed with hard-boiled egg, bacon, and other ingredients, then sliced). The tourist office (4 Pasaje de Chinitas; phone: 52-213445 or 52-228948) can recommend many others.

CHECKING IN

Málaga Palacio Although it has slipped from a once loftier position, this 228-room establishment still features baronial-style public rooms, a rooftop pool, and an outstanding location. Ask for an air conditioned room with a view over the Paseo del Parque. 1 Cortina del Muelle, Málaga (phone: 52-215185). Moderate.

Parador de Gibralfaro On the south side of the Gibralfaro hill, next to the castle. Although it's a 2-mile (3-km) drive from the center, the views over the harbor, bullring, and modern lighthouse of Málaga are worth the inconvenience, as is the good restaurant. None of the 12 rooms is air conditioned. Major credit cards accepted. Monte de Gibralfaro, Málaga (phone: 52-221902; in the US, 212-686-9213; fax: 52-221904). Moderate.

EATING OUT

Antonio Martín A traditional favorite, it has a somewhat erratic reputation but a superb location, especially for lunch outside on the terrace. Closed Mondays. Reservations unnecessary. Major credit cards accepted. 4 Paseo Marítimo, Málaga (phone: 52-222113). Moderate.

La Cancela A pleasant choice, often crowded with tour groups at lunch. Specialties include *fritura malagueña,* or fried seafood, and *ajo blanco,* a cold garlic soup. Closed Sundays. Reservations unnecessary. Major credit

Denis Belgrano, Málaga (phone: 52-223125). Inex-

cards accepted. 3 Calle
pensive.

En Route from Má... Continue 33 miles (53 km) east on N340 to Nerja,
passing a nearly ... nuous wall of resort developments along the way. To
reach the cent... ferja, follow the Balcón de Europa signs.

NERJA This reso... s at the mouth of the Chillar River, on a sloping site
beneath ... ged coastal mountains. The nicest spot in town is the
Balcó... palm-shaded promenade jutting dramatically into the
Me... lt in 1885 and named by King Alfonso XIII, it's lined
... mpposts and old cannon, with one side overlooking a
... me fishing boats. On another side are several cafés with
... d outdoor tables, the place to stop for a cup of *café con*
... the corner sits the parish church, which celebrated its
... y in 1983. The tourist office (2 Puerta del Mar; phone:
... he entrance to the Balcón.

nging to
ve begun
iles (17
n the
kets
a

...m in a beautiful setting atop a bluff overlooking the sea,
... area's best beaches just a stroll away. It has 73 air condi-
... a nice pool, and a restaurant serving international and
... uisine. Major credit cards accepted. 8 Calle Almuñecas,
...ne: 52-520050; in the US, 212-686-9213; fax: 52-521997). Mod-

...UT

...Luque Located on one of the town's loveliest squares, this eatery blends the
traditional (rabbit stew) and the innovative (asparagus mousse). Open
daily. Reservations advised. American Express and Visa accepted. 2 Plaza
Cavana, Nerja (phone: 52-521004). Moderate.

En Route from Nerja Those who like Andalusian villages may want to
detour 4½ miles (7 km) inland along a well-paved road to the *pueblo* of
Frigiliana, a stack of white blocks that was once voted Andalusia's retti-
est village. Go to the Plaza de la Iglesia, where the old-timers hang out, and
drink in the heady scents of orange blossoms, or have a drink and some
tapas at the *Bar-Café Viritudes,* opposite the bus stop and Civil Guard
barracks.

Return to Nerja and head east, stopping 3 miles (5 km) from town, near
the village of Maro, to visit the Cuevas de Nerja. These colossal caves,
discovered in 1959 by boys trying to trap bats, boast the world's longest
stalactite — 295 feet — and prehistoric paintings dating from 20,000 BC.
Over the ages, underground water has worn down rocks and built up

limestone deposits into bizarre shapes that ...
Other highlights include the Hall of the Eleph... are tastefully lit for full effect.
embedded in stone, and the Cataclysm Ch... ant's Tusk and its giant fossil
column fell and shattered millennia ago. An c... mber, where an enormous
and dance, with top classical ballet, unfolds e... anding festival of music
Chamber. The caves are open daily from 10:30 ... ugust in the Cascade
from 10:30 AM to 2 PM and 3:30 to 6 PM in winter; a... u in summer and
52-520076). arge (phone:

Continue east into the province of Granada. Onc...
the highway has been improved and is very scenic: go...
flocks over the scrub-covered hills, old watchtowers ...
cliffs plummeting down to the glittering sea, and slei...
tensely cultivated land painting swathes of green. Few...
courses, and high-rises line this stretch of the Costa del S...
significant settlement, the fishing village of La Herradur...
horseshoe-shape bay, is fully 10 miles (16 km) from Nerja. A...
terraced hillsides and orchards of dark green *chimayo,* a trop...
few miles farther along, Almuñecar appears, its Old Town cl...
lofty hill. Unfortunately, the ravages of modern development h...
to take their toll on what was once an idyllic spot. Proceed 10½ ...
km) farther to Salobreña.

SALOBREÑA On sunny days, this stunning village is nearly blinding fro...
endless layers of whitewash slapped on by old women wielding buc...
and brushes. In the moonlight it becomes a dream town, rising abov...
broad plain, peacefully suspended between the stars and the sea. Its Moo...
ish castle, one of Andalusia's most impressive, occupies an impregnabl...
site that must have seemed like a gift from Allah. From the castle, flat-
roofed houses spill down the hillside to the plain. It's possible to drive
partway up, but park and walk to the top. The final stretch climbs along
Calle Andrés Segovia, named for the renowned guitarist who called Salobreña home. Inside the castle, wander the battlements and catch an eyeful
of coastal scenery (admission charge). Open daily from 9 AM to 7 PM.

CHECKING IN/EATING OUT

Salobreña This little hideaway, a 2-story, 130-room modern structure perched on
a cliff overlooking the Mediterranean, lies 2 miles (3 km) west of the
village. There's a nice pool and a restaurant, but no air conditioning.
Carretera Cádiz, Km 341, Salobreña (phone: 58-610261; fax: 58-610101).
Inexpensive.

En Route from Salobreña Continue on the coastal road for 2 miles (3 km)
to pick up N323 to Granada. The road slices 42 miles (67 km) north
through the rugged Sierra Nevada, following the course of the Guadalfeo
(Ugly River) and leaving the sensuous world of palm trees and tropical

fruit behind. To the east lies a wild region of primitive villages called Las Alpujarras.

Seven miles (11 km) south of Granada a sign is marked Suspiro del Moro. It was from this hill that Boabdil, the last Muslim king in Spain, wept as he took a final look back on his way to exile. From here, it's smooth sailing across a fertile plain to the fabled city of the Moors.

GRANADA At first sight, the city of a thousand and one legends is a disappointing jumble of gray façades and snarling traffic. But Granada's delights are slightly veiled, making discovery more exciting. For full details on sights, hotels, and restaurants, see *Granada* in THE CITIES.

En Route from Granada Leave town on N323 for Jaén, 61 miles (98 km) north, and enter a rolling sea of olive trees ringed by dusty mountains. The road cuts through rough hills to a mountain pass, Puerto de Carretero (3,400 feet high); suddenly, the provincial capital — olive trees at its feet and flanked by gray granite hills and a Moorish castle — appears in the distance. About 6 miles (10 km) before Jaén, another road (N321) veers to the right toward Ubeda. However, if going into Jaén, continue straight ahead on N323.

JAÉN The capital of the province of Jaén sits at the confluence of the Guadalquivir and Guadalbullón rivers. The site was called Auringis by the Romans and became famous for its silver mines and olives. The Moors called it Geen, "way of the caravans," because it lay on the main route between Andalusia and Castile. The Moors were defeated in 1246, but they left behind the chief reason for a visit to Jaén — the 13th-century Castillo de Santa Catalina, a spectacular hilltop fortress whose crumbling ruins have been reconstructed and converted into a government *parador*. Located 2 miles (3 km) from the center of town, the castle sits at the end of a steep, winding road that provides magnificent views of the entire area. In addition to the *parador* (see *Checking In/Eating Out*), visit the former castle parade ground, ringed by defensive towers, and peek into the keep and the Santa Catalina Chapel. Then walk to the far end of the hill to reach a thrilling lookout spot over the town. From this viewpoint, the 16th-century Renaissance Cathedral of Jaén (Plaza de Santa María) looks imposing but a bit odd, its massive façade out of proportion with the surrounding buildings. Some Ribera paintings and a bronze candelabrum with 15 arms are on display in the *Museo de la Catedral,* which is open Fridays through Sundays from 11 AM to 1 PM; admission charge.

Jaén's *Museo Provincial* (27 Paseo de la Estación; phone: 53-250320) is open Tuesdays through Saturdays from 10 AM to 2 PM and from 4 PM to 7 PM; Sundays from 10 AM to 1:30 PM; no admission charge. The town also has several churches of note, particularly the Chapel of San Andrés. For additional information, contact the tourist office (1 Calle Arquitecto Bergés; phone: 53-222737).

CHECKING IN/EATING OUT

Parador de Santa Catalina Incorporating much of Jaén's original Moorish castle, this hostelry has beamed sitting rooms replete with massive chandeliers, tapestries, armor, and coats of arms. Have lunch in the vast dining room with vaulted ceiling or spend the night in a canopied bed. There are 43 air conditioned rooms. Major credit cards accepted. Castillo de Santa Catalina, Jaén (phone: 53-264411; in the US, 212-686-9213; fax: 53-223930). Moderate.

En Route from Jaén Double back on N323 about 6 miles (10 km) to the junction of N321, a two-lane road called the Ruta del Renacimiento (Renaissance Route). Indeed, some of Spain's finest Renaissance architecture lies ahead. Baeza is 30 miles (48 km) from Jaén, Ubeda 35½ miles (57 km).

BAEZA This sleepy little town looks as though its residents closed the gates centuries ago and let time pass them by. Forget about the stark white of most Andalusian towns; Baeza's buildings of golden stone look Italian. A good map for a walking tour is available at the tourist office (Plaza del Pópulo; phone: 53-740444). The most interesting part of Baeza surrounds the 16th-century, late Gothic Cathedral of Santa María and the square of the same name. The cathedral has an outstanding main chapel with gilded relief work and a hexagonal pulpit. A silver monstrance that sits behind a painting is an unusual feature: Put in 25 pesetas and the art rolls up, music commences, and the monstrance revolves in dazzling light. The cathedral is open from 10:30 AM to 1 PM and from 5 to 7 PM in summer; from 10:30 AM to 1 PM and from 4 to 6 PM in winter. Across from the cathedral is the 17th-century Seminario de San Felipe Neri, whose carved main façade is covered with inscriptions written with bull's blood (as was the tradition) by graduates. Nearby is the ornate Palacio de Jabalquinto (Cuesta de San Felipe), built in the early 16th century, with huge studded doors, an interesting main façade, and an interior patio with marble columns. Both buildings are open only sporadically.

CHECKING IN/EATING OUT

Juanito A modest, old-fashioned hostelry on the road to Ubeda, it's better known as a restaurant offering classic Spanish cooking than as a hotel. There's no air conditioning in the 37 rooms. Restaurant reservations advised on weekends. Major credit cards accepted. Av. Arca del Agua, Baeza (phone: 53-740040; fax: 53-742324). Inexpensive.

UBEDA Just 5½ miles (9 km) away from Baeza and even more impressive is historic Ubeda, known as the Florence of Andalusia. Its Plaza Vázquez de Molina is the most architecturally harmonious square in Andalusia, an oasis from another time lined with Renaissance monuments from 16th-century Spain. To reach the square, follow the Conjunto Monumental signs into the town center. Along the way, you'll pass the bustling Plaza de Andalucía, with a graceful clock tower, outdoor tables for relaxing, and a bullet-ridden statue of a Francoist general — in short, everything a small Andalusian town square should have.

Several noteworthy buildings front the shaded Plaza Vázquez de Molina. The 16th-century Renaissance Casa de las Cadenas serves as the Town Hall; its interior patio of slender arches was the work of architect Andrés de Vandelvira, who designed most of old Ubeda. The square's architectural highlight is the Church of San Salvador, whose massive golden façade and sumptuous interior make it one of the best examples of Spanish Renaissance architecture. Built in the early 16th century as the family chapel and mausoleum for Francisco de los Cobos, secretary of the Holy Roman Emperor Charles V, it is still privately owned, but a live-in guide shows visitors the ornate altarpiece crowned by a sculpture of the Transfiguration and an enormous wrought-iron grille. It's open Mondays through Saturdays from 10 AM to 1 PM and from 4 to 7 PM; admission charge.

The Muslim legacy survives here in the traditional crafts of esparto (grass) weaving and pottery making, and the *Exposición de Artesanía Ubetense,* next to the Casa de las Cadenas, displays green Ubeda ceramics, esparto rugs, and other examples of the best of this timeless craftsmanship. Later, visit the San Millán district — especially Calle Valencia — to see artisans at work.

Before the Plaza Vázquez de Molina was completed, a nearby square, the Plaza Primero de Mayo, was the heart of Ubeda; an outdoor market, sports events, and — while the Inquisition reigned — burnings at the stake took place here. On one corner today is the old City Hall, featuring a double row of elegant Gothic arches. Similar touches are found in the Church of San Pablo on the plaza's opposite side, parts of which date from around 1400. Another Ubeda sight, the (former) Hospital de Santiago, a Vandelvira masterpiece, sits on Carrera del Obispo Cobos, far from the historic center. This imposing 16th-century edifice has been called the "Escorial of Andalusia." Note the monumental staircase leading upstairs from the inner courtyard and the woodcarvings in the chapel. Open from 9 AM to 2 PM and from 5 to 8 PM; closed Sundays; no admission charge. The Ubeda Tourist Office is on Plaza del Ayuntamiento (phone: 53-750897).

CHECKING IN/EATING OUT

Parador Condestable Dávalos Antiques and fresh flowers fill the 31 air conditioned rooms (ask for number 12 for the best view) of this converted 16th-century palace. The moderately priced garden restaurant offers excellent traditional cuisine (reservations unnecessary). Major credit cards accepted. 1 Plaza Vázquez de Molina, Ubeda (phone: 53-750345; in the US, 212-686-9213; fax: 53-751259). Moderate.

En Route from Ubeda Our Andalusia tour officially ends in Ubeda. Travelers can return to Castile and Madrid via Bailén, 25½ miles (41 km) west on N322, or proceed northeast toward Valencia via Albacete, also on N322.

Extremadura

Far to the west of Madrid, close to the Portuguese border, lies a remote and often rugged region that played a leading role in one of the most important chapters of Spanish history. During the 15th and 16th centuries, this vast, landlocked area exported its sons to the farthest reaches of the earth to chart unfamiliar and hazardous oceans to discover the New World of the Americas. Extremadura was the cradle of the conquistadores, men such as Francisco Pizarro, an uneducated swineherd who set off to conquer Peru for the Spanish and to plunder the gold of the Inca. Pizarro came from Trujillo, today one of the jewels of Extremadura, a small town rich in fine 16th-century palaces built with gold from the Americas. Also from Trujillo was Francisco de Orellana, the first European to explore the Amazon, while Vasco Núñez de Balboa, who made the first European discovery of the Pacific Ocean, and Hernando de Soto, who colonized Florida for the Spaniards, both hailed from the southern Extremaduran town of Jerez de los Caballeros. Pedro de Valdivia, who conquered present-day Chile, was born and brought up in Villanueva de la Serena.

Today, the names of Extremadura's towns and cities echo all over Latin America. There are Trujillos in Peru, Honduras, and Venezuela. Medellín, the name of the small Extremaduran citadel that produced Hernán Cortés, the European discoverer of Mexico, can be found in Mexico, in Argentina and, most notoriously, in Colombia. Numerous other New World sites, including the Caribbean island of Guadeloupe, take their name from the mountain Monastery of Guadalupe, the place in which Queen Isabella of Spain drew up a contract with Christopher Columbus for his voyage of discovery to America and in which the first Native Americans brought back as prisoners were baptized by their conquerors.

The modern-day sons of Extremadura continue to travel far from home, although now they are more likely to go to the big cities of Spain or the more industrially advanced north of Europe than to cross the Atlantic. This wild corner of the country can still be harsh and primitive, and emigration is an attractive option for young people who aren't drawn to the rustic life.

For the visitor, however, it is precisely this remoteness that gives the region its appeal. Extremadura is an area of immense natural beauty, with vast expanses of rolling countryside broken only occasionally by little whitewashed *pueblos,* or villages, peopled by shepherds and their families. In the north, the fertile plains of wheat, cotton, and tobacco give way to soft hills and tumbling olive groves, then to the snow-capped peaks of the Gredos and Gata mountain ranges. Farther south, the rich red soil is thickly wooded with pungent eucalyptus trees and holm and cork oaks. In spring and early summer, before the heat has burned the landscape brown, carpets of wildflowers stretch for miles.

The region is also rich in architecture and history. The towns, especially Cáceres, Trujillo, and Guadalupe, contain palaces and fine churches — fantastic examples of 16th-century one-upmanship — built by the Spanish nouveaux riches with gold brought back in galleons from their newly discovered territories. Mérida has a museum housing the finest collection of Roman finds in the whole of Spain — fittingly, since Extremadura was one of the chief colonies of the Romans' vast province of Lusitania, and Mérida, founded during the 1st century BC, was Lusitania's capital. The Visigoths, who came later, also left an important heritage, particularly in finely tooled stonework and jewelry. Again, Mérida has some of the best examples of this early Christian civilization.

The Moors arrived during the 8th century and stayed for 500 years, building magnificent castle-fortresses and other structures in their decorative architectural style. Extremadura was next ruled by several orders of knights, who took it upon themselves to chase out the Moors and to protect Christian pilgrims on the long and arduous journey north to the sacred shrine of Santiago de Compostela, in Galicia. They controlled vast areas of land, given to them by grateful Spanish nobles in payment for their services. Alcántara, Monfragüe, Mérida, and Cáceres are still steeped in the history of these crusading orders, which wielded immense political and financial power in the late Middle Ages.

During the 19th century, Napoleon tried to make Extremadura a French province, and the region was the site of fierce fighting until the Spanish, assisted by the British, beat the French back over the Pyrenees.

Today Extremadura is one of Spain's main cattle raising areas; the black bulls seen throughout the countryside may end up in the bullring or in one of the regional dishes. The local fare is good and hearty, with lots of game and meat dishes. The beef, lamb, and pork are all good, and the strong, deep-pink ham is superb. Fish such as trout and tench appear on most menus. Another favorite meal is braised partridge. The region produces some good wines; particularly noteworthy are the strong rosé from Cañamero and the justly renowned, full-bodied red named for the Marqués de Cáceres.

The route outlined below enters the northeast corner of Extremadura, turning off the main N-V highway from Madrid just short of the small town of Navalmoral de la Mata and running down through the foothills of the Sierra de Altamira Mountains to the famous sanctuary town of Guadalupe. From there, it continues west to Trujillo, southwest to Mérida, and west again to Badajoz, a town dominated by the imposing Moorish castle where generations of Muslim kings made their base. The itinerary then proceeds north to Cáceres, richly evocative of Spain's golden age, and on up to Plasencia, a charming town and a good base for trips into the picturesque valleys of the far north of Extremadura. Among these, a visit to the lovely wooded Monastery of Yuste, where the Holy Roman Emperor Charles V spent his last days, is particularly recommended. The total length of the route is between 422 and 453 miles (675/725 km), depending on side excursions.

The roads in Extremadura are generally good (provided you stick to those recommended in the itinerary), except in the remote Las Hurdes area, which can be explored as an optional detour. Distances are often greater than they seem on a map, however, and gas stations can be few and far between, so allow plenty of time and keep the tank full. Don't rely on renting a car locally, because tourism is still new here and there are few car rental offices.

Extremadura is particularly rich in *paradores.* Staying in them is the best way to get a real taste of the region, but be sure to book well in advance; they tend to fill up quickly, even outside the high season. The north of Extremadura is likely to prove more captivating than the south, so it's a good idea to allocate more time for Trujillo, Cáceres, and Guadalupe when planning. Expect to pay $65 or more for a double room in hotels listed as expensive, from $45 to $65 in moderate hotels, and under $40 in the inexpensive ones. Expensive meals are $40 and up for two; moderate, between $25 and $40; and inexpensive, under $25. The telephone numbers listed below include local area codes; when calling from another area in Spain, dial "9" first.

GUADALUPE Entering Extremadura from the east along the main N-V highway from Madrid, take the well-marked turnoff for Guadalupe to the left, 2 miles (3 km) before Navalmoral de la Mata. The road is narrow and often winding, but the drive is spectacular, through olive groves and chestnut woods and, 2½ miles (4 km) outside Guadalupe, past the exquisite Humilladero Hermitage, a small chapel in a panoramic spot where pilgrims of more impressionable times would fall to their knees at the first sight of the Monasterio de Guadalupe below them. The crenelated, turreted extravaganza makes a dramatic sight, nestling in the lee of the Guadalupe mountains, the old village that grew up as an adjunct to it hugging its doorstep. The edifice stands on the site where a small wooden statue of the Virgin Mary, reputedly carved by St. Luke, was found buried in the 13th century. The monastery was founded in the mid-14th century by King Alfonso XI, after he successfully invoked the Virgin's aid in a battle against the Moors in 1340. The conquistadores adopted the shrine as their own and heaped treasures on it from the New World, making it one of the most elaborate and richly decorated monasteries in Spain. Conquered Inca leaders were brought here to be baptized. Freed Christian slaves left their chains here in votive thanks. The monastery was abandoned in the 19th century, then restored and taken over by Franciscan friars in 1908. For the Spanish, it is still one of the most important places of pilgrimage in Christendom, as well as a symbol of *hispanidad,* the cultural and linguistic link between Spain and Spanish America.

A guided tour (Spanish language) takes visitors around the complex (open daily, from 9:30 AM to 1 PM and 3:30 to 6:30 PM; admission charge; phone: 27-367000), including the manuscript room, which houses giant illuminated books of hours, and the sacristy, which has eight paintings by Extremadura's most famous artist, the 17th-century painter Francisco de Zurbarán. The 14th-century church, which was added to in later centuries, has an altarpiece with works by Carducci, Giraldo de Merlo, and Jorge Manuel Theotokópoulos, son of El Greco. One of the main features of the monastery is the 15th-century Mudéjar cloister, unmistakably Moorish in influence and faced with glazed colored tiles (there is a smaller, Gothic cloister in the monastery as well). The tour ends with a visit to the Camarín de la Virgen, where the statue of the Virgin of Guadalupe reposes on a richly worked altar, a casket to one side stuffed full of peseta notes, gifts from grateful or hopeful pilgrims. (For additional details on the monastery, see *Sacred Spain* in DIVERSIONS.)

CHECKING IN

Parador Zurbarán This imposing 15th-century palace is one of the region's most comfortable hotels, with 40 rooms, a swimming pool, and an excellent restaurant serving typical dishes such as *cabrito asado al tomillo* (roast kid with thyme). For additional details, see *Paradores* in DIVERSIONS. 10 Calle Marqués de la Romana, Guadalupe (phone: 27-367075; in the US, 212-686-9213; fax: 27-367076). Expensive.

Hospedería Real Monasterio Housed in the monastery itself and run by the enterprising Franciscan friars, it's not deluxe, but the 46 rooms are arranged around the Gothic cloister and furnished with hand-carved tables and chests. The gardens were recently restored to their original Arab design. Both hotel and restaurant, which serves an excellent fixed-price menu, are very reasonably priced. Plaza Juan Carlos I, Guadalupe (phone: 27-367000; fax: 27-367177). Moderate.

EATING OUT

El Cordero The best restaurant in town, apart from those in the hotels. The house specialty is *cordero asado,* the roast lamb from which the restaurant takes its name. Open daily. Reservations unnecessary. No credit cards accepted. 11 Calle Convento, Guadalupe (phone: 27-367131). Moderate.

En Route from Guadalupe Take the road marked Mérida and follow it down through more olive groves, over a gurgling stream on the valley floor, and on to Cañamero, where it's worth a stop to taste the deservedly famous local wine — but be careful if driving: The pale red liquid is deceptively strong. At Zorita, 32 miles (51 km) from Guadalupe, continue toward Trujillo instead of turning left for Mérida.

TRUJILLO Francisco Pizarro, who waged war on the Inca to win Peru for Spain, was born here, the illegitimate son of a nobleman. A bronze statue of him astride a fiery steed, ready for battle, dominates the pretty Plaza Mayor in the heart of the Old Town. Trujillo's two other famous sons were Diego García de Paredes, who founded another Trujillo in Venezuela, and Francisco de Orellana, the first European to explore the Amazon. The Old Town, perched on a granite hill above the modern one, is full of grand 16th-century mansions financed with wealth brought back from the new territories. Of particular interest is the Palacio de la Conquista, built by Pizarro's half-brother Hernando; it still contains busts of the explorer's family. Theoretically, the palace, located on the Plaza Mayor, is open daily from 10:30 AM to 2 PM and from 4:30 to 6 PM, depending on whether the caretaker is on the premises (be sure to tip him if you do gain entrance). If you can't find him, contact the tourist office in the same square (8 Plaza Mayor; phone: 27-320653). The 13th-century Santa María church holds the tombs of some of the town's most prominent nobles, including García de Paredes, and is also noted for its 15th- to 16th-century Gothic altar (ask the tourist office for admittance). Towering over everything is the impressive Arab-built Castillo — a walk up to its ramparts at sunset gives a spectacular view over the town's rooftops. The people of Trujillo live as they always have, tending sheep and goats, and doing wash by hand. In the evening, the main square is an evocative place to sit and sip a glass of sherry before going on to dine at one of the town's several good restaurants.

CHECKING IN

Parador de Trujillo Beautifully converted from the 16th-century Convent of Santa Clara and tastefully decorated with furniture from that era. Built around a central cloister, it has 46 air conditioned rooms, a small swimming pool, and an excellent restaurant, housed in the old refectory. Try the *morteruelo,* a pâté of chicken, partridge, and rabbit, and the *cochinillo asado,* roast suckling pig. Plaza de Santa Clara, Trujillo (phone: 27-321350; in the US, 212-686-9213; fax: 27-321366). Expensive.

Las Cigüeñas This modern, air conditioned, 78-room hotel doesn't have the charm of the *parador,* but it's a comfortable alternative. It's situated on the main highway from Madrid, a mile (1.6 km) before Trujillo. Carretera N-V, Km 253, Trujillo (phone: 27-321250; fax: 27-321300). Moderate.

EATING OUT

La Cadena Housed in a fine 18th-century palace in the main square, it has whitewashed walls decorated with local ceramics, and serves a very reasonable fixed-price menu. Open daily. No reservations or credit cards accepted. Plaza Mayor, Trujillo (phone: 27-321463). Moderate.

Hostal Pizarro Also in the main square, this restaurant produces some fine local dishes, including *estofado de perdices,* a partridge casserole, and a good *cordero asado,* roast lamb. Open daily. Reservations unnecessary. American Express and Visa accepted. Plaza Mayor, Trujillo (phone: 27-320255). Moderate.

Mesón La Troya Housed in former stables, this restaurant serves some of the best food in Extremadura. Diners receive a complimentary Spanish *tortilla* and a salad as soon as they sit down; other dishes may include *carne con tomate,* beef cooked in a tomato sauce, or *prueba de cerdo,* a wonderfully garlicky pork casserole. Open daily. No reservations or credit cards accepted. Plaza Mayor, Trujillo (phone: 27-321364). Inexpensive.

En Route from Trujillo Take the N-V highway south in the direction of Mérida. After 36 miles (58 km), turn left at the signpost for Santa Amalia, and after another 4½ miles (7 km), turn right at the signpost for Medellín. The road leads over a magnificent 17th-century bridge on the Guadiana River into Medellín, a little town crowned by a well-preserved medieval castle. Hernán Cortés, who was born here in 1485, conquered the Aztec empire and colonized Mexico for his country, and died forgotten in Spain at the age of 62, now has a statue dominating his hometown's Plaza Mayor. If you go to Plaza de España early enough, you can watch a woman frying *churros* (fritters) in a huge vat as the lines form outside the entrance to her small take-out place next to the tobacco shop. The town has a small but bustling market on Thursday mornings. From Medellín, retrace the route to the main N-V and turn left for Mérida.

MÉRIDA Founded by the Romans in 25 BC as Emerita Augusta, a colony for the *emeriti,* or veterans, of the fifth and tenth Roman legions, Mérida quickly grew to be the Spanish Rome, capital of the vast and powerful province of Lusitania. The Roman ruins are among the best in Spain, with top honors going to the Roman theater, which was built by Agrippa, son-in-law of Emperor Augustus, shortly after the city's founding and had seating for 6,000. In summer, classical plays and flamenco dances are performed here. Nearby is a Roman amphitheater that held 14,000 spectators. Both theaters are open daily from 8 AM to 7 PM in the winter and to 9 PM in the summer; admission charge, which includes admittance to the Alcazaba (phone: 24-312530). There's ample parking near the entrance. The *Museo Nacional de Arte Romano* (National Museum of Roman Art; phone: 24-311690), in a building forming part of the theater complex, not only is acknowledged to be the finest repository of Roman artifacts in Spain, but also has drawn kudos for its design. It incorporates a Roman road, discovered when the museum was being built in the early 1980s, and contains a superb collection of statues, glassware, pottery, coins, and mosaics. Open Tuesdays through Saturdays from 10 AM to 2 PM and 4 to 6 PM (afternoon hours in the summer are 5 to 7 PM); Sundays and holidays from 10 AM to 2 PM; admission charge. Two Roman houses near the theaters have been excavated, revealing an intricate water system and some fine mosaics. They're open Tuesdays through Saturdays from 8 AM to 1 PM and 4 to 7 PM; Sundays and holidays from 9 AM to 2 PM; admission charge. Other Roman remains include an exquisite Temple of Diana; the circus, used for chariot racing; the well-preserved Trajan's Arch; the Milagros Aqueduct, the better preserved of two that served the city; and the 60-arched Roman bridge across the Guadiana, the longest bridge ever built in Spain. Information on the ruins is available at the tourist office, located at the entrance to the Roman amphitheater (phone: 24-315353).

Mérida's past as an Arab fiefdom is best seen in the Alcazaba, a Moorish castle built during the 9th century. Inside this fortress, note the cistern, a fine example of sophisticated Arab engineering — its construction assured the Moors a constant supply of water from the Guadiana. Hours are the same as for the Roman amphitheater; admission included in amphitheater ticket.

One last sight not to be missed in Mérida is the Hornito de Santa Eulalia, a shrine dedicated to the little girl who, according to local legend, was baked in an oven (*horno*) in the 4th century, after she spat in the eye of a pagan official rather than renounce Christianity.

CHECKING IN

Parador Vía de la Plata The 16th-century building housing this air conditioned, 82-room *parador* was at first a convent and later a prison. In a quiet but still central part of town, it has a markedly Moorish feel about it, with richly tiled floors and a cool, cloistered courtyard. There's a good restaurant, serving Spanish and Extremaduran specialties. 3 Plaza de Queipo de Llano, Mérida (phone: 24-313800; in the US, 212-686-9213; fax: 24-319208). Expensive.

Emperatriz Right in the heart of town in the main square, this 16th-century palace is now a 41-room hotel, which sports a wonderful Moorish foyer faced with intricate tiles. Its restaurant, popular with local folks, serves such specialties as *tencas fritas con limón* (fried tench) and *gazpacho ajo blanco,* a garlicky Extremaduran version of the Andalusian cold soup. 19 Plaza de España, Mérida (phone: 24-313111; fax: 24-300376). Moderate.

Nova Roma A clean, comfortable, modern hotel with 55 rooms and a restaurant; it's near the Roman theater, amphitheater, and museum. 42 Calle Suárez Somonte, Mérida (phone: 24-311201; fax: 24-300160). Moderate.

EATING OUT

Nicolás Starched linen tablecloths and lots of marble grace this restaurant, which serves a good fixed-price menu with regional specialties. Open daily.

Reservations unnecessary. Major credit cards accepted. Calle Félix Valverde, Mérida (phone: 24-319610). Moderate.

Briz Close to *Nicolás*, but not as chic, this restaurant turns out some fine local dishes, including *perdiz en salsa,* a partridge casserole, and an interesting appetizer of artichokes and chorizo sausage. It also serves an excellent red house wine. Closed Sunday afternoons. Reservations unnecessary. Major credit cards accepted. Calle Félix Valverde, Mérida (phone: 24-319307). Moderate to inexpensive.

Casa Benito Tucked away in a small square off Mérida's main street, this is the best eatery in town, with good regional cooking, an excellent fixed-price lunch menu that changes every day, and friendly service. Very reasonably priced, even in the evening, when the menu goes à la carte. Closed Sundays. Reservations unnecessary. No credit cards accepted. Calle Santa Eulalia, Mérida (phone: 24-315502). Moderate to inexpensive.

En Route from Mérida Leaving Mérida, take the N-V highway west about 39 miles (62 km) to Badajoz.

BADAJOZ The most populous city in Extremadura, with 122,000 residents, and capital of the province of Badajoz, one of the two provinces into which the region is divided (the other is Cáceres), Badajoz was once one of the most important Arab strongholds in western Spain, home to Muslim kings who left behind an impressive castle-fortress and massive ramparts. Today, it's hard not to get the impression that the town has seen better days, hardly surprising considering its troubled history. Its frontier position, just 3 miles (5 km) from the Portuguese border, has made it particularly vulnerable, and it has been torn by just about every war fought on the Iberian Peninsula in the past 500 years. One of the worst scenes of carnage occurred in 1812, during the Peninsular War, when 5,000 of the Duke of Wellington's 15,000 troops died here trying to drive Napoleon's occupying forces back toward France. During the early stages of the Spanish Civil War, Badajoz was the scene of a brutal massacre when Franco's Nationalist forces captured it and then rounded up scores of citizens and herded them into the bullring, where they were executed by machine gun.

Badajoz is not the kind of place in which to spend a great deal of time, but it is fascinating to climb up to the top of the town to get an idea of what it once was. Visit the Alcazaba, the Arab fortress (open daily during daylight hours; no admission charge), and take a closer look at the Torre del Apendiz, known locally as the Torre de Espantaperros, or "Dog Scarer Tower." Inside the fortress is the *Museo Arqueológico* (open Tuesdays through Sundays from 10 AM to 3 PM; admission charge; phone: 24-222314). This vantage point also gives a good view of the Puente de las Palmas, the fine 16th-century bridge that leads across the Guadiana and into town through the crenelated Puerta de las Palmas gate. The area around the Alcazaba is still very Moorish in feeling — a glimpse into the courtyards of some of the houses reveals typically Arabic tiles and ornate columns. Farther down, in the town's main square, Plaza de España, stands a monument to the 16th-century painter Luis de Morales, a native of Badajoz. Several of his paintings can be seen in the *Museo de Bellas Artes* (32 Meléndez Valdez; phone: 24-222845), which is open Mondays through Fridays from 8:30 AM to 2:30 PM; Saturdays from 9 AM to 1 PM; admission charge. The 13th-century Gothic Cathedral of San Juan, which stands in the same square, houses works by Morales, and by Zurbarán and Ribera. The cathedral's museum contains many church relics (open during mass; no admission charge; phone: 24-223999). The Badajoz Tourist Office is at 3 Plaza de Libertad (phone: 24-222763).

CHECKING IN

Zurbarán Badajoz has no outstanding hostelries, but this hotel in the city center is an acceptable place to spend a day or two. It has 215 rooms, air conditioning, a big garden, a swimming pool, and a good restaurant. Paseo de Castelar, Badajoz (phone: 24-223741; fax: 24-220142). Expensive.

Lisboa A comfortable, modern, 176-room, air conditioned hotel that, as its name suggests, is on the road to Portugal, just under a mile (1 km) out of town. 13 Av. de Elvas, Badajoz (phone: 24-272900). Moderate to inexpensive.

EATING OUT

Mesón El Tronco This is the only real restaurant in town (although there are several bars and cafés that serve food) and it's very good. In addition to fixed-price meals, there's a lively bar with an excellent range of *tapas*. Closed Sundays. Reservations unnecessary. Major credit cards accepted. 16 Calle Muñoz Torrero, Badajoz (phone: 24-222076). Moderate.

El Sótano A good place for a quick lunch. The bar has a tempting array of *tapas,* or order something more substantial, such as the *caldereta de cordero,* a typical Extremaduran lamb casserole. Open daily. No reservations. Major credit cards accepted. 6 Calle Virgen de la Soledad, Badajoz (phone: 24-220019). Inexpensive.

CÁCERES The capital of the province of the same name, Cáceres is 57 miles (91 km) northeast of Badajoz via N523. The Roman colony founded here during the 1st century BC was one of the five most important in the province of Lusitania. Destroyed by barbarians, it was rebuilt by the Arabs, who called it Cazris, the forerunner of its modern name. The Moors used it as a fortress town from which to embark on other incursions, and built the walls that still stand today, setting them atop Roman foundations. Surrounded by the Moorish walls, the city's Old Town is so superbly preserved that it has served as a backdrop for more than one film set in the

Middle Ages. A stroll through the sandy-colored maze of narrow streets is like stepping back to the 15th and 16th centuries, when noblemen vied with each other to build more beautiful mansions and palaces with the wealth acquired in their exploits across the Atlantic. Almost every house bears a coat of arms, proudly carved out of the tawny stonework. Until the late 15th century, most of them had battlemented defensive towers as well, but Queen Isabella ordered all but one tower — that of the Casa de las Cigüeñas (House of the Storks) — to be razed in an effort to put a halt to internecine fighting. The tower stands in the Plaza de las Veletas, and is now a military government office that is closed to the public. All is quiet now, and storks nest everywhere in old Cáceres — atop the Church of San Mateo (Plaza de San Mateo), site of a former mosque, and up on the spire of the Church of Santa María. Step inside this latter church, in the main square of the walled city, to see the tombs of some of Cáceres's most famous citizens, marked with their heraldic crests. Also look for the 15th-to-16th-century Palacio de Ovando in the same square; for the intricately carved façade on the 15th-century Palacio de los Golfines de Abajo nearby; and, in a corner of the walled city, for the 16th-century Casa de Toledo-Moctezuma, where Juan Caño, a henchman of Hernán Cortés, lived with his wife, a daughter of Montezuma, the last Aztec emperor. The 16th-century Palacio de Godoy is just outside the walls.

Near Plaza de San Mateo, the 17th-century Casa de las Veletas (House of the Weather Vanes), site of the onetime Moorish Alcázar, today serves as the town's *Museo Arqueológico* (Plaza de las Veletas; phone: 27-247334). It incorporates an interesting Arab cistern and houses collections of Celtic, Roman, and Visigothic remains. It's open Tuesdays through Sundays from 9:30 AM to 2:30 PM; admission charge. Aside from the Casa de las Valetas, the only building in the Old Town that can be visited is the Palacio de Caruajal (Plaza de Santa María; inquire at the tourist office to arrange a tour).

In addition to the Old Town, Cáceres has a much more bustling area at the foot of the walls in the vicinity of the Plaza Mayor, the main square and site of the tourist office (36 Plaza Mayor; phone: 27-246347). Much farther down is the sprawling New Town, which houses most of the shops, hotels, and offices. Two miles (3 km) east of town, on a road that climbs steeply up through olive trees to the peak of the Sierra de la Mosca, stands the Sanctuary of Nuestra Señora de la Montaña (Our Lady of the Mountain). From here, there is a spectacular view over Cáceres, with the Gredos mountains to the north and the Sierra de San Pedro range to the south.

CHECKING IN

Parador de Cáceres Like most of the buildings in the nearly deserted Old Town, this 27-room hostelry, the converted 16th-century Casa de Sánchez de Paredes, is made of undecorated stone. There's a restaurant on the premises. 6 Ancha, Cáceres (phone: 27-211759; in the US, 212-686-9213; fax: 27-211729;). Expensive.

Alcántara In the new part of town — where most of the hotels are located — this comfortable, modern place has 67 air conditioned rooms. No restaurant. 14 Av. Virgen de Guadalupe, Cáceres (phone: 27-228900). Moderate.

Extremadura One of the nicest hotels in town, just opposite the *Alcántara,* with 69 air conditioned rooms, gardens, a swimming pool, and a restaurant. 5 Av. Virgen de Guadalupe, Cáceres (phone: 27-221600; fax: 27-211095). Moderate.

EATING OUT

El Atrio This chic establishment in the new part of town offers haute cuisine. Open daily. Reservations advised. Major credit cards accepted. 30 Av. de España, Bloque 4, Cáceres (phone: 27-242928). Expensive.

La Malvasía Also in the new part of town, this place features regional cooking. For dessert, try the *higo chumbo,* an ice cream made of prickly pear. Closed Sundays. Reservations unnecessary. Visa accepted. 5 Calle Antonio Silva, Cáceres (phone: 27-244609). Expensive.

El Figón One of the most popular restaurants in Cáceres, it serves finely cooked local dishes. Open daily. Reservations advised. Major credit cards accepted. 14 Plaza San Juan, Cáceres (phone: 27-244362). Expensive to moderate.

La Bodega Medieval Hidden away in a quiet alley of the walled Old Town, this eatery has a bodega next door, where customers can drink an aperitif and eat *tapas* before dining. On the menu, watch for *perdiz al estilo Alcántara,* a casserole of partridge with mushrooms, red pepper, and juniper berries. Open daily. Reservations advised. Major credit cards accepted. 1 Calle Orellana, Cáceres (phone: 27-245458). Moderate.

En Route from Cáceres Instead of taking the main road north to Plasencia, head west on N521 toward Valencia de Alcántara, and after 7½ miles (12 km), at Malpartida de Cáceres, turn right onto C523, following it through Brozas to Alcántara. This quiet, peaceful town takes its name from the Arab word for bridge, *al kantara,* specifically referring to the magnificent Roman construction that spans the ravine of the Tagus River just below the town. Alcántara's location close to the Portuguese border has made it an important strategic point throughout history. After the Romans and the Arabs, the military order of the Knights of Alcántara made it their headquarters during the early 13th century, using it as a base for incursions against other Moorish strongholds in the area. The knights' now-crumbling castle can still be seen at the top of the town. Queen Isabella of Spain and her aunt, Beatrice of Portugal, signed a treaty here in 1479, ending years of enmity between the two countries. Napoleon's army occupied the town during the 19th century, billeting troops in the 16th-century Convent of San Benito.

From Alcántara, follow the signs to Mata de Alcántara, and turn left there for Garrovillas. The road passes fields strewn with giant, strangely shaped boulders, clusters of conical stone cattle sheds, and then some wild countryside, relieved only by fig trees and prickly pears, before coming out onto the main N630 highway, where a left turn leads to Plasencia. Along the way, a half-ruined 2nd-century Roman bridge still stands just outside Cañaveral.

PLASENCIA This town's name is derived from the Latin for "may it be pleasing to God and man," which is what Alfonso VIII hoped it would be when he rebuilt it in the 12th century after its recapture from the Moors. With its whitewashed houses, narrow streets, and flowers on almost every wrought-iron balcony, Plasencia is indeed a charming town, as well as an ideal base to explore the north of Extremadura. The town is set in a bend of the Jerte River and is crowned by a splendid cathedral, part 13th-century Romanesque and part late 15th-century Gothic, especially dramatic at sunset. The cathedral museum contains centuries worth of treasures. It's open daily from 9 AM to 12:30 PM and from 4 to 5:30 PM (6:30 PM in summer); admission charge (phone: 27-411612). The 13th-century San Nicolás church is in the vincinity of the cathedral, and the magnificent Church of San Vicente stands in a quiet plaza dotted with orange trees nearby. The porticoed Plaza Mayor, the town's main square, is a pleasant place to have a drink and watch the green mechanical doll on top of the Town Hall at the north end of the square spring into action to strike the hours. If you're here on a Tuesday, visit the market, which has been held in Plasencia since the 13th century.

CHECKING IN

Alfonso VIII The only really good hotel in town. Despite its slightly tatty exterior and location on one of Plasencia's busiest streets, it's comfortable and elegant, with 57 rooms, air conditioning, and a restaurant. 32 Calle Alfonso VIII, Plasencia (phone: 27-410250; fax: 27-418042). Moderate.

EATING OUT

Nykol's A popular place with Plasencians, it serves refined versions of classic Extremaduran dishes. Try the gazpacho with melon and the *solomillo de cerdo crema,* a filet of pork cooked with ham and cheese. Open daily. Reservations advised. MasterCard and Visa accepted. 8 Calle Pedro Isidio, Plasencia (phone: 27-415850). Expensive to moderate.

Florida Well-cooked international dishes and a few local specialties are the fare at this restaurant, about a mile (1.6 km) out of town on the road to Cáceres. Open daily. Reservations advised. Major credit cards accepted. 22 Av. de España, Plasencia (phone: 27-413858). Moderate.

En Route from Plasencia Madrid is 160½ miles (257 km) to the east, Salamanca 82½ miles (132 km) to the north, but if there is time to spare, it's worth spending an extra couple of days in Plasencia and using it as a point from which to explore one or more of the stunningly beautiful valleys to the north of town. Each can be taken in as a day trip, with nights spent in Plasencia.

Those visiting in spring or early summer should be sure to drive up the valley of the Jerte River, taking N110 northeast out of Plasencia and passing through the small towns of Navaconcejo, Cabezuela del Valle, Jerte, and Tornavacas. The valley is one of Spain's main cherry growing areas, and in May and June the fields are a profusion of pink and white blossoms.

The Vera Valley, which also runs northeast of Plasencia, is an idyllic spot any time of the year. Here, hidden among chestnut and pine woods, is the Monasterio de Yuste, the Hieronymite monastery where the great Holy Roman Emperor Charles V retired in 1557 and died the following year. The powerful monarch's rooms can still be seen, along with the chapel where he heard mass (guided tours only; open daily from 9:30 AM to 12:30 PM and from 3:30 to 6:30 PM; admission charge; phone: 27-172130). A restaurant in the monastery serves lunch only. To reach Yuste, follow the signs out of Plasencia and drive 28 miles (45 km) along C501 to the turnoff at the village of Cuacos; the monastery is a mile (1.6 km) farther and is well signposted. Before returning to Plasencia, drive to nearby Garganta la Olla and Aldeanueva de la Vera, picturesque mountain villages with cobbled streets and ornately carved overhanging wooden balconies.

Some of the most remote and most beautiful scenery of Extremadura is in the rugged area known as Las Hurdes. Rolling hills studded with olive trees give way to fir trees and rushing streams, and those traveling early in the morning will see villagers riding their basket-laden mules and donkeys out for a day's work in the fields and women washing clothes in the streams the way their great-grandmothers did.

To reach this area, take the Salamanca road (N630) north from Plasencia and, after 20 miles (32 km), turn left toward Guijo de Granadilla and follow signs for Cerezo and Caminomorisco. Before setting out, pick up one of the maps of the area from the tourist office just off the main square in Plasencia (17 Calle Trujillo; phone: 27-412766). The farther north you go, the more remote and fascinating the villages become. If there is time, the entire circuit can be made, ending in the small mountain town of Hervás — but it's a long drive that will take the better part of a day. There are *hostales* offering good but basic food and accommodations at Cerezo, Caminomorisco, Nuñomoral, and La Alberca. Better still, make a picnic of slices of local ham and cheese, with fresh bread bought from one of the village *panaderías,* and eat it near a Roman bridge, with your feet dangling in the cool waters of one of the many mountain streams.

Hervás is a pretty town, with an interesting and well-preserved Jewish quarter.

From Hervás, just a mile or so off N630, it's a 60-mile (96-km) drive north to Salamanca, or a 28-mile (45-km) drive south back to Plasencia.

CHECKING IN/EATING OUT

Parador Carlos V The imposing 15th-century fortified castle where Charles V stayed for several months, while his rooms were being prepared at the Monastery of Yuste, is today a hotel with 53 air conditioned rooms, a garden, a swimming pool, and a first-rate restaurant. Major credit cards accepted. It's 7½ miles (12 km) beyond the monastery in the direction of Jarandilla de la Vera. Carretera de Plasencia, Jarandilla de la Vera (phone: 27-560117; in the US, 212-686-9213; fax: 27-560088). Expensive.

The Balearic Islands

The Balearic Islands, set in the Mediterranean Sea southeast of Barcelona and east of Valencia, have been invaded repeatedly over the centuries, as the Phoenicians, Greeks, Carthaginians, Romans, Byzantines, Vandals, Moors, French, English, and Spanish successively became the dominant Mediterranean power. These days, however, the only invaders are tourists. While the Balearics (Islas Baleares to the Spanish) are relatively undiscovered by Americans visiting the Continent, as far as the Europeans — and particularly the British and the Germans — are concerned, they are Europe's most popular tourist destination.

Four main islands, aligned in two pairs — Majorca (Mallorca in Spanish) and its smaller neighbor, Minorca (Menorca in Spanish), plus Ibiza and its little sidekick, Formentera — make up the Balearic Archipelago, which also includes several smaller islets. Together, they constitute Spain's Baleares province, with Palma de Mallorca, on Majorca, the provincial capital.

Each island has had its own history, although there are some common threads. Evidence that the archipelago was the home of an advanced megalithic civilization abounds on Majorca and Minorca, in the form of stone monuments whose exact origins and purpose remain a mystery to scholars. Later, the islanders became mercenaries in the armies of Rome and Carthage. Arab incursions began in the 8th century, and by 902 the Moors were securely installed. They remained so, under succeeding dynasties, until James I of Aragon conquered the islands for the Christians, beginning in 1229; about a half-century later, an independent kingdom of Majorca was created (including Montpellier and Roussillon in France as well as the Balearics), which endured until the mid-14th century. Thanks to the islands' position along the main seagoing trading route between northern Italy and northern Europe, these were prosperous times, a virtual Balearic golden age, which continued even after the islands reverted to the kingdom of Aragon in 1343. But early in the 16th century, because of the pirates off their shores, the Balearics were prohibited by the newly united crown of Aragon and Castile from trading with the New World, a ban that cut them off from Spain's golden age and consigned them to a backwater of history.

The islands are closely tied culturally to the region of Catalonia. Two languages are spoken: Castilian Spanish and the Balearic dialect of Catalan, which varies slightly from island to island (thus the confusion of many island place-names, spelled one way in Spanish and another in the local language).

Each island has a distinct personality. Majorca (its name, dating back to the Romans, means "the larger") is the best known and the most developed in terms of the tourist trade. On this small island (about 62 miles from east to west and 47 miles from north to south) is the very Spanish city of Palma, complete with a massive cathedral and a medieval Old Town. On either side of the capital city are beaches endowed with blocks of high-rise hotels, tourist-oriented restaurants, and late-night discos that stretch for miles, much like areas of the Costa del Sol. In the countryside, only a 10-minute drive from the center of Palma, almond and olive groves blanket the landscape, peasants still plow their fields with oxen, and black-clad women can be seen laboring during harvesttime. In one port, the world's most luxurious yachts lie at anchor, while in the next, fishermen drag their boats onto the beach after working through the night.

Majorca has been a magnet for writers, painters, and musicians for more than a century. The trend may have begun in the 1830s when the consumptive composer Frédéric Chopin and his mistress, the author who used the pseudonym George Sand, shivered through an unusually cold winter here in the Valldemosa Carthusian Monastery. Despite his ill health, Chopin was inspired to write some of his finest work. His lover wrote *A Winter in Majorca,* a not exactly flattering account of island life (Majorcan society had not taken kindly to this illicit couple) that was nevertheless enthusiastic about the landscape. It was later translated into English by a 20th-century visitor, the poet and writer Robert Graves. The author of *I, Claudius* and *The White Goddess,* Graves settled in Deya and presided over a virtual artists' and writers' colony. The steady stream of books they generated spread the word of the island's beauty, creating the mass tourism industry that boomed in the 1960s.

Minorca (whose name means "the smaller") is far less developed than either Ibiza or Majorca. Only in the past few years has Minorca entered the tourism competition in earnest, so it still has plenty of undisturbed countryside and isolated beaches. The island is easy to explore — no part of it is more than an hour's drive away from another. Nightlife here is tame by Spanish standards, with only a handful of discos pulsating until dawn. Ancient megaliths and burial grounds provide the major distraction from a very lazy beach existence.

The history of Ibiza (pronounced Ee-*bee*-tha) is not as much in evidence as that of Majorca, with its castles and cathedrals, or Minorca, where cows graze around ancient ruins. The Carthaginians established a colony here during the 7th century BC to exploit the island's salt beds, and the remains of 500 years of this Punic culture are preserved in museum displays and carved in the hillsides as tombs. Ibiza became a haven for writers and artists and a refuge for the counterculture in the 1950s and 1960s; today it serves as a playground for the jet set. Bob Dylan, Bruce Springsteen, *U2,* and Julio Iglesias have all made regular appearances on this small island; a number of performers have cut albums at Ibiza's tucked-away recording studios, and some even maintain sprawling hidden villas here.

The town of Ibiza tumbles down from a cathedral and rampart that overlook the protected harbor. Narrow streets and stairs wind between picture-perfect whitewashed houses, with views of the more modern city and the bay around every corner. Tiny boutiques hawk gaily colored scarves, T-shirts, and postcards, as well as trendy art. Outside of town, there are hundreds of private coves for swimming — some with fine white sand, others with tiny, water-smoothed pebbles — rather than mile-long beaches. High-rise hotels are limited, and the tourist enclaves blend with the island's natural lines. Nightlife begins late, with live entertainment and dancing that slows down only with the dawn. During the winter months, fewer than a dozen of the island's scores of hotels remain open, and the discos pack up the speakers and lights.

Formentera is little more than a spit of sand that lies 4 miles across a strait from Ibiza. This undeveloped island is a tranquil retreat, where what visitors see is what they get. Don't expect any major changes in scenery, though the cliffs at the far end of the island are spectacular. The point here is to relax and lie in the sun. In Formentera, there aren't many distractions from those pursuits.

Sources and Resources

TOURIST INFORMATION

The islands have three types of tourist information offices (provincial, island, city), although in many cases they occupy the same premises. On Majorca, there's the Balearic Government Tourist Office (two locations: in the arrivals area (Terminal B) of the island's San Juan Airport; phone: 71-260803; and in downtown Palma, at 10 Av. Rey Jaime III; phone: 71-712216/712744). These offices provide excellent maps, listings of hotels, and information on a host of other subjects, including golf courses and deserted beaches. There are also 15 municipal tourism offices (Oficinas Municipales de Turismo) on Majorca, one in each major town. The most important are the two in Palma (11 Calle Santo Domingo; phone: 71-724090; and in a booth on Plaza de España, near the train station; phone: 71-711527). These tourist offices have schedules of events, buses, and trains, restaurant listings, and excellent local maps. The hours of all tourist offices in Palma are Monday to Friday from 9 AM to 2:30 PM and from 3 to 8 PM, and Saturday from 10 AM to 1:30 PM; some of the smaller municipal tourist offices are open only in the morning.

On Minorca, the main tourist office (13 Plaza de la Esplanada, Mahón; phone: 71-363790) is open from 9 AM to 2 PM; closed Saturdays. The office distributes maps of the island and brochures outlining the historical sights of interest in Ciudadela and Mahón, as well as the island's archaeological sites. On Ibiza, the main tourist office (13 Paseo Vara de Rey; phone: 71-301900) is open Mondays through Fridays from 9:30 AM to 1 PM and from 4 to 6 PM; and Saturdays from 10AM to 1PM. The office provides a map of the island and of the town of Ibiza that is helpful, although it leaves much to the imagination.

LOCAL COVERAGE Those who read a smattering of Spanish should pick up a copy of the daily *Diario de Mallorca,* which publishes an edition for each island, or of the daily *Ultima Hora,* which provides a good list of activities on Majorca. There is no dearth of information in English, however. The English-language *Majorca Daily Bulletin,* published daily in Palma and sold at newsstands, is packed with timetables and news about happenings around the island. The *Balearic Times,* a glossy magazine published every 2 months with information on upcoming events, nightlife, and restaurant recommendations, is sold at most magazine stands. The *Reader,* published monthly and distributed free through hotels and tourist agencies, has comments on tourist activities and plenty of advertisements for upcoming events.

TELEPHONE

The area code for the Balearic Islands is 71 (note that numbers listed in this chapter include area codes). If calling from elsewhere in Spain, dial "9" first.

CLIMATE

The weather is sparklingly clear, with average high temperatures in the low to mid-80s in July and August, the warmest months, and in the high 50s in January and February, the coldest ones. (Average lows for July and August are in the high 60s to low 70s, and in the mid- to high 40s in January and February.) The temperate climate makes the islands year-round resorts, and even February, when the almonds are in bloom, is beautiful. The swimming season extends from April through October and the average sea temperature, about 60F in April, rises to about 80F in August. Ibiza and Formentera are a bit warmer than the other two islands, and Minorca is the coolest, although the differences are minimal.

GETTING THERE

AIRPLANE Scheduled and charter flights from most major European cities land at Son San Juan Airport on Majorca, but there also are direct flights to Ibiza and Minorca. Inbound flights from Spain are aboard *Iberia* or its subsidiary, *Aviaco.*

The greatest number of daily nonstops to Majorca depart from Barcelona (35 minutes flying time) and Madrid (1 hour, 10 minutes); Alicante, Málaga, Valencia, and Vitoria also have nonstop service, in most cases on a daily basis. In addition, there are direct (not nonstop) flights from the Canary Islands. Nonstop service to Minorca is from Barcelona, Madrid, and Valencia, and there is direct service from Bilbao and Vigo. Nonstop service to Ibiza departs from Barcelona, Madrid, Valencia, and, in summer, Alicante.

The airplane is also the most important form of inter-island hopping, with Palma serving as the hub. *Aviaco* flies several times a day between Palma and Minorca and between Palma and Ibiza, a 30-minute trip in each case. The flights are no more expensive than the same trip by sea.

FERRY Car and passenger ferries operated by *Trasmediterránea* (5 Muelle Viejo, Palma; phone: 71-726740) link the islands with Barcelona and Valencia (and Sète, France) and, via hydrofoil, with Alicante. The company has offices in several cities (2 Vía Laietana, Barcelona; phone: 3-310-2508; 15 Bajo Av. Manuel Soto, Valencia; phone: 6-367-6512 or 6-367-0704; and 2 Explanada de España, Alicante; phone: 6-520-6011). Inter-island service links Palma and Mahón, Minorca, on Sundays, and Palma and Ibiza twice a week year-round by normal steamer, and daily in summer by hydrofoil.

Another ferry company, *Flebasa,* connects Denia on the mainland (between Valencia and Alicante) with Ibiza. The company has offices in Denia (phone: 65-784200 or 65-784011), Ibiza (phone: 71-342871), Madrid (phone: 1-473-2055), and San Sebastián (phone: 43-394891).

SPECIAL EVENTS

The Balearic Government Tourist Office distributes a booklet outlining the traditional festivals that take place throughout the year. For the most part, these are small local events and, except for those mentioned below, not of particular interest to visitors. On Majorca, the *Majorca Open Golf Tournament* is held annually in March at the *Santa Ponsa* course. The *Chopin Festival,* which takes place throughout the month of August, features concerts every Sunday night at the Valldemosa Carthusian Monastery, north of Palma. The *Pollensa Music Festival,* held in August and early September, features classical music on Saturdays in the Convent of Santo Domingo, Pollensa, near the northern tip of the island. (The *Fiesta de Nuestra Señora de los Angeles,* on August 2, during which the Pollensa townfolk reenact a 16th-century battle against invading pirates, is worthwhile for visitors already in the area.) The *Majorca Jazz Festival* brings jazz greats such as Oscar Peterson, Chick Corea, and *Spyro Gyra* to Palma for performances running from mid-November through mid-December.

On Minorca, two music festivals share the season: The *Ciudadela Music Festival* presents classical music in the town square every Monday or Tuesday during July and August, while the *Mahón Music Festival* makes use of the majestic organ of the Santa María church on weekends from late July through mid-September. The *Fiestas de San Juan,* June 23 and 24 in Ciudadela, are the most important of the traditional celebrations: Centuries old, they revolve around horses and include mock jousts and displays of equestrian bravura such as the *jaleo* of prancing horses. Ibiza has two traditional festivals: On March 19, the *Fiesta de San José* includes a procession through the streets of the town of Ibiza; during the first week of September, Santa Eulalia del Río celebrates a *Semana Cultural,* with locals dressed in traditional costumes. Formentera islanders in traditional costume parade through San Francisco Javier, the island capital, on July 25, the *Santiago Apóstol* (Feast of St. James).

SPORTS AND FITNESS

The islands provide opportunities for water sports of all kinds, as well as other spectator and participatory sports.

GOLF There are nine courses — seven on Majorca, one on Minorca, and one on Ibiza. Three of those on Majorca are 18-hole courses: the *Son Vida Club de Golf* (Urbanización Son Vida; phone: 71-791210), about 3 miles/5 km northwest of Palma; the *Club de Golf de Poniente* (Magaluf-Calvía; phone: 71-130148), 7.8 miles (13 km) east along the Andrade highway, exit at Carretera de Calafiguera; and *Golf Santa Ponsa* (Calvía; phone: 71-690211), approximately 10 to 12 miles (16 to 19 km) southwest along the Bay of Palma in the Magaluf area. The 9-hole *Club de Golf de Son Parc* (11 Plaza Bastion, Minorca; phone: 71-363840) is about 14 miles (22 km) north of Mahón. On Ibiza, the *Club de Golf Roca Llisa* (phone: 71-313718), at Santa Eulalia del Río, also has 9 holes.

HANG GLIDING Along with parachuting and flying, this sport is available to the public at the *Royal Flying Club* (at the Aeropuerto de Son Bonet, Marratxi, Majorca; phone: 71-600114). Equipment is available for rental.

HORSE RACING On Majorca, racing takes place regularly at the *Son Pardo Hippodrome* (Carretera de Sóller, Km 3; phone: 71-754031), and at the *Manacor Hippodrome* (Calle Es Pla; phone: 71-550023). But racing holds an even greater fascination for the islanders of Minorca, where trotting races take place every summer on Sundays at tracks in Mahón (phone: 71-363790) and Ciudadela (phone: 71-384132).

SAILING Virtually every hotel on a beach has facilities where small sailboats can be rented and lessons can be arranged. The main sailing school on Majorca is the *Escola Espanyola de Vela Cala Nova* (National Sailing School of Cala Nova) at San Agustín (phone: 71-402512).

SCUBA DIVING Information on scuba diving around Majorca can be picked up at the *Scuba Club* (13 Calle Pedro Alcántara Peña, Palma; phone: 71-463315), or at the *Scuba Club of Santa Ponsa* (84 Vía Rey Jaime; phone: 71-690266).

TENNIS Numerous hotels have their own courts or courts nearby that are open to guests. On Majorca, tennis clubs operating independently of hotels are the *Tenis Club Aeropuerto de Son Bonet* (Marratxi; phone: 71-600114); *Tenis Arenal Son Veri* (1 Calle Costa y Llobera, El Arenal, Palma; phone:

71-263834); and the *Mallorca Club de Tenis* (Calle Mestres d'Aixa, also in Palma; phone: 71-738473).

WINDSURFING Windsurfers (also called sail boards) can be rented at most beach-front hotels.

Majorca

Almost half of Majorca's 320,000 residents live in Palma de Mallorca, a city that has miles of sandy beaches stretching to the east. Those from Ca'n Pastilla to El Arenal, lined by high-rise hotels, restaurants, and discos, are known collectively as the Playa de Palma. To the west, newer tourist developments — their high-rise hotels clustered rather than strung along the sea — have been created on smaller beaches at Cala Mayor, Palma Nova, Illetas, Magaluf, and, beyond the Bay of Palma, Paguera.

At the northern tip of the island is the town of Pollensa, which offers excellent swimming and boating. The rugged Cabo de Formentor (Cape Formentor), at the end of the peninsula curving up around Pollensa Bay, offers spectacular scenery, especially to those who make it to the light-house at the end of the road. Just south of the bay is Alcudia, where a Roman city once stood (and a ruined Roman theater and walls still stand), and, a mile or so south of the village, Alcudia Bay, lined by a 6-mile beach that is much less developed than the Playa de Palma.

Majorca's mountainous western coast is dotted with small villages that have become retreats for those seeking to leave the crowds behind. Sóller is the largest town in this part of the island, and it, along with Puerto de Sóller a few miles away on the coast, does receive its share of tourists via the train that connects the beach with Palma. A bit to the south is Deya, a medieval-looking town built on a small mound between the sea and towering mountains. Still farther south, the villages of Banyalbufar and Estellenchs hug mountainsides that drop steeply to the sea. Valldemosa, where Chopin and George Sand stayed, lies at one of the few passes through the spine of mountains that separate Palma from the coast.

The bulk of Majorca lies to the east of Palma. Most visitors make their way in this direction to visit the Drach Caves and the Hams Caves, in the vicinity of the village of Porto Cristo on the island's eastern coast. They also stop in the city of Manacor, in the interior, 30½ miles (49 km) due east of Palma, where the island's pearl industry is based. Compared with the coasts, the interior of Majorca is a step back in time. Here, the life of the islanders still revolves around farming, shopkeeping, and early-morn-ing markets, rather than around the housing, feeding, and entertaining of tourists. Inca, 17½ miles (28 km) northeast of Palma on the way to Pollensa and Alcudia, is probably the most interesting interior town. A leatherworking center, it also has a large flea market, in full bustle every Thursday morning.

The real beauty of Majorca's countryside is enjoyed by driving —

across the fields, through the mountains, along the coastline. Limit excursions to trips easily completed in a day, since detours to visit unexpected sights constantly crop up. Loop from Palma to Valldemosa, then along the coast to Banyalbufar, Estellenchs, San Telmo, Puerto de Andraitx, Paguera, Magaluf, and back to the city. On another day, go north to Pollensa, then take the narrow road to the tip of Cape Formentor. A visit to a pearl factory in Manacor and to one of the massive caves farther east is another day trip. Or head away from the crowds down to Arenal de la Rapita, a totally undeveloped beach near the southeast corner of the island.

GETTING AROUND

AIRPORT Flights from Europe, mainland Spain, and the other islands arrive at the Aeropuerto de Son San Juan, 7 miles (11 km) to the east of Palma, or a 10-minute ride from the center and hotels along the Playa de Palma. An airport bus links the terminal with Plaza de España, where the bus and train stations are located; taxis to any hotel in the city will cost less than $11.25. For airport information, call 71-264162. The *Iberia* office is at 10 Paseo del Borne, Palma (phone: 71-262647 for information and reservations).

BUS Palma has a well-organized bus system, used primarily by the local population. Two tourist offices (11 Calle Santo Domingo and on Plaza de España) distribute a timetable and route map. (Once a visitor is in the inner city, however, everything is within walking distance.) Buses also link every town on the island, as well as most of the beaches; a schedule is available from a third tourist office (8 Av. Rey Jaime III). The main bus station in Palma is located on Plaza de España (phone: 71-752224).

CAR RENTAL The most extensive rental operations are provided by *Avis* (airport; phone: 71-260910 or 71-260911; and on the Palma waterfront at 16 Paseo Marítimo; phone: 71-730720 or 71-730735; as well as many others throughout the island). Some *Avis* offices are seasonal, so check with them for opening dates and hours. *Hertz* has several offices (at the airport; phone: 71-260809 or 71-264495; and on the Palma waterfront, at 13 Paseo Marítimo; phone: 71-732374). *Europcar* also has two offices (at the airport; phone: 71-263811 or 71-490110; and at 19 Paseo Marítimo; phone: 71-454800 or 71-454400). In addition, there are many small local car rental operations that, in some cases, are significantly less expensive than *Avis* or *Hertz*. Check with your hotel for the closest one or, perhaps, for one offering hotel guests special discounts.

FERRY Daily ferry service connects the island with Barcelona (8 hours) throughout the year; with Valencia (9 hours), 6 days a week; with Mahón on Minorca (6½ hours); and with Ibiza (4½ hours, 2 hours by hydrofoil). There is also ferry service twice a week from Sète, France. *Trasmediterránea* (see "Ferry" in *Getting There*) is the main source, but the ferries dock farther southwest along the bay at the Muelle de Pelaires. In addition to these basic mainland and inter-island services, numerous smaller companies operate around the island, linking the ports of Andraitx and San Telmo at the southwest corner of Majorca with the small offshore island of Dragonera, Palma with Magaluf, and Alcudia with Formentor. The tourist office provides a complete listing of such sailings.

TAXI Plentiful, inexpensive, and much more convenient than buses. Call *Aero-Taxi* (phone: 71-267312), *Radio-Taxi* (phone: 71-755440), or *Taxi Palma Radio* (phone: 71-401414).

TOURS Sightseeing tours by motorcoach reach every corner of the island. They can be booked through tour operators or hotels — tour buses call to pick up participants at their hotels every morning. There are some 20 fairly standard, full-day itineraries, including a tour from Palma to Alcudia Bay, including stops at a local market, the house of Father Junípero Serra in Petra (the Spanish Franciscan, who founded missions in California, was a native Majorcan), and Picafort beach; and a tour to the Drach Caves, with a stop at a pearl factory in Manacor.

TRAIN The island has two railroad lines. One connects Palma with Sóller, one of the most picturesque train rides in Europe. Trains leave five times a day from the station on Calle Eusebio Estrada, off Plaza de España, and wind their way to Sóller, where the journey terminates. Travelers who want to continue to the Puerto and beaches can take a period tramcar, which departs from directly outside the Sóller railway station's main entrance. Another train links Palma with Inca, departing at least every hour from another station next door on Plaza de España.

SPECIAL PLACES

PALMA DE MALLORCA The city's most prominent reminder of the Moorish occupation is the Palacio de la Almudaina, the palace-fortress of the island's Arab rulers, later converted into a royal palace for the Spanish Kings of Majorca and now used, in part, to house the *Museo del Patrimonio Nacional*. It's open weekdays from 10:30 AM to 1:30 PM and from 4 to 6:30 PM; Saturdays from 10:30 AM to 2 PM; closed Sundays and holidays; admission charge (no phone). La Seu, a golden stone Gothic structure and one of Spain's largest cathedrals, was begun in 1230, finished in 1601, and underwent alterations in the early 20th century when it was restored by Antoni Gaudí, the famed Catalan architect. The cathedral chapter house contains a small museum, open Mondays through Fridays from 10 AM to 12:30 PM and from 4 to 6:30 PM, Saturdays from 10 AM to 1:30 PM; admission charge. The cathedral has the same hours and is also open during services.

Palma's cathedral, in Plaza Almoina, stands on high ground at the western edge of the oldest part of the city, which is to the east of the wide, tree-shaded promenade known as El Borne (or Paseo del Borne). The Baños Arabes (Arab Baths), on Calle Serra, remain essentially as they were under the caliphs. They're open daily from 10 AM to 1 PM and from 4 to 6 PM; admission charge (no phone.) Still in the Old Town, in the Portella quarter behind the cathedral, is the *Museo de Mallorca,* housed in an old mansion at 5 Calle de la Portella; it illustrates island history through a collection of archaeological artifacts, documents, paintings, and sculpture. Open from 10 AM to 2 PM and from 4 to 7 PM; closed Sunday afternoons and Mondays; admission charge (no phone). Working your way north, you'll also see the 17th-century Casa Oleza (33 Calle Morey) — known for its inner courtyard — and the 16th-century Gothic and Renaissance Casa Palmer (17 Calle del Sol), before reaching Palma's second-most-renowned church, San Francisco, on the plaza with the same name. Built in the 13th and 14th centuries, it was given a baroque façade in the 17th century. The church is open from 9:30 AM to 1 PM and from 3:30 to 7 PM; closed Sunday afternoons.

Proceed west from St. Francis to reach Santa Eulalia church, a fine example of Majorcan Gothic, built from the 13th to the 15th centuries; behind it (at 2 Calle Zavella) is the 18th-century Casa Vivot, another mansion with a notable courtyard. Still farther west, but still in the Old Town on the east side of El Borne, is Palma's 17th-century Ayuntamiento (Town Hall), standing in a beautiful old square, Plaza Cort.

The Lonja, on the seafront west of El Borne, is one of Palma's star attractions. Built during the 15th century as a stock exchange and commercial building for the city's busy trading merchants, it now serves as an exhibition space for art shows (and is thus open irregularly). Also on the west side of El Borne is the Casa de los Marqueses de Sollerich (10 Calle San Cayetano), an 18th-century mansion with perhaps the finest courtyard in town.

The attractions beyond the center, on the west side of Palma, should not be missed. One of them, the Castillo de Bellver, an unusual round castle built during the 14th century and beautifully preserved, boasts perhaps the best view of Palma and the surrounding area. The adjoining Tower of Homage, looking like a stone rocket ready for blast-off, housed the dungeons. It's open from 8 AM to 10 PM from April through September, to 6 PM the rest of the year; admission charge. The other main attraction, the Pueblo Español (Spanish Village), located across from the Palacio de Congresos, offers a chance to see all of Spain at a glance. Much like its counterpart in Barcelona, this model village contains reproductions of houses and famous buildings from all parts of Spain. It also offers a chance to see Spanish artisans at work and shops where their handiwork can be purchased. The village is open daily from 9 AM to 8 PM; admission charge.

Near the fashionable town of Andraitx, 3 miles (5 km) west of Palma, is the *Fundació Pilar i Joan Miró* (Pilar and Joan Miró Foundation; 35 Juan de Saridakis; phone: 71-405858), a new cultural complex built on the site of the famed artist's former studio. Before Miró's death in 1983, he created a foundation to ensure that his workplace would continue to be used. The foundation mounts changing exhibits from its permanent collection of 5,000 works, including paintings, sculpture, collages, etchings, and lithographs. Some of the artist's correspondence, photographs, and personal objects are also displayed. The complex is open Tuesdays through Saturdays from 11 AM to 6 PM; Sundays and holidays from 11 AM to 3 PM; admission charge.

ELSEWHERE ON THE ISLAND

LA CARTUJA DE VALLDEMOSA (VALLDEMOSA CARTHUSIAN MONASTERY) Set in the mountains 11 miles (18 km) north of Palma, this monastery was founded during the 14th century, although the present buildings are from the 17th and 18th centuries. After the Carthusian monks left it during the 18th century, its cells were rented out to guests, including Frédéric Chopin and George Sand, who spent the winter of 1838–39 here. The Cloister of St. Mary offers beautiful views, and the neo-classical church is decorated with frescoes, an intricately carved choir stall, and rich tapestries. It also features a lovely, well-tended garden area. Open Mondays through Saturdays from 9:30 AM to 1:30 PM and from 3 to 6:30 PM; admission charge (no phone).

DEYA This lovely old village (Deiá in the local language) enjoys an enchanting setting perched loft-like over the sea and backed by evergreen mountains 17 miles (27 km) northwest of Palma. Its natural beauty lured those who made it an artists' and writers' colony — the poet Robert Graves, who lived here until his death in 1985, was probably its most famous long-term resident. He is now buried in the local cemetery, which also has a splendid view of the area.

SÓLLER Almond, lemon, and orange groves surround this town 19 miles (30 km) north of Palma, the largest town on the western side of the island. Like many a settlement on Majorca, the threat of attack from the sea caused it to grow up a few miles inland from its port, Puerto de Sóller, which sits 3 miles (5 km) from the valley on a round, sheltered, beach-lined bay and has become a thriving resort center. Sóller itself has little to see, beyond a cathedral that is among the most elaborate on the island. Most visitors arrive aboard the turn-of-the-century narrow-gauge railroad train from Palma — a wonderfully scenic ride that is well worth the trip — then continue via an extension down to the port for the beach or a bite to eat.

POLLENSA On the northeast coast, 32½ miles (52 km) from Palma, Pollensa (Pollença in the Majorcan dialect), too, is an inland town; Puerto de Pollensa, a fishing village turned resort town, is 4 miles (6 km) away on one of the three largest bays of Majorca, with a big, sweeping beach. On the outskirts of Pollensa is Monte Calvario, a hill crowned by a small chapel reached by car or a climb of 365 steps. In town are the 14th-century parish Church of Nuestra Señora de los Angeles and the 16th-century Santo Domingo convent.

CABO DE FORMENTOR The road from Puerto de Pollensa to Cape Formentor follows the spine of the Sierra de Tramuntana out to sea and provides stunning vistas, particularly at the Mirador d'Es Colomer and at the Formentor lighthouse at the end of the peninsula.

CUEVAS DE ARTÁ (ARTÁ CAVES) These extensive caves are perhaps the most beautiful of the many on the island, yet they are the least visited. They were first explored thoroughly during the 19th century — and are said to have inspired Jules Verne to write *Journey to the Center of the Earth* — but were known as long ago as the 13th century, when they served as a hiding place for Moors after the Reconquest. Open daily; admission charge. On the east coast of the island at Cabo Vermell, 6 miles (10 km) east of Artá (phone: 71-563293).

CUEVAS DEL DRAC (DRACH CAVES) The largest of Majorca's caves are just over a mile long and contain a subterranean lake in addition to four chambers full of fanciful formations in limestone. Visits are guided (English-language tours are possible) and include a concert by floating musicians at the end of the tour. Be warned: The crowds are ridiculous during the summer months. Open daily; admission charge. On the east coast of Majorca, just south of Porto Cristo (phone: 71-570002).

CUEVAS DE ELS HAMS (HAMS CAVES) Virtually next door to the Drach Caves and less impressive, although they are known for the whiteness of their stalactites and stalagmites. Open daily; admission charge. Just west of Porto Cristo (phone: 71-570227).

SHOPPING

Shopping in Palma is concentrated in the city center. Upscale shops, with such names as *Rodier, Gucci,* and *Armani,* tend to be found along Avenida Rey Jaime III. The shopping area that is more likely to be packed with Majorcans and thus with many more bargains is one on the east side of the Paseo del Borne, in small pedestrian streets that climb to the Plaza Mayor and then along Calle Sindicato and Calle San Miguel, which branch out from the square. Leather goods, embroidery, ceramics, and manufactured pearls are all good buys. For general purchases, stop in at *Galerías Preciados* (15 Av. Rey Jaime III), a branch of the Spain-wide department store chain. Majorca also has a well-organized series of open-air markets. The main vegetable and fish market in Plaza Oliver is in operation daily and is worth a visit. An interesting crafts market takes place on Plaza Mayor on Saturday mornings year-round, and more frequently in summer. The *Centro Comercial Plaza Mayor* (Sótanos Plaza Mayor) is a sprawling underground shopping mall containing dozens of stores specializing in leather, suede, and pinewood crafts. Markets in the smaller towns take place once or twice a week; the schedule is printed in the *Balearic Times,* as well as in several tourist office publications. Among the larger markets are the ones in Alcudia on Tuesday and Sunday mornings, in Artá on Tuesday mornings, in Inca on Thursday mornings, in Manacor on Monday mornings, in Pollensa on Sunday mornings, and in Sóller on Saturday mornings. Among the more interesting shops are the following:

BAMUCO Moderately priced leather goods. 19 Palau Reial, Palma de Mallorca (phone: 71-722512).

CASA BONET One of the best embroidery shops on the island. 3 Calle Puigdorfila, Palma de Mallorca (phone: 71-722117).

L'OFRE Better-quality purses and other articles in leather. 28 Paseo del Borne, Palma de Mallorca (phone: 71-223665).

PERLAS MAJÓRICA The island's well-known pearls, of the highest quality, organically manmade (of fish scales), at factory prices (11 Av. Rey Jaime III, Palma de Mallorca; phone: 71-725268). Pearls can also be bought directly from the factory, open daily, except Sundays, just off the main road in Manacor (48 Vía Romana; phone: 71-725268).

SCHEREZADE The best place to buy Lladró porcelain. 5 Calle Brossa, Palma de Mallorca (phone: 71-711974).

NIGHTCLUBS AND NIGHTLIFE

The Balearics have a justly deserved reputation for offering some of the wildest nightlife in the world. Not only does Palma dance all night long, but *BCM* in Magaluf, which has a capacity of over 5,000 revelers, is the world's largest discotheque. Any disco tour of Palma begins in the western part of the city around Plaza Gomila. Here, the stunning glass façade of *Tito's* (phone: 71-237642) faces the sea on the Paseo Marítimo. Glass elevators move party animals between the 4 bars and 5 levels of this extravaganza, and revolving lights present a stunning light show to those on the waterfront. *Alexandra's,* nearby (Plaza Mediterráneo; phone: 71-237810), has the loud music and light shows without the wild setting of *Tito's.* Farther along the bay on the western side of the city, in Cala Mayor, *Pepe's Centre* (322 Av. Joan Miró; phone: 71-403047) and *Disco Liberty,* just down the road (phone: 71-403644), offer excellent late-night dancing and are packed with tourists from every corner of the Continent. Still farther along the bay, Magaluf, a created resort city about a 30-minute drive to the west of Palma, is the area's main disco scene. Here the mega-disco *BCM* (phone: 71-683869) reigns, hosting some of rock's top stars in live performance; *Alexandra's 2 Disco* also packs them in; and plenty of bars percolate with nonstop parties, complete with giant snake dances rolling from one pub into the next. Majorca's *Casino* (Urbanización Sol de Mallorca; phone: 71-680000), featuring American and French roulette, blackjack, and other games of chance, as well as a restaurant and discotheque, is also out this way (take the Cala Figuera turnoff from the Andraitx road).

The Playa de Palma area along the bay to the east of the city also has its complement of nightspots. Try *Riu Palace* (Calle Laud, El Arenal; phone: 71-265704), Majorca's largest disco until the creation of *BCM,* and *Zorba's* (4 Av. Son Rigo; phone: 71-266664), which offers open-air dancing along the beach.

Other tastes can be indulged in downtown Palma. For early-evening drinks, there are *tapas* bars lining Calle Apuntadores. Later, a visit to the *Bar Abaco* (1 Calle San Juan; phone: 71-714939), installed in a former Majorcan palace, is a memorable experience. Guests enter a giant room with wide arches over columns, a bar 30 feet long, Oriental carpets, classical statues, café tables, and baskets of fruit spilling across the floor; upstairs patrons chat on couches surrounding a fireplace while others wander through a reconstructed kitchen and gaze into the garden below, where a small pond shimmers in the light of dozens of giant candles. Classical music plays quietly in the background of this sophisticated establishment, where a mixed drink can cost anywhere from $6 to $12.

CHECKING IN

The majority of the hotels on the islands are dedicated to the group tour trade, but accept individual guests when space is available. The hotels listed below have been selected from more than 1,000 that the island has to offer. Prices are for a double room during high season, from June through September and at *Christmas* and *Easter.* Low-season rates can be 25% less. Expect to pay more than $190 in a hotel listed as very expensive, from $115 to $190 in a hotel listed as expensive, from $55 to $115 in a moderate hotel, and less than $55 in an inexpensive place.

PALMA AND ENVIRONS

VERY EXPENSIVE

Melia Victoria At the western side of the bay, it overlooks the entire city, with one of the best views of the harbor. The 167 rooms all have TV sets, the buffet breakfast is sumptuous, and the location, next to the Plaza Gomila nightclubs, makes it central to Palma nightlife. (The pulsating lights of *Tito's* are next door, so get a room facing the other way to avoid the noise.) There are 2 pools and open-air dancing in summer. 21 Av. Joan Miró, Palma (phone: 71-234342; in the US, 800-336-3542; fax: 71-450824).

Son Vida Located in an old castle, this luxurious, 165-room property boasts lovely grounds, an 18-hole golf course, 2 large pools, 4 outdoor tennis courts, and a good restaurant. Located in the hills a few miles north of

Palma, in Urbanización Son Vida (phone: 71-790000; in New York City, 212-838-3110; elsewhere in the US, 800-223-6800; fax: 71-790017).

Valparaíso Palace Off the beaten tourist path, this modern 138-room establishment offers beautiful gardens, a restaurant, a swimming pool, tennis courts, and a stunning view of the Bay of Palma. In the hills behind Palma, on Francisco Vidal (phone: 71-400411; fax: 71-405904).

EXPENSIVE

Punta Negra A 69-room hotel with bungalows as well, a pool, and virtually a private beach tucked between the rocks at Palma Nova. Carretera Andraitx, Km 12, Palma Nova (phone: 71-680762).

Sol Bellver Half the price of the *Victoria* and not far away from it, it's on the road that rims Palma's harbor. The 393 rooms are simply and sparsely furnished — ask for one with a panoramic view of the yacht harbor. There is a good pool, a restaurant, and a cafeteria. 11 Paseo Marítimo, Palma (phone: 71-238008; fax: 71-284184).

MODERATE

Aquarium In Palma Nova, just across the street from the beach and a short walk from the nightlife, this is a good basic tourist hotel with 109 rooms, a pool, a bar, and a cafeteria. Closed from November through March. Paseo del Mar, Palma Nova (phone: 71-680308).

La Cala Sitting side by side with its sister hotel, the *Santa Ana,* on the Cala Mayor beach, this place is less than half the size (70 rooms) and a bit less expensive. It, too, has a pool, as well as a restaurant. Closed November through March. 4 Calle Gaviota, Cala Mayor (phone: 71-401612; fax: 71-700523).

Costa Azul One of the bargains on the road along Palma's harbor, it has 126 simple rooms, a restaurant, and an indoor-outdoor pool with sliding glass overhead. This is closer to downtown Palma than it is to the Gomila nightlife quarter. Closed in December. 7 Paseo Marítimo, Palma (phone: 71-231940; fax: 71-231971).

Santa Ana Located on Cala Mayor beach, it has 190 simply furnished rooms, most with terraces overlooking the sea, a pool, and a restaurant. 9 Calle Gaviota, Cala Mayor (phone: 71-401512).

INEXPENSIVE

Sol Horizonte Located at the far western end of Palma, near Porto Pí, this is a basic tourist hotel (200 rooms) but the price is right. It has a restaurant and a pool that is open from May to September. It's within a short taxi ride of the Gomila nightlife section and has good views of the bay. 1 Calle Vista Alegre, Palma (phone: 71-400661; fax: 71-400783).

VERY EXPENSIVE

Formentor Occupying a craggy peninsula on the remote northeastern end of the island, this is one of Majorca's most famous hotels. A luxurious, get-away-from-it-all ambience prevails here; among the amenities are 2 outdoor swimming pools, 6 tennis courts (2 of them lit), and 2 fine restaurants. There are 127 rooms, plus miniature golf, riding stables, and a private beach on the premises. The gardens are perhaps the most beautiful on the island. Closed November through March. Playa de Formentor (phone: 71-865300).

La Residencia An old mansion turned into a wondrous, low-key hotel with spectacular views over the sea. It's tucked just off the road leading into Deya from Valldemosa, perched high above the Mediterranean, a 15-minute walk from town. Simple antiques, four-poster beds, and marble floors grace the 27 rooms. There is a swimming pool and tennis, as well as a restaurant. Son Moragues, Deya (phone: 71-639011).

EXPENSIVE

L'Hermitage Virtually a self-contained resort in a mountain setting off the road from Palma to Sóller, far from the crowds and the beach. Rustic elegance is done perfectly here. There are only 20 rooms, with furniture in heavy wood; dining is outside when possible; there are tennis courts, and the swimming pool is surrounded by pines. Carretera de Sollerich, Km 8, Orient (phone: 71-613300; fax: 71-613300).

Vistamar A former manor house still full of Spanish art, this hostelry has 9 double rooms and a suite, all with four-poster beds. It overlooks the sea on one side and is surrounded by olive and almond groves on the other. The restaurant is set on the porticoed terrace. All is magic when lit at night. About 1¾ miles (3 km) from Valldemosa. Carretera Andraitx, Km 2, Valldemosa (phone: 71-612300; fax: 71-612583).

MODERATE

Miramar It's as if time had stopped in the 1930s here. The 69-room hotel is right on the beach at the far north of Majorca and couldn't be more pleasant. It's equipped with only a bar/cafeteria, though. Reserve early. Closed November through March. 39 Paseo Anglada Camarasa, Puerto de Pollensa (phone: 71-531211).

Ses Rotges In the northeast corner of the island, it has 24 rooms, beautiful gardens, a pool, and an outdoor restaurant with a rustic lounge. Closed November through March. 21 Rafael Blanes, Cala Ratjada (phone: 71-564345).

Costa D'Or A small place (42 rooms) just up the road from Deya in Lluch Alcari, with views of the crashing sea below. It's very simple, but the beauty of the spot cannot be improved. There is a restaurant and pool. Closed November through March. Lluch Alcari (phone: 71-639025).

Mar y Vent Near the main highway and about 750 feet above the sea, which lies at the end of a long terraced slope dropping steeply in front of the hotel. It has 19 good, simple rooms, a swimming pool, and great food. Closed in the off-season, usually from December through February. 49 Carrer Mayor, Banyalbufar (phone: 71-610025).

EATING OUT

As with any popular tourist destination, restaurants abound in the Balearic Islands. In addition to German, Scandinavian, and English dining places, there are still scores of restaurants serving up local specialties — fish restaurants and others featuring the lamb, goat, rabbit, chicken, and snail dishes typical of Balearic food. Wines to try are binisalem and felanitx, both from Majorca. Expect to pay $55 and up for a meal for two including an appetizer, main course, dessert, and wine in restaurants listed as expensive; between $25 and $55 at places described as moderate, and between $20 and $25 at inexpensive spots. Because the island economy is extremely seasonal, be sure to call restaurants to make sure they are open, especially off-season.

PALMA AND ENVIRONS

EXPENSIVE

Honoris An excellent French restaurant in the northeastern part of Palma, near the industrial section. Only a handful of well-heeled tourists manage to make the pilgrimage, but those who are serious about eating and have money to spare should try it. Closed Sundays, holidays, *Holy Week,* and August 1–20. Reservations advised. Major credit cards accepted. 76 Carretera Vieja de Bunyola, Palma (phone: 71-290007).

La Lubina Long-established and one of the best fish places in Palma, it's right on the old pier but as upscale and pricey as any place in the city proper. Classical music fills the air, and the atmosphere is hushed and formal. Try the grilled swordfish or the grilled fresh fish of the day. Open daily. Reservations advised. Major credit cards accepted. Muelle Viejo, Palma (phone: 71-723250).

Porto Pí Where King Juan Carlos eats when he comes to Palma — which means almost the top prices in town. It's located in one of Palma's oldest mansions, and the menu features French Basque cooking. The fresh fish here is some of the best on the island — try it baked in pastry, and then try one of the fabulous desserts. Closed Saturdays at lunch, Sundays, and mid-November to mid-December. Reservations necessary. Major credit cards accepted. 174 Av. Joan Miró, Palma (phone: 71-400087).

Real Club Náutico Set in Palma harbor and boasting a panoramic view and alfresco balcony dining, this is one of the most delightful restaurants in the city. Seafood specialities are dominant, ranging from *lubina a la mostaza* (sea bass in mustard sauce) to *paella de langosta* (paella with Mediterranean lobster). Open daily. Reservations advised. Major credit cards accepted. 1 Muelle de San Pedro (phone: 71-718783).

MODERATE

Caballito del Mar Hard to beat for moderately priced outdoor eating along the seafront. On sunny days, the setting couldn't be better, and the food is normally well prepared. Have the fish of the day, perhaps grilled. Closed Sundays. Reservations advised. Major credit cards accepted. 5 Paseo de Sagrera, Palma (phone: 71-721074).

Casa Eduardo Come here just for the fish soup. A noisy, "real people's" fish place, it's located on the pier opposite *La Lubina*. Closed Sundays and Mondays. Reservations unnecessary. No credit cards accepted. 4 Industria Pesquera, on Mollet (phone: 71-721182).

Don Peppone The best Italian food in town, including great antipasti, linguine with shellfish, and osso buco, is served here. It's packed with Palma yuppies, who love it when the roof is rolled back to let the sun shine in. Closed Mondays at lunch and Sundays (except for dinner in the summer). Reservations necessary. Visa accepted. 14 Calle Bayarte, Palma (phone: 71-454242).

Es Parlament In an ornate classical setting in the Balearic Autonomous Parliament building, it's particularly famous for its paella. Closed Sundays and August. Reservations necessary. No credit cards accepted. 11 Calle Conquistador, Palma (phone: 71-726026).

INEXPENSIVE

Ca'n Juanito A basic Spanish eatery with a simple, uninspired decor, it serves excellent local dishes such as rabbit, goat, and lamb. Closed Wednesday evenings. Reservations unnecessary. No credit cards accepted. 11 Av. Aragón, Palma (phone: 71-461065).

Celler Sa Premsa For those who've dreamed of the perfect Spanish restaurant — bullfight posters on the walls, long wooden tables shared with strangers, and great budget food. This is Palma's largest such dining place (seating for 250), and it's usually full. The roast suckling pig is a reliable choice. Closed Saturdays and Sundays. Reservations advised on weekends. Visa accepted. 8 Plaza Obispo Berenguer de Palou, Palma (phone: 71-723529).

ELSEWHERE ON THE ISLAND

MODERATE

Na Burguesa Just outside Palma in the small town of Génova (with a marvelous view of the capital), it serves Majorcan dishes. Try the roast shoulder of lamb or the pork loin. The atmosphere is loud and boisterous, and be prepared to wait for a table. Closed Monday evenings. Reservations essential on weekends. Visa accepted. Mirador de Na Burguesa, Génova (phone: 71-402043).

Celler Ca'n Amer An immense room lined with wine casks, it has gained fame as one of the best spots on the island for local cooking; unfortunately, the prices have increased as its popularity has soared. Closed Sundays in summer, Saturdays and Sundays at other times. Reservations are essential for lunch on Thursdays, when the market brings an overload of hungry folks into town; at other times, reservations are advised. American Express and Visa accepted. 39 Calle Miguel Durán, Inca (phone: 71-501261).

El Guía A simple Spanish place in Sóller, it's a nice choice for lunch after taking the train up from Palma. The food is basic, the seafood excellent. Closed Mondays. Reservations unnecessary. Major credit cards accepted. 12 Calle Castañer, Sóller (phone: 71-630227).

Mandilego In a small town on the Bay of Alcudia, on the north coast of the island, it offers excellent fish dishes, from swordfish steaks to Mediterranean lobsters. Closed Mondays. Reservations advised. No credit cards accepted. 49 Calle Isabel Garau, Ca'n Picafort (phone: 71-527003).

Mesón Ca'n Pedro One of the shrines of Majorcan cooking, this rustic restaurant is also just outside Palma in Génova. Try the *cabrito* (kid) if it's available. Closed Wednesdays. Reservations necessary. Major credit cards accepted. 4 Calle Rector Vives, Génova (phone: 71-402479).

Puig de Sant Miguel Majorcan specialties are featured at this rambling rustic place in the interior, on the road from Montuiri to Manacor. Try suckling pig or leg of lamb, served on wooden tables surrounded with wagon wheels and local pottery. Closed Tuesdays. Reservations advised. No credit cards accepted. Carretera Manacor–Montuiri, Km 31 (phone: 71-646314).

Ses Porxeres This Catalan eatery is best known for its fantastic appetizers. Order the appetizer plate and a good bottle of wine, and have a feast. In fact, for a party of six, four portions will be plenty. Closed Sunday evenings and Mondays. Reservations advised. Visa accepted. Carretera Palma–Sóller, Km 17, Bunyola (phone: 71-613762).

INEXPENSIVE

Ca'n Jaime A simple, tiny, typical restaurant serving excellent food, in the tiny town of Deya. Try the *sopas mallorquinas* (Majorcan soup) and the *arroz brut* ("ugly rice" or "rice in the rough"), and wolf it all down with wine and olives. Closed Mondays except holidays. Reservations unnecessary. No credit cards accepted. 13 Calle Archiduque Luis Salvador, Deya (phone: 71-639029).

Escorca High in the mountain between Sóller and Pollensa, near the Lluch Monastery, this rustic place with a giant fireplace specializes in roast leg of lamb and goat and has wonderful baked apples. Closed Thursdays. Reservations advised. No credit cards accepted. Carretera Pollensa–Sóller, Km 25 (phone: 71-517095).

Es Pouet Francisca In the western mountains, this place is built against a cliff high above Alaro, on the winding unpaved road to the Castillo de Alaro. The roast lamb and the snails are worth every bit of the effort; the homemade *tinto* (red) wine is dark and heavy. Closed Thursdays and Saturdays for lunch. Reservations unnecessary. No credit cards accepted. Leave Alaro on the road to Orient and look for a small sign indicating Espouet, then turn left and begin the climb. The restaurant is the last building accessible by car (phone: 71-510277).

Minorca

The second-largest of the Balearic Islands is the easternmost of the group and also the island farthest from the Spanish mainland. Minorca, which measures about 30 miles from east to west and between 6 and 12 miles north to south, is relatively flat — a hilly plateau with its highest point, Monte Toro, rising just over 1,000 feet in the island's center. The absence of a mountain range such as the one on Majorca means that Minorca is without some of the larger island's spectacular scenery. Yet its outline is rugged and irregular, resulting in roughly 125 miles of coastline blessed with countless small coves and beautiful beaches. More and more tourists are beginning to appreciate Minorca's pleasures, but they haven't inundated the island yet, and agriculture and dairy products remain major industries, along with the making of shoes and costume jewelry.

Traces of past cultures have all but been destroyed on the island, except for the massive megalithic constructions remaining from prehistoric times. Minorca is dotted with hundreds of these stone monuments — cylindrical *talayots,* T-shaped *taulas,* and ship-shaped *navetas* — which are remnants of a so-called *talayotic* Bronze Age culture that may have begun about

2000 BC and was at its height around 1000 BC. Scholars do not yet fully understand the origins of the civilization that raised these monuments, nor have they been able to fathom the structures' exact functions. *Talayots* may have been watchtowers or the houses of chieftains (or the roofs or foundations of such structures). *Taulas,* the form most peculiar to Minorca, may have served a religious purpose. *Navetas,* similar to the conical mounds of the *talayots* but oblong and containing chambers (like the upside-down hull of a ship, whence the name), are thought to have been communal graves. These monuments are found on both government and private land; although some of the sites are easily accessible from the road, others are not.

The largest city on Minorca is its capital, Mahón (population 25,000), a port at the eastern end of the island. Known in the Minorcan language as Maó, it gave the world a favorite local sauce — mayonnaise. The second-largest city and former capital, Ciudadela (Ciutadella in the local language; population 15,000), is at the island's western extreme. The two are starkly different. Mahón shows the influence of 8 decades of 18th-century British rule in its architecture, which sports details such as sash windows and Georgian doors, and caters to predominantly English-speaking visitors. The architecture of Ciudadela, where Germans fill the bungalows of the tourist villages, is classically Spanish. Other towns, such as Alayor, Mercadal, and Ferrerias, are in the interior, along the main road that crosses the island from east to west. Fornells, at one time a fishing village and now a resort town, is on the north coast on a deeply indented bay.

Minorca's beaches are what most visitors come to explore. All are posted with flags due to capricious currents — red signals danger, yellow means caution, and green signifies safety. Son Bou and Santo Tomás, in the center of the southern shore, are the two longest beaches on the island. Cala Santa Galdana, to the west of these, is a beach in a sheltered cove, with very safe and shallow waters, and Cala Blanca, a few miles south of Ciudadela, is a tiny beach surrounded by rocky cliffs. Cala del Pilar, a deserted beach on the north side of the island, is known mainly to locals. To reach it, turn off the main Mahón–Ciudadela road about 3 miles (5 km) past Ferrerias, near the Alputzer farm. Cala Pregonda, east of Cala del Pilar, is also deserted but easier to reach. From Mercadal, take the road northwest toward Ferragut Nou, then walk the last hundred yards to the sea. Es Grao, one of the beaches closest to Mahón, is very shallow, perfect for children. Drive due north from the city to the sea.

GETTING AROUND

AIRPORT Charter flights arrive from most European countries, scheduled flights aboard *Aviaco* from mainland Spain and from Palma de Mallorca. Mahón Airport (phone: 71-360150) is 3 miles (5 km) southwest of the city at San

Clemente. Expect to pay about $4.50 for a taxi ride between the airport and downtown Mahón. The *Aviaco* office is at Mahón Airport (phone: 71-369202 for information and reservations).

BUS Buses depart from Plaza Explanada, Mahón, for Ciudadela a half dozen times a day. Schedules are available from the tourist office (13 Plaza de la Constitución) and are also posted on the square.

CAR RENTAL A rented car is the recommended means of transportation. The island's relatively wide main road runs between Mahón and Ciudadela, and traffic is no problem on the other roads, though parking in the center of Mahón is virtually impossible. *Avis* (at the airport; phone: 71-361576, 71-368976, or 71-381838; and at 53 Plaza Explanada, Mahón; phone: 71-364778) offers the most convenient rentals and has several other locations. *Hertz* has one office (42 Carrer Gran, Villacarlos; phone: 71-364881 or 71-367822). Scores of smaller car rental agencies exist, many associated with hotels. Check with them if a car is needed for only a day or two. (The tourist office has a complete list of all car rental offices on the island.) Note that the best map of the island is the *Archaeological Map of Minorca,* available in local bookstores. It shows not only the roads, including tiny one-lane streets, but also the names of farms in the countryside — invaluable for those who have lost their way, with no road signs for miles, because farm names are clearly marked across the island.

FERRY There are daily ferries from Barcelona between mid-June and mid-September, and then twice a week during the winter; the trip takes 9 hours. Connections between Valencia and Mahón operate only once a week (Valencia, 16 hours, via Palma de Mallorca; and Palma 6½ hours). Most ferries land at Mahón's Estación Marítima; some coming from Alcudia, in Majorca, land at Ciudadela's small harbor. Call *Trasmediterránea* for information (see "Ferry" in *Getting There*).

MOTOR SCOOTER RENTAL Because Minorca is small, many visitors explore it on rented motor scooters or motorcycles. Among the scores of agencies are *Motos Gelabert* (12 Calle José A. Clavé; phone: 71-360614), *Motos Kike* (69 Calle Ciudadela; phone: 71-364120), and *Motos Ramos* (21 Anden de Levante; phone: 71-366813), all in Mahón.

TAXI Cabs do not scurry around the island; you can't hail one on the street. Call *Radio-Taxi* in Mahón (phone: 71-367111) or in Ciudadela (phone: 71-382335 or 71-381197).

SPECIAL PLACES

MAHÓN Throughout most of its history, the capital of modern Minorca was second in importance to Ciudadela. That changed during the 18th century with the arrival of the British, who found Mahón's long, narrow, deep harbor and port facilities preferable to those at the other end of the island.

Mahón, set on a high cliff at the end of the harbor, does not have the wide avenues, majestic buildings, and tree-lined streets of other Spanish capitals, resembling an overgrown fishing village instead. Among the sights is the 18th-century Santa María church, which houses an extraordinary early 19th-century organ that is one of the largest in the world and is considered to be one of the finest (it's the raison d'être of the city's annual summer music festival). Not far away, the marketplace built into the arcaded cloister of a former Carmelite convent is worth a morning visit; otherwise, the town is best enjoyed by wandering through its narrow streets. At night, the port, reached by a steep, winding road called Abundancia, becomes the focus of most nightlife, with dozens of bars and restaurants in the area of the Estación Marítima and several excellent restaurants lining the harbor toward Villacarlos. The British founded this village, southeast of Mahón near the entrance to the harbor, to house the garrison of a nearby fort. Once called Georgetown, it remains even more British in atmosphere than the capital itself.

TREPUCÓ A 13-foot *taula,* the highest on Minorca, and a *talayot* are located at this easily accessible archaeological site a little over a mile south of Mahón.

CIUDADELA Minorca's second-largest city, at the western end of the island, is blessed with a beautiful location and ornate Spanish architecture that attests to its onetime importance as the former capital. Although it was largely destroyed by the Turks during the mid-16th century and then rebuilt, it has a wonderful Old City center with narrow streets and tiny shops. The Cathedral of Santa María, a Gothic church begun during the 14th century, has a crumbling façade, but the interior has been restored and is especially beautiful when the morning light streams through its stained glass window. Outside the church, Calle Quadrado, lined with arcades and shops, leads to Calle Mayor Borne and to Plaza d'es Borne, Ciudadela's main square. Be sure to walk into the Palacio Saura on Calle Santísimo (south of Calle Quadrado and west of the marketplace) to get a sense of an old Minorcan palace with courtyard, staircase, and dome.

NAVETA D'ES TUDONS The restored *naveta* at this accessible site 3 miles (5 km) east of Ciudadela, just south of the road to Mahón, is the best-preserved, the most important, and the most famous megalithic mónument on the island. It is also the *naveta* that looks most like an upside-down ship.

TORRE D'EN GAUMÉS A megalithic settlement covering several acres, it includes *taulas, talayots,* and ancient caves used for habitation; it's easily accessible 2 miles (3 km) south of Alayor, off the road to Son Bou.

SHOPPING

Minorca has a reputation for making excellent leather goods and shoes and is a European leader in the manufacture of costume jewelry. The products of both industries can be bought from factory outlets. Outdoor markets are held on Tuesday and Saturday mornings in Plaza Explanada, Mahón; Friday and Saturday mornings in Ciudadela; Monday and Wednesday mornings in Villacarlos; and Mondays and Wednesdays in San Luis.

CATISA The island's largest costume jewelry factory. 26 Calle Bellavista, Mahón (phone: 71-364545).

MASSA Upscale silver handicrafts. 36 Sant Ferrán, Mahón (phone: 71-364189).

PATRIZIA A prime place for leather goods. 2 Calle Favaller, Ciudadela (phone: 71-380397).

S'ALAMBIC Good for local handicrafts and antique ceramics. 36 Moll de Ponent, Mahón (phone: 71-350707).

SALORD JOVEL A factory outlet that is a good source of leather items. Located in the industrial area along the main road into Ciudadela (phone: 71-382300).

NIGHTCLUBS AND NIGHTLIFE

Nightlife here pales in comparison to that found on Ibiza and Majorca. There are bars and restaurants packed with locals near the Estación Marítima in Mahón and along the harbor to, and including, the port area of Villacarlos. Among the discos on the island is the unique *Cova d'en Xoroi* (no phone), built into a cave on the coast south of Alayor at Cala'n Porter. The cave opens to the sea below a cliff dropping straight to the water. Guests reach the disco via a staircase clinging to the rocks, then strut their stuff on a dance floor 100 feet above the crashing waves. The action starts after midnight and really begins to cook between 2 and 3 AM.

CHECKING IN

The prices listed below are those charged for a double room during the high season, from June through September and at *Christmas* and *Easter*. Low-season rates can be 25% lower. Expect to pay from $110 to $190 for a double in a hotel listed as expensive; from $55 to $110 in a moderate hotel; and less than $55 a night in an inexpensive one.

EXPENSIVE

Port Mahón A grand old hotel overlooking the port, it's within a short walk of both the town center and the port area. The 74 rooms are simply furnished; there is a pool and a restaurant. Av. Fort de l'Eau, Mahón (phone: 71-362600; fax: 71-364595).

MODERATE

Biniali A small *hostal,* much like a country inn, each of its 9 rooms is furnished differently with antiques. The villa, which also has a pool, is about 3 miles

(5 km) south of Mahón, beyond the town of San Luis. Reservations should be made as much in advance as possible. 50 Calle Suestra, San Luis (phone: 71-151724; fax: 71-150352).

Rey Carlos III This modern, 87-room property, with a swimming pool and restaurant, overlooks the harbor at Villacarlos, only a short walk to the port area that is one of the nightlife centers of Minorca. Closed November through April. Miranda de Cala Corp, Villacarlos (phone: 71-363100; fax: 71-363108).

S'Algar A sprawling low building in the middle of the S'Algar resort development on the coast southeast of Mahón and Villacarlos. The 106 rooms have a bungalow feel, with most opening onto a garden area. There is a pool and a restaurant. Closed November through March. Urbanización S'Algar, San Luis (phone: 71-151700; fax: 71-350465).

San Jaime An apartment hotel that's only about 300 yards from the longest beach on the island, Playa Son Bou. Each of the more than 150 apartments has at least one bedroom; there's also a restaurant, 3 pools, and a tennis court. The beach is very quiet — any nightlife entails a half-hour drive. Closed late October through April. Urbanización San Jaime, Playa Son Bou, Alayor (phone: 71-372000).

Sol Club Falco This is a village complex at the far southwest corner of the island. A self-contained resort, it offers accommodations in a series of bungalows, several restaurants and pools, and nightlife, all a short walk from the sea. Closed from November through April. Reservations by the week are preferred. Playa de Son Xoriguer, Cala'n Bosch (phone: 71-384623).

INEXPENSIVE

Hotel del Almirante This Victorian mansion (also known as *Collingwood House*) offers an excellent view of Mahón's port. The 38 rooms are simple but comfortable, and the whole place exudes the mood of a relaxed English country weekend retreat. There are also a number of poolside bungalows for rent, as well as a restaurant on the premises. Closed November through April. Fonduco Puerto de Mahón (phone: 71-362700).

Royal The rooms in this 34-unit apartment hotel are all 1-bedroom with foldout couches. There are a cafeteria and bar downstairs, as well as a swimming pool, and it is only a 5-minute walk to the center of Mahón. 131 Calle del Carmen, Mahón (phone: 71-369534).

EATING OUT

Expect to pay $50 and up for a meal for two including appetizer, main course, dessert, and wine in restaurants listed as expensive; between $25 and $50 at places described as moderate; and between $20 and $25 at inexpensive spots. Because the island economy is extremely seasonal, be sure to call restaurants to make sure they are open, especially off season.

EXPENSIVE

Ca'n Aguedet Perhaps Minorca's best restaurant for Minorcan cooking. In the center of the island, it's family run and quietly elegant, with whitewashed walls and wicker furniture. For appetizers, sample the eggplant stuffed with shrimp or the stuffed onions, then enjoy the peppers stuffed with fish or the rabbit with figs. Open daily. Reservations necessary on weekends. Major credit cards accepted. 23 Calle Lepanto, Mercadal (phone: 71-375391).

Ca's Quintu In the center of Ciudadela, this is a good, simple place serving dishes ranging from fish to Minorcan specialties; try the grilled crayfish. Open daily except for the last 2 weeks in November. Reservations unnecessary. No credit cards accepted. 4 Plaza Alfonso III, Ciudadela (phone: 71-381002).

Casa Manolo The premier fish restaurant in Ciudadela, located at the far end of the port with a great view back to the town. The fish is as fresh and the prices are as high as can be found on the island. Open daily except Sundays in the winter and from December 10 through January 10. Reservations necessary. Major credit cards accepted. 117-121 Marina, Puerto, Ciudadela (phone: 71-380003).

Jágaro In the port area of Mahón, it is closed in by French doors, with lush green plants separating the tables. Definitely upscale, but not too overpriced; the chef is proudest of his fresh fish, either grilled or with sauces. Open daily. Reservations advised. Major credit cards accepted. 334 Moll de Llevant, Mahón (phone: 71-364660/362390).

MODERATE

Ca'n Delio A favorite among the cluster of several similar restaurants set on the romantic Villacarlos harbor, which crawls with tourists during the summer and is locked tighter than a drum from November through March. Reservations advised. No credit cards accepted. 39 Muelle Cala Fons, Villacarlos (phone: 71-369971).

Jardin Marivent A marvelous terrace overlooking the harbor recommends it. The upstairs dining room is used mainly in winter. Try any fish specialty. Closed Mondays in summer, Sundays and at lunch on Mondays in winter. Reservations advised. No credit cards accepted. 314 Moll de Llevant, Mahón (phone: 71-369067).

Moli Des Raco Housed in a converted windmill in Mercadal, on the main road between Mahón and Ciudadela, the Minorcan cooking here is exceptionally popular with locals and plates are heaped with food. Try the lamb or the rabbit and the local wine. Open daily. Reservations necessary. American Express and Visa accepted. 53 Mayor, Mercadal (phone: 71-375392).

Pilar Minorcan specialties in the center of Mahón. This is a tiny eatery, and on most nights its dozen tables are filled with islanders lingering over lamb with parsnips and snails with mayonnaise. Closed Mondays. Reservations unnecessary. American Express and Visa accepted. 61 Forn, Mahón (phone: 71-366817).

INEXPENSIVE

Bar España The gathering place for the town of Villacarlos, and a good part of Mahón as well. Wide open and crowded even in winter, it offers the most reasonable meals on the island — a bit of everything from steaks and veal to fried squid and steamed mussels. The din remains through the evening. Open daily. Reservations unnecessary. No credit cards accepted. 50 Calle Victori, Villacarlos (phone: 71-363299).

Los Bucaneros The most famous of the *chiringuitos* (covered beach restaurants), where crowds eat at long tables just off the sand, it's on the beach in Binibeca, south of Mahón. Great, fresh food is the fare; there is no need for dining protocol. Open in summer only. Reservations unnecessary. No credit cards accepted. Playa de Binibeca (no phone).

Es Caliu Hewn beams, stone walls, the sounds and smells of meat searing over an open fire, and rafters hung with gourds, garlic, and hams combine to make this an all-encompassing dining experience. Try the fried peppers as an appetizer before a choice of either steaks or chops. In winter, open only on weekends. Reservations unnecessary. No credit cards accepted. South of Ciudadela, on the road to Cala Blanca (phone: 71-380165).

Ibiza

The third-largest of the Balearic Islands (about 25 miles east to west and 12 miles north to south) lives up to its reputation as the jet set playground of Europe. Before the 1950s and 1960s, when this once-obscure island began to evolve into an international artists' colony and concourse for the counterculture, word of its existence had hardly seeped beyond the borders of Spain. Then it became almost a household word — and today the island is home away from home to artists and pseudo-artists, movie stars, rock stars, and fashion designers. While Majorca's tourist industry has been leveling off of late, business in Ibiza is booming. The population (about 25,000 year-round) of its capital, Ibiza town, increases nearly tenfold in summer, so don't even think of alighting here in high season without a confirmed and reconfirmed hotel reservation. The hippie nomads of only a decade ago have been replaced by both the young rich and the packaged traveler, and the resulting mix has made the island so cosmopolitan it is virtually impossible to label it Spanish.

The Greeks referred to Ibiza and its southern neighbor, Formentera, as the pine-clad islands. Except for the addition of almond, olive, fig, and other fruit trees, the reference still holds. But Ibiza is also known as the Isla Blanca (White Island), thanks to the brilliance of its square, flat-roofed houses, typically Arabic in style and religiously whitewashed each spring. The local architecture reflects a close affinity to North Africa, a legacy not only of 300 years of Moorish rule, but also of 500 years of colonization by the Carthaginians.

Ibiza town (also known as Eivissa) occupies a hill next to a natural harbor on the southeast coast. The two other main towns are San Antonio Abad (Sant Antoni Abat in the local language) and Santa Eulalia del Río (Santa Eularia del Rio). The former, on a natural harbor, is the epicenter of packaged tourism on the island, with a frenetic nightlife. The latter is a pleasant, quieter resort town at the mouth of the Balearic Islands' only river.

Ibiza's beaches range from those that are backed with hotels and packed with the tourists to stretches of fine white sand lining deserted coves. Beach buses and boats connect the more popular ones to town; a car or a yacht or even a pedal boat allows travelers to discover the more secluded ones. The beaches closest to Ibiza town are Playa Talamanca to the north and Playa Figueretas and Playa d'en Bossa to the south, but anyone seeking to avoid the crowds keeps on riding to Las Salinas, the salt flats farther south, where the beaches include Playa Cavallet, one of the island's official nudist strands — although there is some shedding of bathing suits nearly everywhere. Similarly, the hotels of San Antonio Abad hold many more people than can be accommodated on Playa San Antonio, but within easy reach by bus or boat are the beaches of Port des Torrent, Cala Bassa, Cala Conta, and Cala Tarida, all southwest of town. The beach at Santa Eulalia del Río is also unimpressive, but Playa Llonga to the south and the beaches that stretch northward — Playa d'es Cana, Cala Nova, Cala Lena — are some of the best on the island. Along the north coast are the beaches at the resort development of Portinatx and at Puerto de San Miguel.

GETTING AROUND

AIRPORT Most visitors arrive by air, aboard both regularly scheduled and charter flights that link the island with mainland Spain and, during the summer, with virtually every major city in Europe. *Aviaco* and *Iberia* fly in from mainland Spain; *Aviaco* also provides daily flights from Palma de Mallorca. Ibiza Airport (phone: 71-300300), 5 miles (8 km) southwest of Ibiza town, is equipped to handle jumbo jets and is within a half-hour's drive of virtually every hotel on the island. The *Iberia* office is at 34 Av. de España (phone: 71-300954).

BUS The main bus terminal in Ibiza town is on Avenida Isidoro Macabich. Buses link Ibiza town with San Antonio Abad and Santa Eulalia del Río every half hour during the day. Buses to Portinatx, San Miguel, and the inland villages of San Juan Bautista and San José leave once or twice a day.

CAR RENTAL A rented car is the recommended form of transportation. *Avis* has offices at the airport (phone: 71-302949 or 71-302488) and elsewhere on the island (Rincón Verde, Portinatx; phone: 71-333068; Av. Dr. Fleming, San Antonio; phone: 71-341034; and Apartamentos S'Arenal, Portinatx; phone: 71-333186). *Hertz* has an airport office (phone: 71-300542 or 71-307290) and offices at two other locations (Marina Botafoch, Puerto Deportivo; phone: 71-316723; and Area Servicio, Es Codolar; phone: 71-307822).

FERRY *Trasmediterránea* (see "Ferry" in *Getting There*) connects Ibiza town's Estación Marítima (phone: 71-314513) with Barcelona (9½ hours), Valencia (7 hours), and Palma (4½ hours); there is also a hydrofoil between Alicante and Ibiza (a 2¾-hour trip) and, in summer only, between Palma and Ibiza (a 2-hour trip). Ferries from Barcelona run daily from mid-June to mid-September and then 4 or 5 days a week, depending on the month; ferries from Valencia to Ibiza run once or twice a week. The same company operates a hydrofoil service from Alicante to Ibiza daily year-round. Interisland service links Palma, Majorca, and Ibiza twice a week year-round by normal steamer, and daily in summer by hydrofoil. Ferries to Formentera, operated by *Marítima de Formentera* (phone: 71-320157) and *Transportes Marítimos Pitiusos* (*Transmapi;* Av. Santa Eularia; phone: 71-314486) leave from Ibiza town year-round and take about an hour. *Flebasa* (see "Ferry" in *Getting There*), connects Denia on the mainland (between Valencia and Alicante) with Ibiza, docking at San Antonio Abad rather than at Ibiza town. Departures are daily year-round, and the trip takes 3 hours.

TAXI Taxis operate on a system of fixed destination charges. In Ibiza town, the main taxi stands are on Paseo Vara de Rey (phone: 71-301794) and at Playa de Ses Figueretas (phone: 71-301676). In San Antonio Abad, call 71-340074; in Santa Eulalia del Río, 71-330063.

SPECIAL PLACES

IBIZA Sightseeing on Ibiza really means observing the passing scene, although the island does have its complement of more conventional sights. Most are in the capital, which is divided into a medieval upper town, the Dalt Vila, and a lower town that, at least in the area around the harbor, dates mainly from the mid-19th century. In the lower town, the Barrio de Sa Penya, stretching east from the Estación Marítima, is the fishermen's quarter, full of shops, restaurants, bars, and a lively nightlife. The Marina district to the west of it is the business district, with more shops, restaurants, and bars. Ibiza's main street, Paseo Vara de Rey (the tourist office is at No. 13; phone: 71-301900), is on the western reaches of this district, and still farther west stretch the newer zones of the city, brought about by the boom in tourism.

Dalt Vila is picturesque and compact, an oasis of calm far removed from the hubbub of the rest of the island. An ancient cathedral crowns it, and 16th-century walls that have been declared a national monument enclose it. Enter by the main gateway, the Portal de las Tablas, flanked by Roman statues, and climb the winding cobblestone streets to the cathedral, Santa María de las Nieves, built during the 13th century and restored early in the 18th century. The panoramic view from the terrace is the best in town.

Also in Plaza de la Catedral is the *Museo Arqueológico* (phone: 71-301771), which contains items unearthed on Ibiza and Formentera and is one of the most important museums of Punic (Carthaginian) artifacts in Spain — and in the world. All exhibit identification and information is in Spanish only. The museum is open daily from 10 AM to 1 PM and from 4 to 7 PM; admission charge. Another Dalt Vila museum — the *Museo de Arte Contemporáneo* (Ronda Pintor Narcís Puget; phone: 71-302723) — displays contemporary Spanish paintings and sculpture. It's open from 11 AM to 1 PM and from 6 to 9 PM during summer months, and from 5 to 7 PM winter months; closed Sundays and holidays; admission charge. Visitors whose appetite for pre-Christian artifacts has not been sated should head down to the lower town and to the west of Dalt Vila, to the Punic necropolis of Puig des Molins (Windmill Hill). Because the Carthaginians considered the soil of Ibiza to be especially good for burial purposes, they buried their dead from other colonies here as well, and this necropolis was the largest of several on the island. More than 4,000 tombs were carved into the hillside, and although the graves were pillaged over the centuries, scientific excavations yielded enough to stock the *Museo Monográfico del Puig des Molins,* at the bottom of the hill (31 Vía Romana; phone: 71-301771). The museum is open daily from 10 AM to noon and from 4 to 7 PM. The admission charge includes a visit to the necropolis.

SAN ANTONIO ABAD This former fishing village is now the home of most of the resort development on Ibiza. It's set on a beautiful bay, overlooking an uninhabited rock island, Isla Conejera. Most of the town is a product of the tourist boom, but its 14th-century parish church is the island's second-oldest.

SANTA EULALIA DEL RÍO The much photographed fortress-church, set on a hilltop, is the town's main monument. Built during the 16th century, it contains an ornate Gothic altar screen.

NIGHTCLUBS AND NIGHTLIFE

Never dull, Ibiza's nightlife begins with the nightly *paseo* in Ibiza town, when all those who have spent the day naked or nearly so on the beaches play dress up. Tourist office literature refers to Ibiza's "ad-lib" fashion —

male, female, and unisex — as full of gaiety, freedom, and fun. In truth, the nightly parade of wild and colorful costumes creates almost a carnival atmosphere. Then there are the discos. Ibiza's discos are among the liveliest anywhere, and entire groups of people move from one hot spot to another as the night works its way toward day. Among the largest and best-known discos is *KU* (Carretera Ibiza–San Antonio, Km 6, in San Rafael; phone: 71-314474), which is mainly open-air, with a giant swimming pool set in front of the stage. Name a group and it has probably played here. *Pachá* (Paseo Marítimo in Ibiza town; phone: 71-313612) is not as large as *KU,* but it still holds 2,500 on two dance floors; it opens at midnight. *Amnesia San Rafael* (Carretera Ibiza–San Antonio, Km 5; phone: 71-314136) is for those who still have not had enough after *KU* and *Pachá* have emptied out between 5 and 6 AM. *Gloria's* (Carretera Ibiza–San Antonio, Km 1.5) doesn't even open its doors until 4 AM. There are also scores of bars in Ibiza town, in San Antonio, and in the back streets of Santa Eulalia, where the loud music and the exotically dressed crowds spill out into the streets. A final alternative is the *Casino de Ibiza* (Paseo Marítimo; phone: 71-304850), open from 10 PM to 5 AM.

CHECKING IN

The prices listed below are those charged for a double room during the high season, from June through September and at *Christmas* and *Easter*. Low-season rates can be 25% lower. Expect to pay more than $190 for a double in a hotel listed as very expensive; from $110 to $190 for a double in a hotel listed as expensive; from $55 to $110 in a moderate hotel; and less than $55 a night in an inexpensive one.

VERY EXPENSIVE

Hacienda Na Xamena The ultimate in luxury, this Relais & Châteaux member is isolated in its own world, with views that would inspire an eagle. Set atop a cliff in the northern part of the island, 4 miles (6 km) northwest of San Miguel, this 54-room aerie in white Arabic style has indoor and outdoor swimming pools and tennis courts. The 4th floor restaurant with terraces features — aside from superb food — a splendid bird's-eye view of the beach and village of Puerto de San Miguel and of the pine-forested hills. Closed from November through March. San Juan Bautista (phone: 71-333046; fax: 71-333175).

EXPENSIVE

Pikes In the country, a little over a mile (about 1.6 km) south of San Antonio, the 20 rooms here are individually decorated, but each has a terrace, telephone, and air conditioning. Many of the international stars performing at Ibiza's discos stay here. There is a swimming pool, a tennis court, a poolside bar, and a good restaurant (see *Eating Out*). Closed from late October or mid-November to mid-February or late March, depending on bookings. Children 11 and under must be accompanied by a nanny. Carretera Sa Vorera, Km 12, San Antonio Abad (phone: 71-342222; fax: 71-342312).

Royal Plaza The best hotel in the town center, it has 117 rooms, a rooftop swimming pool, and a bar and coffee shop. 27-29 Calle Pedro Francés, Ibiza (phone: 71-310000).

El Corsario This *hostal* is in the midst of the old section of Ibiza town, with 14 rooms, good views, and a newly renovated restaurant. 5 Calle Poniente, Dalt Vila, Ibiza (phone: 71-301248).

Reco des Sol A reasonable alternative to expensive accommodations in San Antonio, this is a well-run *hostal* with 89 rooms and virtually every amenity, including a pool and a bar/cafeteria. Closed from November through April. 16 Vedra, San Antonio Abad (phone: 71-341104).

Ses Savines It's right on the beach and in the thick of the San Antonio nightlife, with a self-service restaurant, a swimming pool, tennis, and 133 rooms normally packed with British tourists. Playa San Antonio, San Antonio Abad (phone: 71-340066).

EATING OUT

Expect to pay $50 and up for a meal for two including appetizer, main course, dessert, and wine in restaurants listed as expensive; and between $25 and $50 at places described as moderate. Because the island economy is extremely seasonal, be sure to call restaurants to make sure they are open, especially off-season.

Pikes In the hotel of the same name are three unique dining rooms furnished with antiques, plus a terraced garden. The sophisticated yet informal atmosphere and the fact that the restaurant is a bit off the beaten track are some of the reasons why virtually every celebrity who visits the island seems to eat here. The menu is international; try the stuffed smoked salmon in avocado sauce or the hake in a wine cream sauce. Open daily. Reservations essential. Major credit cards accepted. Carretera Sa Vorera, San Antonio Abad (phone: 71-342222 or 71-343511).

Sa Punta The atmosphere here is almost that of a greenhouse. Right on the beach at Santa Eulalia, it serves fresh fish and delicious crunchy vegetables. Closed Sunday evenings, Mondays, and from mid-January through February. Reservations advised. Major credit cards accepted. 36 Calle Isidoro Macabich, Santa Eulalia del Río (phone: 71-330033).

Ca'n Pujol Right on the beach, it serves great seafood and paella. Closed Wednesdays and December. No credit cards accepted. Playa Port des Torrent, San Antonio Abad (phone: 71-341407).

El Naranjo On Santa Eulalia's restaurant row, it is an island favorite. Try the duck with red currants and pepper sauce. Closed Mondays and from mid-December to mid-March. Reservations necessary. Major credit cards accepted. 31 Calle San José, Santa Eulalia del Río (phone: 71-330324).

S'Oficina In the heart of Ibiza town, serving excellent Basque cooking. The fish is good, but for a change of pace, try the beef. Closed Sundays and from mid-December to mid-January. Reservations advised. Major credit cards accepted. 6 Av. de España, Ibiza (phone: 71-300016).

Formentera

The sea is visible from every point on Formentera, which is nearly flat as a pancake except for a lump — the 630-foot-high La Mola "mountain" — at its eastern extremity. Made up of two islets joined by an isthmus, the island measures only about 12 miles from end to end. Ferries arrive at La Sabina, the island harbor, which is on the north coast between two lagoons, Estang de Peix and Estang Pudent (which translate as "fish" and "stinky" lagoon, respectively). The cluster of sparkling white houses down the road from the port is San Francisco Javier, the capital, home to less than half the island's population of 4,500. The next-largest village is San Fernando, 1¼ miles (2 km) to the east. The rest of the island consists of pine forests and salt flats, generously fringed with beaches — Playa de Mitjorn, on the southern coast and 3 miles long, is long enough to escape being crowded. Others include Playa d'Es Pujols, north of San Fernando, which attracts a certain amount of business from package tours; Playa de Ses Illetas and Playa de Llevant, on either side of the Trocadors peninsula, which stretches north from La Sabina; and Cala Sahona, on the western side of the island, still reasonably remote.

The Carthaginians are known to have worked the salt pans, but they left no trace of settlement on the island. The Romans left it its name, a corruption of the Latin Frumentaria — from *frumentum*, or "wheat" — since Formentera served as a granary for the Roman camp on Ibiza. The Arabs were here, too, but when they left after the Reconquest, the island was uninhabited for much of the Middle Ages, due to fear of the marauding pirates who regularly sought refuge from the rough seas on its defenseless shores. Late in the 17th century homesteaders from Ibiza settled; today, their descendants fish, work the fields and the salt pans, and cater to tourists. But Formentera is more tranquil than the other three Balearic Islands and is likely to remain so, since a shortage of fresh water limits development. There are numerous small *hostales* and a couple of large hotels, but they're heavily booked, so anyone planning to stay the night should be sure to have a reservation.

Ferry service from Ibiza town to the Estación Marítima in La Sabina (phone: 71-322703) is frequent, with two lines — *Marítima de Formentera* and *Transportes Marítimos Pitiusos* (*Transmapi*) — providing up to 11 round-trips daily, year-round. A great many visitors, therefore, come over only for the day. One proviso, however: Although the ride across the Es Freus Channel is short (about 1 hour), it's not necessarily sweet, as the sea can be rough and the currents strong. Because ferries are sometimes canceled, make allowance for possible lost time if there's a plane to catch. Taxis line the pier when ferries arrive; they are reasonable, with an entire island tour costing under $20. The island does have bus service, but renting a car or a moped is preferable. *Autos Ibiza,* located in both Ibiza town (phone: 71-314611) and in La Sabina on Formentera (phone: 71-322031), is one of many companies represented. Formentera's Tourist Office (phone: 71-322032), open mornings only, is located in San Francisco Javier.

CHECKING IN

The prices quoted below are those charged during the high season, June through September and *Christmas* and *Easter*. During the low season, prices are generally 25% lower. Expect to pay more than $110 for a double in a hotel listed as expensive, and between $55 and $110 for a double in a moderate hotel.

EXPENSIVE

Iberotel Club la Mola This 328-room resort complex provides the best accommodations on the island, right on its longest beach. Built in Spanish village-style, it offers rooms as well as independent villas, and is equipped with 2 swimming pools, facilities for a variety of water sports, tennis courts, a restaurant, a bar, and a discotheque. Closed from late October through early May. Playa de Mitjorn (phone: 71-328069).

MODERATE

Sa Volta A small *hostal* (18 rooms) near the beach, in the midst of the hottest nightlife on this quiet island. It has no pool, but there's a restaurant. Playa d'Es Pujols (phone: 71-320120).

EATING OUT

Expect to pay anywhere from $25 to more than $50 for a meal for two at the place listed below.

Es Muli des Sal A small eatery on the sand dunes in the northern part of the island; the fresh fish and lobsters are mouth-watering. Open daily. Reservations unnecessary. American Express and Visa accepted. Playa Ses Illetas (no phone).

The Canary Islands

A cluster of seven major and six minor islands in the Atlantic Ocean, the Canary Island archipelago lies about 65 miles off the northwest coast of Africa. The Canaries are aptly called the Fortunate Isles. Bathed by the Gulf Stream and ruffled by the trade winds, they are spread out in a line only about 4° north of the Tropic of Cancer, at roughly the same latitude as Florida, and enjoy a spring-like climate throughout the year — with temperatures mostly in the 70s F. Extremes of heat and cold are unknown in this Spanish archipelago, where European, African, and American influences mingle.

Yet physical contrasts are dramatic, from verdant tropical vegetation to Dantesque, lava-covered lunar landscapes; from towering, snow-capped mountains to rolling desert dunes; from ultramodern tourism complexes to quaint, whitewashed hamlets and recondite valleys populated with tertiary-era flora and fauna. The Canaries attract an ever-increasing number of tourists, but most never venture far from the beaches, leaving the rugged wonders of the islands for more intrepid souls.

There are 13 islands, but only Grand Canary (Gran Canaria in Spanish), Tenerife, Fuerteventura, Lanzarote, La Gomera, El Hierro, and La Palma are of any significant size. Born of volcanic eruptions millions of years ago, the Canaries are dotted with hundreds of volcanoes, and one or two are still smoldering. Because of variations in altitude and climate, some islands have justly been described as miniature continents. On the heights, the vegetation is alpine, and includes Canary pine and broom. On the lower slopes, irrigation of the rich volcanic soils produces an astonishing abundance of tropical and semitropical fruits. Scorching African winds from the Sahara create desert conditions on the easternmost islands of Lanzarote and Fuerteventura, as well as along the eastern coasts of Grand Canary and Tenerife. But lofty volcanic peaks block clouds rolling in from the ocean and create damp, luxuriant conditions elsewhere.

The Canary Islands have piqued the imagination of man since the beginning of recorded history. Homer spoke of them as a privileged kingdom devoid of winter, and Herodotus identified them as the site of the mythical garden of Hesperides (where Atlas stood supporting the weight of the heavens). Plato believed the islands were the remains of the mythical lost continent of Atlantis, and Ptolemy, the 2nd-century geographer, situated his first meridian — 0° longitude — at El Hierro, the most remote of the islands.

When the Spanish attempted to take the islands in the 15th century, they faced fierce resistance from the original inhabitants, the Guanche cave dwellers, who were not conquered until 1496. Little is known about where the Guanche people came from or how. Shepherds and rudimentary farmers, they practiced a cult of the dead, developing a complicated mummification process similar to that used in Egypt. Carvings at the Belmaco Cave in La Palma, yet to be deciphered, promise to reveal much more about this fascinating people. The Guanche who were not killed off by disease, famine, volcanic eruptions, or slavery were absorbed into the Spanish culture. Some of the local people retain the physical characteristics of their forebears (they were tall, fair-skinned, and light-haired), and traces of their existence remain all over the archipelago in the form of ceramics and leather artifacts, geometric cave paintings, mummies, remnants of their language (such place-names as Timanfaya and Tenerife were inherited from the Guanche) and traditions, and their food. Today's islanders have a newly awakened interest in their ancestors, in reaction to what they often feel is neglect from distant Madrid. From time to time, throughout the islands, slogans appear on posters and walls saying *"Godos* go home!" — *Godo,* meaning "Goth" (as in Visigoth), is the islanders' pejorative name for a mainland Spaniard.

For most of their early history, the islands depended on agriculture as the mainstay of their economy, with *malvasía* (malmsey) liquor gaining wide favor in European courts during the 16th century. During the 18th and 19th centuries, sugarcane, muscatel wine, and the cochineal insect brought wealth to the Canaries. The dye obtained from the insect, which lives off the islands' cacti, was exported in large quantities to Britain and France until the invention of artificial colorings. Later, the Canaries prospered with bananas, potatoes, tomatoes, and tobacco. For a long time, trade was monopolized by British firms, which also made the towns of Las Palmas on Grand Canary and Santa Cruz de Tenerife on Tenerife important coaling stations for their ships.

Wealthy Europeans began spending winters in the Canaries during the late 19th century. Today, 5 million tourists visit the islands annually, and although the islands have more than 300,000 hotel beds, it can be extremely difficult to get a room in the better resorts during high season, from December through *Easter.*

The Canary archipelago is one of Spain's 17 autonomous communities. But since 1927, the islands have been split into two provinces, and there is ongoing rivalry between the ports of Las Palmas and Santa Cruz de Tenerife. Las Palmas is the provincial capital of the eastern islands: Grand Canary (the most populated), Fuerteventura (a virtual desert), and Lanzarote (which has the most impressive volcanic scenery). Santa Cruz de Tenerife is the capital of the western group: Tenerife (the largest island), La Palma (the green island), La Gomera, and El Hierro. The archipelago has its own parliament, and each island has its own *cabildo* (council) to look after local affairs.

A mixture of cultures influences Canarian food, which tends to be hearty and simple. *Gofio,* a filling paste made of flour, water, and milk, comes from the Guanche and is an island staple. *Sancocho canario* is fresh fish cooked with both sweet and regular potatoes and served with kneaded *gofio* and *mojo,* an essential Canarian seasoning made with oil, vinegar, garlic, salt, and various spices, such as paprika, coriander, and pepper. *Mojo picón* is a hot seasoning made with peppers; watch out, because it's ubiquitous, and its benign aroma belies its true, incendiary nature. *Papas arrugadas* (literally, wrinkled potatoes), boiled potatoes cooked in their skins and served with *mojo,* are a popular snack. Some of the world's richest fishing grounds lie between the Canaries and the African coast, a plentitude that yields such specialties as stuffed *chicharros* (mackerel) and Tenerife-style *cazuela canaria,* a delectable casserole of fresh or salted fish. Common meat dishes include roast chicken in banana cream, tender roasted kid, and wild boar from Gomera. Most red meat is served with *salmorejo,* a sauce of vinegar, garlic, and assorted spices. Vegetable dishes and stews are usually made with *bubangos* (marrow), cabbage, and watercress.

The tropical and subtropical climate of some of the islands has produced such fresh fruit as avocados, bananas, mangoes, cherimoyas, and papayas. Equally enticing are the desserts, including *frangollo,* a sweet made of corn, milk, and honey, and *gofio turrón,* a nougat candy. Cheese aficionados have a wide variety of cured, raw, and smoked goat and sheep cheeses from which to choose. Meals are often rounded off with *ronmiel,* a punch made of distilled sugarcane and palm sap; *mistela,* coffee laced with sugar and brandy; banana liquor; or the renowned malmsey liquor, which can be a young *verde* (green), *púrpura* (purple-red), *seco* (dry), or *dulce* (sweet), depending on the harvesting period.

Today's Canary Islanders make their living farming, fishing, and producing handicrafts — as well as by working at various jobs in the modern resort developments. They speak Spanish with a musical accent reminiscent of Latin America, a region to which many Canarians have emigrated over the years. Their folk music also has a Latin American rhythm; folk groups play flutes, drums, guitars, and the *timple,* a small stringed instrument. Visitors to the Canary Islands will be charmed not only by the rich tapestry of music, landscape, history, and gastronomy but also by the warm inhabitants.

Sources and Resources

TOURIST INFORMATION

The regional Oficina de Turismo for the Canary Islands is headquartered on the island of Grand Canary (Plaza Ramón Franco in the Parque Santa Catalina, Las Palmas; phone: 28-264623) and is open Mondays through Fridays from 9 AM to 1:30 PM and 5 to 7 PM, Saturdays from 9 AM to 1 PM. The Grand Canary Patronato de Turismo office is centrally located (17 Calle León y Castillo; phone: 28-362222) near the historic Vegueta neighborhood. The new Playa del Inglés Centro Insular de Turismo (corner of Avenida Estados Unidos and Avenida de España; phone: 28-767848) serves as both a tourist information office and a cultural center. Open Mondays through Saturdays from 9 AM to 1 PM and from 4 to 9 PM. Tenerife's tourist office (Plaza de España Bajos del Palacio Insular, Santa Cruz de Tenerife; phone: 22-605586/90) is open Mondays through Fridays from 8 AM to 5:45 PM and Saturdays from 9 AM to 1 a second office (3 Plaza de la Iglesia, Puerto de la Cruz; phone: 22-386000 or 22-384328) is open Mondays through Fridays from 9 AM to 7 and Saturdays from 10 AM to 2 PM. The Patronato de Turismo on Fuerteventura (33 Calle Uno de Mayo, Puerto del Rosario; phone: 28-851024) is open Mondays through Fridays from 9 AM to 2 PM and 4 to 7 PM. The Lanzarote Tourist Office (in the Parque Municipal, Arrecife; phone: 28-913792) is open Mondays through Fridays from 8 AM to 2:30 PM and 5:30 to 7 PM. The La Palma Patronato de Turismo (3 Paseo Marítima, Santa Cruz de La Palma; phone: 22-411641) is open Mondays through Fridays from 8 AM to 3 PM and Saturdays from 9 AM to 1 PM. The El Hierro Patronato de Turismo (1 Calle Licenciado Bueno, Valverde; phone: 22-550078) is open Mondays through Fridays from 8 AM to 5 PM. La Gomera's Tourist Office (20 Calle del Medio, San Sebastián; phone: 22-870752) is open weekdays from 9 AM to 5 PM.

LOCAL COVERAGE Three daily newspapers are published in Las Palmas: *Canarias 7*, *Diario*, and *La Provincia*. In Santa Cruz de Tenerife, *El Día*, *Diario de Avisos*, *La Gaceta de Canarias*, and *Jornada* are also published daily. Newsstands throughout the islands carry a wide range of foreign newspapers and magazines, many of which arrive on the day of publication. A number of English-language publications cater to the needs of tourists and expatriate residents. *Canarias Tourist*, a monthly periodical, is sold on the major islands; published in several languages, it offers information on sights and services. The *Canary Islands Holiday Times*, which provides tourist information in English, German, and Swedish, is published three times a year. *Tenerife Today* provides similar information on Tenerife. The *Island Gazette*, a monthly magazine long published on Tenerife and aimed mainly at long-term visitors and residents, also includes information on Grand Canary. On Lanzarote, the monthly magazine *Lancelot* serves the English-speaking community.

TELEPHONE

The area code for the islands of Grand Canary, Fuerteventura, and Lanzarote is 28. If calling from mainland Spain (or from the Santa Cruz de Tenerife province), dial "9" before the area code and the local number. The area code for the islands of Tenerife, La Palma, La Gomera, and El Hierro is 22. If calling from mainland Spain (or from the Las Palmas province), dial 922 before the local number. The telephone numbers listed in this chapter include area codes; no area code is necessary when dialing within an island or between islands of the same province. Note that the time in the Canaries is 1 hour earlier than on mainland Spain all year.

CLIMATE

The Canaries are subtropical islands situated just above the Tropic of Cancer. They have an agreeable climate year-round, with temperatures ranging from 67 to 83F. Even in the winter, it is rarely necessary to wear more than a sweater in the evening. On Grand Canary and Tenerife, the northern and eastern ends of the islands receive more rain than the mostly arid western and southern regions; the high humidity and heat can make Las Palmas very uncomfortable in August. The more low-lying Lanzarote and Fuerteventura have a desert-like climate, while La Palma's greenness testifies to its higher amount of rainfall.

GETTING THERE

AIRPLANE The Canaries are linked to the Spanish mainland by frequent air service and regular ferry service. *Iberia Airlines* and its associated commuter lines fly direct to the Canaries from several mainland cities, including Barcelona, Madrid, Málaga, and Seville. Frequent daily inter-island flights are provided by *Iberia* and *Binter,* the Canaries' regional carrier. Air traffic is heavy during the peak tourist season (between December and *Easter*); plane reservations should be made well in advance.

FERRY *Trasmediterránea* (26-27 Av. Ramón de Carranza, Cádiz; phone: 56-284311; and 2 Calle Pedro Muñoz Seca, Madrid; phone: 1-431-0700) operates passenger and vehicle ferries several times a week between Cádiz and Santa Cruz de Tenerife, Las Palmas on Grand Canary, and Arrecife on Lanzarote. The trip from Cádiz to Tenerife takes about 36 hours and costs a minumum of $100 per person, one way. *Trasmediterránea* also has frequent inter-island ferry and hydrofoil service. On the islands, *Trasmediterránea* maintains two offices (at 59 Calle de la Marina, Santa Cruz de Tenerife; phone: 22-277300; and at Muelle Ribera Oeste, Las Palmas; phone: 28-267766).

SPECIAL EVENTS

Camels, bands, and lavishly dressed islanders participate in the *Cabalgata de los Tres Reyes* (Cavalcade of the Three Kings), which takes place on January 5 or 6 in several towns throughout the islands, most notably Las Palmas and Santa Cruz de Tenerife. Also celebrated on all the islands with astonishing exuberance is February's *Carnaval;* Santa Cruz de Tenerife and Las Palmas compete to outdo each other with dazzling and outrageous parades, costumes, and nonstop music and dancing. *Semana Santa* (Holy Week), from *Palm Sunday* through *Easter Sunday,* is observed with solemn processions throughout the islands. In addition, each town has a fiesta to honor its patron saint (exact dates can vary from year to year). During the last 2 weeks of April, Tegueste, near La Laguna, Tenerife, combines its *romería* (flower-bedecked oxcart procession) with a show of 15,000 bottles of wine from 20 Spanish bodegas. On Tenerife in June, carpets of flowers are arranged on the streets of La Laguna and La Orotava for *Corpus Christi* processions. Early in May, the *Día de la Cruz* (Day of the Cross) is the occasion for one of the year's most lighthearted fiestas, particularly on the island of El Hierro. During September, San Sebastián on La Gomera holds its *Semana de Colón* (Columbus Week) celebrations (commemorating his passage through the islands in 1492, the first stop on his historic voyage of discovery to the New World). September 8 is a big day on Grand Canary, when a colorful procession pays homage to Nuestra Señora del Pino (Our Lady of the Pine) in Teror. The port town of Puerto de la Cruz in Tenerife hosts an annual ecological film festival during the third week of November. Once every 5 years, La Palma holds its *Fiestas Lustrales,* a 2-week festival in Santa Cruz de la Palma held in honor of *Nuestra Señora de las Nieves (Our Lady of the Snows),* in which the highlight is the *Danza de los Enanos* (Dwarfs' Dance); the next celebration will be held in 1995. Finally, Las Palmas hosts the *Festival de Opera* in February and March, and in La Laguna, on Tenerife, the *International Festival of Theater and Dance* takes place from March through May.

SPORTS AND FITNESS

The ideal climate makes the Canary Islands an outdoors lovers' paradise, and a wide range of sports and fitness facilities is available. Spectator sports include the *juego de palo*, a fencing bout in which two contestants jostle one another with large, flexible poles. Awesome pole-jumping feats are accomplished on the island of La Palma, where young men — propelled by 2.5-meter-long poles — hurdle across and over the treacherous countryside at breakneck speed. Another local favorite is *lucha canaria* — a primitive and colorful form of wrestling. Cock fighting is legal and is usually held on Sundays from December to May; the *López Socas Stadium* (Calle Ortiz de Sarate; no phone) is the venue in Las Palmas. Soccer is also popular, and anyone watching a clash between Santa Cruz de Tenerife and Las Palmas may wonder whether this isn't a blood sport, too. Those seeking a good corrida, however, have come to the wrong place: Bullfighting was officially banned in the Canary Islands in 1991.

BOATING The Canaries have a variety of well-equipped marinas; a number of yachtsmen use the islands as a starting point for their transatlantic crossings. Lateen sailing is a Canarian specialty, and regular regattas are held in the summer. Grand Canary's yachting clubs include the *Real Club Náutico de Gran Canaria* (phone: 28-266690 or 28-245202) in Las Palmas, one of Spain's oldest, with a wide range of sports facilities; *Puerto Deportivo de Puerto Rico* (phone: 28-745331), on the southern part of the island, which offers sea excursions and yacht rentals; and *Club de Yates Pasito Blanco* (phone: 28-762259) in Maspalomas.

FISHING Swordfish, stingray, tunny, grouper, conger eel, and giant ray are some of the 1,500 species that thrive in the waters surrounding the Canaries. Craft and equipment rentals are available at most harbors, and fine catches are also possible by casting off the islands' many rock cliffs or beaches. Fishing excursions are organized from Puerto Rico on Grand Canary. *Nautisport* (phone: 22-791459) runs shark fishing trips from Los Cristianos quay on Tenerife (about $40 per person, including lunch and drinks), and daily fishing excursions are organized from Los Gigantes harbor, Santiago de Tiede, in southeast Tenerife (phone: 22-867179 or 22-867332). For deep-sea fishing from Corralejo on Fuerteventura, contact *Escualo* in Jandía (phone: 28-852293) or *Pez Velero* (phone: 28-866173).

GOLF Canary Island golf courses boast challenging conditions amid spectacular and unusual scenery. On Grand Canary, the *Club de Golf Las Palmas* (Carretera de Bandama, Km 5; phone: 28-351050), Spain's oldest golf club, offers beautiful surroundings 9 miles (14 km) south of Las Palmas on the edge of a volcanic crater, while the greens at *Campo de Golf, Maspalomas* (near the *Iberotel Maspalomas Oasis;* phone: 28-762581) are carpeted with Bermuda turf. Tenerife's offerings include the 18-hole championship course (plus another 9 holes) at *Club del Sur* (San Miguel de Abona; phone: 22-704555), laid out around lava fields; the *Club de Golf de Tenerife* (La Laguna; phone: 22-250240); and the *Amarilla Golf and Country Club* (Costa del Silencio, Arona; phone: 22-103422).

HORSEBACK RIDING Horses can be rented from a number of hotels and stables throughout the islands. On Grand Canary, try *Picadero del Club de Golf de Bandama* (Carretera Bandama, Posada; phone: 28-351290) or *Picadero del Oasis de Maspalomas* (Playa de Maspalomas; phone: 28-762378), both in Las Palmas. On Tenerife, the *Amarilla Golf and Country Club* (Costa del Silencio, Arona; phone: 22-103422) has an equestrian center.

JEEP SAFARIS *Unisafari,* on Grand Canary (21 Calle Dr. Grau Bassas, Las Palmas; phone: 28-277100), is one of several companies that run off-road driving safaris through the wilder parts of the islands.

SCUBA DIVING AND SNORKELING The islands boast clear, warm waters and myriad exotic fish. One of the best spots for diving lies between the northern tip of Fuerteventura and the southern tip of Lanzarote, around the Isla de los Lobos. The *Diving Center Miguel Abella Cerdá* (Apartado 8, Corralejo, Fuerteventura; phone: 28-866243) offers a variety of boat trips and scuba courses with English-speaking instructors and dive masters. On Grand Canary, Heinz Lange, a German expatriate dive master, runs a scuba school in Maspalomas (phone: 28-765244); the *Club Sun Sub* (at the *Buenaventura Hotel,* Plaza Ansite, Playa del Inglés; phone: 28-761650, ext.

925) offers a variety of courses and reef trips, as does the *Club Canario de Investigaciones y Actividades Subacuáticas* (67 Calle Pío XII, Las Palmas; phone: 28-246810). On Tenerife, try the *Las Palmeras* hotel (Av. Marítima, Playa de las Américas; phone: 22-790911).

SKY DIVING The strong trade winds that fan the archipelago provide ideal conditions for free-fall and sky diving. The *Paraclub de Gran Canaria* (phone: 28-247393) and the *Escuela Club Tamaran* (phone: 28-243540) specialize in sky diving and free-falls, respectively. Both are located at 244 León y Castillo, Grand Canary.

SUBMARINE EXCURSIONS The clear waters, full of exotic fish, surrounding the Grand Canary port town of Puerto de Mogan are ideal to explore by submarine. Book this underwater adventure via *Undersea S.L.* (389 Puerto de Mogan; phone: 28-565108) or *Top Action* (96 Puerto de Mogan; phone: 28-566146).

SWIMMING AND SUNNING Sunbathing is *the* "sport" of the Canaries, and many of the islands' beaches (those away from the huge resort areas) are as yet virtually untouched by mass tourism. Miles of uncrowded golden sands can be found on Fuerteventura (at the northeastern tip and parts of the southern coast) and Lanzarote (on the southern coast). The most crowded of the islands' beaches are on Grand Canary and Tenerife. Topless bathing is more the rule than the exception, and nude bathing is very common in many of the secluded areas.

TENNIS Most of the islands' larger hotels and resorts have tennis courts, and many new sports-oriented complexes are springing up. Tennis clubs on Grand Canary include the *Club Sun Sub* (*Buenaventura Hotel,* Plaza Ansite, Playa del Inglés; phone: 28-761650, ext. 925); *Club de Tenis Biarritz* (18 Av. de Bonn, San Agustín; phone: 28-760356); and *Club de Tenis Helga Masthoff* (Carretera de los Palmitos, El Tablero; phone: 28-761436). Clubs on Tenerife include the *Club Británico de Juegos* (British Sports Club; Carretera de Taoro, Puerto de la Cruz; phone: 22-384823), and *Oceánico Tenis Club* (Carretera de Fuerteventura, Puerto de la Cruz; phone: 22-380018).

WATER SKIING Water skiing schools operate from the more popular beaches on Grand Canary, Tenerife, and Lanzarote.

WINDSURFING Steady breezes make the Canaries an ideal spot for this increasingly popular sport. Enthusiasts trek here from all over Europe, and the islands have hosted several world championships. Instruction is available and boards can be rented, for about $25 a day, on many of the islands' beaches. Popular Grand Canary windsurfing schools and centers include the *Mistral Windsurfing Club* (at the *Bahía Feliz Hotel,* Playa de Tarajalillo; phone: 28-763332), the *Escuela Territorial de Vela de Puerto Rico* (Puerto Rico; phone: 28-745331), and the *Luis Molina Windsurfing School*

(Playa del Inglés; phone: 28-761524). El Médano Beach, near Reina Sofía Airport on Tenerife, is a favorite windsurfing site; *Looping Windsurf School* (Costa Teguise; phone: 22-815796) is the place to learn how to windsurf on Lanzarote. The beaches at Corralejo, Cotillo, and Jandía are the best spots for riding the wind and the waves off Fuerteventura.

Grand Canary

Grand Canary, the most heavily populated of the Canary Islands, covers only 592 square miles, but it encompasses a variety of landscapes and climates. When it is cool and cloudy along the northern slopes — where tomatoes, potatoes, sugarcane, and bananas flourish — sunbathers will be soaking up the rays on beaches in the cloudless south. At the same time, chill winds may be sweeping over this circular island's 6,400-foot central heights, ruffling the upland forests of laurel, pine, and eucalyptus. Sheer ravines cut into the volcanic mountains of the center, and agriculture flourishes because of intricate irrigation schemes. While ever-increasing numbers of sun-hungry visitors flock to the fine beaches of the southern coast, most of the island's 600,000 inhabitants live in the north in the bustling capital of Las Palmas. Stretched along a strip of seafront at the island's northeastern tip, Las Palmas is the largest city in the archipelago, with 350,000 inhabitants, a major port, a fading tourist resort, and a shopping center.

In the interior of the island, southwest of Las Palmas along narrow, mountain roads, is Tejeda, standing about 4,800 feet above sea level amid a bleak, volcanic landscape. The setting, described by the Spanish poet Miguel de Unamuno as a "petrified storm," is awesome. More soothing is the Maspalomas–Playa del Inglés–San Agustín resort area, sometimes called the Costa Canaria, along the island's southern coast. The area stretches for miles, embracing three resort developments, excellent beaches, and a mini-Sahara of spectacular sand dunes.

More secluded, quainter spots are opening up in the coves west of Maspalomas–Playa del Inglés. The tiny fishing community of Puerto de Mogan is fast becoming the retreat of the yachting set, who are attracted by its charming marina and enchanting canal-cooled Mediterranean village.

GETTING AROUND

AIRPORT Scheduled flights connect Grand Canary with Alicante, Asturias (Oviedo), Barcelona, Bilbao, Granada, Jerez de la Frontera, Madrid, Málaga, Santiago de Compostela, Seville, and Valencia on the Spanish mainland, as well as with Palma de Mallorca in the Balearics. There are also daily flights to and from Fuerteventura, El Hierro, Lanzarote, La Palma, and Tenerife. Grand Canary's airport, Gando, is located about 14 miles (22 km) from Las Palmas and 15½ miles (25 km) from San Agustín.

The No. 60 bus runs hourly to downtown Las Palmas; a taxi ride costs about $25. The *Iberia* office in Las Palmas is at 8 Calle Alcalde Ramírez Béthencourt (phone: 28-372111).

BUS The central bus station is next to Salcai, Parque San Telmo. *Avenida Rafael Cabrera* (phone: 28-368631) covers the southern part of the island and *Utinsa* (phone: 28-360179) handles the northern part. The most useful route is the No. 1, or Teatro–Puerto route, which runs day and night along Calle León y Castillo from the resort area to the historic quarter.

CAR RENTAL Major rental car companies are *Avis* (13 Calle Juan Manuel Durán, Las Palmas; phone: 28-265532 or 28-265567; Carretera Las Palmas a Mogan, phone: 28-25572; Playa del Inglés, phone: 28-760963; and at Gando Airport, phone: 28-700158); *Hertz* (in Las Palmas; phone: 28-264576; at Playa del Inglés; phone: 28-762572; and at the airport; phone: 28-700084); and *Europcar* (24 Calle Los Martínez de Escobar, Las Palmas; phone: 28-275997; Edificio Bayuca, Playa del Inglés; phone: 28-765500; and at the airport; phone: 28-700147).

FERRY *Trasmediterránea* (Muelle Santa Catalina, Las Palmas; phone: 28-260070) operates car and passenger ferries between Las Palmas and Cádiz and between Las Palmas and the six other major Canaries, and jetfoils (28-273884) between Las Palmas and the other islands.

MOPEDS AND MOTORCYCLES Throughout the island, mopeds are available for about $11.25 a day, motorcycles for about $20. Try *Motos Rent-Puig* (4 Calle Montevideo, Las Palmas; phone: 28-274901) or *Med-Ped* (Edificio Barbados, Av. Tirajana, Playa del Inglés; phone: 28-764434).

PLANES Planes with pilots can be chartered to island hop. The largest charter company is *Naysa, S.A.* (53 Av. Béthencourt, Las Palmas (phone: 28-36144).

TAXI Taxis in Las Palmas use meters; elsewhere on the island, it is best to agree on a rate with the driver before the trip. Las Palmas has numerous cab-stands, as well as radio cabs (phone: 28-762871 or 28-277712). For a radio cab in the Maspalomas area, call 28-762871 or 28-760293.

SPECIAL PLACES

LAS PALMAS The city stretches from La Isleta peninsula and the Puerto de la Luz area, where cruise liners and merchant vessels dock, south along a narrow isthmus. The Castillo de la Luz, on the Isleta on Calle Juan Rejón, was built in 1494 to protect the town from pirates and other invaders (which included the English fleet of Sir Francis Drake) and has been restored to serve as a cultural center. Just south of the Isleta, on the western side of the isthmus, begins a 2-mile beach, Playa de las Canteras. Running parallel to the beach is the Paseo de las Canteras, a promenade boasting numerous bars, cafés, and a variety of restaurants: not just Spanish but Swedish, Italian, Chinese, Finnish, Mexican, Indian, and German. Most resort hotels are in this strip as well. These, however, have suffered from a tourist exodus to the south of the island. The bulk are shabby and frayed, and serve the lower end of the package circuit. The public market, located in the southern fringes of the barrio, is still appealing. It occupies an entire block at the corner of Calle Néstor de la Torre and Calle Galicia.

To the south are the palm trees and fountains of Parque Doramas, containing a zoo, a swimming pool, the no-longer-charming *Santa Catalina* hotel, and the Pueblo Canario. The latter is an unusual replica of a Canarian village, designed by the local painter and sculptor Néstor de la Torre (1888–1938). It offers a pleasant open-air café, craft shops, and regular folk dancing and singing performances (Sundays from 11:45 AM to 1:15 PM and Thursdays from 5:30 to 7 PM). It also contains the artist's house, now the *Museo Néstor* (phone: 28-245135), displaying his paintings and memorabilia. It's open Mondays through Fridays from 10 AM to noon and from 4 to 7 PM; Saturdays from 10 AM to noon; Sundays and holidays from 10:30 AM to 1:30 PM; admission charge. Any bus traveling along Calle León y Castillo at Parque Santa Catalina also goes to Parque Doramas. Another park, Parque de San Telmo, is farther south, where the broad, bustling shopping street, Calle Mayor de Triana, begins and leads south to the Vegueta, the city's Old Quarter. Parallel to Triana is the *Casa-Museo Pérez Galdós* (6 Calle Caño; phone: 28-366976), the former home of a 19th- and 20th-century writer and campaigner against social injustice. It's open Mondays through Saturdays from 9 AM to 1 PM; closed Sundays; admission charge.

The Vegueta, the city's historic center, an area of peaceful cobbled streets, old balconied buildings, and pleasant squares, is a bit farther south (from the Isleta or Puerto de la Luz area, take a taxi or bus No. 1). Here, fronting the noble Plaza de Santa Ana, is the 15th-century cathedral, Gothic in origin, with a later, neo-classical exterior. The cathedral's *Museo Diocesano de Arte Sacro* (31 Calle Doctor Chil; phone: 28-310872) boasts a collection of magnificent Flemish and Castilian paintings. The museum is open weekdays, except Wednesdays, from 9 AM to 2 PM and 4 to 6 PM; weekends from 10 AM to 1:30 PM; admission charge.

Directly across the street from the cathedral is the *Casa-Museo Colón* (1 Calle Colón; phone: 28-311255), the former governors' residence. This dignified mansion housed Christopher Columbus for a short time in 1502 before he headed to the Americas on one of his later voyages. It now functions as a small museum, containing objects from the period of Columbus's explorations, including heavy cannon, faded maps, and models of the explorer's vessels. It's open weekdays from 9:30 AM to 2:30 PM; Saturdays from 9:30 AM to 1 PM; admission charge. Nearby is the *Museo Canario* (2 Calle Doctor Verneau; phone: 28-315600), displaying ceramics and implements of the original island inhabitants. The first floor has glass cases containing hundreds of skulls of the Guanche, some showing evidence of trepanation techniques used in primitive medicine. Most striking are the mummified remains of entire bodies. The museum is open daily from 10 AM to 1 PM and from 3 to 6 PM; admission charge.

THE NORTH Cenobio de Valerón, a remarkable archaeological site, is 15½ miles (25 km) west of Las Palmas via the C810 coastal highway. Here the rock is honeycombed with caves where once, it is believed, young daughters of the Guanche nobility were kept as vestal virgins. From nearby Guía, a road zigags inland and back eastward through fertile terraced farmland, to Moya and Arucas. The latter, 10½ miles (17 km) out of Las Palmas, has a somber Gothic-style church, built during this century, which stands out against the town's white houses. There are spectacular views from the observation deck at the top of the nearby Montaña de Arucas. Continue south to Teror, 13 miles (21 km) from Las Palmas, whose wooden-balconied mansions are a marvel of traditional, harmonious architecture. At its heart is the 18th-century basilica Nuestra Señora del Pino (Our Lady of the Pine), which houses the much-venerated statue of Grand Canary's patron saint, said to have been found in a pine tree in 1481. The statue is the object of the island's annual pilgrimage on September 8.

THE INTERIOR Drive south on C811 to Tafira, a green residential area overlooking Las Palmas, and follow signs beyond to the *mirador* (belvedere) on Pico de Bandama, a 1,865-foot peak that looks down on a perfect volcanic crater, more than 3,000 feet across and 650 feet deep. Continue toward Tejeda to San Mateo. There, the *Casa-Museo Cho Zacarías* is a rustically charming old house with rooms full of old furniture and implements, and a restaurant serving simple, moderately priced meals between 1 and 4 PM (closed Mondays; no phone). From San Mateo, a road winds up into pinewoods and stark mountains. At Cruz de Tejeda, 26 miles (42 km) from Las Palmas and more than 4,825 feet above sea level, there are impressive views of a tortured landscape, including a vast amphitheater and the isolated Roque Nublo, a rock said to have been worshiped by the Guanches. The *Hostería la Cruz de Tejeda* (phone: 28-658050), part of the *parador* chain, is a good place to stop for lunch (open daily; moderate).

THE SOUTH The Maspalomas–Playa del Inglés–San Agustín resort area, about 34½ miles (55 km) via a toll-free freeway from Las Palmas and 15½ miles (25 km) from Gando Airport, lures most of Grand Canary's visitors. At Maspalomas, the southernmost part of the area, are spectacular sand dunes, a 4-mile beach, a sprawl of elegant resort hotels, and a lighthouse. San Agustín, the northernmost part, with another beach, also has luxury hotels, but tends to be more residential, while between the two, the endless high-rise hotels and apartment blocks of Playa del Inglés (Englishman's Beach) attract large numbers of visitors on inexpensive packages. Most of the island's sports facilities and a variety of nightlife and other attractions are in this area. There's even Ciudad del Oueste, a Western show town, where cowboys and Indians fight it out twice daily, and the *Three Stars Saloon* (Calle Cañon del Aguila, San Agustín; phone: 28-762573 or 28-762982) serves meals to the twang of country-and-western music. At Playa del Inglés is Palmitos Park (no phone), home of 230 species of exotic birds and hundreds of varieties of tropical butterflies. It's open daily from 9 AM to 6 PM. About a mile (1.6 km) to the west of the Maspalomas lighthouse, Playa Pasito Blanco has a deep-water harbor with a marina where deep-sea charters can be hired. Also west of Maspalomas, just 20 miles (32 km) away, is the Puerto Rico apartment-condominium development, with a marina, a beach, swimming pools, restaurants, shopping, and playgrounds.

THE WEST The Puerto de Mogan marina, about 15 miles (25 km) from the Maspalomas–Playa del Inglés–San Agustín area, is the quaintest beachfront spot on the island and home to its most tasteful tourist development. The complex is composed of a tiny Mediterrenean-style village with Venetian-inspired canals crisscrossed by tiny 2-story apartments (for rent) and stone-paved alleys with arches festooned with bougainvillea. The marina, with its stylish outdoor cafés and tall sailing ships, looks out on the colorful fishing fleet and port. A small municipal fish market on the west end thrives, supplying the marina restaurants with the daily catch. The original whitewashed fishing village sits on a hill to the north, providing a rustic backdrop to the newer, sleeker enclave below. A ferry ride to neighboring Puerto Rico and Arguineguin (service six times daily from the port; buy tickets on board) is a pleasant, leisurely way to study the underlying coast.

SHOPPING

Las Palmas is a well-known shopper's paradise, offering a dazzling variety of products minus the IVA, or value added tax, found on the mainland. Each island does, however, impose its own luxury tax on imports. This means that products at the lower end of the market are less expensive than elsewhere — tobacco and liquor are particularly low-priced — but costlier goods may be no less expensive than on the mainland or elsewhere in Europe. As the European Economic Community gradually removes duties on the internal movement of goods around the Continent, there will be less variation in prices among the Canaries, mainland Spain, and the rest of Europe, except for goods coming from outside the EC.

Large stores and small boutiques stock everything from the latest designer clothing to top-quality leather goods, sold at nonnegotiable prices, while in hundreds of shops known as bazaars, it's possible to bargain over the cost of electronic goods, precious and semi-precious stones, jewelry, and local handicrafts. It's a good idea to know the range of prices of items under consideration throughout the city before actually buying. It's also a good idea to know the price of luxury goods at home; although items such as cameras, computers, and video and sound equipment may be less expensive than in European capitals, they often sell for less in the US, with more possibility of redress if a purchase proves faulty. (Be sure to know the model number of the item you're looking for.) As for crafts, open-worked embroidery is a Canarian specialty; intricately hand-embroidered blouses, table linen, and bedspreads are especially appealing. Make sure the product is authentic, not a mass-produced imitation. Other interesting buys include the *timple,* the small guitar-like instrument featured in island folk music, and pottery — particularly the simple designs made without the use of a potter's wheel.

In Las Palmas, the traditional shopping street is Calle Mayor de Triana (or just Triana), while the larger stores and newer boutiques are found on Avenida Mesa y López, near the port. The bazaars are found mostly around the Parque Santa Catalina district. Shops are generally open from 9 AM to 1 PM and from 4:15 to 7:30 PM. The rival Spanish department stores have branches opposite each other: *El Corte Inglés* (18 Av. Mesa y López; phone: 28-272600 or 28-263000), and *Galerías Preciados* (15 Av. Mesa y López; phone: 28-233055).

FATAGA ARTESANÍA CANARIA The place for high-quality island handicrafts. Pueblo Canario, Las Palmas (phone: 28-243911).

MAYA Everything from jade and porcelain giftware to computers and stereo equipment. 105-107 Calle Triana, Las Palmas (phone: 28-367167 or 28-372049).

MIKEL Ceramics and other gifts. In the Edificio Vera Cruz, just off the Plaza de España, Las Palmas (phone: 28-274606).

LAS PERLAS Precious stones, cultured pearls, and gold and silver jewelry. 32 Calle Luis Morote, Las Palmas (phone: 28-269701).

SAPHIR A wide selection of Swiss watches, precious stones, cultured pearls, and silver and porcelain gift items. 97 Calle Triana (phone: 28-362388) and 70 Calle Sagasta, Las Palmas (phone: 28-275964).

NIGHTCLUBS AND NIGHTLIFE

After-dark activity in the Canaries hits its stride in Las Palmas. Although nightspots are not in abundance, there are some discos, and a few of the hotels have casinos. For dancing, try *Cupé* (65 Calle Nicholás Estévanez), *Amnesia* (39 Calle Los Martínez Escobar), *Dinos* (in the *Los Bardinos Hotel,* 3 Calle Eduardo Benot; phone: 28-266100), *Reina Isabel* in the *Reina Isabel* hotel (see *Checking In*), and *Toca-Toca* (53 Calle Secretario Artiles). The Las Palmas chic frequent the *Utopia* pub (Calle de Tomás Miller), while the jet and yachting set gravitate to the ultraposh *Panchá* pub (Parque Santa Catalina). The nearby café *Terraza Derby* (Parque de

Santa Catalina) is also popular for late nights. The *Santa Catalina* hotel and the *Melia Tamarindos* hotel both have casinos (see *Checking In*).

CHECKING IN

Hotels are concentrated in Las Palmas and the more desirable resort areas around Maspalomas and beyond, where there are also many apartments for rent at reasonable prices. From November through *Easter,* bookings are heavy and reservations are advisable; in summer, rooms generally do not sell out and advance reservations are not needed. After *Easter,* many establishments offer discounts of 20% to 30% off their high-season rates. Most hotels cater to large tour groups — from northern Europe during winter, from Spain in summer. Expect to pay $150 or more for a double room at hotels listed as expensive, between $55 and $110 at establishments listed as moderate, and under $40 at places listed as inexpensive.

LAS PALMAS

EXPENSIVE

Melia Las Palmas Formerly the *Cristina Sol,* this large and luxurious property overlooking Las Canteras beach is a favorite of businesspeople. The 316 air conditioned rooms feature glass-enclosed balconies, color TV sets, VCRs, and mini-bars. There are also 2 swimming pools and a bather's terrace, which overlooks the beach, as well as 2 fine restaurants, a discotheque, and lovely gardens. 6 Calle Gomera, Las Palmas (phone: 28-267600; in the US, 800-336-3542; fax: 28-268411).

Reina Isabel Although relatively modern in decor and furnishings, this once-luxurious property could stand some renovations. Still, it's right on Las Canteras beach, and all 234 rooms are air conditioned and have color TV sets and private balconies. Other features include 24-hour room service, a fine restaurant, a popular terrace bar, a rooftop, a heated swimming pool (with an adjoining disco), a solarium, and a beachfront esplanade. 40 Calle Alfredo L. Jones, Paseo de las Canteras, Las Palmas (phone: 28-260100).

Santa Catalina Most of the city's hotels are modern, but this Spanish colonial fantasy, with carved wood balconies, bucks the trend. Spacious and charmingly old-fashioned, it stands in the middle of the flowers of Parque Doramas. The 200 renovated rooms are large, with balconies, traditional furnishings, air conditioning, mini-bars, and color TV sets. Other facilities include a casino, a large swimming pool, tennis courts, a restaurant, a bar, and a shopping arcade. Doramas, Las Palmas (phone: 28-243040; fax: 28-242764).

MODERATE

Astoria This establishment attracts many visitors who arrive by boat, and because of its location next to the busy port (rather than near the beach), the first-rate accommodations come at a very reasonable rate. Facilities include a squash court, a gym, sauna, pool, a restaurant, and terrace bar. 54 Fernando Evananteme, Las Palmas (phone: 28-222750; fax: 28-272499).

N.H. Imperial Playa A luxury hotel on the eastern end of Las Canteras beach, popular with the briefcase crowd. Its 142 rooms provide fine views of the bay and active beachfront esplanade. Amenities include state-of-the-art convention facilities, a gym, a restaurant, and a sauna. Calle Ferreira, Playa de la Cantera, Las Palmas (phone: 28-264854; fax: 28-269442).

INEXPENSIVE

Villa Blanca For those on a tight budget, this 45-room hotel is comfortable, clean, and functional, and does not feature a restaurant. Located near Las Canteras beach, across the street from the *Reina Isabel*. 35 Calle Alfredo L. Jones, Las Palmas (phone: 28-260016).

MASPALOMAS AREA

EXPENSIVE

Gloria Palace An ultramodern luxury behemoth situated between Playa del Inglés and Maspalomas, it has 448 air conditioned rooms with mini-bars and sea views. Facilities include 4 pools, a snack bar, a garden restaurant and a rooftop restaurant, 3 tennis courts, a health club, and a casino. Calle Las Margaritas, Maspalomas (phone: 28-768300; 28-767929).

Iberotel Maspalomas Oasis This busy, large, luxury resort near the lighthouse has 342 air conditioned, stylishly designed rooms. Tennis, archery, a children's nursery, and nightly entertainment are among the facilities. Excellent international food is served in *Le Jardin* grill. This is a popular place with tour groups, particularly German travelers. Plaza Palmeras, Playa de Maspalomas (phone: 28-141448; fax: 28-141192).

Melia Tamarindos Surrounded by beautiful gardens, this hotel rivals the best of them in decor, grounds, and facilities. Its 2 swimming pools and beach make it a good place for simple lounging in the sun, although tennis, miniature golf, archery, bowling, and casino gambling are all available. There are 318 air conditioned rooms, several bars, a restaurant, and a disco. 3 Calle Retama, Playa de San Agustín (phone: 28-762600; in the US, 800-336-3542; fax: 28-762264).

Riu Palace The newest, most palatial, and best-located luxury hotel in the area, this white, colonial-style establishment sits at the juncture between the Maspalomas and Playa del Inglés beaches, overlooking the magnificent Sahara-like dunes and blue Atlantic waters beyond. The spacious 352 air conditioned rooms and 16 suites are outfitted with all the modern luxuries. Other attractions include a tropical terrace bar fronting a palm-fronded pool, a solarium, a luxury shopping arcade, and a complete fitness center with gym, sauna, climated pool, and beauty center. Meals are served in a glass, marble, and velvet dining room. There's live music nightly in the ballroom. 1 Plaza de Fuerteventura, Playa del Inglés (phone: 28-764362; fax: 28-764854).

MODERATE

IFA Beach A comfortable, well-run, property fronting the San Agustin beach, with all the amenities, including a restaurant. There's an emphasis on water sports during the summer. 25 Los Jazmines, Playa de San Agustín (phone: 28-765100; fax: 28-768599).

MOGAN

MODERATE

Sol Club de Mar An attractive, Mediterranean-style hotel and apartment complex in the heart of Puerto de Mogan's marina. The hotel has 56 rustically decorated rooms with ocean or marina-facing terraces, a poolside bar, and an outdoor restaurant with an ocean view (see *Eating Out*). An additional 110 fully equipped apartments available for rent are nearby. 35140 Puerto de Mogan (phone: 28-565065; fax: 28-565438).

EATING OUT

Diners on cosmopolitan Grand Canary can enjoy a wide range of international dishes, as well as local specialties and various Spanish offerings. Expect to pay $55 or more for a meal for two at places listed as expensive, between $30 and $40 at restaurants in the moderate category, and under $20 at inexpensive ones. Prices do not include drinks, wine, or tips.

LAS PALMAS

EXPENSIVE

El Aqueducto A fine meat and fish grill in a restored colonial building near the Playa de la Canteras beach. There's a lively bar and rustic dining room on the ground floor; more elegant second-floor rooms have Art Deco touches. Open daily. Reservations not necessary. Visa and Diners Club accepted. 45 Sargento Llagas (phone: 28-264242).

Churchill In an old colonial-style building that houses the *British Club* upstairs, this restaurant features a menu that makes good use of imaginative recipes from a variety of countries. Specialties include pâtés, roast baby lamb, and home-baked pies. Closed Saturday afternoons, Sundays, and holidays. Reservations necessary. Major credit cards accepted. 274 Calle León y Castillo, Las Palmas (phone: 28-249192).

MODERATE

Bla Donau This warm, family-run Hungarian restaurant serves both international and Hungarian entrées, including beef Stroganoff and goulash.

There's lively gypsy music on weekend nights from October to April. Open daily. Reservations advised on weekends. Major credit cards accepted. 37 Calle Sargento Llagas (phone: 28-274486).

Bodegón A longtime favorite for Canarian cooking, especially seafood. Try the *cazuela canaria* (fish casserole) or the *sancocho de pescado* (fish stew). Closed Mondays. Reservations unnecessary. No credit cards accepted. Pueblo Canario, Parque Doramas, Las Palmas (phone: 28-242985).

El Cortijo This wood-beamed replica of a Castilian inn serves mighty portions of roast suckling pig, lamb chops, and Segovia sausage in a hearty and informal atmosphere. Ask for a local delicacy called *queso de flor,* a yellow cheese made from sheep's and goat's milk that's been fermented with an extract of thistles; the spicy taste complements the local white wines. Open daily. Reservations unnecessary. Visa accepted. 3 Calle Diderot, Las Palmas (phone: 28-275955).

Mesón La Paella Authentic Catalan cooking and excellent Middle Eastern rice dishes are the specialties in this eatery, one of the few places in the Canaries offering good paella. Closed Saturday evenings, Sundays, and holidays. Reservations unnecessary. Visa accepted. 47 Calle Juan Manuel Durán, Las Palmas (phone: 28-271640).

El Pote A popular spot for cooking in the style of Galicia — the Galician pork chops and Santiago tart make for tasty eating. Closed Sundays. Reservations unnecessary. MasterCard and Visa accepted. 41 Calle Juan Manuel Durán, Las Palmas (phone: 28-278058).

INEXPENSIVE

El Gallo Feliz Its Danish owner attracts Scandinavians with plates of herring and smoked eel on toast with scrambled eggs. Friendly, fast service in a cozy room. Open evenings only, November through April. Reservations unnecessary. No credit cards accepted. 35 Paseo de las Canteras, Las Palmas (no phone).

MASPALOMAS AREA

EXPENSIVE

Rias Bajas An elegant spot featuring the flavors of Galicia. Fish dishes are a specialty; for dessert, try the *tarta de Santiago* (almond tart). Open daily. Reservations necessary. Visa and American Express accepted. Edificio Playa Sol, Av. Tirajana, Playa del Inglés (phone: 28-764033).

San Agustín Beach Club This restaurant, with an African decor, enjoys a striking setting overlooking the beach. The quality of food, which consists primarily of fish and meat dishes, has slipped somewhat recently, but the ambience and view remain impressive. Closed during May and June. Reservations advised. Major credit cards accepted. Playa de los Cocoteros, San Agustín (phone: 28-760370).

La Toja On the ground floor of an undistinguished apartment building, but very comfortable and welcoming inside. Seafood is featured here. Try the prawn crêpes, dill-marinated salmon, hake, or angler. Closed Sundays for lunch. Reservations unnecessary. Major credit cards accepted. 17 Av. Tirajana, Playa del Inglés (phone: 28-761196).

MODERATE

Casa Pepe El Breca II The most traditional authentic Canary Island dining spot in the area, serving *papas arrugadas* (wrinkled potatoes) and *gofio* (a paste of flour, water, and milk). Fish specialties include steamed mussels and fried octopus. Closed Sundays. Reservations unnecessary. No credit cards accepted. On a hill above Maspalomas on the road to Fataga. El Lomo, Maspalomas (phone: 28-772637).

Tenderete II Seafood and Canarian specialties, such as *papas arrugadas con mojo* (wrinkled potatoes in a piquant sauce), are this place's forte. Open daily. Reservations unnecessary. Major credit cards accepted. Just opposite the *Rey Carlos* hotel in the Edificio Aloe, Av. San Bartolomé de Tirajana, Playa del Inglés (phone: 28-761460).

INEXPENSIVE

La Casa Vieja Grilled meats are the specialty at this down-to-earth place, where diners sit on rustic wooden benches and can watch their meals being prepared at the huge grill in the middle of the dining room. Open daily. No reservations. No credit cards accepted. 139 El Lomo, Carretera de Fataga, Maspalomas (phone: 28-762736).

MOGAN AREA

MODERATE

Acaymo This popular dining spot, located about 4 miles (7 km) north of the port in the mountainous town of Mogan, serves typical island bistro fare — grilled meats and fish. A sunny terrace with a sweeping view of the Mogan Valley is a bonus. Closed Tuesdays. Reservations unnecessary. Visa and MasterCard accepted. Carretera a Mogan, Valle de Mogan (phone: 28-740263)..

Marina Occupying a prime spot in the marina, this Irish-owned restaurant and pub serves such diverse entrées as steaks and paella. The staff is attentive, and an Irish bartender guarantees the authenticity of the Irish coffee. Guests can dine indoors or on the terrace overlooking the marina. Open

daily. Reservations unnecessary. Major credit cards accepted. Local
X-113, Puerto de Mogan (phone: 28-565095 or 28-5655224).

Sol Club de Mar At the hotel of the same name, guests can choose casual poolside
dining at lunch, or a more romantic indoor setting, with views of Puerto
de Mogan's beach and cove. Fresh fish is the house staple. Open daily.
Reservations unnecessary. Major credit cards accepted. 35140 Puerto de
Mogan (phone: 28-565066).

Tenerife

At 793 square miles, the largest of the Canary Islands is only 20 minutes
by air west of Las Palmas and is also accessible by flights from Madrid in
a little over 2 hours. Local legend has it that God put so much effort into
creating the beaches of Grand Canary that night fell before he could finish
the mountains. When he came to Tenerife, he began with the mountains,
and this time darkness fell before he could get around to the beaches. Thus
Tenerife has fewer beaches than its neighbor and the sand is black. Still,
there is enough to attract the visitor. Towering above Tenerife's mixture
of lush vegetation and arid desert is the massive dormant volcano, Pico del
Teide, Spain's highest peak at 12,200 feet — the island's name is believed
to have evolved from a Guanche word meaning snow-capped mountain.

Because it receives more rain than its neighbors, Tenerife is the archipelago's main agricultural center, producing most of its vegetables. The
northern and northwestern corners receive the most rainfall, which en-
courages forests and colorful vegetation, while the south is arid and desolate. Also in the north are the settlements of long standing: Santa Cruz de
Tenerife, the provincial capital; La Laguna, site of one of Spain's oldest
seats of learning; and Puerto de la Cruz, once important as a fruit- and
wine-exporting port and now a prestigious tourism resort. Around southern beaches at Los Cristianos and Playa de las Américas, the all-year
sunshine has fostered a development boom, covering tracts of desert with
apartments and hotels. These resorts, and the nearby Reina Sofía Airport,
are linked with Santa Cruz by a fast four-lane highway, while another
autoroute speeds traffic up to Puerto de la Cruz. Interior roads, in contrast, are narrow, winding, and tiring to drive.

GETTING AROUND

AIRPORT Tenerife has direct air service with Alicante, Asturias (Oviedo), Barcelona, Bilbao, Granada, Jerez de la Frontera, Madrid, Málaga, Santiago
de Compostela, Seville, and Valencia, on the mainland, as well as with
Palma de Mallorca in the Balearic Islands. There are also regular connections with Fuerteventura, Grand Canary, El Hierro, Lanzarote, and La
Palma. National and international flights arrive and depart from Reina
Sofía Airport, on the island's southern coast, about 37½ miles (60 km)
from Santa Cruz de Tenerife. Most inter-island flights use Los Rodeos

Airport (Aeropuerto del Norte), 8 miles (13 km) from Santa Cruz. *Iberia* has several Tenerife offices (23 Av. de Anaga, Santa Cruz; phone: 22-288000; Av. de Venezuela, Puerto de la Cruz; phone: 22-380050; and at the airport; phone: 22-252340). Buses run between Reina Sofía Airport and Santa Cruz, and there are regular buses from between Los Rodeos Airport and Santa Cruz and Puerto de la Cruz. The taxi fare from Reina Sofía to Santa Cruz is about $40, from Los Rodeos, about $11.25.

BUS There is frequent bus service to all of the island's major centers. The main bus station in Santa Cruz is on Avenida 3 de Mayo (phone: 22-218122 or 22-219399); in Puerto de la Cruz, on Calle del Pozo, just opposite the post office (phone: 22-382814). At Los Cristianos, buses stop at the main taxi stand opposite the Cepsa gas station (for information, call 22-770606).

CAR RENTAL Major rental car companies are *Avis* (21 Imelda Seris, Santa Cruz; phone: 22-241294; Av. de Venezuela, Puerto de la Cruz; phone: 22-384552; at Reina Sofía Airport; phone: 22-770656; and at Los Rodeos Airport, La Laguna; phone: 22-259090); *Hertz* (Av. de Anaga, Santa Cruz; phone: 22-274805; Plaza Augustín de Béthencourt, Puerto de la Cruz; phone: 22-384719 or 22-384560; at Reina Sofía Airport; phone: 22-384719; at Los Rodeos Airport, La Laguna; phone: 22-384719 or 22-384560; and at Playa de las Américas, Grupo Urbania; phone: 22-790861); and *Europcar* (Edificio Portofino, Puerto de la Cruz; phone: 22-381804 or 22-381928; Centro Comercial Teneguía, Calle José Campos y Arenas; phone: 22-381777 or 22-380738; Vía Litoral, Playa de las Américas; phone: 22-791150 or 22-791154; and at Reina Sofía Airport; phone: 22-771150).

FERRY *Trasmediterránea* (59 Calle Marina, Santa Cruz; phone: 22-277300) has regular sailings between Cádiz and Santa Cruz, as well as between Tenerife and many of the other islands. The company also runs a jet foil, which is an extra-fast hydrofoil, from Santa Cruz to Las Palmas, Grand Canary (operating 5 to 7 days a week, 3 to 4 times a day), and to Morro Jable, Fuerteventura (with departures on Mondays and Saturdays at 9 AM), as well as a hydrofoil service between Los Cristianos and San Sebastián, on the neighboring island of La Gomera, stopping occasionally at Las Palmas (Muelle de los Cristianos; phone: 22-796178; operating 4 times a day). Regular ferry service between Los Cristianos and San Sebastián is operated by *Ferry Gomera* (Edificio Rascacielos, Av. 3 de Mayo, Santa Cruz; phone: 22-219244; and Muelle de los Cristianos; phone: 22-790556). These ferries run three times a day except Tuesdays, when they offer only once-a-day service.

MOPEDS AND MOTORCYCLES These can be rented from *Moped Santos* (Playa Azul, Playa de las Américas; phone: 22-791639) for about $60 to $190 per week, $20 to $30 per day; hourly rates are also available.

TAXI Cabs can be requested by telephone in Santa Cruz (phone: 22-641459 or 22-615111), Puerto de la Cruz (phone: 22-384910 or 22-385818), Playa de las Américas (phone: 22-791407 or 22-791669), and Los Cristianos (phone: 22-790352, 22-795459, or 22-795509).

SPECIAL PLACES

SANTA CRUZ DE TENERIFE AND THE NORTH Backed by sawtooth mountains, this provincial capital is an important port, with over 200,000 inhabitants and many modern buildings. More Spanish in character and aesthetically more pleasing than Las Palmas, it has no beaches to speak of, and is primarily a city of shops, with boutique-lined Calle del Castillo closed to traffic but filled with hordes of shoppers. Plaza de España, where this pedestrian area begins, is next to the port and is noteworthy for its memorial to the men of Tenerife who died in the Spanish Civil War. Visible from quite a distance, the towering monument also serves as a directional marker for tourists making their way back to the center of town. Just off the Plaza de España, on the third floor of the Palacio Insular, is the *Museo Arqueológico y Antropológico* (5 Calle Bravo Murillo; phone: 22-242090), which has a collection of 100 Guanche mummies, more than 1,000 skulls and 300,000 bones, and other artifacts of the Canary Islands' original inhabitants. The museum is open Mondays through Saturdays from 9 AM to 1 PM and from 4 to 8 PM in the winter months; 9 AM to 2 PM in the summer months; closed Sundays and holidays; admission charge. North of the port, along Avenida de Anaga, where flame trees and palms provide a pleasant tropical air, is the Castillo de Paso Alto, a 17th-century fortress that now houses a regional military museum (no phone). The museum is open Tuesdays through Sundays from 10 AM to 2 PM.

Five miles (8 km) north of town lies Playa de las Teresitas, which claims to be the world's largest artificial beach; the golden sand covering this mile-long stretch — a pleasant place for swimming, sunbathing, or a quick snack at one of its many inexpensive restaurants — was imported from the Sahara. From here, the road turns inland and corkscrews steeply upward to the Anaga headland, a dramatic area of knife-edge ridges, ravines, and dense evergreen woods. At El Bailadero pass, the picturesquely situated village of Taganana can be seen down below, but the road continues west along the crest of the range to the Pico del Inglés Belvedere, a lookout point 3,300 feet above sea level, from which there is a spectacular view of Pico del Teide rising in the distance. Soon after, the road descends to La Laguna, the university town and former island capital, which has an interesting old section highlighted by the Plaza del Adelantado, the 16th-century Church of the Concepción (now a national monument), and a 20th-century cathedral with a neo-classical façade.

PUERTO DE LA CRUZ West of Santa Cruz, on the rocky Atlantic coast where the lush Orotava Valley meets the sea, Puerto de la Cruz is a major resort center, and has been a cosmopolitan place for centuries. The last eruption of El Teide destroyed the harbor at Garachico, 20½ miles (33 km) to the west, giving added importance to the port here. European traders of many nationalities settled in, and wealthy British tourists began arriving to enjoy the mild winter climate during the last century. Today the town has many foreign residents and almost 100 hotels catering to visitors. Banana plantations, tropical fruits, jasmine, and bougainvillea flourish along the steeply terraced coast, behind which El Teide towers, often girded by clouds and covered with snow in winter.

The town has pleasant squares, especially the Plaza de la Iglesia, with its gardens and old buildings. Straw-hatted women in traditional bright embroidered skirts sell flowers near the Ayuntamiento (Town Hall) on Calle de Santo Domingo. Next to this street, Calle de San Telmo, the bustling main thoroughfare, runs along the waterfront, with a bevy of shops, hotels, and bistros. Follow San Telmo until it becomes Avenida de Colón. The town's centerpiece, the Lago de Martiánez leisure complex, is located here. Don't miss this series of beautifully landscaped seawater pools, promenades, and lounging areas set in and around rocky volcanic outcroppings that extend offshore for hundreds of yards. Besides being a perfect sunbathing spot, the complex, designed by the late Lanzarote artist César Manrique, includes a gymnasium, a restaurant, bars, and a nightclub. Just opposite, on Avenida de Colón, is the *Café de Paris,* a popular meeting place where patrons eat and drink amid palms, mirrors, and wrought iron, a piano tinkling in the background. Until a couple of years ago, this complex — plus the swimming pools scattered throughout the area — had to make up for the resort's lack of suitable beaches. Now, however, the town boasts a lavish new beach and esplanade designed by Manrique, who included fountains, lush vegetation, and a layer of golden sand shipped from the Sahara Desert. The beach is a 5-minute walk east of Calle de San Telmo, on Paseo Luis Lavaggi.

Also visit the *Jardín Botánico* (Botanical Gardens; phone: 22-383572), located on Carretera del Botánico at the eastern entrance to town. Rated among the world's finest, the gardens were created by order of King Carlos III in 1788, and cover 5 acres with thousands of varieties of tropical plants, including a 200-year-old rubber tree. The gardens are open daily from 9 AM to 7 PM. Admission charge. Another attraction, at the opposite end of town and reached by a free bus from Playa de Martiánez, is Loro Parque, a tropical park with an orchid garden, plus a dolphin show and 1,300 parrots — some of which ride bicycles and do other tricks in a parrot show. The park is open from 9 AM to 6 PM; admission charge. On Sundays at 11 AM, typical Canaries folk dancing and singing, plus an exhibition of local wrestling, take place on the grounds of the *Tigaiga* hotel (16 Parque de Taoro; phone: 22-383500 or 22-383251). The Parque de Taoro also houses the *Taoro Casino* (phone: 22-382819) which offers slot machines, blackjack, and roulette tables, complemented by sweeping views of the town and the ocean. The casino is open from 6 PM to 3 AM in the winter; from 7 PM to 4 AM in the summer; open later on Friday and Saturday nights; passport required for admission.

LA OROTAVA In a valley of the same name, overlooking Puerto de la Cruz, which is 6 miles (10 km) away and 1,000 feet below, La Orotava occupies a site that was once a Guanche capital and is among the most compelling settings on the island. One of the oldest towns on Tenerife, it has steep cobbled streets and handsome homes with exquisite balconies, red roofs, and interior patios. The 18th-century Church of the Concepción, now a museum, is a highlight, as is *Artesanía La Casa de los Balcones* (3 Calle San Francisco; phone: 22-380629), an arts and crafts center in an old balconied house with a flower-filled patio. Here visitors will find the delicate *calado,* or drawn-thread embroidery, used for everything from handkerchiefs to tablecloths and manufactured by women working at wooden looms. The annual *Corpus Christi* festival in June is a celebration of the religious fervor, energy, and artistry of the town's residents. Although the feast day is celebrated throughout the Canaries, the festivities are at their most colorful here. Before the procession, the town's squares and streets are covered with carpets made of hundreds of thousands of flower petals — bougainvillea, dahlias, geraniums, carnations — as well as crushed leaves, pine needles, and colorful designs in sand. The largest and most intricate carpet is laid on the Plaza del Ayuntamiento.

PICO DEL TEIDE This is one excursion not to be missed on any visit to the Canaries. Mt. Teide, which towers 12,200 feet above sea level and overlooks a sea of clouds, is situated in the Parque Nacional de las Cañadas del Teide (phone: 22-330701), a beautiful forest of heather, evergreens, eucalyptus, and Canarian pine at an altitude of some 6,500 feet. The park is reached via the town and the valley of La Orotava, where corn, chestnuts, and bananas are raised in abundance. It's open daily during daylight hours; no admission charge. Beyond La Orotava, the road leads to a desolate, treeless amphitheater. This is Las Cañadas, an ancient volcanic crater some 47 miles in diameter, from the center of which surges the great bulk of El Teide, a newer volcano and the tallest mountain in Spain. Las Cañadas is scarred and strewn with boulders; the last eruption in 1798 destroyed a peak that was even larger than El Teide. A cable car takes 35 passengers on a 10-minute journey to the base of the cone. From there it is a 25-minute hike to the edge, from where most of the Canaries and even the coast of Africa are visible on a clear day. Those short of breath should take care, as the air is quite rarefied at this altitude. Dedicated climbers can spend the night near the peak at the *Cueva de Hielo,* a mountain shelter (literally, the "Ice Cave"); for less adventurous sorts, there is a rustic *parador* (see *Checking In*) near the cable car. Free guided tours depart the visitors' center at 9:30 AM, 11:30 AM, and 1:30 PM daily (phone: 22-259903). Avoid Sundays and holidays, when the park is crowded. The cable car (phone: 22-383711) runs from 9 AM to 4:30 PM daily and costs about $4.50 each way.

ICOD DE LOS VINOS West of Puerto de la Cruz, a road winds above sea-whipped rocks and black sand coves to this small town, the center of the island's wine- and malmsey-grape-producing area. The town's proudest possession is the *drago,* Tenerife's oldest dragon tree, said to be more than 1,000 years old. From Icod, a drive through banana plantations leads to the nearby beach resort of San Marcos, amid black cliffs.

SHOPPING

The Puerto de la Cruz area has the most varied goods. The main shopping streets in Santa Cruz are found in a square zone formed by Calle del Castillo, Calle Valentín Sanz, Calle Emilio Calzadillo, and the ocean; as in Las Palmas, the shopkeepers are willing to negotiate but are not about to give anything away. Clothing, toys, watches, crafts, and lots more, including junk, are sold every Sunday morning at *El Rastro,* the open-air market on Avenida de Anaga in Santa Cruz. A crafts fair is held on the first Sunday of the month along the Garachico promenade, 20 miles (32 km) south along the coast from Puerto de la Cruz (in winter, it usually is held in the patio of the San Francisco convent). A shopping center with 50 shops selling a broad range of goods is located under the *Vallemar* hotel (2 Av. de Colón, Puerto de la Cruz).

B. CHOITRAM Carries Lladró porcelain, jewelry, and fine crystal. 3 Calle Sargento Cáceres, Puerto de la Cruz (phone: 22-380420).

CASA IRIARTE Local handicrafts, including beautiful embroidery and Toledo ware. 21 Calle San Juan, Puerto de la Cruz (phone: 22-383993).

CASA ROMY A typical bazaar, stocking everything from binoculars to semi-precious stones. 2 Calle San Juan, Puerto de la Cruz (phone: 22-380651).

JOYERÍA PURRILOS Fine watches, crystal, and leather goods. 14 Calle Quintana, Puerto de la Cruz (phone: 22-384432).

MARI PETRI Authentic hand-embroidered items, including blouses, shawls, and skirts. Two locations: 4 Calle Obispo Pérez Cáceres, Puerto de la Cruz (phone: 22-381711), and 3 San Antonio, Puerto de la Cruz (phone: 22-387416).

REGALOS EROS A range of gifts, including Lladró porcelain. 22 Calle Santo Domingo, Puerto de la Cruz (phone: 22-380299).

CHECKING IN

Most of Tenerife's best hotels are concentrated in Puerto de la Cruz, where there is a large selection in all price ranges. Phenomenal development has taken place in the southern beach area around Playa de las Américas, where there are numerous apartment blocks, as well as hotels providing accommodations for package tours. Expect to pay $150 or more for a double room at a hotel listed as expensive, and $50 to $110 at a place described as moderate.

PUERTO DE LA CRUZ

EXPENSIVE

Melia Botánico Set amid lush tropical gardens, this 282-room top-of-the-line establishment, with an attentive, English-speaking staff, is just a step away from the Botanical Gardens, about a mile from downtown. Rooms are air conditioned and tastefully furnished, with color TV sets, VCRs, mini-bars, and hair dryers. Other facilities include fine shops, a discotheque, tennis courts, a swimming pool, and a poolside restaurant. Calle Richard J. Yeoward, Puerto de la Cruz (phone: 22-381400; in the US, 800-336-3542; fax: 22-381504).

Melia San Felipe A modern seafront hotel with an elegant marble lobby, conveniently situated near the hub of the island's activities. Its 260 air conditioned rooms have views of the sea or mountains. Tennis courts, a large pool, a playground, and a lively entertainment program make it a fine resort choice. 22 Av. de Colón, Puerto de la Cruz (phone: 22-383311; in the US, 800-336-3542; fax: 22-387697).

Parque San Antonio Tucked away in a veritable botanical garden all its own, this hotel is a 5-minute bus ride from the center of Puerto de la Cruz. All 211 rooms are air conditioned. There is also a restaurant. Carretera de las Arenas, Puerto de la Cruz (phone: 22-384851).

La Paz Situated in an upscale residential area of Puerto de la Cruz, this 167-room hotel features a tasteful Spanish decor. All of the rooms are air conditioned and attractive. There is also a swimming pool and tennis courts. The staff speaks English and is very attentive and friendly. Urbanización La Paz, Puerto de la Cruz (phone: 22-385011).

Semiramis This 15-story property is imaginatively built into the cliff edge. All 275 air conditioned rooms have terraces overlooking the ocean, color TV sets, VCRs, mini-bars, and refrigerators; some have complete kitchens. A good dining room, a tropical garden, 3 swimming pools (2 heated), a tennis court, and shops are among the attractions. 12 Calle Leopoldo Cologán, Puerto de la Cruz (phone: 22-385551; fax: 22-385253).

MODERATE

Marquesa Historic charm and modern comforts are combined in this 88-room hotel in the old section of Puerto de la Cruz. A leafy patio, a swimming pool, and a popular terrace and restaurant are among the facilities. 11 Calle Quintana, Puerto de la Cruz (phone: 22-383151; fax: 22-386950).

Monopol A landmark since 1742 and in business since 1888, this hotel is worth a visit even for those not staying here, if only to see the handsome carved wooden balconies overlooking the lovely Plaza de la Iglesia. There's a charming old wicker-and-wood patio, and 100 simple and well-kept rooms — some with views and balconies — as well as a modest outdoor pool, a gameroom, 2 bars, and a small dining room. 15 Calle Quintana, Puerto de la Cruz (phone: 22-384611; fax: 22-370310).

ELSEWHERE ON THE ISLAND

EXPENSIVE

Mencey Part of the elegant CIGA chain and by far the finest hotel on Tenerife, this old yellow building is located in the heart of the capital. Its former grandeur has survived modernization, and the 275 air conditioned rooms have been splendidly refurbished; there's also a wing with motel-type units. There are 2 swimming pools, tennis courts, a bar, a poolside buffet, and lovely gardens. 38 Av. José Naveiras, Santa Cruz de Tenerife (phone: 22-276700; in the US, 800-221-2340; fax: 22-280017).

MODERATE

Bouganville Playa Large and modern, this 481-room property has 2 swimming pools (1 for children), 4 bars, squash and tennis courts, a fitness center, a large sauna, and conference facilities. All rooms are air conditioned and have terraces with sea views. Urbanización San Eugenio, Playa de las Américas, Adeje (phone: 22-790200).

Gran Tenerife Open terraces and spacious gardens give a pleasant air to this well-maintained establishment on a black sand beach. The 356 air conditioned rooms are attractively furnished; 52 one-bedroom garden bungalows are also available. There are 3 ocean-fed saltwater swimming pools, tennis courts, and a nightly cabaret show. Playa de las Américas, Adeje (phone: 22-791200).

Los Hibiscos This pleasant low-rise development of 138 studio apartments and 180 hotel rooms surrounds a series of gardens and a swimming pool. Guests use the facilities of the adjacent *Bouganville Playa* hotel. Urbanización San Eugenio, Playa de las Américas, Adeje (phone: 22-791462).

Parador de las Cañadas del Teide Ideal for those seeking tranquillity and fresh mountain air, this place is about an hour drive from Puerto de la Cruz. More than 7,000 feet above sea level, it sits in the crater of an extinct volcano and offers remarkable views of lava fields and of El Teide, Spain's highest peak. The 16 large, spotlessly clean rooms are furnished in simple rustic style, there's a swimming pool, a lounge with a fireplace, and a restaurant. Reservations are required well in advance. Las Cañadas del Teide (phone: 22-332304; in the US, 212-686-9213).

EATING OUT

Restaurants on Tenerife feature Canarian and international dishes. The better places, with the most extensive menus, are found in Puerto de la Cruz. For typical Canarian fare at good prices, try the smaller eateries in the narrow streets near the Plaza del Charco. Expect to pay $55 or more for dinner for two in restaurants listed as expensive, between $30 and $40 in places listed as moderate, and $20 or less in inexpensive restaurants. Prices do not include drinks, wine, or tips.

PUERTO DE LA CRUZ

EXPENSIVE

La Magnolia A light and airy restaurant with a garden, it serves Catalan and international dishes. Specialties include a delicious *zarzuela* (fish stew) and stuffed partridge. Closed Mondays and May. Reservations advised. Major credit cards accepted. 5 Carretera del Botánico, Puerto de la Cruz (phone: 22-385614).

MODERATE

La Papaya Each guest is greeted with a complimentary glass of sherry in this converted old Canarian house. Local dishes are the specialty here; be sure to top off the meal with a dish of homemade ice cream. Open daily. Reservations unnecessary. No credit cards accepted. 14 Calle Lomo, Puerto de la Cruz (phone: 22-382811).

El Pescado The name means "the fish," and that's what guests will find on the menu, prepared in a variety of intriguing ways. Closed Wednesdays and May through September. Reservations unnecessary. No credit cards accepted. 3-A Av. de Venezuela, Puerto de la Cruz (phone: 22-382806).

Sagar Nestled on a quiet back street behind the quaint Plaza de la Iglesia, this Indian restaurant offers a romantic setting and excellent service. The amiable English-speaking owner is a willing guide to the extensive menu and wine cellar. Open daily. Reservations advised. Major credit cards accepted. 6 Calle Cologán, Puerto de la Cruz (phone: 22-380444).

INEXPENSIVE

La Marina International dishes, with a strong emphasis on fish, are served in a nautical setting near the port. Closed Saturdays and from June through mid-July. No reservations or credit cards accepted. 2 Calle San Juan, Puerto de la Cruz (phone: 22-385401).

Patio Canario Enjoy local specialties in this rustic Canarian house with a timber and tiled roof, and lots of potted plants and fresh flowers. Try *conejo en* *salmorejo* (rabbit in a tasty sauce) or a hearty *potaje canario de verduras* (vegetable soup). Closed Thursdays. Reservations unnecessary. Major credit cards accepted. 4 Calle Lomo, Puerto de la Cruz (phone: 22-380451).

ELSEWHERE ON THE ISLAND

EXPENSIVE

Las Folías Situated in a traditionally designed shopping center by the sea, the emphasis here is on fresh ingredients. Try the crab salad, roast lamb, or chateaubriand. Soft lamplight gives the dining room an intimate atmosphere. Closed Sundays. Reservations advised. Major credit cards accepted. *Centro Comercial Pueblo Canario,* Playa de las Américas (phone: 22-792269).

La Riviera Snazzy continental dishes are the hallmark of this chic, tastefully decorated restaurant. Closed Sundays and mid-August through mid-September. Reservations advised. Major credit cards accepted. 155 Rambla General Franco, Santa Cruz de Tenerife (phone: 22-275812).

MODERATE

La Caseta de Madera This popular eatery in an old wooden building specializes in Canarian cooking with a Tenerife twist. The emphasis is on seafood, but the daily specials are also worth a try. Closed Saturday evenings and Sundays. Reservations unnecessary. Major credit cards accepted. Calle Regla, Barrio Los Llanos, Santa Cruz de Tenerife (phone: 22-210023).

Mesón del Orgaz Seafood and Segovia-style roast meat cooked in a wood-fired oven are the specialties of this place, in the same shopping center as *Las Folías.* The dining room boasts a beamed ceiling and plush red seats. Closed Wednesdays in summer. Reservations unnecessary. No credit cards accepted. *Centro Comercial Pueblo Canario,* Playa de las Américas (phone: 22-793169).

L'Scala Near Los Cristianos Beach, with an outside terrace, this restaurant serves authentic Castilian dishes, such as roast suckling pig, in agreeable surroundings. Closed Tuesdays. Reservations unnecessary. No credit cards accepted. 7 Calle La Paloma, Los Cristianos (phone: 22-791051).

Lanzarote

An eerie, burnt-out island pockmarked by hundreds of extinct volcanoes, Lanzarote is the most physically astonishing of the Canaries. Its bizarrely spectacular landscape evokes in first-time visitors the sense of having been transported to the very beginning — or end — of time. A 1- or 2-day visit is enough to see this awe-inspiring scenery, but many travelers are tempted to linger longer on some of the island's white sand beaches. Set 85 miles northeast of Las Palmas and only 65 miles from the coast of Morocco,

Lanzarote has some 300 volcanoes, and petrified seas of lava — known as *malpaís* — writhe across parts of the island. Nevertheless, its farms produce sumptuous melons, figs, onions, and tomatoes, thanks to a remarkable system of cultivation. Local farmers spread *picón* (black volcanic ash) on their fields to absorb and retain moisture, and thus manage to coax an abundant harvest in a land that has no running water and sparse rainfall. They also produce a notable wine from the *malvasía,* or malmsey, grape, which is grown on vines planted in walled hollows to protect them from the hot, searing winds.

By such ingenuity and persistence, the native population (now 50,000) managed to survive from approximately the time when the Genoese navigator Lancelotto Malocello landed here in the 14th century (and gave the island its name) until mass tourism hit in the 1980s. Some 700,000 visitors now set foot in this easternmost of the Canaries annually, and hotels and apartment blocks abound, as well as desalinization plants to provide water. Fortunately, new buildings may be no higher than 3 stories, billboards are banned, and construction is confined to three main zones. Except for Arrecife, the undistinguished, traffic-clogged capital on the island's eastern coast, and three "artificial" resort areas — Costa Teguise (north of Arrecife, and popular with royalty and the international jet set), Puerto del Carmen (south of both Arrecife and the airport, the most-developed area and center of nightlife), and Playa Blanca (still farther south, facing Fuerteventura, where some of the best beaches are) — the island largely retains its magical quality. For this, much credit is due to the late artist and environmentalist César Manrique, who was responsible for the development of various island sites.

GETTING AROUND

AIRPORT The Aeropuerto de Lanzarote is 4 miles (6 km) from Arrecife. *Iberia* offers direct service between the island and Alicante, Barcelona, Bilbao, Madrid, Málaga, and Seville, as well as inter-island service with Grand Canary, Tenerife, and Fuerteventura. *Iberia*'s Arrecife office is at 2 Av. Rafael González (phone: 28-810354).

BUS Service throughout the island is provided by *Arrecife Bus* (phone: 28-811546 or 28-810116) and *Lanzarote Bus* (phone: 28-812458 or 28-811546). A guided bus tour of the volcanoes runs about $30 ($45 with lunch).

CAR RENTAL Major rental car companies are *Avis* (Tías; phone: 28-512400; *Club Resort Los Zocos,* Costa Teguise; phone: 28-816439, ext. 377; *Lanzarote Palace* hotel, Playa de los Pocillos; phone: 28-512400; and at the airport, Arrecife; phone: 28-812256); *Hertz* (at the airport; phone: 28-813711; and at the *Arrecife Gran* hotel; phone: 28-813711); and *Europcar* (at the airport, Arrecife; phone: 28-814440 or 28-802657; *Centro Comercial La Olita,* Teguise; phone: 28-813976; and at the *Centro Comercial,* Punta Limones, Playa Blanca; phone: 28-517077 or 28-517078).

FERRY *Trasmediterránea* ferries sail regularly between Arrecife and Cádiz, as well as to Las Palmas, Grand Canary, Santa Cruz de Tenerife, and Puerto del Rosario, Fuerteventura. In addition, the company operates a jet foil between Playa Blanca and Corralejo and Puerto del Rosario on Fuerteventura. *Alisur, a Trasmediterránea* subsidiary, runs a ferry between Playa Blanca, Lanzarote, and Corralejo, Fuerteventura, 4 times daily. It also has twice-a-day ferry service from Orzola, on the north end of the island, to the quaint fishing village of Caleta del Cebo, on the lovely, unspoiled island of La Graciosa, known for its golden Sahara sand beaches and home to a protected natural park. In Arrecife, contact *Trasmediterránea* (90 Calle José Antonio; phone: 28-811188) and *Alisur* (1 Calle La Esperanza; phone: 28-814272).

TAXI Taxis are available on call in Arrecife (phone: 28-811680 and 28-810283) and in Puerto del Carmen (phone: 28-825034). Hiring a car and driver for a tour of the volcanoes costs about $40.

SPECIAL PLACES

LAS MONTAÑAS DEL FUEGO (FIRE MOUNTAINS) Between 1730 and 1736, a series of terrifying eruptions devastated the western part of Lanzarote, burying farmland and a number of villages under volcanic debris. This area now makes up the Parque Nacional de Timanfaya. Entering from Yaiza, a typical, whitewashed village in the south, 14½ miles (23 km) from Arrecife, visitors come to the Echadero de los Camellos, where dromedaries wait to carry people on short journeys over the lava (there is a charge for this, in addition to the park admission). The main road through the park winds up a hill known as Islote de Hilario, where subsurface temperatures reach upward of 800F. Twigs placed in a hollow catch fire within seconds, and when a park ranger pours water down a vent in the earth's surface, a steam geyser instantly erupts. A tour bus cruises "The Route of the Volcanoes" (with commentary in English) for a close view of this lunar-like landscape, where virtually no living creature exists. Before departing, try a volcano-broiled steak at *El Diablo,* the park restaurant (see *Eating Out*). The park is open daily from 9 AM to 5 PM; admission charge. *Note:* Strong footwear is recommended to explore the lava fields, and those with cameras should remember to bring a blower brush to clean off the dust.

La Gería, the area around the village of Uga, 1½ miles (3 km) east of Yaiza, is one of the island's main wine producing centers. A short detour off the main raod to Arrecife, north toward Mashache, offers views of the peculiar horseshoe-shaped stone structures in which the grapevines thrive. South of Yaiza, the coast contains a variety of natural wonders: the Salinas de Janubio salt flats; the dancing waters of Los Hervideros, which are jets of seawater shooting out of volcanic rock; and the El Gofo green lagoon, separated from the sea by a large crater, where vendors sell semi-precious olivine stones collected in the area.

THE NORTH An 18-mile (29-km) drive north of Arrecife leads to Jameos del Agua, a beautiful grotto carved by nature out of black volcanic rock, with a lagoon — formed when molten lava met the sea — inhabited by blind white crabs. The grotto has been transformed into a natural, partially enclosed entertainment and shopping complex; at one end is a beautifully landscaped outdoor pool area. Folk music shows, with dinner and dancing; a terraced top floor bar with sweeping ocean views; and a mini-museum dedicated to volcanoes, including a large rock collection and a state-of-the-art video on volcanology, are some of the features here. The entertainment grotto is open daily from 11 AM to 8 PM (later for the show); admission charge (phone: 28-835010). Some 300 yards away is the *Cueva de los Verdes* (Green Cave), the world's largest volcanic tunnel, a place where the Guanche and later inhabitants took refuge from invaders. Extending nearly 4 miles to the sea, it was created by cooling lava. Open from 11 AM to 6 PM daily; tours depart on the hour, sometimes with an English-speaking guide; admission charge. At the northernmost tip of the island, 7 miles (11 km) farther along, is the Mirador del Río, a lookout point atop old fortifications where there is a breathtaking view of some of the smaller Canaries — Graciosa, Montaña Clara, and Alegranza.

Returning southward, the road passes Haría, a village of white houses in a green valley dotted with hundreds of palms, and the last home of architect César Manrique (who was killed in a car accident in 1992). The town is the most picturesque and authentic of the island's villages. One of Lazarote's most breathtaking views if from the heights of the Mirador de Haria, 3 miles (5 km) to the south. Farther on lies Teguise, the former island capital. Set on top of an extinct volcano, Teguise has a castle, the Castillo de Guanapay, perched on top of the cone, which has the best views in town of some of the smaller Canaries. The town's colonial appearance, convents, churches, and Espinolas palace (now the seat of the local government) make it a worthwhile stop. The island's current capital, Arrecife, is not particularly interesting, but it does have two castles, the 16th-century Castillo de San Gabriel (open weekdays from 9 AM to 2 PM; admission charge) and the 18th-century Castillo de San José. The latter, renovated by César Manrique, is now the home of the *Museo de Artes de Contemporáneo* (International Museum of Contemporary Art; open daily from 11 AM to 5 PM; no admission charge; phone: 28-812321) and of the deluxe *Castillo de San José* restaurant (see *Eating Out*). Except for the hotel bars, there is very little nightlife activity.

Another way to explore the work of César Manrique is by visiting the *Fundación César Manrique* (phone: 28-810138) in the village of Taro, on the eastern end of Tahiche. The foundation, located in one of Manrique's former homes, illustrates the talent and tastes of the artist, who took advantage of an existing network of lava formations to create an impressive living space. It houses a bookshop, souvenir store, and a snack bar, and is open weekdays from 10 AM to 7 PM; weekends from 10 AM to 2 PM; admission charge.

CHECKING IN

Until recently, there were only a few spartan pensions on the island, but modern hotels and apartments now offer a wide range of accommodations, primarily in Costa Teguise and Puerto del Carmen. Expect to pay $150 or more for a double room in hotels listed as expensive, and between $55 and $110 in hotels listed as moderate.

EXPENSIVE

La Gería An attractive establishment facing the sea, situated 2 miles (3 km) east of Puerto del Carmen. The black marble steps from the lobby lead to a large circular bar and a huge heated swimming pool. All 244 rooms are air conditioned and have terraces with ocean views. Playa de los Pocillos, Puerto del Carmen (phone: 28-510441).

Melia Salinas Looking like a giant spacecraft in a tropical paradise, this property, decorated by César Manrique, offers 310 modern air conditioned rooms, each with a private terrace facing the sea. Outdoor delights include a private beach, free-form pool, large gardens, tennis courts, and equipment for scuba diving and sailing, in addition to restaurants, bars, massage services, a sauna, a cinema, and a disco. Calle Sur Teguise, Costa Teguise (phone: 28-813040; in the US, 800-336-3542; fax: 28-813390).

Teguise Playa A large pyramid-shaped establishment on its own beach, only a short distance from the *Costa Teguise Golf Club*, it boasts 324 air conditioned rooms, all with sea views, and has 2 pools, a bar, and a restaurant. Good service and a good value. Urbanización, Costa Teguise (phone: 28-816654; in the US, 800-332-4872; fax: 28-810979).

MODERATE

Aparthotel Don Paco and Apartamentos Castilla This resort complex near the beach, a few minutes drive from Arrecife and the airport, offers 228 spacious rooms and apartments with attractive pinewood fittings, color TV sets, and fully equipped kitchens; all have ocean views. Facilities include 2 swimming pools, squash courts, a gymnasium, 2 restaurants, a bar, and a disco. Playa de los Pocillos, Puerto del Carmen (phone: 28-511034 for the hotel; 28-511618 for the apartments).

Arrecife Gran A contemporary resort overlooking Arrecife harbor, with 148 air conditioned rooms, a large pool and sun deck, tennis courts, gym, and sauna. Its most unusual feature is a restaurant on an island in the middle of a small lake that can be reached only by boat. Av. Mancomunidad, Arrecife (phone: 28-811250; fax: 28-814259).

Los Fariones Surrounded by tropical gardens, this friendly 237-room hotel fronts a small beach and features a heated swimming pool and tennis courts. The rooms are air conditioned, comfortable, and functional. Urbanización Playa Blanca, Puerto del Carmen (phone: 28-825175; fax: 28-510202).

EATING OUT

The tourist influx has spurred the establishment of restaurants offering international dishes, particularly along the busy Puerto del Carmen beachfront, but a few places continue to serve authentic Canaries cooking. One local specialty is creamy *queso conejero* ("rabbit cheese" — although it's actually made from goat's milk, molded inside woven palm fronds). Try the local wine, made from the *malvasía,* or malmsey, grape, grown in the lava fields. The El Grifo Bodega label has been a favorite since 1775. Expect to pay $55 or more for dinner for two in restaurants listed as expensive, between $30 and $40 in restaurants listed as moderate, and $20 or less in inexpensive places. Prices do not include drinks, tax, or tips.

EXPENSIVE

Castillo de San José In the cellar of an old castle that now houses the *Museo de Artes de Contemporáneo* (International Museum of Contemporary Art), this is one of the most beautiful restaurants on the island, serving an international cuisine. Open daily. Reservations advised. Major credit cards accepted. A bit over a mile (2 km) northeast of Arrecife on the road to Las Caletas (phone: 28-812321).

Malvasía Grill Bright checkered tablecloths, a rustic atmosphere, and efficient and friendly service make for pleasant dining in this restaurant in the *Los Zocos* resort. The menu offers a varied sampling of international dishes and a good selection of international wines. Open for dinner only; closed holidays. Reservations advised. Major credit cards accepted. *Los Zocos,* Playa de las Cucharas, Costa Teguise (phone: 28-816436).

MODERATE

Acatife This centuries-old house in the old town of Teguise is the place for international cooking at reasonable prices. Open for dinner only; closed Sundays and Mondays. Reservations unnecessary. Major credit cards accepted. Plaza de la Iglesia, Teguise (phone: 28-845027).

La Bohème International dishes are the specialty here, served at tables illuminated by cozy lamplight. It has the best selection of wine on the island. Open daily. Reservations unnecessary. No credit cards accepted. 51 Av. de las Playas, Puerto del Carmen (phone: 28-825915).

La Marina Canarian and South American fare highlight the menu in this promenade restaurant with a nautical air. Don't pass up the grilled lamb chops. Closed Tuesdays. Reservations unnecessary. No credit cards accepted. Av. Marítimo de las Playas, Puerto del Carmen (phone: 28-826096).

INEXPENSIVE

La Casa Roja Good, simple seafood dishes are served at this popular place overlooking the little harbor in Puerto del Carmen. Open daily. Reservations unnecessary. No credit cards accepted. 22 Plaza Varadero, Puerto del Carmen (phone: 28-826515).

El Diablo This glass-enclosed eatery, designed by César Manrique, stands amid the Montañas del Fuego, the island's live volcanic Fire Mountains. Patrons can feast on volcano-broiled steak from seats offering panoramic views of the crater-pocked park and the Atlantic Ocean to the south. Open daily for lunch only. No reservations or credit cards accepted. Parque Nacional de Timanfaya (phone: 28-840057).

Playa Blanca There is no menu; the excellent seafood dishes offered depend on the catch of the day. Open daily. No reservations or credit cards accepted. Yaiza (no phone).

Fuerteventura

With the longest shoreline, plenty of spacious, empty beaches, and an arid climate that guarantees year-round sunshine, Fuerteventura is just the spot for windsurfers, beach bums, sun lovers, anglers, and those seeking total seclusion. It is the island closest to Africa — only 59 miles offshore — and the dramatic, howling winds and impressive sand dunes never let visitors forget it.

Most of the island's 30,000 residents live in Puerto del Rosario, the capital, located about midway along the eastern coast. Atlantic rollers break against the rocky western coast, while the best beaches extend along the southeast coast, and Jandía, for instance, and in the north near Corralejo, once a quiet fishing village and now a growing resort. Fishing, from the beaches or a boat, is excellent.

The island can be toured in a day, taking in the rugged interior including Betancuria, a secluded oasis chosen by Béthencourt (a Frenchman who settled Fuerteventura), as the island's original capital in 1404. An enjoyable excursion can be made from Corralejo over translucent waters to the offshore Isla de los Lobos.

GETTING AROUND

AIRPORT Fuerteventura's airport is located 3 miles (5 km) from Puerto del Rosario. *Iberia* (11 Calle Uno de Mayo; phone: 28-851250; airport; phone: 28-851250) has direct service to and from Barcelona, Bilbao, Málaga, Madrid and Seville, as well as Grand Canary, Tenerife, and Lanzarote.

BUS The main bus station is located at 25 Calle Alfonso XIII, Puerto del Rosario (phone: 28-850951).

CAR RENTAL Major rental car companies are *Avis* (8 Calle Primero de Mayo, Puerto Rosario; phone: 28-850261; *Casa Atlántica Hotel,* on Playa Jandía, Morro del Jable; phone: 28-876017; and 18 Calle La Oliva, Juan de Austria, Corralejo; phone: 28-866388); *Hertz* (Av. Generalísimo, Corralejo; phone: 28-866259, 28-866432, and 28-866436; at the airport; phone: 28-866259; *Centro Comercial Tennis Center,* Playa Paraíso, Morro Jable-Jandía; phone: 28-876126; and *Centro Comercial,* El Matorral, Morro Jable-Jandía; phone: 28-876138); and *Europcar* (27 Calle El Cosco, Puerto del Rosario; phone: 28-852436 or 28-852438; at the airport; phone: 28-852436; *Centro Comercial Barqueros,* Corralejo; phone: 28-866167; *Apartamentos Tinojay,* Caleta de Fuste; phone: 28-852436; Complejo Sotavento, Costa Calma; phone: 28-871041; and Edificio Esmeraldo Local 1, Jandía; phone: 28-877044).

FERRY *Trasmediterránea* (46 Calle León y Castillo, Puerto del Rosario; phone: 28-850877) has regular sailings from Puerto del Rosario to Las Palmas, Grand Canary, Arrecife, and Lanzarote, and from Morro Jable (at the southern tip of Fuerteventura) to Santa Cruz de Tenerife. The company also operates a jet foil between Morro Jable and Las Palmas and between Puerto del Rosario and Corralejo and Playa Blanca, Lanzarote. *Ferry Betancuria,* a subsidiary of *Ferry Gomera* headquartered at Edificio Rascacielos (Av. 3 de Mayo, Santa Cruz de Tenerife; phone: 22-221040), has three daily sailings between Corralejo and Playa Blanca, Lanzarote, while *Alisur* (1 Calle La Esperanza, Arrecife; phone: 28-814272) covers the same route four times daily.

TAXI Taxis sometimes can be hailed on the streets in Puerto del Rosario, or they can be requested by calling 28-850059.

CHECKING IN

Frenzied construction in recent years has added hundreds of hotel and apartment rooms to previously meager accommodations. Large hotels around Jandía in the south attract mainly German guests; inexpensive apartments are available in Corralejo. Expect to pay $150 or more for a double room in a hotel listed as expensive, and between $70 and $110 at a place described as moderate.

EXPENSIVE

Iberotel Tres Islas This spiffy luxury establishment on a remote golden sand beach is surrounded by tropical gardens. All 365 rooms are air conditioned, with TV sets and mini-bars, and there are three restaurants, a large saltwater swimming pool, tennis courts, and a fitness center. Playa de Corralejo (phone: 28-866000; fax: 28-866154).

Robinson Club Centrally located on the desirable southeast coast, this beachside hotel has a clubby look and feel. Most of the 213 air conditioned rooms have water views; other pluses range from manicured lawns and a tropical bar to miniature golf, tennis, a pool, and a restaurant for guests only. Morro del Jable, Paraja (phone: 28-541375; fax: 28-541025).

Los Gorriones A member of the Sol chain, this 309-room hotel is on a secluded beach in the south of the island. Completely air conditioned, it is functional and comfortable, and includes a restaurant, a pool, tennis courts, and windsurfing facilities. Playa de la Barca, Gran Tarajal (phone: 28-547025; in the US, 800-336-3542; fax: 28-870825).

Iberotel Oliva Beach A more modest version of its sister hotel, the *Ibertol Tres Islas,* this place has 410 rooms and good views of the area's spectacular dunes. It has a restaurant, a pool, and tennis courts. Playa de Corralejo (phone: 28-866100; fax: 28-866154).

Parador de Fuerteventura Standing on the edge of the ocean about 2 miles (3 km) south of the capital, this modern *parador,* 2 decades old, is the most splendid hotel on the island. A pleasant place, with polished wood floors and oil paintings, it has 50 air conditioned rooms, a swimming pool, and a good restaurant. Playa Blanca, Puerto del Rosario (phone: 28-851150; in the US, 212-686-9213; fax: 28-851158).

EATING OUT

Be sure to try the *queso majorero,* a spicy goat cheese preserved with a mixture of oil, hot pepper, and *gofio* flour. A moderately priced meal for two on Fuerteventura will cost between $20 and $35, not including drinks, wine, or tips.

Casa Juan The day's catch is proudly displayed in a rowboat full of ice at this seafood house, where fried and baked fish are the specialties. Open daily. Reservations unnecessary. No credit cards accepted. 5 Calle General Linares, Corralejo (phone: 28-866219).

El Patio Whitewashed arches, a timber roof, and a floor of old tiles provide a cozy air to this quaint eatery near the harbor. Try the fish stew, the baked kid, and the banana flambé. Closed Mondays. Reservations unnecessary. No credit cards accepted. Calle Lepanto, Corralejo (phone: 28-866668).

La Palma

One of the few islands to have escaped inundation by tourists, possibly because it is short on good beaches, La Palma has sufficient numbers of other attractions to justify a visit. Shaped like a leaf, it measures approximately 13 miles by 29 miles and is possibly the most beautiful island of the archipelago — which is why it is known as the "Isla Bonita," or "Pretty Island." It's also the greenest isle in the group, hence its other nickname, the "Isla Verde" ("Green Island"). A massive crater, the Caldera de Taburiente, occupies the center of the island, with ravines and streams running down to the rugged coastline. At over 6,000 feet, La Palma is the world's highest island. Below its pine-forested heights are intensely cultivated, terraced fields producing tropical and other fruits (as well as tobacco plants, originally imported from Cuba, from which the island's noted cigars are made). The capital, Santa Cruz de la Palma, was once the third most important port of the Spanish empire. It still retains picturesque colonial-style homes and a 16th-century City Hall. Today, with 18,000 inhabitants, it is one of the most pleasant towns in the Canaries. Although facilities and services for tourists are not as well developed on La Palma as on Grand Canary or Tenerife, it does attract Europeans who prefer quiet vacations.

GETTING AROUND

AIRPORT La Palma's small airport is located 5 miles (8 km) from Santa Cruz de La Palma. *Iberia* (1 Calle Apurón; phone: 22-411345) has direct flights to Barcelona and Madrid, to Grand Canary and Tenerife, as well as to El Hierro in the summer.

CAR RENTAL Major rental car companies are *Avis* (32 Calle O'Daly; phone: 22-411480 or 22-413742); *Hertz* (18 Av. Puente; phone: 22-413676); and *Europcar* (39 Calle O'Daly, Santa Cruz de La Palma; phone: 22-414338; and at the airport; 22-428042).

FERRY *Trasmediterránea* (2 Calle Pérez de Brito, Santa Cruz de La Palma; phone: 22-412415) offers regular sailings to Grand Canary, Tenerife, El Hierro, and La Gomera.

SPECIAL PLACES

SANTA CRUZ DE LA PALMA Standing at the foot of a colossal cliff, which is part of an eroded crater, the island capital has an unhurried Old World atmosphere. Along its quiet streets are excellent examples of the architecture of the Canary Islands. Particularly noteworthy are the Ayuntamiento (City Hall), with a beautiful Renaissance façade, and El Salvador, a 16th-century church with a fine coffered ceiling. Also of interest is the *Museo Naval* (Calle Barco de la Virgen; no phone), a maritime museum in a life-size replica of Christopher Columbus's *Santa María*. It's open Mondays through Saturdays from 10 AM to 1 PM and from 4 to 7 PM; admission charge.

LA CALDERA DE TABURIENTE A half-hour's drive west of the capital is the Mirador de la Concepción, a wonderful spot from which to gaze down on the coast and Santa Cruz de La Palma. The road then proceeds upward and through a tunnel, from where a road to the right winds up amid pinewoods to La Cumbrecita, a lookout point offering a breathtaking panorama of the 5-mile-wide crater, a world of tumbled rock, craggy heights, and forest. The crater bottom can be visited by driving along a dirt track from Llanos de Aridane, a town in the island's western interior, up the Barranco de las Angustias, a giant cleft. A rock sacred to the Guanche stands in the crater, and it was here that the last of the original inhabitants held out against the Spaniards. Not far from Llanos is El Time, a cliff whose top affords a tremendous view up the yawning Angustias chasm and down on banana plantations climbing in steps from the ocean. On the northern edge of the crater, at El Roque de los Muchachos, the island's highest point (7,950 feet), stands an astronomical station, built by several European nations. (Permission to visit must be obtained from the Observatorio Astrofísico de Canarias, Edificio Tynabana, Av. Puente, Santa Cruz de La Palma; phone: 22-413510). To reach El Roque, take the Barlovento road out of Santa Cruz de La Palma and turn left after 2 miles (3 km); it is another 22 miles (35 km) through impressive scenery.

FUENCALIENTE In the southern part of the island, near the village of Fuencaliente, stand the San Antonio and Teneguía volcanoes. Teneguía last erupted in 1971, sending molten lava flowing down to the sea. Sulfurous vapors rise from the crater, and water that pours down the fissures shoots back up as steam.

CHECKING IN

A moderately priced double room at the hotels listed below will cost between $50 and $90.

Marítimo A 4-story, seafront hotel, with 69 air conditioned rooms complete with color TV sets, mini-bars, and terraces. 75 Av. Marítimo, Santa Cruz de la Palma (phone: 22-420222 or 22-416340; fax: 22-414302).

Parador de Santa Cruz de la Palma This place occupies a building that is typically Canarian in style, down to the characteristic wooden balconies, in an ideal seafront location. The 32 rooms are very comfortable; the restaurant specializes in international and local dishes. 34 Av. Marítima, Santa Cruz de la Palma (phone: 22-412340; in the US, 212-686-9213; fax: 22-411856).

EATING OUT

Expect to pay between $25 and $45 for a meal for two at the moderately priced restaurants listed below. Prices do not include drinks, wine, or tips.

La Abuela Canarian and international specialties are served in this agreeable old tiled house, which has a large fireplace and a worn wooden floor. It stands just below the Mirador de la Concepción, along a rutted road. Closed Mondays. Reservations unnecessary. No credit cards accepted. 107 Buena Vista de Abajo, Breña Alta (phone: 22-415106).

La Fontana Situated in a modern apartment block just off the beach south of Santa Cruz de La Palma, this eatery has a bar and terrace, where patrons enjoy such delights as sirloin steaks cooked in whiskey and prawns fried in garlic. Closed Mondays. Reservations unnecessary. Major credit cards accepted. Urbanización Adelfas, Los Cancajos, Breña Baja (phone: 22-434250).

El Parral With its red tablecloths and fresh flowers, this eating spot opposite the Santa Catalina castle is the perfect place to sample baked fresh salmon, followed by strawberries and cream or a *rapadura,* a honey cone with almonds. Try the *queso de la isla,* a smoked goat cheese with dry *opuncias* (prickly pears) and almonds. Closed Mondays. Reservations unnecessary. Visa accepted. 7 Calle Castillete, Santa Cruz de la Palma (phone: 22-413915).

San Petronio As the name suggests, this restaurant on the island's west coast serves Italian dishes. Closed Mondays. Reservations unnecessary. No credit cards accepted. Llanos de Aridane (phone: 22-462403).

La Gomera

Although it measures only 146 square miles, this round island rises steeply from a precipitous shoreline to nearly 5,000 feet at its central peak, Mount Garajonay. The craggy seacoast and mountainous terrain make transportation from one valley to the next so difficult that the islanders have developed a whistling language to communicate with one another over great distances. Situated about 20 miles across the water from Tenerife's southwestern coast, La Gomera is usually visited as a day trip by tourists vacationing on one of the larger Canary Islands. Christopher Columbus, who stopped here in 1492 to procure water and provisions on his first voyage of discovery, is reputed to have spent some memorable days with the mistress of the island, the widow Beatriz de Peraza, Countess of Gomera; his visit is a source of great local pride. In San Sebastián, the island's tiny, picturesque capital, is Nuestra Señora de la Asunción, where Columbus and his crews heard mass before setting off for parts unknown. The church, on Calle del Medio near the tourist office, was restored in 1992 in honor of the 500th anniversary of Columbus's discovery of the New World. The house in which the explorer is said to have slept, called the *Casa de Colón,* is now a museum housing a permanent collection of pre-Columbian art, and the Torre del Conde (Count's Tower), an old fortress standing near the sea, has been declared a national historic monument. For shopping, stroll along Main Street, an ideal place to pick up the local red-clay pottery.

The island's Garajonay National Park, encompassing the peak and surrounding woodlands — some 10,000 acres — is a UNESCO Natural World Heritage Site, home to over 850 species of plants and flowers. The rare *laurisilva,* an ancient, tertiary-era laurel plant whose lovely petals once graced the whole of the Mediterranean region, can be found at Garajonay, its last outpost. The Centro de Visitantes (Visitors' Center) is located northeast of San Sebastián, at Juego de Bolas. Turn off the main road to Vallehermoso (signposted) at Las Rosas and head south. To arrange for a free guide, call a week in advance (phone: 22-800993). There are signposted walking trails and free maps available. The park is open Mondays through Saturdays from 9:30 AM to 4:30 PM, but dense fog tends to creep in during the afternoon, so try to visit before 3 PM.

A worthwhile excursion out of San Sebastián is to the Valle Gran Rey, a spectacular ravine on the opposite side of the island, reached by hair-raising roads. Other highlights of the island are its several banana plantations and orchards; beaches of black and red volcanic sand; Playa de Santiago, a fishing village with a pebble beach; and the whistling Gomerans themselves. Boat trips around the island leave from the tiny harbor at Playa de Santiago and can be booked at the *Canaexpress* travel agency in the *Tecina* hotel (phone: 22-870400). The most popular excursion features a visit to "Los Orangos," thousands of basalt columns rising from the sea like giant organ pipes.

GETTING AROUND

CAR RENTAL Major rental car companies are *Avis* (21 Caseta del Muelle, San Sebastián; phone: 22-870461), *Hertz* (6 Av. Fred Olsen, San Sebastián; phone: 22-870924 or 22-870751), and *Europcar* (7 Av. Fred Olsen, San Sebastián; phone: 22-870055).

FERRY *Trasmediterránea* (35 General Franco, San Sebastián; phone: 22-871300) has regular sailings to Grand Canary, Tenerife, La Palma, and El Hierro, as well as hydrofoil service between San Sebastián and Los Cristianos, Tenerife. *Ferry Gomera* (Av. Fred Olsen, San Sebastián; phone: 22-871007) has three daily departures between San Sebastián and Los Cristianos (except Tuesdays, when there are two departures).

CHECKING IN

A double room at a La Gomera hotel in the expensive category runs from $110 to $150; and at a hotel described as moderate, from $65 to $105.

EXPENSIVE

Tecina Perched on a hill overlooking Playa de Santiago, this self-contained village of whitewashed cabañas contains 485 rooms. The pool and its tropical island bar have a Caribbean look, and there's a modern gym with sauna, tennis, and squash. There is a poolside restaurant that serves buffet-style meals. Lomada de Tecina, San Sebastián (phone/fax: 22-895050).

MODERATE

Parador Conde de la Gomera Perched majestically on a rocky crest overlooking San Sebastián, the mountains, and the ocean, this splendid 43-room inn is surrounded by tropical gardens. Try to get a room that faces south (overlooking the gardens) or one on the ground floor (each has a cool patio, decorated with local pottery). The grand salon, with antique furniture and replicas of famous ships, offers guests a small library. There's also a swimming pool with a bar and grill. The dining room serves good food, too (see *Eating Out*). Accommodations on the island are very limited and the rooms here are much in demand, so make reservations early. San Sebastián de la Gomera (phone: 22-871100; in the US, 212-686-9213; fax: 22-871116).

Pensión Colón A clean and simple establishment lodged in a picturesque townhouse with a patio, it's steps away from the Nuestra Señora de la Asunción church, where Columbus and his crews heard mass. The most desirable of the 9 rooms look out onto the courtyard. There is a restaurant inside. No credit cards accepted. 59 Calle Real, San Sebastián (phone: 22-870245).

EATING OUT

Expect to pay between $50 and $60 for a meal for two at an expensive restaurant, between $35 and $45 at a moderate establishment, and $35 or less at an inexpensive spot. Prices do not include drinks, taxes, or tips.

EXPENSIVE

Parador Conde de la Gomera Located in the *parador* of the same name, this is the most elegant and traditional restaurant in town, boasting a fine Spanish and local menu, plus a substantial wine list. If it's on the *menú del día,* try the *potaje de berros* (watercress stew). Open daily. Reservations advised. Major credit cards accepted. San Sebastián (phone: 22-871100).

MODERATE

La Casa del Mar This is the best seafood restaurant in town, serving super-fresh fish with exotic island spices. Try the *san cochadas* (parrot fish) or the *viejas fritas* (tiny, tender white fish that are deep-fried and served with sweet and white potatoes, *mojo* sauce, and kneaded *gofio*). Open daily. No reservations or credit cards accepted. Av. Fred Olsen (phone: 22-871219).

Marqués de Oristan Ensconced in a 200-year-old house, once thought to be the residence of its namesake, this place features Italian fare in several indoor dining rooms or an outdoor courtyard. The cozy bar is a popular nightspot. Open daily. Reservations unnecessary. Major credit cards accepted. 26 Calle del Medio, San Sebastián (phone: 22-870022).

INEXPENSIVE

La Cabaña In this simple setting, meat and poultry dishes typical of the Canaries — wild boar, roast kid and lamb, and chicken in banana sauce — are the order of the day. Save room for the spicy *queso curado,* a cured cheese made from blended goat's and sheep's milk and smoked with heather. No reservations or credit cards accepted. In the tiny barrio of El Langreo, northwest of San Sebastián on the Carretera del Barranco (no phone).

Rincón del Cedro A quaint, family-run pizzeria decorated in pine wood and red tiles. Open daily. No reservations or credit cards accepted. Near the town center, at Plaza de la Constitución, San Sebastián (no phone).

El Hierro

The smallest and least inhabited of the archipelago's major islands, El Hierro is the harshest of all, with black volcanic soil, steep massifs, deep craters, barren mountains, and a serious dearth of springwater. Its name means "the iron one," and the island really does appear to be lost in the Iron Age. Inhabited by prehistoric fauna and giant lizards, this rocky 107 square miles is the ideal spot for those who appreciate solitude and nature at its most dramatic.

The farthest west of the islands, El Hierro appears grim and unfriendly from the sea, since its coasts are of black lava dotted with cactus. Clouds often shroud its central area, a plateau 4,900 feet above sea level. Not all of the island is stark, however; tiny pockets of emerald green glitter in the mountainous interior, providing pasture for flocks of sheep. Their milk, combined with cow's and/or goat's milk, is an essential ingredient of the popular *queso herreño,* a slightly sour-tasting smoked cheese.

The hardy Bimbache, El Hierro's original inhabitants, solved the problem of the island's lack of springwater by harvesting water from the evergreen leaves of the garoe tree. The trees were so important to the islanders that, until fairly recently, the ownership of one tree was a communal affair, with different branches belonging to different proprietors. The island's inhospitable conditions eventually forced much of the population to emigrate to South America.

About 3,500 of the current 7,000 residents live in the capital, Valverde, which is known for its wine. From Valverde, visitors can make short excursions to such natural wonders as La Dehesa, a huge igneous desert whose rolling slopes create the hypnotic illusion of a continual wave. Towering over this calm expanse is the El Sanctuario de Nuestra Señora de Los Reyes (Sanctuary of Our Lady of the Catholic Monarchs), which every 4 years is the focal point of a great pilgrimage (the next will take place in 1995). During these processions, the image of the Virgin Mary is borne for 19 miles along harsh, windy roads to the capital, accompanied by pilgrims, some bearing candles, some playing native music.

The island's tiny airport handles *Iberia's* flights to Grand Canary, Tenerife, Madrid, and Valencia. *Trasmediterránea* (Puerto de la Estaca, Valverde; phone: 22-550129) has regular ferry service to Grand Canary, Tenerife, La Palma, and Gomera. Though El Hierro usually is visited as a day trip by tourists vacationing on one of the larger islands, accommodations and meals are available at the moderately priced *Parador de El Hierro* (phone: 22-550101; in the US, 212-686-9213) in Las Playas, 12 miles (20 km) south of Valverde. Modern, but traditionally styled, it has 47 rooms, a black sand beach, a pool, and a restaurant.

Index